JO

was born in Dublin in 1667. A man of vast contradictions, his was the keenest mind and sharpest tongue in an age marked by intellectual brilliance; his personal life, however, was characterized by frustration and defeat. Swift's political ambition, which took him to England, ended with the downfall of the Tory ministry in 1714, and he returned to Ireland as Dean of St. Patrick's Cathedral. But his energy and wit could not be stifled, and it was in this period that he wrote his ironic masterpiece, GULLIVER'S TRAVELS. Swift died on October 19, 1745, and was buried beneath the Latin epitaph he himself composed. It reads, in English: "He has gone where savage indignation can lacerate his heart no more."

THE AENEID OF VIRGIL Translated by Allen Mandelbaum
THE BROTHERS KARAMAZOV by Fyodor Dostoevsky
BARABBAS by Pär Lagerkvist
CANDIDE by Voltaire
COLLECTED SHORT STORIES by Aldous Huxley
THE COMPLETE SHORT STORIES OF MARK TWAIN
   Edited by Charles Neider
A COUNTRY DOCTOR'S NOTEBOOK by Mikhail Bulgakov
CRIME AND PUNISHMENT by Fyodor Dostoevsky
FAR FROM THE MADDING CROWD by Thomas Hardy
FATHERS AND SONS by Ivan Turgenev
50 GREAT AMERICAN SHORT STORIES Edited by Milton Crane
FOUR SHORT NOVELS by Herman Melville
GREEN MANSIONS by W. H. Hudson
GULLIVER'S TRAVELS AND OTHER STORIES by Jonathan Swift
HEART OF DARKNESS and THE SECRET SHARER by Joseph Conrad
THE HUNCHBACK OF NOTRE DAME by Victor Hugo
THE IDIOT by Fyodor Dostoevsky
THE IMMORALIST by André Gide
LORD JIM by Joseph Conrad
MADAME BOVARY by Gustave Flaubert
THE METAMORPHOSIS AND OTHER STORIES BY FRANZ KAFKA
   Edited by Stanley Corngold
NOTES FROM UNDERGROUND by Fyodor Dostoyevsky
NOTES OF A NATIVE SON by James Baldwin
THE OCTOPUS by Frank Norris
THE ODYSSEY by Homer
SADNESS by Donald Barthelme
75 SHORT MASTERPIECES Edited by Roger Goodman
SISTER CARRIE by Theodore Dreiser
A SPY IN THE HOUSE OF LOVE by Anaïs Nin
THOREAU: WALDEN AND OTHER WRITINGS Edited by Joseph Wood Krutch
THREE SHORT NOVELS by Joseph Conrad
WAR AND PEACE by Leo Tolstoy
WE by Yevgeny Zamiatin

Swift:

GULLIVER'S TRAVELS
AND OTHER WRITINGS

Edited and with an introduction by
MIRIAM KOSH STARKMAN

BANTAM BOOKS · TORONTO · NEW YORK · LONDON

SWIFT: GULLIVER'S TRAVELS AND OTHER WRITINGS

A Bantam Classic / November 1962

2nd printing .... August 1965	5th printing ..... August 1968
3rd printing .... October 1966	6th printing .... October 1969
4th printing .... August 1967	7th printing .. September 1970
Bantam edition /	*December 1971*
9th printing ..... August 1973	10th printing ...... May 1975
11th printing .. December 1976	

Library of Congress Catalog Card Number: 62-20941

ISBN 0-553-10547-7

Published simultaneously in the United States and Canada

Bantam Books are published by Bantam Books, Inc. Its trade-
mark, consisting of the words "Bantam Books" and the por-
trayal of a bantam, is registered in the United States Patent
Office and in other countries. Marca Registrada. Bantam
Books, Inc., 666 Fifth Avenue, New York, New York 10019.

PRINTED IN THE UNITED STATES OF AMERICA

CONTENTS

INTRODUCTION

I

Of satire in general and of Jonathan Swift in particular, this may safely be prognosticated—that they will endure. Satire seems to require categorically only two conditions: a subject and a satirist. Given our post-lapsarian state, frailty and fallibility are sufficient subjects, and the details abound. But of the shaping hand of the satirist, qualifications are to be made. For satire is a strict art, despite all the difficulties we may encounter in defining that art neatly. We are all often indignant, and sometimes witty about our indignations, but we do not thereby turn satirists. For it is not only the anger and the involvement, the idealism and the wit, but the manipulations of them, how they are turned to formful, organic use that constitute the satiric art.

Among the genres of literature, satire exerts a perennial fascination, the fascination of the forbidden. Often hostile, shocking, or destructive, satire tends to approach the thin end of cynicism and misanthropy, to frighten or disgust. But the positive purpose that impels the satirist neutralizes, justifies, and heals by his intention to correct and reform, by his essential moralism. Thus the nature of satire is ambivalent, complex, and elusive.

Rhetorically, satire challenges from the beginning, for, strictly speaking, it cannot be defined; it is not accurately a genre, though we often call it so; yet it seems to usurp other genres and function as though it were one. A satirical novel, a satirical sonnet, for example, become primarily satire, and the novel or sonnet characteristics more often than not become subsidiary to the satiric intention. Yet if satire is only a mode, a tone, a manner of speaking, does it thereby function as a kind of pervasive metaphor, so crucial that it determines the characteristics of the genre within which it is operating? For operate satire does within almost any genre, in all kinds of lyric poetry from epic to song, in tragedy as well as comedy, in prose as well as in poetry. But satire flourishes just as comfortably in the non-formal areas of composition in prose and poetry—in sermon, tract, broadside, in the most occasional rhymed squib.

Historically, then, any rhetorical system, whether clearly enunciated or tacit, seems to have allowed satire ample growth. Nor has satire any clearly differentiating logical imperatives of its own; any subversion of any logic, any incursion on the rule of common sense will support it. Nevertheless, however difficult the definition of satire may be in the formal terms of rhetoric or logic, the history of satire is proof of its viability, from Aristophanes to Thurber. Heroic poetry may die, indeed it may already have done so, but satire remains, a friend to man.

And the more deeply it strikes at the core of our human condition, the more effective it is. Satire is bred of dissatisfaction with vice and folly; the positive purpose, however deeply subsumed, that impels the satirist's aggressions is the amelioration of the human creature and his lot on earth. Between the status quo and ideal perfection lies the discrepancy which the satirist resolves by means of wit; and wit is the condition of satire, the primary tool of the satirist. Wit, by its nature, allows for, indeed demands, a maximum of cerebration. But the emotional tone of satire is crucial, too: a maximum involvement, though that involvement may encompass the whole spectrum of emotion from the comic to the tragic, be as controlled, contemplative, and urbane as Horace's, or as wild, open, and savage as Juvenal's, and, on occasion, Swift's.

Perhaps the most crucial of the ways in which the satirist manipulates his art is in the assumption by the writer of a role within his work, a role that has been called the persona or the mask. That role is a satirist's role, but it is not identical with the satirist who is the author of the work. Aside from biographical considerations, this differentiation between satirist and his persona or personae is important in our understanding of any particular satire in question, for the satirist-speaker, the persona, is a fictional device which helps the work to manifest itself. Now, the persona in satire is frequently angry, carping, difficult, captious, even savage. At other times he may be comic and ingenuous to the point of simple-mindedness. But one cannot, or should not, deduce the personality of the author from his personae, any more than one should interpret the personae of a satire by the biography of its author. The author need only be capable of creating his persona. Each is both more and less than the other.

In Swift studies, the confusion of author and persona has been rampant. Swift's life has been read as identical with his works, his biography interpreted in terms of his works, and his works, in circular fashion, in terms of this often hypothe-sized biography. This kind of biographical fallacy is not uncommon, but the satirist is particular susceptible to it because his fictional personae, when used most artistically, are most persuasive and thus give the illusion of historical rather than fictional truth. Certainly it is easier not to misread Achilles as Homer than it is not to misread Gulliver as Swift. Nevertheless, the obligation remains not to do either.

Nevertheless, too, Homer must have had a considerable predisposition to the heroic ideal to have conceived his Achilles. Just so, the satirist must, by nature and training, be predisposed to the satiric mode rather than to another. To have emerged as a satirist in the first place, Swift, the man, required a sufficiently strong and balanced combination of anger and love, indignation and concern. His anger is everywhere apparent, and his life provided him with more than ample justification for anger. His concern lay in his earnest, and as it happens his Christian, belief that mankind is not only susceptible of salvation but worthy of being saved. Swift spoke very meaningfully when he claimed to "hate and detest that animal called man," but to "heartily love John, Peter, Thomas, and so forth"; for his professed hatred of the animal called man spells his dissatisfaction with man-kind, and his love for the individual, his hope for mankind. The tension between the two is controlled by his wit, his ability to keep both hatred and love, dismay and hope, in dynamic suspension—a sane and productive resolution, both biographically and artistically.

The word "sane" is a controversial word in respect to Swift, for one of the pervasive myths beclouding both Swift's life and works is the myth of the mad, angry Dean. That myth, essentially a Romantic fabrication, is sufficiently exploded not to warrant serious attention as a biographical fact. The problem remains that modern psychological and psychoanalyti-cal interpretations have ended up not very far from the same conclusion: "It is submitted on the basis of such a study of *Gulliver's Travels* that Swift was a neurotic who exhibited psychosexual infantilism, with a particular showing of copro-philia, associated with misogyny, misanthropy, mysophilia and mysophobia." [Phyllis Greenacre.] Inasmuch as our concern at the moment is not with Swift's biography but with his art, it may be pertinent to suggest that if Swift was neurotic—and he may very well have been so—a point-by-point rela-tionship does not necessarily exist between life and work.

Indeed, if our generic approach to Swift be just, that point-by-point relationship could not exist. Within a theory of art as neurosis, satire as a type lends more support to the analyst than do the verse epistle, let us say, or the didactic couplet. Even so, it would seem more fruitful, in general, to psychoanalyze Swift's personae rather than Jonathan Swift.

A recent approach to Swift makes such an effort to use the insights and methods of psychoanalysis on Swift's works rather than on his life. Concentrating on Swift's "excremental vision," as it has been called, which has affronted and puzzled readers from Swift's day to our own, the theory suggests that Swift's preoccupation with anality is not so much an individual neurosis as an intuitive understanding between anality and culture, an understanding of the theory of sublimation, an attack on social neurosis. That is, Swift is describing the cultural level man has reached rather than his own neurotic development. "The thesis . . . is that if we are willing to listen to Swift we will find startling anticipations of Freudian theorems about anality, about sublimation, and about the universal neurosis of mankind. . . . Swiftian psychoanalysis differs from the Freudian in that the vehicle for the exploration of the unconscious is not psychoanalysis but wit." [Norman O. Brown, *Life against Death*.]

Whatever the psychoanalytic implications may be, the fact is that Swift's satires fit neatly into the history of Western satire, show clear lines of relationship to Aristophanes and Juvenal, and more immediately to the satires of the sixteenth century, to the Restoration, and to the satires of Swift's own contemporaries. When Swift chose to be buried under the legend, "Here lies Jonathan Swift where savage indignation can no longer lacerate his heart," so far as his works are concerned he effectively described the two components of his vision: his indignation and his heart. Any one of his contemporaries would have recognized the "savage" as traditional and Juvenalian.

II

Biographically, Swift poses many problems to his students. Jonathan Swift was born in Dublin on November 30, 1667, the son of Abigail Errick Swift, and of Jonathan Swift the elder, who died some eight months before his son's birth, leaving his widow and two children to the support of his elder brother Godwin. In his first year the infant Jonathan was abducted to England by his nurse and was not returned for about three years. Soon after his return to Ireland, he went into the household of his uncle Godwin, where he remained until he was sent to the Kilkenny School at the age of six. He remained at Kilkenny until he was fourteen. In 1682 he proceeded to Trinity College, Dublin, where he distinguished himself in no way except by receiving his degree *speciali gratia* in 1685. He remained at Trinity studying for his M.A. until 1689, when, in the face of a threatened invasion of Ireland by the king's forces, the college was permitted to withdraw. Swift left Dublin for England, visited his mother in Leicestershire, and that same year began his career as secretary to Sir William Temple, at Moor Park.

The problems in interpreting these facts begin immediately with the question of his paternity, with either Sir William Temple or his father John Temple being chief contenders for the honor of having been Swift's illegitimate father. There is in fact little evidence to support either claim, or to question his legitimacy in the first place, except that either supposed father serves to provide an answer, however tenuous, to solve the problem of Swift's anomalous relationship with Esther Johnson, his Stella; for if Stella was illegitimately a Temple, too—also a highly suppositious assumption—then one or another degree of consanguinity prevented the marriage of Swift and Stella. What seems more pertinent to our under-standing of Swift's complex personality is the fact that Swift was fatherless from the beginning of his life, and motherless for some of the most crucial years of his life. It would have been odd indeed had not these deprivations markedly influenced his growing personality. Swift's ingratitude, even hostility, toward his uncle teases one's understanding. Swift's special degree, too, is anomalous, though it may be interpreted as an administrative rather than a disciplinary action. The fact is that no amount of sensationalism can possibly make Swift any more interesting than he already is by reason of his works, nor can any amount of biographical conventionality detract from the complex fascination of the mind and art of Jonathan Swift.

The next decade in Swift's life, from 1689 to 1699, centers around his service to Sir William Temple and his life in the household at Moor Park. It was during this period that Swift expected to establish a career through political prefer-ment, but when Sir William died in 1699, Swift was left disappointed in his hopes and faced by the necessity of carv-ing out a career at the relatively advanced age of thirty-two.

For when Swift came to Moor Park it was as to a temporary refuge, and, indeed, when he left after about six months, it was with a letter of recommendation to Sir Robert Southwell, the Secretary for Ireland, which, however, had no practical results. Back again at Moor Park, Swift continued as secretary to Sir William until 1694, when, growing impatient with Temple's dilatoriness in helping him secure a prebendary and follow a career in the Church, Swift returned to Ireland. He was ordained a priest in the Anglican Church in 1695 and through the efforts of his Irish kinsmen was appointed to the obscure parish of Kilroot near Belfast. In 1696 Swift was back with Temple again, but upon Temple's death he was left disappointed of his legitimate hopes and expectations: political place or preferment in the Church.

But the period at Moor Park had been more than a series of frustrations for Swift. It was a period of self-education, the fixing of his talent and his temperament. The physical milieu could scarcely have been more felicitous, nor could the social. In addition to Sir William Temple, an urbane, cultivated, experienced statesman and philosopher, two notable ladies, Lady Temple and Lady Gifford, graced the household. And Swift's Stella, Esther Johnson, lived at Moor Park, eight years old when Swift arrived and eighteen when he left; Swift was to be closely associated with her for the rest of her life. But most important, Moor Park was the milieu in which Swift began to write poetry and in which he conceived and wrote the first of his great satires, *Tale of a Tub* and the *Battle of the Books*. Though almost a quarter of a century elapsed between these works and *Gulliver's Travels,* there is the closest relationship among them. For by the time Swift left Moor Park he had already assumed his characteristic stance; his genius as a satirist was fixed. Much was to be added to his depth and to his range, but he had already found his métier. If Moor Park was a disappointment from a practical point of view, Swift left it already embarked upon a great career—as a satirist.

But that career was not the one Swift sought. Indeed his major satires, by reason of which he enters the realm of belles-lettres, were the incidental by-products of his life as churchman, political journalist, and wit. For the latter half of his life Swift achieved considerable fame as a public, political writer, but always in the service of others. Never deeply committed to the Whig position, he spent twelve years as a Whig pamphleteer. With the accession of the Harley ministry, he began a stint as a Tory journalist, and again was in no way commensurately rewarded for his efforts. As a churchman, his rewards were too little and too late; when he was finally awarded a clerical post somewhat commensurate with his status and services, it was in Ireland, where he felt himself in exile, with the Deanery of St. Patrick's. With the fall of Robert Harley, head of the Tory ministry, he returned to Ireland, whence he emerged only twice again for any length of time. He became the great champion of the Irish people, and even as he raged against England for her exploitation of the Irish, he reviled the Irish for submitting to the exploitation. Never was love expressed with more rage. Thus the outward circumstances of Swift's life were not felicitous, and for all his fame he was repeatedly frustrated in his hopes. In his end Swift was as unfortunate as in his beginning. Afflicted by the degenerative diseases of old age, Swift was declared incompetent in 1742 and died, in darkness and in sorrow, on October 19, 1745.

The history of Swift's life from the time he returned to Ireland from Moor Park until his death is, in a sense, the history of his political journalism. These tracts, written on the behalf first of the Whigs, then of the Tories, and then of the Irish people, constitute a long and honorable chapter in eighteenth-century political thought and repay the closest attention not only from a historical point of view, but from the point of view of Swift's own mind, art, and personality. A detailed study of Swift must necessarily include them. But for a brief survey of Jonathan Swift, satirist, it will perhaps suffice to indicate how, on occasion, Swift's journalism achieved such a high pitch of virtuosity that topical journalism became universal satire. A protest against the wretched state of Ireland, a land of "beggars, thieves, oppressors, fools, and knaves," "nation of slaves, who sell themselves for nothing," *A Modest Proposal for preventing the children of poor people in Ireland from being a burden to their parents or country, and for making them beneficial to the public,* is only one of many of Swift's Irish protests, and only one of many modest proposals for the amelioration of social ills. But in its brilliant satire—its parody of the new science of political arithmetic, of current differentiations between the deserving and the undeserving poor, in its ironic reversal of the tenet that the wealth of a nation lay in its population, in its ironic conclusion that cannibalism is the only humane alternative to Ireland's exploitation—*A Modest Proposal* reaches a moral indignation that has seldom been equaled in satire. Thus economics became belles-lettres.

In another sense, the history of Swift's life may be traced through his social relationships, among which his relationships with women are complex and susceptible of the most sensational interpretations. In 1696, in Kilroot, Swift met Jane Waring, Varina as he called her, whom he wooed and by whom he was rejected. For four years thereafter, correspondence ensued between them, until Varina, now the pursuer, was rejected by Swift in a letter which has all the reasonable, cruel arrogance of someone whose feelings have been seriously wounded. To some critics Varina's original rejection has appeared to mark a traumatic turning away from women on Swift's part from which he never recovered. The long relationship with Stella, dating from 1689 until her death in 1728, and the fact that Stella came to live near Swift in Ireland in 1700 and remained thereafter, is indeed anomalous. Even in Swift's lifetime there were rumors that Swift and Mistress Esther Johnson were secretly married, but that it was a marriage in name only. Whether there was a marriage, why there was none if there was none, what the nature of the relationship was, are all unresolved questions. What is clear is the fact that Stella was the recipient, source, or inspiration of many of Swift's poems, letters, and particularly of his *Journal to Stella,* the last a remarkable account, written in a coded private language, of Swift's activities in England from 1710 to 1713 when he was at the height of his political effectiveness. And the relationship with Stella is often obscured by the facts of Swift's relationship with Vanessa, Esther Vanhomrigh, whom Swift met in 1707 and with whom he was closely involved until her death in 1723. There is reason to suppose that Swift, twice Vanessa's age, was somewhat uncomfortably caught in conflicting loyalties between Vanessa and Stella.

Among the men who figure in Swift's life are numbered some of the greatest names of his day: Congreve, Addison, Steele, Bolingbroke, Oxford, Pope, Gay, Prior, Arbuthnot. These relationships are significant not only in that they depict a highly social and urbane Swift, but in that they also indicate another large area of Swift's writings (aside from his journalistic pamphlets), the so-called *jeux d'esprits,* composed for the private delectation of his friends. Among these witty, occasional writings may be numbered Swift's poems. When John Dryden prognosticated that Cousin Swift would never be a poet, in a sense he spoke truly. For Swift lacks the authentic voice of the poet, the sensibility and the vision—except on some few occasions when he surpasses himself as in "Cadenus and Vanessa." For though Swift is more personality than poet, he is a remarkably skillful versifier. His verse is accomplished *vers de société*—parodic, moralistic, complimentary, always anti-romantic and sometimes outrageous.

The range of Swift's prose *jeux* is greater. Some are serious moralistic and didactic pieces, like the *Proposal for Correcting, Improving, and Ascertaining the English Tongue,* or the literary *Tatler* papers, or the *Thoughts on Various Subjects.* But the great majority are satirical pieces in which Swift seems to be whetting his pen, carefully practicing his rhetorical art and working out his medium, prose satire. They range from the early *Meditation on a Broomstick,* a parody on Robert Boyle's serious meditations which completely fooled Lady Berkeley for whom the joke was perpetrated, to the heady spoofing of astrology of the *Bickerstaff Papers,* to the animus of *Mr. Collins's Discourse of Freethinking; put into plain English by way of Abstract, for the Use of the Poor,* to the brilliant effrontery of the *Argument against Abolishing Christianity.* Even the least promising of them, like the lengthy *Polite Conversation,* shows in its preface a technique and intention that are seriously mindful of the artistic exigencies of satire. There is indeed some cause for question whether Swift as a wit, the writer of prose and verse *jeux,* was merely practicing his art with his left hand in preparation for his great work, or whether on two occasions, in his *Tale of a Tub* volume and in *Gulliver's Travels,* the *jeux* reached such a height of excellence that they stole, through the back door, into the realm of English belles-lettres.

III

The *Tale of a Tub* volume, which contained also the *Battle of the Books* and the *Mechanical Operation of the Spirit,* and was published in 1704, has something of the quality of an Athena sprung full blown. It is astonishing that so young a man—Swift was in his twenties when he wrote it—should have been capable of such virtuosity of matter and method, of such broad and encompassing knowledge, and of such inventiveness of satiric techniques. Of the three pieces, the greatest is *Tale of a Tub;* it is perhaps also the most difficult of Swift's works, and certainly it makes the most taxing demands upon the reader. Its complexity is immediately heralded in Swift's double theme: a satire on the corruptions in religion *and* learning. Taken together and interwoven in complicated and contrapuntal pattern, each theme manifests and supports the other. Of the two themes, the satire on the abuses in religion is given about one-third of the space in the work. Alternating these sections of the religious allegory, and announced by a series of six prefatory items, is the satire on the abuses in learning, in which category Swift, taking all knowledge to be his province, proceeds to satirize abuses in criticism, science, and philosophy. The whole forms what seems to be a chaotic and formless, sprawling work, the very formlessness of which, however, is an elaborate parody of seventeenth-century writing.

The satire on abuses in religion is carried brilliantly by the allegory of the three brothers, Peter, Martin, and Jack, standing respectively for Catholicism, Established Protestantism, and Dissent, as they rent the cloaks of original Christianity given to them by the father. The brothers' exploits constitute a satiric history of Christianity up to Swift's time; and the satire is inventive and telling, with Peter emerging as knave, Jack as madman, and Martin as a temperate but by no means perfect fool. For Swift's devotion to his satiric pattern never obliterates his sense of reality; though he sets up satiric norms, he never succumbs to them.

Considerably more complex is Swift's satire on contemporary abuses in learning, a welter of prefatory sections, footnotes, digressions and conclusions, the whole immediately parodic of the chaos Swift finds modern learning to be. Of the ideas controlling *Tale of a Tub,* the basic one revolves around the war between Ancients and Moderns, which turns on the simple question of whether the old learning is superior to the new. Though that war is a perennial one, it is more sharply articulated in some periods than in others; and in the seventeenth century, particularly with the growth of the new science, it was especially virulent. That war was more than a theoretical one, and upon one's position in it lay one's direction in belles-lettres, criticism, science, and philosophy. Each of these subjects constituted a separate battle in the war; the battle of the books in which the whole question of imitation and the rules was involved, the battle over the new experimental science, the battle over the old Aristotelian versus the new mechanistic philosophy were all at stake. In a sense, even the religious allegory in *Tale of a Tub* is related to the war between the Ancients and Moderns, the choice being between Martin and Jack. Except for the *Battle of the Books, Tale of a Tub* encompasses the whole of the Ancients-Moderns controversy, and Swift's position is uncompromisingly Ancient. The fact is that Swift was by temperament and belief, here as elsewhere, consistently conservative. And there is perhaps some cause for rejoicing that he was so, for the Ancient position is always more comfortable for the satirist; the new, the amorphous, the incomplete always provide better grist for the satiric mill than the old, the tried, the proven.

A moralist of a conservative, pessimistic, and angry temper, seriously devoted to the Christian ideal, Jonathan Swift, looked about him, and everywhere he found vice and folly, madness and depravity. Meanwhile the Moderns were busy promulgating an intoxicating faith in the Idea of Progress, a consuming belief in the utility of knowledge, a confidence in the invariability of the laws of Nature and the ability of science and philosophy to explain these laws. Nor was it only the theories of the Moderns, their pride and presumption that appalled Swift, it was their practice, too, their experiments and projects, in societies and academies, their personnel, their wits, projectors, and virtuosos. Confronting the new learning with the old, Swift finds the new science silly, the new philosophy mad, the new criticism pedantic; his new philosopher is a madman, his scientist a plebeian pedant, and his new critic a pedant, plebeian, and fool.

These satiric themes in *Tale of a Tub,* however, do not emerge in orderly sequence in separate sections, but indirectly through "A Digression Concerning Critics," "A Digression Concerning Madness," "A Digression in Praise of Digressions," and through the prefatory materials, indeed through the religious allegory on occasion. Just as Enthusiastic Jack as founder of Aeolism carries the satire of the new philosophy, so Catholic Peter is pre-eminently the scientist, the projector and virtuoso who carries the satire on science until he grows mad with "pride, projects, and knavery." His universal pickle, though primarily satirical of holy water, is simultaneously satirical of the quackery of seventeenth-century medicine in its search for universal panaceas. Again, inasmuch as Epicureanism in the seventeenth century was essentially a Modern system, the "Digression on Madness" in the *Tale* contains an elaborate anatomy of the Epicurean doctrine of happiness as the greatest good: "the sublime and refined point of felicity, called the possession of being well-deceived; the serene peaceful state of being a fool among knaves." For his satire on Modern criticism, Swift sets up the person of the mechanick-critic, a pedant without wit or taste, an ass of the ancient vintage of asses, the very antithesis of the Ancient scholar and gentleman. With the skill of the most adept metaphysician, Swift attacks metaphysical speculation; an exponent of reason, he attacks the rationalism of the Moderns; and with the most virtuoso-like intellect, he attacks intellectualism.

These, then, are some of the ideas controlling *Tale of a Tub,* but they do not begin to suggest the brilliant technique nor the encyclopedic range of his frame of reference. Since so much of Swift's satire is, at the primary level, topical, the reader is called upon to possess an intimate knowledge of seventeenth-century learning. And the agility required of the reader in hopping along with Swift's satiric movements— from parody to invective, to lampoon, to irony, to sarcasm, from shift to shift of persona—is no less taxing. Within the last ten years scholarship has made great progress in deciphering the mysteries that *Tale of a Tub* often poses, but there is much yet to be achieved. Swift was never to surpass himself in this great work.

It will have been noted that Swift fights no battle of the books in *Tale of a Tub,* although all other areas of modern learning are attacked. The reason for the omission is that Swift fought that battle in a separate work in the same volume, in *A Full and True Account of the Battle Fought Last Friday Between the Ancient and the Modern Books in St. James's Library,* commonly referred to as the *Battle of the Books.* If, however, the *Tale* is to be seen complete, the *Battle* is to be read as a chapter of it, as if the *Battle* were to have been called "A Digression on the Battle of the Books Fought Last Friday, etc." After *Tale of a Tub, Battle of the Books* is a relief, easy and direct, a mock-heroic piece in which it seems obvious that Swift is adapting the poetic form of the mock-heroic epic to the exigencies of prose. The subject is direct: a formidable battle takes place between the Ancient and Modern books in St. James's Library for the possession of the higher peak in Helicon, traditionally claimed by the Ancients and now claimed by the Moderns. Though the Ancients are clearly the victors, the account is left unfinished.

The armies of the Moderns are vast, a "confused multitude," consisting of "stink-pot-flingers," mercenaries, "rogues and ragamuffins." On the other hand, "The army of the Ancients was much fewer in number; Homer led the horse, and Pindar the light-horse; Euclid was chief engineer; Plato and Aristotle commanded the bowmen; Herodotus and Livy the foot; Hippocrates the dragoons. The allies led by Vossius and Temple brought up the rear." Most ludicrous of the newest Moderns are Wotton and Bentley, but they are repulsed by Aesop and Phalaris and destroyed by Swift's contemporary Ancients, Temple and Boyle.

To understand the significance of the personnel of the *Battle* requires of the reader a certain familiarity with the immediate occasion which bred Swift's satire. It begins with the publication in 1690 of Sir William Temple's *Essay on Ancient and Modern Learning* in which, in the process of objecting to the pride of the Moderns and rejecting the the theory of progress, Sir William happens to urge the greatness of Aesop and Phalaris among the Ancients. Refuting Temple, in his *Reflections upon Ancient and Modern Learning* in 1694, William Wotton, a Cambridge don, enthusiastically defends the Modern learning and repudiates authority when it clashes with reason. The Phalaris tangent of the controversy begins the following year with Charles Boyle's edition of *Phalaris,* in which, incidentally, he rebukes the scholarly Richard Bentley, the keeper of St. James's Library, but primarily upholds the authenticity of Phalaris. That authenticity is in turn seriously disputed, on sixteen counts, by Bentley in his *Dissertation upon the Epistles of Phalaris, Themistocles, Socrates, Euripides, etc., and Aesop's Fables,* which, as it happened, was appended to the second edition of Wotton's *Reflections.* In 1698 Bentley's *Dissertation* is *Examined* by Charles Boyle, and rejected. By 1699 the whole controversy is satirized in William King's *Dialogues of the Dead.* But the classic and final satire on the subject is to be found in Swift's *Battle of the Books.* Thus we see why in the *Battle* Temple and Boyle are the ancient defenders, why Wotton and Bentley are so sharply ridiculed, and why Aesop and Phalaris are so prominent among the Ancient defenders.

Stemming also from Temple is Swift's most telling figure in the *Battle of the Books,* the fable of the Ancient bee and the Modern spider: "So that in short the question comes to all this; which is the nobler being of the two, that which by a lazy contemplation of four inches round, by an overweening pride, feeding and engendering on itself, turns all into excrement and venom, producing nothing at last, but fly-bane and a cobweb; or that which by an universal range, with long search, much study, true judgment and distinction of things, brings home honey and wax." And the answer is: "that instead of Dirt and poison, we [the Ancients] have rather chosen to fill our hives with honey and wax, thus furnishing mankind with the two noblest of things, which are sweetness and light." *Battle of the Books* is one of Swift's most well-tempered satires, as if he felt that the battle was so certainly a victory for the Ancients that it did not earn his wrath.

As *Battle of the Books* is a digression to *Tale of a Tub,* so *A Discourse Concerning the Mechanical Operation of the Spirit* is a footnote to it, particularly to the Aeolist system of Section VIII and to the "Digression Concerning Madness." It is a separate treatise on the nature of religious Enthusiasm, its origin, theory and practice. A parody on scientific treatises, the *Mechanical Operation* is cast in the form of an epistle of the sort communicated to the Royal Society. It proceeds allegorically, according to which system explanation is made of how the Ass, standing for the Enthusiastic preacher, bears his Rider, the fanatic auditory, to heaven. But when more specific explanation comes due, Swift retires like any arcane philosopher to a sidenote: "Here the whole scheme of spiritual mechanism was deduced and explained with an appearance of great reading and observation; but it was thought neither safe nor convenient to print it," and a whole paragraph of asterisks ensues. But the argument emerges clearly enough: since the generation of zeal comes through the corruption of the senses, the mystery of Enthusiasm is actually nothing more nor less than a vast collective orgasm. The connections between sex and Enthusiasm were scarcely original with Swift; the distinction of the *Mechanical Operation of the Spirit* is that Swift raises the connection to a system. *Mechanical Operation* has the hilarity of *Tale of a Tub,* but it is only a fragment.

Written almost a quarter of a century later than the *Tale of a Tub* volume, *Gulliver's Travels* exhibits the same vigor of mind, the intensity, often violence, of emotion; the same brilliant virtuosity of satiric technique. The ideas in *Gulliver,* too, will be familiar to the reader of the *Tale:* Swift's championing of reason; his mistrust of the passions, particularly pride; his anti-rationalism, his rejection of projects and experiments— metaphysical preoccupations that obscure the revealed truths of Christianity. As for the form of *Gulliver,* though in a sense it is as custom made for its occasion as the form of the *Tale,* its components are more familiar. A satire of universal as well as topical scope, *Gulliver's Travels* supports the themes of travel fiction (of the extraordinary, imaginary, philosophic, cosmic, and fantastic voyages) and of the Utopia. Its implications are political, scientific, philosophical, and, some have thought, theological. Though much of *Gulliver's Travels* is rewarding to the most ingenuous reader, it amply repays the most searching analysis.

Books I and II were written in 1721–2; Book IV in 1723; and Book III in 1724–5. The whole manuscript was revised in 1726, surrounded by anonymity and obfuscation—as was Swift's habit. The first improved edition was not published until 1735, by Faulkner. It is significant to note that portions of Books I and III may stem from Swift's contribution to the *Memoirs of Martinus Scriblerus* of 1714, a collective *jeu d'esprit* of the Scriblerus Club of which Swift, Pope, Gay, and Arbuthnot were members. This early inception would account for some of the inconsistencies and infelicities in the narrative.

Books I and II are all but perfect in themselves and in relation to one another—the giant Gulliver among the pygmy Lilliputians changes easily into pygmy Gulliver among the giant Brobdingnagians. The scale of proportions, 12 to 1, is carefully preserved; the relativity of vision, Gulliver's telescopic eye as it reflects the Lilliputians, and his microscopic eye as he surveys the Brobdingnagians, is brilliantly ingenious, however much it may owe to Berkeley's *Theory of Vision* (except for certain inconsistencies of tone in Chapters 1, 2, and 6 of Book I, possibly to be accounted for by an earlier inception). Book I is, for the most part, perfect satire, the diminution operating with complete consistency and telling force both physically and figuratively. There is a great deal of topical satire implicit in Book I, largely of a political nature (and the exact details of that satire are in much dispute), but it is always viable on a universal level. Gulliver's cool, rational eye telescopes the absurdity of man in all his foolish, petty preoccupations, and the total effect is simultaneously ingenious, biting, and charming. But the satire grows mordant in Book II, the eye mercilessly microscopic, and Gulliver, now a dwarf, on the basis of his own evidence, is found along with his kind "to be the most pernicious race of little vermin that Nature ever suffered to crawl upon the earth," by the King of the Brobdingnagians. The emphasis is now principally on the moral nature of man, and disgust pervades the conclusions. The miniature charm of the Lilliputians has been replaced by a large indignation.

That indignation reaches savage proportions in Book IV. But between Books II and IV stands Book III, a kind of major digression which, for whatever exigencies, breaks the perfection of the form of *Gulliver's Travels* as a whole. In themselves, too, these series of fragments that constitute Book III lack range and force. The first, the voyage to Leputa, topical in its satire of English exploitation of the Irish in the flying island and of the Newtonian mathematics, is most inventive. The voyage to Balnibarbi, particularly in the Academy of Lagado, is direct and undisguised satire of the Royal Society. The new criticism, literary and historical, is the object of satire of the third voyage; the voyage to Glubbdubdrib. Only the fourth, the voyage to Luggnagg, in its dismaying depiction of the immortal Struldbrugs, achieves depth and force in a profound disillusion. So much for your immortality, Swift seems to be saying, it would be a catastrophe and a show. Although the frame of reference of these voyages in Book III is not dissimilar to that of *Tale of a Tub,* these *jeux* never rise above themselves into the realm of satire. Nevertheless, they do provide a pause, a kind of breather, between the intensity of Book II and the intensity of Book IV of *Gulliver's Travels*.

Upon Book IV of *Gulliver's Travels* the problem of the interpretation of the whole centers. What exactly did Swift mean to tell us in Book IV? And this question has been approached with a greater than academic intensity for two hundreds years, for upon the answer rests Swift's ultimate answer as to the nature and destiny of man. Almost immediately upon Swift's death (the book was greeted with acclaim upon publication), a long history of invective against Book IV began, which reached its climax in an outraged self-righteousness and rejection by the nineteenth century. Witness Thackeray, who found Swift "a monster gibbering shrieks and gnashing imprecations against mankind—tearing down all shreds of modesty, past all sense of manliness and shame; filthy in word, filthy in thought, furious, raging, obscene." But beyond his impropriety, it is Swift's apparent misanthropy that has disturbed his critics. Did Swift, who so often teetered on the edge of misanthropy, finally succumb to it in Book IV? The criticism of our own century has been considerably more temperate and searching in answering this question, though a great diversity of opinion still continues to rage.

First of all, it would be well to remember that in *Gulliver's Travels* we are in the presence of a satire, not a sermon, that Gulliver is not Swift but a persona, and that satire operates as metaphor or scheme. In that scheme, then, it becomes necessary to come to terms with the working symbols, the Houyhnhnms and the Yahoos as they represent the extremes of Swift's fable, and to watch the operation of the wit as it weaves between and mediates the love and hate that they respectively represent. Of the Yahoos, the reprehensible, disgusting, excremental beasts of Swift's fable, we know considerably more than we know of the more negatively developed Houyhnhnms. But it is safe to assume that by and large they represent passion and reason, respectively. It is how Swift intends us to construe this passion and reason that constitutes the problem.

Some modern critics have found the Houyhnhnms in their passionless perfection only little more acceptable than the Yahoos in their abandoned bestiality. They have seen in the Houyhnhnms a generally colorless, unattractive, or untenable Reason that marks Swift's battle against a rising tide of optimism, benevolence, and Deism, precisely as he battled them in his sermons; some critics have gone so far as to see in the Houyhnhnms a direct attack against Bolingbroke's defense of Deism. Other critics, stressing the Christian element in *Gulliver's Travels,* have turned the book into a kind of sermon in which the Yahoos represent the unclean, odious, and fallen flesh of man, and the Houyhnhnms the pride of rationalist man unguided by divine revelation, a defense of Augustinian Christianity against Deism. Thus the answer lies neither in Houyhnhnm nor Yahoo, but in Don Pedro, the satiric norm.

Perhaps a more fruitful approach lies in equating Swift's satiric metaphor with the time-honored metaphor of the universe as a great chain of being in which the various forms of creation are encompassed in the separate links of the chain which stretches from God to the least considerable speck of the created universe. In this chain, man, occupying a middle link between angel and beast, partakes of the qualities of both, at his highest potential a little less than angel, at his lowest a little more than beast. Subvert the chain, displace the links, and "heark what discord follows!" The beast, acting at his highest potential, seems to become superior, or at least acts as though he were superior, to man; the horse (Houyhnhnm) becomes a reasonable creature, man (Yahoo) becomes a bestial one.

However, having accepted Swift's metaphor, we are obliged to keep it intact; we cannot proceed to change the terms and read *Gulliver's Travels* allegorically, to turn it into another *Pilgrim's Progress*. We cannot ask ourselves whether, because we recognize the rational perfection of the Houyhnhnms, we would therefore be willing to have our children reared communally like the Houyhnhnms' foals. The satiric system once drawn operates only within its enclosed system; the alternatives, which are by no means literalistic, are between passion and reason, very real alternatives for Swift and his contemporaries. Yahoo man only figuratively throws around excrement; Houyhnhnm man only figuratively always retains his equanimity. There is, furthermore, a mock-heroic quality about *Gulliver's Travels* as there is about all Swift's satires.

It is important, too, to remember Swift's habit of commenting ironically upon his own metaphor, winking at the reader in the process of his horseplay, like Martin's nonsense for all that he stands for Protestantism in *Tale of a Tub*. So it is with the perfect Houyhnhnms: their name on the page orthographically looking the way a horse's whinny sounds, a snort of dubeity exactly equivalent to the wink of an eye, *Hmn, Hmn*. Nor is the snort entirely comic; it has its pathetic overtones, too.

And it is with a snort of both comic and pathetic relief that we follow Gulliver back to England, where he finds it necessary to retire to the stench of the stable as respite from the stink of his wife and children. Don Pedro, the good man, begins the modulation back to the world of reality. The metaphor is resolved. The *reductio ad absurdum* has encompassed a *reductio ad perfectem*.

Nor is there any need to minimize the savagery of the attack in Book IV, for all our recognition of the operation of the fable. The savage Yahoos are indeed a savage condemnation of mankind, revolting to the strongest sensibility. The very scheme of *Gulliver's Travels* is a set of savage alternatives; and the resolution, by any system, is scarcely optimistic. The Gulliver of the end of Book IV is not calculated to fill one with complacency; he is scarcely Swift, but he is extremely uncomfortable; he has enjoyed the benefits of a revelation he is ill-equipped to digest. Rejecting the Yahoos and rejected by the Houyhnhnms, he is left suspended in a middle state; like man's middle state between the angels and the beasts, it is, by definition, an anomalous one. If this is misanthropy, we can only make the most of it.

The temptation to tidy up Swift's life and works into neat systems is strong; it is probably just as misguided. In the final analysis the key to understanding him is his moral intensity; it is also the measure of his greatness.

VOLUME III.

Of the AUTHOR's

WORKS.

CONTAINING,

TRAVELS

INTO SEVERAL

Remote Nations of the WORLD.

In Four PARTS, viz.

I. A Voyage to LIL-
LIPUT.

II. A Voyage to BROB-
DINGNAG.

III. A Voyage to LA-

PUTA, BALNIBARBI,
LUGGNAGG, GLUBB-
DUBDRIB and JAPAN.

IV. A Voyage to the
COUNTRY of the
HOUYHNHNMS.

By *LEMUEL GULLIVER*, first a Surgeon,
and then a CAPTAIN of several SHIPS.

——— Retroq;
Vulgus abhorret ab his.

In this Impreſſion ſeveral Errors in the *London* and *Dublin*
Editions are corrected.

DUBLIN:

Printed by and for GEORGE FAULKNER, Printer
and Bookſeller, in *Eſſex-Street*, oppoſite to the
Bridge. MDCCXXXV.

The text used in this edition is substantially that of the 1735 edition; the punctuation has been somewhat modified, and capitalization and italics have been made conformable to modern usage.

A LETTER FROM CAPT. GULLIVER
TO HIS COUSIN SYMPSON [1]

I hope you will be ready to own publicly, whenever you shall be called to it, that by your great and frequent urgency you prevailed on me to publish a very loose and uncorrect account of my travels; with direction to hire some young gentlemen of either university to put them in order, and correct the style, as my cousin Dampier [2] did by my advice, in his book called *A Voyage round the World*. But I do not remember I gave you power to consent, that any thing should be omitted, and much less that any thing should be inserted: therefore, as to the latter, I do here renounce every thing of that kind; particularly a paragraph about her Majesty the late Queen Anne, of most pious and glorious memory; although I did reverence and esteem her more than any of human species. But you, or your interpolator, ought to have considered, that as it was not my inclination, so was it not decent to praise any animal of our composition before my master Houyhnhnm; and besides, the fact was altogether false; for to my knowledge, being in England during some part of her Majesty's reign, she did govern by a chief minister; nay, even by two successively; the first whereof was the Lord of Godolphin, and the second the Lord of Oxford; so that you have made me *say the thing that was not.* Likewise, in the account of the Academy of Projectors, and several passages of my discourse to my master Houyhnhnm, you have either omitted some material circumstances, or minced or changed them in such a manner, that I do hardly know mine own work. When I formerly hinted to you something of this in a letter, you were pleased to answer, that you were afraid of giving offence; that people in power were very watchful over the press, and apt not only to interpret, but to punish every thing which looked like an *innuendo* (as I think you called it). But pray, how could that which I spoke so many years ago, and at above five thousand leagues distance, in another reign, be applied to any of the Yahoos who now are said to govern the herd; especially at a time when I little thought on or feared the unhappiness of

[1] Cousin Sympson is a fiction, but the letter allows Swift to comment upon the circumstances of the publication of his work and to object to the inaccuracies of the first edition. As in *Tale of a Tub,* the use of prefatory apparatus is satirical of current practice.
[2] A popular explorer and writer of travel books (1652–1715).

living under them? Have not I the most reason to complain, when I see these very Yahoos carried by Houyhnhnms in a vehicle, as if these were brutes, and those the rational creatures? And, indeed, to avoid so monstrous and detestable a sight was one principal motive of my retirement hither.

Thus much I thought proper to tell you in relation to your self, and to the trust I reposed in you.

I do in the next place complain of my own great want of judgment, in being prevailed upon by the intreaties and false reasonings of you and some others, very much against mine own opinion, to suffer my travels to be published. Pray bring to your mind how often I desired you to consider, when you insisted on the motive of public good, that the Yahoos were a species of animals utterly incapable of amendment by precepts or examples, and so it hath proved; for instead of seeing a full stop put to all abuses and corruption, at least in this little island, as I had reason to expect: behold, after above six months' warning, I cannot learn that my book hath produced one single effect according to mine intentions: I desired you would let me know by a letter, when party and faction were extinguished; judges learned and upright; pleaders honest and modest, with some tincture of commonsense; and Smithfield [1] blazing with pyramids of law-books; the young nobility's education entirely changed; the physicians banished; the female Yahoos abounding in virtue, honour, truth and good sense; courts and levees of great ministers thoroughly weeded and swept; wit, merit and learning rewarded; all disgracers of the press in prose and verse condemned to eat nothing but their own cotton, and quench their thirst with their own ink. These, and a thousand other reformations, I firmly counted upon by your encouragement; as indeed they were plainly deducible from the precepts delivered in my book. And, it must be owned, that seven months were a sufficient time to correct every vice and folly to which Yahoos are subject, if their natures had been capable of the least disposition to virtue or wisdom; yet so far have you been from answering mine expectation in any of your letters, that on the contrary you are loading our carrier every week with libels, and keys, and reflections, and memoirs, and second parts; wherein I see myself accused of reflecting upon great states-folk; of degrading human nature (for so they have still the confidence to style it), and of abusing the female sex. I find likewise, that the writers of those bundles are not agreed among themselves; for some of them

[1] In London; notable as the site for the burning of heretics and martyrs.

will not allow me to be author of mine own travels; and others make me author of books to which I am wholly a stranger.[1]

I find likewise that your printer hath been so careless as to confound the times, and mistake the dates of my several voyages and returns, neither assigning the true year, or the true month, or day of the month; and I hear the original manuscript is all destroyed since the publication of my book. Neither have I any copy left; however, I have sent you some corrections, which you may insert if ever there should be a second edition: and yet I cannot stand to them, but shall leave that matter to my judicious and candid readers, to adjust it as they please.

I hear some our sea-Yahoos find fault with my sea-language, as not proper in many parts, nor now in use. I cannot help it. In my first voyages, while I was young, I was instructed by the oldest mariners, and learned to speak as they did. But I have since found that the sea-Yahoos are apt, like the land ones, to become new-fangled in their words; which the latter change every year, insomuch as I remember upon each return to mine own country, their old dialect was so altered that I could hardly understand the new. And I observe, when any Yahoo comes from London out of curiosity to visit me at mine own house, we neither of us are able to deliver our conceptions in a manner intelligible to the other.

If the censure of Yahoos could any way affect me, I should have great reason to complain that some of them are so bold as to think my book of travels a mere fiction out of mine own brain; and have gone so far as to drop hints that the Houyhnhnms and Yahoos have no more existence than the inhabitants of Utopia.

Indeed I must confess, that as to the people of Lilliput, Brobdingrag (for so the word should have been spelt, and not erroneously 'Brobdingnag') and Laputa, I have never yet heard of any Yahoo so presumptuous as to dispute their being, or the facts I have related concerning them; because the truth immediately strikes every reader with conviction. And is there less probability in my account of the Houyhnhnms or Yahoos, when it is manifest as to the latter, there are so many thousands even in this city, who only differ from their brother brutes in Houyhnhnmland, because they use a sort of a jabber, and do not go naked? I wrote for their amendment,

---

[1] Imitations, continuations, and "second parts" began to appear almost immediately after the publication of *Gulliver*. Swift, who almost always published anonymously, was often accused of the authorship of works in which he had no part.

and not their approbation. The united praise of the whole race would be of less consequence to me than the neighing of those two degenerate Houyhnhnms I keep in my stable; because from these, degenerate as they are, I still improve in some virtues, without any mixture of vice.

Do these miserable animals presume to think that I am so far degenerated as to defend my veracity? Yahoo as I am, it is well known through all Houyhnhnmland, that by the instructions and example of my illustrious master, I was able in the compass of two years (although I confess with the utmost difficulty) to remove that infernal habit of lying, shuffling, deceiving, and equivocating, so deeply rooted in the very souls of all my species, especially the Europeans.

I have other complaints to make upon this vexatious occasion; but I forbear troubling myself or you any further. I must freely confess, that since my last return, some corruptions of my Yahoo nature have revived in me by conversing with a few of your species, and particularly those of mine own family, by an unavoidable necessity; else I should never have attempted so absurd a project as that of reforming the Yahoo race in this kingdom; but I have now done with all such visionary schemes for ever.

April 2, 1727.

THE PUBLISHER TO THE READER.

The author of these *Travels*, Mr. Lemuel Gulliver,[1] is my ancient and intimate friend; there is likewise some relation between us by the mother's side. About three years ago Mr. Gulliver, growing weary of the concourse of curious people coming to him at his house in Redriff, made a small purchase of land, with a convenient house, near Newark in Nottinghamshire, his native country; where he now lives retired, yet in good esteem among his neighbours.

Although Mr. Gulliver was born in Nottinghamshire, where his father dwelt, yet I have heard him say, his family came from Oxfordshire; to confirm which, I have observed in the churchyard at Banbury, in that county, several tombs and monuments of the Gullivers.

Before he quitted Redriff, he left the custody of the following papers in my hands, with the liberty to dispose of them as I should think fit. I have carefully perused them three times: the style is very plain and simple; and the only fault I find is, that the author, after the manner of travellers, is a little too circumstantial. There is an air of truth apparent through the whole; and indeed, the author was so distinguished for his veracity, that it became a sort of proverb among his neighbours at Redriff, when any one affirmed a thing, to say, it was as true as if Mr. Gulliver had spoke it.

By the advice of several worthy persons, to whom, with the author's permission, I communicated these papers, I now venture to send them into the world, hoping they may be at least, for some time, a better entertainment to our young noblemen than the common scribbles of politics and party.

This volume would have been at least twice as large, if I had not made bold to strike out innumerable passages relating to the winds and tides, as well as to the variations and bearings in the several voyages; together with the minute descriptions of the management of the ship in storms, in the style of sailors: likewise the account of the longitudes and latitudes; wherein I have reason to apprehend that Mr. Gulliver may be a little dissatisfied: but I was resolved to fit the work as much as possible to the general capacity of readers. However, if my own ignorance in sea-affairs shall have led me to commit some mistakes, I alone am answerable for them: and if any traveller hath a curiosity to see the whole work at large,

[1] Note the implications of *gullible* inherent in the name *Gulliver*.

as it came from the hand of the author, I will be ready to gratify him.

As for any further particulars relating to the author, the reader will receive satisfaction from the first pages of the book.

RICHARD SYMPSON.

THE

CONTENTS.

PART I.

[A VOYAGE TO LILLIPUT]

PART II.

[A VOYAGE TO BROBDINGNAG]

PART III.

[A VOYAGE TO LAPUTA, BALNIBARBI, GLUBBDUBDRIB, LUGGNAGG, AND JAPAN]

PART IV.

[A VOYAGE TO THE COUNTRY OF THE HOUYHNHNMS]

TRAVELS.

PART I.

A VOYAGE TO LILLIPUT [1]

CHAPTER I.

The author gives some account of himself and family; his first inducements to travel. He is shipwrecked, and swims for his life, gets safe on shore in the country of Lilliput, is made a prisoner, and carried up the country.

MY father had a small estate in Nottinghamshire; I was the third of five sons. He sent me to Emanuel College in Cambridge at fourteen years old, where I resided three years, and applied my self close to my studies: but the charge of maintaining me (although I had a very scanty allowance) being too great for a narrow fortune, I was bound apprentice to Mr. James Bates, an eminent surgeon in London, with whom I continued four years; and my father now and then sending me small sums of money, I laid them out in learning navigation, and other parts of the mathematics, useful to those who intend to travel, as I always believed it would be some time or other my fortune to do. When I left Mr. Bates, I went down to my father; where, by the assistance of him and my uncle John, and some other relations I got forty pounds, and a promise of thirty pounds a year to maintain me at Leyden: [2] there I studied physic two years and seven months, knowing it would be useful in long voyages.

Soon after my return from Leyden, I was recommended, by my good master Mr. Bates, to be surgeon to the *Swallow*, Captain Abraham Pannell commander; with whom I continued three years and a half, making a voyage or two into the Levant, [3] and some other parts. When I came back, I resolved to settle in London, to which Mr. Bates, my master, encouraged me; and by him I was recommended to several patients. I

---

[1] *Lilliput* has been construed as a combination of *lilli* (*little,* according to the coded, private, "little language" of Swift's *Journal to Stella*) and *put* (connoting vice, as in the Spanish *puta* or Italian *putta;* see *Laputa* in Book III of *Gulliver*).

[2] A famous medical university in Holland; *physic* is *medicine.*

[3] The eastern Mediterranean.

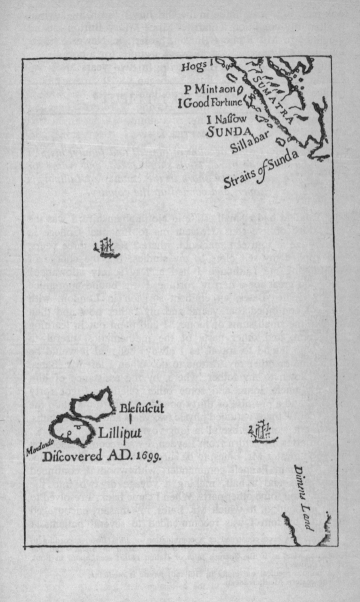

took part of a small house in the Old Jury,[1] and being advised to alter my condition, I married Mrs.[2] Mary Burton, second daughter to Mr. Edmond Burton, hosier, in Newgate Street, with whom I received four hundred pounds for a portion.

But, my good master Bates dying in two years after, and I having few friends, my business began to fail; for my conscience would not suffer me to imitate the bad practice of too many among my brethren. Having therefore consulted with my wife, and some of my acquaintance, I determined to go again to sea. I was surgeon successively in two ships, and made several voyages, for six years, to the East and West Indies, by which I got some addition to my fortune. My hours of leisure I spent in reading the best authors, ancient and modern, being always provided with a good number of books; and when I was ashore, in observing the manners and dispositions of the people, as well as learning their language, wherein I had a great facility by the strength of my memory.

The last of these voyages not proving very fortunate, I grew weary of the sea, and intended to stay at home with my wife and family. I removed from the Old Jury to Fetter Lane, and from thence to Wapping, hoping to get business among the sailors; but it would not turn to account. After three years' expectation that things would mend, I accepted an advantageous offer from Captain William Prichard, master of the *Antelope*, who was making a voyage to the South Sea. We set sail from Bristol, May 4th, 1699, and our voyage at first was very prosperous.

It would not be proper, for some reasons, to trouble the reader with the particulars of our adventures in those seas: let it suffice to inform him, that in our passage from thence to the East Indies, we were driven by a violent storm to the northwest of Van Diemen's Land.[3] By an observation, we found ourselves in the latitude of 30 degrees 2 minutes south. Twelve of our crew were dead by immoderate labour, and ill food; the rest were in a very weak condition. On the fifth of November, which was the beginning of summer in those parts, the weather being very hazy, the seamen spied a rock, within half a cable's length of the ship; but the wind was so strong, that we were driven directly upon it, and immediately split. Six of the crew, of whom I was one, having let down the boat into the sea, made a shift to get clear of the

---

[1] The old Jewry, the Jewish quarter in London in the Middle Ages.
[2] An abbreviation for Mistress, used for the married and unmarried women alike.
[3] Tasmania, supposedly part of the Australian mainland.

ship, and the rock. We rowed by my computation about three leagues, till we were able to work no longer, being already spent with labour while we were in the ship. We therefore trusted ourselves to the mercy of the waves; and in about half an hour the boat was overset by a sudden flurry from the north. What became of my companions in the boat, as well as of those who escaped on the rock, or were left in the vessel, I cannot tell; but conclude they were all lost. For my own part, I swam as fortune directed me, and was pushed forward by wind and tide. I often let my legs drop, and could feel no bottom: but when I was almost gone and able to struggle no longer, I found myself within my depth; and by this time the storm was much abated. The declivity was so small, that I walked near a mile before I got to the shore, which I conjectured was about eight o'clock in the evening. I then advanced forward near half a mile, but could not discover any sign of houses or inhabitants; at least I was in so weak a condition, that I did not observe them. I was extremely tired, and with that, and the heat of the weather, and about half a pint of brandy that I drank as I left the ship, I found myself much inclined to sleep. I lay down on the grass, which was very short and soft, where I slept sounder than ever I remember to have done in my life, and, as I reckoned, above nine hours; for when I awaked, it was just daylight. I attempted to rise, but was not able to stir: for as I happened to lie on my back, I found my arms and legs were strongly fastened on each side to the ground; and my hair, which was long and thick, tied down in the same manner. I likewise felt several slender ligatures across my body, from my armpits to my thighs. I could only look upwards; the sun began to grow hot, and the light offended my eyes. I heard a confused noise about me, but, in the posture I lay, could see nothing except the sky. In a little time I felt something alive moving on my left leg, which advancing gently forward over my breast, came almost up to my chin; when, bending my eyes downwards as much as I could, I perceived it to be a human creature not six inches high,[1] with a bow and arrow in his hands, and a quiver at his back. In the mean time, I felt at least forty more of the same kind (as I conjectured) following the first. I was in the utmost astonishment, and roared so loud, that they all ran back in a fright; and some of them, as I was afterwards told, were hurt with the falls they got by leaping from my sides upon the ground. However,

[1] Swift's scale in Lilliput is consistently 1 to 12; in Brobdingnag 12 to 1.

they soon returned, and one of them, who ventured so far as to get a full sight of my face, lifting up his hands and eyes by way of admiration, cried out in a shrill, but distinct voice, *Hekinah degul:* [1] the others repeated the same words several times, but I then knew not what they meant. I lay all this while, as the reader may believe, in great uneasiness: at length, struggling to get loose, I had the fortune to break the strings and wrench out the pegs that fastened my left arm to the ground; for, by lifing it up to my face, I discovered the methods they had taken to bind me; and, at the same time, with a violent pull, which gave me excessive pain, I a little loosened the strings that tied down my hair on the left side, so that I was just able to turn my head about two inches. But the creatures ran off a second time, before I could seize them; whereupon there was a great shout in a very shrill accent, and after it ceased, I heard one of them cry aloud, *Tolgo phonac;* when in an instant I felt above a hundred arrows discharged on my left hand, which pricked me like so many needles; and besides they shot another flight into the air, as we do bombs in Europe, whereof many, I suppose, fell on my body (though I felt them not) and some on my face, which I immediately covered with my left hand. When this shower of arrows was over, I fell a groaning with grief and pain, and then striving again to get loose, they discharged another volley larger than the first, and some of them attempted with spears to stick me in the sides; but, by good luck, I had on me a buff jerkin, which they could not pierce. I thought it the most prudent method to lie still, and my design was to continue so till night, when, my left hand being already loose, I could easily free myself: and as for the inhabitants, I had reason to believe I might be a match for the greatest armies they could bring against me, if they were all of the same size with him that I saw. But fortune disposed otherwise of me. When the people observed I was quiet, they discharged no more arrows: but by the noise increasing, I knew their numbers were greater; and about four yards from me, over-against my right ear, I heard a knocking for above an hour, like people at work; when, turning my head that way, as well as the pegs and strings would permit me; I saw a stage erected about a foot and a half from the ground,

[1] The languages of the countries of the Travels have been either discounted as deliberate nonsense, or insisted upon as careful, elaborate constructions, coded words based on a system of substitutions and anagrams like the system of the *Journal to Stella.* (For an explanation of the system, see Paul Odell Clark, "A Gulliver Dictionary," *Studies in Philology,* vol. 50 (1953), 592–624.) Clark reads *Hekinah degul* as *What in the devil.*

capable of holding four of the inhabitants, with two or three
ladders to mount it: from whence one of them, who seemed
to be a person of quality, made me a long speech, whereof I
understood not one syllable. But I should have mentioned,
that before the principal person began his oration, he cried out
three times, *Langro dehul san:* (these words and the former
were afterwards repeated and explained to me). Whereupon
immediatly about fifty of the inhabitants came, and cut the
strings that fastened the left side of my head, which gave me
the liberty of turning it to the right, and of observing the
person and gesture of him who was to speak. He appeared to
be of a middle age, and taller than any of the other three
who attended him, whereof one was a page who held up his
train, and seemed to be somewhat longer than my middle
finger; the other two stood one on each side to support him.
He acted every part of an orator, and I could observe many
periods of threatenings, and others of promises, pity and
kindness. I answered in a few words, but in the most submissive manner, lifting up my left hand and both eyes to the
sun, as calling him for a witness; and being almost famished
with hunger, having not eaten a morsel for some hours before I left the ship, I found the demands of nature so strong
upon me, that I could not forbear showing my impatience
(perhaps against the strict rules of decency) by putting
my finger frequently on my mouth to signify that I wanted
food. The *Hurgo* (for so they call a great lord, as I afterwards
learnt) understood me very well. He descended from the
stage, and commanded that several ladders should be applied to my sides, on which above an hundred of the inhabitants mounted, and walked towards my mouth, laden
with baskets full of meat, which had been provided and
sent thither by the King's orders upon the first intelligence
he received of me. I observed there was the flesh of several
animals, but could not distinguish them by the taste. There
were shoulders, legs and loins shaped like those of mutton,
and very well dressed, but smaller than the wings of a lark.
I ate them by two or three at a mouthful, and took three
loaves at a time, about the bigness of musket bullets. They
supplied me as fast as they could, showing a thousand marks
of wonder and astonishment at my bulk and appetite. I
then made another sign that I wanted drink. They found by
my eating that a small quantity would not suffice me; and
being a most ingenious people, they slung up with great
dexterity one of their largest hogsheads, then rolled it towards

my hand, and beat out the top; I drank it off at a draught, which I might well do, for it hardly held half a pint, and tasted like a small wine of Burgundy, but much more delicious. They brought me a second hogshead, which I drank in the same manner, and made signs for more, but they had none to give me. When I had performed these wonders, they shouted for joy, and danced upon my breast, repeating several times as they did at first, *Hekinah degul*. They made me a sign that I should throw down the two hogsheads, but first warned the people below to stand out of the way, crying aloud, *Borach mivola;* and when they saw the vessels in the air, there was an universal shout of *Hekinah degul*. I confess I was often tempted, while they were passing backwards and forwards on my body, to seize forty or fifty of the first that came in my reach, and dash them against the ground. But the remembrance of what I had felt, which probably might not be the worst they could do, and the promise of honour I made them, for so I interpreted my submissive behaviour, soon drove out those imaginations. Besides, I now considered my self as bound by the laws of hospitality to a people who had treated me with so much expense and magnificence. However, in my thoughts I could not sufficiently wonder at the intrepidity of these diminutive mortals, who durst venture to mount and walk on my body, while one of my hands was at liberty, without trembling at the very sight of so prodigious a creature as I must appear to them. After some time, when they observed that I made no more demands for meat, there appeared before me a person of high rank from his Imperial Majesty. His Excellency, having mounted on the small of my right leg, advanced forwards up to my face, with about a dozen of his retinue. And producing his credentials under the Signet Royal, which he applied close to my eyes, spoke about ten minutes, without any signs of anger, but with a kind of determinate resolution; often pointing forwards, which, as I afterwards found, was towards the capital city, about half a mile distant, whither it was agreed by his Majesty in council that I must be conveyed. I answered in few words, but to no purpose, and made a sign with my hand that was loose, putting it to the other (but over his Excellency's head, for fear of hurting him or his train) and then to my own head and body, to signify that I desired my liberty. It appeared that he understood me well enough, for he shook his head by way of disapprobation, and held his hand in a posture to show that I must be carried as a prisoner. However, he made other signs to let me understand that I should have meat and drink enough, and very good treatment. Whereupon I once more thought of attempting to break my bonds; but again, when I felt the smart of their arrows upon my face and hands, which were all in blisters, and many of the darts still sticking in them, and observing likewise that the number of my enemies encreased, I gave tokens to let them know that they might do with me what they pleased. Upon this the *Hurgo* and his train withdrew, with much civility and cheerful countenances. Soon after I heard a general shout, with frequent repetitions of the words, *Peplom selan,* and I felt great numbers of the people on my left side relaxing the cords to such a degree, that I was able to turn upon my right, and to ease myself with making water; which I very plentifully did, to the great astonishment of the people, who conjecturing by my motions what I was going to do, immediately opened to the right and left on that side to avoid the torrent which fell with such noise and violence from me. But before this, they had daubed my face and both my hands with a sort of ointment very pleasant to the smell, which in a few minutes removed all the smart of their arrows. These circumstances, added to the refreshment I had received by their victuals and drink, which were very nourishing, disposed me to sleep. I slept about eight hours, as I was afterwards assured; and it was no wonder, for the physicians, by the Emperor's order, had mingled a sleeping potion in the hogsheads of wine.

It seems that upon the first moment I was discovered sleeping on the ground after my landing, the Emperor had early notice of it by an express, and determined in council that I should be tied in the manner I have related (which was done in the night while I slept), that plenty of meat and drink should be sent me, and a machine prepared to carry me to the capital city.

This resolution perhaps may appear very bold and dangerous, and I am confident would not be imitated by any prince in Europe on the like occasion; however, in my opinion, it was extremely prudent as well as generous. For supposing these people had endeavoured to kill me with their spears and arrows while I was asleep, I should certainly have awaked with the first sense of smart, which might so far have roused my rage and strength, as to enable me to break the strings wherewith I was tied; after which, as they were not able to make resistance, so they could expect no mercy.

These people are most excellent mathematicians, and

arrived to a great perfection in mechanics by the countenance and encouragement of the Emperor, who is a renowned patron of learning. This prince hath several machines fixed on wheels, for the carriage of trees and other great weights. He often builds his largest men of war, whereof some are nine foot long, in the woods where the timber grows, and has them carried on these engines three or four hundred yards to the sea. Five hundred carpenters and engineers were immediately set at work to prepare the greatest engine they had. It was a frame of wood raised three inches from the ground, about seven foot long and four wide, moving upon twenty-two wheels. The shout I heard was upon the arrival of this engine,[1] which, it seems, set out in four hours after my landing. It was brought parallel to me as I lay. But the principal difficulty was to raise and place me in this vehicle. Eighty poles, each of one foot high, were erected for this purpose, and very strong cords of the bigness of packthread were fastened by hooks to many bandages, which the workmen had girt round my neck, my hands, my body, and my legs. Nine hundred of the strongest men were employed to draw up these cords by many pulleys fastened on the poles, and thus, in less than three hours, I was raised and slung into the engine, and there tied fast. All this I was told, for while the whole operation was performing, I lay in a profound sleep, by the force of that soporiferous medicine infused into my liquor. Fifteen hundred of the Emperor's largest horses, each about four inches and a half high, were employed to draw me towards the metropolis, which, as I said, was half a mile distant.

About four hours after we began our journey, I awaked by a very ridiculous accident; for, the carriage being stopped a while to adjust something that was out of order, two or three of the young natives had the curiosity to see how I looked when I was asleep; they climbed up into the engine, and advancing very softly to my face, one of them, an officer in the guards, put the sharp end of his half-pike a good way up into my left nostril, which tickled my nose like a straw, and made me sneeze violently: whereupon they stole off unperceived, and it was three weeks before I knew the cause of my awaking so suddenly. We made a long march the remaining part of the day, and rested at night with five hundred guards on each side of me, half with torches, and half with bows and arrows, ready to shoot me if I should

[1] A mechanical contrivance, or any machine.

offer to stir. The next morning at sunrise we continued our march, and arrived within two hundred yards of the city gates about noon. The Emperor and all his court came out to meet us, but his great officers would by no means suffer his Majesty to endanger his person by mounting on my body.

At the place where the carriage stopped, there stood an ancient temple, esteemed to be the largest in the whole kingdom, which having been polluted some years before by an unnatural murder, was, according to the zeal of those people, looked on as profane, and therefore had been applied to common use, and all the ornaments and furniture carried away. In this edifice it was determined I should lodge. The great gate fronting to the north was about four foot high, and almost two foot wide, through which I could easily creep. On each side of the gate was a small window not above six inches from the ground: into that on the left side, the King's smiths conveyed fourscore and eleven chains, like those that hang to a lady's watch in Europe, and almost as large, which were locked to my left leg with six and thirty padlocks. Over against this temple, on the other side of the great highway, at twenty foot distance, there was a turret at least five foot high. Here the Emperor ascended with many principal lords of his court, to have an opportunity of viewing me, as I was told, for I could not see them. It was reckoned that above an hundred thousand inhabitants came out of the town upon the same errand; and in spite of my guards, I believe there could not be fewer than ten thousand, at several times, who mounted upon my body by the help of ladders. But a proclamation was soon issued to forbid it upon pain of death. When the workmen found it was impossible for me to break loose, they cut all the strings that bound me; whereupon I rose up with as melancholy a disposition as ever I had in my life. But the noise and astonishment of the people at seeing me rise and walk are not to be expressed. The chains that held my left leg were about two yards long, and gave me not only the liberty of walking backwards and forwards in a semicircle; but, being fixed within four inches of the gate, allowed me to creep in, and lie at my full length in the temple.

Chapter II.

The Emperor of Lilliput, attended by several of the nobility, comes to see the author in his confinement. The Emperor's person and habit described. Learned men appointed to teach the author their language. He gains favour by his mild disposition. His pockets are searched, and his sword and pistols taken from him.

When I found myself on my feet, I looked about me, and must confess I never beheld a more entertaining prospect. The country round appeared like a continued garden, and the inclosed fields, which were generally forty foot square, resembled so many beds of flowers. These fields were intermingled with woods of half a stang,[1] and the tallest trees, as I could judge, appeared to be seven foot high. I viewed the town on my left hand, which looked like the painted scene of a city in a theatre.

I had been for some hours extremely pressed by the necessities of nature; which was no wonder, it being almost two days since I had last disburthened myself. I was under great difficulties between urgency and shame. The best expedient I could think on, was to creep into my house, which I accordingly did; and shutting the gate after me, I went as far as the length of my chain would suffer, and discharged my body of that uneasy load. But this was the only time I was ever guilty of so uncleanly an action; for which I cannot but hope the candid reader will give some allowance, after he hath maturely and impartially considered my case, and the distress I was in. From this time my constant practice was, as soon as I rose, to perform that business in open air, at the full extent of my chain, and due care was taken every morning before company came, that the offensive matter should be carried off in wheelbarrows by two servants appointed for that purpose. I would not have dwelt so long upon a circumstance, that perhaps at first sight may appear not very momentous, if I had not thought it necessary to justify my character in point of cleanliness to the world; which I am told some of my maligners have been pleased, upon this and other occasions, to call in question.

When this adventure was at an end, I came back out of my

[1] A quarter of an acre.

house, having occasion for fresh air. The Emperor [1] was already descended from the tower, and advancing on horseback towards me, which had like to have cost him dear; for the beast, although very well trained, yet wholly unused to such a sight, which appeared as if a mountain moved before him, reared up on his hinder feet: but that prince, who is an excellent horseman, kept his seat, until his attendants ran in, and held the bridle, while his Majesty had time to dismount. When he alighted, he surveyed me round with great admiration, but kept beyond the length of my chains. He ordered his cooks and butlers, who were already prepared, to give me victuals and drink, which they pushed forward in a sort of vehicles upon wheels until I could reach them. I took these vehicles, and soon emptied them all; twenty of them were filled with meat, and ten with liquor; each of the former afforded me two or three good mouthfuls, and I emptied the liquor of ten vessels, which was contained in earthen vials, into one vehicle, drinking it off at a draught; and so I did with the rest. The Empress, and young princes of the blood, of both sexes, attended by many ladies, sat at some distance in their chairs; but upon the accident that happened to the Emperor's horse, they alighted, and came nearer his person, which I am now going to describe. He is taller, by almost the breadth of my nail, than any of his court, which alone is enough to strike an awe into the beholders. His features are strong and masculine, with an Austrian lip and arched nose, his complexion olive, his countenance erect, his body and limbs well proportioned, all his motions graceful, and his deportment majestic. He was then past his prime, being twenty-eight years and three quarters old, of which he had reigned about seven, in great felicity, and generally victorious. For the better convenience of beholding him, I lay on my side, so that my face was parallel to his, and he stood but three yards off: however, I have had him since many times in my hand, and therefore cannot be deceived in the description. His dress was very plain and simple, and the fashion of it between the Asiatic and the

---

[1] The political allegory in *Gulliver's Travels* is inescapable and extensive, if not always consistent or even decipherable. Generally speaking, Book I is satirical of events in England from 1708-1715, the end of the reign of Queen Anne and the beginning of the reign of George I, particularly of the period when Oxford (Robert Harley) and Bolingbroke (Henry St. John) between them led the Tory government, and to both of whom Swift, as spokesman for the Tories, was loyal both personally and politically. Thus Gulliver is sometimes Oxford, sometimes Bolingbroke. (See Arthur E. Case, "Personal and Political Satire in *Gulliver's Travels*," in *Four Essays on Gulliver's Travels*, 1945, 1958, pp. 69-96. I am primarily indebted to Case for the annotations on the political satire which follow.)

European; but he had on his head a light helmet of gold, adorned with jewels, and a plume on the crest. He held his sword drawn in his hand, to defend himself, if I should happen to break loose; it was almost three inches long, the hilt and scabbard were gold enriched with diamonds. His voice was shrill, but very clear and articulate, and I could distinctly hear it when I stood up. The ladies and courtiers were all most magnificently clad, so that the spot they stood upon seemed to resemble a petticoat spread on the ground, embroidered with figures of gold and silver. His Imperial Majesty spoke often to me, and I returned answers, but neither of us could understand a syllable. There were several of his priests and lawyers present (as I conjectured by their habits) who were commanded to address themselves to me, and I spoke to them in as many languages as I had the least smattering of, which were High and Low Dutch, Latin, French, Spanish, Italian, and Lingua Franca,[1] but all to no purpose. After about two hours the court retired, and I was left with a strong guard, to prevent the impertinence, and probably the malice of the rabble, who were very impatient to crowd about me as near as they durst; and some of them had the impudence to shoot their arrows at me as I sat on the ground by the door of my house, whereof one very narrowly missed my left eye. But the colonel ordered six of the ringleaders to be seized, and thought no punishment so proper as to deliver them bound into my hands, which some of his soldiers accordingly did, pushing them forwards with the butt-ends of their pikes into my reach; I took them all in my right hand, put five of them into my coat-pocket, and as to the sixth, I made a countenance as if I would eat him alive. The poor man squalled terribly, and the colonel and his officers were in much pain, especially when they saw me take out my penknife: but I soon put them out of fear; for, looking mildly, and immediately cutting the strings he was bound with, I set him gently on the ground, and away he ran. I treated the rest in the same manner, taking them one by one out of my pocket, and I observed both the soldiers and people were highly obliged at this mark of my clemency, which was represented very much to my advantage at court.

Towards night I got with some difficulty into my house, where I lay on the ground, and continued to do so about a fortnight; during which time the Emperor gave orders to have

---

[1] High Dutch is German; Low Dutch is Dutch; Lingua Franca is a polyglot jargon spoken in the ports of the Mediterranean.

a bed prepared for me. Six hundred beds of the common
measure were brought in carriages, and worked up in my
house; an hundred and fifty of their beds sewn together made
up the breadth and length, and these were four double, which
however kept me but very indifferently from the hardness of
the floor, that was of smooth stone. By the same computation
they provided me with sheets, blankets, and coverlets, tolerable
enough for one who had been so long enured to hardships
as I.

As the news of my arrival spread through the kingdom, it
brought prodigious numbers of rich, idle, and curious people
to see me; so that the villages were almost emptied, and
great neglect of tillage and household affairs must have
ensued, if his Imperial Majesty had not provided by several
proclamations and orders of state against this inconveniency.
He directed that those who had already beheld me should
return home, and not presume to come within fifty yards of
my house without license from court; whereby the secretaries
of state got considerable fees.

In the mean time, the Emperor held frequent councils to debate what course should be taken with me; and I was afterwards assured by a particular friend, a person of great quality,
who was as much in the secret as any, that the court was under
many difficulties concerning me. They apprehended my breaking loose, that my diet would be very expensive, and might
cause a famine. Sometimes they determined to starve me, or
at least to shoot me in the face and hands with poisoned
arrows, which would soon dispatch me: but again they considered, that the stench of so large a carcase might produce
a plague in the metropolis, and probably spread through the
whole kingdom. In the midst of these consultations, several
officers of the army went to the door of the great council-
chamber; and two of them being admitted, gave an account
of my behaviour to the six criminals above-mentioned, which
made so favourable an impression in the breast of his Majesty
and the whole board in my behalf, that an imperial commission was issued out, obliging all the villages nine hundred yards
round the city to deliver in every morning six beeves, forty
sheep, and other victuals for my sustenance; together with a
proportionable quantity of bread, and wine, and other liquors:
for the due payment of which his Majesty gave assignments
upon his treasury. For this prince lives chiefly upon his own
demesnes, seldom except upon great occasions raising any sub-
sidies upon his subjects, who are bound to attend him in his

wars at their own expense. An establishment was also made of six hundred persons to be my domestics, who had board-wages allowed for their maintenance, and tents built for them very conveniently on each side of my door. It was likewise ordered, that three hundred tailors should make me a suit of clothes after the fashion of the country: that six of his Majesty's greatest scholars should be employed to instruct me in their language: and, lastly, that the Emperor's horses, and those of the nobility and troops of guards, should be exercised in my sight, to accustom themselves to me. All these orders were duly put in execution, and in about three weeks I made a great progress in learning their language; during which time the Emperor frequently honoured me with his visits, and was pleased to assist my masters in teaching me. We began already to converse together in some sort; and the first words I learnt were to express my desire that he would please to give me my liberty, which I every day repeated on my knees. His answer, as I could apprehend was, that this must be a work of time, not to be thought on without the advice of his council, and that first I must *lumos kelmin pesso desmar lon emposo;* that is swear a peace with him and his kingdom. However, that I should be used with all kindness, and he advised me to acquire, by my patience, and discreet behaviour, the good opinion of himself and his subjects. He desired I would not take it ill, if he gave orders to certain proper officers to search me; for probably I might carry about me several weapons, which must needs be dangerous things, if they answered the bulk of so pro-digious a person. I said, his Majesty should be satisfied, for I was ready to strip myself, and turn up my pockets before him. This I delivered part in words, and part in signs. He replied, that by the laws of the kingdom I must be searched by two of his officers; that he knew this could not be done without my consent and assistance; that he had so good an opinion of my generosity and justice, as to trust their persons in my hands: that whatever they took from me should be returned when I left the country, or paid for at the rate which I would set upon them. I took up the two officers in my hands, put them first into my coat-pockets, and then into every other pocket about me, except my two fobs, and another secret pocket which I had no mind should be searched, wherein I had some little neces-saries of no consequence to any but myself. In one of my fobs there was a silver watch, and in the other a small quantity of gold in a purse. These gentlemen, having pen, ink and paper about them, made an exact inventory of every thing they saw;

and when they had done, desired I would set them down, that they might deliver it to the Emperor. This inventory I afterwards translated into English, and is word for word as follows.[1]

Imprimis, In the right coat-pocket of the Great Man-Mountain (for so I interpret the words *Quinbus Flestrin*) after the strictest search, we found only one great piece of coarse cloth, large enough to be a foot-cloth for your Majesty's chief room of state. In the left pocket, we saw a huge silver chest, with a cover of the same metal, which we, the searchers, were not able to lift. We desired it should be opened, and one of us, stepping into it, found himself up to the midleg in a sort of dust, some part whereof, flying up to our faces, set us both a sneezing for several times together. In his right waistcoat-pocket, we found a prodigious bundle of white thin substances, folded one over another, about the bigness of three men, tied with a strong cable, and marked with black figures; which we humbly conceive to be writings, every letter almost half as large as the palm of our hands. In the left, there was a sort of engine, from the back of which were extended twenty long poles, resembling the palisados before your Majesty's court; wherewith we conjecture the Man-Mountain combs his head, for we did not always trouble him with questions, because we found it a great difficulty to make him understand us. In the large pocket on the right side of his middle cover (so I translate the word *ranfu-lo,* by which they meant my breeches) we saw a hollow pillar of iron, about the length of a man, fastened to a strong piece of timber, larger than the pillar; and upon one side of the pillar were huge pieces of iron sticking out, cut into strange figures, which we know not what to make of. In the left pocket, another engine of the same kind. In the smaller pocket on the right side, were several round flat pieces of white and red metal, of different bulk; some of the white, which seemed to be silver, were so large and heavy, that my comrade and I could hardly lift them. In the left pocket were two black pillars irregularly shaped: we could not, without difficulty, reach the top of them as we stood at the bottom of his pocket. One of them was covered, and seemed all of a piece; but at the upper end of the other, there appeared a white round substance, about twice the bigness of our heads.

[1] The search of Gulliver and its results may be taken to refer to the activities of the Committee of Secrecy of 1715, a Whig group investigating the recently defeated Tory ministry, particularly Oxford and Bolingbroke; they were accused of Jacobitism and of favoring France in the Treaty of Utrecht which brought the War of the Spanish Succession, in which France and England were the primary contenders, to a close.

Within each of these were inclosed a prodigious plate of steel; which, by our orders, we obliged him to show us, because we apprehended they might be dangerous engines. He took them out of their cases, and told us, that in his own country his practice was to shave his beard with one of these, and to cut his meat with the other. There were two pockets which we could not enter: these he called his fobs; they were two large slits cut into the top of his middle cover, but squeezed close by the pressure of his belly. Out of the right fob hung a great silver chain, with a wonderful kind of engine at the bottom. We directed him to draw out whatever was at the end of that chain; which appeared to be a globe, half silver, and half of some transparent metal: for on the transparent side we saw certain strange figures circularly drawn, and thought we could touch them, until we found our fingers stopped with that lucid substance. He put this engine to our ears, which made an incessant noise like that of a watermill. And we conjecture it is either some unknown animal, or the god that he worships: but we are more inclined to the latter opinion, because he assured us (if we understood him right, for he expressed himself very imperfectly), that he seldom did any thing without consulting it. He called it his oracle, and said it pointed out the time for every action of his life. From the left fob he took out a net almost large enough for a fisherman, but contrived to open and shut like a purse, and served him for the same use: we found therein several massy pieces of yellow metal, which, if they be of real gold, must be of immense value.

Having thus, in obedience to your Majesty's commands, diligently searched all his pockets, we observed a girdle about his waist made of the hide of some prodigious animal; from which, on the left side, hung a sword of the length of five men, and on the right, a bag or pouch divided into two cells, each cell capable of holding three of your Majesty's subjects. In one of these cells were several globes or balls of a most ponderous metal, about the bigness of our heads, and required a strong hand to lift them: the other cell contained a heap of certain black grains, but of no great bulk or weight, for we could hold above fifty of them in the palms of our hands.

This is an exact inventory of what we found about the body of the Man-Mountain, who used us with great civility, and due respect to your Majesty's commission. Signed and sealed on the fourth day of the eighty-ninth moon of your Majesty's auspicious reign.

CLEFREN FRELOCK, MARSI FRELOCK.

When this inventory was read over to the Emperor, he directed me to deliver up the several particulars. He first called for my scimitar, which I took out, scabbard and all. In the mean time he ordered three thousand of his choicest troops (who then attended him) to surround me at a distance, with their bows and arrows just ready to discharge: but I did not observe it, for my eyes were wholly fixed upon his Majesty. He then desired me to draw my scimitar, which, although it had got some rust by the sea-water, was in most parts exceeding bright. I did so, and immediately all the troops gave a shout between terror and surprise; for the sun shone clear, and the reflection dazzled their eyes as I waved the scimitar to and fro in my hand. His Majesty, who is a most magnanimous prince, was less daunted than I could expect; he ordered me to return it into the scabbard, and cast it on the ground as gently as I could, about six foot from the end of my chain. The next thing he demanded was one of the hollow iron pillars, by which he meant my pocket-pistols. I drew it out, and at his desire, as well as I could, expressed to him the use of it; and charging it only with powder, which by the closeness of my pouch happened to escape wetting in the sea (an inconvenience that all prudent mariners take special care to provide against), I first cautioned the Emperor not to be afraid, and then I let it off in the air. The astonishment here was much greater than at the sight of my scimitar. Hundreds fell down as if they had been struck dead; and even the Emperor, although he stood his ground, could not recover himself in some time. I delivered up both my pistols in the same manner as I had done my scimitar, and then my pouch of powder and bullets; begging him that the former might be kept from the fire, for it would kindle with the smallest spark, and blow up his imperial palace into the air. I likewise delivered up my watch, which the Emperor was very curious to see, and commanded two of his tallest yeomen of the guards to bear it on a pole upon their shoulders, as draymen in England do a barrel of ale. He was amazed at the continual noise it made, and the motion of the minute-hand, which he could easily discern; for their sight is much more acute than ours: he asked the opinions of his learned men about him, which were various and remote, as the reader may well imagine without my repeating; although indeed I could not very perfectly understand them. I then gave up my silver and copper money, my purse with nine large pieces of gold, and some smaller ones; my knife and razor, my comb and silver snuff-box, my handkerchief and journal book.

My scimitar, pistols, and pouch, were conveyed in carriages to his Majesty's stores; but the rest of my goods were returned me.

I had, as I before observed, one private pocket which escaped their search, wherein there was a pair of spectacles (which I sometimes use for the weakness of my eyes), a pocket perspective, and several other little conveniences; which, being of no consequence to the Emperor, I did not think my self bound in honour to discover, and I apprehended they might be lost or spoiled if I ventured them out of my possession.

Chapter III.

The author diverts the Emperor and his nobility of both sexes in a very uncommon manner. The diversions of the court of Lilliput described. The author hath his liberty granted him upon certain conditions.

My gentleness and good behaviour had gained so far on the Emperor and his court, and indeed upon the army and people in general, that I began to conceive hopes of getting my liberty in a short time. I took all possible methods to cultivate this favourable disposition. The natives came by degrees to be less apprehensive of any danger from me. I would sometimes lie down, and let five or six of them dance on my hand. And at last the boys and girls would venture to come and play at hide and seek in my hair. I had now made a good progress in understanding and speaking their language. The Emperor had a mind one day to entertain me with several of the country shows, wherein they exceed all nations I have known, both for dexterity and magnificence. I was diverted with none so much as that of the rope-dancers, performed upon a slender white thread, extended about two foot, and twelve inches from the ground. Upon which I shall desire liberty, with the reader's patience, to enlarge a little.

This diversion is only practised by those persons who are candidates for great employments, and high favour, at court. They are trained in this art from their youth, and are not always of noble birth, or liberal education. When a great office is vacant either by death or disgrace (which often happens) five or six of those candidates petition the Emperor to entertain his Majesty and the court with a dance on the rope, and whoever jumps the highest without falling, succeeds in the office. Very often the chief ministers themselves are commanded to show their skill, and to convince the Emperor that they have not lost their faculty. Flimnap,[1] the Treasurer, is allowed to cut a caper on the strait rope, at least an inch higher than any other lord in the whole empire. I have seen him do the summerset several times together upon a trencher fixed on the rope, which is no thicker than a common packthread in England. My friend Reldresal,[2] principal Secretary for Private Affairs, is, in my opinion, if I am not partial, the second after the Treasurer; the rest of the great officers are much upon a par.

These diversions are often attended with fatal accidents, whereof great numbers are on record. I my self have seen two or three candidates break a limb. But the danger is much greater when the ministers themselves are commanded to show their dexterity; for by contending to excel themselves and their fellows, they strain so far, that there is hardly one of them who hath not received a fall, and some of them two or three. I was assured that a year or two before my arrival, Flimnap would have infallibly broke his neck, if one of the King's cushions, that accidentally lay on the ground, had not weakened the force of his fall.[3]

There is likewise another diversion, which is only shown before the Emperor and Empress, and first minister, upon particular occasions. The Emperor lays on a table three fine silken threads of six inches long. One is blue, the other red, and the third green.[4] These threads are proposed as prizes for those persons whom the Emperor hath a mind to distinguish by a peculiar mark of his favour. The ceremony is performed in his Majesty's great chamber of state, where the candidates are to undergo a trial of dexterity very different from the former, and such as I have not observed the least resemblance of in any other country of the old or the new world. The Emperor holds a stick [5] in his hands, both ends parallel to the horizon, while the candidates, advancing one by one, sometimes leap over the stick, sometimes creep under it backwards and forwards several times, according as the stick is advanced or depressed.

1 Sir Robert Walpole, leader of the Whigs and chairman of the Committee of Secrecy.
2 Possibly the Duke of Marlborough, who was a Whig; possibly the Earl of Stanhope, Walpole's successor.
3 The Duchess of Kendall, mistress of George I, who helped restore Walpole in 1721 after his fall.
4 The Orders of the Garter, Bath, and Thistle.
5 When Walpole received the Order of the Bath in 1725, Swift wrote: "And he who'll leap over a stick for the King, / Is qualified best for a dog on a string."

Sometimes the Emperor holds one end of the stick, and his first minister the other; sometimes the minister has it entirely to himself. Whoever performs his part with most agility, and holds out the longest in leaping and creeping, is rewarded with the blue-coloured silk; the red is given to the next, and the green to the third, which they all wear girt twice round about the middle; and you see few great persons about this court who are not adorned with one of these girdles.

The horses of the army, and those of the royal stables, having been daily led before me, were no longer shy, but would come up to my very feet without starting. The riders would leap them over my hand as I held it on the ground, and one of the Emperor's huntsmen, upon a large courser, took my foot, shoe and all; which was indeed a prodigious leap. I had the good fortune to divert the Emperor one day, after a very extraordinary manner. I desired he would order several sticks of two foot high, and the thickness of an ordinary cane, to be brought me; whereupon his Majesty commanded the master of his woods to give directions accordingly, and the next morning six woodmen arrived with as many carriages, drawn by eight horses to each. I took nine of these sticks, and fixing them firmly in the ground in a quadrangular figure, two foot and a half square, I took four other sticks, and tied them parallel at each corner, about two foot from the ground; then I fastened my handkerchief to the nine sticks that stood erect, and extended it on all sides till it was as tight as the top of a drum; and the four parallel sticks, rising about five inches higher than the handkerchief, served as ledges on each side. When I had finished my work, I desired the Emperor to let a troop of his best horse, twenty-four in number, come and exercise upon this plain. His Majesty approved of the proposal, and I took them up one by one in my hands, ready mounted and armed, with the proper officers to exercise them. As soon as they got into order, they divided into two parties, performed mock skirmishes, discharged blunt arrows, drew their swords, fled and pursued, attacked and retired, and in short discovered the best military discipline I ever beheld. The parallel sticks secured them and their horses from falling over the stage; and the Emperor was so much delighted, that he ordered this entertainment to be repeated several days, and once was pleased to be lifted up, and give the word of command; and, with great difficulty, persuaded even the Empress her self to let me hold her in her close chair within two yards of the stage, from whence she was able to take a full view of the whole performance. It was my good fortune that no ill accident happened in these entertainments; only once a fiery horse that belonged to one of the captains pawing with his hoof struck a hole in my handkerchief, and his foot slipping, he overthrew his rider and himself; but I immediately relieved them both, for covering the hole with one hand, I set down the troop with the other, in the same manner as I took them up. The horse that fell was strained in the left shoulder, but the rider got no hurt, and I repaired my handkerchief as well as I could; however, I would not trust to the strength of it any more in such dangerous enterprises.

About two or three days before I was set at liberty, as I was entertaining the court with these kinds of feats, there arrived an express to inform his Majesty that some of his subjects, riding near the place where I was first taken up, had seen a great black substance lying on the ground, very oddly shaped, extending its edges round as wide as his Majesty's, bedchamber, and rising up in the middle as high as a man: that it was no living creature, as they at first apprehended, for it lay on the grass without motion, and some of them had walked round it several times; that by mounting upon each others' shoulders, they had got to the top, which was flat and even, and stamping upon it they found it was hollow within; that they humbly conceived it might be something belonging to the Man-Mountain, and if his Majesty pleased, they would undertake to bring it with only five horses. I presently knew what they meant, and was glad at heart to receive this intelligence. It seems upon my first reaching the shore after our shipwreck, I was in such confusion, that before I came to the place where I went to sleep, my hat, which I had fastened with a string to my head while I was rowing, and had stuck on all the time I was swimming, fell off after I came to land; the string, as I conjecture, breaking by some accident which I never observed, but thought my hat had been lost at sea. I intreated his Imperial Majesty to give orders it might be brought to me as soon as possible, describing to him the use and the nature of it: and the next day the waggoners arrived with it, but not in a very good condition; they had bored two holes in the brim, within an inch and half of the edge, and fastened two hooks in the holes; these hooks were tied by a long cord to the harness, and thus my hat was dragged along for above half an English mile: but the ground in that country being extremely smooth and level, it received less damage than I expected.

Two days after this adventure, the Emperor having ordered

that part of his army which quarters in and about his metropolis to be in a readiness, took a fancy of diverting himself in a very singular manner. He desired I would stand like a colossus, with my legs as far asunder as I conveniently could. He then commanded his general (who was an old experienced leader, and a great patron of mine) to draw up the troops in close order, and march them under me, the foot by twenty-four in a breast, and the horse by sixteen, with drums beating, colours flying, and pikes advanced. This body consisted of three thousand foot, and a thousand horse. His Majesty gave orders, upon pain of death, that every soldier in his march should observe the strictest decency with regard to my person; which, however, could not prevent some of the younger officers from turning up their eyes as they passed under me. And, to confess the truth, my breeches were at that time in so ill a condition, that they afforded some opportunities for laughter and admiration.

I had sent so many memorials and petitions for my liberty, that his Majesty at length mentioned the matter, first in the cabinet, and then in a full council; where it was opposed by none, except Skyresh Bolgolam,[1] who was pleased, without any provocation, to be my mortal enemy. But it was carried against him by the whole board, and confirmed by the Emperor. That minister was *Galbet,* or Admiral of the Realm, very much in his master's confidence, and a person well versed in affairs, but of a morose and sour complexion. However, he was at length persuaded to comply; but prevailed that the articles and conditions upon which I should be set free, and to which I must swear, should be drawn up by himself. These articles were brought to me by Skyresh Bolgolam in person, attended by two under-secretaries, and several persons of distinction. After they were read, I was demanded to swear to the performance of them; first in the manner of my own country, and afterwards in the method prescribed by their laws; which was to hold my right foot in my left hand, to place the middle finger of my right hand on the crown of my head, and my thumb on the tip of my right ear. But because the reader may perhaps be curious to have some idea of the style and manner of expression peculiar to that people, as well as to know the articles upon which I recovered my liberty, I have made a translation of the whole instrument word for word, as near as I was able, which I here offer to the public.

[1] The Earl of Nottingham, First Lord of the Admiralty from 1680–1684, who, as an independent Tory, tried to restrict the power of the Tory ministry in 1711.

GOLBASTO MOMAREN EVLAME GURDILO SHEFIN MULLY ULLY GUE, most mighty Emperor of Lilliput, delight and terror of the universe, whose dominions extend five thousand blustrugs (about twelve miles in circumference) to the extremities of the globe; monarch of all monarchs, taller than the sons of men; whose feet press down to the center, and whose head strikes against the sun; at whose nod the princes of the earth shake their knees; pleasant as the spring, comfortable as the summer, fruitful as autumn, dreadful as winter. His most sublime Majesty proposeth to the Man-Mountain, lately arrived at our celestial dominion, the following articles, which by a solemn oath he shall be obliged to perform.

First, The Man-Mountain shall not depart from our dominions, without our licence under our great seal.

Secondly, He shall not presume to come into our metropolis, without our express order; at which time the inhabitants shall have two hours warning to keep within their doors.

Thirdly, The said Man-Mountain shall confine his walks to our principal high roads, and not offer to walk or lie down in a meadow or field of corn.

Fourthly, As he walks the said roads, he shall take the utmost care not to trample upon the bodies of any of our loving subjects, their horses, or carriages, nor take any of our said subjects into his hands, without their own consent.

Fifthly, If an express require extraordinary dispatch, the Man-Mountain shall be obliged to carry in his pocket the messenger and horse a six days' journey once in every moon, and return the said messenger back (if so required) safe to our Imperial Presence.

Sixthly, He shall be our ally against our enemies in the island of Blefuscu,[1] and do his utmost to destroy their fleet, which is now preparing to invade us.

Seventhly, That the said Man-Mountain shall, at his times of leisure, be aiding and assisting to our workmen, in helping to raise certain great stones, towards covering the wall of the principal park, and other our royal buildings.

Eighthly, That the said Man-Mountain shall, in two moons' time, deliver in an exact survey of the circumference of our dominions by a computation of his own paces round the coast.

Lastly, That upon his solemn oath to observe all the above

[1] France.

articles, the said Man-Mountain shall have a daily allowance of meat and drink sufficient for the support of 1728
of our subjects, with free access to our Royal Person, and
other marks of our favour. Given at our palace at Belfa-
borac the twelfth day of the ninety-first moon of our reign.

I swore and subscribed to these articles with great cheerful-
ness and content, although some of them were not so honourable as I could have wished; which proceeded wholly from the
malice of Skyresh Bolgolam the High Admiral: whereupon my
chains were immediately unlocked, and I was at full liberty;
the Emperor himself in person did me the honour to be by at
the whole ceremony. I made my acknowledgements by pros-
trating myself at his Majesty's feet: but he commanded me to
rise; and after many gracious expressions, which, to avoid the
censure of vanity, I shall not repeat, he added, that he hoped
I should prove a useful servant, and well deserve all the favours he had already conferred upon me, or might do for the
future.

The reader may please to observe, that in the last article for
the recovery of my liberty, the Emperor stipulates to allow me
a quantity of meat and drink sufficient for the support of 1728
Lilliputians. Some time after, asking a friend at court how
they came to fix on that determinate number, he told me, that
his Majesty's mathematicians, having taken the height of my
body by the help of a quadrant, and finding it to exceed theirs
in the proportion of twelve to one, they concluded from the
similarity of their bodies, that mine must contain at least 1728
of theirs, and consequently would require as much food as was
necessary to support that number of Lilliputians. By which the
reader may conceive an idea of the ingenuity of that people,
as well as the prudent and exact œconomy of so great a prince.

Chapter IV.

*Mildendo,[1] the metropolis of Lilliput, described, together with
the Emperor's palace. A conversation between the author
and a principal secretary, concerning the affairs of that
empire; the author's offers to serve the Emperor in his
wars.*

The first request I made after I had obtained my liberty,
was, that I might have licence to see Mildendo, the metrop-

[1] London.

olis; which the Emperor easily granted me, but with a special charge to do no hurt, either to the inhabitants or their houses. The people had notice by proclamation of my design to visit the town. The wall which encompassed it is two foot and an half high, and at least eleven inches broad, so that a coach and horses may be driven very safely round it; and it is flanked with strong towers at ten foot distance. I stepped over the great western gate, and passed very gently, and sideling through the two principal streets, only in my short waistcoat, for fear of damaging the roofs and eaves of the houses with the skirts of my coat. I walked with the utmost circumspection, to avoid treading on any stragglers, who might remain in the streets, although the orders were very strict, that all people should keep in their houses, at their own peril. The garret windows and tops of houses were so crowded with spectators, that I thought in all my travels I had not seen a more populous place. The city is an exact square, each side of the wall being five hundred foot long. The two great streets, which run cross and divide it into four quarters, are five foot wide. The lanes and alleys, which I could not enter, but only viewed them as I passed, are from twelve to eighteen inches. The town is capable of holding five hundred thousand souls. The houses are from three to five stories. The shops and markets well provided.

The Emperor's palace is in the center of the city, where the two great streets meet. It is inclosed by a wall of two foot high, and twenty foot distant from the buildings. I had his Majesty's permission to step over this wall; and the space being so wide between that and the palace, I could easily view it on every side. The outward court is a square of forty foot, and includes two other courts: in the inmost are the royal apartments, which I was very desirous to see, but found it extremely difficult; for the great gates, from one square into another, were but eighteen inches high and seven inches wide. Now the buildings of the outer court were at least five foot high, and it was impossible for me to stride over them without infinite damage to the pile, although the walls were strongly built of hewn stone, and four inches thick. At the same time the Emperor had a great desire that I should see the magnificence of his palace; but this I was not able to do till three days after, which I spent in cutting down with my knife some of the largest trees in the royal park, about an hundred yards distant from the city. Of these trees I made two stools, each about three foot high, and strong enough to bear my weight. The people having received notice a second time, I went again through the city to the palace, with my two stools in my hands. When I came to the side of the outer court, I stood upon one stool, and took the other in my hand: this I lifted over the roof, and gently set it down on the space between the first and second court, which was eight foot wide. I then stepped over the buildings very conveniently from one stool to the other, and drew up the first after me with a hooked stick. By this contrivance I got into the inmost court; and lying down upon my side, I applied my face to the windows of the middle stories, which were left open on purpose, and discovered the most splendid apartments that can be imagined. There I saw the Empress, and the young princes in their several lodgings, with their chief attendants about them. Her Imperial Majesty was pleased to smile very graciously upon me, and gave me out of the window her hand to kiss.

But I shall not anticipate the reader with farther descriptions of this kind, because I reserve them for a greater work, which is now almost ready for the press; containing a general description of this empire, from its first erection, through a long series of princes, with a particular account of their wars and politics, laws, learning, and religion; their plants and animals, their peculiar manners and customs, with other matters very curious and useful; my chief design at present being only to relate such events and transactions as happened to the public, or to myself, during a residence of about nine months in that empire.

One morning, about a fortnight after I had obtained my liberty, Reldresal, Principal Secretary (as they style him) of Private Affairs, came to my house, attended only by one servant. He ordered his coach to wait at a distance, and desired I would give him an hour's audience; which I readily consented to, on account of his quality, and personal merits, as well as of the many good offices he had done me during my solicitations at court. I offered to lie down, that he might the more conveniently reach my ear; but he chose rather to let me hold him in my hand during our conversation. He began with compliments on my liberty; said he might pretend to some merit in it; but, however, added, that if it had not been for the present situation of things at court, perhaps I might not have obtained it so soon. For, said he, as flourishing a condition as we appear to be in to foreigners, we labour under two mighty evils; a violent faction at home, and the danger of an invasion by a most potent enemy from abroad. As to the first, you are to understand, that for above seventy moons past, there have been two struggling parties in the empire, under the names of *Tramecksan* and *Slamecksan*,[1] from the high and low heels on their shoes, by which they distinguish themselves.

It is alleged indeed, that the high heels are most agreeable to our ancient constitution: but however this be, his Majesty hath determined to make use of only low heels in the administration of the government and all offices in the gift of the crown, as you cannot but observe; and particularly, that his Majesty's imperial heels are lower at least by a *drurr* than any of his court,[2] (*drurr* is a measure about the fourteenth part of an inch). The animosities between these two parties run so high, that they will neither eat nor drink, nor talk with each other. We compute the *Tramecksan,* or High-Heels, to exceed us in number; but the power is wholly on our side. We apprehend his Imperial Highness, the heir to the crown, to have some tendency towards the High-Heels; at least we can plainly discover one of his heels higher than the other, which gives him a hobble in his gait. Now, in the midst of these intestine disquiets, we are threatened with an invasion from the island of Blefuscu, which is the other great empire of the universe, almost as large and powerful as this of his Majesty.[3] For as to what we have heard you affirm, that there are other kingdoms and states in the world, inhabited by human creatures as large as yourself, our philosophers are in much doubt, and would rather conjecture that you dropped from the moon, or one of the stars; because it is certain, that an hundred mortals of your bulk would, in a short time, destroy all the fruits and cattle of his Majesty's dominions. Besides, our histories of six thousand moons make no mention of any other regions, than the two great empires of Lilliput and Blefuscu. Which two mighty powers have, as I was going to tell you, been engaged in a most obstinate war for six and thirty moons past. It began upon the following occasion. It is allowed on all hands, that the primitive way of breaking eggs before we eat them, was upon the larger end: but his present Majesty's grandfather, while he was a boy, going to eat an egg, and breaking it according to the ancient practice, happened to cut one of his fingers. Whereupon the Emperor his father published an edict, com-

---

[1] The Tory (High Church) and the Whig (Low Church) political parties.
[2] George I was more sympathetic to the Whigs than to the Tories; the Prince of Wales, later George II, hobnobbed with the discontented of both parties. *Drurr* has been read as *dirt* or *turd*.
[3] France and England were the main contenders in the War of the Spanish Succession (1701–1713).

manding all his subjects, upon great penalties, to break the smaller end of their eggs. The people so highly resented this law, that our histories tell us there have been six rebellions raised on that account; wherein one emperor lost his life, and another his crown.[1] These civil commotions were constantly fomented by the monarchs of Blefuscu; and when they were quelled, the exiles always fled for refuge to that empire. It is computed, that eleven thousand persons have, at several times, suffered death, rather than submit to break their eggs at the smaller end. Many hundred large volumes have been published upon this controversy: but the books of the Big-Endians have been long forbidden, and the whole party rendered incapable by law of holding employments.[2] During the course of these troubles, the emperors of Blefuscu did frequently expostulate by their ambassadors, accusing us of making a schism in religion, by offending against a fundamental doctrine of our great prophet Lustrog, in the fifty-fourth chapter of the *Brundecral* (which is their Alcoran). This, however, is thought to be a mere strain upon the text: for the words are these; *That all true believers shall break their eggs at the convenient end:* and which is the convenient end, seems, in my humble opinion, to be left to every man's conscience, or at least in the power of the chief magistrate to determine. Now the Big-Endian exiles have found so much credit in the Emperor of Blefuscu's court, and so much private assistance and encouragement from their party here at home, that a bloody war hath been carried on between the two empires for six and thirty moons with various success; during which time we have lost forty capital ships, and a much greater number of smaller vessels, together with thirty thousand of our best seamen and soldiers; and the damage received by the enemy is reckoned to be somewhat greater than ours. However, they have now equipped a numerous fleet, and are just preparing to make a descent upon us; and his Imperial Majesty, placing great confidence in your valour and strength, hath commanded me to lay this account of his affairs before you.

I desired the Secretary to present my humble duty to the Emperor, and to let him know, that I thought it would not become me, who was a foreigner, to interfere with parties; but

[1] The Big Endians and the Little Endians represent the Catholics and Protestants; they also suggest England and Rome in the reign of King Henry VIII; the controversy between the two also suggests the Civil Wars in England in the 1640s when Charles I was beheaded and James II exiled.

[2] The Test Act, which Swift militantly supported, demanding the repudiation of belief in Transubstantiation, was used to prevent public employment of Catholics and Nonconformists.

I was ready, with the hazard of my life, to defend his person and state against all invaders.

CHAPTER V

The author by an extraordinary stratagem prevents an invasion. A high title of honour is conferred upon him. Ambassadors arrive from the Emperor of Blefuscu, and sue for peace. The Empress's apartment on fire by an accident; the author instrumental in saving the rest of the palace.

The empire of Blefuscu is an island situated to the north-northeast side of Lilliput, from whence it is parted only by a channel of eight hundred yards wide. I had not yet seen it, and upon this notice of an intended invasion, I avoided appearing on that side of the coast, for fear of being discovered by some of the enemy ships, who had received no intelligence of me, all intercourse between the two empires having been strictly forbidden during the war, upon pain of death, and an embargo laid by our Emperor upon all vessels whatsoever. I communicated to his Majesty a project I had formed of seizing the enemy's whole fleet; which, as our scouts assured us, lay at anchor in the harbour ready to sail with the first fair wind. I consulted the most experienced seamen upon the depth of the channel, which they had often plumbed; who told me, that in the middle at high water it was seventy *glumgluffs* deep, which is about six foot of European measure; and the rest of it fifty *glumgluffs* at most. I walked to the northeast coast over against Blefuscu; where, lying down behind a hillock, I took out my small pocket perspective-glass, and viewed the enemy's fleet at anchor, consisting of about fifty men of war, and a great number of transports: I then came back to my house, and gave order (for which I had a warrant) for a great quantity of the strongest cable and bars of iron. The cable was about as thick as packthread, and the bars of the length and size of a knitting-needle. I trebled the cable to make it stronger, and for the same reason I twisted three of the iron bars together, bending the extremities into a hook. Having thus fixed fifty hooks to as many cables, I went back to the northeast coast, and putting off my coat, shoes, and stockings, walked into the sea in my leathern jerkin, about half an hour before high water. I waded with what haste I could, and swam in the middle about thirty yards until I felt ground; I arrived at the fleet in less than half an hour. The enemy was so frighted when they saw me, that they leaped out of their ships, and swam to shore, where there could not be fewer than thirty thousand souls. I then took my tackling, and fastening a hook to the hole at the prow of each, I tied all the cords together at the end. While I was thus employed, the enemy discharged several thousand arrows, many of which stuck in my hands and face; and besides the excessive smart, gave me much disturbance in my work. My greatest apprehension was for my eyes, which I should have infallibly lost, if I had not suddenly thought of an expedient. I kept among other little necessaries a pair of spectacles in a private pocket, which, as I observed before, had escaped the Emperor's searchers. These I took out and fastened as strongly as I could upon my nose, and thus armed went on boldly with my work in spite of the enemy's arrows, many of which struck against the glasses of my spectacles, but without any other effect, further than a little to discompose them. I had now fastened all the hooks, and taking the knot in my hand, began to pull; but not a ship would stir, for they were all too fast held by their anchors, so that the boldest part of my enterprise remained. I therefore let go the cord, and leaving the hooks fixed to the ships, I resolutely cut with my knife the cables that fastened the anchors, receiving above two hundred shots in my face and hands; then I took up the knotted end of the cables to which my hooks were tied, and with great ease drew fifty of the enemy's largest men-of-war after me.

The Blefuscudians, who had not the least imagination of what I intended, were at first confounded with astonishment. They had seen me cut the cables, and thought my design was only to let the ships run adrift, or fall foul on each other: but when they perceived the whole fleet moving in order, and saw me pulling at the end, they set up such a scream of grief and despair, that it is almost impossible to describe or conceive. When I had got out of danger, I stopped a while to pick out the arrows that stuck in my hands and face, and rubbed on some of the same ointment that was given me at my first arrival, as I have formerly mentioned. I then took off my spectacles, and waiting about an hour until the tide was a little fallen, I waded through the middle with my cargo, and arrived safe at the royal port of Lilliput.[1]

[1] The Whigs claimed that the Treaty of Utrecht which ended the war of the Spanish Succession, as negotiated by the Tories, was favorable to France rather than to England; the Tories claimed that they had safeguarded the naval supremacy of England; hence Gulliver's safe arrival with the fleet of Blefuscu.

The Emperor and his whole court stood on the shore expecting the issue of this great adventure. They saw the ships move forward in a large half-moon, but could not discern me, who was up to my breast in water. When I advanced to the middle of the channel, they were yet more in pain, because I was under water to my neck. The Emperor concluded me to be drowned, and that the enemy's fleet was approaching in a hostile manner: but he was soon eased of his fears; for, the channel growing shallower every step I made, I came in a short time within hearing, and holding up the end of the cable by which the fleet was fastened, I cried in a loud voice, *Long live the most puissant Emperor of Lilliput!* This great prince received me at my landing with all possible encomiums, and created me a *Nardac* upon the spot, which is the highest title of honour among them.

His Majesty desired I would take some other opportunity of bringing all the rest of his enemy's ships into his ports. And so unmeasurable is the ambition of princes, that he seemed to think of nothing less than reducing the whole empire of Blefuscu into a province, and governing it by a viceroy; of destroying the Big-Endian exiles, and compelling that people to break the smaller end of their eggs, by which he would remain sole monarch of the whole world. But I endeavoured to divert him from this design, by many arguments drawn from the topics of policy as well as justice: and I plainly protested, that I would never be an instrument of bringing a free and brave people into slavery. And when the matter was debated in council, the wisest part of the ministry were of my opinion.

This open bold declaration of mine was so opposite to the schemes and politics of his Imperial Majesty, that he could never forgive me; he mentioned it in a very artful manner at council, where I was told that some of the wisest appeared, at least, by their silence, to be of my opinion; but others, who were my secret enemies, could not forbear some expressions, which by a side-wind reflected on me. And from this time began an intrigue between his Majesty and a junto of ministers maliciously bent against me, which broke out in less than two months, and had like to have ended in my utter destruction. Of so little weight are the greatest services to princes, when put into the balance with a refusal to gratify their passions.

About three weeks after this exploit, there arrived a solemn embassy from Blefuscu, with humble offers of a peace; which was soon concluded upon conditions very advantageous to our Emperor, wherewith I shall not trouble the reader. There were six ambassadors, with a train of about five hundred persons, and their entry was very magnificent, suitable to the grandeur of their master, and the importance of their business. When their treaty was finished, wherein I did them several good offices by the credit I now had, or at least appeared to have at court, their Excellencies, who were privately told how much I had been their friend, made me a visit in form. They began with many compliments upon my valour and generosity, invited me to that kingdom in the Emperor their master's name, and desired me to show them some proofs of my prodigious strength, of which they had heard so many wonders; wherein I readily obliged them, but shall not interrupt the reader with the particulars.

When I had for some time entertained their Excellencies to their infinite satisfaction and surprise, I desired they would do me the honour to present my most humble respects to the Emperor their master, the renown of whose virtues had so justly filled the whole world with admiration, and whose royal person I resolved to attend before I returned to my own country. Accordingly, the next time I had the honour to see our Emperor, I desired his general licence to wait on the Blefuscudian monarch, which he was pleased to grant me, as I could plainly perceive, in a very cold manner; but could not guess the reason, till I had a whisper from a certain person, that Flimnap and Bolgolam had represented my intercourse with those ambassadors as a mark of disaffection, from which I am sure my heart was wholly free.[1] And this was the first time I began to conceive some imperfect idea of courts and ministers.

It is to be observed, that these ambassadors spoke to me by an interpreter, the languages of both empires differing as much from each other as any two in Europe, and each nation priding itself upon the antiquity, beauty, and energy of their own tongues, with an avowed contempt for that of their neighbour; yet our Emperor, standing upon the advantage he had got by the seizure of their fleet, obliged them to deliver their credentials, and make their speech, in the Lilliputian tongue. And it must be confessed, that from the great intercourse of trade and commerce between both realms, from the continual reception of exiles, which is mutual among them, and from the custom in each empire to send their young nobility and richer gentry to the other, in order to polish themselves, by seeing the world, and understanding men and manners; there are few

---

[1] Bolingbroke's visit, as Secretary of State, to France was regarded with suspicion, and he was accused of Jacobite sympathies. See Chapter VII, in which Gulliver is accused of treason.

persons of distinction, or merchants, or seamen, who dwell in the maritime parts, but what can hold conversation in both tongues; as I found some weeks after, when I went to pay my respects to the Emperor of Blefuscu, which in the midst of great misfortunes, through the malice of my enemies, proved a very happy adventure to me, as I shall relate in its proper place.

The reader may remember, that when I signed those articles upon which I recovered my liberty, there were some which I disliked upon account of their being too servile, neither could any thing but an extreme necessity have forced me to submit. But being now a *Nardac*, of the highest rank in that empire, such offices were looked upon as below my dignity, and the Emperor (to do him justice) never once mentioned them to me. However, it was not long before I had an opportunity of doing his Majesty, at least as I then thought, a most signal service. I was alarmed at midnight with the cries of many hundred people at my door; by which being suddenly awaked, I was in some kind of terror. I heard the word *burglum* repeated incessantly: several of the Emperor's court, making their way through the crowd, intreated me to come immediately to the palace, where her Imperial Majesty's apartment was on fire, by the carelessness of a maid of honour, who fell asleep while she was reading a romance. I got up in an instant; and orders being given to clear the way before me, and it being likewise a moonshine night, I made a shift to get to the palace without trampling on any of the people. I found they had already applied ladders to the walls of the apartment, and were well provided with buckets, but the water was at some distance. These buckets were about the size of a large thimble, and the poor people supplied me with them as fast as they could; but the flame was so violent that they did little good. I might easily have stifled it with my coat, which I unfortunately left behind me for haste, and came away only in my leathern jerkin. The case seemed wholly desperate and deplorable, and this magnificent palace would have infallibly been burnt down to the ground, if, by a presence of mind, unusual to me, I had not suddenly thought of an expedient. I had the evening before drank plentifully of a most delicious wine, called *glimigrim* (the Blefuscudians call it *flunec*, but ours is esteemed the better sort), which is very diuretic. By the luckiest chance in the world, I had not discharged myself of any part of it. The heat I had contracted by coming very near the flames, and by my labouring to quench them, made the wine begin to operate by urine; which I voided in such a quantity, and applied so well to the proper places, that in three minutes the fire was wholly extinguished, and the rest of that noble pile, which had cost so many ages in erecting, preserved from destruction.

It was now daylight, and I returned to my house, without waiting to congratulate with the Emperor; because, although I had done a very eminent piece of service, yet I could not tell how his Majesty might resent the manner by which I had performed it: for, by the fundamental laws of the realm, it is capital in any person, of what quality soever, to make water within the precincts of the palace. But I was a little comforted by a message from his Majesty, that he would give orders to the Grand Justiciary for passing my pardon in form; which, however, I could not obtain. And I was privately assured, that the Empress, conceiving the greatest abhorrence of what I had done, removed to the most distant side of the court, firmly resolved that those buildings should never be repaired for her use; and, in the presence of her chief confidents, could not forbear vowing revenge.[1]

CHAPTER VI.[2]

Of the inhabitants of Lilliput; their learning, laws and customs; the manner of educating their children. The author's way of living in that country. His vindication of a great lady.

Although I intend to leave the description of this empire to a particular treatise, yet in the mean time I am content to gratify the curious reader with some general ideas. As the common size of the natives is somewhat under six inches, so there is an exact proportion in all other animals, as well as plants and trees: for instance, the tallest horses and oxen are between four and five inches in height, the sheep an inch

[1] This episode, the extinguishing of the palace fire, has usually been taken to refer to Swift's publication of *Tale of a Tub*, which offended Queen Anne, who then refused to grant him a bishopric. More recently it has been read as the Treaty of Utrecht, which stopped the war but by questionable means. The Tories began negotiations with France without the approval of England's allies in the War and against the opposition of the Whigs. Oxford, who led the negotiations, was also vulnerable on personal grounds, in his gross and indecorous behavior to Queen Anne, who dismissed him.

[2] The Utopian elements in Chapter VI, somewhat inconsistent with the satirical depiction of Lilliput in the preceding and following sections, have been accounted for by the early inception of Book I, when Swift was writing as a Scriblerian.

and a half, more or less; their geese about the bigness of a sparrow, and so the several gradations downwards, till you come to the smallest, which, to my sight, were almost invisible; but nature hath adapted the eyes of the Lilliputians to all objects proper for their view: they see with great exactness, but at no great distance. And to show the sharpness of their sight towards objects that are near, I have been much pleased with observing a cook pulling a lark, which was not so large as a common fly; and a young girl threading an invisible needle with invisible silk. Their tallest trees are about seven foot high; I mean some of those in the great royal park, the tops whereof I could but just reach with my fist clenched. The other vegetables are in the same proportion; but this I leave to the reader's imagination.

I shall say but little at present of their learning, which for many ages hath flourished in all its branches among them, but their manner of writing is very peculiar, being neither from the left to the right, like the European; nor from the right to the left, like the Arabians; nor from up to down, like the Chinese; nor from down to up, like the Cascagians,[1] but aslant from one corner of the paper to the other, like ladies in England.

They bury their dead with their heads directly downwards, because they hold an opinion that in eleven thousand moons they are all to rise again, in which period the earth (which they conceive to be flat) will turn upside down, and by this means they shall, at their resurrection, be found ready standing on their feet. The learned among them confess the absurdity of this doctrine, but the practice still continues, in compliance to the vulgar.

There are some laws and customs in this empire very peculiar, and if they were not so directly contrary to those of my own dear country, I should be tempted to say a little in their justification. It is only to be wished, that they were as well executed. The first I shall mention relates to informers. All crimes against the state are punished here with the utmost severity; but if the person accused maketh his innocence plainly to appear upon his trial, the accuser is immediately put to an ignominious death; and out of his goods or lands, the innocent person is quadruply recompensed for the loss of his time, for the danger he underwent, for the hardship of his imprisonment, and for all the charges he hath been at

---

[1] Possibly a coded word for *Cantonese*, who, like the Chinese, would be, according to contemporary opinion, writing oddly.

in making his defence. Or, if that fund be deficient, it is largely supplied by the crown. The Emperor doth also confer on him some public mark of his favour, and proclamation is made of his innocence through the whole city.

They look upon fraud as a greater crime than theft, and therefore seldom fail to punish it with death; for they allege, that care and vigilance, with a very common understanding, may preserve a man's goods from thieves, but honesty hath no fence against superior cunning; and since it is necessary that there should be a perpetual intercourse of buying and selling, and dealing upon credit, where fraud is permitted and connived at, or hath no law to punish it, the honest dealer is always undone, and the knave gets the advantage. I remember when I was once interceding with the King for a criminal who had wronged his master of a great sum of money, which he had received by order, and ran away with; and happening to tell his Majesty, by way of extenuation, that it was only a breach of trust; the Emperor thought it monstrous in me to offer, as a defence, the greatest aggravation of the crime: and truly I had little to say in return, farther than the common answer, that different nations had different customs; for, I confess, I was heartily ashamed.

Although we usually call reward and punishment the two hinges upon which all government turns, yet I could never observe this maxim to be put in practice by any nation except that of Lilliput. Whoever can there bring sufficient proof that he hath strictly observed the laws of his country for seventy-three moons, hath a claim to certain privileges, according to his quality and condition of life, with a proportionable sum of money out of a fund appropriated for that use: he likewise acquires the title of *Snilpall*, or *Legal*, which is added to his name, but doth not descend to his posterity. And these people thought it a prodigious defect of policy among us, when I told them that our laws were enforced only by penalties, without any mention of reward. It is upon this account that the image of Justice, in their courts of judicature, is formed with six eyes, two before, as many behind, and on each side one, to signify circumspection; with a bag of gold open in her right hand, and a sword sheathed in her left, to show she is more disposed to reward than to punish.

In choosing persons for all employments, they have more regard to good morals than to great abilities; for, since government is necessary to mankind, they believe that the common size of human understandings is fitted to some station or other; and that Providence never intended to make the management of public affairs a mystery, to be comprehended only by a few persons of sublime genius, of which there seldom are three born in an age: but they suppose truth, justice, temperance, and the like, to be in every man's power; the practice of which virtues, assisted by experience and a good intention, would qualify any man for the service of his country, except where a course of study is required. But they thought the want of moral virtues was so far from being supplied by superior endowments of the minds, that employments could never be put into such dangerous hands as those of persons so qualified; and at least, that the mistakes committed by ignorance in a virtuous disposition would never be of such fatal consequence to the public weal, as the practices of a man whose inclinations led him to be corrupt, and had great abilities to manage, to multiply, and defend his corruptions.

In like manner, the disbelief of a divine Providence renders a man uncapable of holding any public station; for since kings avow themselves to be deputies of Providence, the Lilliputians think nothing can be more absurd than for a prince to employ such men as disown the authority under which he acts.

In relating these and the following laws, I would only be understood to mean the original institutions, and not the most scandalous corruptions into which these people are fallen by the degenerate nature of man. For as to that infamous practice of acquiring great employments by dancing on the ropes, or badges of favour and distinction by leaping over sticks, and creeping under them, the reader is to observe, that they were first introduced by the grandfather [1] of the Emperor now reigning, and grew to the present height by the gradual increase of party and faction.

Ingratitude is among them a capital crime, as we read it to have been in some other countries; for they reason thus, that whoever makes ill returns to his benefactor, must needs be a common enemy to the rest of mankind, from whom he hath received no obligation, and therefore such a man is not fit to live.

Their notions relating to the duties of parents and children differ extremely from ours. For, since the conjunction of male and female is founded upon the great law of nature, in order to propagate and continue the species, the Lilliputians will

---

[1] James I was given to prolific bestowal of titles, new and old, to swell the treasury.

needs have it, that men and women are joined together like other animals, by the motives of concupiscence; and that their tenderness towards their young proceeds from the like natural principle: for which reason they will never allow, that a child is under any obligation to his father for begetting him, or to his mother for bringing him into the world; which, considering the miseries of human life, was neither a benefit in itself, nor intended so by his parents, whose thoughts in their love-encounters were otherwise employed. Upon these, and the like reasonings, their opinion is, that parents are the last of all others to be trusted with the education of their own children: and therefore they have in every town public nurseries, where all parents, except cottagers and labourers, are obliged to send their infants of both sexes to be reared and educated when they come to the age of twenty moons, at which time they are supposed to have some rudiments of docility. These schools are of several kinds, suited to different qualities, and to both sexes. They have certain professors well skilled in preparing children for such a condition of life as befits the rank of their parents, and their own capacities as well as inclinations. I shall first say something of the male nurseries, and then of the female.

The nurseries for males of noble or eminent birth are provided with grave and learned professors, and their several deputies. The clothes and food of the children are plain and simple. They are bred up in the principles of honour, justice, courage, modesty, clemency, religion, and love of their country; they are always employed in some business, except in the times of eating and sleeping, which are very short, and two hours for diversions, consisting of bodily exercises. They are dressed by men until four years of age, and then are obliged to dress themselves, although their quality be ever so great; and the women attendants, who are aged proportionately to ours at fifty, perform only the most menial offices. They are never suffered to converse with servants, but go together in small or greater numbers to take their diversions, and always in the presence of a professor, or one of his deputies; whereby they avoid those early bad impressions of folly and vice to which our children are subject. Their parents are suffered to see them only twice a year; the visit is not to last above an hour; they are allowed to kiss the child at meeting and parting; but a professor, who always stands by on those occasions, will not suffer them to whisper, or use any fondling expressions, or bring any presents of toys, sweetmeats, and the like.

The pension from each family for the education and enter-tainment of a child, upon failure of due payment, is levied by the Emperor's officers.

The nurseries for children of ordinary gentlemen, merchants, traders, and handicrafts, are managed proportionably after the same manner; only those designed for trades are put out apprentices at seven years old, whereas those of persons of quality continue in their nurseries till fifteen, which answers to one and twenty with us: but the confinement is gradually lessened for the last three years.

In the female nurseries, the young girls of quality are edu-cated much like the males, only they are dressed by orderly servants of their own sex, but always in the presence of a professor or deputy, until they come to dress themselves, which is at five years old. And if it be found that these nurses ever presume to entertain the girls with frightful or foolish stories, or the common follies practiced by chamber-maids among us, they are publicly whipped thrice about the city, imprisoned for a year, and banished for life to the most desolate parts of the country. Thus the young ladies there are as much ashamed of being cowards and fools as the men, and despise all personal ornaments beyond decency and cleanli-ness; neither did I perceive any difference in their education, made by their difference of sex, only that the exercises of the females were not altogether so robust; and that some rules were given them relating to domestic life, and a smaller compass of learning was enjoined them: for their maxim is, that among people of quality, a wife should be always a reasonable and agreeable companion, because she cannot always be young. When the girls are twelve years old, which among them is the marriageable age, their parents or guardians take them home, with great expressions of gratitude to the professors, and seldom without tears of the young lady and her companions.

In the nurseries of females of the meaner sort, the children are instructed in all kinds of works proper for their sex, and their several degrees: those intended for apprentices are dismissed at seven years old, the rest are kept to eleven.

The meaner families who have children at these nurseries are obliged, besides their annual pension, which is as low as possible, to return to the steward of the nursery a small monthly share of their gettings, to be a portion for the child; and therefore all parents are limited in their expenses by the law. For the Lilliputians think nothing can be more unjust,

than that people, in subservience to their own appetites,
should bring children into the world, and leave the burthen
of supporting them on the public. As to persons of quality,
they give security to appropriate a certain sum for each child,
suitable to their condition; and these funds are always managed
with good husbandry, and the most exact justice.

The cottagers and labourers keep their children at home,
their business being only to till and cultivate the earth, and
therefore their education is of little consequence to the public;
but the old and diseased among them are supported by
hospitals: for begging is a trade unknown in this empire.

And here it may perhaps divert the curious reader, to give
some account of my domestic, and my manner of living in this
country, during a residence of nine months and thirteen days.
Having a head mechanically turned, and being likewise forced
by necessity, I had made for myself a table and chair convenient enough, out of the largest trees in the royal park.
Two hundred sempstresses were employed to make me shirts,
and linen for my bed and table, all of the strongest and
coarsest kind they could get; which, however, they were forced
to quilt together in several folds, for the thickest was some
degrees finer than lawn. Their linen is usually three inches
wide, and three foot make a piece. The sempstresses took my
measure as I lay on the ground, one standing at my neck,
and another at my midleg, with a strong cord extended,
that each held by the end, while the third measured the length
of the cord with a rule of an inch long. Then they measured
my right thumb, and desired no more; for by a mathematical
computation, that twice round the thumb is once round the
wrist, and so on to the neck and the waist, and by the help
of my old shirt, which I displayed on the ground before them
for a pattern, they fitted me exactly. Three hundred tailors
were employed in the same manner to make me clothes; but
they had another contrivance for taking my measure. I
kneeled down, and they raised a ladder from the ground to my
neck; upon this ladder one of them mounted, and let fall a
plumb-line from my collar to the floor, which just answered
the length of my coat; but my waist and arms I measured
myself. When my clothes were finished, which was done in
my house, (for the largest of theirs would not have been able
to hold them) they looked like the patchwork made by the
ladies in England, only that mine were all of a colour.

I had three hundred cooks to dress my victuals, in little
convenient huts built about my house, where they and their

families lived, and prepared me two dishes apiece. I took up
twenty waiters in my hand, and placed them on the table; an
hundred more attended below on the ground, some with
dishes of meat, and some with barrels of wine, and other
liquors, slung on their shoulders; all which the waiters above
drew up as I wanted, in a very ingenious manner, by certain
cords, as we draw the bucket up a well in Europe. A dish of
their meat was a good mouthful, and a barrel of their liquor
a reasonable draught. Their mutton yields to ours, but their
beef is excellent. I have had a sirloin so large, that I have been
forced to make three bites of it; but this is rare. My servants
were astonished to see me eat it bones and all, as in our
country we do the leg of a lark. Their geese and turkeys I
usually ate at a mouthful, and I must confess they far exceed
ours. Of their smaller fowl I could take up twenty or thirty
at the end of my knife.

One day his Imperial Majesty, being informed of my way
of living, desired that himself and his royal consort, with the
young princes of the blood of both sexes, might have the
happiness (as he was pleased to call it) of dining with me.
They came accordingly, and I placed them upon chairs of
state on my table, just over-against me, with their guards
about them. Flimnap the Lord High Treasurer attended there
likewise, with his white staff; and I observed he often looked
on me with a sour countenance, which I would not seem to
regard, but ate more than usual, in honour to my dear country, as well as to fill the court with admiration. I have some
private reasons to believe, that this visit from his Majesty
gave Flimnap an opportunity of doing me ill offices to his
master. That minister had always been my secret enemy,
although he outwardly caressed me more than was usual to
the moroseness of his nature. He represented to the Emperor
the low condition of his treasury; that he was forced to take up
money at great discount; that exchequer bills would not circulate under nine per cent below par; that I had cost his
Majesty above a million and a half of *sprugs* (their greatest
gold coin, about the bigness of a spangle); and upon the
whole, that it would be advisable in the Emperor to take the
first fair occasion of dismissing me.

I am here obliged to vindicate the reputation of an excellent
lady,[1] who was an innocent sufferer upon my account. The
Treasurer took a fancy to be jealous of his wife, from the

[1] Walpole's wife, Catherine Shorter, was accused of notorious infidelity, at
which her husband winked.

malice of some evil tongues, who informed him that her Grace had taken a violent affection for my person; and the court-scandal ran for some time, that she once came privately to my lodging. This I solemnly declare to be a most infamous falsehood, without any grounds, farther than that her Grace was pleased to treat me with all innocent marks of freedom and friendship. I own she came often to my house, but always publicly, nor ever without three more in the coach, who were usually her sister and young daughter, and some particular acquaintance; but this was common to many other ladies of the court. And I still appeal to my servants round, whether they at any time saw a coach at my door without knowing what persons were in it. On those occasions, when a servant had given me notice, my custom was to go immediately to the door; and, after paying my respects, to take up the coach and two horses very carefully in my hands (for if there were six horses, the postillion always unharnessed four) and place them on a table, where I had fixed a moveable rim quite round, of five inches high, to prevent accidents. And I have often had four coaches and horses at once on my table full of company, while I sat in my chair leaning my face towards them; and when I was engaged with one set, the coachmen would gently drive the others round my table. I have passed many an afternoon very agreeably in these conversations. But I defy the Treasurer, or his two informers (I will name them, and let them make their best of it) Clustril and Drunlo,[1] to prove that any person ever came to me *incognito,* except the Secretary Reldresal, who was sent by express command of his Imperial Majesty, as I have before related. I should not have dwelt so long upon this particular, if it had not been a point wherein the reputation of a great lady is so nearly concerned, to say nothing of my own; although I had the honour to be a *Nardac,* which the Treasurer himself is not; for all the world knows he is only a *Clumglum,* a title inferior by one degree, as that of a marquis is to a duke in England; yet I allow he preceded me in right of his post. These false informations, which I afterwards came to the knowledge of, by an accident not proper to mention, made the Treasurer show his lady for some time an ill countenance, and me a worse; for although he was at last undeceived and reconciled to her, yet I lost all credit with him, and found my interest decline very fast

---

[1] Possibly informers used by Walpole in the trial of the Bishop of Rochester; (see p. 188, note 2).

with the Emperor himself, who was indeed too much governed by that favourite.

Chapter VII.

The author, being informed of a design to accuse him of high treason, makes his escape to Blefuscu. His reception there.

Before I proceed to give an account of my leaving this kingdom, it may be proper to inform the reader of a private intrigue which had been for two months forming against me.

I had been hitherto all my life a stranger to courts, for which I was unqualified by the meanness of my condition. I had indeed heard and read enough of the dispositions of great princes and ministers; but never expected to have found such terrible effects of them in so remote a country, governed, as I thought, by very different maxims from those in Europe.

When I was just preparing to pay my attendance on the Emperor of Blefuscu, a considerable person at court [1] (to whom I had been very serviceable at a time when he lay under the highest displeasure of his Imperial Majesty) came to my house very privately at night in a close chair, and without sending his name, desired admittance: the chairmen were dismissed; I put the chair, with his Lordship in it, into my coat-pocket; and giving orders to a trusty servant to say I was indisposed and gone to sleep, I fastened the door of my house, placed the chair on the table, according to my usual custom, and sat down by it. After the common salutations were over, observing his Lordship's countenance full of concern, and enquiring into the reason, he desired I would hear him with patience in a matter that highly concerned my honour and my life. His speech was to the following effect, for I took notes of it as soon as he left me.

You are to know, said he, that several committees of council have been lately called in the most private manner on your account; and it is but two days since his Majesty came to a full resolution.

You are very sensible that Sgyresh Bolgolam (*Galbet,* or High Admiral) hath been your mortal enemy almost ever since your arrival. His original reasons I know not, but his hatred is much encreased since your great success against

[1] Probably the Duke of Marlborough, who connived to have Bolingbroke flee to France.

Blefuscu, by which his glory, as Admiral, is obscured. This lord, in conjunction with Flimnap the High Treasurer, whose enmity against you is notorious on account of his lady, Limtoc the General, Lalcon the Chamberlain, and Balmuff the Grand Justiciary,[1] have prepared articles of impeachment against you, for treason, and other capital crimes.

This preface made me so impatient, being conscious of my own merits and innocence, that I was going to interrupt; when he entreated me to be silent, and thus proceeded.

Out of gratitude for the favours you have done me, I procured information of the whole proceedings, and a copy of the articles, wherein I venture my head for your service.

Articles of Impeachment against Quinbus Flestrin (the Man-Mountain).

ARTICLE I.

Whereas, by a statute made in the reign of his Imperial Majesty Calin Deffar Plune, it is enacted, that whoever shall make water within the precincts of the royal palace shall be liable to the pains and penalties of high treason: notwithstanding, the said Quinbus Flestrin, in open breach of the said law, under colour of extinguishing the fire kindled in the apartment of his Majesty's most dear imperial consort, did maliciously, traitorously, and devilishly, by discharge of his urine, put out the said fire kindled in the said apartment, lying and being within the precincts of the said royal palace, against the statute in that case provided, etc., against the duty, etc.

ARTICLE II.

That the said Quinbus Flestrin, having brought the imperial fleet of Blefuscu into the royal port, and being afterwards commanded by his Imperial Majesty to seize all the other ships of the said empire of Blefuscu, and reduce that empire to a province, to be governed by a viceroy from hence, and to destroy and put to death not only all the Big-Endian exiles, but likewise all the people of that empire who would not

---

[1] The lords who drafted the Articles of Impeachment, that is the charges of the Committee of Secrecy against Bolingbroke and Oxford, have been identified as follows: Bolgolam as the Earl of Nottingham; Flimnap as Robert Walpole, Chairman of the Committee of Secrecy; Limtoc as General Stanhope, Secretary of War; Lalcon as the Lord Steward, Duke of Devonshire; Balmuff as the Lord Chancellor, Lord Cowper. They were either Whigs or dissident Tories objecting to the negotiations of the Treaty of Utrecht.

immediately forsake the Big-Endian heresy: he, the said
Flestrin, like a false traitor against his most Auspicious,
Serene, Imperial Majesty, did petition to be excused from the
said service, upon pretence of unwillingness to force the
consciences, or destroy the liberties and lives of an innocent
people.

ARTICLE III.

That, whereas certain ambassadors arrived from the court
of Blefuscu to sue for peace in his Majesty's court: he, the
said Flestrin, did, like a false traitor, aid, abet, comfort, and
divert the said ambassadors, although he knew them to be
servants to a prince who was lately an open enemy to his
Imperial Majesty, and in open war against his said Majesty.

ARTICLE IV.

That the said Quinbus Flestrin, contrary to the duty of a
faithful subject, is now preparing to make a voyage to the
court and empire of Blefuscu, for which he hath received
only verbal licence from his Imperial Majesty; and under
colour of the said licence, doth falsely and traitorously intend
to take the said voyage, and thereby to aid, comfort, and
abet the Emperor of Blefuscu, so late an enemy, and in open
war with his Imperial Majesty aforesaid.

There are some other articles, but these are the most
important, of which I have read you an abstract.

In the several debates upon this impeachment, it must be
confessed that his Majesty gave many marks of his great lenity,
often urging the services you had done him, and endeavouring
to extenuate your crimes. The Treasurer and Admiral insisted
that you should be put to the most painful and ignominious
death, by setting fire on your house at night; and the General
was to attend with twenty thousand men armed with poisoned
arrows to shoot you on the face and hands. Some of your
servants were to have private orders to strew a poisonous
juice on your shirts and sheets, which would soon make you
tear your own flesh, and die in the utmost torture. The General
came into the same opinion, so that for a long time there
was a majority against you. But his Majesty resolving, if possible, to spare your life, at last brought off the Chamberlain.

Upon this incident, Reldresal, Principal Secretary for
Private Affairs, who always approved himself your true
friend, was commanded by the Emperor to deliver his opinion,

which he accordingly did; and therein justified the good
thoughts you have of him. He allowed your crimes to be
great, but that still there was room for mercy, the most
commendable virtue in a prince, and for which his Majesty
was so justly celebrated. He said the friendship between you
and him was so well known to the world, that perhaps the
most honourable board might think him partial: however, in
obedience to the command he had received, he would freely
offer his sentiments. That if his Majesty, in consideration of
your services, and pursuant to his own merciful disposition,
would please to spare your life, and only give order to put
out both your eyes, he humbly conceived that by this expedient justice might in some measure be satisfied, and all the
world would applaud the lenity of the Emperor, as well as the
fair and generous proceedings of those who have the honour
to be his counsellors. That the loss of your eyes would be no
impediment to your bodily strength, by which you might still
be useful to his Majesty.[1] That blindness is an addition to
courage, by concealing dangers from us; that the fear you had
for your eyes was the greatest difficulty in bringing over the
enemy's fleet, and it would be sufficient for you to see by the
eyes of the ministers, since the greatest princes do no more.

This proposal was received with the utmost disapprobation
by the whole board. Bolgolam, the Admiral, could not preserve
his temper; but rising up in fury, said, he wondered how the
Secretary durst presume to give his opinion for preserving the
life of a traitor: that the services you had performed were, by
all true reasons of state, the great aggravation of your crimes;
that you, who were able to extinguish the fire by discharge of
urine in her Majesty's apartment (which he mentioned with
horror), might, at another time, raise an inundation by the
same means, to drown the whole palace; and the same strength
which enabled you to bring over the enemy's fleet might
serve, upon the first discontent, to carry it back: that he had
good reasons to think you were a Big-Endian in your heart;
and as treason begins in the heart before it appears in overt
acts, so he accused you as a traitor on that account, and
therefore insisted you should be put to death.

The Treasurer was of the same opinion; he showed to what
straits his Majesty's revenue was reduced by the charge of
maintaining you, which would soon grow insupportable: that

---

[1] In the impeachment proceedings (see p. 79, note 1) some Whigs suggested
that Bolingbroke and Oxford be accused of misdemeanors rather than treason,
by means of which they would forfeit their civil and property rights rather
than their lives.

the Secretary's expedient of putting out your eyes was so far
from being a remedy against this evil, that it would probably
increase it, as it is manifest from the common practice of
blinding some kind of fowl, after which they fed the faster,
and grew sooner fat: that his sacred Majesty, and the council,
who are your judges, were in their own consciences fully
convinced of your guilt, which was a sufficient argument to
condemn you to death, without the formal proofs required
by the strict letter of the law.

But his Imperial Majesty, fully determined against capital
punishment, was graciously pleased to say, that since the council
thought the loss of your eyes too easy a censure, some other
may be inflicted hereafter. And your friend the Secretary
humbly desiring to be heard again, in answer to what the
Treasurer had objected concerning the great charge his
Majesty was at in maintaining you, said that his Excellency,
who had the sole disposal of the Emperor's revenue, might
easily provide against this evil, by gradually lessening your
establishment; by which, for want of sufficient food, you
would grow weak and faint, and lose your appetite, and
consequently decay and consume in a few months; neither
would the stench of your carcass be then so dangerous, when
it should become more than half diminished; and immediately
upon your death, five or six thousand of his Majesty's subjects
might, in two or three days, cut your flesh from your bones,
take it away by cart-loads, and bury it in distant parts to
prevent infection, leaving the skelton · as a monument of
admiration to posterity.

Thus by the great friendship of the Secretary, the whole
affair was compromised. It was strictly enjoined, that the
project of starving you by degrees should be kept a secret, but
the sentence of putting out your eyes was entered on the
books; none dissenting except Bolgolam the Admiral, who
being a creature of the Empress, was perpetually instigated
by her Majesty to insist upon your death, she having borne
perpetual malice against you, on account of that infamous and
illegal method you took to extinguish the fire in her apartment.

In three days your friend the Secretary will be directed to
come to your house, and read before you the articles of impeachment; and then to signify the great lenity and favour of
his Majesty and council, whereby you are only condemned to
the loss of your eyes, which his Majesty doth not question

you will gratefully and humbly submit to; and twenty of his Majesty's surgeons will attend, in order to see the operation well performed, by discharging very sharp-pointed arrows into the balls of your eyes, as you lie on the ground.

I leave to your prudence what measures you will take; and to avoid suspicion, I must immediately return in as private a manner as I came.

His Lordship did so, and I remained alone, under many doubts and perplexities of mind.

It was a custom introduced by this prince and his ministry (very different, as I have been assured, from the practices of former times) that after the court had decreed any cruel execution, either to gratify the monarch's resentment, or the malice of a favourite, the Emperor always made a speech to his whole council, expressing his great lenity and tenderness, as qualities known and confessed by all the world. This speech was immediately published through the kingdom; nor did any thing terrify the people so much as those encomiums on his Majesty's mercy; because it was observed, that the more these praises were enlarged and insisted on, the more inhuman was the punishment, and the sufferer more innocent. Yet as to myself, I must confess, having never been designed for a courtier either by my birth or education, I was so ill a judge of things, that I could not discover the lenity and favour of this sentence, but conceived it (perhaps erroneously) rather to be rigorous than gentle. I sometimes thought of standing my trial, for although I could not deny the facts alleged in the several articles, yet I hoped they would admit of some extenuations. But having in my life perused many state trials, which I ever observed to terminate as the judges thought fit to direct, I durst not rely on so dangerous a decision, in so critical a juncture, and against such powerful enemies. Once I was strongly bent upon resistance, for while I had liberty, the whole strength of that empire could hardly subdue me, and I might easily with stones pelt the metropolis to pieces; but I soon rejected that project with horror, by remembering the oath I had made to the Emperor, the favours I received from him, and the high title of *Nardac* he conferred upon me. Neither had I so soon learned the gratitude of courtiers, to persuade myself that his Majesty's present severities acquitted me of all past obligations.

At last I fixed upon a resolution, for which it is probable I may incur some censure, and not unjustly; for I confess I owe the preserving my eyes, and consequently my liberty, to my own great rashness and want of experience: because if I had then known the nature of princes and ministers, which I have since observed in many other courts, and their methods of treating criminals less obnoxious than myself, I should with great alacrity and readiness have submitted to so easy a punishment. But hurried on by the precipitancy of youth, and having his Imperial Majesty's licence to pay my attendance upon the Emperor of Blefuscu, I took this opportunity, before the three days were elapsed, to send a letter to my friend the Secretary, signifying my resolution of setting out that morning for Blefuscu [1] pursuant to the leave I had got; and without waiting for an answer, I went to that side of the island where our fleet lay. I seized a large man of war, tied a cable to the prow, and, lifting up the anchors, I stripped myself, put my clothes (together with my coverlet, which I carried under my arm) into the vessel, and drawing it after me between wading and swimming, arrived at the royal port of Blefuscu, where the people had long expected me; they lent me two guides to direct me to the capital city, which is of the same name. I held them in my hand until I came within two hundred yards of the gate, and desired them to signify my arrival to one of the secretaries, and let him know, I there waited his Majesty's commands. I had an answer in about an hour, that his Majesty, attended by the royal family, and great officers of the court, was coming out to receive me. I advanced a hundred yards. The Emperor, and his train, alighted from their horses, the Empress and ladies from their coaches, and I did not perceive they were in any fright or concern. I lay on the ground to kiss his Majesty's and the Empress's hand. I told his Majesty that I was come according to my promise, and with the licence of the Emperor my master, to have the honour of seeing so mighty a monarch, and to offer him any service in my power, consistent with my duty to my own prince; not mentioning a word of my disgrace, because I had hitherto no regular information of it, and might suppose myself wholly ignorant of any such design; neither could I reasonably conceive that the Emperor would discover the secret while I was out of his power: wherein, however, it soon appeared I was deceived.

I shall not trouble the reader with the particular account of my reception at this court, which was suitable to the generosity of so great a prince; nor of the difficulties I was in for

---

[1] Just before his trial for treason Bolingbroke, doubting the justice he would receive, fled to France.

want of a house and bed, being forced to lie on the ground, wrapped up in my coverlet.

Chapter VIII.

The author, by a lucky accident, finds means to leave Blefuscu; and, after some difficulties, returns safe to his native country.

Three days after my arrival, walking out of curiosity to the northeast coast of the island, I observed, about half a league off, in the sea, somewhat that looked like a boat overturned. I pulled off my shoes and stockings, and wading two or three hundred yards, I found the object to approach nearer by force of the tide, and then plainly saw it to be a real boat, which I supposed might, by some tempest, have been driven from a ship; whereupon I returned immediately towards the city, and desired his Imperial Majesty to lend me twenty of the tallest vessels he had left after the loss of his fleet, and three thousand seamen under the command of his Vice-Admiral. This fleet sailed round, while I went back the shortest way to the coast where I first discovered the boat; I found the tide had driven it still nearer. The seamen were all provided with cordage, which I had beforehand twisted to a sufficient strength. When the ships came up, I stripped myself, and waded till I came within an hundred yards of the boat, after which I was forced to swim till I got up to it. The seamen threw me the end of the cord, which I fastened to a hole in the fore-part of the boat, and the other end to a man of war; but I found all my labour to little purpose; for being out of my depth, I was not able to work. In this necessity, I was forced to swim behind, and push the boat forwards as often as I could, with one of my hands; and the tide favouring me, I advanced so far, that I could just hold up my chin and feel the ground. I rested two or three minutes, and then gave the boat another shove, and so on till the sea was no higher than my armpits; and now the most laborious part being over, I took out my other cables, which were stowed in one of the ships, and fastening them first to the boat, and then to nine of the vessels which attended me; the wind being favourable the seamen towed, and I shoved till we arrived within forty yards of the shore: and waiting till the tide was out, I got dry to the boat, and by the assistance of two thousand men, with ropes and engines, I made a shift to turn it on its bottom, and found it was but little damaged.

I shall not trouble the reader with the difficulties I was under by the help of certain paddles, which cost me ten days making, to get my boat to the royal port of Blefuscu, where a mighty concourse of people appeared upon my arrival, full of wonder at the sight of so prodigious a vessel. I told the Emperor that my good fortune had thrown this boat in my way, to carry me to some place from whence I might return into my native country, and begged his Majesty's orders for getting materials to fit it up, together with his licence to depart; which, after some kind expostulations, he was pleased to grant.

I did very much wonder, in all this time, not to have heard of any express relating to me from our Emperor to the court of Blefuscu. But I was afterwards given privately to understand, that his Imperial Majesty, never imagining I had the least notice of his designs, believed I was only gone to Blefuscu in performance of my promise, according to the licence he had given me, which was well known at our court, and would return in a few days when that ceremony was ended. But he was at last in pain at my long absence; and after consulting with the Treasurer, and the rest of that cabal, a person of quality was dispatched with the copy of the articles against me. This envoy had instructions to represent to the monarch of Blefuscu the great lenity of his master, who was content to punish me no further than with the loss of mine eyes; that I had fled from justice, and if I did not return in two hours, I should be deprived of my title of *Nardac,* and declared a traitor. The envoy further added, that in order to maintain the peace and amity between both empires, his master expected, that his brother of Blefuscu would give orders to have me sent back to Lilliput, bound hand and foot, to be punished as a traitor.

The Emperor of Blefuscu, having taken three days to consult, returned an answer consisting of many civilities and excuses. He said, that as for sending me bound, his brother knew it was impossible; that although I had deprived him of his fleet, yet he owed great obligations to me for many good offices I had done him in making the peace. That however both their Majesties would soon be made easy; for I had found a prodigious vessel on the shore, able to carry me on the sea, which he had given order to fit up with my own assistance and direction, and he hoped in a few weeks both empires would be freed from so insupportable an incumbrance.

With this answer the envoy returned to Lilliput, and the monarch of Blefuscu related to me all that had passed, offering me at the same time (but under the strictest confidence) his gracious protection if I would continue in his service; wherein although I believed him sincere, yet I resolved never more to put any confidence in princes or ministers, where I could possibly avoid it; and therefore, with all due acknowledgements for his favourable intentions, I humbly begged to be excused. I told him, that since fortune, whether good or evil, had thrown a vessel in my way, I was resolved to venture myself in the ocean, rather than be an occasion of difference between two such mighty monarchs. Neither did I find the Emperor at all displeased; and I discovered by a certain accident, that he was very glad of my resolution, and so were most of his ministers.

These considerations moved me to hasten my departure somewhat sooner than I intended; to which the court, impatient to have me gone, very readily contributed. Five hundred workmen were employed to make two sails to my boat, according to my directions, by quilting thirteen fold of their strongest linen together. I was at the pains of making ropes and cables, by twisting ten, twenty or thirty of the thickest and strongest of theirs. A great stone that I happened to find, after a long search by the seashore, served me for an anchor. I had the tallow of three hundred cows for greasing my boat, and other uses. I was at incredible pains in cutting down some of the largest timber trees for oars and masts, wherein I was, however, much assisted by his Majesty's ship-carpenters, who helped me in smoothing them, after I had done the rough work.

In about a month, when all was prepared, I sent to receive his Majesty's commands, and to take my leave. The Emperor and royal family came out of the palace; I lay down on my face to kiss his hand, which he very graciously gave me; so did the Empress, and young princes of the blood. His Majesty presented me with fifty purses of two hundred *sprugs* apiece, together with his picture at full length, which I put immediately into one of my gloves, to keep it from being hurt. The ceremonies at my departure were too many to trouble the reader with at this time.

I stored the boat with the carcasses of an hundred oxen, and three hundred sheep, with bread and drink proportionable, and as much meat ready dressed as four hundred cooks could provide. I took with me six cows and two bulls alive, with as many ewes and rams, intending to carry them into my own country, and propagate the breed. And to feed them on board, I had a good bundle of hay, and a bag of corn. I would gladly have taken a dozen of the natives, but this was a thing the Emperor would by no means permit; and besides a diligent search into my pockets, his Majesty engaged my honour not to carry away any of his subjects, although with their own consent and desire.

Having thus prepared all things as well as I was able, I set sail on the twenty-fourth day of September, 1701, at six in the morning; and when I had gone about four leagues to the northward, the wind being at southeast, at six in the evening, I descried a small island about half a league to the northwest. I advanced forward, and cast anchor on the lee-side of the island, which seemed to be uninhabited. I then took some refreshment, and went to my rest. I slept well, and as I conjecture at least six hours, for I found the day broke in two hours after I awaked. It was a clear night. I ate my breakfast before the sun was up; and heaving anchor, the wind being favourable, I steered the same course that I had done the day before, wherein I was directed by my pocket-compass. My intention was to reach, if possible, one of those islands which I had reason to believe lay to the northeast of Van Diemen's Land. I discovered nothing all that day; but upon the next, about three in the afternoon, when I had by my computation made twenty-four leagues from Blefuscu, I descried a sail steering to the southeast; my course was due east. I hailed her, but could get no answer; yet I found I gained upon her, for the wind slackened. I made all the sail I could, and in half an hour she spied me, then hung out her ancient, and discharged a gun. It is not easy to express the joy I was in upon the unexpected hope of once more seeing my beloved country, and the dear pledges I had left in it. The ship slackened her sails, and I came up with her between five and six in the evening, September 26; but my heart leapt within me to see her English colours. I put my cows and sheep into my coat-pockets, and got on board with all my little cargo of provisions. The vessel was an English merchantman, returning from Japan by the North and South Seas; the captain, Mr. John Biddel of Deptford, a very civil man, and an excellent sailor. We were now in the latitude of 30 degrees south; there were about fifty men in the ship; and here I met an old comrade of mine, one Peter Williams, who gave me a good character to the captain. This gentleman treated me with kindness, and desired I would let

him know what place I came from last, and whither I was
bound; which I did in few words; but he thought I was raving,
and that the dangers I underwent had disturbed my head;
whereupon I took my black cattle and sheep out of my pocket,
which, after great astonishment, clearly convinced him of my
veracity. I then showed him the gold given me by the Emperor of Blefuscu, together with his Majesty's picture at full
length, and some other rarities of that country. I gave him
two purses of two hundred *sprugs* each, and promised, when
we arrived in England, to make him a present of a cow and a
sheep big with young.

I shall not trouble the reader with a particular account of
this voyage, which was very prosperous for the most part. We
arrived in the Downs on the 13th of April, 1702. I had only
one misfortune, that the rats on board carried away one of my
sheep; I found her bones in a hole, picked clean from the
flesh. The rest of my cattle I got safe on shore, and set them
a grazing in a bowling-green at Greenwich, where the fineness
of the grass made them feed very heartily, though I had always
feared the contrary; neither could I possibly have preserved
them in so long a voyage, if the captain had not allowed me
some of his best biscuit, which, rubbed to powder, and mingled with water, was their constant food. The short time I
continued in England, I made a considerable profit by showing my cattle to many persons of quality, and others: and
before I began my second voyage, I sold them for six hundred
pounds. Since my last return, I find the breed is considerably
increased, especially the sheep; which I hope will prove much
to the advantage of the woollen manufacture, by the fineness
of the fleeces.

I stayed but two months with my wife and family; for my
insatiable desire of seeing foreign countries would suffer me
to continue no longer. I left fifteen hundred pounds with my
wife, and fixed her in a good house at Redriff. My remaining
stock I carried with me, part in money, and part in goods, in
hopes to improve my fortunes. My eldest uncle, John, had
left me an estate in land, near Epping, of about thirty pounds
a year; and I had a long lease of the Black Bull in Fetter
Lane, which yielded me as much more; so that I was not in
any danger of leaving my family upon the parish. My son
Johnny, named so after his uncle, was at the grammar school,
and a towardly child. My daughter Betty (who is now well
married, and has children) was then at her needlework. I took
leave of my wife, and boy and girl, with tears on both sides,

and went on board the *Adventure,* a merchant-ship of three
hundred tons, bound for Surat, Captain John Nicholas of
Liverpool, commander. But my account of this voyage must
be referred to the second part of my *Travels.*

THE END OF THE FIRST PART.

TRAVELS.

Part II.

A VOYAGE TO BROBDINGNAG.

Chapter I.

*A great storm described. The longboats sent to fetch water,
the author goes with it to discover the country. He is left
on shore, is seized by one of the natives, and carried to a
farmer's house. His reception there, with several accidents
that happened there. A description of the inhabitants.*

Having been condemned by nature and fortune to an active
and restless life, in two months after my return I again
left my native country, and took shipping in the Downs on
the 20th day of June, 1702, in the *Adventure*, Capt. John
Nicholas, a Cornish man, commander, bound for Surat. We
had a very prosperous gale till we arrived at the Cape of Good
Hope, where we landed for fresh water, but discovering a leak,
we unshipped our goods, and wintered there; for the captain
falling sick of an ague, we could not leave the Cape till
the end of March. We then set sail, and had a good voyage
till we passed the Straits of Madagascar; but having got northward of that island, and to about five degrees south latitude,
the winds, which in those seas are observed to blow a constant
equal gale between the north and west from the beginning of
December to the beginning of May, on the 19th of April began to blow with much greater violence, and more westerly
than usual, continuing so for twenty days together, during
which time we were driven a little to the east of the Molucca
Islands, and about three degrees northward of the Line, as our
captain found by an observation he took the 2nd of May, at
which time the wind ceased, and it was a perfect calm, whereat
I was not a little rejoiced. But he, being a man well experienced in the navigation of those seas, bid us all prepare against
a storm, which accordingly happened the day following: for
a southern wind, called the southern monsoon, began to set in.

Finding it was like to overblow, we took in our spritsail,
and stood by to hand the foresail; but making foul weather,

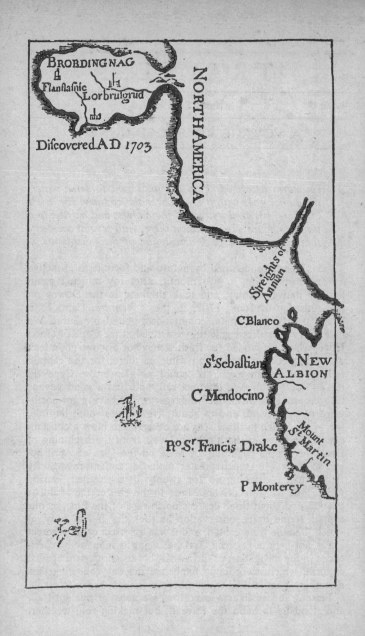

we looked the guns were all fast, and handed the missen. The
ship lay very broad off, so we thought it better spooning before the sea, than trying or hulling. We reefed the foresail and
set him, we hauled aft the fore-sheet; the helm was hard a
weather. The ship wore bravely. We belayed the fore-down-
haul; but the sail was split, and we hauled down the yard, and
got the sail into the ship, and unbound all the things clear of it.
It was a very fierce storm; the sea broke strange and dangerous. We hauled off upon the lanyard of the whipstaff, and
helped the man at helm. We would not get down our topmast,
but let all stand, because she scudded before the sea very well,
and we knew that the topmast being aloft, the ship was the
wholesomer, and made better way through the sea, seeing we
had searoom. When the storm was over, we set foresail and
mainsail, and brought the ship to. Then we set the missen,
main-topsail and the fore-topsail. Our course was east-north-
east, the wind was at southwest. We got the starboard tacks
aboard, we cast off our weatherbraces and lifts; we set in the
lee braces, and hauled forward by the weather bowlings, and
hauled them tight, and belayed them, and hauled over the
missen tack to windward, and kept her full and by as near as
she would lie.[1]

During this storm, which was followed by a strong wind
west-southwest, we were carried by my computation about
five hundred leagues to the east, so that the oldest sailor on
board could not tell in what part of the world we were. Our
provisions held out well, our ship was staunch, and our crew
all in good health; but we lay in the utmost distress for water.
We thought it best to hold on the same course rather than turn
more northerly, which might have brought us to the northwest
parts of Great Tartary, and into the frozen sea.

On the 16th day of June, 1703, a boy on the topmast discovered land. On the 17th we came in full view of a great
island or continent, (for we knew not whether) on the south
side whereof was a small neck of land jutting out into the sea,
and a creek too shallow to hold a ship of above one hundred
tons. We cast anchor within a league of this creek, and our
captain sent a dozen of his men well armed in the longboat,
with vessels for water if any could be found. I desired his
leave to go with them, that I might see the country, and make
what discoveries I could. When we came to land we saw no

[1] This paragraph is taken almost verbatim from Samuel Sturmy's *Mariners
Magazine* of 1679, probably to achieve both a realistic nautical description and
satire on travel book terminology in general.

river or spring, nor any sign of inhabitants. Our men therefore wandered on the shore to find out some fresh water near the sea, and I walked alone about a mile on the other side, where I observed the country all barren and rocky. I now began to be weary, and seeing nothing to entertain my curiosity, I returned gently down towards the creek; and the sea being full in my view, I saw our men already got into the boat, and rowing for life to the ship. I was going to hollow after them, although it had been to little purpose, when I observed a huge creature walking after them in the sea, as fast as he could: he waded not much deeper than his knees, and took prodigious strides: but our men had the start of him half a league, and the sea thereabouts being full of sharp pointed rocks, the monster was not able to overtake the boat. This I was afterwards told, for I durst not stay to see the issue of that adventure; but ran as fast as I could the way I first went; and then climbed up a steep hill which gave me some prospect of the country. I found it fully cultivated; but that which first surprised me was the length of the grass, which in those grounds that seemed to be kept for hay was above twenty foot high.

I fell into a high road, for so I took it to be, although it served to the inhabitants only as a footpath through a field of barley. Here I walked on for some time, but could see little on either side, it being now near harvest, and the corn rising at least forty foot. I was an hour walking to the end of this field, which was fenced in with a hedge of at least one hundred and twenty foot high, and the trees so lofty that I could make no computation of their altitude. There was a stile to pass from this field into the next; it had four steps, and a stone to cross over when you came to the uppermost. It was impossible for me to climb this stile, because every step was six foot high, and the upper stone above twenty. I was endeavouring to find some gap in the hedge, when I discovered one of the inhabitants in the next field advancing towards the stile, of the same size with him whom I saw in the sea pursuing our boat. He appeared as tall as an ordinary spire-steeple, and took about ten yards at every stride, as near as I could guess. I was struck with the utmost fear and astonishment, and ran to hide my self in the corn, from whence I saw him at the top of the stile, looking back into the next field on the right hand, and heard him call in a voice many degrees louder than a speaking-trumpet; but the noise was so high in the air, that at first I certainly thought it was thunder. Whereupon seven monsters like himself came towards him with reaping-hooks in their hands, each hook about the largeness of six scythes. These people were not so well clad as the first, whose servants or labourers they seemed to be. For, upon some words he spoke, they went to reap the corn in the field where I lay. I kept from them at as great a distance as I could, but was forced to move with extreme difficulty, for the stalks of the corn were sometimes not above a foot distant, so that I could hardly squeeze my body betwixt them. However, I made a shift to go forward till I came to a part of the field where the corn had been laid by the rain and wind. Here it was impossible for me to advance a step; for the stalks were so interwoven that I could not creep through, and the beards of the fallen ears so strong and pointed that they pierced through my clothes into my flesh. At the same time I heard the reapers not above an hundred yards behind me. Being quite dispirited with toil, and wholly overcome by grief and despair, I lay down between two ridges, and heartily wished I might there end my days. I bemoaned my desolate widow, and fatherless children. I lamented my own folly and wilfulness in attempting a second voyage against the advice of all my friends and relations. In this terrible agitation of mind I could not forbear thinking of Lilliput, whose inhabitants looked upon me as the greatest prodigy that ever appeared in the world; where I was able to draw an imperial fleet in my hand, and perform those other actions which will be recorded for ever in the chronicles of that empire, while posterity shall hardly believe them, although attested by millions. I reflected what a mortification it must prove to me to appear as inconsiderable in this nation as one single Lilliputian would be among us. But this I conceived was to be the least of my misfortunes: for, as human creatures are observed to be more savage and cruel in proportion to their bulk, what could I expect but to be a morsel in the mouth of the first among these enormous barbarians who should happen to seize me? Undoubtedly philosophers are in the right when they tell us, that nothing is great or little otherwise than by comparison.[1] It might have pleased fortune to let the Lilliputians find some nation, where the people were as diminutive with respect to them, as they were to me. And who knows but that even this prodigious race of mortals might be equally overmatched in some distant part of the world, whereof we have yet no discovery?

[1] Swift's comments recall the theory of the relativity of vision as expounded in Berkeley's *Theory of Vision* of 1709.

Scared and confounded as I was, I could not forbear going on with these reflections, when one of the reapers, approaching within ten yards of the ridge where I lay, made me apprehend that with the next step I should be squashed to death under his foot, or cut in two with his reaping hook. And therefore, when he was again about to move, I screamed as loud as fear could make me. Whereupon the huge creature trod short, and looking round about under him for some time, at last espied me as I lay on the ground. He considered a while with the caution of one who endeavours to lay hold on a small dangerous animal in such a manner that it shall not be able either to scratch or to bite him, as I my self have sometimes done with a weasel in England. At length he ventured to take me up behind by the middle between his forefinger and thumb, and brought me within three yards of his eyes, that he might behold my shape more perfectly. I guessed his meaning, and my good fortune gave me so much presence of mind, that I resolved not to struggle in the least as he held me in the air above sixty foot from the ground, although he grievously pinched my sides, for fear I should slip through his fingers. All I ventured was to raise my eyes towards the sun, and place my hands together in a supplicating posture, and to speak some words in an humble melancholy tone, suitable to the condition I then was in. For I apprehended every moment that he would dash me against the ground, as we usually do any little hateful animal which we have a mind to destroy. But my good star would have it, that he appeared pleased with my voice and gestures, and began to look upon me as a curiosity, much wondering to hear me pronounce articulate words, although he could not understand them. In the mean time I was able to forbear groaning and shedding tears, and turning my head towards my sides; letting him know, as well as I could, how cruelly I was hurt by the pressure of his thumb and finger. He seemed to apprehend my meaning; for, lifting up the lappet of his coat, he put me gently into it, and immediately ran along with me to his master, who was a substantial farmer, and the same person I had first seen in the field.

The farmer, having (as I supposed by their talk) received such an account of me as his servant could give him, took a piece of a small straw, about the size of a walking staff, and therewith lifted up the lappets of my coat; which it seems he thought to be some kind of covering that nature had given me. He blew my hairs aside to take a better view of my face. He called his hinds about him, and asked them (as I afterwards learned) whether they had ever seen in the fields any little creature that resembled me. He then placed me softly on the ground upon all four, but I got immediately up, and walked slowly backwards and forwards, to let those people see I had no intent to run away. They all sat down in a circle about me, the better to observe my motions. I pulled off my hat, and made a low bow towards the farmer. I fell on my knees, and lifted up my hands and eyes, and spoke several words as loud as I could: I took a purse of gold out of my pocket, and humbly presented it to him. He received it on the palm of his hand, then applied it close to his eye, to see what it was, and afterwards turned it several times with the point of a pin (which he took out of his sleeve), but could make nothing of it. Whereupon I made a sign that he should place his hand on the ground. I then took the purse, and opening it, poured all the gold into his palm. There were six Spanish pieces of four pistoles each, beside twenty or thirty smaller coins. I saw him wet the tip of his little finger upon his tongue, and take up one of my largest pieces, and then another, but he seemed to be wholly ignorant what they were. He made me a sign to put them again into my purse, and the purse again into my pocket, which after offering to him several times, I thought it best to do.

The farmer by this time was convinced I must be a rational creature. He spoke often to me, but the sound of his voice pierced my ears like that of a watermill; yet his words were articulate enough. I answered as loud as I could, in several languages, and he often laid his ear within two yards of me, but all in vain, for we were wholly unintelligible to each other. He then sent his servants to their work, and taking his handkerchief out of his pocket, he doubled and spread it on his left hand, which he placed flat on the ground, with the palm upwards, making me a sign to step into it, as I could easily do, for it was not above a foot in thickness. I thought it my part to obey, and for fear of falling, laid my self at full length upon the handkerchief, with the remainder of which he lapped me up to the head for further security, and in this manner carried me home to his house. There he called his wife, and showed me to her; but she screamed and ran back as women in England do at the sight of a toad or a spider. However, when she had a while seen my behaviour, and how well I observed the signs her husband made, she was soon reconciled, and by degrees grew extremely tender of me.

It was about twelve at noon, and a servant brought in din-

ner. It was only one substantial dish of meat (fit for the plain
condition of an husbandman) in a dish of about four and
twenty foot diameter. The company were the farmer and his
wife, three children, and an old grandmother: when they were
sat down, the farmer placed me at some distance from him on
the table, which was thirty foot high from the floor. I was in
a terrible fright, and kept as far as I could from the edge for
fear of falling. The wife minced a bit of meat, then crumbled
some bread on a trencher, and placed it before me. I made
her a low bow, took out my knife and fork, and fell to eat,
which gave them exceeding delight. The mistress sent her maid
for a small dram cup, which held about two gallons, and filled
it with drink; I took up the vessel with much difficulty in both
hands, and in a most respectful manner drank to her ladyship's
health, expressing the words as loud as I could in English,
which made the company laugh so heartily, that I was almost
deafened with the noise. This liquor tasted like a small cider,
and was not unpleasant. Then the master made me a sign to
come to his trencher side; but as I walked on the table, being
in great surprise all the time, as the indulgent reader will easily
conceive and excuse, I happened to stumble against a crust,
and fell flat on my face, but received no hurt. I got up immediately, and observing the good people to be in much concern, I took my hat (which I held under my arm out of good
manners) and waving it over my head, made three huzzas to
show I had got no mischief by the fall. But advancing forwards
toward my master (as I shall henceforth call him) his youngest son who sat next him, an arch boy of about ten years old,
took me up by the legs, and held me so high in the air, that I
trembled every limb; but his father snatched me from him,
and at the same time gave him such a box on the left ear, as
would have felled an European troop of horse to the earth,
ordering him to be taken from the table. But being afraid the
boy might owe me a spite, and well remembering how mischievous all children among us naturally are to sparrows, rabbits, young kittens, and puppy dogs, I fell on my knees, and
pointing to the boy, made my master understand, as well as I
could, that I desired his son might be pardoned. The father
complied, and the lad took his seat again; whereupon I went
to him and kissed his hand, which my master took, and made
him stroke me gently with it.

In the midst of dinner, my mistress's favourite cat leapt into
her lap. I heard a noise behind me like that of a dozen stock-
ing-weavers at work; and turning my head I found it pro-

ceeded from the purring of this animal, who seemed to be three times larger than an ox, as I computed by the view of her head, and one of her paws, while her mistress was feeding and stroking her. The fierceness of this creature's countenance altogether discomposed me; although I stood at the further end of the table, above fifty foot off, and although my mistress held her fast for fear she might give a spring, and seize me in her talons. But it happened there was no danger; for the cat took not the least notice of me when my master placed me within three yards of her. And as I have been always told, and found true by experience in my travels, that flying, or discovering fear before a fierce animal, is a certain way to make it pursue or attack you, so I resolved in this dangerous juncture to show no manner of concern. I walked with intrepidity five or six times before the very head of the cat, and came within half a yard of her; whereupon she drew her self back, as if she were more afraid of me: I had less apprehension concerning the dogs, whereof three or four came into the room, as it is usual in farmers' houses; one of which was a mastiff equal in bulk to four elephants, and a greyhound somewhat taller than the mastiff, but not so large.

When dinner was almost done, the nurse came in with a child of a year old in her arms, who immediately spied me, and began a squall that you might have heard from London Bridge to Chelsea, after the usual oratory of infants, to get me for a plaything. The mother out of pure indulgence took me up, and put me towards the child, who presently seized me by the middle, and got my head in his mouth, where I roared so loud that the urchin was frighted, and let me drop, and I should infallibly have broke my neck if the mother had not held her apron under me. The nurse to quiet her babe made use of a rattle, which was a kind of hollow vessel filled with great stones, and fastened by a cable to the child's waist; but all in vain, so that she was forced to apply the last remedy by giving it suck. I must confess no object ever disgusted me so much as the sight of her monstrous breast, which I cannot tell what to compare with, so as to give the curious reader an idea of its bulk, shape and colour. It stood prominent six foot, and could not be less than sixteen in circumference. The nipple was about half the bigness of my head, and the hue both of that and the dug so varified with spots, pimples and freckles, that nothing could appear more nauseous: for I had a near sight of her, she sitting down the more conveniently to give suck, and I standing on the table. This made me reflect upon the fair skins of our English ladies, who appear so beautiful to us, only because they are of our own size, and their defects not to be seen but through a magnifying glass, where we find by experiment that the smoothest and whitest skins look rough and coarse, and ill coloured.[1]

I remember when I was at Lilliput, the complexions of those diminutive people appeared to me the fairest in the world; and talking upon this subject with a person of learning there, who was an intimate friend of mine, he said that my face appeared much fairer and smoother when he looked on me from the ground, than it did upon a nearer view when I took him up in my hand, and brought him close, which he confessed was at first a very shocking sight. He said he could discover great holes in my skin, that the stumps of my beard were ten times stronger than the bristles of a boar, and my complexion made up of several colours altogether disagreeable: although I must beg leave to say for my self, that I am as fair as most of my sex and country, and very little sunburnt by all my travels. On the other side, discoursing of the ladies in that emperor's court, he used to tell me, one had freckles, another too wide a mouth, a third too large a nose, nothing of which I was able to distinguish. I confess this reflection was obvious enough; which however I could not forbear, lest the reader might think those vast creatures were actually deformed: for I must do them justice to say they are a comely race of people; and particularly the features of my master's countenance, although he were but a farmer, when I beheld him from the height of sixty foot, appeared very well proportioned.

When dinner was done, my master went out to his labourers, and, as I could discover by his voice and gesture, gave his wife a strict charge to take care of me. I was very much tired and disposed to sleep, which my mistress perceiving, she put me on her own bed, and covered me with a clean white handkerchief, but larger and coarser than the mainsail of a man of war.

I slept about two hours and dreamed I was at home with my wife and children, which aggravated my sorrows when I awaked and found my self alone in a vast room, between two and three hundred foot wide, and above two hundred high,

[1] Swift's simultaneous fascination and disgust with Gulliver's microscopic description of the Brobdingnagians reflects contemporary preoccupation with the newly discovered microscope. Like the more recently discovered telescope, the microscope fired the imaginations of the public, which soon turned both instruments into fashionable fads. Swift himself bought a microscope for Stella.

lying in a bed twenty yards wide. My mistress was gone about her household affairs, and had locked me in. The bed was eight yards from the door. Some natural necessities required me to get down; I durst not presume to call, and if I had, it would have been in vain with such a voice as mine at so great a distance from the room where I lay to the kitchen where the family kept. While I was under these circumstances, two rats crept up the curtains, and ran smelling backwards and forwards on the bed. One of them came up almost to my face, whereupon I rose in a fright, and drew out my hanger to defend my self. These horrible animals had the boldness to attack me on both sides, and one of them held his fore-feet at my collar; but I had the good fortune to rip up his belly before he could do me any mischief. He fell down at my feet, and the other, seeing the fate of his comrade, made his escape, but not without one good wound on the back, which I gave him as he fled, and made the blood run trickling from him. After this exploit, I walked gently to and fro on the bed, to recover my breath and loss of spirits. These creatures were of the size of a large mastiff, but infinitely more nimble and fierce; so that if I had taken off my belt before I went to sleep, I must have infallibly been torn to pieces and devoured. I measured the tail of the dead rat, and found it to be two yards long wanting an inch; but it went against my stomach to drag the carcass off the bed, where it lay still bleeding; I observed it had yet some life, but with a strong slash cross the neck I thoroughly dispatched it.

Soon after, my mistress came into the room, who seeing me all bloody, ran and took me up in her hand. I pointed to the dead rat, smiling and making other signs to show I was not hurt; whereat she was extremely rejoiced, calling the maid to take up the dead rat with a pair of tongs, and throw it out of the window. Then she set me on a table, where I showed her my hanger all bloody, and wiping it on the lappet of my coat, returned it to the scabbard. I was pressed to do more than one thing which another could not do for me, and therefore endeavoured to make my mistress understand that I desired to be set down on the floor; which after she had done, my bashfulness would not suffer me to express my self farther than by pointing to the door, and bowing several times The good woman with much difficulty at last perceived what I would be at, and taking me up again in her hand, walked into the garden, where she set me down. I went on one side about two hundred yards, and beckoning to her not to look or to follow

me, I hid myself between two leaves of sorrel, and there discharged the necessities of nature.

I hope the gentle reader will excuse me for dwelling on
these and the like particulars, which, however insignificant
they may appear to grovelling vulgar minds, yet will certainly
help a philosopher to enlarge his thoughts and imagination,
and apply them to the benefit of public as well as private life,
which was my sole design in presenting this and other accounts of my travels to the world; wherein I have been chiefly
studious of truth, without affecting any ornaments of learning
or of style. But the whole scene of this voyage made so strong
an impression on my mind, and is so deeply fixed in my memory, that in committing it to paper I did not omit one material circumstance: however, upon a strict review, I blotted out
several passages of less moment which were in my first copy,
for fear of being censured as tedious and trifling, whereof
travellers are often, perhaps not without justice, accused.

CHAPTER II.

*A description of the farmer's daughter. The author carried to
a market-town, and then to the metropolis. The particulars of his journey.*

My mistress had a daughter nine years old, a child of
forward parts for her age, very dextrous at her needle,
and skilful in dressing her baby. Her mother and she contrived to fit up the baby's [1] cradle for me against night: the
cradle was put into a small drawer of a cabinet, and the drawer
placed upon a hanging shelf for fear of the rats. This was my
bed all the time I stayed with those people, although made
more convenient by degrees, as I began to learn their language,
and make my wants known. This young girl was so handy,
that after I had once or twice pulled off my clothes before her,
she was able to dress and undress me, although I never gave
her that trouble when she would let me do either my self. She
made me seven shirts, and some other linen, of as fine cloth
as could be got, which indeed was coarser than sackcloth; and
these she constantly washed for me with her own hands. She
was likewise my school-mistress to teach me the language:
when I pointed to any thing, she told me the name of it in
her own tongue, so that in a few days I was able to call for

[1] Doll's.

whatever I had a mind to. She was very good natured, and not above forty foot high, being little for her age. She gave me the name of *Grildrig*,[1] which the family took up, and afterwards the whole kingdom. The word imports what the Latins call *nanunculus*, the Italians *homunceletino*, and the English *mannikin*. To her I chiefly owe my preservation in that country: we never parted while I was there; I called her my *glumdalclitch*, or 'little nurse': and I should be guilty of great ingratitude if I omitted this honourable mention of her care and affection towards me, which I heartily wish it lay in my power to requite as she deserves, instead of being the innocent but unhappy instrument of her disgrace, as I have too much reason to fear.

It now began to be known and talked of in the neighbourhood, that my master had found a strange animal in the field, about the bigness of a *splackmuck*, but exactly shaped in every part like a human creature, which it likewise imitated in all its actions; seemed to speak in a little language of its own, had already learned several words of theirs, went erect upon two legs, was tame and gentle, would come when it was called, do whatever it was bid, had the finest limbs in the world, and a complexion fairer than a nobleman's daughter of three years old. Another farmer who lived hard by, and was a particular friend of my master, came on a visit on purpose to enquire into the truth of this story. I was immediately produced, and placed upon a table, where I walked as I was commanded, drew my hanger, put it up again, made my reverence to my master's guest, asked him in his own language how he did, and told him he was welcome, just as my little nurse had instructed me. This man, who was old and dim-sighted, put on his spectacles to behold me better, at which I could not forbear laughing very heartily, for his eyes appeared like the full moon shining into a chamber at two windows. Our people, who discovered the cause of my mirth, bore me company in laughing, at which the old fellow was fool enough to be angry and out of countenance. He had the character of a great miser, and to my misfortune he well deserved it, by the cursed advice he gave my master to show me as a sight upon a market-day in the next town, which was half an hour's riding, about two and twenty miles from our house. I guessed there was some mischief contriving, when I observed my master and

---

[1] *Grildrig* has been interpreted as *Girl-thing*. *Glumdalclitch*, read as *clutching the doll grimly*, has been read as implying Stella, whom Swift knew from her childhood.

his friend whispering long together, sometimes pointing at me; and my fears made me fancy that I overheard and understood some of their words. But the next morning Glumdalclitch, my little nurse, told me the whole matter, which she had cunningly picked out from her mother. The poor girl laid me on her bosom, and fell a weeping with shame and grief. She apprehended some mischief would happen to me from rude vulgar folks, who might squeeze me to death, or break one of my limbs by taking me in their hands. She had also observed how modest I was in my nature, how nicely I regarded my honour, and what an indignity I should conceive it to be exposed for money as a public spectacle [1] to the meanest of the people. She said, her papa and mamma had promised that Grildrig should be hers, but now she found they meant to serve her as they did last year, when they pretended to give her a lamb, and yet, as soon as it was fat, sold it to a butcher. For my own part, I may truly affirm that I was less concerned than my nurse. I had a strong hope, which never left me, that I should one day recover my liberty; and as to the ignominy of being carried about for a monster, I considered my self to be a perfect stranger in the country, and that such a misfortune could never be charged upon me as a reproach if ever I should return to England, since the King of Great Britain himself, in my condition, must have undergone the same distress.

My master, pursuant to the advice of my friend, carried me in a box the next market-day to the neighbouring town, and took along with him his little daughter, my nurse, upon a pillion behind him. The box was close on every side, with a little door for me to go in and out, and a few gimlet-holes to let in air. The girl had been so careful to put the quilt of her baby's bed into it, for me to lie down on. However, I was terribly shaken and discomposed in this journey, although it were but of half an hour. For the horse went about forty foot at every step, and trotted so high, that the agitation was equal to the rising and falling of a ship in a great storm, but much more frequent: our journey was somewhat further than from London to St. Albans. My master alighted at an inn which he used to frequent; and after consulting a while with the innkeeper, and making some necessary preparations, he hired the *Grultrud,* or crier, to give notice through the town of a

---

[1] The contemporary practice of exhibiting oddities is related not only to showmanship but to the interest in collections and museums fostered by the new science in its attempt to organize knowledge.

strange creature to be seen at the Sign of the Green Eagle, not so big as a *splacknuck* (an animal in that country very finely shaped, about six foot long) and in every part of the body resembling an human creature, could speak several words, and perform an hundred diverting tricks.

I was placed upon a table in the largest room of the inn, which might be near three hundred foot square. My little nurse stood on a low stool close to the table, to take care of me, and direct what I should do. My master, to avoid a crowd, would suffer only thirty people at a time to see me. I walked about on the table as the girl commanded; she asked me questions as far as she knew my understanding of the language reached, and I answered them as loud as I could. I turned about several times to the company, paid my humble respects, said they were welcome, and used some other speeches I had been taught. I took up a thimble filled with liquor, which Glumdalclitch had given me for a cup, and drank their health. I drew out my hanger, and flourished with it after the manner of fencers in England. My nurse gave me part of a straw, which I exercised as a pike, having learned the art in my youth. I was that day shown to twelve sets of company, and as often forced to go over again with the same fopperies, till I was half dead with weariness and vexation. For those who had seen me made such wonderful reports, that the people were ready to break down the doors to come in. My master for his own interest would not suffer any one to touch me except my nurse; and, to prevent danger, benches were set round the table at such a distance as put me out of every body's reach. However, an unlucky school-boy aimed a hazel nut directly at my head, which very narrowly missed me; otherwise, it came with so much violence that it would have infallibly knocked out my brains, for it was almost as large as a small pumpion: [1] but I had the satisfaction to see the young rogue well beaten, and turned out of the room.

My master gave public notice, that he would show me again the next market-day, and in the mean time he prepared a more convenient vehicle for me, which he had reason enough to do; for I was so tired with my first journey, and with entertaining company for eight hours together, that I could hardly stand upon my legs, or speak a word. It was at least three days before I recovered my strength; and that I might have no rest at home, all the neighbouring gentlemen from an hundred miles round, hearing of my fame, came to see me at my

[1] Pumpkin.

master's own house. There could not be fewer than thirty persons with their wives and children (for the country is very populous); and my master demanded the rate of a full room whenever he showed me at home, although it were only to a single family. So that for some time I had but little ease every day of the week (except Wednesday, which is their Sabbath), although I were not carried to the town.

My master, finding how profitable I was like to be, resolved to carry me to the most considerable cities of the kingdom. Having therefore provided himself with all things necessary for a long journey, and settled his affairs at home, he took leave of his wife, and upon the 17th of August, 1703, about two months after my arrival, we set out for the metropolis, situated near the middle of that empire, and about three thousand miles distance from our house: my master made his daughter Glumdalclitch ride behind him. She carried me on her lap in a box tied about her waist. The girl had lined it on all sides with the softest cloth she could get, well quilted underneath, furnished it with her baby's bed, provided me with linen and other necessaries, and made every thing as convenient as she could. We had no other company but a boy of the house, who rode after us with the luggage.

My master's design was to show me in all the towns by the way, and to step out of the road for fifty or an hundred miles, to any village or person of quality's house where he might expect custom. We made easy journeys of not above seven or eight-score miles a day: for Glumdalclitch, on purpose to spare me, complained she was tired with the trotting of the horse. She often took me out of my box at my own desire, to give me air, and show me the country, but always held me fast by leading-strings. We passed over five or six rivers many degrees broader and deeper than the Nile or the Ganges; and there was hardly a rivulet so small as the Thames at London Bridge. We were ten weeks in our journeys, and I was shown in eighteen large towns, besides many villages and private families.

On the 26th day of October, we arrived at the metropolis, called in their language *Lorbrulgrud*,[1] or *Pride of the Universe*. My master took a lodging in the principal street of the city, not far from the royal palace, and put out bills in the usual form, containing an exact description of my person and parts. He hired a large room between three and four hundred foot wide. He provided a table sixty foot in diameter, upon

[1] Probably London.

which I was to act my part, and palisadoed it round three feet
from the edge, and as many high, to prevent my falling over.
I was shown ten times a day to the wonder and satisfaction
of all people. I could now speak the language tolerably well,
and perfectly understood every word that was spoken to me.
Besides, I had learnt their alphabet, and could make a shift
to explain a sentence here and there; for Glumdalclitch had
been my instructor while we were at home, and at leisure
hours during our journey. She carried a little book in her
pocket, not much larger than a Sanson's *Atlas;* it was a common treatise for the use of young girls, giving a short account
of their religion; out of this she taught me my letters, and
interpreted the words.

Chapter III.

*The author sent for to court. The Queen buys him of his mas-
ter the farmer, and presents him to the King. He disputes
with his Majesty's great scholars. An apartment at court
provided for the author. He is in high favour with the
Queen. He stands up for the honour of his own country.
His quarrels with the Queen's dwarf.*

The frequent labours I underwent every day made in a few
weeks a very considerable change in my health: the more
my master got by me, the more unsatiable he grew. I had quite
lost my stomach, and was almost reduced to a skeleton. The
farmer observed it, and concluding I soon must die, resolved
to make as good a hand of me as he could. While he was thus
reasoning and resolving with himself, a *slardral,* or gentleman
usher, came from court, commanding my master to bring me
immediately thither for the diversion of the Queen and her
ladies. Some of the latter had already been to see me, and
reported strange things of my beauty, behaviour, and good
sense. Her Majesty and those who attended her were beyond
measure delighted with my demeanor. I fell on my knees, and
begged the honour of kissing her imperial foot; but this gracious princess held out her little finger towards me (after I
was set on a table) which I embraced in both my arms, and
put the tip of it, with the utmost respect, to my lip. She made
me some general questions about my country and my travels,
which I answered as distinctly and in as few words as I could.
She asked whether I would be content to live at court. I bowed

down to the board of the table, and humbly answered that I was my master's slave, but if I were at my own disposal, I should be proud to devote my life to her Majesty's service. She then asked my master whether he were willing to sell me at a good price. He, who apprehended I could not live a month, was ready enough to part with me, and demanded a thousand pieces of gold, which were ordered him on the spot, each piece being about the bigness of eight hundred moidores; but, allowing for the proportion of all things between that country and Europe, and the high price of gold among them, was hardly so great a sum as a thousand guineas would be in England. I then said to the Queen, since I was now her Majesty's most humble creature and vassal, I must beg the favour, that Glumdalclitch, who had always tended me with so much care and kindness, and understood to do it so well, might be admitted into her service, and continue to be my nurse and instructor. Her Majesty agreed to my petition, and easily got the farmer's consent, who was glad enough to have his daughter preferred at court: and the poor girl herself was not able to hide her joy. My late master withdrew, bidding me farewell, and saying he had left me in a good service; to which I replied not a word, only making him a slight bow.

The Queen observed my coldness, and when the farmer was gone out of the apartment, asked me the reason. I made bold to tell her Majesty that I owed no other obligation to my late master, than his not dashing out the brains of a poor harmless creature found by chance in his field; which obligation was amply recompensed by the gain he had made in showing me through half the kingdom, and the price he had now sold me for. That the life I had since led was laborious enough to kill an animal of ten times my strength. That my health was much impaired by the continual drudgery of entertaining the rabble every hour of the day, and that if my master had not thought my life in danger, her Majesty perhaps would not have got so cheap a bargain. But as I was out of all fear of being ill treated under the protection of so great and good an empress, the Ornament of Nature, the Darling of the World, the Delight of her Subjects, the Phœnix of the Creation; so, I hoped, my late master's apprehensions would appear to be groundless, for I already found my spirits to revive by the influence of her most august presence.

This was the sum of my speech, delivered with great improprieties and hesitation; the latter part was altogether framed in the style peculiar to that people, whereof I learned some phrases from Glumdalclitch, while she was carrying me to court.

The Queen, giving great allowance for my defectiveness in speaking, was however surprised at so much wit and good sense in so diminutive an animal. She took me in her own hand, and carried me to the King, who was then retired to his cabinet. His Majesty, a prince of much gravity, and austere countenance, not well observing my shape at first view, asked the Queen after a cold manner, how long it was since she grew fond of a *splackmuck;* for such it seems he took me to be, as I lay upon my breast in her Majesty's right hand. But this princess, who hath an infinite deal of wit and humour, set me gently on my feet upon the scrutore, and commanded me to give his Majesty an account of my self, which I did in a very few words; and Glumdalclitch, who attended at the cabinet door, and could not endure I should be out of her sight, being admitted, confirmed all that had passed from my arrival at her father's house.

The King, although he be as learned a person as any in his dominions, had been educated in the study of philosophy,[1] and particularly mathematics; yet when he observed my shape exactly, and saw me walk erect, before I began to speak, conceived I might be a piece of clock-work (which is in that country arrived to a very great perfection), contrived by some ingenious artist. But, when he heard my voice, and found what I delivered to be regular and rational, he could not conceal his astonishment. He was by no means satisfied with the relation I gave him of the manner I came into his kingdom, but thought it a story concerted between Glumdalclitch and her father, who had taught me a set of words to make me sell at a higher price. Upon this imagination he put several other questions to me, and still received rational answers, no otherwise detective than by a foreign accent, and an imperfect knowledge in the language, with some rustic phrases which I had learned at the farmer's house, and did not suit the polite style of a court.

His Majesty sent for three great scholars who were then in their weekly waiting (according to the custom in that country). These gentlemen, after they had a while examined my shape with much nicety, were of different opinions concerning me. They all agreed that I could not be produced according to the regular laws of nature, because I was not framed with

---

[1] Recently the King of the Brobdingnagians has been equated with Sir William Temple, Swift's patron.

a capacity of preserving my life, either by swiftness, or climbing of trees, or digging holes in the earth. They observed by my teeth, which they viewed with great exactness, that I was a carnivorous animal; yet most quadrupeds being an overmatch for me, and field mice, with some others, too nimble, they could not imagine how I should be able to support my self, unless I fed upon snails and other insects, which they offered by many learned arguments to evince that I could not possibly do. One of them seemed to think that I might be an embryo, or abortive birth. But this opinion was rejected by the other two, who observed my limbs to be perfect and finished, and that I had lived several years, as it was manifested from my beard, the stumps whereof they plainly discovered through a magnifying-glass. They would not allow me to be a dwarf, because my littleness was beyond all degrees of comparison; for the Queen's favourite dwarf, the smallest ever known in that kingdom, was near thirty foot high. After much debate, they concluded unanimously that I was only *relplum scalcath*,[1] which is interpreted literally, *lusus naturæ;*[2] a determination exactly agreeable to the modern philosophy of Europe, whose professors, disdaining the old evasion of occult causes, whereby the followers of Aristotle endeavour in vain to disguise their ignorance, have invented this wonderful solution of all difficulties to the unspeakable advancement of human knowledge.

After this decisive conclusion, I entreated to be heard a word or two. I applied myself to the King, and assured his Majesty that I came from a country which abounded with several millions of both sexes, and of my own stature; where the animals, trees, and houses were all in proportion, and where by consequence I might be as able to defend my self, and to find sustenance, as any of his Majesty's subjects could do here; which I took for a full answer to those gentlemen's arguments. To this they only replied with a smile of contempt, saying, that the farmer had instructed me very well in my lesson. The King, who had a much better understanding, dismissing his learned men, sent for the farmer, who by good fortune was not yet gone out of town; having therefore first examined him privately, and then confronted him with me and the young girl, his Majesty began to think that what we told him might possibly be true. He desired the Queen to order that a particular care should be taken of me, and was of opinion, that Glumdalclitch should still continue in her office of tend-

---

[1] This phrase has been decoded as *real prime carcass*.
[2] A freak of nature.

ing me, because he observed we had a great affection for each
other. A convenient apartment was provided for her at court;
she had a sort of governess appointed to take care of her education, a maid to dress her, and two other servants for menial
offices; but the care of me was wholly appropriated to her
self. The Queen commanded her own cabinet-maker to contrive a box that might serve me for a bed-chamber, after the
model that Glumdalclitch and I should agree upon. This man
was a most ingenious artist, and according to my directions,
in three weeks finished for me a wooden chamber of sixteen
foot square, and twelve high, with sash-windows, a door, and
two closets, like a London bed-chamber. The board that made
the ceiling was to be lifted up and down by two hinges, to put
in a bed ready furnished by her Majesty's upholsterer, which
Glumdalclitch took out every day to air, made it with her own
hands, and letting it down at night, locked up the roof over
me. A nice workman, who was famous for little curiosities,
undertook to make me two chairs, with backs and frames, of a
substance not unlike ivory, and two tables, with a cabinet to
put my things in. The room was quilted on all sides; as well as
the floor and the ceiling, to prevent any accident from the
carelessness of those who carried me, and to break the force
of a jolt when I went in a coach. I desired a lock for my door
to prevent rats and mice from coming in: the smith after several attempts made the smallest that was ever seen among
them, for I have known a larger at the gate of a gentleman's
house in England. I made a shift to keep the key in a pocket
of my own, fearing Glumdalclitch might lose it. The Queen
likewise ordered the thinnest silks that could be gotten, to
make me clothes, not much thicker than an English blanket,
very cumbersome till I was accustomed to them. They were
after the fashion of the kingdom, partly resembling the Persian, and partly the Chinese, and are a very grave decent habit.

The Queen became so fond of my company, that she could
not dine without me. I had a table placed upon the same at
which her Majesty ate, just at her left elbow, and a chair to sit
on. Glumdalclitch stood upon a stool on the floor, near my
table, to assist and take care of me. I had an entire set of silver
dishes and plates, and other necessaries, which, in proportion to those of the Queen, were not much bigger than what
I have seen in a London toy-shop, for the furniture of a baby-
house; these my little nurse kept in her pocket, in a silver box,
and gave me at meals as I wanted them, always cleaning them
her self. No person dined with the Queen but the two prin-

cesses royal, the elder sixteen years old, and the younger at that time thirteen and a month. Her Majesty used to put a bit of meat upon one of my dishes, out of which I carved for my self; and her diversion was to see me eat in miniature. For the Queen (who had indeed but a weak stomach) took up at one mouthful as much as a dozen English farmers could eat at a meal, which to me was for some time a very nauseous sight. She would craunch the wing of a lark, bones and all, between her teeth, although it were nine times as large as that of a full-grown turkey; and put a bit of bread in her mouth, as big as two twelve-penny loaves. She drank out of a golden cup, above a hogshead at a draught. Her knives were twice as long as a scythe set straight upon the handle. The spoons, forks, and other instruments were all in the same proportion. I remember when Glumdalclitch carried me out of curiosity to see some of the tables at court, where ten or a dozen of these enormous knives and forks were lifted up together, I thought I had never till then beheld so terrible a sight.

It is the custom that every Wednesday (which, as I have before observed, was their Sabbath), the King and Queen, with the royal issue of both sexes, dine together in the apartment of his Majesty, to whom I was now become a favourite, and at these times my little chair and table were placed at his left hand before one of the salt-cellars. This prince took a pleasure in conversing with me, enquiring into the manners, religion, laws, government, and learning of Europe, wherein I gave him the best account I was able. His apprehension was so clear, and his judgment so exact, that he made very wise reflections and observations upon all I said. But I confess, that after I had been a little too copious in talking of my own beloved country, of our trade, and wars by sea and land, of our schisms in religion, and parties in the state, the prejudices of his education prevailed so far, that he could not forbear taking me up in his right hand, and stroking me gently with the other, after an hearty fit of laughing, asked me whether I were a Whig or a Tory. Then turning to his first minister, who waited behind him with a white staff, near as tall as the main-mast of the *Royal Sovereign*,[1] he observed how contemptible a thing was human grandeur, which could be mimicked by such diminutive insects as I: and yet, said he, I dare engage, those creatures have their titles and distinctions of honour, they contrive little nests and burrows, that they call houses and

[1] The name of one of the largest ships in the English navy in the seventeenth century.

cities; they make a figure in dress and equipage; they love, they fight, they dispute, they cheat, they betray. And thus he continued on, while my colour came and went several times, with indignation to hear our noble country, the mistress of arts and arms, the scourge of France, the arbitress of Europe, the seat of virtue, piety, honour and truth, the pride and envy of the world, so contemptuously treated.

But, as I was not in a condition to resent injuries, so, upon mature thoughts, I began to doubt whether I were injured or no. For, after having been accustomed several months to the sight and converse of this people, and observed every object upon which I cast my eyes to be of proportionable magnitude, the horror I had first conceived from their bulk and aspect was so far worn off, that if I had then beheld a company of English lords and ladies in their finery, and birthday clothes,[1] act-ing their several parts in the most courtly manner of strutting, and bowing, and prating, to say the truth, I should have been strongly tempted to laugh as much at them as this king and his grandees did at me. Neither indeed could I forbear smiling at my self, when the Queen used to place me upon her hand towards a looking-glass, by which both our persons appeared before me in full view together; and there could nothing be more ridiculous than the comparison: so that I really began to imagine my self dwindled many degrees below my usual size.

Nothing angered and mortified me so much as the Queen's dwarf,[2] who being of the lowest stature that was ever in that country (for I verily think he was not full thirty foot high), became so insolent at seeing a creature so much beneath him, that he would always affect to swagger and look big as he passed by me in the Queen's antechamber, while I was standing on some table talking with the lords or ladies of the court, and he seldom failed of a smart word or two upon my little-ness; against which I could only revenge my self by calling him brother, challenging him to wrestle, and such repartees as are usual in the mouths of court pages. One day at dinner this malicious little cub was so nettled with something I had said to him, that raising himself upon the frame of her Majesty's chair, he took me up by the middle, as I was sitting down, not thinking any harm, and let me drop into a large silver bowl of cream, and then ran away as fast as he could. I fell over

---

[1] New clothes were customarily worn on the occasion of royal birthdays.
[2] Swift is satirizing the custom of keeping dwarfs, like monkeys, as pets at court.

head and ears, and if I had not been a good swimmer, it might have gone very hard with me; for Glumdalclitch in that instant happened to be at the other end of the room, and the Queen was in such a fright that she wanted presence of mind to assist me. But my little nurse ran to my relief, and took me out, after I had swallowed above a quart of cream. I was put to bed; however I received no other damage than the loss of a suit of clothes, which was utterly spoiled. The dwarf was soundly whipped, and as a further punishment, forced to drink up the bowl of cream into which he had thrown me; neither was he ever restored to favour: for, soon after, the Queen bestowed him to a lady of high quality, so that I saw him no more, to my very great satisfaction, for I could not tell to what extremities such a malicious urchin might have carried his resentment.

He had before served me a scurvy trick, which set the Queen a laughing, although at the same time she were heartily vexed, and would have immediately cashiered him, if I had not been so generous as to intercede. Her Majesty had taken a marrowbone upon her plate, and after knocking out the marrow, placed the bone again in the dish erect as it stood before; the dwarf watching his opportunity, while Glumdalclitch was gone to the sideboard, mounted the stool she stood on to take care of me at meals, took me up in both hands, and squeezing my legs together, wedged them into the marrow-bone above my waist, where I stuck for some time, and made a very ridiculous figure. I believe it was near a minute before any one knew what was become of me, for I thought it below me to cry out. But, as princes seldom get their meat hot, my legs were not scalded, only my stockings and breeches in a sad condition. The dwarf at my entreaty had no other punishment than a sound whipping.

I was frequently rallied by the Queen upon account of my fearfulness, and she used to ask me whether the people of my country were as great cowards as my self. The occasion was this. The kingdom is much pestered with flies in summer, and these odious insects, each of them as big as a Dunstable lark, hardly gave me any rest while I sat at dinner, with their continual humming and buzzing about my ears. They would sometimes alight upon my victuals, and leave their loathsome excrement or spawn behind, which to me was very visible, although not to the natives of that country, whose large optics were not so acute as mine in viewing smaller objects. Sometimes they would fix upon my nose or forehead, where they stung me to the quick, smelling very offensively; for I could easily trace that viscous matter, which our naturalists tell us enables those creatures to walk with their feet upwards upon a ceiling. I had much ado to defend my self against these detestable animals, and could not forbear starting when they came on my face. It was the common practice of the dwarf to catch a number of these insects in his hand as schoolboys do among us, and let them out suddenly under my nose on purpose to frighten me, and divert the Queen. My remedy was to cut them in pieces with my knife as they flew in the air, wherein my dexterity was much admired.

I remember one morning when Glumdalclitch had set me in my box upon a window, as she usually did in fair days to give me air (for I durst not venture to let the box be hung on a nail out of the window, as we do with cages in England), after I had lifted up one of my sashes, and sat down at my table to eat a piece of sweet cake for my breakfast; above twenty wasps, allured by the smell, came flying into the room, humming louder than the drones of as many bagpipes. Some of them seized my cake, and carried it piecemeal away; others flew about my head and face, confounding me with the noise, and putting me in the utmost terror of their stings. However I had the courage to rise and draw my hanger, and attack them in the air. I dispatched four of them, but the rest got away, and I presently shut my window. These insects were as large as partridges: I took out their stings, found them an inch and a half long, and as sharp as needles. I carefully preserved them all, and having since shown them with some other curiosities in several parts of Europe, upon my return to England I gave three of them to Gresham College,[1] and kept the fourth for my self.

CHAPTER IV.

The country described. A proposal for correcting modern maps. The King's palace, and some account of the metropolis. The author's way of travelling. The chief temple described.

I now intend to give the reader a short description of this country, as far as I travelled in it, which was not above two thousand miles round Lorbrulgrud the metropolis. For the

[1] The original name of the Royal Society.

Queen, whom I always attended, never went further when she accompanied the King in his progresses, and there stayed till his Majesty returned from viewing his frontiers. The whole extent of this prince's dominions reacheth about six thousand miles in length, and from three to five in breadth. From whence I cannot but conclude that our geographers of Europe are in a great error, by supposing nothing but sea between Japan and California; for it was ever my opinion, that there must be a balance of earth to counterpoise the great continent of Tartary; and therefore they ought to correct their maps and charts, by joining this vast tract of land to the northwest parts of America, wherein I shall be ready to lend them my assistance.

The kingdom is a peninsula, terminated to the northeast by a ridge of mountains thirty miles high, which are altogether impassable by reason of the volcanoes upon the tops. Neither do the most learned know what sort of mortals inhabit beyond these mountains, or whether they be inhabited at all. On the three other sides it is bounded by the ocean. There is not one seaport in the whole kingdom, and those parts of the coasts into which the rivers issue are so full of pointed rocks, and the sea generally so rough, that there is no venturing with the smallest of their boats; so that these people are wholly excluded from any commerce with the rest of the world. But the large rivers are full of vessels, and abound with excellent fish, for they seldom get any from the sea, because the sea-fish are of the same size with those in Europe, and consequently not worth catching; whereby it is manifest, that nature in the production of plants and animals of so extraordinary a bulk is wholly confined to this continent, of which I leave the reasons to be determined by philosophers. However, now and then they take a whale that happens to be dashed against the rocks, which the common people feed on heartily. These whales I have known so large that a man could hardly carry one upon his shoulders; and sometimes for curiosity they are brought in hampers to Lorbrulgrud: I saw one of them in a dish at the King's table, which passed for a rarity, but I did not observe he was fond of it; for I think indeed the bigness disgusted him, although I have seen one somewhat larger in Greenland.

The country is well inhabited, for it contains fifty-one cities, near an hundred walled towns, and a great number of villages. To satisfy my curious reader, it may be sufficient to describe Lorbrulgrud. This city stands upon almost two equal parts on each side the river that passes through. It contains above eighty thousand houses. It is in length three *glonglungs* (which make about fifty-four English miles) and two and a half in breadth, as I measured it my self in the royal map made by the King's order, which was laid on the ground on purpose for me, and extended an hundred feet; I paced the diameter and circumference several times barefoot, and computing by the scale, measured it pretty exactly.

The King's palace is no regular edifice, but an heap of buildings about seven miles round: the chief rooms are generally two hundred and forty foot high, and broad and long in proportion. A coach was allowed to Glumdalclitch and me, wherein her governess frequently took her out to see the town, or go among the shops; and I was always of the party, carried in my box; although the girl at my own desire would often take me out, and hold me in her hand, that I might more conveniently view the houses and the people as we passed along the streets. I reckoned our coach to be about a square of Westminster Hall, but not altogether so high, however, I cannot be very exact. One day the governess ordered our coachman to stop at several shops, where the beggars, watching their opportunity, crowded to the sides of the coach, and gave me the most horrible spectacles that ever an European eye beheld. There was a woman with a cancer in her breast, swelled to a monstrous size, full of holes, in two or three of which I could have easily crept, and covered my whole body. There was a fellow with a wen in his neck, larger than five woolpacks, and another with a couple of wooden legs, each about twenty foot high. But the most hateful sight of all was the lice crawling on their clothes: I could see distinctly the limbs of these vermin with my naked eye, much better than those of an European louse through a microscope, and their snouts with which they rooted like swine. They were the first I had ever beheld, and I should have been curious enough to dissect one of them, if I had proper instruments (which I unluckily left behind me in the ship) although indeed the sight was so nauseous, that it perfectly turned my stomach.

Beside the large box in which I was usually carried, the Queen orderd a smaller one to be made for me, of about twelve foot square, and ten high, for the convenience of travelling, because the other was somewhat too large for Glumdalclitch's lap, and cumbersome in the coach; it was made by the same artist, whom I directed in the whole contrivance. This travelling closet was an exact square with a window in

the middle of three of the squares, and each window was lat-
ticed with iron wire on the outside, to prevent accidents in
long journeys. On the fourth side, which had no window, two
strong staples were fixed, through which the person that carried me, when I had a mind to be on horseback, but in a
leathern belt, and buckled it about his waist. This was always
the office of some grave trusty servant to whom I could confide, whether I attended the King and Queen in their progresses, or were disposed to see the gardens, or pay a visit to
some great lady or minister of state in the court, when Glumdalclitch happened to be out of order: for I soon began to be
known and esteemed among the greatest officers, I suppose
more upon account of their Majesties' favour than any merit
of my own. In journeys, when I was weary of the coach, a
servant on horseback would buckle my box, and place it on
a cushion before him; and there I had a full prospect of the
country on three sides from my three windows. I had in this
closet a field-bed and a hammock hung from the ceiling, two
chairs and a table, neatly screwed to the floor, to prevent being
tossed about by the agitation of the horse or the coach. And
having been long used to sea-voyages, those motions, although
sometimes very violent, did not much discompose me.

Whenever I had a mind to see the town, it was always in my
travelling-closet, which Glumdalclitch held in her lap in a
kind of open sedan, after the fashion of the country, borne by
four men, and attended by two others in the Queen's livery.
The people, who had often heard of me, were very curious
to crowd about the sedan, and the girl was complaisant enough
to make the bearers stop, and to take me in her hand that I
might be more conveniently seen.

I was very desirous to see the chief temple, and particularly
the tower belonging to it, which is reckoned the highest in the
kingdom. Accordingly one day my nurse carried me thither,
but I may truly say I came back disappointed; for the height
is not above three thousand foot, reckoning from the ground
to the highest pinnacle top; which, allowing for the difference
between the size of those people and us in Europe is no great
matter for admiration, nor at all equal in proportion (if I
rightly remember) to Salisbury steeple. But, not to detract
from a nation to which during my life I shall acknowledge my
self extremely obliged, it must be allowed that whatever this
famous tower wants in height is amply made up in beauty and
strength. For the walls are near an hundred foot thick, built
of hewn stone, whereof each is about forty foot square, and

adorned on all sides with statues of gods and emperors cut in marble larger than the life, placed in their several niches. I measured a little finger which had fallen down from one of these statues, and lay unperceived among some rubbish, and found it exactly four foot and an inch in length. Glumdal-clitch wrapped it up in a handkerchief, and carried it home in her pocket to keep among other trinkets, of which the girl was very fond, as children at her age usually are.

The King's kitchen is indeed a noble building, vaulted at top, and about six hundred foot high. The great oven is not so wide by ten paces as the cupola at St. Paul's: for I measured the latter on purpose after my return. But if I should describe the kitchen-grate, the prodigious pots and kettles, the joints of meat turning on the spits, with many other particulars, perhaps I should be hardly believed; at least a severe critic would be apt to think I enlarged a little, as travellers are often suspected to do. To avoid which censure, I fear I have run too much into the other extreme; and that if this treatise should happen to be translated into the language of Brobdingnag [1] (which is the general name of that kingdom) and transmitted thither, the King and his people would have reason to complain that I had done them an injury by a false and diminutive representation.

His Majesty seldom keeps above six hundred horses in his stables: they are generally from fifty-four to sixty foot high. But, when he goes abroad on solemn days, he is attended for state by a militia guard of five hundred horse, which indeed I thought was the most splendid sight that could be ever beheld, till I saw part of his army in battalia, whereof I shall find another occasion to speak.

CHAPTER V.

Several adventures that happened to the author. The execution of a criminal. The author shows his skill in navigation.

I should have lived happy enough in that country, if my littleness had not exposed me to several ridiculous and troublesome accidents, some of which I shall venture to relate. Glumdalclitch often carried me into the gardens of the court in my smaller box, and would sometimes take me out of it

[1] *Brobdingnag* has been decoded *England* with overtones of *grand* and *big*.

and hold me in her hand, or set me down to walk. I remember, before the dwarf left the Queen, he followed us one day into those gardens; and my nurse having set me down, he and I being close together, near some dwarf apple-trees, I must needs show my wit by a silly allusion between him and the trees, which happens to hold in their language as it doth in ours. Whereupon, the malicious rogue, watching his opportunity, when I was walking under one of them, shook it directly over my head, by which a dozen apples, each of them near as large as a Bristol barrel, came tumbling about my ears; one of them hit me on the back as I chanced to stoop, and knocked me down flat on my face, but I received no other hurt, and the dwarf was pardoned at my desire, because I had given the provocation.

Another day Glumdalclitch left me on a smooth grass-plot to divert my self while she walked at some distance with her governess. In the mean time there suddenly fell such a violent shower of hail, that I was immediately by the force of it struck to the ground: and when I was down, the hailstones gave me such cruel bangs all over the body, as if I had been pelted with tennis-balls; however I made a shift to creep on all four, and shelter my self by lying flat on my face on the lee-side of a border of lemon thyme, but so bruised from head to foot that I could not go abroad in ten days. Neither is this at all to be wondered at, because nature in that country observing the same proportion through all her operations, a hailstone is near eighteen hundred times as large as one in Europe, which I can assert upon experience, having been so curious to weigh and measure them.

But a more dangerous accident happened to me in the same garden, when my little nurse, believing she had put me in a secure place, which I often entreated her to do, that I might enjoy my own thoughts, and having left my box at home to avoid the trouble of carrying it, went to another part of the gardens with her governess and some ladies of her acquaintance. While she was absent and out of hearing, a small white spaniel belonging to one of the chief gardeners, having got by accident into the garden, happened to range near the place where I lay. The dog, following the scent, came directly up, and taking me in his mouth ran straight to his master, wagging his tail, and set me gently on the ground. By good fortune he had been so well taught, that I was carried between his teeth without the least hurt, or even tearing my clothes. But the poor gardener, who knew me well, and had a great kindness for me, was in a terrible fright. He gently took me up in both his hands, and asked me how I did; but I was so amazed and out of breath, that I could not speak a word. In a few minutes I came to my self, and he carried me safe to my little nurse, who by this time had returned to the place where she left me, and was in cruel agonies when I did not appear, nor answer when she called: she severely reprimanded the gardener on account of his dog. But the thing was hushed up, and never known at court; for the girl was afraid of the Queen's anger; and truly as to my self, I thought it would not be for my reputation that such a story should go about.

This accident absolutely determined Glumdalclitch never to trust me abroad for the future out of her sight. I had been long afraid of this resolution, and therefore concealed from her some little unlucky adventures that happened in those times when I was left by my self. Once a kite hovering over the garden made a stoop [1] at me, and if I had not resolutely drawn my hanger, and run under a thick espalier, he would have certainly carried me away in his talons. Another time, walking to the top of a fresh mole-hill, I fell to my neck in the hole through which that animal had cast up the earth, and coined some lie not worth remembering, to excuse my self for spoiling my clothes. I likewise broke my right shin against the shell of a snail, which I happened to stumble over, as I was walking alone, and thinking on poor England.

I cannot tell whether I were more pleased or mortified to observe in those solitary walks, that the smaller birds did not appear to be at all afraid of me, but would hop about within a yard distance, looking for worms and other food with as much indifference and security as if no creature at all were near them. I remember a thrush had the confidence to snatch out of my hand with his bill a piece of cake that Glumdalclitch had just given me for my breakfast. When I attempted to catch any of these birds, they would boldly turn against me, endeavouring to pick my fingers, which I durst not venture within their reach; and then they would hop back unconcerned to hunt for worms or snails, as they did before. But one day I took a thick cudgel, and threw it with all my strength so luckily at a linnet, that I knocked him down, and seizing him by the neck with both my hands, ran with him in triumph to my nurse. However, the bird, who had only been stunned, recovering himself, gave me so many boxes with his

[1] Swoop.

wings on both sides of my head and body, although I held him at arm's length, and was out of the reach of his claws, that I was twenty times thinking to let him go. But I was soon relieved by one of our servants, who wrung off the bird's neck, and I had him next day for dinner by the Queen's command. This linnet, as near as I can remember, seemed to be somewhat larger than an English swan.

The maids of honour often invited Glumdalclitch to their apartments, and desired she would bring me along with her, on purpose to have the pleasure of seeing and touching me. They would often strip me naked from top to toe, and lay me at full length in their bosoms; wherewith I was much disgusted; because, to say the truth, a very offensive smell came from their skins; which I do not mention or intend to the disadvantage of those excellent ladies, for whom I have all manner of respect; but I conceive that my sense was more acute in proportion to my littleness, and that those illustrious persons were no more disagreeable to their lovers, or to each other, than people of the same quality are with us in England. And, after all, I found their natural smell was much more supportable than when they used perfumes, under which I immediately swooned away. I cannot forget that an intimate friend of mine in Lilliput took the freedom, in a warm day, when I had used a good deal of exercise, to complain of a strong smell about me, although I am as little faulty that way as most of my sex: but I suppose his faculty of smelling was as nice with regard to me, as mine was to that of this people. Upon this point, I cannot forbear doing justice to the Queen my mistress, and Glumdalclitch my nurse, whose persons were as sweet as those of any lady in England.

That which gave me most uneasiness among these maids of honour, when my nurse carried me to visit them, was to see them use me without any manner of ceremony, like a creature who had no sort of consequence. For they would strip themselves to the skin, and put on their smocks in my presence, while I was placed on their toilet directly before their naked bodies, which, I am sure, to me was very far from being a tempting sight, or from giving me any other emotions than those of horror and disgust. Their skins appeared so coarse and uneven, so variously coloured, when I saw them near, with a mole here and there as broad as a trencher, and hairs hanging from it thicker than pack-threads, to say nothing further concerning the rest of their persons. Neither did they at all scruple while I was by to discharge what they had drunk, to the quantity of at least two hogsheads, in a vessel that held above three tuns. The handsomest among these maids of honour, a pleasant frolicsome girl of sixteen, would sometimes set me astride upon one of her nipples, with many other tricks, wherein the reader will excuse me for not being over particular. But I was so much displeased, that I entreated Glumdalclitch to contrive some excuse for not seeing that young lady any more.

One day a young gentleman, who was nephew to my nurse's governess, came and pressed them both to see an execution. It was of a man who had murdered one of that gentleman's intimate acquaintance. Glumdalclitch was prevailed on to be of the company, very much against her inclination, for she was naturally tender-hearted: and as for my self, although I abhorred such kind of spectacles, yet my curiosity tempted me to see something that I thought must be extraordinary. The malefactor was fixed in a chair upon a scaffold erected for the purpose, and his head cut off at one blow with a sword of about forty foot long. The veins and arteries spouted up such a prodigious quantity of blood, and so high in the air, that the great *jet d'eau* at Versailles was not equal for the time it lasted; and the head, when it fell on the scaffold floor, gave such a bounce as made me start, although I was at least an English mile distant.

The Queen, who often used to hear me talk of my sea-voyages, and took all occasions to divert me when I was melancholy, asked me whether I understood how to handle a sail or an oar, and whether a little exercise of rowing might not be convenient for my health. I answered that I understood both very well. For although my proper employment had been to be surgeon or doctor to the ship, yet often, upon a pinch, I was forced to work like a common mariner. But I could not see how this could be done in their country, where the smallest wherry was equal to a first rate man of war among us, and such a boat as I could manage would never live in any of their rivers: her Majesty said, if I would contrive a boat, her own joiner should make it, and she would provide a place for me to sail in. The fellow was an ingenious workman, and by my instructions in ten days finished a pleasure-boat with all its tackling, able conveniently to hold eight Europeans. When it was finished, the Queen was so delighted, that she ran with it in her lap to the King, who ordered it to be put in a cistern full of water, with me in it, by way of trial, where I could not manage my two sculls or little oars for want of room. But the

Queen had before contrived another project. She ordered the joiner to make a wooden trough of three hundred foot long, fifty broad, and eight deep; which being well pitched to prevent leaking, was placed on the floor along the wall, in an outer room of the palace. It had a cork near the bottom to let out the water when it began to grow stale, and two servants could easily fill it in half an hour. Here I often used to row for my diversion, as well as that of the Queen and her ladies, who thought themselves agreeably entertained with my skill and agility. Sometimes I would put up my sail, and then my business was only to steer, while the ladies gave me a gale with their fans; and when they were weary, some of the pages would blow my sail forward with their breath, while I showed my art by steering starboard or larboard as I pleased. When I had done, Glumdalclitch always carried back my boat into her closet, and hung it on a nail to dry.

In this exercise I once met an accident which had like to have cost me my life. For, one of the pages having put my boat into the trough, the governess who attended Glumdalclitch very officiously lifted me up to place me in the boat; but I happened to slip through her fingers, and should have infallibly fallen down forty foot upon the floor if, by the luckiest chance in the world, I had not been stopped by a corking-pin that stuck in the good gentlewoman's stomacher; the head of the pin passed between my shirt and the waistband of my breeches, and thus I was held by the middle in the air till Glumdalclitch ran to my relief.

Another time, one of the servants, whose office it was to fill my trough every third day with fresh water, was so careless to net a huge frog (not perceiving it) slip out of his pail. The frog lay concealed till I was put into my boat, but then seeing a resting place, climbed up, and made it lean so much on one side, that I was forced to balance it with all my weight on the other, to prevent overturning. When the frog was got in, it hopped at once half the length of the boat, and then over my head, backwards and forwards, daubing my face and clothes with its odious slime. The largeness of its features made it appear the most deformed animal that can be conceived. However, I desired Glumdalclitch to let me deal with it alone. I banged it a good while with one of my sculls, and at last forced it to leap out of the boat.

But the greatest danger I ever underwent in that kingdom was from a monkey, who belonged to one of the clerks of the kitchen. Glumdalclitch had locked me up in her closet, while

she went somewhere upon business or a visit. The weather
being very warm, the closet window was left open, as well as
the windows and the door of my bigger box, in which I usually lived, because of its largeness and conveniency. As I sat
quietly meditating at my table, I heard something bounce in
at the closet window, and skip about from one side to the
other; whereat, although I were much alarmed, yet I ventured
to look out, but not stirring from my seat; and then I saw this
frolicsome animal, frisking and leaping up and down till at
last he came to my box, which he seemed to view with great
pleasure and curiosity, peeping in at the door and every window. I retreated to the farther corner of my room, or box, but
the monkey, looking in at every side, put me into such a
fright, that I wanted presence of mind to conceal my self
under the bed, as I might easily have done. After some time
spent in peeping, grinning, and chattering, he at last espied
me, and reaching one of his paws in at the door, as a cat does
when she plays with a mouse, although I often shifted place
to avoid him; he at length seized the lappet of my coat (which
being made of that country silk, was very thick and strong)
and dragged me out. He took me up in his right forefoot, and
held me as a nurse does a child she is going to suckle, just as
I have seen the same sort of creature do with a kitten in
Europe: and when I offered to struggle, he squeezed me so
hard, that I thought it more prudent to submit. I have good
reason to believe that he took me for a young one of his own
species, by his often stroking my face very gently with his
other paw. In these diversions he was interrupted by a noise at
the closet door, as if some body were opening it; whereupon
he suddenly leaped up to the window at which he had come
in, and thence upon the leads and gutters, walking upon three
legs, and holding me in the fourth, till he clambered up to a
roof that was next to ours. I heard Glumdalclitch give a shriek
at the moment he was carrying me out. The poor girl was
almost distracted: that quarter of the palace was all in an
uproar; the servants ran for ladders; the monkey was seen by
hundreds in the court sitting upon the ridge of a building,
holding me like a baby in one of his fore-paws, and feeding
me with the other, by cramming into my mouth some victuals
he had squeezed out of the bag on one side of his chaps, and
patting me when I would not eat; whereat many of the rabble
below could not forbear laughing; neither do I think they
justly ought to be blamed, for without question the sight was
ridiculous enough to every body but my self. Some of the

people threw up stones, hoping to drive the monkey down; but this was strictly forbidden, or else very probably my brains had been dashed out.

The ladders were now applied, and mounted by several men, which the monkey observing, and finding himself almost encompassed, not being able to make speed enough with his three legs, let me drop on a ridge tile, and made his escape. Here I sat for some time five hundred yards from the ground, expecting every moment to be blown down by the wind, or to fall by my own giddiness, and come tumbling over and over from the ridge to the eaves. But an honest lad, one of my nurse's footmen, climbed up, and putting me into his breeches pocket, brought me down safe.

I was almost choked with the filthy stuff the monkey had crammed down my throat; but my dear little nurse picked it out of my mouth with a small needle, and then I fell a vomiting, which gave me great relief. Yet I was so weak and bruised in the sides with the squeezes given me by this odious animal, that I was forced to keep my bed a fortnight. The King, Queen and all the court sent every day to enquire after my health, and her Majesty made me several visits during my sickness. The monkey was killed, and an order made that no such animal should be kept about the palace.

When I attended the King after my recovery, to return him thanks for his favours, he was pleased to rally me a good deal upon this adventure. He asked me what my thoughts and speculations were while I lay in the monkey's paw; how I liked the victuals he gave me, his manner of feeding; and whether the fresh air on the roof had sharpened my stomach. He desired to know what I would have done upon such an occasion in my own country. I told his Majesty, that in Europe we had no monkeys, except such as were brought for curiosities from other places, and so small, that I could deal with a dozen of them together, if they presumed to attack me. And as for that monstrous animal with whom I was so lately engaged (it was indeed as large as an elephant), if my fears had suffered me to think so far as to make use of my hanger (looking fiercely and clapping my hand upon the hilt as I spoke) when he poked his paw into my chamber, perhaps I should have given him such a wound as would have made him glad to withdraw it with more haste than he put it in. This I delivered in a firm tone, like a person who was jealous lest his courage should be called in question. However, my speech produced nothing else besides a loud laughter, which all the respect due to his Majesty from those about him could not make them contain. This made me reflect how vain an attempt it is for a man to endeavour doing himself honour among those who are out of all degree of equality or comparison with him. And yet I have seen the moral of my own behaviour very frequent in England since my return, where a little contemptible varlet, without the least title to birth, person, wit, or common sense, shall presume to look with importance, and put himself upon a foot with the greatest persons of the kingdom.

I was every day furnishing the court with some ridiculous story; and Glumdalclitch, although she loved me to excess, yet was arch enough to inform the Queen whenever I committed any folly that she thought would be diverting to her Majesty. The girl, who had been out of order, was carried by her governess to take the air about an hour's distance, or thirty miles from town. They alighted out of the coach near a small footpath in a field, and Glumdalclitch setting down my travelling box, I went out of it to walk. There was a cow-dung in the path, and I must needs try my activity by attempting to leap over it. I took a run, but unfortunately jumped short, and found my self just in the middle up to my knees. I waded through with some difficulty, and one of the footmen wiped me as clean as he could with his handkerchief; for I was filthily bemired, and my nurse confined me to my box till we returned home; where the Queen was soon informed of what had passed, and the footmen spread it about the court, so that all the mirth, for some days, was at my expense.

CHAPTER VI.

Several contrivances of the author to please the King and Queen. He shows his skill in music. The King enquires into the state of Europe, which the author relates to him. The King's observations thereon.

I used to attend the King's levee once or twice a week, and had often seen him under the barber's hand, which indeed was at first very terrible to behold. For the razor was almost twice as long as an ordinary scythe. His Majesty according to the custom of the country was only shaved twice a week. I once prevailed on the barber to give me some of the suds or lather, out of which I picked forty or fifty of the strongest stumps of hair. I then took a piece of fine wood, and cut it like the back of a comb, making several holes in it at equal distance with as small a needle as I could get from Glumdalclitch. I fixed in the stumps so artificially, scraping and sloping them with my knife towards the points, that I made a very tolerable comb; which was a seasonable supply, my own being so much broken in the teeth, that it was almost useless, neither did I know any artist in that country so nice and exact, as would undertake to make me another.

And this puts me in mind of an amusement wherein I spent many of my leisure hours. I desired the Queen's woman to save for me the combings of her Majesty's hair, whereof in time I got a good quantity, and consulting with my friend the cabinet-maker, who had received general orders to do little jobs for me, I directed him to make two chair frames, no larger than those I had in my box, and then to bore little holes with a fine awl round those parts where I designed the backs and seats; through these holes I wove the strongest hairs I could pick out, just after the manner of cane-chairs in England. When they were finished, I made a present of them to her Majesty, who kept them in her cabinet, and used to show them for curiosities, as indeed they were the wonder of every one who beheld them. The Queen would have had me sit upon one of these chairs, but I absolutely refused to obey her, protesting I would rather die a thousand deaths than place a dishonourable part of my body on those precious hairs that once adorned her Majesty's head. Of these hairs (as I had always a mechanical genius) I likewise made a neat little purse about five foot long, with her Majesty's name deciphered in gold letters, which I gave to Glumdalclitch, by the Queen's consent. To say the truth, it was more for show than use, being not of strength to bear the weight of the larger coins, and therefore she kept nothing in it, but some little toys that girls are fond of.

The King, who delighted in music, had frequent consorts at court, to which I was sometimes carried, and set in my box on a table to hear them: but the noise was so great, that I could hardly distinguish the tunes. I am confident that all the drums and trumpets of a royal army, beating and sounding together just at your ears, could not equal it. My practice was to have my box removed from the places where the performers sat, as far as I could, then to shut the doors and windows of it, and draw the window curtains; after which I found their music not disagreeable.

I had learned in my youth to play a little upon the spinet; Glumdalclitch kept one in her chamber, and a master attended twice a week to teach her: I call it a spinet, because it somewhat resembled that instrument, and was played upon in the same manner. A fancy came into my head that I would entertain the King and Queen with an English tune upon this instrument. But this appeared extremely difficult: for the spinet was near sixty foot long, each key being almost a foot wide, so that, with my arms extended, I could not reach to above five keys, and to press them down required a good smart stroke with my fist, which would be too great a labour, and to no purpose. The method I contrived was this. I prepared two round sticks about the bigness of common cudgels; they were thicker at one end than the other, and I covered the thicker ends with a piece of a mouse's skin, that by rapping on them I might neither damage the tops of the keys, nor interrupt the sound. Before the spinet a bench was placed about four foot below the keys, and I was put upon the bench. I ran sideling upon it that way and this, as fast as I could, banging the proper keys with my two sticks, and made a shift to play a jig to the great satisfaction of both their Majesties: but it was the most violent exercise I ever underwent, and yet I could not strike above sixteen keys, nor, consequently, play the bass and treble together, as other artists do; which was a great disadvantage to my performance.

The King, who, as I before observed, was a prince of excellent understanding, would frequently order that I should be brought in my box, and set upon the table in his closet. He would then command me to bring one of my chairs out of the box, and sit down within three yards distance upon the top of the cabinet, which brought me almost to a level with his face. In this manner I had several conversations with him. I one day took the freedom to tell his Majesty, that the contempt he discovered towards Europe, and the rest of the world, did not seem answerable to those excellent qualities of mind he was master of. That reason did not extend it self with the bulk of the body: on the contrary, we observed in our country that the tallest persons were usually least provided with it. That among other animals, bees and ants had the reputation of more industry, art and sagacity than many of the larger kinds. And that, as inconsiderable as he took me to be, I hoped I might live to do his Majesty some signal service. The King heard me with attention, and began to conceive a much better opinion of me than he had ever before. He desired I would

give him as exact an account of the government of England as
I possibly could; because, as fond as princes commonly are of
their own customs (for so he conjectured of other monarchs
by my former discourses), he should be glad to hear of any
thing that might deserve imitation.

Imagine with thy self, courteous reader, how often I then
wished for the tongue of Demosthenes or Cicero, that might
have enabled me to celebrate the praise of my own dear native
country in a style equal to its merits and felicity.

I began my discourse by informing his Majesty that our
dominions consisted of two islands, which composed three
mighty kingdoms under one sovereign, besides our plantations [1] in America. I dwelt long upon the fertility of our
soil, and the temperature of our climate. I then spoke at
large upon the constitution of an English parliament, partly
made up of an illustrious body called the House of Peers,
persons of the noblest blood, and of the most ancient and
ample patrimonies. I described that extraordinary care always
taken of their education in arts and arms, to qualify them for
being counsellors born to the king and kingdom, to have a
share in the legislature, to be members of the highest court
of judicature from whence there could be no appeal; and
to be champions always ready for the defence of their prince
and country by their valour, conduct and fidelity. That these
were the ornament and bulwark of the kingdom, worthy
followers of their most renowned ancestors, whose honour
had been the reward of their virtue, from which their
posterity were never once known to degenerate. To these were
joined several holy persons, as part of that assembly, under
the title of bishops, whose peculiar business it is to take care
of religion, and of those who instruct the people therein.
These were searched and sought out through the whole nation,
by the prince and wisest counsellors, among such of the
priesthood as were most deservedly distinguished by the
sanctity of their lives, and the depth of their erudition; who
were indeed the spiritual fathers of the clergy and the people.

That the other part of the parliament consisted of an
assembly called the House of Commons, who were all
principal gentlemen, freely picked and culled out by the
people themselves, for their great abilities, and love of their
country, to represent the wisdom of the whole nation. And
these two bodies make up the most august assembly in Europe,

[1] Colonies.

to whom, in conjunction with the prince, the whole legislature is committed.

I then descended to the courts of justice, over which the judges, those venerable sages and interpreters of the law, presided, for determining the disputed rights and properties of men, as well as for the punishment of vice, and protection of innocence. I mentioned the prudent management of our treasury, the valour and achievements of our forces by sea and land. I computed the number of our people, by reckoning how many millions there might be of each religious sect, or political party among us. I did not omit even our sports and pastimes, or any other particular which I thought might redound to the honour of my country. And I finished all with a brief historical account of affairs and events in England for about an hundred years past.

This conversation was not ended under five audiences, each of several hours, and the King heard the whole with great attention, frequently taking notes of what I spoke, as well as memorandums of what questions he intended to ask me.

When I had put an end to these long discourses, his Majesty in a sixth audience, consulting his notes, proposed many doubts, queries, and objections, upon every article. He asked, what methods were used to cultivate the minds and bodies of our young nobility, and in what kind of business they commonly spent the first and teachable part of their lives. What course was taken to supply that assembly when any noble family became extinct. What qualifications were necessary in those who are to be created new lords: whether the humour of the prince, a sum of money to a court-lady, or a prime minister, or a design of strengthening a party opposite to the public interest, ever happened to be motives in those advancements. What share of knowledge these lords had in the laws of their country, and how they came by it, so as to enable them to decide the properties of their fellow-subjects in the last resort. Whether they were always so free from avarice, partialities, or want, that a bribe, or some other sinister view, could have no place among them. Whether those holy lords I spoke of were constantly promoted to that rank upon account of their knowledge in religious matters, and the sanctity of their lives, had never been compliers with the times while they were common priests; or slavish prostitute chaplains to some nobleman, whose opinions they continued servilely to follow after they were admitted into that assembly.

He then desired to know what arts were practised in electing those whom I called commoners. Whether a stranger with a strong purse might not influence the vulgar voters to choose him before their own landlords, or the most considerable gentleman in the neighbourhood. How it came to pass, that people were so violently bent upon getting into this assembly, which I allowed to be a great trouble and expense, often to the ruin of their families, without any salary or pension: because this appeared such an exalted strain of virtue and public spirit, that his Majesty seemed to doubt it might possibly not be always sincere: and he desired to know whether such zealous gentlemen could have any views of refunding themselves for the charges and trouble they were at, by sacrificing the public good to the designs of a weak and vicious prince, in conjunction with a corrupted ministry. He multiplied his questions, and sifted me thoroughly upon every part of this head, proposing numberless enquiries and objections, which I think it not prudent or convenient to repeat.

Upon what I said in relation to our courts of justice, his Majesty desired to be satisfied in several points: and this I was the better able to do, having been formerly almost ruined by a long suit in chancery, which was decreed for me with costs. He asked, what time was usually spent in determining between right and wrong, and what degree of expense. Whether advocates and orators had liberty to plead in causes manifestly known to be unjust, vexatious, or oppressive. Whether party in religion or politics were observed to be of any weight in the scale of justice. Whether those pleading orators were persons educated in the general knowledge of equity, or only in provincial, national, and other local customs. Whether they or their judges had any part in penning those laws, which they assumed the liberty of interpreting and glossing upon at their pleasure. Whether they had ever at different times pleaded for and against the same cause, and cited precedents to prove contrary opinions. Whether they were a rich or a poor corporation. Whether they received any pecuniary reward for pleading or delivering their opinions. And particularly whether they were ever admitted as members in the lower senate.

He fell next upon the management of our treasury; and said, he thought my memory had failed me, because I computed our taxes at about five or six millions a year, and when I came to mention the issues, he found they sometimes amounted to more than double; for the notes he had taken were very particular in this point, because he hoped, as he told me, that the knowledge of our conduct might be useful to him, and he could not be deceived in his calculations. But, if what I told him were true, he was still at a loss how a kingdom could run out of its estate like a private person. He asked me, who were our creditors; and where we found money to pay them. He wondered to hear me talk of such chargeable and extensive wars; that certainly we must be a quarrelsome people, or live among very bad neighbours, and that our generals must needs be richer than our kings.[1] He asked what business we had out of our own islands, unless upon the score of trade or treaty, or to defend the coasts with our fleet. Above all, he was amazed to hear me talk of a mercenary standing army in the midst of peace,[2] and among a free people. He said if we were governed by our own consent in the persons of our representatives, he could not imagine of whom we were afraid, or against whom we were to fight; and would hear my opinion, whether a private man's house might not better be defended by himself, his children, and family, than by a half a dozen rascals picked up at a venture in the streets, for small wages, who might get an hundred times more by cutting their throats.

He laughed at my odd kind of arithmetic (as he was pleased to call it) in reckoning the numbers of our people by a computation drawn from the several sects among us in religion and politics. He said, he knew no reason, why those who entertain opinions prejudicial to the public should be obliged to change, or should not be obliged to conceal them. And as it was tyranny in any government to require the first, so it was weakness not to enforce the second: for a man may be allowed to keep poisons in his closets, but not to vend them about as cordials.

He observed, that among the diversions of our nobility and gentry I had mentioned gaming. He desired to know at what age this entertainment was usually taken up, and when it was laid down. How much of their time it employed; whether it ever went so high as to affect their fortunes. Whether mean vicious people, by their dexterity in that art, might not arrive at great riches, and sometimes keep our very nobles in dependence, as well as habituate them to vile companions,

[1] This sentence possibly has implications of Marlborough, who was said to have made a tidy profit from the War of the Spanish Succession.
[2] The Bill of Rights of 1689 prohibited the maintaining of a mercenary army; George I protected some of his Hanoverian possessions by means of mercenaries.

wholly take them from the improvement of their minds, and force them, by the losses they received, to learn and practice that infamous dexterity upon others.

He was perfectly astonished with the historical account I gave him of our affairs during the last century, protesting it was only an heap of conspiracies, rebellions, murders, massacres, revolutions, banishments; the very worst effects that avarice, faction, hypocrisy, perfidiousness, cruelty, rage, madness, hatred, envy, lust, malice, and ambition could produce.

His Majesty in another audience was at the pains to recapitulate the sum of all I had spoken, compared the questions he made with the answers I had given; then taking me into his hands, and stroking me gently, delivered himself in these words, which I shall never forget, nor the manner he spoke them in: My little friend Grildrig, you have made a most admirable panegyric upon your country. You have clearly proved that ignorance, idleness and vice are the proper ingredients for qualifying a legislator. That laws are best explained, interpreted, and applied by those whose interest and abilities lie in perverting, confounding, and eluding them. I observe among you some lines of an institution, which in its original might have been tolerable, but these half erased, and the rest wholly blurred and blotted by corruptions. It doth not appear from all you have said, how any one perfection is required towards the procurement of any one station among you; much less that men are ennobled on account of their virtue, that priests are advanced for their piety or learning, soldiers for their conduct or valour, judges for their integrity, senators for the love of their country, or counsellors for their wisdom. As for yourself (continued the King) who have spent the greatest part of your life in travelling, I am well disposed to hope you may hitherto have escaped many vices of your country. But, by what I have gathered from your own relation, and the answers I have with much pains wringed and extorted from you, I cannot but conclude the bulk of your natives to be the most pernicious race of little odious vermin that nature ever suffered to crawl upon the surface of the earth.

Chapter VII.

The author's love of his country. He makes a proposal of much advantage to the King, which is rejected. The King's great ignorance in politics. The learning of that country very imperfect and confined. Their laws, and military affairs, and parties in the state.

Nothing but an extreme love of truth could have hindered me from concealing this part of my story. It was in vain to discover my resentments, which were always turned into ridicule: and I was forced to rest with patience while my noble and most beloved country was so injuriously treated. I am heartily sorry as any of my readers can possibly be, that such an occasion was given: but this prince happened to be so curious and inquisitive upon every particular, that it could not consist either with gratitude or good manners to refuse giving him what satisfaction I was able. Yet thus much I may be allowed to say in my own vindication, that I artfully eluded many of his questions, and gave to every point a more favourable turn by many degrees than the strictness of truth would allow. For I have always borne that laudable partiality to my own country, which Dionysius Halicarnassensis [1] with so much justice recommends to an historian. I would hide the frailties and deformities of my political mother, and place her virtues and beauties in the most advantageous light. This was my sincere endeavour in those many discourses I had with that mighty monarch, although it unfortunately failed of success.

But great allowances should be given to a king who lives wholly secluded from the rest of the world, and must therefore be altogether unacquainted with the manners and customs that most prevail in other nations: the want of which knowledge will ever produce many prejudices, and a certain narrowness of thinking, from which we and the politer countries of Europe are wholly exempted. And it would be hard indeed, if so remote a prince's notions of virtue and vice were to be offered as a standard for all mankind.

To confirm what I have now said, and further to show the miserable effects of a confined education, I shall here insert a passage which will hardly obtain belief. In hopes to ingratiate my self farther into his Majesty's favour, I told him of an

[1] A Greek writer, who lived in Rome, and expounded the true greatness of Rome in his *Archaeologia*.

invention discovered between three and four hundred years
ago, to make a certain powder,[1] into an heap of which the
smallest spark of fire falling, would kindle the whole in a
moment, although it were as big as a mountain, and make it
all fly up in the air together, with a noise and agitation greater
than thunder. That a proper quantity of this powder rammed
into an hollow tube of brass or iron, according to its bigness,
would drive a ball of iron or lead with such violence and
speed as nothing was able to sustain its force. That the largest
balls, thus discharged, would not only destroy whole ranks of
an army at once, but batter the strongest walls to the ground,
sink down ships, with a thousand men in each, to the bottom
of the sea; and when linked together by a chain, would cut
through masts and rigging, divide hundreds of bodies in the
middle, and lay all waste before them. That we often put this
powder into large hollow balls of iron, and discharged them by
an engine into some city we were besieging, which would rip
up the pavement, tear the houses to pieces, burst and throw
splinters on every side, dashing out the brains of all who
came near. That I knew the ingredients very well, which were
cheap, and common; I understood the manner of com-
pounding them, and could direct his workmen how to make
those tubes of a size proportionable to all other things in his
Majesty's kingdom, and the largest need not be above two
hundred foot long; twenty or thirty of which tubes, charged
with the proper quantity of powder and balls, would batter
down the walls of the strongest town in his dominions in a
few hours, or destroy the whole metropolis, if ever it should
pretend to dispute his absolute commands. This I humbly
offered to his Majesty as a small tribute of acknowledgment
in return of so many marks that I had received of his royal
favour and protection.

The King was struck with horror at the description I had
given of those terrible engines, and the proposal I had made.
He was amazed how so impotent and groveling an insect as I
(these were his expressions) could entertain such inhuman
ideas, and in so familiar a manner as to appear wholly unmoved at all the scenes of blood and desolation, which I had
painted as the common effects of those destructive machines,
whereof he said, some evil genius, enemy to mankind, must
have been the first contriver. As for himself, he protested,
that although few things delighted him so much as new

[1] In *Tale of a Tub* Swift satirizes modern inventions, among them gunpowder.

discoveries in art or in nature, yet he would rather lose half his kingdom than be privy to such a secret, which he commanded me, as I valued my life, never to mention any more.

A strange effect of narrow principles and short views! that a prince possessed of every quality which procures veneration, love, and esteem; of strong parts, great wisdom and profound learning, endued with admirable talents for government, and almost adored by his subjects, should from a nice unnecessary scruple, whereof in Europe we can have no conception, let slip an opportunity put into his hands, that would have made him absolute master of the lives, the liberties, and the fortunes of his people. Neither do I say this with the least intention to detract from the many virtues of that excellent king, whose character I am sensible will on this account be very much lessened in the opinion of an English reader: but I take this defect among them to have risen from their ignorance, by not having hitherto reduced politics into a science, as the more acute wits of Europe have done. For I remember very well, in a discourse one day with the King, when I happened to say there were several thousand books among us written upon the art of government, it gave him (directly contrary to my intention) a very mean opinion of our understandings. He professed both to abominate and despise all mystery, refinement, and intrigue, either in a prince or a minister. He could not tell what I meant by secrets of state, where an enemy or some rival nation were not in the case. He confined the knowledge of governing within very narrow bounds; to common sense and reason, to justice and lenity, to the speedy determination of civil and criminal causes; with some other obvious topics which are not worth considering. And he gave it for his opinion, that whoever could make two ears of corn, or two blades of grass to grow upon a spot of ground where only one grew before, would deserve better of mankind, and do more essential service to his country, than the whole race of politicians put together.

The learning of this people is very defective, consisting only in morality, history, poetry, and mathematics, wherein they must be allowed to excel. But the last of these is wholly applied to what may be useful in life, to the improvement of agriculture and all mechanical arts; so that among us it would be little esteemed. And as to ideas, entities, abstractions and transcendentals, I could never drive the least conception into their heads.

No law of that country must exceed in words the number of

letters in their alphabet, which consists only of two and
twenty. But indeed, few of them extend even to that length.
They are expressed in the most plain and simple terms,
wherein those people are not mercurial enough to discover
above one interpretation. And to write a comment upon any
law is a capital crime. As to the decision of civil causes, or
proceedings against criminals, their precedents are so few,
that they have little reason to boast of any extraordinary skill
in either.

They have had the art of printing, as well as the Chinese,
time out of mind. But their libraries are not very large; for
that of the King's, which is reckoned the largest, doth not
amount to above a thousand volumes, placed in a gallery of
twelve hundred foot long, from whence I had liberty to borrow
what books I pleased. The Queen's joiner had contrived in
one of Glumdalclitch's rooms a kind of wooden machine
five and twenty foot high, formed like a standing ladder; the
steps were each fifty foot long: it was indeed a moveable
pair of stairs, the lowest end placed at ten foot distance from
the wall of the chamber. The book I had a mind to read was
put up leaning against the wall. I first mounted to the upper
step of the ladder, and turning my face towards the book,
began at the top of the page, and so walking to the right and
left about eight or ten paces, according to the length of the
lines, till I had gotten a little below the level of my eyes, and
then descending gradually till I came to the bottom: after
which I mounted again, and began the other page in the same
manner, and so turned over the leaf, which I could easily
do with both my hands, for it was as thick and stiff as a pasteboard, and in the largest folios not above eighteen or twenty
foot long.

Their style is clear, masculine, and smooth, but not florid,
for they avoid nothing more than multiplying unnecessary
words, or using various expressions. I have perused many of
their books, especially those in history and morality. Among
the latter I was much diverted with a little old treatise, which
always lay in Glumdalclitch's bedchamber, and belonged to
her governess, a grave elderly gentlewoman, who dealt in
writings of morality and devotion. The book treats of the
weakness of human kind, and is in little esteem except among
women and the vulgar. However, I was curious to see what
an author of that country could say upon such a subject.
This writer went through all the usual topics of European
moralists, showing how diminutive, contemptible, and helpless

an animal was man in his own nature; how unable to defend himself from the inclemencies of the air, or the fury of wild beasts. How much he was excelled by one creature in strength, by another in speed, by a third in foresight, by a fourth in industry. He added, that nature was degenerated in these latter declining ages of the world, and could now produce only small abortive births in comparison of those in ancient times.[1] He said it was very reasonable to think, not only that the species of men were originally much larger, but also that there must have been giants in former ages, which, as it is asserted by history and tradition, so it hath been confirmed by huge bones and skulls casually dug up in several parts of the kingdom, far exceeding the common dwindled race of man in our days. He argued, that the very laws of nature absolutely required we should have been made, in the beginning, of a size more large and robust, not so liable to destruction from every little accident of a tile falling from an house, or a stone cast from the hand of a boy, or of being drowned in a little brook. From this way of reasoning the author drew several moral applications useful in the conduct of life, but needless here to repeat. For my own part, I could not avoid reflecting how universally this talent was spread of drawing lectures in morality, or indeed rather matter of discontent and repining, from the quarrels we raise with nature. And, I believe, upon a strict enquiry those quarrels might be shown as ill-grounded among us as they are among that people.

As to their military affairs, they boast that the King's army consists of an hundred and seventy-six thousand foot, and thirty-two thousand horse, if that may be called an army which is made up of tradesmen in the several cities, and farmers in the country, whose commanders are only the nobility and gentry without pay or reward. They are indeed perfect enough in their exercises, and under very good discipline, wherein I saw no great merit: for how should it be otherwise, where every farmer is under the command of his own landlord, and every citizen under that of the principal men in his own city, chosen after the manner of Venice by ballot?

I have often seen the militia of Lorbrulgrud drawn out to

[1] Swift here expounds the Theory of Nature's Decay in rejection of which the Theory of Progress was formulated. In refutation of the image of the Ancients as giants, the Moderns claimed that, even if they themselves were dwarfs seated upon the shoulders of the giant, the dwarf is taller and can see farther, inasmuch as knowledge is cumulative.

exercise in a great field near the city, of twenty miles square.
They were in all not above twenty-five thousand foot, and six
thousand horse; but it was impossible for me to compute their
number, considering the space of ground they took up. A
cavalier mounted on a large steed might be about ninety foot
high. I have seen this whole body of horse upon the word of
command draw their swords at once, and brandish them in the
air. Imagination can figure nothing so grand, so surprising
and so astonishing. It looked as if ten thousand flashes of
lightning were darting at the same time from every quarter
of the sky.

I was curious to know how this prince, to whose dominions
there is no access from any other country, came to think of
armies, or to teach his people the practice of military discipline. But I was soon informed, both by conversation, and
reading their histories. For in the course of many ages they
have been troubled with the same disease to which the whole
race of mankind is subject; the nobility often contending for
power, the people for liberty, and the King for absolute
dominion. All which, however happily tempered by the laws
of that kingdom, have been sometimes violated by each of
the three parties, and have more than once occasioned civil
wars, the last whereof was happily put an end to by this
prince's grandfather in a general composition; and the militia
then settled with common consent hath been ever since kept
in the strictest duty.

CHAPTER VIII.

*The King and Queen make a progress to the frontiers. The
author attends them. The manner in which he leaves
the country very particularly related. He returns to
England.*

I had always a strong impulse that I should sometime recover my liberty, although it was impossible to conjecture by
what means, or to form any project with the least hope of
succeeding. The ship in which I sailed was the first ever
known to be driven within sight of that coast, and the King
had given strict orders, that if at any time another appeared,
it should be taken ashore, and with all its crew and passengers
brought in a tumbril to Lorbrulgrud. He was strongly bent
to get me a woman of my own size, by whom I might propagate the breed: but I think I should rather have died than

undergone the disgrace of leaving a posterity to be kept in cages like tame canary birds, and perhaps in time sold about the kingdom to persons of quality for curiosities. I was indeed treated with much kindness; I was the favourite of a great king and queen, and the delight of the whole court, but it was upon such a foot as ill became the dignity of human kind. I could never forget those domestic pledges I had left behind me. I wanted to be among people with whom I could converse upon even terms, and walk about the streets and fields without fear of being trod to death like a frog or young puppy. But my deliverance came sooner than I expected, and in a manner not very common: the whole story and circumstances of which I shall faithfully relate.

I had now been two years in this country; and about the beginning of the third, Glumdalclitch and I attended the King and Queen in progress to the south coast of the kingdom. I was carried as usual in my travelling-box, which, as I have already described, was a very convenient closet of twelve foot wide. I had ordered a hammock to be fixed by silken ropes from the four corners at the top, to break the jolts, when a servant carried me before him on horseback, as I sometimes desired, and would often sleep in my hammock while we were upon the road. On the roof of my closet, just over the middle of the hammock, I ordered the joiner to cut out a hole of a foot square to give me air in hot weather as I slept, which hole I shut at pleasure with a board that drew backwards and forwards through a groove.

When we came to our journey's end, the King thought proper to pass a few days at a palace he hath near Flanflasnic,[1] a city within eighteen English miles of the seaside. Glumdalclitch and I were much fatigued; I had gotten a small cold, but the poor girl was so ill as to be confined to her chamber. I longed to see the ocean, which must be the only scene of my escape, if ever it should happen. I pretended to be worse than I really was, and desired leave to take the fresh air of the sea, with a page whom I was very fond of, and who had sometimes been trusted with me. I shall never forget with what unwillingness Glumdalclitch consented, nor the strict charge she gave the page to be careful of me, bursting at the same time into a flood of tears, as if she had some foreboding of what was to happen. The boy took me out in my box about half an hour's walk from the palace towards the rocks on the seashore. I ordered him to set me down, and

[1] Has been decoded as *fantastic*.

lifting up one of my sashes, cast many a wistful melancholy look towards the sea. I found my self not very well, and told the page that I had a mind to take a nap in my hammock, which I hoped would do me good. I got in, and the boy shut the window close down to keep out the cold. I soon fell asleep, and all I can conjecture is, that while I slept, the page, thinking no danger could happen, went among the rocks to look for birds' eggs, having before observed him from my window searching about, and picking up one or two in the clefts. Be that as it will; I found my self suddenly awaked with a violent pull upon the ring which was fastened at the top of my box for the conveniency of carriage. I felt the box raised very high in the air, and then borne forward with prodigious speed. The first jolt had like to have shaken me out of my hammock, but afterwards the motion was easy enough. I called out several times as loud as I could raise my voice, but all to no purpose. I looked towards my windows, and could see nothing but the clouds and sky. I heard a noise just over my head like the clapping of wings, and then began to perceive the woeful condition I was in; that some eagle had got the ring of my box in his beak, with an intent to let it fall on a rock like a tortoise in a shell, and then pick out my body and devour it. For the sagacity and smell of this bird enable him to discover his quarry at a great distance, although better concealed than I could be within a two-inch board.

In a very little time I observed the noise and flutter of wings to encrease very fast, and my box was tossed up and down like a signpost in a windy day. I heard several bangs or buffets, as I thought, given to the eagle (for such I am certain it must have been that held the ring of my box in his beak) and then all on a sudden felt my self falling perpendicularly down for above a minute, but with such incredible swiftness that I almost lost my breath. My fall was stopped by a terrible squash, that sounded louder to my ears than the cataract of Niagara; after which I was quite in the dark for another minute, and then my box began to rise so high that I could see light from the tops of my windows. I now perceived that I was fallen into the sea. My box, by the weight of my body, the goods that were in, and the broad plates of iron fixed for strength at the four corners of the top and bottom, floated about five foot deep in water. I did then, and do now suppose that the eagle which flew away with my box was pursued by two or three others, and forced to let me drop while he was defending himself against the rest, who hoped to share in the prey. The plates of iron fastened at the bottom of the box (for those were the strongest) preserved the balance while it fell, and hindered it from being broken on the surface of the water. Every joint of it was well grooved, and the door did not move on hinges, but up and down like a sash, which kept my closet so tight that very little water came in. I got with much difficulty out of my hammock, having first ventured to draw back the slip-board on the roof already mentioned, contrived on purpose to let in air, for want of which I found my self almost stifled.

How often did I then wish my self with my dear Glumdalclitch, from whom one single hour had so far divided me! And I may say with truth, that in the midst of my own misfortune, I could not forbear lamenting my poor nurse, the grief she would suffer for my loss, the displeasure of the Queen, and the ruin of her fortune. Perhaps many travellers have not been under greater difficulties and distress than I was at this juncture, expecting every moment to see my box dashed in pieces, or at least overset by the first violent blast, or a rising wave. A breach in one single pane of glass would have been immediate death: nor could any thing have preserved the windows but the strong lattice wires placed on the outside against accidents in travelling. I saw the water ooze in at several crannies, although the leaks were not considerable, and I endeavoured to stop them as well as I could. I was not able to lift up the roof of my closet, which otherwise I certainly should have done, and sat on the top of it, where I might at least preserve my self from being shut up, as I may call it, in the hold. Or, if I escaped these dangers for a day or two, what could I expect but a miserable death of cold and hunger! I was four hours under these circumstances, expecting and indeed wishing every moment to be my last.

I have already told the reader, that there were two strong staples fixed upon the side of my box which had no window, and into which the servant who used to carry me on horseback would put a leathern belt, and buckle it about his waist. Being in this disconsolate state, I heard, or at least thought I heard some kind of grating noise on that side of my box where the staples were fixed, and soon after I began to fancy that the box was pulled or towed along in the sea; for I now and then felt a sort of tugging which made the waves rise near the tops of my windows, leaving me almost in the dark. This gave me some faint hopes of relief, although I was not able to imagine how it could be brought about. I ventured to unscrew one of my chairs, which were always fastened to the floor; and having made a hard shift to screw it down again directly under the slipping-board that I had lately opened, I mounted on the chair, and putting my mouth as near as I could to the hole, I called for help in a loud voice, and in all the languages I understood. I then fastened my handkerchief to a stick I usually carried, and thrusting it up the hole, waved it several times in the air, that if any boat or ship were near, the seamen might conjecture some unhappy mortal to be shut up in the box.

I found no effect from all I could do, but plainly perceived my closet to be moved along; and in the space of an hour, or better, that side of the box where the staples were, and had no window, struck against something that was hard. I apprehended it to be a rock, and found my self tossed more than ever. I plainly heard a noise upon the cover of my closet, like that of a cable, and the grating of it as it passed through the ring. I then found my self hoisted up by degrees at least three foot higher than I was before. Whereupon I again thrust up my stick and handkerchief, calling for help till I was almost hoarse. In return to which, I heard a great shout repeated three times, giving me such transports of joy as are not to be conceived but by those who feel them. I now heard a trampling over my head, and somebody calling through the hole with a loud voice in the English tongue: If there be any body below, let them speak. I answered, I was an Englishman, drawn by ill fortune into the greatest calamity that ever any creature underwent, and begged, by all that was moving, to be delivered out of the dungeon I was in. The voice replied, I was safe, for my box was fastened to their ship; and the carpenter should immediately come, and saw an hole in the cover, large enough to pull me out. I answered, that was needless, and would take up too much time, for there was no more to be done, but let one of the crew put his finger into the ring, and take the box out of the sea into the ship, and so into the captain's cabin. Some of them upon hearing me talk so wildly thought I was mad; others laughed; for indeed it never came into my head that I was now got among people of my own stature and strength. The carpenter came, and in a few minutes sawed a passage about four foot square, then let down a small ladder, upon which I mounted, and from thence was taken into the ship in a very weak condition.

The sailors were all in amazement, and asked me a thousand questions, which I had no inclination to answer. I was equally confounded at the sight of so many pigmies, for such I took them to be, after having so long accustomed my eyes to the monstrous objects I had left. But the captain, Mr. Thomas Wilcocks, an honest worthy Shropshire man, observing I was ready to faint, took me into his cabin, gave me a cordial to comfort me, and made me turn in upon his own bed, advising me to take a little rest, of which I had great need. Before I went to sleep I gave him to understand that I had some valuable furniture in my box, too good to be lost; a fine hammock, an handsome field-bed, two chairs, a table and a cabinet: that my closet was hung on all sides, or rather quilted, with silk and cotton: that if he would let one of the crew bring my closet into his cabin, I would open it there before him, and show him my goods. The captain, hearing me utter these absurdities, conluded I was raving: however (I suppose to pacify me), he promised to give order as I desired, and going upon deck sent some of his men down into my closet, from whence (as I afterwards found) they drew up all my goods, and stripped off the quilting; but the chairs, cabinet and bedstead, being screwed to the floor, were much damaged by the ignorance of the seamen, who tore them up by force. Then they knocked off some of the boards for the use of the ship, and when they had got all they had a mind for, let the hulk drop into the sea, which, by reason of many breaches made in the bottom and sides, sunk to rights. And indeed I was glad not to have been a spectator of the havoc they made; because I am confident it would have sensibly touched me, by bringing former passages into my mind, which I had rather forget.

I slept some hours, but perpetually disturbed with dreams of the place I had left, and the dangers I had escaped. However, upon waking I found my self much recovered. It was now about eight o'clock at night, and the captain ordered supper immediately, thinking I had already fasted too long. He entertained me with great kindness, observing me not to look wildly, or talk inconsistently; and when we were left alone, desired I would give him a relation of my travels, and by what accident I came to be set adrift in that monstrous wooden chest. He said, that about twelve o'clock at noon, as he was looking through his glass, he spied it at a distance, and thought it was a sail, which he had a mind to make, being not much out of his course, in hopes of buying some biscuit,

his own beginning to fall short. That upon coming nearer,
and finding his error, he sent out his longboat to discover what
I was; that his men came back in a fright, swearing they
had seen a swimming house. That he laughed at their folly,
and went himself in the boat, ordering his men to take a
strong cable along with them. That the weather being calm,
he rowed round me several times, observed my windows, and
the wire lattices that defended them. That he discovered two
staples upon one side, which was all of boards, without any
passage for light. He then commanded his men to row up to
that side, and fastening a cable to one of the staples, ordered
his men to tow my chest (as he called it) towards the ship.
When it was there, he gave directions to fasten another cable
to the ring fixed in the cover; and to raise up my chest with
pulleys, which all the sailors were not able to do above two
or three foot. He said, they saw my stick and handkerchief
thrust out of the hole, and concluded that some unhappy
man must be shut up in the cavity. I asked whether he or the
crew had seen any prodigious birds in the air about the time
he first discovered me: to which he answered, that discoursing this matter with the sailors while I was asleep, one
of them said he had observed three eagles flying towards the
north, but remarked nothing of their being larger than the
usual size, which I suppose must be imputed to the great
height they were at: and he could not guess the reason of my
question. I then asked the captain how far he reckoned we
might be from land; he said, by the best computation he
could make, we were at least an hundred leagues. I assured
him, that he must be mistaken by almost half, for I had
not left the country from whence I came above two hours before I dropped into the sea. Whereupon he began again to
think that my brain was disturbed, of which he gave me a hint,
and advised me to go to bed in a cabin he had provided. I
assured him I was well refreshed with his good entertainment and company, and as much in my senses as ever I was
in my life. He then grew serious, and desired to ask me freely
whether I were not troubled in mind by the consciousness of
some enormous crime, for which I was punished at the command of some prince, by exposing me in that chest, as
great criminals in other countries have been forced to sea in
a leaky vessel without provisions: for although he should
be sorry to have taken so ill a man into his ship, yet he
would engaged his word to set me safe on shore in the first
port where we arrived. He added, that his suspicions were

much increased by some very absurd speeches I had delivered
at first to the sailors, and afterwards to himself, in relation
to my closet or chest, as well as by my odd looks and
behaviour while I was at supper.

I begged his patience to hear me tell my story, which I
faithfully did from the last time I left England to the moment
he first discovered me. And, as truth always forceth its way
into rational minds, so this honest worthy gentleman, who
had some tincture of learning, and very good sense, was
immediately convinced of my candor and veracity. But further
to confirm all I had said, I entreated him to give order that
my cabinet should be brought, of which I kept the key in my
pocket (for he had already informed me how the seamen
disposed of my closet); I opened it in his presence, and
showed him the small collection of rarities I made in the
country from whence I had been so strangely delivered. There
was the comb I had contrived out of the stumps of the King's
beard, and another of the same materials, but fixed into a
paring of her Majesty's thumb-nail, which served for the
back. There was a collection of needles and pins from a foot
to half a yard long. Four wasp-stings, like joiners' tacks: some
combings of the Queen's hair: a gold ring which one day
she made me a present of in a most obliging manner, taking it
from her little finger, and throwing it over my head like a collar. I desired the captain would please to accept this ring
in return of his civilities, which he absolutely refused. I showed
him a corn that I had cut off with my own hand from a maid
of honour's toe; it was about the bigness of a Kentish pippin,
and grown so hard, that when I returned to England, I got
it hollowed into a cup and set in silver. Lastly, I desired him
to see the breeches I had then on, which were made of a
mouse's skin.

I could force nothing on him but a footman's tooth, which
I observed him to examine with great curiosity, and found
he had a fancy for it. He received it with abundance of
thanks, more than such a trifle could deserve. It was drawn
by an unskilful surgeon in a mistake from one of Glumdalclitch's men, who was afflicted with the toothache, but it
was as sound as any in his head. I got it cleaned, and put
it into my cabinet. It was about a foot long, and four inches
in diameter.

The captain was very well satisfied with this plain relation
I had given him; and said, he hoped, when we returned to
England I would oblige the world by putting it in paper, and

making it public. My answer was, that I thought we were already overstocked with books of travels: that nothing could now pass which was not extraordinary, wherein I doubted some authors less consulted truth than their own vanity or interest, or the diversion of ignorant readers. That my story could contain little besides common events, without those ornamental descriptions of strange plants, trees, birds, and other animals, or of the barbarous customs and idolatry of savage people, with which most writers abound. However, I thanked him for his good opinion, and promised to take the matter into my thoughts.

He said he wondered at one thing very much, which was to hear me speak so loud, asking me whether the King or Queen of that country were thick of hearing. I told him it was what I had been used to for above two years past, and that I admired as much at the voices of him and his men, who seemed to me only to whisper, and yet I could hear them well enough. But when I spoke in that country, it was like a man talking in the street to another looking out from the top of a steeple, unless when I was placed on a table, or held in any person's hand. I told him I had likewise observed another thing, that when I first got into the ship, and the sailors stood all about me, I thought they were the most little contemptible creatures I had ever beheld. For, indeed, while I was in that prince's country, I could never endure to look in a glass after my eyes had been accustomed to such prodigious objects, because the comparison gave me so despicable a conceit of my self. The captain said, that while we were at supper, he observed me to look at every thing with a sort of wonder, and that I often seemed hardly able to contain my laughter, which he knew not well how to take, but imputed it to some disorder in my brain. I answered, it was very true, and I wondered how I could forbear, when I saw his dishes of the size of a silver threepence, a leg of pork hardly a mouthful, a cup not so big as a nutshell: and so I went on, describing the rest of his household-stuff and provisions after the same manner. For although the Queen had ordered a little equipage of all things necessary for me while I was in her service, yet my ideas were wholly taken up with what I saw on every side of me, and I winked at my own littleness as people do at their own faults. The captain understood my raillery very well, and merrily replied with the old English proverb, that he doubted my eyes were bigger than my belly, for he did not observe my stomach so good, although I had fasted all day: and continuing in his mirth, protested he would have gladly given an hundred pounds to have seen my closet in the eagle's bill, and afterwards in its fall from so great an height into the sea; which would certainly have been a most astonishing object, worthy to have the description of it transmitted to future ages: and the comparison of Phaeton was so obvious, that he could not forbear applying it, although I did not much admire the conceit.

The captain, having been at Tonquin,[1] was in his return to England driven northeastward to the latitude of 44 degrees, and of longitude 143. But meeting a trade wind two days after I came on board him, we sailed southward a long time, and coasting New Holland kept our course west-southwest, and then south-southwest till we doubled the Cape of Good Hope. Our voyage was very prosperous, but I shall not trouble the reader with a journal of it. The captain called in at one or two ports and sent in his longboat for provisions and fresh water, but I never went out of the ship till we came into the Downs, which as on the 3d day of June, 1706, about nine months after my escape. I offered to leave my goods in security for payment of my freight; but the captain protested he would not receive one farthing. We took kind leave of each other, and I made him promise he would come to see me at my house in Redriff. I hired a horse and guide for five shillings, which I borrowed of the captain.

As I was on the road, observing the littleness of the houses, the trees, the cattle and the people, I began to think my self in Lilliput. I was afraid of trampling on every traveller I met, and often called aloud to have them stand out of the way, so that I had like to have gotten one or two broken heads for my impertinence.

When I came to my own house, for which I was forced to enquire, one of the servants opening the door, I bent down to go in (like a goose under a gate) for fear of striking my head. My wife ran out to embrace me, but I stooped lower than her knees, thinking she could otherwise never be able to reach my mouth. My daughter kneeled to ask me blessing, but I could not see her till she arose, having been so long used to stand with my head and eyes erect to above sixty foot; and then I went to take her up with one hand, by the waist. I looked down upon the servants and one or two friends who were in the house, as if they had been pigmies, and I a giant. I told my wife she had been too thrifty, for I found she

[1] A French Indochina port, Tongking.

had starved herself and her daughter to nothing. In short, I behaved my self so unaccountably, that they were all of the captain's opinion when he first saw me, and concluded I had lost my wits. This I mention as an instance of the great power of habit and prejudice.

In a little time I and my family and friends came to a right understanding: but my wife protested I should never go to sea any more; although my evil destiny so ordered that she had not power to hinder me, as the reader may know hereafter. In the mean time I here conclude the second part of my unfortunate voyages.

THE END OF THE SECOND PART.

TRAVELS.

PART III.

A VOYAGE TO LAPUTA, BALNIBARBI, LUGGNAGG, GLUBBDUBDRIB, AND JAPAN.

CHAPTER I.

The author sets out on his third voyage. Is taken by pirates. The malice of a Dutchman. His arrival at an island. He is received into Laputa.

I had not been at home above ten days, when Captain William Robinson, a Cornish man, commander of the *Hopewell,* a stout ship of three hundred tons, came to my house. I had formerly been surgeon of another ship where he was master, and a fourth part owner, in a voyage to the Levant. He had always treated me more like a brother than an inferior officer, and hearing of my arrival made me a visit, as I apprehended, only out of friendship, for nothing passed more than what is usual after long absence. But repeating his visits often, expressing his joy to find me in good health, asking whether I were now settled for life, adding that he intended a voyage to East Indies, in two months, at last plainly invited me, although with some apologies, to be surgeon of the ship; that I should have another surgeon under me besides our two mates; that my salary should be double to the usual pay; and that having experienced my knowledge in sea-affairs to be at least equal to his, he would enter into any engagement to follow my advice, as much as if I had share in the command.

He said so many other obliging things, and I knew him to be so honest a man, that I could not reject his proposal; the thirst I had of seeing the world, notwithstanding my past misfortunes, continuing as violent as ever. The only difficulty that remained was to persuade my wife, whose consent however I at last obtained, by the prospect of advantage she proposed to her children.

Parts Unknown

LAND OF
IESSO

St James Bay
Robbin I

C. Patience

Salmonb.

Straits of the Vries

Companys

Land

Staits I

Ucanal

Sea of Corea

Sanda I
Torgut
Huao Jedo
Cinaca Tonengo
I APON

Yonsa I
Bungo I
Dimenis Straits
I Tanaxuma

Poualco
Tou Pt
Rsd Pt
Bosho Pt

Barnevelt

Ongeluckig I

South I

Siato

Glangurn

Maldoneda

I Deserta

Glubdubdrib

Urat
Timal

LUGN-AGG
the Maldopad

Clamrynig

Laputa

BALNIBARBI

Lagado

Dicovered A.D 1701

We set out the 5th day of August, 1706, and arrived at Fort St. George [1] the 11th of April, 1707. We stayed there three weeks to refresh our crew, many of whom were sick. From thence we went to Tonquin, where the captain resolved to continue some time, because many of the goods he intended to buy were not ready, nor could he expect to be dispatched in several months. Therefore in hopes to defray some of the charges he must be at, he bought a sloop, loaded it with several sorts of goods, wherewith the Tonquinese usually trade to the neighbouring islands; and putting fourteen men on board, whereof three were of the country, he appointed me master of the sloop, and gave me power to traffic while he transacted his affairs at Tonquin.

We had not sailed above three days, when, a great storm arising, we were driven five days to the north-northeast, and then to the east, after which we had fair weather, but still with a pretty strong gale from the west. Upon the tenth day we were chased by two pirates, who soon overtook us; for my sloop was so deep loaden, that she sailed very slow, neither were we in a condition to defend our selves.

We were boarded about the same time by both the pirates, who entered furiously at the head of their men, but finding us all prostrate upon our faces (for so I gave order), they pinioned us with strong ropes, and setting a guard upon us, went to search the sloop.

I observed among them a Dutchman, who seemed to be of some authority, although he was not commander of either ship. He knew us by our countenances to be Englishmen, and jabbering to us in his own language, swore we should be tied back to back, and thrown into the sea. I spoke Dutch tolerably well; I told him who we were, and begged him in consideration of our being Christians and Protestants, of neighbouring countries, in strict alliance,[2] that he would move the captains to take some pity on us. This inflamed his rage; he repeated his threatenings, and turning to his companions, spoke with great vehemence, in the Japanese language, as I suppose, often using the word *Christianos*.

The largest of the two pirate ships was commanded by a Japanese captain, who spoke a little Dutch, but very imperfectly. He came up to me, and after several questions, which I answered in great humility, he said we should not die. I made

<hr/>

[1] Madras.

[2] England and Holland were united in the Grand Alliance against France in the War of the Spanish Succession, but economically they continued to be rivals.

the captain a very low bow, and then turning to the Dutch-man, said, I was sorry to find more mercy in a heathen, than in a brother Christian. But I had soon reason to repent those foolish words; for that malicious reprobate, having often endeavoured in vain to persuade both the captains that I might be thrown into the sea (which they would not yield to after the promise made me, that I should not die), however prevailed so far as to have a punishment inflicted on me, worse in all human appearance than death it self. My men were sent by an equal division into both the pirate ships, and my sloop new manned. As to my self, it was determined that I should be set adrift in a small canoe, with paddles and a sail, and four days' provisions, which last the Japanese captain was so kind to double out of his own stores, and would permit no man to search me. I got down into the canoe, while the Dutchman, standing upon the deck, loaded me with all the curses and injurious terms his language could afford.

About an hour before we saw the pirates, I had taken an observation, and found we were in the lattitude of 46 N. and of longitude 183. When I was at some distance from the pirates, I discovered by my pocket-glass several islands to the southeast. I set up my sail, the wind being fair, with a design to reach the nearest of those islands, which I made a shift to do in about three hours. It was all rocky; however I got many birds' eggs, and striking fire I kindled some heath and dry seaweed, by which I roasted my eggs. I ate no other supper, being resolved to spare my provisions as much as I could. I passed the night under the shelter of a rock, strowing some heath under me, and slept pretty well.

The next day I sailed to another island, and thence to a third and fourth, sometimes using my sail, and sometimes my paddles. But not to trouble the reader with a particular account of my distresses, let it suffice that on the 5th day I arrived at the last island in my sight, which lay south-south-east to the former.

This island was at a greater distance than I expected, and I did not reach it in less than five hours. I encompassed it almost round before I could find a convenient place to land in, which was a small creek, about three times the wideness of my canoe. I found the island to be all rocky, only a little intermingled with tufts of grass, and sweet-smelling herbs. I took out my small provisions, and after having refreshed myself, I secured the remainder in a cave, whereof there were great numbers. I gathered plenty of eggs upon the rocks, and

got a quantity of dry seaweed, and parched grass, which I
designed to kindle the next day, and roast my eggs as well as
I could. (For I had about me my flint, steel, match, and
burning-glass.) I lay all night in the cave where I had lodged
my provisions. My bed was the same dry grass and seaweed
which I intended for fuel. I slept very little for the disquiets
of my mind prevailed over my weariness, and kept me awake.
I considered how impossible it was to preserve my life in so
desolate a place, and how miserable my end must be. Yet I
found my self so listless and desponding, that I had not the
heart to rise, and before I could get spirits enough to creep
out of my cave, the day was far advanced. I walked a while
among the rocks; the sky was perfectly clear, and the sun so
hot, that I was forced to turn my face from it: when all on a
sudden it became obscured, as I thought, in a manner very
different from what happens by the interposition of a cloud.
I turned back, and perceived a vast opaque body between me
and the sun, moving forwards towards the island: [1] it seemed
to be about two miles high, and hid the sun six or seven minutes, but I did not observe the air to be much colder, or the
sky more darkened, than if I had stood under the shade of a
mountain. As it approached nearer over the place where I was,
it appeared to be a firm substance, the bottom flat, smooth,
and shining very bright from the reflection of the sea below.
I stood upon a height about two hundred yards from the shore,
and saw this vast body descending almost to a parallel with
me, at less than an English mile distance. I took out my pock-
et-perspective, and could plainly discover numbers of people
moving up and down the sides of it, which appeared to be
sloping, but what those people were doing I was not able to
distinguish.

The natural love of life gave me some inward motions of
joy, and I was ready to entertain a hope, that this adventure
might some way or other help to deliver me from the desolate place and condition I was in. But at the same time the
reader can hardly conceive my astonishment, to behold an
island in the air, inhabited by men, who were able (as it
should seem) to raise, or sink, or put it into a progressive
motion, as they pleased. But not being at that time in a disposition to philosophize upon this phenomenon, I rather chose
to observe what course the island would take, because it
seemed for a while to stand still. Yet soon after it advanced
nearer, and I could see the sides of it, encompassed with sev-

[1] See p. 164, note 2.

eral gradations of galleries, and stairs, at certain intervals, to
descend from one to the other. In the lowest gallery, I beheld
some people fishing with long angling rods, and others looking on. I waved my cap (for my hat was long since worn out)
and my handkerchief towards the island; and upon its nearer
approach, I called and shouted with the utmost strength of my
voice; and then looking circumspectly, I beheld a crowd gathered to that side which was most in my view. I found by their
pointing towards me and to each other, that they plainly
discovered me, although they made no return to my shouting.
But I could see four or five men running in great haste up the
stairs to the top of the island, who then disappeared. I happened rightly to conjecture, that these were sent for orders to
some person in authority upon this occasion.

The number of people increased, and in less than half an
hour the island was moved and raised in such a manner, that
the lowest gallery appeared in a parallel of less than an hundred yards' distance from the height where I stood. I then put
my self into the most supplicating postures, and spoke in the
humblest accent, but received no answer. Those who stood
nearest over-against me seemed to be persons of distinction,
as I supposed by their habit. They conferred earnestly with
each other, looking often upon me. At length one of them
called out in a clear, polite, smooth dialect, not unlike in
sound to the Italian; and therefore I returned an answer in that
language, hoping at least that the cadence might be more
agreeable to his ears. Although neither of us understood the
other, yet my meaning was easily known, for the people saw
the distress I was in.

They made signs for me to come down from the rock, and
go towards the shore, which I accordingly did; and the flying
island being raised to a convenient height, the verge directly
over me, a chain was let down from the lowest gallery, with
a seat fastened to the bottom, to which I fixed my self, and
was drawn up by pulleys.

CHAPTER II.

The humours and dispositions of the Laputans described. An account of their learning. Of the King and his court. The author's reception there. The inhabitants subject to fears and disquietudes. An account of the women.

At my alighting I was surrounded by a crowd of people, but those who stood nearest seemed to be of better quality. They beheld me with all the marks and circumstances of wonder; neither indeed was I much in their debt, having never till then seen a race of mortals so singular in their shapes, habits, and countenances. Their heads were all reclined either to the right, or the left; one of their eyes turned inward, and the other directly up to the zenith. Their outward garments were adorned with the figures of suns, moons, and stars, interwoven with those of fiddles, flutes, harps, trumpets, guitars, harpsichords, and many more instruments of music, unknown to us in Europe.[1] I observed here and there many in the habits of servants, with a blown bladder fastened like a flail to the end of a short stick, which they carried in their hands. In each bladder was a small quantity of dried pease or little pebbles (as I was afterwards informed). With these bladders they now and then flapped the mouths and ears of those who stood near them, of which practice I could not then conceive the meaning. It seems, the minds of these people are so taken up with intense speculations, that they neither can speak, nor attend to the discourses of others, without being roused by some external taction upon the organs of speech and hearing; for which reason those persons who are able to afford it always keep a flapper (the original is *climenole*) in their family, as one of their domestics, nor ever walk abroad or make visits without him. And the business of this officer is, when two or more persons are in company, gently to strike with his bladder the mouth of him who is to speak, and the right ear of him

[1] Swift satirizes the Modern scientists' preoccupations with scientific formulations of music, "musico-mathematics" as it has been called. Thus he embroiders the clothes the Laputans wear with musical instruments, and later turns the food they eat into musical shapes. (See: Marjorie Hope Nicolson, "The Scientific Background of Swift's 'Voyage to Laputa,'" in *Science and Imagination*, 1956, pp. 110–154, to which I am indebted for most of the annotations on the science satire that follow.)

In addition, the substantial amount of political satire in Book III should be noted, in which Swift focuses on the Whig ministry under George I; he considers the Whigs political projectors whose experiments in government he satirizes as no less ludicrous than the scientific experiments reported in the *Transactions of the Royal Society*. When read against the political and scientific backgrounds both, Book III becomes most meaningful.

or them to whom the speaker addresseth himself. This flapper
is likewise employed diligently to attend his master in his
walks, and upon occasion to give him a soft flap on his eyes,
because he is always so wrapped up in cogitation, that he is in
manifest danger of falling down every precipice, and bouncing
his head against every post, and in the streets, of jostling
others or being jostled himself into the kennel.[1]

It was necessary to give the reader this information, without which he would be at the same loss with me, to understand the proceedings of these people, as they conducted me
up the stairs, to the top of the island, and from thence to the
royal palace. While we were ascending, they forgot several
times what they were about, and left me to my self, till their
memories were again roused by their flappers; for they appeared altogether unmoved by the sight of my foreign habit
and countenance, and by the shouts of the vulgar, whose
thoughts and minds were more disengaged.

At last we entered the palace, and proceeded into the
chamber of presence, where I saw the King seated on his
throne, attended on each side by persons of prime quality.[2]
Before the throne was a large table filled with globes and
spheres, and mathematical instruments of all kinds. His Majesty took not the least notice of us, although our entrance
was not without sufficient noise, by the concourse of all persons belonging to the court. But he was then deep in a problem, and we attended at least an hour before he could solve
it. There stood by him, on each side, a young page, with flaps
in their hands, and when they saw he was at leisure, one of
them gently struck his mouth, and the other his right ear; at
which he started like one awaked on the sudden, and looking
towards me, and the company I was in, recollected the occasion of our coming, whereof he had been informed before.
He spoke some words, whereupon immediately a young man
with a flap came up to my side, and flapped me gently on the
right ear; but I made signs as well as I could, that I had no
occasion for such an instrument; which as I afterwards found
gave his Majesty and the whole court a very mean opinion of
my understanding. The King, as far as I could conjecture,
asked me several questions, and I addressed my self to him in

[1] Gutter. Some have supposed that Swift here satirizes Sir Isaac Newton,
whom he disliked not only for his mathematics but also for his championing of Wood's half-pence in opposition to which Swift wrote his *Drapier's
Letters*.

[2] Swift may be satirizing George I who, though a patron of music and
science, knew little about either.

all the languages I had. When it was found that I could neither understand nor be understood, I was conducted by his order to an apartment in his palace (this prince being distinguished above all his predecessors for his hospitality to strangers),[1] where two servants were appointed to attend me. My dinner was brought, and four persons of quality, whom I remembered to have seen very near the King's person, did me the honour to dine with me. We had two courses, of three dishes each. In the first course there was a shoulder of mutton, cut into an equilateral triangle, a piece of beef into a rhomboides, and a pudding into a cycloid. The second course was two ducks, trussed up into the form of fiddles; sausages and puddings resembling flutes and hautboys, and a breast of veal in the shape of a harp. The servants cut our bread into cones, cylinders, parallelograms, and several other mathematical figures.

While we were at dinner, I made bold to ask the names of several things in their language; and those noble persons, by the assistance of their flappers, delighted to give me answers, hoping to raise my admiration of their great abilities, if I could be brought to converse with them. I was soon able to call for bread and drink, or whatever else I wanted.

After dinner my company withdrew, and a person was sent to me by the King's order, attended by a flapper. He brought with him pen, ink, and paper, and three or four books, giving me to understand by signs, that he was sent to teach me the language. We sat together four hours, in which time I wrote down a great number of words in columns, with the translations over against them. I likewise made a shift to learn several short sentences. For my tutor would order one of my servants to fetch something, to turn about, to make a bow, to sit, or stand, or walk and the like. Then I took down the sentence in writing. He showed me also in one of his books the figures of the sun, moon, and stars, the zodiac, the tropics, and polar circles, together with the denominations of many figures of planes and solids. He gave me the names and descriptions of all the musical instruments, and the general terms of art in playing on each of them. After he had left me, I placed all my words with their interpretations in alphabetical order. And thus in a few days, by the help of a very faithful memory, I got some insight into their language.

The word which I interpret the *Flying* or *Floating Island* is in the original *Laputa*, whereof I could never learn the true

[1] George I's hospitality to strangers, chiefly Hanoverians, called attention to itself. He tended to give them lucrative posts in England.

etymology.[1] *Lap* in the old obsolete language signifieth *high*, and *untuh* a *governor*, from which they say by corruption was derived *Laputa,* from *Lapuntuh.* But I do not approve of this derivation, which seems to be a little strained. I ventured to offer to the learned among them a conjecture of my own, that *Laputa* was *quasi Lap outed; Lap* signifying properly the dancing of the sunbeams in the sea, and *outed* a wing, which however I shall not obtrude, but submit to the judicious reader.

Those to whom the King had entrusted me, observing how ill I was clad, ordered a tailor to come next morning, and take my measure for a suit of clothes. This operator did his office after a different manner from those of his trade in Europe. He first took my altitude by a quadrant, and then, with rule and compasses, described the dimensions and outlines of my whole body, all which he entered upon paper, and in six days brought my clothes very ill made, and quite out of shape, by happening to mistake a figure in the calculation.[2] But my comfort was, that I observed such accidents very frequent and little regarded.

During my confinement for want of clothes, and by an indisposition that held me some days longer, I much enlarged my dictionary; and when I went next to court, was able to understand many things the King spoke, and to return him some kind of answers. His Majesty had given orders that the island should move northeast and by east, to the vertical point over Lagado,[3] the metropolis of the whole kingdom below upon the firm earth. It was about ninety leagues distant, and our voyage lasted four days and an half. I was not in the least sensible of the progressive motion made in the air by the island. On the second morning about eleven o'clock, the King himself in person, attended by his nobility, courtiers, and officers, having prepared all their musical instruments, played on them for three hours without intermission, so that I was quite stunned with the noise; neither could I possibly guess the meaning till my tutor informed me. He said that the people of their island had their ears adapted to hear the music of the spheres, which always played at certain periods, and the court

---

[1] Swift here satirizes the new philology and probably Dr. Richard Bentley, its most distinguished exponent.

[2] Swift may be satirizing a well-known error made by the printer of Newton's calculations concerning the distance of the sun from the earth, which made Newton appear ridiculous. More generally he is satirizing current preoccupations with astronomical calculations and surveying and measuring instruments, as they were the subjects of many papers published in the *Philosophical Transactions of the Royal Society.* Note that the word *philosophy* in the period is synonymous with our use of the word *science.*

[3] London.

was now prepared to bear their part in what ever instrument they most excelled.

In our journey towards Lagado, the capital city, his Majesty ordered that the island should stop over certain towns and villages, from whence he might receive the petitions of his subjects. And to this purpose, several packthreads were let down with small weights at the bottom. On these packthreads the people strung their petitions, which mounted up directly like the scraps of paper fastened by schoolboys at the end of the string that holds their kite. Sometimes we received wine and victuals from below, which were drawn up by pulleys.

The knowledge I had in mathematics gave me great assistance in acquiring their phraseology, which depended much upon that science and music; and in the latter I was not unskilled. Their ideas are perpetually conversant in lines and figures. If they would, for example, praise the beauty of a woman or any other animal, they describe it by rhombs, circles, parallelograms, ellipses, and other geometrical terms, or else by words of art drawn from music, needless here to repeat. I observed in the King's kitchen all sorts of mathematical and musical instruments, after the figures of which they cut up the joints that were served to his Majesty's table.[1]

Their houses are very ill built, the walls bevil, without one right angle in any apartment; and this defect ariseth from the contempt they bear for practical geometry, which they despise as vulgar and mechanic, those instructions they give being too refined for the intellectuals of their workmen, which occasions perpetual mistakes. And although they are dextrous enough upon a piece of paper in the management of the rule, the pencil, and the divider, yet in the common actions and behaviour of life I have not seen a more clumsy, awkward, and unhandy people, nor so slow and perplexed in their conceptions upon all other subjects, except those of mathematics and music. They are very bad reasoners, and vehemently given to opposition, unless when they happen to be of the right opinion, which is seldom their case. Imagination, fancy, and invention, they are wholly strangers to, nor have any words in their language by which those ideas can be expressed; the whole compass of their thoughts and mind being shut up within the two forementioned sciences.

Most of them, and especially those who deal in the astronomical part, have great faith in judicial astrology, although they are ashamed to own it publicly. But what I chiefly ad-

[1] See p. 50, note 1.

mired, and thought altogether unaccountable, was the strong disposition I observed in them towards news and politics, perpetually enquiring into public affairs, giving their judgments in matters of state, and passionately disputing every inch of a party opinion. I have indeed observed the same disposition among most of the mathematicians I have known in Europe, although I could never discover the least analogy between the two sciences; unless those people suppose, that because the smallest circle hath as many degrees as the largest, therefore the regulation and management of the world require no more abilities than the handling and turning of a globe. But I rather take this quality to spring from a very common infirmity of human nature, inclining us to be more curious and conceited in matters where we have least concern, and for which we are least adapted either by study or nature.

These people are under continual disquietudes, never enjoying a minute's peace of mind; and their disturbances proceed from causes which very little affect the rest of mortals. Their apprehensions arise from several changes they dread in the celestial bodies. For instance; that the earth, by the continual approaches of the sun towards it, must in course of time be absorbed or swallowed up. That the face of the sun will by degrees be encrusted with its own effluvia, and give no more light to the world. That the earth very narrowly escaped a brush from the tail of the last comet, which would have infallibly reduced it to ashes; and that the next, which they have calculated for one and thirty years hence, will probably destroy us. For, if in its perihelion it should approach within a certain degree of the sun (as by their calculations they have reason to dread), it will conceive a degree of heat ten thousand times more intense than that of red-hot glowing iron, and in its absence from the sun, carry a blazing tail ten hundred thousand and fourteen miles long; through which if the earth should pass at the distance of one hundred thousand miles from the nucleus or main body of the comet, it must in its passage be set on fire, and reduce to ashes. That the sun daily spending its rays without any nutriment to supply them, will at last be wholly consumed and annihilated; which must be attended with the destruction of this earth, and of all the planets that receive their light from it.[1]

<hr />

[1] In this paragraph and the following one, Swift is satirizing several scientific preoccupations of the period: Newton's theory that the earth might be absorbed or otherwise destroyed by the sun; contemporary concern that Halley's comet (due to appear in 1758) might catapult into the earth and reduce it to ashes; and contemporary theories on the nature of sun spots.

They are so perpetually alarmed with the apprehensions of these and the like impending dangers, that they can neither sleep quietly in their beds, nor have any relish for the common pleasures or amusements of life. When they meet an acquaintance in the morning, the first question is about the sun's health, how he looked at his setting and rising, and what hopes they have to avoid the stroke of the approaching comet. This conversation they are apt to run into with the same temper that boys discover in delighting to hear terrible stories of sprites and hobgoblins, which they greedily listen to, and dare not go to bed for fear.

The women of the island have abundance of vivacity; they contemn their husbands, and are exceedingly fond of strangers, whereof there is always a considerable number from the continent below, attending at court, either upon affairs of the several towns and corporations, or their own particular occasions, but are much despised, because they want the same endowments. Among these the ladies choose their gallants: but the vexation is, that they act with too much ease and security, for the husband is always so rapt in speculation, that the mistress and lover may proceed to the greatest familiarities before his face, if he be but provided with paper and implements, and without his flapper at his side.

The wives and daughters lament their confinement to the island, although I think it the most delicious spot of ground in the world; and although they live here in the greatest plenty and magnificence, and are allowed to do whatever they please, they long to see the world, and take the diversions of the metropolis, which they are not allowed to do without a particular licence from the King; and this is not easy to be obtained because the people of quality have found by frequent experience how hard it is to persuade their women to return from below. I was told that a great court lady, who had several children, is married to the prime minister, the richest subject in the kingdom, a very graceful person, extremely fond of her, and lives in the finest palace of the island, went down to Lagado, on the pretence of health, there hid her self for several months, till the King sent a warrant to search for her; and she was found in an obscure eating house all in rags, having pawned her clothes to maintain an old deformed footman, who beat her every day, and in whose company she was taken much against her will. And although her husband received her with all possible kindness, and without the least reproach, she

soon after contrived to steal down again with all her jewels, to
the same gallant, and hath not been heard of since.

This may perhaps pass with the reader rather for an European or English story, than for one of a country so remote.
But he may please to consider, that the caprices of womankind
are not limited by any climate or nation, and that they are
much more uniform than can be easily imagined.

In about a month's time I had made a tolerable proficiency
in their language, and was able to answer most of the King's
questions, when I had the honour to attend him. His Majesty
discovered not the least curiosity to enquire into the laws,
government, history, religion, or manners of the countries
where I had been, but confined his questions to the state of
mathematics, and received the account I gave him with great
contempt and indifference, though often roused by his flapper
on each side.

CHAPTER III.

*A phenomenon solved by modern philosophy and astronomy.
The Laputans' great improvements in the latter. The
King's method of suppressing insurrections.*

I desired leave of this prince to see the curiosities of the island, which he was graciously pleased to grant, and ordered my tutor to attend me. I chiefly wanted to know to
what cause in art or in nature it owed its several motions,
whereof I will now give a philosophical account [1] to the reader.

The Flying or Floating Island [2] is exactly circular, its diameter 7,837 yards, or about four miles and an half, and consequently contains ten thousand acres. It is three hundred yards
thick. The bottom or under surface, which appears to those
who view it from below, is one even regular plate of adamant,
shooting up to the height of about two hundred yards. Above
it lie the several minerals in their usual order, and over all is
a coat of rich mould ten or twelve foot deep. The declivity of

[1] The "philosophical account" is a direct parody of the language of the
Philosophical Transactions of the Royal Society.
[2] Swift's flying island is a combination of satire on voyages to the moon
(here reversed to a voyage of the moon to the earth) and of flying machines.
The mathematical figures assume significance when collated with William
Gilbert's figures in his *De Maguete.* Swift's flying island works by the principles of terrestrial magnetism. (See Marjorie Hope Nicolson, *Voyages to the
Moon,* 1960, pp. 189–195.) In addition, Swift's island is satirical of the exploitation of Ireland by England in all its punitive and controlling measures.

the upper surface, from the circumference to the center, is the natural cause why all the dews and rains which fall upon the island are conveyed in small rivulets towards the middle, where they are emptied into four large basins, each of about half a mile in circuit, and two hundred yards distant from the center. From these basins the water is continually exhaled by the sun in the day time, which effectually prevents their overflowing. Besides, as it is in the power of the monarch to raise the island above the region of clouds and vapours, he can prevent the falling of dews and rains whenever he pleases. For the highest clouds cannot rise above two miles, as naturalists agree, at least they were never known to do so in that country.

At the center of the island there is a chasm about fifty yards in diameter, from whence the astronomers descend into a large dome, which is therefore called *Flandona Gagnole,* or the *Astronomer's Cave,* situated at the depth of an hundred yards beneath the upper surface of the adamant. In this cave are twenty lamps continually burning, which from the reflection of the adamant cast a strong light into every part. The place is stored with great variety of sextants, quadrants, telescopes, astrolabes, and other astronomical instruments. But the greatest curiosity, upon which the fate of the island depends, is a loadstone of a prodigious size, in shape resembling a weaver's shuttle. It is in length six yards, and in the thickest part at least three yards over. This magnet is sustained by a very strong axle of adamant passing through its middle, upon which it plays, and is poised so exactly that the weakest hand can turn it. It is hooped round with an hollow cylinder of adamant, four foot deep, as many thick, and twelve yards in diameter, placed horizontally, and supported by eight adamantine feet, each six yards high. In the middle of the concave side there is a groove twelve inches deep, in which the extremities of the axle are lodged, and turned round as there is occasion.

The stone cannot be moved from its place by any force, because the hoop and its feet are one continued piece with that body of adamant which constitutes the bottom of the island.

By means of this loadstone, the island is made to rise and fall, and move from one place to another. For, with respect to that part of the earth over which the monarch presides, the stone is endued at one of its sides with an attractive power, and at the other with a repulsive. Upon placing the magnet

erect with its attracting end towards the earth, the island de-
scends; but when the repelling extremity points downwards,
the island mounts directly upwards. When the position of the
stone is oblique, the motion of the island is so too. For in this
magnet the forces always act in lines parallel to its direction.

By this oblique motion the island is conveyed to different
parts of the monarch's dominions. To explain the manner of
its progress, let A B represent a line drawn cross the dominions of Balnibarbi, let the line c d represent the loadstone, of
which let d be the repelling end, and c the attracting end, the
island being over C; let the stone be placed in the position c d
with its repelling end downwards; then the island will be
driven upwards obliquely towards D. When it is arrived at D,
let the stone be turned upon its axle till its attracting end points
towards E, and then the island will be carried obliquely towards E; where if the stone be again turned upon its axle till
it stands in the position E F, with its repelling point downwards, the island will rise obliquely towards F, where by directing the attracting end towards G, the island may be carried to G, and from G to H, by turning the stone, so as to
make its repelling extremity point directly downwards. And
thus by changing the situation of the stone as often as there is
occasion, the island is made to rise and fall by turns in an
oblique direction, and by those alternate risings and fallings
(the obliquity being not considerable) is conveyed from one
part of the dominions to the other.

But it must be observed, that this island cannot move beyond the extent of the dominions below, nor can it rise above
the height of four miles. For which the astronomers (who
have written large systems concerning the stone) assign the
following reason: that the magnetic virtue does not extend
beyond the distance of four miles, and that the mineral which
acts upon the stone in the bowels of the earth, and in the sea
about six leagues distant from the shore, is not diffused
through the whole globe, but terminated with the limits of the
King's dominions: and it was easy, from the great advantage
of such a superior situation, for a prince to bring under his
obedience whatever country lay within the attraction of that
magnet.

When the stone is put parallel to the plane of the horizon,
the island standeth still; for in that case, the extremities of it,
being at equal distance from the earth, act with equal force,
the one in drawing downwards, the other in pushing upwards,
and consequently no motion can ensue.

This loadstone is under the care of certain astronomers, who from time to time give it such positions as the monarch directs. They spend the greatest part of their lives in observing the celestial bodies, which they do by the assistance of glasses far excelling ours in goodness. For although their largest telescopes do not exceed three feet, they magnify much more than those of a hundred with us, and at the same time show the stars with greater clearness. This advantage hath enabled them to extend their discoveries much farther than our astronomers in Europe. They have made a catalogue of ten thousand fixed stars, whereas the largest of ours do not contain above one third part of that number. They have likewise discovered two lesser stars, or 'satellites', which revolve about Mars,[1] whereof the innermost is distant from the center of the primary planet exactly three of his diameters, and the outermost five; the former revolves in the space of ten hours, and the latter in twenty-one and an half; so that the squares of their periodical times are very near in the same proportion with the cubes of their distance from the center of Mars; which evidently shows them to be governed by the same law of gravitation, that influences the other heavenly bodies.

They have observed ninety-three different comets, and settled their periods with great exactness. If this be true (and they affirm it with great confidence), it is much to be wished that their observations were made public, whereby the theory of comets, which at present is very lame and defective, might be brought to the same perfection with other parts of astronomy.

The King would be the most absolute prince in the universe, if he could but prevail on a ministry to join with him; but these having their estates below on the continent, and considering that the office of a favourite hath a very uncertain tenure, would never consent to the enslaving their country.

If any town should engage in rebellion or mutiny, fall into violent factions, or refuse to pay the usual tribute, the King hath two methods of reducing them to obedience. The first and the mildest course is by keeping the island hovering over such a town, and the lands about it, whereby he can deprive them of the benefit of the sun and the rain, and consequently afflict the inhabitants with dearth and diseases. And if the crime deserve it, they are at the same time pelted from above with great stones, against which they have no defence but by

---

[1] Swift happens to have guessed correctly; in 1899 two satellites of Mars were discovered.

creeping into cellars or caves, while the roofs of their houses are beaten to pieces. But if they still continue obstinate, or offer to raise insurrections, he proceeds to the last remedy, by letting the island drop directly upon their heads, which makes a universal destruction both of houses and men.[1] However, this is an extremity to which the prince is seldom driven, neither indeed is he willing to put it in execution; nor dare his ministers advise him to an action which, as it would render them odious to the people, so it would be a great damage to their own estates, that lie all below, for the island is the King's demesne.

But there is still indeed a more weighty reason, why the kings of this country have been always averse from executing so terrible an action, unless upon the utmost necessity. For if the town intended to be destroyed should have in it any tall rocks, as it generally falls out in the larger cities, a situation probably chosen at first with a view to prevent such a catastrophe; or if it abound in high spires or pillars of stone,[2] a sudden fall might endanger the bottom or under surface of the island, which although it consist, as I have said, of one entire adamant two hundred yards thick, might happen to crack by too great a shock, or burst by approaching too near the fires from the houses below, as the backs both of iron and stone will often do in our chimneys. Of all this the people are well apprised, and understand how far to carry their obstinacy, where their liberty or property is concerned. And the King, when he is highest provoked, and most determined to press a city to rubbish, orders the island to descend with great gentleness, out of a pretence of tenderness to his people, but indeed for fear of breaking the adamantine bottom; in which case it is the opinion of all their philosophers, that the loadstone could no longer hold it up, and the whole mass would fall to the ground.

About three years before my arrival among them,[3] while the King was in his progress over his dominions, there happened an extraordinary accident which had like to have put a

---

[1] The satire turns to political channels as Swift satirizes English domination of Ireland; he implies economic exploitation like Wood's half-pence, punitive legislative action, and military violence.

[2] The spires, rocks, and stones which deter the flying island from landing have been interpreted as the Church, the nobility, and the citizenry which support Ireland; the fear of breaking the adamantine bottom is the fear of revolution.

[3] This paragraph and the four following it were omitted from all editions of *Gulliver* until 1899; the revolutionary implications of the Irish agitation against Wood's half-pence in this passage would have made Swift (the Drapier) vulnerable to charges.

period to the fate of that monarchy, at least as it is now instituted. Lindaloin,[1] the second city in the kingdom, was the first
his Majesty visited in his progress. Three days after his departure, the inhabitants, who had often complained of great
oppressions, shut the town gates, seized on the governor, and
with incredible speed and labour erected four large towers,
one at every corner of the city (which is an exact square),
equal in height to a strong pointed rock that stands directly in
the center of the city.[2] Upon the top of each tower, as well as
upon the rock, they fixed a great loadstone, and in case their
design should fail, they had provided a vast quantity of the
most combustible fuel, hoping to burst therewith the adamantine bottom of the island, if the loadstone project should miscarry.

It was eight months before the King had perfect notice that
the Lindalinians were in rebellion. He then commanded that
the island should be wafted over the city. The people were
unanimous, and had laid in store of provisions, and a great
river runs through the middle of the town. The King hovered
over them several days to deprive them of the sun and the
rain. He ordered many packthreads to be let down, yet not a
person offered to send up a petition, but instead thereof, very
bold demands, the redress of all their grievances, great im-
munities, the choice of their own governor, and other the like
exorbitances. Upon which his Majesty commanded all the inhabitants of the island to cast great stones from the lower
gallery into the town; but the citizens had provided against
this mischief by conveying their persons and effects into the
four towers, and other strong buildings, and vaults underground.

The King being now determined to reduce this proud people, ordered that the island should descend gently within forty
yards of the top of the towers and rock. This was accordingly
done; but the officers employed in that work found the descent
much speedier than usual, and by turning the loadstone could
not without great difficulty keep it in a firm position, but
found the island inclining to fall. They sent the King immediate intelligence of this astonishing event and begged his Majesty's permission to raise the island higher; the King consented, a general council was called, and the officers of the

---

[1] Dublin or Ireland.
[2] The tower has been interpreted as the Church in Ireland (St. Patrick's
Cathedral), the four towers as the four chief agencies of the Irish government, and the combustible fuel as the incendiary pamphlets against the English, among them Swift's *Drapier's Letters*.

loadstone ordered to attend. One of the oldest and expertest among them obtained leave to try an experiment. He took a strong line of an hundred yards, and the island being raised over the town above the attracting power they had felt, he fastened a piece of adamant to the end of his line which had in it a mixture of iron mineral, of the same nature with that whereof the bottom or lower surface of the island is composed, and from the lower gallery let it down slowly towards the top of the towers. The adamant was not descended four yards, before the officer felt it drawn so strongly downwards, that he could hardly pull it back. He then threw down several small pieces of adamant, and observed that they were all violently attracted by the top of the tower. The same experiment was made on the other three towers, and on the rock with the same effect.

This incident broke entirely the King's measures and (to dwell no longer on other circumstances) he was forced to give the town their own conditions.

I was assured by a great minister, that if the island had descended so near the town as not to be able to raise it self, the citizens were determined to fix it for ever, to kill the King and all his servants, and entirely change the government.

By a fundamental law of this realm, neither the King nor either of his two elder sons are permitted to leave the island, nor the Queen, till she is past child-bearing.[1]

CHAPTER IV.

The author leaves Laputa, is conveyed to Balnibarbi,[2] arrives at the metropolis. A description of the metropolis and the country adjoining. The author hospitably received by a great lord. His conversation with that lord.

Although I cannot say that I was ill treated in this island, yet I must confess I thought my self too much neglected, not without some degree of contempt. For neither prince nor people appeared to be curious in any part of knowledge, except mathematics and music, wherein I was far their inferior, and upon that account very little regarded.

[1] A possible thrust at George I and his frequent sorties from England to his Hanoverian possessions. The Act of Settlement (1701) denied the king the right to leave England without specific permission of the Parliament.

[2] *Balnibarbi* has been decoded as *Barbary*, which would connote *uncivilized* to contemporary readers.

On the other side, after having seen all the curiosities of the island, I was very desirous to leave it, being heartily weary of those people. They were indeed excellent in two sciences for which I have great esteem, and wherein I am not unversed, but at the same so abstracted and involved in speculation that I never met with such disagreeable companions. I conversed only with women, tradesmen, flappers, and court-pages, during two months of my abode there, by which at last I rendered my self extremely contemptible; yet these were the only people from who I could ever receive a reasonable answer.

I had obtained by hard study a good degree of knowledge in their language; I was weary of being confined to an island where I received so little countenance, and resolved to leave it with the first opportunity.

There was a great lord at court, nearly related to the King,[1] and for that reason alone used with respect. He was universally reckoned the most ignorant and stupid person among them. He had performed many eminent services for the crown, had great natural and acquired parts, adorned with integrity and honour, but so ill an ear for music, that his detractors reported he had been often known to beat time in the wrong place; neither could his tutors without extreme difficulty teach him to demonstrate the most easy proposition in the mathematics. He was pleased to show me many marks of favour, often did me the honour of a visit, desired to be informed in the affairs of Europe, the laws and customs, the manners and learning of the several countries where I had travelled. He listened to me with great attention, and made very wise observations on all I spoke. He had two flappers attending him for state, but never made use of them except at court, and in visits of ceremony, and would always command them to withdraw when we were alone together.

I intreated this illustrious person to intercede in my behalf with his Majesty for leave to depart, which he accordingly did, as he was pleased to tell me, with regret: for indeed he had made me several offers very advantageous, which however I refused with expressions of the highest acknowledgement.

On the 16th day of February, I took leave of his Majesty and the court. The King made me a present to the value of

[1] The Prince of Wales, later George II, was unpopular at court and notable for his lack of interest in science and music. But though he "hobbled" between the Whigs and Tories, he was substantially a Tory and thus is made to reject Whig political projects; the Tories built their hopes on his succession. Thus he is sympathetic to Gulliver and dispenses with a "flapper."

about two hundred pounds English, and my protector his kinsman as much more, together with a letter of recommendation to a friend of his in Lagado, the metropolis; the island being then hovering over a mountain about two miles from it, I was let down from the lowest gallery, in the same manner as I had been taken up.

The continent, as far as it is subject to the monarch of the Flying Island, passes under the general name of Balnibarbi, and the metropolis, as I said before, is called Lagado. I felt some little satisfaction in finding my self on firm ground. I walked to the city without any concern, being clad like one of the natives, and sufficiently instructed to converse with them. I soon found out the person's house to whom I was recommended, presented my letter from his friend the grandee in the island, and was received with much kindness. This great lord, whose name was Munodi,[1] ordered me an apartment in his own house, where I continued during my stay, and was entertained in a most hospitable manner.

The next morning after my arrival he took me in his chariot to see the town, which is about half the bigness of London, but the houses very strangely built, and most of them out of repair. The people in the streets walked fast, looked wild, their eyes fixed, and were generally in rags. We passed through one of the town gates, and went about three miles into the country, where I saw many labourers working with several sorts of tools in the ground, but was not able to conjecture what they were about; neither did I observe any expectation either of corn or grass, although the soil appeared to be excellent. I could not forbear admiring at these odd appearances both in town and country, and I made bold to desire my conductor, that he would be pleased to explain to me what could be meant by so many busy heads, hands, and faces, both in the streets and the fields, because I did not discover any good effects they produced; but on the contrary, I never knew a soil so unhappily cultivated, houses so ill contrived and so ruinous, or a people whose countenances and habit expressed so much misery and want.[2]

---

[1] Munodi has been taken as Bolingbroke or Oxford, both of whom retired from public life and represented the good old Tory cause.

[2] The satire generally is directed against Modern scientific methods of architecture and husbandry as, respectively, ugly and fruitless. The economic implications concern the South Sea Bubble which broke in 1720. Oxford, when minister, had vouched for the South Sea Company by which the government was considerably enriched; when it went bankrupt the public, which had invested in it heavily, was defrauded and Oxford was held responsible, though in fact he was not.

This Lord Munodi was a person of the first rank, and had been some years Governor of Lagado, but by a cabal of ministers was discharged for insufficiency. However, the King treated him with tenderness, as a well-meaning man, but of a low contemptible understanding.

When I gave that free censure of the country and its inhabitants, he made no further answer than by telling me that I had not been long enough among them to form a judgment, and that the different nations of the world had different customs, with other common topics to the same purpose. But when we returned to his palace, he asked me how I liked the building, what absurdities I observed, and what quarrel I had with the dress and looks of his domestics. This he might safely do, because every thing about him was magnificent, regular, and polite. I answered that his Excellency's prudence, quality, and fortune had exempted him from those defects which folly and beggary had produced in others. He said if I would go with him to his country house, about twenty miles distant, where his estate lay, there would be more leisure for this kind of conversation. I told his Excellency that I was entirely at his disposal, and accordingly we set out next morning.

During our journey, he made me observe the several methods used by farmers in managing their lands, which to me were wholly unaccountable: for, except in some very few places, I could not discover one ear of corn or blade of grass. But in three hours travelling the scene was wholly altered; we came into a most beautiful country; the farmers' houses at small distances, neatly built, the fields enclosed, containing vineyards, corn-grounds and meadows. Neither do I remember to have seen a more delightful prospect. His Excellency observed my countenance to clear up; he told me with a sigh, that there his estate began, and would continue the same till we should come to his house. That his countrymen ridiculed and despised him for managing his affairs no better, and for setting so ill an example to the kingdom, which however was followed by very few, such as were old and wilful, and weak like himself.

We came at length to the house, which was indeed a noble structure, built according to the best rules of ancient architecture. The fountains, gardens, walks, avenues, and groves were all disposed with exact judgment and taste. I gave due praises to every thing I saw, wherof his Excellency took not the least notice till after supper, when, there being no third companion, he told me with a very melancholy air, that he doubted he must throw down his houses in town and country, to rebuild them after the present mode, destroy all his plantations, and cast others into such a form as modern usage required, and give the same directions to all his tenants, unless he would submit to incur the censure of pride, singularity, affectation, ignorance, caprice, and perhaps encrease his Majesty's displeasure.

That the admiration I appeared to be under would cease or diminish when he had informed me of some particulars, which probably I never heard of at court, the people there being too much taken up in their own speculations to have regard to what passed here below.

The sum of his discourse was to this effect. That about forty years ago, certain persons went up to Laputa either upon business or diversion, and after five months continuance came back with a very little smattering in mathematics, but full of volatile spirits acquired in that airy region. That these persons upon their return began to dislike the management of every thing below, and fell into schemes of putting all arts, sciences, languages, and mechanics upon a new foot. To this end they procured a royal patent for erecting an academy of PROJECTORS in Lagado; [1] and the humour prevailed so strongly among the people, that there is not a town of any consequence in the kingdom without such an academy. In these colleges the professors contrive new rules and methods of agriculture and building, and new instruments and tools for all trades and manufactures, whereby, as they undertake, one man shall do the work of ten; a palace may be built in a week, of materials so durable as to last for ever without repairing. All the fruits of the earth shall come to maturity at whatever season we think fit to choose, and increase an hundred fold more than they do at present, with innumerable other happy proposals. The only inconvenience is, that none of these projects are yet brought to perfection; and in the mean time the whole country lies miserably waste, the houses in ruins, and the people without food or clothes. By all which, instead of being discouraged, they are fifty times more violently bent upon prosecuting their schemes, driven equally on by hope

[1] Swift's academy is immediately satiric of the Royal Society and many lesser societies and academies which projected large schemes for the advancement of knowledge, which Swift found vain and foolish in their aims, methods, and personnel There is very possibly an implication of political projecting here too, in the schemes of the Whigs for the improvement of the political and economic status of England.

and despair: that as for himself, being not of an enterprising spirit, he was content to go on in the old forms, to live in the houses his ancestors had built, and act as they did in every part of life without innovation. That some few other persons of quality and gentry had done the same, but were looked on with an eye of contempt and ill will, as enemies to art, ignorant, and ill commonwealth's-men, preferring their own ease and sloth before the general improvement of their country.

His Lordship added, that he would not by any further particulars prevent the pleasure I should certainly take in viewing the Grand Academy, whither he was resolved I should go. He only desired me to observe a ruined building upon the side of a mountain about three miles distant, of which he gave me this account. That he had a very convenient mill within half a mile of his house, turned by a current from a large river, and sufficient for his own family as well as a great number of his tenants. That about seven years ago a club of those projectors came to him with proposals to destroy this mill, and build another on the side of that mountain, on the long ridge whereof a long canal must be cut for a repository of water, to be conveyed up by pipes and engines to supply the mill: because the wind and air upon a height agitated the water, and thereby made it fitter for motion: and because the water descending down a declivity would turn the mill with half the current of a river whose course is more upon a level. He said, that being then not very well with the court, and pressed by many of his friends, he complied with the proposal; and after employing an hundred men for two years, the work miscarried, the projectors went off, laying the blame entirely upon him, railing at him ever since, and putting others upon the same experiment, with equal assurance of success, as well as equal disappointment.[1]

In a few days we came back to town, and his Excellency, considering the bad character he had in the Academy, would not go with me himself, but recommended me to a friend of his to bear me company thither. My Lord was pleased to represent me as a great admirer of projects, and a person of much curiosity and easy belief, which indeed was not with-

[1] Swift appears to be satirizing experiments by Hawksbee and Jurin on the nature of capillary action, the relationship between the height and flow of a stream, the effect of gravity on flow and the relationship between motion and altitude, all neatly and mathematically presented to the Royal Society.

Politically, the old mill may represent the fiscal system of England as it was destroyed by the political projectors with their South Sea and other bubbles; Munodi (Oxford) is left with the blame.

out truth, for I had my self been a sort of projector in my younger days.

Chapter V.

The author permitted to see the Grand Academy of Lagado.[1] The Academy largely described. The arts wherein the professors employ themselves.

This academy is not an entire single building, but a continuation of several houses on both sides of a street, which growing waste was purchased and applied to that use.[2]

I was received very kindly by the Warden, and went for many days to the Academy. Every room hath in it one or more projectors, and I believe I could not be in fewer than five hundred rooms.

The first man I saw was of a meagre aspect, with sooty hands and face, his hair and beard long, ragged and singed in several places. His clothes, shirt, and skin were all of the same colour. He had been eight years upon a project for extracting sunbeams out of cucumbers, which were to be put into vials hermetically sealed, and let out to warm the air in raw inclement summers.[3] He told me, he did not doubt in eight years more he should be able to supply the Governor's gardens with sunshine at a reasonable rate; but he complained that his stock was low, and entreated me to give him something as an encouragement to ingenuity, especially since this had been a very dear season for cucumbers. I made him a small present, for my Lord had furnished me with money on purpose, because he knew their practice of begging from all who go to see them.

I went into another chamber, but was ready to hasten back, being almost overcome with a horrible stink. My conductor pressed me forward, conjuring me in a whisper to give no offence, which would be highly resented, and therefore I durst not so much as stop my nose. The projector of this cell was the most ancient student of the Academy. His face and beard were of a pale yellow; his hands and clothes daubed over with

---

[1] According to his letter to Stella of Dec. 13, 1710, Swift visited Gresham College in person.

[2] Swift's description suits the government buildings in Whitehall better than the actual Royal Society, which lends support to the political reading of Book III.

[3] Hales's experiments on plant and animal respiration appear to be the source of this satire; apples rather than cucumbers figure in Hales's account.

filth. When I was presented to him, he gave me a very close embrace (a compliment I could well have excused). His employment from his first coming into the Academy was an operation to reduce human excrement to its original food, by separating the several parts, removing the tincture which it receives from the gall, making the odour exhale, and scumming off the saliva.[1] He had a weekly allowance from the society of a vessel filled with human ordure, about the bigness of a Bristol barrel.

I saw another at work to calcine ice into gunpowder,[2] who likewise showed me a treatise he had written concerning the malleability of fire, which he intended to publish.

There was a most ingenious architect who had contrived a new method for building houses, by beginning at the roof and working downwards to the foundation,[3] which he justified to me by the like practice of those two prudent insects, the bee and the spider.

There was a man born blind, who had several apprentices in his own condition: their employment was to mix colours for painters, which their master taught them to distinguish by feeling and smelling.[4] It was indeed my misfortune to find them at that time not very perfect in their lessons, and the professor himself happened to be generally mistaken: this artist is much encouraged and esteemed by the whole fraternity.

In another apartment I was highly pleased with a projector, who had found a device of plowing the ground with hogs, to save the charges of plows, cattle, and labour.[5] The method is this: in an acre of ground you bury, at six inches distance, and eight deep, a quantity of acorns, dates, chestnuts, and other mast or vegetables whereof these animals are fondest; then you drive six hundred or more of them into the field, where in a few days they will root up the whole ground in

---

[1] One of the few instances when the satire in Book III has a literary rather than scientific source; the source here is Rabelais.

[2] This detail is possibly satirical of Boyle's experiments on heat and cold, to which Swift adds gunpowder.

[3] The literary source for this detail may be Tom Brown's *Amusements;* it should be noted that there were some similar experiments reported to the Royal Society.

[4] Although this detail is intended to show the lunacy of the projectors, a not dissimilar observation is made in Robert Boyle's *Experiments and Observations upon Colour.*

[5] Swift may be recalling such works as the Archbishop of Dublin's *On the Manuring of Lands by Sea-shells in Ireland,* or *Culture of Tobacco in Zeylan* in which buffaloes rather than hogs manure the ground; both were reported in the *Philosophical Transactions.*

search of their food, and make it fit for sowing, at the same
time manuring it with their dung. It is true upon experiment
they found the charge and trouble very great, and they had
little or no crop. However, it is not doubted that this invention
may be capable of great improvement.

I went into another room, where the walls and ceiling were
all hung round with cobwebs, except a narrow passage for
the artist to go in and out. At my entrance he called aloud
to me not to disturb his webs.[1] He lamented the fatal mistake
the world had been so long in of using silkworms, while we
had such plenty of domestic insects, who infinitely excelled
the former, because they understood how to weave as well as
spin. And he proposed farther, that by employing spiders, the
charge of dyeing silks would be wholly saved; whereof I was
fully convinced when he showed me a vast number of flies
most beautifully coloured, wherewith he fed his spiders,
assuring us that the webs would take a tincture from them;
and as he had them of all hues, he hoped to fit every body's
fancy, as soon as he could find proper food for the flies, of
certain gums, oils, and other glutinous matter, to give a
strength and consistence to the threads.

There was an astronomer who had undertaken to place a
sundial upon the great weathercock on the town-house, by
adjusting the annual and diurnal motions of the earth and
sun, so as to answer and coincide with all accidental turnings
by the wind.[2]

I was complaining of a small fit of the colic, upon which
my conductor led me into a room, where a great physician
resided, who was famous for curing that disease by contrary
operations from the same instrument.[3] He had a large pair of
bellows with a long slender muzzle of ivory. This he conveyed eight inches up the anus, and drawing in the wind,
he affirmed he could make the guts as lank as a dried bladder.
But when the disease was more stubborn and violent, he let
in the muzzle while the bellows were full of wind, which
he discharged into the body of the patient, then withdrew the

[1] In 1710 a M. Bon reported in the *Philosophical Transactions* that he had
spun stockings and gloves from the webs of spiders. From another experiment
on natural coloration Swift takes the colored flies fed to the spiders to color
their webs.

[2] Sir Christopher Wren made a wind-recording machine that operated on
much the same principle.

[3] Swift here is generally satiric of experiments with respiration and
artificial respiration, particularly of St. Andre's account in the *Philosophical
Transactions* of "An Extraordinary Effect of the Cholick"; the principle
in both is the inducement of reverse peristalsis.

instrument to replenish it, clapping his thumb strongly against
the orifice of the fundament; and this being repeated three
or four times, the adventitious wind would rush out, bringing
the noxious along with it (like water put into a pump) and
the patient recovers. I saw him try both experiments upon a
dog, but could not discern any effect from the former. After
the latter, the animal was ready to burst, and made so violent
a discharge, as was very offensive to me and my companions.
The dog died on the spot, and we left the doctor endeavouring
to recover him by the same operation.

I visited many other apartments, but shall not trouble my
reader with all the curiosities I observed, being studious of
brevity.

I had hitherto seen only one side of the Academy, the other
being appropriated to the advancers of speculative learning,
of whom I shall say something when I have mentioned one
illustrious person more, who is called among them 'the universal artist'. He told us he had been thirty years employing
his thoughts for the improvement of human life.[1] He had two
large rooms full of wonderful curiosities, and fifty men at
work. Some were condensing air into a dry tangible substance,
by extracting the nitre, and letting the aqueous or fluid particles percolate; others softening marble for pillows and pin-
cushions; others petrifying the hoofs of a living horse to
preserve them from foundering. The artist himself was at
that time busy upon two great designs: the first, to sow land
with chaff, wherein he affirmed the true seminal virtue to
be contained, as he demonstrated by several experiments
which I was not skilful enough to comprehend. The other
was, by a certain composition of gums, minerals, and vegetables outwardly applied to prevent the growth of wool upon
two young lambs; and he hoped in a reasonble time to propagate the breed of naked sheep all over the kingdom.

We crossed a walk to the other part of the Academy, where,
as I have already said, the projectors in speculative learning
resided.

The first professor I saw was in a very large room, with forty
pupils about him. After salutation, observing me to look earnestly upon a frame, which took up the greatest part of both
the length and breadth of the room, he said perhaps I might
wonder to see him employed in a project for improving specu-

[1] Particularly, Swift seems to imply Sir Robert Boyle; generally, he
strikes at Modern pretentiousness in attempting to arrive at universal
systems of knowledge. The following half-dozen paragraphs set up Swift's
own universal system.

lative knowledge by practical and mechanical operations.[1] But the world would soon be sensible of its usefulness, and he flattered himself that a more noble, exalted thought never sprang in any other man's head. Every one knows how laborious the usual method is of attaining to arts and sciences; whereas by his contrivance, the most ignorant person at a reasonable charge, and with a little bodily labour, may write books in philosophy, poetry, politics, law, mathematics and theology, without the least assistance from genius or study. He then led me to the frame, about the sides whereof all his pupils stood in ranks. It was twenty foot square, placed in the middle of the room. The superficies was composed of several bits of wood, about the bigness of a die, but some larger than others. They were all linked together by slender wires. These bits of wood were covered on every square with papers pasted on them; and on these papers were written all the words of their language in their several moods, tenses, and declensions, but without any order. The professor then desired me to observe, for he was going to set his engine at work. The pupils at his command took each of them hold of an iron handle, whereof there were forty fixed round the edges of the frame, and giving them a sudden turn, the whole disposition of the words was entirely changed. He then commanded six and thirty of the lads to read the several lines softly as they appeared upon the frame; and where they found three or four words together that might make part of a sentence, they dictated to the four remaining boys who were scribes. This work was repeated three or four times, and at every turn the engine was so contrived, that the words shifted into new places, as the square bits of wood moved upside down.

Six hours a day the young students were employed in this labour, and the professor showed me several volumes in large folio already collected, of broken sentences, which he intended to piece together, and out of those rich materials to give the world a complete body of all arts and sciences; which however might be still improved, and much expedited, if the public would raise a fund for making and employing five hundred such frames in Lagado, and oblige the managers to contribute in common their several collections.

[1] No scientific source has been found for the frame; a political reading has been suggested which cites the speculation mania of the "South Sea Year," 1720, as source for the experiments. Among the speculations floated was one for the manufacture of a perpetual-motion wheel and a device for manuring farm lands.

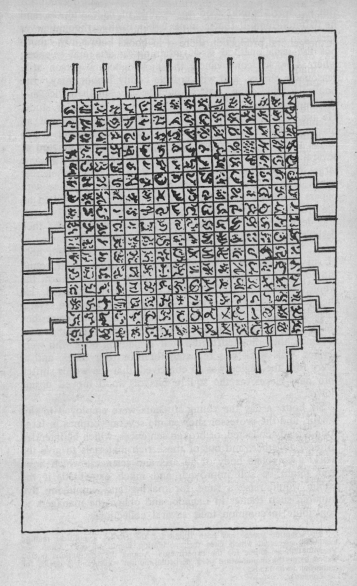

He assured me, that this invention had employed all his thoughts from his youth; that he had emptied the whole vocabulary into his frame, and made the strictest computation of the general proportion there is in books between the numbers of particles, nouns, and verbs, and other parts of speech.

I made my humblest acknowledgements to this illustrious person for his great communicativeness, and promised if ever I had the good fortune to return to my native country, that I would do him justice, as the sole inventor of this wonderful machine; the form and contrivance of which I desired leave to delineate upon paper as in the figure here annexed. I told him, although it were the custom of our learned in Europe to steal inventions from each other, who had thereby at least this advantage, that it became a controversy which was the right owner; yet I would take such caution, that he should have the honour entire without a rival.

We next went to the school of languages,[1] where three professors sat in consultation upon improving that of their own country.

The first project was to shorten discourse by cutting polysyllables into one, and leaving out verbs and participles, because in reality all things imaginable are but nouns.

The other was a scheme for entirely abolishing all words whatsoever; and this was urged as a great advantage in point of health as well as brevity. For it is plain, that every word we speak is in some degree a diminution of our lungs by corrosion, and consequently contributes to the shortening of our lives. An expedient was therefore offered, that since words are only names for *things,* it would be more convenient for all men to carry about them such *things* as were necessary to express the particular business they are to discourse on. And this invention would certainly have taken place, to the great ease as well as health of the subject, if the women in conjunction with the vulgar and illiterate had not threatened to raise a rebellion, unless they might be allowed the liberty to speak with their tongues, after the manner of their forefathers: such constant irreconcilable enemies to science are the common people. However, many of the most learned and wise adhere to the new scheme of expressing themselves by *things,* which hath only this inconvenience attending it, that

---

[1] Swift refers to contemporary attempts to create a universal language, to reform English, and provide a language that would be useful for the dissemination of scientific truths. The attempt was begun by Bacon, defended by Sprat in his *History of the Royal Society,* and received its fullest expression in John Wilkins's essay towards a *Real Character and Philosophical Language,* 1668.

if a man's business be very great, and of various kinds,
he must be obliged in proportion to carry a greater bundle of
things upon his back, unless he can afford one or two strong
servants to attend him. I have often beheld two of those sages
almost sinking under the weight of their packs, like pedlars
among us; who when they met in the streets would lay down
their loads, open their sacks and hold conversation for an
hour together; then put up their implements, help each other
to resume their burthens, and take their leave.

But for short conversations a man may carry implements
in his pockets and under his arms, enough to supply him, and
in his house he cannot be at a loss; therefore the room where
company meet who practise this art is full of all *things* ready
at hand, requisite to furnish matter for this kind of artificial
converse.

Another great advantage proposed by this invention was
that it would serve as an universal language to be understood
in all civilised nations, whose goods and utensils are generally
of the same kind, or nearly resembling, so that their uses
might easily be comprehended. And thus ambassadors would
be qualified to treat with foreign princes or ministers of state,
to whose tongues they were utter strangers.

I was at the mathematical school, where the master taught
his pupils after a method scarce imaginable to us in Europe.
The proposition and demonstration were fairly written on a thin
wafer, with ink composed of a cephalic tincture. This the student was to swallow upon a fasting stomach, and for three
days following eat nothing but bread and water. As the wafer
digested, the tincture mounted to his brain, bearing the proposition along with it. But the success hath not hitherto been
answerable, partly by some error in the *quantum* or composition, and partly by the perverseness of lads, to whom this bolus
is so nauseous that they generally steal aside, and discharge
it upwards before it can operate; neither have they been yet
persuaded to use so long an abstinence as the prescription
requires.

CHAPTER VI.

*A further account of the Academy. The author proposes some
improvements which are honourably received.*

In the school of political projectors I was but ill entertained,
the professors appearing in my judgment wholly out of their

senses, which is a scene that never fails to make me melancholy. These unhappy people were proposing schemes for persuading monarchs to choose favourites upon the score of their wisdom, capacity and virtue; of teaching ministers to consult the public good; of rewarding merit, great abilities and eminent services; of instructing princes to know their true interest by placing it on the same foundation with that of their people: of choosing for employments persons qualified to exercise them; with many other wild impossible chimæras, that never entered before into the heart of man to conceive, and confirmed in me the old observation, that there is nothing so extravagant and irrational which some philosophers have not maintained for truth.

But, however, I shall so far do justice to this part of the Academy, as to acknowledge that all of them were not so visionary. There was a most ingenious doctor who seemed to be perfectly versed in the whole nature and system of government. This illustrious person had very usefully employed his studies in finding out effectual remedies for all diseases and corruptions to which the several kinds of public administration are subject by the vices or infirmities of those who govern, as well as by the licentiousness of those who are to obey. For instance: whereas all writers and reasoners have agreed, that there is a strict universal resemblance between the natural and the political body; can there be any thing more evident, than that the health of both must be preserved, and the diseases cured by the same prescriptions? It is allowed that senates and great councils are often troubled with redundant, ebullient, and other peccant humours, with many diseases of the head, and more of the heart; with strong convulsions, with grievous contractions of the nerves and sinews in both hands, but especially the right; with spleen, flatus, vertigos and deliriums; with scrofulous tumours full of fœtid purulent matter; with sour frothy ructations, with canine appetites and crudeness of digestion, besides many others needless to mention. This doctor therefore proposed, that upon the meeting of a senate, certain physicians should attend at the three first days of their sitting, and, at the close of each day's debate, feel the pulses of every senator; after which, having maturely considered, and consulted upon the nature of the several maladies, and the methods of cure, they should on the fourth day return to the senate house, attended by their apothecaries stored with proper medicines; and before the members sat, administer to each of them lenitives, aperitives, abstersives,

corrosives, restringents, palliatives, laxatives, cephalalgics, ic-
terics, apophlegmatics, acoustics, as their several cases required; and according as these medicines should operate,
repeat, alter, or omit them at the next meeting.

This project could not be of any great expense to the public,
and might, in my opinion, be of much use for the dispatch
of business in those countries where senates have any share in
the legislative power; beget unanimity, shorten debates, open
a few mouths which are now closed, and close many more
which are now open; curb the petulancy of the young, and
correct the positiveness of the old; rouse the stupid, and damp
the pert.

Again, because it is a general complaint that the favourites
of princes are troubled with short and weak memories, the
same doctor proposed, that whoever attended a first minister,
after having told his business with the utmost brevity, and in
the plainest words, should at his departure give the said
minister a tweak by the nose, or a kick in the belly, or tread
on his corns, or lug him thrice by both ears, or run a pin into
his breech, or pinch his arm black and blue, to prevent
forgetfulness: and at every levee day repeat the same operation, till the business were done or absolutely refused.

He likewise directed, that every senator in the great council of a nation, after he had delivered his opinion, and argued
in the defence of it, should be obliged to give his vote directly
contrary; because if that were done, the result would infallibly
terminate in the good of the public.

When parties in a state are violent, he offered a wonderful
contrivance to reconcile them. The method is this. You take
an hundred leaders of each party; you dispose them into
couples of such whose heads are nearest of a size; then let two
nice operators saw off the occiput of each couple at the same
time, in such a manner that the brain may be equally divided.
Let the occiputs thus cut off be interchanged, applying each to
the head of his opposite party-man. It seems indeed to be a
work that requireth some exactness, but the professor assured
us, that if it were dextrously performed the cure would be
infallible. For he argued thus; that the two half brains being
left to debate the matter between themselves within the space
of one skull, would soon come to a good understanding, and
produce that moderation, as well as regularity of thinking, so
much to be wished for in the heads of those who imagine
they came into the world only to watch and govern its
motion: and as to the difference of brains in quantity or

quality, among those who are directors in faction, the doctor assured us from his own knowledge, that it was a perfect trifle.

I heard a very warm debate between two professors, about the most commodious and effectual ways and means of raising money without grieving the subject. The first affirmed the justest method would be to lay a certain tax upon vices and folly, and the sum fixed upon every man to be rated after the fairest manner by a jury of his neighbours. The second was of an opinion directly contrary, to tax those qualities of body and mind for which men chiefly value themselves, the rate to be more or less according to the degrees of excelling, the decision whereof should be left entirely to their own breast. The highest tax was upon men who are the greatest favourites of the other sex, and the assessments according to the number and natures of the favours they have received; for which they are allowed to be their own vouchers. Wit, valour, and politeness were likewise proposed to be largely taxed, and collected in the same manner, by every person's giving his own word for the quantum of what he possessed. But as to honour, justice, wisdom and learning, they should not be taxed at all, because they are qualifications of so singular a kind, that no man will either allow them in his neighbour, or value them in himself.

The women were proposed to be taxed according to their beauty and skill in dressing, wherein they had the same privilege with the men, to be determined by their own judgment. But constancy, chastity, good sense, and good nature were not rated, because they would not bear the charge of collecting.

To keep senators in the interest of the crown, it was proposed that the members should raffle for employments, every man first taking an oath, and giving security that he would vote for the court, whether he won or no, after which the losers had in their turn the liberty of raffling upon the next vacancy. Thus hope and expectation would be kept alive; none would complain of broken promises, but impute their disappointments wholly to Fortune, whose shoulders are broader and stronger than those of a ministry.

Another professor showed me a large paper of instructions for discovering plots and conspiracies against the government. He advised great statesmen to examine into the diet of all suspected persons; their times of eating; upon which side they lay in bed; with which hand they wiped their posteriors; to take a strict view of their excrements, and from the colour, the odour, the taste, the consistence, the crudeness or maturity of digestion, form a judgment of their thoughts and designs. Because men are never so serious, thoughtful, and intent, as when they are at stool, which he found by frequent experiment: for in such conjunctures, when he used merely as a trial to consider which was the best way of murdering the King, his ordure would have a tincture of green, but quite different when he thought only of raising an insurrection or burning the metropolis.

The whole discourse was written with great acuteness, containing many observations both curious and useful for politicians, but as I conceived not altogether complete. This I ventured to tell the author, and offered if he pleased to supply him with some additions. He received my proposition with more compliance than is usual among writers, especially those of the projecting species, professing he would be glad to receive farther information.

I told him, that in the kingdom of Tribnia, by the natives called Langden,[1] where I had long sojourned, the bulk of the people consisted wholly of discoverers, witnesses, informers, accusers, prosecutors, evidences, swearers, together with their several subservient and subaltern instruments, all under the colours, the conduct, and pay of ministers and their deputies. The plots in that kingdom are usually the workmanship of those persons who desire to raise their own characters of profound politicians; to restore new vigour to a crazy administration; to stifle or divert general discontents; to fill their coffers with forfeitures; and raise or sink the opinion of public credit, as either shall best answer their private advantage. It is first agreed and settled among them what suspected persons shall be accused of a plot: then effectual care is taken to secure all their letters and other papers, and put the owners in chains. These papers are delivered to a set of artists, very dextrous in finding out the mysterious meanings of words, syllables, and letters. For instance, they can decipher a close-stool to signify a privy-council, a flock of geese a senate, a lame dog an invader,[2] a codshead a ———, the plague a stand-

---

[1] *Tribnia* and *Langden* are anagrams for *Britain* and *England*.

[2] In the trial of Francis Atterbury, Bishop of Rochester, for treason, evidence of treasonous correspondence between the Bishop and the Pretender was found in the Bishop's close-stool, or toilet; it was in code and the evidence was questionable. A lame dog, Harlequin, also figured in the evidence. (See Swift's poem: "Upon the Horrid Plot discovered by Harlequin, the Bishop of Rochester's French dog.") Swift, a friend of Atterbury, believed in his innocence.

ing army, a buzzard a minister, the gout a high priest, a gibbet a secretary of state, a chamberpot a committee of grandees, a sieve a court lady, a broom a revolution, a mousetrap an employment, a bottomless pit the treasury, a sink a court, a cap and bells a favourite, a broken reed a court of justice, an empty tun a general, a running sore the administration.

When this method fails, they have two others more effectual, which the learned among them call acrostics and anagrams. First they can decipher all initial letters into political meanings. Thus N shall signify a plot, B a regiment of horse, L a fleet at sea. Or secondly, by transposing the letters of the alphabet in any suspected paper, they can lay open the deepest designs of a discontented party. So, for example, if I should say in a letter to a friend, Our Brother Tom has just got the piles, a man of skill in this art would discover how the same letters which compose that sentence may be analyzed into the following words: Resist—a plot is brought home—The Tour.[1] And this is the anagrammatic method.

The professor made me great acknowledgments for communicating these observations, and promised to make honourable mention of me in his treatise.

I saw nothing in this country that could invite me to a longer continuance, and began to think of returning home to England.

Chapter VII.

The author leaves Lagado, arrives at Maldonada.[2] No ship ready. He takes a short voyage to Glubbdubdrib. His reception by the Governor.

The continent of which this kingdom is a part extends itself, as I have reason to believe, eastward to that unknown tract of America, westward of California, and north to the Pacific Ocean, which is not above an hundred and fifty miles from Lagado;[3] where there is a good port and much commerce with the great island of Luggnagg, situated to the northwest about 29 degrees north latitude, and 140 longitude. This island of Luggnagg stands southeastwards of Japan,

---

[1] *The Tour* is a signature; besides implying the Tower of London, a prison, it recalls *La Tour*, the name by which Bolingbroke was known in France during his exile.
[2] Dublin.
[3] London.

about an hundred leagues distant. There is a strict alliance
between the Japanese Emperor and the King of Luggnagg,
which affords frequent opportunities of sailing from one
island to the other. I determined therefore to direct my
course this way in order to my return to Europe. I hired two
mules with a guide to show me the way, and carry my small
baggage. I took leave of my noble protector, who had shown
me so much favour, and made me a generous present at my
departure.

My journey was without any accident or adventure worth
relating. When I arrived at the port of Maldonada (for so it is
called), there was no ship in the harbour bound for Luggnagg,
nor like to be in some time. The town is about as large as
Portsmouth. I soon fell into some acquaintance, and was very
hospitably received. A gentleman of distinction said to me,
that since the ships bound for Luggnagg could not be ready
in less than a month, it might be no disagreeable amusement
for me to take a trip to the little island of Glubbdubdrib,
about five leagues off to the southwest. He offered himself
and a friend to accompany me, and that I should be provided
with a small convenient barque for the voyage.

Glubbdubdrib, as nearly as I can interpret the word, signifies The Island of *Sorcerers* or *Magicians*. It is about one
third as large as the Isle of Wight, and extremely fruitful: it
is governed by the head of a certain tribe, who are all
magicians. This tribe marries only among each other, and
the eldest in succession is prince or governor. He hath a
noble palace and a park of about three thousand acres,
surrounded by a wall of hewn stone twenty foot high. In
this park are several smaller inclosures for cattle, corn, and
gardening.

The Governor and his family are served and attended by
domestics of a kind somewhat unusual. By his skill in necromancy, he hath power of calling whom he pleaseth from the
dead, and commanding their service for twenty-four hours,
but no longer; nor can he call the same persons up again in
less than three months, except upon very extraordinary occasions.

When we arrived at the island, which was about eleven in
the morning, one of the gentlemen who accompanied me went
to the Governor, and desired admittance for a stranger, who
came on purpose to have the honour of attending on his
Highness. This was immediately granted, and we all three
entered the gate of the palace between two rows of guards,

armed and dressed after a very antic manner, and something in their countenances that made my flesh creep with a horror I cannot express. We passed through several apartments between servants of the same sort, ranked on each side as before, till we came to the chamber of presence, where, after three profound obeisances, and a few general questions, we were permitted to sit on three stools near the lowest step of his Highness's throne. He understood the language of Balnibarbi, although it were different from that of his island. He desired me to give him some account of my travels; and to let me see that I should be treated without ceremony, he dismissed all his attendants with a turn of his finger, at which to my great astonishment they vanished in an instant, like visions in a dream, when we awake on a sudden. I could not recover my self in some time, till the Governor assured me that I should receive no hurt; and observing my two companions to be under no concern, who had been often entertained in the same manner, I began to take courage, and related to his Highness a short history of my several adventures, yet not without some hesitation, and frequently looking behind me to the place where I had seen those domestic spectres. I had the honour to dine with the Governor, where a new set of ghosts served up the meat, and waited at table. I now observed my self to be less terrified than I had been in the morning. I stayed till sunset, but humbly desired his Highness to excuse me for not accepting his invitation of lodging in the palace. My two friends and I lay at a private house in the town adjoining, which is the capital of this little island; and the next morning we returned to pay our duty to the Governor, as he was pleased to command us.

After this manner we continued in the island for ten days, most part of every day with the Governor, and at night in our lodging. I soon grew so familiarized to the sight of spirits, that after the third or fourth time they gave me no emotion at all; or if I had any apprehensions left, my curiosity prevailed over them. For his Highness the Governor ordered me to call up whatever persons I would choose to name, and in whatever numbers among all the dead from the beginning of the world to the present time, and command them to answer any questions I should think fit to ask; with this condition, that my questions must be confined within the compass of the times they lived in. And one thing I might depend upon, that they would certainly tell me truth, for lying was a talent of no use in the lower world.

I made my humble acknowledgements to his Highness for so great a favour. We were in a chamber, from whence there was a fair prospect into the park. And because my first inclination was to be entertained with scenes of pomp and magnificence, I desired to see Alexander the Great, at the head of his army just after the battle of Arbela, which upon a motion of the Governor's finger immediately appeared in a large field under the window, where we stood. Alexander was called up into the room: it was with great difficulty that I understood his Greek, and had but little of my own. He assured me upon his honour that he was not poisoned, but died of a fever by excessive drinking.[1]

Next I saw Hannibal passing the Alps, who told me he had not a drop of vinegar in his camp.[2]

I saw Cæsar and Pompey at the head of their troops, just ready to engage. I saw the former in his great triumph. I desired that the Senate of Rome might appear before me in one large chamber, and a modern representative, in counterview, in another. The first seemed to be an assembly of heroes and demigods; the other a knot of pedlars, pickpockets, highwaymen and bullies.

The Governor at my request gave the sign for Cæsar and Brutus to advance towards us. I was struck with a profound veneration at the sight of Brutus, and could easily discover the most consummate virtue, the greatest intrepidity and firmness of mind, the truest love of his country and general benevolence for mankind in every lineament of his countenance. I observed with much pleasure that these two persons were in good intelligence with each other; and Cæsar freely confessed to me, that the greatest actions of his own life were not equal by many degrees to the glory of taking it away. I had the honour to have much conversation with Brutus; and was told, that his ancestor Junius, Socrates, Epaminondas, Cato the younger, Sir Thomas More and himself were perpetually together: a *sextumvirate* to which all the ages of the world cannot add a seventh.

It would be tedious to trouble the reader with relating what vast numbers of illustrious persons were called up, to gratify that insatiable desire I had to see the world in every period of antiquity placed before me. I chiefly fed my eyes with behold-

---

[1] Plutarch's *Lives* disputes the legend that Alexander the Great was poisoned, stating that he died of a fever in 323 B.C.
[2] According to Livy, Hannibal succeeded in crossing the Alps by building a fire on an impassable rock and saturating it in vinegar.

ing the destroyers of tyrants and usurpers, and the restorers of
liberty to oppressed and injured nations. But it is impossible
to express the satisfaction I received in my own mind, after
such a manner as to make it a suitable entertainment to the
reader.

CHAPTER VIII.

*A further account of Glubbdubdrib. Ancient and modern his-
tory corrected.*

Having a desire to see those ancients, who were most renowned for wit and learning, I set apart one day on purpose. I proposed that Homer and Aristotle might appear at the
head of all their commentators; but these were so numerous
that some hundreds were forced to attend in the court and
outward rooms of the palace. I knew and could distinguish
those two heroes at first sight, not only from the crowd, but
from each other. Homer was the taller and comelier person
of the two, walked very erect for one of his age, and his eyes
were the most quick and piercing I ever beheld. Aristotle
stooped much, and made use of a staff. His visage was meager,
his hair lank and thin, and his voice hollow. I soon discovered
that both of them were perfect strangers to the rest of the
company, and had never seen or heard of them before. And I
had a whisper from a ghost, who shall be nameless, that these
commentators always kept in the most distant quarters from
their principals in the lower world, through a consciousness
of shame and guilt, because they had so horribly misrepresented the meaning of those authors to posterity. I introduced
Didymus and Eustathius [1] to Homer, and prevailed on him
to treat them better than perhaps they deserved, for he soon
found they wanted a genius to enter into the spirit of a poet.
But Aristotle was out of all patience with the account I gave
him of Scotus and Ramus,[2] as I presented them to him, and
he asked them whether the rest of the tribe were as great
dunces as themselves.

I then desired the Governor to call up Descartes [3] and Gas-

[1] Tenth- and eleventh-century A.D. commentators on Homer; Homer was
a key figure in the *Battle of the Books*.
[2] Duns Scotus (d. 1308) was a scholastic philosopher; Peter Ramus
(16th c.) in *Animadversions* revised the Aristotelian logic. Note that Swift
does not criticize Aristotle, only Aristotelians.
[3] For Swift, René Descartes was a "type" of the Modern philosopher;
in *Tale of a Tub* he found Descartes' theory of vortices "romantic."

sendi,[1] with whom I prevailed to explain their systems to
Aristotle. This great philosopher freely acknowledged his own
mistakes in natural philosophy, because he proceeded in many
things upon conjecture, as all men must do; and he found that
Gassendi, who had made the doctrine of Epicurus as palatable
as he could, and the *vortices* of Descartes, were equally exploded. He predicted the same fate to *attraction*,[2] whereof the
present learned are such zealous asserters. He said, that new
systems of nature were but new fashions, which would vary
in every age; and even those who pretend to demonstrate them
from mathematical principles would flourish but a short period
of time, and be out of vogue when that was determined.

I spent five days in conversing with many others of the ancient learned. I saw most of the first Roman emperors. I prevailed on the Governor to call up Eliogabalus's [3] cooks to
dress us a dinner, but they could not show us much of their
skill, for want of materials. A helot of Agesilaus made us a
dish of Spartan broth, but I was not able to get down a second
spoonful.

The two gentlemen who conducted me to the island were
pressed by their private affairs to return in three days, which
I employed in seeing some of the modern dead who had made
the greatest figure for two or three hundred years past in our
own and other countries of Europe; and having been always
a great admirer of old illustrious families, I desired the Governor would call up a dozen or two of kings with their ancestors in order, for eight or nine generations. But my disappointment was grievous and unexpected. For instead of a long train
with royal diadems, I saw in one family, two fiddlers, three
spruce courtiers, and an Italian prelate. In another, a barber,
an abbot, and two cardinals. I have too great a veneration for
crowned heads to dwell any longer on so nice a subject: but
as to counts, marquesses, dukes, earls, and the like, I was not
so scrupulous. And I confess it was not without some pleasure
that I found my self able to trace the particular features, by
which certain families are distinguished, up to their originals.
I could plainly discover from whence one family derives a
long chin, why a second hath abounded with knaves for two
generations, and fools for two more; why a third happened to

---

[1] Pierre Gassendi (1592–1655) helped turn Epicureanism into a "Modern"
system. Note that Swift found speculative philosophy in general vain and
foolish, for ultimate truth lay in Christian revelation.

[2] Newton's theory of gravitation.

[3] A third-century Roman emperor proverbial for his gluttony.

be crack-brained, and a fourth to be sharpers. Whence it came what Polydore Virgil says of a certain great house, *Nec vir fortis, nec fœmina casta*.[1] How cruelty, falsehood, and cowardice grew to be characteristics by which certain families are distinguishd as much as by their coat of arms. Who first brought the pox into a noble house, which hath lineally descended in scrofulous tumours to their posterity. Neither could I wonder at all this, when I saw such an interruption of lineages by pages, lackeys, valets, coachmen, gamesters, fiddlers, players, captains, and pickpockets.

I was chiefly disgusted with modern history.[2] For having strictly examined all the persons of greatest name in the course of princes for an hundred years past, I found how the world had been misled by prostitute writers, to ascribe the greatest exploits in war to cowards, the wisest counsel to fools, sincerity to flatterers, Roman virtue to betrayers of their country, piety to atheists, chastity to sodomites, truth to informers. How many innocent and excellent persons had been condemned to death or banishment, by the practising of great ministers upon the corruption of judges, and the malice of factions. How many villains had been exalted to the highest places of trust, power, dignity, and profit: how great a share in the motions and events of courts, councils, and senates might be challenged by bawds, whores, pimps, parasites, and buffoons: how low an opinion I had of human wisdom and integrity, when I was truly informed of the springs and motives of great enterprises and revolutions in the world, and of the contemptible accidents to which they owed their success.

Here I discovered the roguery and ignorance of those who pretend to write *anecdotes*, or secret history; who send so many kings to their graves with a cup of poison; will repeat the discourse between a prince and chief minister, where no witness was by; unlock the thoughts and cabinets of ambassadors and secretaries of state; and have the perpetual misfortune to be mistaken. Here I discovered the true causes of many great events that have surprised the world: how a whore can govern the back-stairs, the back-stairs a council, and the council a senate. A general confessed in my presence, that he got a victory purely by the force of cowardice and ill conduct:

[1] "Neither were their men strong nor their women chaste." Actually the phrase does not occur in Polydore Virgil, a sixteenth-century author of a Latin history of England.
[2] Note that Modern historians are the "mercenaries" of the *Battle of the Books*.

and an admiral that for want of proper intelligence, he beat
the enemy to whom he intended to betray the fleet.[1] Three
kings [2] protested to me, that in their whole reigns they did
never once prefer any person of merit, unless by mistake or
treachery of some minister in whom they confided: neither
would they do it if they were to live again; and they showed
with great strength of reason, that the royal throne could not
be supported without corruption, because that positive, confident, restive temper, which virtue infused into man, was a
perpetual clog to public business.

I had the curiosity to enquire in a particular manner, by
what method great numbers had procured to themselves high
titles of honour, and prodigious estates; and I confined my
enquiry to a very modern period: however, without grating
upon present times, because I would be sure to give no offence
even to foreigners (for I hope the reader need not be told
that I do not in the least intend my own country in what I say
upon this occasion), a great number of persons concerned were
called up, and upon a very slight examination, discovered
such a scene of infamy, that I cannot reflect upon it without
some seriousness. Perjury, oppression, subornation, fraud,
pandarism, and the like infirmities, were amongst the most
excusable arts they had to mention, and for these I gave, as it
was reasonable, due allowance. But when some confessed they
owed their greatness and wealth to sodomy or incest; others
to the prostituting of their own wives and daughters; others
to the betraying their country or their prince; some to poisoning, more to the perverting of justice in order to destroy the
innocent: I hope I may be pardoned if these discoveries inclined me a little to abate of that profound veneration which
I am naturally apt to pay to persons of high rank, who ought
to be treated with the utmost respect due to their sublime dignity, by us their inferiors.

I had often read of some great services done to princes and
states, and desired to see the persons by whom those services
were performed. Upon enquiry I was told that their names
were to be found on no record, except a few of them whom
history hath represented as the vilest rogues and traitors. As to
the rest, I had never once heard of them. They all appeared
with dejected looks, and in the meanest habit, most of them
telling me they died in poverty and disgrace, and the rest on
a scaffold or a gibbet.

---

[1] Possibly Admiral Russell, who was suspected of treason in the Battle
of La Hague in 1692.
[2] Generally taken to be Charles II, James II, and William III.

Among others there was one person whose case appeared a little singular. He had a youth about eighteen years old standing by his side. He told me he had for many years been commander of a ship, and in the sea fight at Actium had the good fortune to break through the enemy's great line of battle, sink three of their capital ships, and take a fourth, which was the sole cause of Antony's flight, and of the victory that ensued; that the youth standing by him, his only son, was killed in the action. He added, that upon the confidence of some merit, the war being at an end, he went to Rome, and solicited at the court of Augustus to be preferred to a greater ship, whose commander had been killed; but without any regard to his pretensions, it was given to a boy who had never seen the sea, the son of a Libertina, who waited on one of the Emperor's mistresses. Returning back to his own vessel, he was charged with neglect of duty, and the ship given to a favourite page of Publicola the Vice-Admiral; whereupon he retired to a poor farm, at a great distance from Rome, and there ended his life.[1] I was so curious to know the truth of this story, that I desired Agrippa might be called, who was admiral in that fight. He appeared and confirmed the whole account, but with much more advantage to the captain, whose modesty had extenuated or concealed a great part of his merit.

I was surprised to find corruption grown so high and so quick in that empire, by the force of luxury so lately introduced; which made me less wonder at many parallel cases in other countries, where vices of all kinds have reigned so much longer, and where the whole praise as well as pillage hath been engrossed by the chief commander, who perhaps had the least title to either.

As every person called up made exactly the same appearance he had done in the world, it gave me melancholy reflections to observe how much the race of human kind was degenerate among us, within these hundred years past. How the pox under all its consequences and denominations had altered every lineament of an English countenance, shortened the size of bodies, unbraced the nerves, relaxed the sinews and muscles, introduced a sallow complexion, and rendered the flesh loose and rancid.

I descended so low as to desire that some English yeomen

[1] The story may bear reference to the Earl of Peterborough, who fought valiantly in the War of the Spanish Succession, but was called home in disgrace partly through the machinations of the young Emperor Charles, who then replaced him as Admiral. On the Earl's journey home, he witnessed the death of his young son.

of the old stamp might be summoned to appear, once so famous for the simplicity of their manners, diet and dress, for justice in their dealings, for their true spirit of liberty, for their valour and love of their country. Neither could I be wholly unmoved after comparing the living with the dead, when I considered how all these pure native virtues were prostituted for a piece of money by their grandchildren, who in selling their votes, and managing at elections, have acquired every vice and corruption that can possibly be learned in a court.

CHAPTER IX.

The author's return to Maldonada. Sails to the kingdom of Luggnagg. The author confined. He is sent for to court. The manner of his admittance. The King's great lenity to his subjects.

The day of our departure being come, I took leave of his Highness the Governor of Glubbdubdrib, and returned with my two companions to Maldonada, where after a fortnight's waiting, a ship was ready to sail for Luggnagg. The two gentlemen and some others were so generous and kind as to furnish me with provisions, and see me on board. I was a month in this voyage. We had one violent storm, and were under a necessity of steering westward to get into the trade wind, which holds for above sixty leagues. On the 21st of April, 1709, we sailed in the river of Clumegnig, which is a seaport town, at the southeast point of Luggnagg. We cast anchor within a league of the town, and made a signal for a pilot. Two of them came on board in less than half an hour, by whom we were guided between certain shoals and rocks, which are very dangerous in the passage, to a large basin, where a fleet may ride in safety within a cable's length of the town wall.

Some of our sailors, whether out of treachery or inadvertence, had informed the pilots that I was a stranger and a great traveller, whereof these gave notice to a custom-house officer, by whom I was examined very strictly upon my landing. This officer spoke to me in the language of Balnibarbi, which by the force of much commerce is generally understood in that town, especially by seamen, and those employed in the customs. I gave him a short account of some particulars, and made my story as plausible and consistent as I could; but I thought it necessary to disguise my country, and call my self a Hollander, because my intentions were for Japan, and I knew the Dutch were the only Europeans permitted to enter into that kingdom. I therefore told the officer, that having been shipwrecked on the coast of Balnibarbi, and cast on a rock, I was received up into Laputa, or the Flying Island (of which he had often heard) and was now endeavouring to get to Japan, from whence I might find a convenience of returning to my own country. The officer said I must be confined till he could receive orders from court, for which he would write immediately, and hoped to receive an answer in a fortnight. I was carried to a convenient lodging, with a sentry placed at the door; however I had the liberty of a large garden, and was treated with humanity enough, being maintained all the time at the King's charge. I was visited by several persons, chiefly out of curiosity, because it was reported I came from countries very remote, of which they had never heard.

I hired a young man who came in the same ship to be an interpreter; he was a native of Luggnagg, but had lived some years at Maldonada, and was a perfect master of both languages. By his assistance I was able to hold a conversation with those that came to visit me; but this consisted only of their questions, and my answers.

The dispatch came from court about the time we expected. It contained a warrant for conducting me and my retinue to Traldragdubh or Trildrogdrib (for it is pronounced both ways as near as I can remember) by a party of ten horse. All my retinue was that poor lad for an interpreter, whom I persuaded into my service. At my humble request, we had each of us a mule to ride on. A messenger was dispatched half a day's journey before us, to give the King notice of my approach, and to desire that his Majesty would please to appoint a day and hour, when it would be his gracious pleasure that I might have the honour to *lick the dust before his footstool*. This is the court style, and I found it to be more than matter of form: for upon my admittance two days after my arrival, I was commanded to crawl up on my belly, and lick the floor as I have advanced; but on account of my being a stranger, care was taken to have it so clean that the dust was not offensive. However, this was a peculiar grace, not allowed to any but persons of the highest rank, when they desire an admittance. Nay, sometimes the floor is strewed with dust on purpose, when the person to be admitted happens to have powerful enemies at court: and I have seen a great lord with his mouth so crammed, that when he had crept to the proper distance from the throne, he was not able to speak a word. Neither is

there any remedy, because it is capital for those who receive
an audience to spit or wipe their mouths in his Majesty's presence. There is indeed another custom, which I cannot altogether approve of. When the King hath a mind to put any of
his nobles to death in a gentle indulgent manner, he commands
to have the floor strewed with a certain brown powder, of a
deadly composition, which being licked up infallibly kills him
in twenty-four hours. But in justice to this prince's great
clemency, and the care he hath of his subjects' lives (wherein
it were much to be wished that the monarchs of Europe would
imitate him), it must be mentioned for his honour, that strict
orders are given to have the infected parts of the floor well
washed after every such execution, which if his domestics
neglect, they are in danger of incurring his royal displeasure.
I my self heard him give directions, that one of his pages
should be whipped, whose turn it was to give notice about
washing the floor after an execution, but maliciously had
omitted it; by which neglect a young lord of great hopes coming to an audience, was unfortunately poisoned, although the
King at that time had no design against his life. But this good
prince was so gracious as to forgive the page his whipping,
upon promise that he would do so no more, without special
orders.

To return from this digression; when I had crept within four
yards of the throne, I raised my self gently upon my knees,
and then striking my forehead seven times against the ground,
I pronounced the following words, as they had been taught me
the night before. *Ickpling gloffthrobb squutserumm blhiop
mlashnalt, zwin, tnodbalkguff slhiophad gurdlubh asht.*[1] This
is the compliment established by the laws of the land for all
persons admitted to the King's presence. It may be rendered
into English thus: *May your Cœlestial Majesty outlive the sun,
eleven moons and an half.* To this the King returned some answer, which although I could not understand, yet I replied as
I had been directed: *Fluft drin yalerick dwuldum prastrad
mirplush,* which properly signifies, *My tongue is in the mouth
of my friend,* and by this expression was meant that I desired
leave to bring my interpreter; whereupon the young man
already mentioned was accordingly introduced, by whose intervention I answered as many questions as his Majesty could
put in above an hour. I spoke in the Balnibarbian tongue, and
my interpreter delivered my meaning in that of Luggnagg.

---

[1] The implications of these words, which seem intended to be very
respectful, are actually obscene. Note the decipherable *lick, belly, swine,
ass,* and half a dozen lines down *prostrate, mire.*

The King was much delighted with my company, and ordered his *Bliffmarklub* or high chamberlain to appoint a lodging in the court for me and my interpreter, with a daily allowance for my table, and a large purse of gold for my common expenses.

I stayed three months in this country out of perfect obedience to his Majesty, who was pleased highly to favour me, and made me very honourable offers. But I thought it more consistent with prudence and justice to pass the remainder of my days with my wife and family.

CHAPTER X.

The Luggnaggians commended. A particular description of the Struldbruggs, with many conversations between the auhor and some eminent persons upon that subject.

The Luggnaggians are a polite and generous people, and although they are not without some share of that pride which is peculiar to all eastern countries, yet they show themselves courteous to strangers, especially such who are countenanced by the court. I had many acquaintances among persons of the best fashion, and being always attended by my interpreter, the conversation we had was not disagreeable.

One day in much good company I was asked by a person of quality, whether I had seen any of their *Struldbruggs* [1] or *immortals*. I said I had not, and desired he would explain to me what he meant by such an appellation applied to a mortal creature. He told me, that sometimes, although very rarely, a child happened to be born in a family with a red circular spot in the forehead, directly over the left eyebrow, which was an infallible mark that it should never die. The spot, as he described it, was about the compass of a silver threepence, but in the course of time grew larger, and changed its colour; for at twelve years old it became green, so continued till five and twenty, then turned to a deep blue; at five and forty it grew coal black, and as large as an English shilling, but never admitted any farther alteration. He said these births were so rare, that he did not believe there could be above eleven hundred *Struldbruggs* of both sexes in the whole kingdom, of

---

[1] *Struldbrugg* has been decoded as *stir dull blood*. Note that Swift's immortality theme is a composite of the literary preoccupation with everlasting life without youth (as in the Tithonus myth) and scientific concern with longevity, a frequent theme in the travel literature of the period. To an orthodox Christian the quest for eternal life was blasphemous as well as foolish.

which he computed about fifty in the metropolis, and among the rest a young girl born about three years ago. That these productions were not peculiar to any family, but a mere effect of chance, and the children of the *Struldbruggs* themselves were equally mortal with the rest of the people.

I freely own my self to have been struck with inexpressible delight upon hearing this account: and the person who gave it me happening to understand the Balnibarbian language, which I spoke very well, I could not forbear breaking out into expressions perhaps a little too extravagant. I cried out as in a rapture: Happy nation where every child hath at least a chance for being immortal! Happy people who enjoy so many living examples of ancient virtue, and have masters ready to instruct them in the wisdom of all former ages! But happiest beyond all comparison are those excellent *Struldbruggs,* who being born exempt from that universal calamity of human nature, have their minds free and disengaged, without the weight and depression of spirits caused by the continual apprehension of death. I discovered my admiration that I had not observed any of these illustrious persons at court, the black spot on the forehead being so remarkable a distinction, that I could not have easily overlooked it: and it was impossible that his Majesty, a most judicious prince, should not provide himself with a good number of such wise and able counsellors. Yet perhaps the virtue of those reverend sages was too strict for the corrupt and libertine manners of a court. And we often find by experience that young men are too opinionative and volatile to be guided by the sober dictates of their seniors. However, since the King was pleased to allow me access to his royal person, I was resolved upon the very first occasion to deliver my opinion to him on this matter freely, and at large by the help of my interpreter; and whether he would please to take my advice or no, yet in one thing I was determined, that his Majesty having frequently offered me an establishment in this country, I would with great thankfulness accept the favour, and pass my life here in the conversation of those superior beings the *Struldbruggs,* if they would please to admit me.

The gentleman to whom I addressed my discourse, because (as I have already observed) he spoke the language of Balnibarbi, said to me with a sort of a smile, which usually ariseth from pity to the ignorant, that he was glad of any occasion to keep me among them, and desired my permission to explain to the company what I had spoke. He did so, and they talked together for some time in their own language, whereof

I understood not a syllable, neither could I observe by their countenances what impression my discourse had made on them. After a short silence the same person told me, that his friends and mine (so he thought fit to express himself) were very much pleased with the judicious remarks I had made on the great happiness and advantages of immortal life: and they were desirous to know in a particular manner, what scheme of living I should have formed to my self, if it had fallen to my lot to have been born a *Struldbrugg*.

I answered, it was easy to be eloquent on so copious and delightful a subject, especially to me who have been often apt to amuse my self with visions of what I should do if I were a king, a general, or a great lord; and upon this very case I had frequently run over the whole system how I should employ my self and pass the time if I were sure to live for ever.

That if it had been my good fortune to come into the world a *Struldbrugg*, as soon as I could discover my own happiness by understanding the difference between life and death, I would first resolve by all arts and methods whatsoever to procure my self riches: in the pursuit of which by thrift and management, I might reasonably expect in about two hundred years to be the wealthiest man in the kingdom. In the second place, I would from my earliest youth apply myself to the study of arts and sciences, by which I should arrive in time to excel all others in learning. Lastly, I would carefully record every action and event of consequence that happened in the public, impartially draw the characters of the several successions of princes, and great ministers of state, with my own observations on every point. I would exactly set down the several changes in customs, languages, fashions of dress, diet and diversions. By all which acquirements, I should be a living treasury of knowledge and wisdom, and certainly become the oracle of the nation.

I would never marry after threescore, but live in an hospitable manner, yet still on the saving side. I would entertain myself in forming and directing the minds of hopeful young men, by convincing them from my own remembrance, experience and observation, fortified by numerous examples, of the usefulness of virtue in public and private life. But my choice and constant companions should be a set of my own immortal brotherhood, among whom I would elect a dozen from the most ancient down to my own contemporaries. Where any of these wanted fortunes, I would provide them with convenient lodges round my own estate, and have some of them always at my table, only mingling a few of the most valuable among you mortals, whom length of time would harden me to lose with little or no reluctance, and treat your posterity after the same manner, just as a man diverts himself with the annual succession of pinks and tulips in his garden, without regretting the loss of those which withered the preceding year.

These *Struldbruggs* and I would mutually communicate our observations and memorials through the course of time, remark the several gradations by which corruption steals into the world, and oppose it in every step, by giving perpetual warning and instruction to mankind; which, added to the strong influence of our own example, would probably prevent that continual degeneracy of human nature so justly complained of in all ages.

Add to all this, the pleasure of seeing the various revolutions of states and empires,[1] the changes in the lower and upper world, ancient cities in ruins, and obscure villages become the seats of kings. Famous rivers lessening into shallow brooks, the ocean leaving one coast dry, and overwhelming another; the discovery of many countries yet unknown. Barbarity overrunning the politest nations, and the most barbarous becoming civilized. I should then see the discovery of the longitude,[2] the perpetual motion,[3] the universal medicine,[4] and many other great inventions brought to the utmost perfection.

What wonderful discoveries should we make in astronomy, by outliving and confirming our own predictions, by observing the progress and returns of comets, with the changes of motion in the sun, moon and stars.

I enlarged upon many other topics, which the natural desire of endless life and sublunary happiness could easily furnish me with. When I had ended, and the sum of my discourse had been interpreted as before to the rest of the company, there was a good deal of talk among them in the language of the country, not without some laughter at my expense. At last the same gentleman who had been my interpreter said, he was desired by the rest to set me right in a few mistakes, which I

---

[1] Swift was early exposed to Sir William Temple's cyclical theory of history; it was opposed both to the theory of nature's decay and to the idea of progress.

[2] Swift satirizes contemporary attempts to discover an easy method for determining longitude at sea.

[3] The quest for perpetual motion had already begun with Bacon; it becomes a type of the vanity of Modern science for Swift.

[4] The "universal medicine" was sought by the occultists as a means to achieve immortality. For Swift there was no great difference between the methods and aims of occult science and philosophy and their more orthodox counterparts.

had fallen into through the common imbecility of human nature, and upon that allowance was less answerable for them. That this breed of *Struldbruggs* was peculiar to their country, for there were no such people either in Balnibarbi or Japan, where he had the honour to be ambassador from his Majesty, and found the natives in both those kingdoms very hard to believe that the fact was possible; and it appeared from my astonishment when he first mentioned the matter to me, that I received it as a thing wholly new, and scarcely to be credited. That in the two kingdoms above mentioned, where during his residence he had conversed very much, he observed long life to be the universal desire and wish of mankind. That whoever had one foot in the grave was sure to hold back the other as strongly as he could. That the oldest had still hopes of living one day longer, and looked on death as the greatest evil, from which nature always prompted him to retreat; only in this island of Luggnagg the appetite for living was not so eager, from the continual example of the *Struldbruggs* before their eyes.

That the system of living contrived by me was unreasonable and unjust, because it supposed a perpetuity of youth, health, and vigour, which no man could be so foolish to hope, however extravagant he might be in his wishes. That the question therefore was not whether a man would choose to be always in the prime of youth, attended with prosperity and health, but how he would pass a perpetual life under all the usual disadvantages which old age brings along with it. For although few men will avow their desires of being immortal upon such hard conditions, yet in the two kingdoms before-mentioned of Balnibarbi and Japan, he observed that every man desired to put off death for some time longer, let it approach ever so late, and he rarely heard of any man who died willingly, except he were incited by the extremity of grief or torture. And he appealed to me whether in those countries I had travelled, as well as my own, I had not observed the same general disposition.

After this preface, he gave me a particular account of the *Struldbruggs* among them. He said they commonly acted like mortals, till about thirty years old, after which by degrees they grew melancholy and dejected, increasing in both till they came to fourscore. This he learned from their own confession; for otherwise there not being above two or three of that species born in an age, they were too few to form a general observation by. When they came to fourscore years, which is reckoned the extremity of living in this country, they had not only all the follies and infirmities of other old men, but many more which arose from the dreadful prospect of never dying. They were not only opinionative, peevish, covetous, morose, vain, talkative, but uncapable of friendship, and dead to all natural affection, which never descended below their grandchildren. Envy and impotent desires are their prevailing passions. But those objects against which their envy seems principally directed, are the vices of the younger sort, and the deaths of the old. By reflecting on the former, they find themselves cut off from all possibility of pleasure; and whenever they see a funeral, they lament and repine that others are gone to an harbour of rest, to which they themselves never can hope to arrive. They have no remembrance of any thing but what they learned and observed in their youth and middle age, and even that is very imperfect: and for the truth or particulars of any fact, it is safer to depend on common traditions than upon their best recollections. The least miserable among them appear to be those who turn to dotage and entirely lose their memories; these meet with more pity and assistance, because they want many bad qualities which abound in others.

If a *Struldbrugg* happen to marry one of his own kind, the marriage is dissolved of course by the courtesy of the kingdom, as soon as the younger of the two comes to be fourscore. For the law thinks it a reasonable indulgence, that those who are condemned without any fault of their own to a perpetual continuance in the world, should not have their misery doubled by the load of a wife.

As soon as they have completed the term of eighty years, they are looked on as dead in law; their heirs immediately succeed to their estates, only a small pittance is reserved for their support, and the poor ones are maintained at the public charge. After that period they are held incapable of any employment of trust or profit; they cannot purchase lands or take leases, neither are they allowed to be witnesses in any cause, either civil or criminal, not even for the decision of meers and bounds.

At ninety they lose their teeth and hair; they have at that age no distinction of taste, but eat and drink whatever they can get, without relish or appetite. The diseases they were subject to still continue without encreasing or diminishing. In talking they forget the common appellation of things, and the names of persons, even of those who are their nearest friends and relations. For the same reason they never can amuse themselves with reading, because their memory will not serve to carry them from the beginning of a sentence to the end; and by this defect they are deprived of the only entertainment whereof they might otherwise be capable.

The language of this country being always upon the flux, the *Struldbruggs* of one age do not understand those of another; neither are they able after two hundred years to hold any conversation (farther than by a few general words) with their neighbours the mortals; and thus they lie under the disadvantage of living like foreigners in their own country.

This was the account given me of the *Struldbruggs*, as near as I can remember. I afterwards saw five or six of different ages, the youngest not above two hundred years old, who were brought to me at several times by some of my friends; but although they were told that I was a great traveller, and had seen all the world, they had not the least curiosity to ask me a question; only desired I would give them *slumskudask*, or a token of remembrance; which is a modest way of begging, to avoid the law that strictly forbids it, because they are provided for by the public, although indeed with a very scanty allowance.

They are despised and hated by all sorts of people: when one of them is born, it is reckoned ominous, and their birth is recorded very particularly; so that you may know their age by consulting the registry, which however hath not been kept above a thousand years past, or at least hath been destroyed by time or public disturbances. But the usual way of computing how old they are, is by asking them what kings or great persons they can remember, and then consulting history, for infallibly the last prince in their mind did not begin his reign after they were fourscore years old.

They were the most mortifying sight I ever beheld, and the women more horrible than the men. Besides the usual deformities in extreme old age, they acquired an additional ghastliness in proportion to their number of years, which is not to be described, and among half a dozen I soon distinguished which was the eldest, although there was not above a century or two between them.

The reader will easily believe, that from what I had heard and seen, my keen appetite for perpetuity of life was much abated. I grew heartily ashamed of the pleasing visions I had formed, and thought no tyrant could invent a death into which I would not run with pleasure from such a life. The King heard of all that had passed between me and my friends upon this occasion, and rallied me very pleasantly, wishing I would send a couple of *Struldbruggs* to my own country, to arm our people against the fear of death; but this it seems is forbidden by the fundamental laws of the kingdom, or else I should have been well content with the trouble and expense of transporting them.

I could not but agree that the laws of this kingdom, relating to the *Struldbruggs,* were founded upon the strongest reasons, and such as any other country would be under the necessity of enacting in the like circumstances. Otherwise, as avarice is the necessary consequent of old age, those immortals would in time become proprietors of the whole nation, and engross the civil power, which, for want of abilities to manage, must end in the ruin of the public.

CHAPTER XI.

The author leaves Luggnagg and sails to Japan. From thence he returns in a Dutch ship to Amsterdam, and from Amsterdam to England.

I thought this account of the *Struldbruggs* might be some entertainment to the reader, because it seems to be a little out of the common way; at least, I do not remember to have met the like in any book of travels that hath come to my hands: and if I am deceived, my excuse must be, that it is necessary for travellers who describe the same country very often to agree in dwelling on the same particulars, without deserving the censure of having borrowed or transcribed from those who wrote before them.

There is indeed a perpetual commerce between this kingdom and the great empire of Japan, and it is very probable that the Japanese authors may have given some account of the *Struldbruggs;* but my stay in Japan was so short, and I was so entirely a stranger to the language, that I was not qualified to make any enquiries. But I hope the Dutch upon this notice will be curious and able enough to supply my defects.

His Majesty having often pressed me to accept some employment in his court, and finding me absolutely determined to return to my native country, was pleased to give me his licence to depart, and honoured me with a letter of recommendation under his own hand to the Emperor of Japan. He likewise presented me with four hundred forty-four large pieces of gold (this nation delighting in even numbers) and a red diamond which I sold in England for eleven hundred pounds.

On the 6th day of May, 1709, I took a solemn leave of his Majesty, and all my friends. This prince was so gracious as to order a guard to conduct me to Glanguenstald, which is a royal port to the southwest part of the island. In six days I found a vessel ready to carry me to Japan, and spent fifteen days in the voyage. We landed at a small port-town called Xamoschi, situated on the southeast part of Japan. The town lies on the western part where there is a narrow strait, leading northward into a long arm of the sea, upon the northwest part of which Yedo,[1] the metropolis stands. At landing I showed the custom-house officers my letter from the King of Luggnagg to his Imperial Majesty: they knew the seal perfectly well; it was as broad as the palm of my hand. The impression was, *a king lifting up a lame beggar from the earth*. The magistrates of the town, hearing of my letter, received me as a public minister; they provided me with carriages and servants, and bore my charges to Yedo, where I was admitted to an audience, and delivered my letter; which was opened with great ceremony, and explained to the Emperor by an interpreter, who gave me notice of his Majesty's order, that I should signify my request, and whatever it were, it should be granted for the sake of his royal brother of Luggnagg. This interpreter was a person employed to transact affairs with the Hollanders; he soon conjectured by my countenance that I was an European, and therefore repeated his Majesty's commands in Low Dutch, which he spoke perfectly well. I answered (as I had before determined) that I was a Dutch merchant, shipwrecked in a very remote country, from whence I travelled by sea and land to Luggnagg, and then took shipping for Japan, where I knew my countrymen often traded, and with some of these I hoped to get an opportunity of returning into Europe: I therefore most humbly entreated his royal favour to give order, that I should be conducted in safety to Nangasac. To this I added another petition, that for the sake of my patron the King of Luggnagg, his Majesty would condescend to excuse my performing the ceremony imposed on my countrymen of *trampling upon the crucifix*,[2] because I had been thrown into his kingdom by my misfortunes, without any

---

[1] Tokyo.

[2] "Figure-treading" (upon the crucifix) was a form of inquisition by which Japanese discovered Christian converts.

intention of trading. When this latter petition was interpreted
to the Emperor, he seemed a little surprised, and said he believed I was the first of my countrymen who ever made any
scruple in this point, and that he began to doubt whether I
was a real Hollander or no; but rather suspected I must be a
Christian.[1] However, for the reasons I had offered, but chiefly
to gratify the King of Luggnagg, by an uncommon mark of
his favour, he would comply with the singularity of my humour; but the affair must be managed with dexterity, and his
officers should be commanded to let me pass as it were by
forgetfulness. For he assured me, that if the secret should be
discovered by my countrymen, the Dutch, they would cut my
throat in the voyage. I returned my thanks by the interpreter
for so unusual a favour; and some troops being at that time
on their march to Nangasac, the commanding officer had orders to convey me safe thither, with particular instructions
about the business of the crucifix.

On the 9th day of June, 1709, I arrived at Nangasac, after
a very long and troublesome journey. I soon fell into company of some Dutch sailors belonging to the *Amboyna*[2] of
Amsterdam, a stout ship of 450 tons. I had lived long in
Holland, pursuing my studies at Leyden, and I spoke Dutch
well. The seamen soon knew from whence I came last; they
were curious to enquire into my voyages and course of life. I
made up a story as short and probable as I could, but concealed the greatest part. I knew many persons in Holland; I
was able to invent names for my parents, whom I pretended to
be obscure people in the province of Gelderland. I would have
given the captain (one Theodorus Vangrult) what he pleased
to ask for my voyage to Holland; but understanding I was a
surgeon, he was contented to take half the usual rate, on condition that I would serve him in the way of my calling. Before
we took shipping, I was often asked by some of the crew,
whether I had performed the ceremony above-mentioned. I
evaded the question by general answers, that I had satisfied
the Emperor and court in all particulars. However, a malicious
rogue of a skipper went to an officer, and pointng to me, told
him, I had not yet *trampled on the crucifix:* but the other,
who had received instructions to let me pass, gave the rascal
twenty strokes on the shoulders with a bamboo, after which
I was no more troubled with such questions.

[1] Current antipathy to Holland stemmed from its commercial rivalry
with England, its religious libertarianism, and its political republicanism.
[2] The ship is named after the massacre at Amboyna in the East Indies
in 1623, in which English citizens were tortured and massacred.

Nothing happened worth mentioning in this voyage. We sailed with a fair wind to the Cape of Good Hope, where we stayed only to take in fresh water. On the 6th of April we arrived safe at Amsterdam, having lost only three men by sickness in the voyage, and a fourth who fell from the foremast into the sea, not far from the coast of Guinea. From Amsterdam I soon after set sail for England in a small vessel belonging to that city.

On the 10th of April, 1710, we put in at the Downs. I landed the next morning, and saw once more my native country after an absence of five years and six months complete. I went straight to Redriff, where I arrived the same day at two in the afternoon, and found my wife and family in good health.

THE END OF THE THIRD PART

Nuyts Land

Edels Land
Lewins Land

I St Francot

I St Pider

Sweers I

I Maelsuyker
De Wits I

HOUYHNHNMS LAND

Discovered AD 1711

TRAVELS.

PART IV.

A Voyage to the Country of the Houyhnhnms.

CHAPTER I.

The author sets out as captain of a ship. His men conspire against him, confine him a long time to his cabin, set him on shore in an unknown land. He travels up in the country. The Yahoos, a strange sort of animal, described. The author meets two Houyhnhnms.

I continued at home with my wife and children about five months in a very happy condition, if I could have learned the lesson of knowing when I was well. I left my poor wife big with child, and accepted an advantageous offer made me to be captain of the *Adventure,* a stout merchantman of 350 tons: for I understood navigation well, and being grown weary of a surgeon's employment at sea, which however I could ex- ericse upon occasion, I took a skilful young man of that call- ing, one Robert Purefoy, into my ship. We set sail from Ports- mouth upon the 7th day of September, 1710; on the 14th, we met with Captain Pocock of Bristol, at Tenariff, who was going to the bay of Campechy, to cut logwood. On the 16th, he was parted from us by a storm; I heard since my return that his ship foundered, and none escaped, but one cabin-boy. He was an honest man, and a good sailor, but a little too positive in his own opinions, which was the cause of his destruction, as it hath been of several others. For if he had followed my advice, he might at this time have been safe at home with his family as well as myself.

I had several men died in my ship of calentures, so that I was forced to get recruits out of Barbadoes, and the Leeward Islands, where I touched by the direction of the merchants who employed me, which I had soon too much cause to repent; for I found afterwards that most of them had been buccaneers. I had fifty hands on board, and my orders were, that I should trade with the Indians in the South Sea, and make what discoveries I could. These rogues whom I had picked up debauched my other men, and they all formed a conspiracy to seize the ship and secure me; which they did one morning, rushing into my cabin, and binding me hand and foot, threatening to throw me overboard if I offered to stir. I told them, I was their prisoner, and would submit. This they made me swear to do, and then unbound me, only fastening one of my legs with a chain near my bed, and placed a sentry at my door with his piece charged, who was commanded to shoot me dead if I attempted my liberty. They sent me down victuals and drink, and took the government of the ship to themselves. Their design was to turn pirates, and plunder the Spaniards, which they could not do till they got more men. But first they resolved to sell the goods in the ship, and then go to Madagascar for recruits, several among them having died since my confinement. They sailed many weeks, and traded with the Indians, but I knew not what course they took, being kept close prisoner in my cabin, and expecting nothing less than to be murdered, as they often threatened me.

Upon the 9th day of May, 1711, one James Welch came down to my cabin; and said he had orders from the captain to set me ashore. I expostulated with him, but in vain; neither would he so much as tell me who their new captain was. They forced me into the long-boat, letting me put on my best suit of clothes, which were as good as new, and a small bundle of linen, but no arms except my hanger; and they were so civil as not to search my pockets, into which I conveyed what money I had, with some other little necessaries. They rowed about a league, and then set me down on a strand. I desired them to tell me what country it was: they all swore, they knew no more than myself, but said, that the captain (as they called him) was resolved, after they had sold the lading, to get rid of me in the first place where they discovered land. They pushed off immediately, advising me to make haste, for fear of being overtaken by the tide, and bade me farewell.

In this desolate condition I advanced forward, and soon got upon firm ground, where I sat down on a bank to rest myself, and consider what I had best to do. When I was a little refreshed, I went up into the country, resolving to deliver myself to the first savages I should meet, and purchase my life from them by some bracelets, glass rings, and other toys, which sailors usually provide themselves with in those

voyages, and whereof I had some about me: the land was
divided by long rows of trees, not regularly planted, but
naturally growing; there was great plenty of grass, and several
fields of oats. I walked very circumspectly for fear of being
surprised, or suddenly shot with an arrow from behind or
on either side. I fell into a beaten road, where I saw many
tracks of human feet, and some of cows, but most of horses.
At last I beheld several animals [1] in a field, and one or two
of the same kind sitting in trees. Their shape was very singular,
and deformed, which a little discomposed me, so that I lay
down behind a thicket to observe them better. Some of them
coming forward near the place where I lay, gave me an
opportunity of distinctly marking their form. Their heads and
breasts were covered with a thick hair, some frizzled and
others lank; they had beards like goats, and a long ridge
of hair down their backs, and the foreparts of their legs and
feet, but the rest of their bodies were bare, so that I might see
their skins, which were of a brown buff colour. They had
no tails, nor any hair at all on their buttocks, except about
the anus; which, I presume, nature had placed there to defend
them as they sat on the ground; for this posture they used,
as well as lying down, and often stood on their hind feet.
They climbed high trees, as nimbly as a squirrel, for they had
strong extended claws before and behind, terminating in
sharp points, and hooked. They would often spring, and
bound, and leap with prodigious agility. The females were not
so large as the males; they had long lank hair on their heads,
and only a sort of down on the rest of their bodies, except
about the anus, and pudenda. Their dugs hung between their
fore-feet, and often reached almost to the ground as they
walked. The hair of both sexes was of several colours, brown,
red, black, and yellow. Upon the whole, I never beheld in all
my travels so disagreeable an animal, or one against which I
naturally conceived so strong antipathy. So that thinking I had
seen enough, full of contempt and aversion, I got up and
pursued the beaten road, hoping it might direct me to the
cabin of some Indian. I had not gone far when I met one
of these creatures full in my way, and coming up directly
to me. The ugly monster, when he saw me, distorted several
ways every feature of his visage, and stared as at an object
he had never seen before; then approaching nearer, lifted up

[1] *Yahoo* has been explained as composed of *yah* and *ugh*, both interjections
implying disgust. Their description may derive from contemporary accounts
in travel books of apes and Hottentots.

his forepaw, whether out of curiosity or mischief, I could not tell: but I drew my hanger, and gave him a good blow with the flat side of it, for I durst not strike him with the edge, fearing the inhabitants might be provoked against me, if they should come to know that I had killed or maimed any of their cattle. When the beast felt the smart, he drew back, and roared so loud, that a herd of at least forty came flocking about me from the next field, howling and making odious faces; but I ran to the body of a tree, and leaning my back against it, kept them off, by waving my hanger. Several of this cursed brood getting hold of the branches behind leaped up into the tree, from whence they began to discharge their excrements on my head: however, I escaped pretty well, by sticking close to the stem of the tree, but was almost stifled with the filth, which fell about me on every side.

In the midst of this distress, I observed them all to run away on a sudden as fast as they could, at which I ventured to leave the tree, and pursue the road, wondering what it was that could put them into this fright. But looking on my left hand, I saw a horse walking softly in the field, which my persecutors having sooner discovered, was the cause of their flight. The horse started a little when he came near me, but soon recovering himself, looked full in my face with manifest tokens of wonder: he viewed my hands and feet, walking round me several times. I would have pursued my journey, but he placed himself directly in the way, yet looking with a very mild aspect, never offering the least violence. We stood gazing at each other for some time; at last I took the boldness to reach my hand towards his neck, with a design to stroke it, using the common style and whistle of jockeys when they are going to handle a strange horse. But this animal, seeming to receive my civilities with disdain, shook his head, and bent his brows, softly raising up his left forefoot to remove my hand. Then he neighed three or four times, but in so different a cadence, that I almost began to think he was speaking to himself in some language of his own.

While he and I were thus employed, another horse came up; who applying himself to the first in a very formal manner, they gently struck each other's right hoof before, neighing several times by turns, and varying the sound, which seemed to be almost articulate. They went some paces off, as if it were to confer together, walking side by side, backward and forward, like persons deliberating upon some affair of weight, but often turning their eyes towards me, as it were to watch that I might

not escape. I was amazed to see such actions and behaviour in
brute beasts, and concluded with myself, that if the inhabitants of this country were endued with a proportionable degree
of reason, they must needs be the wisest people upon earth.
This thought gave me so much comfort, that I resolved to go
forward until I could discover some house or village, or meet
with any of the natives, leaving the two horses to discourse
together as they pleased. But the first, who was a dapple grey,
observing me to steal off, neighed after me in so expressive
a tone, that I fancied myself to understand what he meant;
whereupon I turned back, and came near him, to expect his
farther commands; but concealing my fear as much as I could,
for I began to be in some pain, how this adventure might
terminate; and the reader will easily believe I did not much
like my present situation.

The two horses came up close to me, looking with great
earnestness upon my face and hands. The grey steed rubbed
my hat all round with his right fore-hoof, and discomposed it
so much, that I was forced to adjust it better, by taking it
off, and settling it again; whereat both he and his companion
(who was a brown bay) appeared to be much surprised; the
latter felt the lappet of my coat, and finding it to hang loose
about me, they both looked with new signs of wonder.[1] He
stroked my right hand, seeming to admire the softness, and
colour; but he squeezed it so hard between his hoof and his
pastern, that I was forced to roar; after which they both
touched me with all possible tenderness. They were under
great perplexity about my shoes and stockings, which they
felt very often, neighing to each other, and using various
gestures, not unlike those of a philosopher, when he would
attempt to solve some new and difficult phænomenon.

Upon the whole, the behaviour of these animals was so
orderly and rational, so acute and judicious, that I at last
concluded, they must needs be magicians, who had thus
metamorphosed themselves upon some design, and seeing
a stranger in the way, were resolved to divert themselves with
him; or perhaps were really amazed at the sight of a man
so very different in habit, feature, and complexion from
those who might probably live in so remote a climate. Upon
the strength of this reasoning, I ventured to address them in
the following manner: Gentlemen, if you be conjurers, as I

---

[1] The relationship of clothes to the man, an analogue of the relationship
of body to soul, fascinated Swift; see his "clothes philosophy" in *Tale of
a Tub*.

have good cause to believe, you can understand any language; therefore I make bold to let your Worships know, that I am a poor distressed Englishman, driven by his misfortunes upon your coast, and I entreat one of you, to let me ride upon his back, as if he were a real horse, to some house or village, where I can be relieved. In return of which favour, I will make you a present of this knife and bracelet (taking them out of my pocket). The two creatures stood silent while I spoke, seeming to listen with great attention; and when I had ended, they neighed frequently towards each other, as if they were engaged in serious conversation. I plainly observed, that their language expressed the passions very well, and the words might with little pains be resolved into an alphabet more easily than the Chinese.

I could frequently distinguish the word *Yahoo*, which was repeated by each of them several times; and although it was impossible for me to conjecture what it meant, yet while the two horses were busy in conversation, I endeavoured to practice this word upon my tongue; and as soon as they were silent, I boldly pronounced *Yahoo* in a loud voice, imitating, at the same time, as near as I could, the neighing of a horse; at which they were both visibly surprised, and the grey repeated the same word twice, as if he meant to teach me the right accent, wherein I spoke after him as well as I could, and found myself perceivably to improve every time, although very far from any degree of perfection. Then the bay tried me with a second word, much harder to be pronounced; but reducing it to the English orthography, may be spelt thus, *Houyhnhnm*.[1] I did not succeed in this so well as the former, but after two or three farther trials, I had better fortune; and they both appeared amazed at my capacity.

After some farther discourse, which I then conjectured might relate to me, the two friends took their leaves, with the same compliment of striking each other's hoof; and the grey made me signs that I should walk before him, wherein I thought it prudent to comply, till I could find a better director. When I offered to slacken my pace, he would cry *hhuun*,

[1] *Houyhnhnm*, generally pronounced *hwínnim*, strongly suggests a whinny, which becomes the basic principle of the language of the rational horses. The satiric system here sharply departs from the system of the languages of the other three books, which are, after all, spoken by men. The nasal quality of the Houyhnhnms' language may be satiric of the nasality and slovenly carelessness of contemporary aristocratic English enunciation. *Hhuun, hhuun*, accordingly, may be read as *run, run*. It has been suggested that *Yahoo* is an anagram of *Houyhnhnm* with the nasality left out, as is appropriate for low-bred creatures.

hhuun; I guessed his meaning, and gave him to understand, as well as I could, that I was weary, and not able to walk faster; upon which he would stand a while to let me rest.

CHAPTER II.

The author conducted by a Houyhnhnm to his house. The house described. The author's reception. The food of the Houyhnhnms. The author in distress for want of meat, is at last relieved. His manner of feeding in that country.

Having travelled about three miles, we came to a long kind of building, made of timber stuck in the ground, and wattled across; the roof was low, and covered with straw. I now began to be a little comforted, and took out some toys, which travellers usually carry for presents to the savage Indians of America and other parts, in hopes the people of the house would be thereby encouraged to receive me kindly. The horse made me a sign to go in first; it was a large room with a smooth clay floor, and a rack and manger extending the whole length on one side. There were three nags, and two mares, not eating, but some of them sitting down upon their hams, which I very much wondered at; but wondered more to see the rest employed in domestic business. They seemed but ordinary cattle; however, this confirmed my first opinion, that a people who could so far civilize brute animals must needs excel in wisdom all the nations of the world. The grey came in just after, and thereby prevented any ill treatment which the others might have given me. He neighed to them several times in a style of authority, and received answers.

Beyond this room there were three others, reaching the length of the house, to which you passed through three doors, opposite to each other, in the manner of a vista; we went through the second room towards the third; here the grey walked in first, beckoning me to attend: I waited in the second room, and got ready my presents for the master and mistress of the house: they were two knives, three bracelets of false pearl, a small looking-glass and a bead necklace. The horse neighed three or four times, and I waited to hear some answers in a human voice, but I heard no other returns than in the same dialect, only one or two a little shriller than his. I began to think that this house must belong to some person of great note among them, because there appeared so much ceremony before I could gain admittance. But that a man of quality should be served all by horses was beyond my comprehension. I feared my brain was disturbed by my sufferings and misfortunes: I roused myself, and looked about me in the room where I was left alone; this was furnished as the first, only after a more elegant manner. I rubbed my eyes often, but the same objects still occurred. I pinched my arms and sides, to awake myself, hoping I might be in a dream. I then absolutely concluded, that all these appearances could be nothing else but necromancy and magic. But I had no time to pursue these reflections; for the grey horse came to the door, and made me a sign to follow him into the third room, where I saw a very comely mare, together with a colt and foal, sitting on their haunches, upon mats of straw, not unartfully made, and perfectly neat and clean.

The mare, soon after my entrance, rose from her mat, and coming up close, after having nicely observed my hands and face, gave me a most contemptuous look; then turning to the horse, I heard the word *Yahoo* often repeated betwixt them; the meaning of which word I could not then comprehend, although it were the first I had learned to pronounce; but I was soon better informed, to my everlasting mortification: for the horse beckoning to me with his head, and repeating the word *hhuun, hhuun,* as he did upon the road, which I understood was to attend him, led me out into a kind of court, where was another building at some distance from the house. Here we entered, and I saw three of those detestable creatures, which I first met after my landing, feeding upon roots, and the flesh of some animals, which I afterwards found to be that of asses and dogs, and now and then a cow dead by accident or disease. They were all tied by the neck with strong withes, fastened to a beam; they held their food between the claws of their forefeet, and tore it with their teeth.

The master horse ordered a sorrel nag, one of his servants, to untie the largest of these animals, and take him into the yard. The beast and I were brought close together, and our countenances diligently compared, both by master and servant, who thereupon repeated several times the word *Yahoo*. My horror and astonishment are not to be described, when I observed, in this abominable animal, a perfect human figure; the face of it indeed was flat and broad, the nose depressed, the lips large, and the mouth wide. But these differences are common to all savage nations, where the lineaments of the countenance are distorted by the natives suffering their infants to lie grovelling on the earth, or by carrying them on their backs, nuzzling with their face against the mother's shoulders. The forefeet of the Yahoo differed from my hands in nothing else but the length of the nails, the coarseness and brownness of the palms, and the hairiness on the backs. There was the same resemblance between our feet, with the same differences, which I knew very well, although the horses did not, because of my shoes and stockings; the same in every part of our bodies, except as to hairiness and colour, which I have already described.

The great difficulty that seemed to stick with the two horses, was to see the rest of my body so very different from that of a Yahoo, for which I was obliged to my clothes, whereof they had no conception: the sorrel nag offered me a root, which he held (after their manner, as we shall describe in its proper place) between his hoof and pastern; I took it in my hand, and having smelt it, returned it to him as civilly as I could. He brought out of the Yahoo's kennel a piece of ass's flesh, but it smelt so offensively that I turned from it with loathing: he then threw it to the Yahoo, by whom it was greedily devoured. He afterwards showed me a wisp of hay, and a fetlock full of oats; but I shook my head, to signify, that neither of these were food for me. And indeed, I now apprehended, that I must absolutely starve, if I did not get to some of my own species: for as to those filthy Yahoos, although there were few greater lovers of mankind, at that time, than myself, yet I confess I never saw any sensitive being so detestable on all accounts; and the more I came near them, the more hateful they grew, while I stayed in that country. This the master horse observed by my behaviour, and therefore sent the Yahoo back to his kennel. He then put his fore-hoof to his mouth, at which I was much surprised, although he did it with ease, and with a motion that appeared perfectly natural, and made other signs to know what I would eat; but I could not return him such an answer as he was able to apprehend; and if he had understood me, I did not see how it was possible to contrive any way for finding myself nourishment. While we were thus engaged, I observed a cow passing by, whereupon I pointed to her, and expressed a desire to let me go and milk her. This had its effect; for he led me back into the house, and ordered a mare-servant to open a room, where a good store of milk lay in earthen and wooden vessels, after a very orderly and cleanly manner. She gave me a large bowl full, of which I drank very heartily, and found myself well refreshed.

About noon I saw coming towards the house a kind of vehicle drawn like a sledge by four Yahoos. There was in it an old steed, who seemed to be of quality; he alighted with his hind feet forward, having by accident got a hurt in his left forefoot. He came to dine with our horse, who received him with great civility. They dined in the best room, and had oats boiled in milk for the second course, which the old horse ate warm, but the rest cold. Their mangers were placed circular in the middle of the room, and divided into several partitions, round which they sat on their haunches upon bosses of straw. In the middle was a large rack with angles answering to every partition of the manger. So that each horse and mare ate their own hay, and their own mash of oats and milk, with much decency and regularity. The behaviour of the young colt and foal appeared very modest, and that of the master and mistress extremely cheerful and compaisant to their guest. The grey ordered me to stand by him and much discourse passed between him and his friend concerning me, as I found by the stranger's often looking on me, and the frequent repetition of the word *Yahoo*.

I happened to wear my gloves, which the master grey observing, seemed perplexed, discovering signs of wonder what I had done to my forefeet; he put his hoof three or four times to them, as if he would signify, that I should reduce them to their former shape, which I presently did, pulling off both my gloves, and putting them into my pocket. This occasioned farther talk, and I saw the company was pleased with my behaviour, whereof I soon found the good effects. I was ordered to speak the few words I understood, and while they were at dinner, the master taught me the names for oats, milk, fire, water, and some others: which I could readily pronounce after him, having from my youth a great facility in learning languages.

When dinner was done, the master horse took me aside, and by signs and words made me understand the concern he was in, that I had nothing to eat. Oats in their tongue are called *hlunnh*. This word I pronounced two or three times; for although I had refused them at first, yet upon second thoughts, I considered that I could contrive to make of them a kind of bread, which might be sufficient with milk to keep me alive, till I could make my escape to some other country, and to creatures of my own species. The horse immediately ordered a white mare-servant of his family to bring me a good quantity of oats in a sort of wooden tray. These I heated before the fire as well as I could, and rubbed them till the husks came off, which I made a shift to winnow from the grain; I ground and beat them between two stones, then took water, and made them into a paste or cake, which I toasted at the fire, and ate with warm milk.[1] It was at first a very insipid diet, although common enough in many parts of Europe, but grew tolerable by time; and having been often reduced to hard fare in my life, this was not the first experiment I had made how easily nature is satisfied. And I cannot but observe, that I never had one hour's sickness, while I stayed in this island. It is true, I sometimes made a shift to catch a rabbit, or bird, by springes made of Yahoos' hairs, and I often gathered wholesome herbs, which I boiled, or ate as salads with my bread, and now and then, for a rarity, I made a little butter, and drank the whey. I was at first at a great loss for salt;[2] but custom soon reconciled the want of it; and I am confident that the frequent use of salt among us is an effect of luxury, and was first introduced only as a provocative to drink; except where it is necessary for preserving of flesh in long voyages, or in places remote from great markets. For we observe no animal to be fond of it but man: and as to myself, when I left this country, it was a great while before I could endure the taste of it in anything that I ate.

This is enough to say upon the subject of my diet, wherewith other travellers fill their books, as if the readers were personally concerned whether we fared well or ill. However, it was necessary to mention this matter, lest the world should think it impossible that I could find sustenance for three years in such a country, and among such inhabitants.

When it grew towards evening, the master horse ordered a place for me to lodge in; it was but six yards from the house, and separated from the stable of the Yahoos. Here I got some straw, and covering myself with my own clothes, slept very sound. But I was in a short time better accommodated, as the reader shall know hereafter, when I come to treat more particularly about my way of living.

[1] The detail is probably meant to suggest the temperance of the Houyhnhnms.
[2] An error on Swift's, or Gulliver's part; many animals like salt.

Chapter III.

The author studious to learn the language, the Houyhnhnm his master assists in teaching him. The language described. Several Houyhnhnms of quality come out of curiosity to see the author. He gives his master a short account of his voyage.

My principal endeavour was to learn the language, which my master (for so I shall henceforth call him) and his children, and every servant of his house were desirous to teach me. For they looked upon it as a prodigy that a brute animal should discover such marks of a rational creature. I pointed to every thing, and enquired the name of it, which I wrote down in my journal-book when I was alone, and corrected my bad accent, by desiring those of the family to pronounce it often. In this employment, a sorrel nag, one of the under servants, was very ready to assist me.

In speaking, they pronounce through the nose and throat, and their language approaches nearest to the High Dutch or German, of any I know in Europe; but is much more graceful and significant. The Emperor Charles V made almost the same observation, when he said, that if he were to speak to his horse, it should be in High Dutch.[1]

The curiosity and impatience of my master were so great, that he spent many hours of his leisure to instruct me. He was convinced (as he afterwards told me) that I must be a Yahoo, but my teachableness, civility and cleanliness astonished him; which were qualities altogether so opposite to those animals. He was most perplexed about my clothes, reasoning sometimes with himself, whether they were a part of my body; for I never pulled them off till the family were asleep, and got them on before they waked in the morning. My master was eager to learn from whence I came, how I acquired those appearances of reason which I discovered in all my action; and to know my story from my own mouth, which he hoped he should soon do by the great proficiency I made in learning and pronouncing their words and sentences. To help my memory, I formed all I learned into the English alphabet, and writ the words down with the translations. This last, after some time, I ventured to do in my master's presence. It cost me much

---

[1] German; Charles V reputedly addressed his God in Spanish, his mistress in Italian, and his horse in German.

trouble to explain to him what I was doing; for the inhabitants have not the least idea of books or literature.

In about ten weeks time I was able to understand most of his questions, and in three months could give him some tolerable answers. He was extremely curious to know from what part of the country I came, and how I was taught to imitate a rational creature, because the Yahoos (whom he saw I exactly resembled in my head, hands and face, that were only visible), with some appearance of cunning, and the strongest disposition to mischief, were observed to be the most unteachable of all brutes. I answered, that I came over the sea, from a far place, with many others of my own kind, in a great hollow vessel made of the bodies of trees: that my companions forced me to land on this coast, and then left me to shift for myself. It was with some difficulty, and by the help of many signs, that I brought him to understand me. He replied, that I must needs be mistaken, or that I 'said the thing which was not.' (For they have no words in their language to express lying or falsehood.) He knew it was impossible that there could be a country beyond the sea, or that a parcel of brutes could move a wooden vessel whither they pleased upon water. He was sure no Houyhnhnm alive could make such a vessel, or would trust Yahoos to manage it.

The word *Houyhnhnm*, in their tongue, signifies a *horse*, and in its etymology, *the perfection of nature*. I told my master that I was at a loss for expression, but would improve as fast as I could; and hoped in a short time I should be able to tell him wonders: he was pleased to direct his own mare, his colt and foal, and the servants of the family to take all opportunities of instructing me, and every day for two or three hours he was at the same pains himself: several horses and mares of quality in the neighbourhood came often to our house upon the report spread of a wonderful Yahoo, that could speak like a Houyhnhnm, and seemed in his words and actions to discover some glimmerings of reason. These delighted to converse with me; they put many questions, and received such answers as I was able to return. By all which advantages, I made so great a progress, that in five months from my arrival I understood whatever was spoke, and could express myself tolerably well.

The Houyhnhnms who came to visit my master, out of a design of seeing and talking with me, could hardly believe me to be a right Yahoo, because my body had a different covering from others of my kind. They were astonished to observe me without the usual hair or skin except on my head, face, and hands; but I discovered that secret to my master, upon an accident, which happened about a fortnight before.

I have already told the reader, that every night, when the family were gone to bed, it was my custom to strip and cover myself with my clothes: it happened one morning early, that my master sent for me, by the sorrel nag, who was his valet; when he came, I was fast asleep, my clothes fallen off on one side, and my shirt above my waist. I awaked at the noise he made, and observed him to deliver his message in some disorder; after which he went to my master, and in a great fright gave him a very confused account of what he had seen: this I presently discovered; for going, as soon as I was dressed, to pay my attendance upon his Honour, he asked me the meaning of what his servant had reported, that I was not the same thing when I slept as I appeared to be at other times; that his valet assured him, some part of me was white, some yellow, at least not so white, and some brown.

I had hitherto concealed the secret of my dress, in order to distinguish myself as much as possible from that cursed race of Yahoos; but now I found it in vain to do so any longer. Besides, I considered that my clothes and shoes would soon wear out, which already were in a declining condition, and must be supplied by some contrivance from the hides of Yahoos or other brutes; whereby the whole secret would be known. I therefore told my master, that in the country from whence I came those of my kind always covered their bodies with the hairs of certain animals prepared by art, as well for decency, as to avoid inclemencies of air both hot and cold; of which, as to my own person, I would give him immediate conviction, if he pleased to command me; only desiring his excuse, if I did not expose those parts that nature taught us to conceal. He said my discourse was all very strange, but especially the last part; for he could not understand why nature should teach us to conceal what nature had given. That neither himself nor family were ashamed of any parts of their bodies; but however I might do as I pleased. Whereupon, I first unbuttoned my coat, and pulled it off. I did the same with my waistcoat; I drew off my shoes, stockings, and breeches. I let my shirt down to my waist, and drew up the bottom, fastening it like a girdle about my middle to hide my nakedness.

My master observed the whole performance with great signs of curiosity and admiration. He took up all my clothes in his pastern, one piece after another, and examined them diligently; he then stroked my body very gently and looked round me several times, after which he said, it was plain I must be a perfect Yahoo; but that I differed very much from the rest of my species, in the whiteness and smoothness of my skin, my want of hair in several parts of my body, the shape and shortness of my claws behind and before, and my affectation of walking continually on my two hinder feet. He desired to see no more, and gave me leave to put on my clothes again, for I was shuddering with cold.

I expressed my uneasiness at his giving me so often the appellation of *Yahoo,* an odious animal, for which I had so utter an hatred and contempt. I begged he would forbear applying that word to me, and take the same order in his family, and among his friends whom he suffered to see me. I requested likewise, that the secret of my having a false covering to my body might be known to none but himself, at least as long as my present clothing should last; for as to what the sorrel nag his valet had observed, his Honour might command him to conceal it.

All this my master very graciously consented to, and thus the secret was kept till my clothes began to wear out, which I was forced to supply by several contrivances, that shall hereafter be mentioned. In the mean time, he desired I would go on with my utmost diligence to learn their language, because he was more astonished at my capacity for speech and reason than at the figure of my body, whether it were covered or no; adding, that he waited with some impatience to hear the wonders which I promised to tell him.

From thenceforward he doubled the pains he had been at to instruct me; he brought me into all company, and made them treat me with civility, because, as he told them privately, this would put me into good humour, and make me more diverting.

Every day when I waited on him, beside the trouble he was at in teaching, he would ask me several questions concerning myself, which I answered as well as I could; and by those means he had already received some general ideas, although very imperfect. It would be tedious to relate the several steps by which I advanced to a more regular conversation: but the first account I gave of myself in any order and length, was to this purpose:

That I came from a very far country, as I already had attempted to tell him, with about fifty more of my own species;

that we travelled upon the seas, in a great hollow vessel made of wood, and larger than his Honour's house. I described the ship to him in the best terms I could, and explained by the help of my handkerchief displayed, how it was driven forward by the wind. That upon a quarrel among us, I was set on shore on this coast, where I walked forward without knowing whither, till he delivered me from the persecution of those execrable Yahoos. He asked me, who made the ship, and how it was possible that the Houyhnhnms of my country would leave it to the management of brutes? My answer was, that I durst proceed no farther in my relation, unless he would give me his word and honour that he would not be offended, and then I would tell him the wonders I had so often promised. He agreed; and I went on by assuring him, that the ship was made by creatures like myself, who in all the countries I had travelled, as well as in my own, were the only governing, rational animals; and that upon my arrival hither, I was as much astonished to see the Houyhnhnms act like rational beings, as he or his friends could be in finding some marks of reason in a creature he was pleased to call a Yahoo, to which I owned my resemblance in every part, but could not account for their degenerate and brutal nature. I said farther, that if good fortune ever restored me to my native country, to relate my travels hither, as I resolved to do, every body would believe that I 'said the thing which was not'; that I invented the story out of my own head; and with all possible respect to himself, his family and friends, and under his promise of not being offended, our countrymen would hardly think it probable, that a Houyhnhnm should be the presiding creature of a nation, and a Yahoo the brute.

CHAPTER IV.

The Houyhnhnms' notion of truth and falsehood. The author's discourse disapproved by his master. The author gives a more particular account of himself, and the accidents of his voyage.

My master heard me with great appearances of uneasiness in his countenance, because *doubting* or *not believing,* are so little known in this country, that the inhabitants cannot tell how to behave themselves under such circumstances. And I remember in frequent discourses with my master concerning the nature of manhood, in other parts of the world, having occasion to talk of *lying* and *false representation,* it was with much difficulty that he comprehended what I meant, although he had otherwise a most acute judgment. For he argued thus; that the use of speech was to make us understand one another, and to receive information of facts; now if any one *said the thing which was not,* these ends were defeated; because I cannot properly be said to understand him, and I am so far from receiving information, that he leaves me worse than in ignorance, for I am led to believe a thing *black* when it is *white,* and *short* when it is *long.* And these were all the notions he had concerning that faculty of *lying,* so perfectly well understood, and so universally practised among human creatures.

To return from this digression; when I asserted that the Yahoos were the only governing animals in my country, which my master said was altogether past his conception, he desired to know, whether we had Houyhnhnms among us, and what was their employment: I told him, we had great numbers, that in summer they grazed in the fields, and in winter were kept in houses, with hay and oats, where Yahoo servants were employed to rub their skins smooth, comb their manes, pick their feet, serve them with food, and make their beds. I understand you well, said my master, it is now very plain, from all you have spoken, that whatever share of reason the Yahoos pretend to, the Houyhnhnms are your masters; I heartily wish our Yahoos would be so tractable. I begged his Honour would please to excuse me from proceeding any farther, because I was very certain that the account he expected from me would be highly displeasing. But he insisted in commanding me to let him know the best and the worst: I told him, he should be obeyed. I owned, that the Houyhnhnms among us, whom we called horses, were the most generous and comely animal we had, that they excelled in strength and swiftness; and when they belonged to persons of quality, employed in travelling, racing, and drawing chariots, they were treated with much kindness and care, till they fell into diseases, or became foundered in the feet; but then they were sold, and used to all kind of drudgery till they died; after which their skins were stripped and sold for what they were worth, and their bodies left to be devoured by dogs and birds of prey. But the common race of horses had not so good fortune, being kept by farmers and carriers and other mean people, who put them to greater labour, and feed them worse. I described, as well as I could, our way of riding, the shape and use of a bridle, a saddle, a spur, and a whip, of harness and wheels. I added, that we fastened plates of a certain hard substance called 'iron' at the bottom of their feet, to preserve their hoofs from being broken by the stony ways on which we often travelled.

My master, after some expressions of great indignation, wondered how we dared to venture upon a Houyhnhnm's back, for he was sure that the weakest servant in his house would be able to shake off the strongest Yahoo, or by lying down, and rolling upon his back, squeeze the brute to death. I answered, that our horses were trained up from three or four years old to the several uses we intended them for; that if any of them proved intolerably vicious, they were employed for carriages, that they were severely beaten while they were young, for any mischievous tricks; that the males, designed for the common use of riding or draught, were generally castrated about two years after their birth, to take down their spirits, and make them more tame and gentle; that they were indeed sensible of rewards and punishments; but his Honour would please to consider, that they had not the least tincture of reason any more than the Yahoos in this country.

It put me to the pains of my circumlocutions to give my master a right idea of what I spoke; for their language doth not abound in variety of words, because their wants and passions are fewer than among us. But it is impossible to express his noble resentment at our savage treatment of the Houyhnhnm race, particularly after I had explained the manner and use of castrating horses among us, to hinder them from propagating their kind, and to render them more servile. He said, if it were possible there could be any country where Yahoos alone were endued with reason, they certainly must be the governing animal, because reason will in time always prevail against brutal strength. But, considering the frame of our bodies, and especially of mine, he thought no creature of equal bulk was so ill contrived for employing that reason in the common offices of life; whereupon he desired to know whether those among whom I lived resembled me or the Yahoos of his country. I assured him, that I was as well shaped as most of my age; but the younger and the females were much more soft and tender, and the skins of the latter generally as white as milk. He said, I differed indeed from other Yahoos, being much more cleanly, and not altogether so deformed, but in point of real advantage he thought I differed for the worse. That my nails were of no use either to my fore or hinder feet; as to my forefeet, he could not properly call them by that name, for he never observed me to walk upon them; that they were too soft to bear the ground; that I generally went with them uncovered, neither was the covering I sometimes wore on them of the same shape or so strong as that on my feet behind. That I could not walk with any security, for if either of my hinder feet slipped, I must inevitably fall. He then began to find fault with other parts of my body, the flatness of my face, the prominence of my nose, my eyes placed directly in front, so that I could not look on either side without turning my head: that I was not able to feed myself without lifting one of my forefeet to my mouth: and therefore nature had placed those joints to answer that necessity. He knew not what could be the use of those several clefts and divisions in my feet behind; that these were too soft to bear the hardness and sharpness of stones without a covering made from the skin of some other brute; that my whole body wanted a fence against heat and cold, which I was forced to put on and off every day with tediousness and trouble. And lastly, that he observed every animal in this country naturally to abhor the Yahoos, whom the weaker avoided, and the stronger drove from them. So that supposing us to have the gift of reason, he could not see how it were possible to cure that natural antipathy which every creature discovered against us; nor consequently, how we could tame and render them serviceable. However, he would (as he said) debate the matter no farther, because he was more desirous to know my own story, the country where I was born, and the several actions and events of my life before I came hither.

I assured him how extremely desirous I was that he should be satisfied in every point; but I doubted much, whether it would be possible for me to explain myself on several subjects whereof his Honour could have no conception, because I saw nothing in his country to which I could resemble them. That however, I would do my best, and strive to express myself by similitudes, humbly desiring his assistance when I wanted proper words, which he was pleased to promise me.

I said, my birth was of honest parents, in an island called England, which was remote from this country as many days' journey as the strongest of his Honour's servants could travel in the annual course of the sun. That I was bred a surgeon, whose trade is to cure wounds and hurts in the body, got by accident or violence. That my country was governed by a female man, whom we called *queen*. That I left it to get riches, whereby I might maintain myself and family when I should return. That in my last voyage I was commander of the ship, and had about fifty Yahoos under me, many of which died at sea, and I was forced to supply them by others picked out from several nations. That our ship was twice in danger of being sunk; the first time by a great storm, and the second, by striking against a rock. Here my master interposed, by asking me, how I could persuade strangers out of different countries to venture with me, after the losses I had sustained, and the hazards I had run. I said, they were fellows of desperate fortunes, forced to fly from the places of their birth, on account of their poverty or their crimes. Some were undone by lawsuits; others spent all they had in drinking, whoring, and gaming; others fled for treason; many for murder, theft, poisoning, robbery, perjury, forgery, coining false money; for committing rapes or sodomy; for flying from their colours, or deserting to the enemy; and most of them had broken prison; none of these durst return to their native countries for fear of being hanged, or of starving in a jail; and therefore were under a necessity of seeking a livelihood in other places.

During this discourse, my master was pleased often to interrupt me; I had made use of many circumlocutions in describing to him the nature of the several crimes, for which most of our crew had been forced to fly their country. This labour took up several days' conversation before he was able to comprehend me. He was wholly at a loss to know what could be the use or necessity of practising those vices. To clear up which I endeavoured to give him some ideas of the desire of power and riches; of the terrible effects of lust, intemperance, malice and envy. All this I was forced to define and describe by putting of cases, and making suppositions. After which, like one whose imagination was struck with something never seen or heard of before, he would lift up his eyes with amazement and indignation. Power, government, war, law, punishment, and a thousand other things had no terms wherein that language could express them, which made the difficulty almost insuperable to give my master any conception of what I meant. But being of an excellent understanding, much improved by contemplation and converse, he at last arrived at a competent knowledge of what human nature in our parts of the world is capable to perform, and desired I would give him some particular account of that land which we call Europe, especially of my own country.

CHAPTER V.

The author, at his master's commands, informs him of the state of England. The causes of war among the princes of Europe. The author begins to explain the English constitution.

The reader may please to observe, that the following extract of many conversations I had with my master contains a summary of the most material points which were discoursed at several times for above two years; his Honour often desiring fuller satisfaction as I farther improved in the Houyhnhnm tongue. I laid before him, as well as I could, the whole state of Europe; I discoursed of trade and manufactures, of arts and sciences; and the answers I gave to all the questions he made, as they arose upon several subjects, were a fund of conversation not to be exhausted. But I shall here only set down the substance of what passed between us concerning my own country, reducing it into order as well as I can, without any regard to time or other circumstances, while I strictly adhere to truth. My only concern is, that I shall hardly be able to do justice to my master's arguments and expressions, which must needs suffer by my want of capacity, as well as by a translation into our barbarous English.

In obedience therefore to his Honour's commands, I related to him the Revolution under the Prince of Orange; the long war with France entered into by the said prince, and renewed by his successor the present queen, wherein the greatest powers of Christendom were engaged, and which still continued: I computed, at his request, that about a million of Yahoos might have been killed in the whole progress of it, and perhaps a hundred or more cities taken, and five times as many ships burnt or sunk.

He asked me what were the usual causes or motives that made one country go to war with another. I answered they were innumerable, but I should only mention a few of the chief. Sometimes the ambition of princes, who never think they have land or people enough to govern: sometimes the corruption of ministers, who engage their master in a war in order to stifle or divert the clamour of the subjects against their evil administration. Difference in opinions hath cost many millions of lives: for instance, whether *flesh* be *bread*, or *bread* be *flesh*: whether the juice of a certain *berry* be *blood* or *wine;* whether *whistling* be a vice or a virtue; whether it be better to *kiss a post*, or throw it into the fire; what is the best colour for a *coat*, whether *black, white, red,* or *grey;* and whether it should be *long* or *short, narrow* or *wide, dirty* or *clean,* with many more.[1] Neither are any wars so furious and bloody, or of so long continuance, as those occasioned by difference in opinion, especially if it be in things indifferent.

Sometimes the quarrel between two princes is to decide which of them shall dispossess a third of his dominions, where neither of them pretend to any right. Sometimes one prince quarrelleth with another, for fear the other should quarrel with him. Sometimes a war is entered upon, because the enemy is too *strong,* and sometimes because he is too *weak.* Sometimes our neighbours *want* the things which we *have,* or *have* the things which we *want;* and we both fight, till they take ours or give us theirs. It is a very justifiable cause of war to invade a country after the people have been wasted by famine, destroyed by pestilence, or embroiled by factions amongst themselves. It is justifiable to enter into a war against our nearest ally, when one of his towns lies convenient for us, or a territory of land, that would render our dominions round and compact. If a prince send forces into a nation where the people are poor and ignorant, he may lawfully put half of them to death, and make slaves of the rest, in order to civilize and reduce them from their barbarous way of living. It is a very kingly, honourable, and frequent practice, when one prince desires the assistance of another to secure him against an invasion, that the assistant, when he hath driven out the invader, should seize on the dominions himself, and kill, imprison or banish the prince he came to relieve. Alliance by blood or marriage is a sufficient cause of war between princes, and the nearer the kindred is, the greater is their disposition to quarrel: *poor* nations are *hungry,* and *rich* nations are *proud;* and the pride and hunger will ever be at variance. For these reasons, the trade of a soldier is held the most honourable of all others: because a soldier is a Yahoo hired to kill in cold blood as many of his own species, who have never offended him, as possibly he can.

There is likewise a kind of beggarly princes in Europe, not able to make war by themselves, who hire out their troops to richer nations, for so much a day to each man; of which they

[1] In the seventeenth century Anglican was split from Puritan, and later High Church was split from Low Church, on four basic practices: the controversy over the Eucharist, the place of music in the church service, the veneration of the crucifix, and the appropriateness of certain ecclesiastical vestments.

keep three fourths to themselves, and it is the best part of their maintenance; such are those in Germany and many northern parts of Europe.[1]

What you have told me (said my master) upon the subject of war, does indeed discover most admirably the effects of that reason you pretend to: however, it is happy that the *shame* is greater than the *danger;* and that nature hath left you utterly uncapable of doing much mischief. For your mouths lying flat with your faces, you can hardly bite each other to any purpose, unless by consent. Then as to the claws upon your feet before and behind, they are so short and tender, that one of our Yahoos would drive a dozen of yours before him. And therefore in recounting the numbers of those who have been killed in battle, I cannot but think that you have *said the thing which is not*.

I could not forbear shaking my head and smiling a little at his ignorance. And being no stranger to the art of war, I gave him a description of cannons, culverins, muskets, carabines, pistols, bullets, powder, swords, bayonets, battles, sieges, retreats, attacks, undermines, countermines, bombardments, sea-fights; ships sunk with a thousand men; twenty thousand killed on each side; dying groans, limbs flying in the air; smoke, noise, confusion, trampling to death under horses' feet; flight, pursuit, victory; fields strewed with carcasses left for food to dogs, and wolves, and birds of prey; plundering, stripping, ravishing, burning and destroying. And to set forth the valour of my own dear countrymen, I assured him, that I had seen them blow up a hundred enemies at once in a siege, and as many in a ship, and beheld the dead bodies drop down in pieces from the clouds, to the great diversion of all the spectators.

I was going on to more particulars, when my master commanded me silence. He said, whoever understood the nature of Yahoos might easily believe it possible for so vile an animal to be capable of every action I had named, if their strength and cunning equalled their malice. But as my discourse had increased his abhorrence of the whole species, so he found it gave him a disturbance in his mind, to which he was wholly a stranger before. He thought his ears being used to such abominable words, might by degrees admit them with less detestation. That although he hated the Yahoos of this country, yet he no more blamed them for their odious qualities,

---

[1] George I, while still Elector of Hanover, hired mercenaries to protect his holdings.

than he did a *gnnayh* (a bird of prey) for its cruelty, or a sharp stone for cutting his hoof. But when a creature pretending to reason could be capable of such enormities, he dreaded lest the corruption of that faculty might be worse than brutality itself. He seemed therefore confident, that instead of reason, we were only possessed of some quality fitted to increase our natural vices; as the reflection from a troubled stream returns the image of an ill-shapen body, not only *larger,* but more *distorted.*

He added, that he had heard too much upon the subject of war, both in this and some former discourses. There was another point which a little perplexed him at present. I had said, that some of our crew left their country on account of being ruined by *law;* that I had already explained the meaning of the word; but he was at a loss how it should come to pass, that the *law* which was intended for *every* man's preservation, should be any man's ruin. Therefore he desired to be farther satisfied what I meant by *law,* and the dispensers thereof according to the present practice in my own country: because he thought nature and reason were sufficient guides for a reasonable animal, as we pretended to be, in showing us what we ought to do, and what to avoid.

I assured his Honour, that law was a science wherein I had not much conversed, further than by employing advocates in vain, upon some injustices that had been done me. However, I would give him all the satisfaction I was able.

I said there was a society of men among us, bred up from their youth in the art of proving by words multiplied for the purpose, that white is black and black is white, according as they are paid. To his society all the rest of the people are slaves.

For example, if my neighbour hath a mind to my cow, he hires a lawyer to prove that he ought to have my cow from me. I must then hire another to defend my right, it being against all rules of law that any man should be allowed to speak for himself. Now in this case, I who am the true owner lie under two great disadvantages. First, my lawyer, being practiced almost from his cradle in defending falsehood, is quite out of his element when he would be an advocate for justice, which as an office unnatural, he always attempts with great awkwardness, if not with ill will. The second disadvantage is, that my lawyer must proceed with great caution: or else he will be reprimanded by the judges, and abhorred by his brethren, as one who would lessen the practice of the law.

And therefore I have but two methods to preserve my cow. The first is to gain over my adversary's lawyer with a double fee, who will then betray his client by insinuating that he hath justice on his side. The second way is for my lawyer to make my cause appear as unjust as he can, by allowing the cow to belong to my adversary; and this if it be skilfully done will certainly bespeak the favour of the bench.

Now, your Honour is to know that these judges are persons appointed to decide all controversies of property, as well as for the trial of criminals, and picked out from the most dextrous lawyers who are grown old or lazy: and having been biassed all their lives against truth and equity, lie under such a fatal necessity of favouring fraud, perjury, and oppression, that I have known several of them refuse a large bribe from the side where justice lay, rather than injure the faculty [1] by doing any thing unbecoming their nature or their office.

It is a maxim among these lawyers, that whatever hath been done before may legally be done again: and therefore they take special care to record all the decisions formerly made against common justice and the general reason of mankind. These, under the name of *precedents,* they produce as authorities, to justify the most iniquitous opinions; and the judges never fail of decreeing accordingly.

In pleading, they studiously avoid entering into the *merits* of the cause, but are loud, violent, and tedious in dwelling upon all *circumstances* which are not to the purpose. For instance, in the case already mentioned: they never desire to know what claim or title my adversary hath to my cow, but whether the said cow were red or black, her horns long or short; whether the field I graze her in be round or square, whether she was milked at home or abroad, what diseases she is subject to, and the like; after which they consult precedents, adjourn the cause from time to time, and in ten, twenty, or thirty years come to an issue.

It is likewise to be observed that this society hath a peculiar cant and jargon of their own, that no other mortal can understand, and wherein all their laws were written, which they take special care to multiply; whereby they have wholly confounded the very essence of truth and falsehood, of right and wrong; so that it will take thirty years to decide whether the field left me by my ancestors for six generations belongs to me or to a stranger three hundred miles off.

In the trial of persons accused for crimes against the state

[1] The legal profession.

the method is much more short and commendable: the judge
first sends to sound the disposition of those in power, after
which he can easily hang or save the criminal, strictly preserving all due forms of law.

Here my master, interposing, said it was a pity, that creatures endowed with such prodigious abilities of mind as these
lawyers, by the description I gave of them, must certainly be,
were not rather encouraged to be instructors of others in wisdom and knowledge. In answer to which I assured his Honour, that in all points out of their own trade they were usually
the most ignorant and stupid generation among us, the most
despicable in common conversation, avowed enemies to all
knowledge and learning, and equally disposed to pervert the
general reason of mankind in every other subject of discourse,
as in that of their own profession.

Chapter VI.

*A continuation of the state of England under Queen Anne.
The character of a first minister in the courts of Europe.*

My master was yet wholly at a loss to understand what motives could incite this race of lawyers to perplex, disquiet, and
weary themselves by engaging in a confederacy of injustice,
merely for the sake of injuring their fellow-animals, neither
could be comprehend what I meant in saying they did it for
hire. Whereupon I was at much pains to describe to him the
use of money, the materials it was made of, and the value of
the metals; that when a Yahoo had got a great store of this
precious substance, he was able to purchase whatever he had
a mind to, the finest clothing, the noblest houses, great tracts
of land, the most costly meats and drinks, and have his choice
of the most beautiful females. Therefore since money alone
was able to perform all these feats, our Yahoos thought they
could never have enough of it to spend or to save, as they
found themselves inclined from their natural bent either to
profusion or avarice. That the rich man enjoyed the fruit of
the poor man's labour, and the latter were a thousand to one
in proportion to the former. That the bulk of our people were
forced to live miserably, by labouring every day for small
wages to make a few live plentifully. I enlarged myself much
on these and many other particulars to the same purpose: but
his Honour was still to seek, for he went upon a supposition

that all animals had a title to their share in the productions of the earth, and especially those who presided over the rest. Therefore he desired I would let him know what these costly meats were, and how any of us happened to want them. Whereupon I enumerated as many sorts as came into my head, with the various methods of dressing them, which could not be done without sending vessels by sea to every part of the world, as well for liquors to drink, as for sauces, and innumerable other conveniences. I assured him, that this whole globe of earth must be at least three times gone round, before one of our better female Yahoos could get her breakfast, or a cup to put it in.[1] He said, that must needs be a miserable country which cannot furnish food for its own inhabitants. But what he chiefly wondered at was how such vast tracts of ground as I described should be wholly without fresh water, and the people put to the necessity of sending over the sea for drink. I replied, that England (the dear place of my nativity) was computed to produce three times the quantity of food more than its inhabitants are able to consume, as well as liquors extracted from grain, or pressed out of the fruit of certain trees, which made excellent drink; and the same proportion in every other convenience of life. But in order to feed the luxury and intemperance of the males, and the vanity of the females, we sent away the greatest part of our necessary things to other countries, from whence in return we brought the materials of diseases, folly, and vice, to spend among ourselves. Hence it follows of necessity that vast numbers of our people are compelled to seek their livelihood by begging, robbing, stealing, cheating, pimping, forswearing, flattering, suborning, forging, gaming, lying, fawning, hectoring, voting, scribbling, star-gazing, poisoning, whoring, canting, libelling, free-thinking, and the like occupations: every one of which terms, I was at much pains to make him understand.

That wine was not imported among us from foreign countries to supply the want of water or other drinks, but because it was a sort of liquid which made us merry, by putting us out of our senses; diverted all melancholy thoughts, begat wild extravagant imaginations in the brain, raised our hopes, and banished our fears; suspended every office of reason for a time, and deprived us of the use of our limbs, until we fell into a profound sleep; although it must be confessed, that we always

---

[1] Swift objected to the importation of luxuries, such as china, coffee and tea, as weakening the economy, particularly of such an impoverished country as Ireland.

awaked sick and dispirited, and that the use of this liquor
filled us with diseases, which made our lives uncomfortable
and short.

But beside all this, the bulk of our people supported themselves by furnishing the necessities or conveniences of life to
the rich, and to each other. For instance, when I am at home
and dressed as I ought to be, I carry on my body the workmanship of an hundred tradesmen; the building and furniture of
my house employ as many more; and five times the number to
adorn my wife.

I was going on to tell him of another sort of people, who get
their livelihood by attending the sick, having upon some occasions informed his Honour that many of my crew had died of
diseases. But here it was with the utmost difficulty that I
brought him to apprehend what I meant. He could easily conceive that a Houyhnhnm grew weak and heavy a few days
before his death, or by some accident might hurt a limb. But
that Nature, who works all things to perfection, should suffer
any pains to breed in our bodies, he thought impossible, and
desired to know the reason of so unaccountable an evil. I told
him, we fed on a thousand things which operated contrary to
each other; that we ate when we were not hungry, and drank
without the provocation of thirst; that we sat whole nights
drinking strong liquors without eating a bit, which disposed
us to sloth, enflamed our bodies, and precipitated or prevented
digestion. That prostitute female Yahoos acquired a certain
malady, which bred rottenness in the bones of those who fell
into their embraces; that this and many other diseases were
propagated from father to son, so that great numbers come
into the world with complicated maladies upon them; that it
would be endless to give him a catalogue of all diseases incident to human bodies; for they could not be fewer than five or
six hundred, spread over every limb and joint; in short, every
part, external and intestine, having diseases appropriated to
each. To remedy which, there was a sort of people bred up
among us, in the profession or pretence of curing the sick.
And because I had some skill in the faculty, I would, in gratitude to his Honour, let him know the whole mystery and
method by which they proceed.

Their fundamental is, that all diseases arise from repletion,
from whence they conclude that a great evacuation of the body
is necessary, either through the natural passage, or upwards
at the mouth. Their next business is, from herbs, minerals,
gums, oils, shells, salts, juices, seaweed, excrements, barks of

trees, serpents, toads, frogs, spiders, dead men's flesh and bones, birds, beasts and fishes, to form a composition for smell and taste the most abominable, nauseous and detestable that they can possibly contrive, which the stomach immediately rejects with loathing; and this they call a vomit. Or else from the same storehouse, with some other poisonous additions, they command us to take in at the orifice above or below (just as the physician then happens to be disposed) a medicine equally annoying and disgustful to the bowels, which, relaxing the belly, drives down all before it, and this they call a purge or a clyster. For nature (as the physicians allege) having intended the superior anterior orifice only for the intromission of solids and liquids, and the inferior posterior for ejection, these artists ingeniously considering that in all diseases Nature is forced out of her seat; therefore to replace her in it, the body must be treated in a manner directly contrary, by interchanging the use of each orifice, forcing solids and liquids in at the anus, and making evacuations at the mouth.

But besides real diseases we are subject to many that are only imaginary, for which the physicians have invented imaginary cures; these have their several names, and so have the drugs that are proper for them, and with these our female Yahoos are always infested.

One great excellency in this tribe is their skill at prognostics, wherein they seldom fail; their predictions in real diseases, when they rise to any degree of malignity, generally portending death, which is always in their power, when recovery is not: and therefore, upon any unexpected signs of amendment, after they have pronounced their sentence, rather than be accused as false prophets, they know how to approve their sagacity to the world by a seasonable dose.

They are likewise of special use to husbands and wives who are grown weary of their mates, to eldest sons, to great ministers of state, and often to princes.

I had formerly upon occasion discoursed with my master upon the nature of our government in general, and particularly of our own excellent constitution, deservedly the wonder and envy of the whole world. But having here accidentally mentioned a 'minister of state', he commanded me some time after to inform him, what species of Yahoo I particularly meant by that appellation.

I told him that a first or chief minister of state, who was the person I intended to describe, was a creature wholly exempt from joy and grief, love and hatred, pity and anger; at least makes use of no other passions but a violent desire of wealth, power, and titles; that he applies his words to all uses, except to the indication of his mind: that he never tells a *truth,* but with an intent that you should take it for a *lie;* nor a *lie,* but with a design that you should take it for a *truth;* that those he speaks worst of behind their backs are in the surest way to preferment; and whenever he begins to praise you to others or to yourself, you are from that day forlorn. The worst mark you can receive is a *promise,* especially when it is confirmed with an oath; after which every wise man retires, and gives over all hopes.

There are three methods by which a man may rise to be chief minister: the first is, by knowing how with prudence to dispose of a wife, a daughter, or a sister: the second, by betraying or undermining his predecessor: and the third is, by a *furious zeal* in public assemblies against the corruptions of the court. But a wise prince would rather choose to employ those who practise the last of these methods; because such zealots prove always the most obsequious and subservient to the will and passions of their master. That these 'ministers' having all employment at their disposal, preserve themselves in power by bribing the majority of a senate or great council; and at last, by an expedient called an 'act of indemnity' (whereof I described the nature to him) they secure themselves from after reckonings, and retire from the public, laden with the spoils of the nation.

The palace of a chief minister is a seminary to breed up others in his own trade: the pages, lackeys, and porter, by imitating their master, become ministers of state in their several districts, and learn to excel in the three principal *ingredients,* of *insolence, lying,* and *bribery.* Accordingly, they have a *subaltern* court paid to them by persons of the best rank, and sometimes by the force of dexterity and impudence arrive through several gradations to be successors to their lord.

He is usually governed by a decayed wench or favourite footman, who are the tunnels through which all graces are conveyed, and may properly be called, *in the last resort,* the governors of the kingdom.

One day my master, having heard me mention the nobility of my country, was pleased to make me a compliment which I could not pretend to deserve: that he was sure I must have been born of some noble family, because I far exceeded in shape, colour, and cleanliness, all the Yahoos of his nation, although I seemed to fail in strength and agility, which must be imputed to my different way of living from those other brutes, and besides, I was not only endowed with the faculty of speech, but likewise with some rudiments of reason, to a degree that with all his acquaintance I passed for a prodigy.

He made me observe, that among the Houyhnhnms, the *white*, the *sorrel*, and the *iron-grey*, were not so exactly shaped as the *bay*, the *dapple-grey*, and the *black;* nor born with equal talents of the mind, or a capacity to improve them; and therefore continued always in the condition of servants, without ever aspiring to match out of their own race, which in that country would be reckoned monstrous and unnatural.

I made his Honour my most humble acknowledgments for the good opinion he was pleased to conceive of me; but assured him at the same time that my birth was of the lower sort, having been born of plain honest parents, who were just able to give me a tolerable education: that *nobility* among us was altogether a different thing from the idea he had of it; that our young noblemen are bred from their childhood in idleness and luxury; that as soon as years will permit, they consume their vigor and contract odious diseases among lewd females; and when their fortunes are almost ruined, they marry some woman of mean birth, disagreeable person, and unsound constitution, merely for the sake of money, whom they hate and despise. That the productions of such marriages are generally scrofulous, ricketty, or deformed children, by which means the family seldom continues above three generations, unless the wife takes care to provide a healthy father among her neighbours or domestics, in order to improve and continue the breed. That a weak diseased body, a meager countenance, and sallow complexion are the true marks of noble blood; and a healthy robust appearance is so disgraceful in a man of quality, that the world concludes his real father to have been a groom, or a coachman. The imperfections of his mind run parallel with those of his body, being a composition of spleen, dullness, ignorance, caprice, sensuality, and pride.

Without the consent of this *illustrious body* no law can be enacted, repealed, or altered, and these nobles have likewise the decision of all our possessions without appeal.

CHAPTER VII.

The author's great love of his native country. His master's observations upon the constitution and administration of England, as described by the author, with parallel cases and comparisons. His master's observations upon human nature.

The reader may be disposed to wonder how I could prevail on myself to give so free a representation of my own species, among a race of mortals who were already too apt to conceive the vilest opinion of human kind from that entire congruity betwixt me and their Yahoos. But I must freely confess, that the many virtues of those excellent quadrupeds, placed in opposite view to human corruptions, had so far opened my eyes and enlarged my understanding, that I began to view the actions and passions of man in a very different light, and to think the honour of my own kind not worth managing; which, besides, it was impossible for me to do before a person of so acute a judgment as my master, who daily convinced me of a thousand faults in myself, whereof I had not the least perception before, and which with us would never be numbered even among human infirmities. I had likewise learned from his example an utter detestation of all falsehood or disguise; and truth appeared so amiable to me, that I determined upon sacrificing every thing to it.

Let me deal so candidly with the reader as to confess, that there was yet a much stronger motive for the freedom I took in my representation of things. I had not been a year in this country before I contracted such a love and veneration for the inhabitants, that I entered on a firm resolution never to return to human kind, but to pass the rest of my life among these admirable Houyhnhnms in the contemplation and practice of every virtue; where I could have no example or incitement to vice. But it was decreed by Fortune, my perpetual enemy, that so great a felicity should not fall to my share. However, it is now some comfort to reflect, that in what I said of my countrymen I extenuated their faults as much as I durst before so strict an examiner, and upon every article gave as favourable a turn as the matter would bear. For, indeed, who is there alive that will not be swayed by his bias and partiality to the place of his birth?

I have related the substance of several conversations I had with my master, during the greatest part of the time I had the honour to be in his service, but have indeed for brevity sake omitted much more than is here set down.

When I had answered all his questions, and his curiosity seemed to be fully satisfied, he sent for me one morning early, and commanding me to sit down at some distance (an honour which he had never before conferred upon me), he said, he had been very seriously considering my whole story, as far as it related both to myself and my country: that he looked upon us as a sort of animals to whose share, by what accident he could not conjecture, some small pittance of *reason* had fallen, whereof we made no other use than by its assistance to aggravate our *natural* corruptions, and to acquire new ones which Nature had not given us. That we disarmed ourselves of the few abilities she had bestowed, had been very successful in multiplying our original wants, and seemed to spend our whole lives in vain endeavours to supply them by our own inventions. That as to myself, it was manifest I had neither the strength or agility of a common Yahoo, that I walked infirmly on my hinder feet, had found out a contrivance to make my claws of no use or defence, and to remove the hair from my chin, which was intended as a shelter from the sun and the weather. Lastly, that I could neither run with speed, nor climb trees like my brethren (as he called them) the Yahoos in this country.

That our institutions of government and law were plainly owing to our gross defects in *reason*, and by consequence, in *virtue;* because *reason* alone is sufficient to govern a *rational* creature; which was therefore a character we had no pretence to challenge, even from the account I had given of my own people, although he manifestly perceived, that in order to favour them I had concealed many particulars, and often *said the thing which was not.*

He was the more confirmed in this opinion, because he observed, that as I agreed in every feature of my body with other Yahoos, except where it was to my real disadvantage in point of strength, speed, and activity, the shortness of my claws, and some other particulars where nature had no part; so from the representation I had given him of our lives, our manners, and our actions, he found as near a resemblance in the disposition of our minds. He said the Yahoos were known to hate one another more than they did any different species of animals; and the reason usually assigned was the odiousness of their shape, which all could see in the rest, but not in themselves. He had therefore begun to think it not unwise in us to cover our bodies, and, by that invention, conceal many of our deformities from each other, which would else be hardly supportable. But he now found he had been mistaken, and that the dissensions of those brutes in his country were owing to the same cause with ours, as I had described them. For if (said he) you throw among five Yahoos as much food as would be sufficient for fifty, they will, instead of eating peaceably, fall together by the ears, each single one impatient to have all to itself; and therefore a servant was usually employed to stand by while they were feeding abroad, and those kept at home were tied at a distance from each other. That if a cow died of age or accident, before a Houyhnhnm could secure it for his own Yahoos, those in the neighbourhood would come in herds to seize it, and then would ensue such a battle as I had described, with terrible wounds made by their claws on both sides, although they seldom were able to kill one another, for want of such convenient instruments of death as we had invented. At other times the like battles have been fought between the Yahoos of several neighbourhoods without any visible cause; those of one district watching all opportunities to surprise the next before they are prepared. But if they find their project hath miscarried, they return home, and, for want of enemies, engage in what I call a civil war among themselves.

That in some fields of his country there are certain shining stones of several colours, whereof the Yahoos are violently fond, and when part of these stones are fixed in the earth, as it sometimes happeneth, they will dig with their claws for whole days to get them out, carry them away, and hide them by heaps in their kennels; but still looking round with great caution, for fear their comrades should find out their treasure. My master said, he could never discover the reason of this unnatural appetite, or how these stones could be of any use to a Yahoo; but now he believed it might proceed from the same principle of avarice which I had ascribed to mankind; that he had once, by way of experiment, privately removed a heap of these stones from the place where one of his Yahoos had buried it: whereupon the sordid animal, missing his treasure, by his loud lamenting brought the whole herd to the place, there miserably howled, then fell to biting and tearing the rest, began to pine away, would neither eat, nor sleep, nor work, till he ordered a servant privately to convey the stones into the same hole and hide them as before; which when his Yahoo had found, he presently recovered his spirits and good humour, but took care to remove them to a better hiding-place, and hath ever since been a very serviceable brute.

My master farther assured me, which I also observed myself, that in the fields where these shining stones abound, the fiercest and most frequent battles are fought, occasioned by perpetual inroads of the neighbouring Yahoos.

He said, it was common, when two Yahoos discovered such a stone in a field, and were contending which of them should be the proprietor, a third would take the advantage, and carry it away from them both; which my master would needs contend to have some resemblance with our *suits at law;* wherein I thought it for our credit not to undeceive him; since the decision he mentioned was much more equitable than many decrees among us: because the plaintiff and defendant there lost nothing beside the stone they contended for, whereas our *courts of equity* would never have dismissed the cause while either of them had any thing left.

My master, continuing his discourse, said, there was nothing that rendered the Yahoos more odious than their undistinguishing appetite to devour every thing that came in their way, whether herbs, roots, berries, corrupted flesh of animals, or all mingled together: and it was peculiar in their temper, that they were fonder of what they could get by rapine or stealth at a greater distance, than much better food provided for them at home. If their prey held out, they would eat till they were ready to burst, after which Nature had pointed out to them a certain root that gave them a general evacuation.

There was also another kind of root very juicy, but somewhat rare and difficult to be found, which the Yahoos sought for with much eagerness, and would suck it with great delight; it produced in them the same effects that wine hath upon us. It would make them sometimes hug, and sometimes tear one another; they would howl and grin, and chatter, and reel, and tumble, and then fall asleep in the mud.

I did indeed observe, that the Yahoos were the only animals in this country subject to any diseases; which, however, were much fewer than horses have among us, and contracted not by any ill treatment they meet with, but by the nastiness and greediness of that sordid brute. Neither has their language any more than a general appellation for those maladies, which is borrowed from the name of the beast, and called *hnea-yahoo,* or the *yahoo's evil,* and the cure prescribed is a mixture of their own dung and urine forcibly put down the Yahoo's throat. This I have since often known to have been taken with success: and do here freely recommend it to my country-men, for the public good, as an admirable specific against all diseases produced by repletion.

As to learning, government, arts, manufactures, and the like, my master confessed he could find little or no resemblance between the Yahoos of that country and those in ours. For he only meant to observe what parity there was in our natures. He had heard indeed some curious Houyhnhnms observe, that in most herds there was a sort of ruling Yahoo (as among us there is generally some leading or principal stag in a park), who was always more *deformed* in body, and *mischievous in disposition*, than any of the rest. That this *leader* had usually a favourite as *like himself* as he could get, whose employment was to *lick his master's feet and posteriors, and drive the fe-male Yahoos to his kennel;* for which he was now and then rewarded with a piece of ass's flesh. This *favourite* is hated by the whole herd, and therefore, to protect himself, keeps always near the person of his leader. He usually continues in office till a worse can be found; but the very moment he is dis-carded, his successor, at the head of all the Yahoos in that district, young and old, male and female, come in a body, and discharge their excrements upon him from head to foot. But how far this might be applicable to our *courts* and *favourites*, and *ministers of state*, my master said I could best determine.

I durst make no return to this malicious insinuation, which debased human understanding below the sagacity of a com-mon *hound*, who has judgment enough to distinguish and follow the cry of the *ablest dog in the pack*, without being ever mistaken.

My master told me, there were some qualities remarkable in the Yahoos, which he had not observed me to mention, or at least very slightly, in the accounts I had given him of human kind. He said, those animals, like other brutes, had their females in common; but in this they differed, that the she-Yahoo would admit the male while she was pregnant, and that the hees would quarrel and fight with the females as fiercely as with each other. Both which practices were such degrees of infamous brutality, that no other sensitive creature ever arrived at.

Another thing he wondered at in the Yahoos was their strange disposition to nastiness and dirt; whereas there appears to be a natural love of cleanliness in all other animals. As to the two former accusations, I was glad to let them pass without any reply, because I had not a word to offer upon them in defence of my species, which otherwise I certainly had done from my own inclinations. But I could have easily vindicated human kind from the imputation of singularity upon the last article, if there had been any *swine* in that country (as unluckily for me there were not), which, although it may be a *sweeter quadruped* than a Yahoo, cannot, I humbly conceive, in justice pretend to more cleanliness; and so his Honour himself must have owned, if he had seen their filthy way of feeding, and their custom of wallowing and sleeping in the mud.

My master likewise mentioned another quality which his servants had discovered in several Yahoos, and to him was wholly unaccountable. He said, a fancy would sometimes take a Yahoo to retire into a corner, to lie down and howl, and groan, and spurn away all that came near him, although he were young and fat, and wanted neither food nor water; nor did the servants imagine what could possibly ail him. And the only remedy they found was to set him to hard work, after which he would infallibly come to himself. To this I was silent out of partiality to my own kind; yet here I could plainly discover the true seeds of *spleen*,[1] which only seizeth on the *lazy*, the *luxurious*, and the *rich*; who, if they were forced to undergo the *same regimen*, I would undertake for the cure.

His Honour had farther observed, that a female Yahoo would often stand behind a bank or a bush, to gaze on the young males passing by, and then appear, and hide, using many antic gestures and grimaces, at which time it was observed, that she had a most offensive smell; and when any of the males advanced, would slowly retire, looking often back, and with a counterfeit show of fear, run off into some convenient place where she knew the male would follow her.

At other times if a female stranger came among them, three or four of her own sex would get about her, and stare and chatter, and grin, and smell her all over, and then turn off with gestures that seemed to express contempt and disdain.

Perhaps my master might refine a little in these speculations, which he had drawn from what he observed himself, or had been told him by others: however, I could not reflect without some amazement, and much sorrow, that the rudiments of *lewdness, coquetry, censure,* and *scandal,* should have place by instinct in womankind.

---

[1] A fashionable disease in the eighteenth century, like melancholy in the seventeenth; Queen Anne suffered from the spleen. It seems to have been a state which we would generally call neurasthenic.

I expected every moment that my master would accuse the Yahoos of those unnatural appetites in both sexes, so common among us. But Nature, it seems, hath not been so expert a school-mistress; and these politer pleasures are entirely the productions of art and reason, on our side of the globe.

CHAPTER VIII.

The author relates several particulars of the Yahoos. The great virtues of the Houyhnhnms. The education and exercise of their youth. Their general assembly.

As I ought to have understood human nature much better than I supposed it possible for my master to do, so it was easy to apply the character he gave of the Yahoos to myself and my countrymen, and I believed I could yet make farther discoveries from my own observation. I therefore often begged his Honour to let me go among the herds of Yahoos in the neighbourhood, to which he always very graciously consented, being perfectly convinced that the hatred I bore those brutes would never suffer me to be corrupted by them; and his Honour ordered one of his servants, a strong sorrel nag, very honest and good-natured, to be my guard, without whose protection I durst not undertake such adventures. For I have already told the reader how much I was pestered by those odious animals upon my first arrival. And I afterwards failed very narrowly three or four times of falling into their clutches, when I happened to stray at any distance without my hanger. And I have reason to believe they had some imagination that I was of their own species, which I often assisted myself, by stripping up my sleeves, and showing my naked arms and breast in their sight, when my protector was with me: at which times they would approach as near as they durst, and imitate my actions after the manner of monkeys, but ever with great signs of hatred, as a tame jackdaw, with cap and stockings, is always persecuted by the wild ones, when he happens to be got among them.

They are prodigiously nimble from their infancy; however, I once caught a young male of three years old, and endeavoured by all marks of tenderness to make it quiet; but the little imp fell a squalling, and scratching, and biting with such violence, that I was forced to let it go, and it was high time, for a whole troop of old ones came about us at the noise, but finding the cub was safe (for away it ran), and my sorrel nag being by, they durst not venture near us. I observed the young animal's flesh to smell very rank, and the stink was somewhat between a weasel and a fox, but much more disagreeable. I forgot another circumstance (and perhaps I might have the reader's pardon if it were wholly omitted) that while I held the odious vermin in my hands, it voided its filthy excrements of a yellow liquid substance all over my clothes; but by good fortune there was a small brook hard by, where I washed myself as clean as I could, although I durst not come into my master's presence, until I were sufficiently aired.

By what I could discover, the Yahoos appear to be the most unteachable of all animals, their capacities never reaching higher than to draw or carry burthens. Yet I am of opinion this defect ariseth chiefly from a perverse, restive disposition. For they are cunning, malicious, treacherous and revengeful. They are strong and hardy, but of a cowardly spirit, and by consequence insolent, abject, and cruel. It is observed, that the *redhaired* of both sexes are more libidinous and mischievous than the rest, whom yet they much exceed in strength and activity.

The Houyhnhnms keep the Yahoos for present use in huts not far from the house; but the rest are sent abroad to certain fields, where they dig up roots, eat several kinds of herbs, and search about for carrion, or sometimes catch weasels and *luhimuhs* (a sort of wild rat), which they greedily devour. Nature hath taught them to dig deep holes with their nails on the side of a rising ground, wherein they lie by themselves; only the kennels of the females are larger, sufficient to hold two or three cubs.

They swim from their infancy like frogs, and are able to continue long under water, where they often take fish, which the females carry home to their young. And upon this occasion, I hope the reader will pardon my relating an odd adventure.

Being one day abroad with my protector the sorrel nag, and the weather exceeding hot, I entreated him to let me bathe in a river that was near. He consented, and I immediately stripped myself stark naked, and went down softly into the stream. It happened that a young female Yahoo, standing behind a bank, saw the whole proceeding, and inflamed by desire, as the nag and I conjectured, came running with all speed, and leaped into the water within five yards of the place where I bathed. I was never in my life so terribly frightened; the nag was grazing at some distance, not suspecting any harm. She embraced me after a most fulsome manner; I roared as loud as I could, and the nag came galloping towards me, whereupon she quitted her grasp, with the utmost reluctancy, and leaped upon the opposite bank, where she stood gazing and howling all the time I was putting on my clothes.

This was matter of diversion to my master and his family, as well as of mortification to myself. For now I could no longer deny that I was a real Yahoo in every limb and feature, since the females had a natural propensity to me as one of their own species: neither was the hair of this brute of a red colour (which might have been some excuse for an appetite a little irregular) but black as a sloe, and her countenance did not make an appearance altogether so hideous as the rest of the kind; for, I think she could not be above eleven years old.

Having already lived three years in this country, the reader I suppose will expect that I should, like other travellers, give him some account of the manners and customs of its inhabitants, which it was indeed my principal study to learn.

As these noble Houyhnhnms are endowed by nature with a general disposition to all virtues, and have no conceptions or ideas of what is evil in a rational creature, so their grand maxim is to cultivate *reason*, and to be wholly governed by it. Neither is *reason* among them a point problematical as with us, where men can argue with plausibility on both sides of a question; but strikes you with immediate conviction; as it must needs do where it is not mingled, obscured, or discoloured by passion and interest. I remember it was with extreme difficulty that I could bring my master to understand the meaning of the word *opinion*, or how a point could be disputable; because *reason* taught us to affirm or deny only where we are certain; and beyond our knowledge we cannot do either. So that controversies, wranglings, disputes, and positiveness in false or dubious propositions are evils unknown among the Houyhnhnms. In the like manner, when I used to explain to him our several systems of *natural philosophy*, he would laugh that a creature pretending to *reason* should value itself upon the knowledge of other people's conjectures, and in things where that knowledge, if it were certain, could be of no use. Wherein he agreed entirely with the sentiments of Socrates, as Plato delivers them; which I mention as the highest honour I can do that prince of philosophers. I have often since reflected what destruction such a doctrine would make in the libraries of Europe, and how many paths to fame would be then shut up in the learned world.

Friendship and *benevolence* are the two principal virtues among the Houyhnhnms, and these not confined to particular objects, but universal to the whole race. For a stranger from the remotest part is equally treated with the nearest neighbour, and wherever he goes, looks upon himself as at home. They preserve *decency* and *civility* in the highest degrees, but are altogether ignorant of *ceremony*. They have no fondness for their colts or foals, but the care they take in educating them proceeds entirely from the dictates of *reason*. And I observed my master to show the same affection to his neighbour's issue that he had for his own. They will have it that *Nature* teaches them to love the whole species, and it is *reason* only that maketh a distinction of persons, where there is a superior degree of virtue.

When the matron Houyhnhnms have produced one of each sex, they no longer accompany with their consorts, except they lose one of their issue by some casualty, which very seldom happens: but in such a case they meet again; or when the like accident befalls a person whose wife is past bearing, some other couple bestows on him one of their own colts, and then go together a second time till the mother be pregnant. This caution is necessary to prevent the country from being overburthened with numbers. But the race of inferior Houyhnhnms bred up to be servants is not so strictly limited upon this article; these are allowed to produce three of each sex, to be domestics in the noble families.

In their marriages they are exactly careful to choose such colours as will not make any disagreeable mixture in the breed. *Strength* is chiefly valued in the male, and *comeliness* in the female, not upon the account of *love,* but to preserve the race from degenerating: for where a female happens to excel in *strength,* a consort is chosen with regard to *comeliness.* Courtship, love, presents, jointures, settlements, have no place in their thoughts, or terms whereby to express them in their language. The young couple meet and are joined, merely because it is the determination of their parents and friends: it is what they see done every day, and they look upon it as one of the necessary actions in a reasonable being. But the violation of marriage, or any other unchastity, was never heard of: and the married pair pass their lives with the same friendship and mutual benevolence that they bear to all others of the same species who come in ther way; without jealousy, fondness, quarrelling, or discontent.

In educating the youth of both sexes, their method is admirable, and highly deserves our imitation. These are not suffered to taste a grain of oats, except upon certain days, till eighteen years old; nor milk, but very rarely; and in summer they graze two hours in the morning, and as many in the evening, which their parents likewise observe; but the servants are not allowed above half that time; and a great part of the grass is brought home, which they eat at the most convenient hours, when they can be best spared from work.

Temperance, industry, exercise and *cleanliness,* are the lessons equally enjoined to the young ones of both sexes: and my master thought it monstrous in us to give the females a different kind of education from the males, except in some articles of domestic management; whereby, as he truly observed, one half of our natives were good for nothing but bringing children into the world: and to trust the care of their children to such useless animals, he said, was yet a greater instance of brutality.

But the Houyhnhnms train up their youth to strength, speed, and hardiness, by exercising them in running races up and down steep hills, or over hard stony grounds, and when they are all in a sweat, they are ordered to leap over head and ears into a pond or a river. Four times a year the youth of certain districts meet to show their proficiency in running and leaping, and other feats of strength or agility, where the victor is rewarded with a song made in his or her praise. On this festival the servants drive a herd of Yahoos into the field, laden with hay, and oats, and milk for a repast to the Houyhnhnms; after which these brutes are immediately driven back again, for fear of being noisome to the assembly.

Every fourth year, at the vernal equinox, there is a representative council of the whole nation, which meets in a plain about twenty miles from our house, and continues about five or six days. Here they inquire into the state and condition of the several districts; whether they abound or be deficient in hay or oats, or cows or Yahoos. And wherever there is any want (which is but seldom) it is immediately supplied by unanimous consent and contribution. Here likewise the regulation of children is settled: as for instance, if a Houyhnhnm hath two males, he changeth one of them with another who hath two females: and when a child hath been lost by any casualty, where the mother is past breeding, it is determined what family in the district shall breed another to supply the loss.

CHAPTER IX.

A grand debate at the general assembly of the Houyhnhnms, and how it was determined. The learning of the Houyhnhnms. Their buildings. Their manner of burials. The defectiveness of their language.

One of these grand assemblies was held in my time, about three months before my departure, whither my master went as the representative of our district. In this council was resumed their old debate, and indeed, the only debate that ever happened in their country; whereof my master after his return gave me a very particular account.

The question to be debated was, whether the Yahoos should be exterminated from the face of the earth. One of the members for the affirmative offered several arguments of great strength and weight, alleging, that as the Yahoos were the most filthy, noisome, and deformed animal which nature ever produced, so they were the most restive and indocible, mischievous and malicious: they would privately suck the teats of the Houyhnhnms' cows, kill and devour their cats, trample down their oats and grass, if they were not continually watched, and commit a thousand other extravagances. He took notice of a general tradition, that Yahoos had not been always in their country: but that many ages ago two of these brutes appeared together upon a mountain, whether produced by the heat of the sun upon corrupted mud and slime, or from the ooze and froth of the sea, was never known. That these Yahoos engendered, and their brood in a short time grew so numerous as to overrun and infest the whole nation. That the Houyhnhnms, to get rid of this evil, made a general hunting, and at last enclosed the whole herd; and destroying the older, every Houyhnhnm kept two young ones in a kennel, and brought them to such a degree of tameness, as an animal so savage by nature can be capable of acquiring; using them for draught and carriage. That there seemed to be much truth in this tradition, and that those creatures could not be *ylnhniamshy* (or *aborigines* of the land) because of the violent hatred the Houyhnhnms, as well as all other animals, bore them; which although their evil disposition sufficiently deserved, could never have arrived at so high a degree, if they had been aborigines, or else they would have long since been rooted out. That the inhabitants taking a fancy to use the service of the Yahoos, had very imprudently neglected to cultivate the breed of asses, which were a comely animal, easily kept, more tame and orderly, without any offensive smell, strong enough for labour, although they yield to the other in agility of body; and if their braying be no agreeable sound, it is far preferable to the horrible howlings of the Yahoos.

Several others declared their sentiments to the same purpose, when my master proposed an expedient to the assembly, whereof he had indeed borrowed the hint from me. He approved of the tradition, mentioned by the 'honourable member' who spoke before, and affirmed, that the two Yahoos said to be first seen among them had been driven thither over the sea; that coming to land, and being forsaken by their companions, they retired to the mountains, and degenerating by degrees, became in process of time much more savage than those of their own species in the country from whence these two originals came. The reason of his assertion was, that he had now in his possession a certain wonderful Yahoo (meaning myself) which most of them had heard of, and many of them had seen. He then related to them how he first found me; that my body was all covered with an artificial composure of the skins and hairs of other animals: that I spoke in a language of my own, and had thoroughly learned theirs: that I had related to him the accidents which brought me thither: that when he saw me without my covering, I was an exact Yahoo in every part, only of a whiter colour, less hairy, and with shorter claws. He added, how I had endeavoured to persuade him, that in my own and other countries the Yahoos acted as the governing, rational animal, and held the Houyhnhnms in servitude: that he observed in me all the qualities of a Yahoo, only a little more civilized by some tincture of reason, which however was in a degree as far inferior to the Houyhnhnm race as the Yahoos of their country were to me: that, among other things, I mentioned a custom we had of castrating Houyhnhnms when they were young, in order to render them tame; that the operation was easy and safe; that it was no shame to learn wisdom from brutes, as industry is taught by the ant, and building by the swallow. (For so I translate the word *lyhannh,* although it be a much larger fowl.) That this invention might be practised upon the younger

Yahoos here, which, besides rendering them tractable and fitter for use, would in an age put an end to the whole species without destroying life. That in the mean time the Houyhnhnms should be *exhorted* to cultivate the breed of asses, which, as they are in all respects more valuable brutes, so they have this advantage, to be fit for service at five years old, which the others are not till twelve.

This was all my master thought fit to tell me at that time of what passed in the grand council. But he was pleased to conceal one particular, which related personally to myself, whereof I soon felt the unhappy effect, as the reader will know in its proper place, and from whence I date all the succeeding misfortunes of my life.

The Houyhnhnms have no letters, and consequently their knowledge is all traditional. But there happening few events of any moment among a people so well united, naturally disposed to every virtue, wholly governed by reason, and cut off from all commerce with other nations, the historical part is easily preserved without burthening their memories. I have already observed, that they are subject to no diseases, and therefore can have no need of physicians. However, they have excellent medicines composed of herbs, to cure accidental bruises and cuts in the pastern or frog of the foot by sharp stones, as well as other maims and hurts in the several parts of the body.

They calculate the year by the revolution of the sun and the moon, but use no subdivisions into weeks. They are well enough acquainted with the motions of those two luminaries, and understand the nature of eclipses; and this is the utmost progress of their astronomy.

In poetry they must be allowed to excel all other mortals; wherein the justness of their similes, and the minuteness, as well as exactness of their descriptions, are indeed inimitable. Their verses abound very much in both of these, and usually contain either some exalted notions of friendship and benevolence, or the praises of those who were victors in races and other bodily exercises. Their buildings, although very rude and simple, are not inconvenient, but well contrived to defend them from all injuries of cold and heat. They have a kind of tree, which at forty years old loosens in the root, and falls with the first storm; it grows very straight, and being pointed like stakes with a sharp stone (for the Houyhnhnms know not the use of iron), they stick them erect in the ground about ten inches asunder, and then weave in oat-straw, or sometimes wattles betwixt them. The roof is made after the same manner, and so are the doors.

The Houyhnhnms use the hollow part between the pastern and the hoof of their forefeet as we do our hands, and this with greater dexterity than I could at first imagine. I have seen a white mare of our family thread a needle (which I lent her on purpose) with that joint. They milk their cows, reap their oats, and do all the work which require hands, in the same manner. They have a kind of hard flints, which, by grinding against other stones, they form into instruments, that serve instead of wedges, axes, and hammers. With tools made of these flints they likewise cut their hay, and reap their oats, which there groweth naturally in several fields: the Yahoos draw home the sheaves in carriages, and the servants tread them in certain covered huts, to get out the grain, which is kept in stores. They make a rude kind of earthen and wooden vessels, and bake the former in the sun.

If they can avoid casualties, they die only of old age, and are buried in the obscurest places that can be found, their friends and relations expressing neither joy nor grief at their departure; nor does the dying person discover the least regret that he is leaving the world, any more than if he were upon returning home from a visit to one of his neighbours: I remember my master having once made an appointment with a friend and his family to come to his house upon some affair of importance; on the day fixed, the mistress and her two children came very late; she made two excuses, first for her husband, who, as she said, happened that very morning to *lhnuwnh*. The word is strongly expressive in their language, but not easily rendered into English: it signifies, 'to retire to his first mother'. Her excuse for not coming sooner was, that her husband dying late in the morning, she was a good while consulting her servants about a convenient place where his body should be laid; and I observed she behaved herself at our house as cheerfully as the rest: she died about three months after.

They live generally to seventy or seventy-five years, very seldom to fourscore: some weeks before their death they feel a gradual decay, but without pain. During this time they are much visited by their friends, because they cannot go abroad with their usual ease and satisfaction. However, about ten days before their death, which they seldom fail in computing, they return the visits that have been made them by those who are nearest in the neighbourhood, being carried in a convenient sledge drawn by Yahoos; which vehicle they use, not only upon this occasion, but when they grow old, upon long journeys, or when they are lamed by any accident. And therefore when the dying Houyhnhnms return those visits, they take a solemn leave of their friends, as if they were going to some remote part of the country, where they designed to pass the rest of their lives.

I know not whether it may be worth observing, that the Houyhnhnms have no word in their language to express any thing that is evil, except what they borrow from the deformities or ill qualities of the Yahoos. Thus they denote the folly of a servant, an omission of a child, a stone that cuts their feet, a continuance of foul or unseasonable weather, and the like, by adding to each the epithet of *yahoo*. For instance, *hhnm yahoo, whnaholm yahoo, ynhnmawihlma yahoo,* and an ill-contrived house *ynholmhnmrohlnw yahoo.*

I could with great pleasure enlarge farther upon the manners and virtues of this excellent people; but intending in a short time to publish a volume by itself expressly upon that subject, I refer the reader thither. And in the mean time, proceed to relate my own sad catastrophe.

CHAPTER X.

The author's œconomy and happy life among the Houyhnhnms. His great improvement in virtue, by conversing with them. Their conversations. The author has notice given him by his master that he must depart from the country. He falls into a swoon for grief, but submits. He contrives and finishes a canoe, by the help of a fellow-servant, and puts to sea at a venture.

I had settled my little œconomy to my own heart's content. My master had ordered a room to be made for me after their manner, about six yards from the house, the sides and floors of which I plastered with clay, and covered with rush mats of my own contriving; I had beaten hemp, which there grows wild, and made of it a sort of ticking: this I filled with the feathers of several birds I had taken with springes made of Yahoos' hairs, and were excellent food. I had worked two chairs with my knife, the sorrel nag helping me in the grosser and more laborious part. When my clothes were worn to rags,

I made myself others with the skins of rabbits, and of a certain beautiful animal about the same size, called *nnuhnoh*, the
skin of which is covered with a fine down. Of these I likewise
made very tolerable stockings. I soled my shoes with wood
which I cut from a tree, and fitted to the upper leather, and
when this was worn out, I supplied it with the skins of Yahoos
dried in the sun. I often got honey out of hollow trees, which
I mingled with water, or ate it with my bread. No man could
more verify the truth of these two maxims, *That nature is very
easily satisfied;* and *That necessity is the mother of invention.*
I enjoyed perfect health of body and tranquillity of mind; I
did not feel the treachery or inconstancy of a friend, nor the
injuries of a secret or open enemy. I had no occasion of
bribing, flattering or pimping to procure the favour of any
great man or of his minion. I wanted no fence against fraud or
oppression; here was neither physician to destroy my body,
nor lawyer to ruin my fortune; no informer to watch my
words and actions, or forge accusations against me for hire:
here were no gibers, censurers, backbiters, pickpockets, highwaymen, housebreakers, attorneys, bawds, buffoons, gamesters,
politicians, wits, splenetics, tedious talkers, controvertists,
ravishers, murderers, robbers, virtuosos: no leaders or followers of party and faction: no encouragers to vice, by seduce-
ment or examples: no dungeon, axes, gibbets, whipping-posts,
or pillories: no cheating shopkeepers or mechanics: no pride,
vanity, or affectation: no fops, bullies, drunkards, strolling
whores, or poxes: no ranting, lewd, expensive wives: no stupid,
proud pedants: no importunate, overbearing, quarrelsome,
noisy, roaring, empty, conceited, swearing companions: no
scoundrels, raised from the dust upon the merit of their vices,
or nobility thrown into it on account of their virtues: no lords,
fiddlers, judges or dancing-masters.

I had the favour of being admitted to several Houyhnhnms,
who came to visit or dine with my master; where his Honour
graciously suffered me to wait in the room, and listen to their
discourse. Both he and his company would often descend to
ask me questions, and receive my answers. I had also sometimes the honour of attending my master in his visits to others.
I never presumed to speak, except in answer to a question, and
then I did it with inward regret, because it was a loss of so
much time for improving myself: but I was infinitely delighted
with the station of an humble auditor in such conversations,
where nothing passed but what was useful, expressed in the
fewest and most significant words: where (as I have already

said) the greatest decency was observed, without the least degree of ceremony; where no person spoke without being pleased himself, and pleasing his companions; where there was no interruptions, tediousness, heat, or difference of sentiments. They have a notion, that when people are met together, a short silence doth much improve conversation: this I found to be true; for during those little intermissions of talk, new ideas would arise in their minds, which very much enlivened the discourse. Their subjects are generally on friendship and benevolence; or order and œconomy; sometimes upon the visible operations of nature, or ancient traditions; upon the bounds and limits of virtue; upon the unerring rules of reason; or upon some determinations to be taken at the next great assembly; and often upon the various excellencies of poetry. I may add without vanity, that my presence often gave them sufficient matter for discourse, because it afforded my master an occasion of letting his friends into the history of me and my country, upon which they were all pleased to descant in a manner not very advantageous to human kind; and for that reason I shall not repeat what they said: only I may be allowed to observe, and his Honour, to my great admiration, appeared to understand the nature of Yahoos much better than myself. He went through all our vices and follies, and discovered many which I had never mentioned to him, by only supposing what qualities a Yahoo of their country, with a small proportion of reason, might be capable of exerting: and concluded, with too much probability, how vile as well as miserable such a creature must be.

I freely confess, that all the little knowledge I have of any value was acquired by the lectures I received from my master, and from hearing the discourses of him and his friends; to which I should be prouder to listen, than to dictate to the greatest and wisest assembly in Europe. I admired the strength, comeliness, and speed of the inhabitants; and such a constellation of virtues in such amiable persons produced in me the highest veneration. At first, indeed, I did not feel that natural awe which the Yahoos and all other animals bear towards them; but it grew upon me by degrees, much sooner than I imagined, and was mingled with a respectful love and gratitude, that they would condescend to distinguish me from the rest of my species.

When I thought of my family, my friends, my countrymen, or human race in general, I considered them as they really were, Yahoos in shape and disposition, only a little more civilized, and qualified with the gift of speech, but making no other use of reason than to improve and multiply those vices, whereof their brethren in his country had only the share that nature allotted them. When I happened to behold the reflection of my own form in a lake or fountain, I turned away my face in horror and detestation of myself, and could better endure the sight of a common Yahoo, than of my own person. By conversing with the Houyhnhnms, and looking upon them with delight, I fell to imitate their gait and gesture, which is now grown into a habit, and my friends often tell me in a blunt way that I 'trot like a horse,' which, however, I take for a great compliment: neither shall I disown, that in speaking I am apt to fall into the voice and manner of the Houyhnhnms, and hear myself ridiculed on that account without the least mortification.

In the midst of all this happiness, when I looked upon myself to be fully settled for life, my master sent for me one morning a little earlier than his usual hour. I observed by his countenance that he was in some perplexity, and at a loss how to begin what he had to speak. After a short silence, he told me, he did not know how I would take what he was going to say; that in the last general assembly, when the affair of the Yahoos was entered upon, the representatives had taken offence at his keeping a Yahoo (meaning myself) in his family more like a Houyhnhnm than a brute animal. That he was known frequently to converse with me, as if he could receive some advantage or pleasure in my company: that such a practice was not agreeable to reason or nature, or a thing ever heard of before among them. The assembly did therefore *exhort* him, either to employ me like the rest of my species, or command me to swim back to the place from whence I came. That the first of these expedients was utterly rejected by all the Houyhnhnms who had ever seen me at his house or their own: for they alleged, that because I had some rudiments of reason, added to the natural pravity of those animals, it was to be feared, I might be able to seduce them into the woody and mountainous parts of the country, and bring them in troops by night to destroy the Houyhnhnms' cattle, as being naturally of the ravenous kind, and averse from labour.

My master added, that he was duly pressed by the Houyhnhnms of the neighbourhood to have the assembly's *exhortation* executed, which he could not put off much longer. He doubted it would be impossible for me to swim to another country, and therefore wished I would contrive some sort of vehicle resembling those I had described to him, that might carry me on the sea; in which work I should have the assistance of his own servants, as well as those of his neighbours. He concluded, that for his own part he could have been content to keep me in his service as long as I lived, because he found I had cured myself of some bad habits and dispositions, by endeavouring, as far as my inferior nature was capable, to imitate the Houyhnhnms.

I should here observe to the reader, that a decree of the general assembly in this country is expressed by the word *hnhloayn,* which signifies an *exhoration,* as near as I can render it: for they have no conception how a rational creature can be *compelled,* but only advised or *exhorted,* because no person can disobey reason, without giving up his claim to be a rational creature.

I was struck with the utmost grief and despair at my master's discourse, and being unable to support the agonies I was under, I fell into a swoon at his feet: when I came to myself he told me, that he concluded I had been dead. (For these people are subject to no such imbecilities of nature.) I answered, in a faint voice, that death would have been too great an happiness; that although I could not blame the assembly's *exhortation,* or the urgency of his friends; yet, in my weak and corrupt judgment, I thought it might consist with reason to have been less rigorous. That I could not swim a league, and probably the nearest land to theirs might be distant above an hundred; that many materials, necessary for making a small vessel to carry me off, were wholly wanting in this country, which, however, I would attempt in obedience and gratitude to his Honour, although I concluded the thing to be impossible, and therefore looked on my self as already devoted to destruction. That the certain prospect of an unnatural death was the least of my evils: for, supposing I should escape with life by some strange adventure, how could I think with temper [1] of passing my days among Yahoos, and relapsing into my old corruptions, for want of examples to lead and keep me within the paths of virtue? That I knew too well upon what solid reasons all the determinations of the wise Houyhnhnms were founded, not to be shaken by arguments of mine, a miserable Yahoo; and therefore, after presenting him with my humble thanks for the offer of his servants' assistance in making a vessel, and desiring a reasonable time for so difficult a work, I told him I would endeavour to preserve a wretched

[1] Equanimity.

being; and, if ever I returned to England, was not without hopes of being useful to my own species, by celebrating the praises of the renowned Houyhnhnms, and proposing their virtues to the imitation of mankind.

My master in a few words made me a very gracious reply, allowed me the space of two months to finish my boat; and ordered the sorrel nag, my fellow-servant (for so at this distance I may presume to call him) to follow my instructions, because I told my master, that his help would be sufficient, and I knew he had a tenderness for me.

In his company my first business was to go to that part of the coast where my rebellious crew had ordered me to be set on shore. I got upon a height, and looking on every side into the sea, fancied I saw a small island, towards the northeast: I took out my pocket-glass, and could then clearly distinguish it about five leagues off, as I computed, but it appeared to the sorrel nag to be only a blue cloud: for as he had no conception of any country beside his own, so he could not be as expert in distinguishing remote objects at sea as we who so much converse in that element.

After I had discovered this island, I considered no farther; but resolved it should, if possible, be the first place of my banishment, leaving the consequence to fortune.

I returned home, and consulting with the sorrel nag, we went into a copse at some distance, where I with my knife, and he with a sharp flint fastened very artificially [1] after their manner, to a wooden handle, cut down several oak wattles about the thickness of a walking-staff, and some larger pieces. But I shall not trouble the reader with a particular description of my own mechanics: let it suffice to say that in six weeks' time, with the help of the sorrel nag, who performed the parts that required most labour, I finished a sort of Indian canoe, but much larger, covering it with the skins of Yahoos well stitched together, with hempen threads of my own making. My sail was likewise composed of the skins of the same animal; but I made use of the youngest I could get, the older being too tough and thick, and I likewise provided myself with four paddles. I laid in a stock of boiled flesh, of rabbits and fowls, and took with me two vessels, one filled with milk, and the other with water.

I tried my canoe in a large pond near my master's house, and then corrected in it what was amiss; stopping all the chinks with Yahoos' tallow, till I found it staunch, and able

[1] Artfully.

to bear me and my freight. And when it was as complete as I could possibly make it, I had it drawn on a carriage very gently by Yahoos to the seaside, under the conduct of the sorrel nag and another servant.

When all was ready, and the day came for my departure, I took leave of my master and lady, and the whole family, my eyes flowing with tears, and my heart quite sunk with grief. But his Honour, out of curiosity, and perhaps (if I may speak it without vanity) partly out of kindness, was determined to see me in my canoe, and got several of his neighbouring friends to accompany him. I was forced to wait above an hour for the tide, and then observing the wind very fortunately bearing towards the island, to which I intended to steer my course, I took a second leave of my master: but as I was going to prostrate myself to kiss his hoof, he did me the honour to raise it gently to my mouth. I am not ignorant how much I have been censured for mentioning this last particular. Detractors are pleased to think it improbable, that so illustrious a person should descend to give so great a mark of distinction to a creature so inferior as I. Neither have I forgot how apt some travellers are to boast of extraordinary favours they have received. But if these censurers were better acquainted with the noble and courteous disposition of the Houyhnhnms, they would soon change their opinion.

I paid my respects to the rest of the Houyhnhnms in his Honour's company; then getting into my canoe, I pushed off from shore.

CHAPTER XI.

The author's dangerous voyage. He arrives at New Holland, hoping to settle there. Is wounded with an arrow by one of the natives. Is seized and carried by force into a Portuguese ship. The great civilities of the captain. The author arrives at England.

I began this desperate voyage on February 15, 1714–5, at 9 o'clock in the morning. The wind was very favourable, however, I made use at first only of my paddles, but considering I should soon be weary, and that the wind might probably chop about, I ventured to set up my little sail; and thus with the help of the tide I went at the rate of a league and a half an hour, as near as I could guess. My master and his friends continued on the shore till I was almost out of sight; and I often heard the sorrel nag (who always loved me) crying out, *Hnuy illa nyha maiah Yahoo*,[1] Take care of thyself, gentle Yahoo.

My design was, if possible, to discover some small island uninhabited, yet sufficient by my labour to furnish me with the necessaries of life, which I would have thought a greater happiness than to be first minister in the politest court of Europe; so horrible was the idea I conceived of returning to live in the society and under the government of Yahoos. For in such a solitude as I desired, I could at least enjoy my own thoughts, and reflect with delight on the virtues of those inimitable Houyhnhnms, without any opportunity of degenerating into the vices and corruptions of my own species.

The reader may remember what I related when my crew conspired against me, and confined me to my cabin. How I continued there several weeks, without knowing what course we took, and when I was put ashore in the long-boat, how the sailors told me with oaths, whether true or false, that they knew not in what part of the world we were. However, I did then believe us to be about ten degrees southward of the Cape of Good Hope, or about 45 degrees southern latitude, as I gathered from some general words I overheard among them, being I supposed to the southeast in their intended voyage to Madagascar. And although this were but little better than conjecture, yet I resolved to steer my course eastward, hoping to reach the southwest coast of New Holland, and perhaps some such island as I desired, lying westward of it. The wind was full west, and by six in the evening I computed I had gone eastward at least eighteen leagues, when I spied a very small island about half a league off, which I soon reached. It was nothing but a rock, with one creek, naturally arched by the force of tempests. Here I put in my canoe, and climbing a part of the rock, I could plainly discover land to the east, extending from south to north. I lay all night in my canoe, and repeating my voyage early in the morning, I arrived in seven hours to the southeast point of New Holland. This confirmed me in the opinion I have long entertained, that the maps and charts place this country at least three degrees more to the east than it really is; which thought I communicated many years ago to my worthy friend Mr. Herman Moll,[2] and gave him my reasons for it, although he hath rather chosen to follow other authors.

[1] The phrase has been read literally as, *No ill nigh my Yahoo*.
[2] A famous mapmaker.

I saw no inhabitants in the place where I landed, and being unarmed, I was afraid of venturing far into the country. I found some shellfish on the shore, and ate them raw, not daring to kindle a fire, for fear of being discovered by the natives. I continued three days feeding on oysters and limpets, to save my own provisions, and I fortunately found a brook of excellent water, which gave me great relief.

On the fourth day, venturing out early a little too far, I saw twenty or thirty natives upon a height, not above five hundred yards from me. They were stark naked, men, women, and children, round a fire, as I could discover by the smoke. One of them spied me, and gave notice to the rest; five of them advanced towards me, leaving the women and children at the fire. I made what haste I could to the shore, and getting into my canoe, shoved off: the savages observing me retreat, ran after me; and before I could get far enough into the sea, discharged an arrow which wounded me deeply on the inside of my left knee (I shall carry the mark to my grave). I apprehended the arrow might be poisoned, and paddling out of the reach of their darts (being a calm day), I made a shift to suck the wound, and dress it as well as I could.

I was at a loss what to do, for I durst not return to the same landing-place, but stood to the north, and was forced to paddle; for the wind, although very gentle, was against me, blowing northwest. As I was looking about for a secure landing-place, I saw a sail to the north-northeast, which appearing every minute more visible, I was in some doubt, whether I should wait for them or no; but at last my detestation of the Yahoo race prevailed, and turning my canoe, I sailed and paddled together to the south, and got into the same creek from whence I set out in the morning, choosing rather to trust myself among these barbarians, than live with European Yahoos. I drew up my canoe as close as I could to the shore, and hid myself behind a stone by the little brook, which, as I have already said, was excellent water.

The ship came within a half a league of this creek, and sent out her long-boat with vessels to take in fresh water (for the place it seems was very well known) but I did not observe it until the boat was almost on shore, and it was too late to seek another hiding-place. The seamen at their landing observed my canoe, and rummaging it all over, easily conjectured that the owner could not be far off. Four of them well armed searched every cranny and lurking-hole, till at last they found me flat on my face behind the stone. They gazed a while in

admiration at my strange uncouth dress, my coat made of
skins, my wooden-soled shoes, and my furred stockings; from
whence, however, they concluded I was not a native of the
place, who all go naked. One of the seamen in Portuguese bid
me rise, and asked who I was. I understood that language very
well, and getting upon my feet, said, I was a poor Yahoo, banished from the Houyhnhnms, and desired they would please
to let me depart. They admired to hear me answer them in
their own tongue, and saw by my complexion I must be an
European; but were at loss to know what I meant by Yahoos
and Houyhnhnms, and at the same time fell a laughing at my
strange tone in speaking, which resembled the neighing of a
horse. I trembled all the while betwixt fear and hatred: I again
desired leave to depart, and was gently moving to my canoe;
but they laid hold on me, desiring to know, what country I
was of, whence I came, with many other questions. I told
them I was born in England, from whence I came above five
years ago, and then their country and ours were at peace. I
therefore hoped they would not treat me as an enemy, since
I meant them no harm, but was a poor Yahoo, seeking some
desolate place where to pass the remainder of his unfortunate
life.

When they began to talk, I thought I never heard or saw
any thing so unnatural; for it appeared to me as monstrous as
if a dog or a cow should speak in England, or a Yahoo in
Houyhnhnmland. The honest Portuguese were equally amazed
at my strange dress, and the odd manner of delivering my
words, which however they understood very well. They spoke
to me with great humanity, and said they were sure their captain would carry me *gratis* to Lisbon, from whence I might
return to my own country; that two of the seamen would go
back to the ship, inform the captain of what they had seen,
and receive his orders; in the mean time, unless I would give
my solemn oath not to fly, they would secure me by force. I
thougth it best to comply with their proposal. They were very
curious to know my story, but I gave them very little satisfaction; and they all conjectured that my misfortunes had in-
paired my reason. In two hours the boat which went loaden
with vessels of water, returned with the captain's commands
to fetch me on board. I fell on my knees to preserve my liberty; but all was in vain, and the men having tied me with
cords, heaved me into the boat, from whence I was taken into
the ship, and from thence into the captain's cabin.

His name was Pedro de Mendez; he was a very courteous

and generous person; he entreated me to give some account of my self, and desired to know what I would eat or drink; said, I should be used as well as himself, and spoke so many obliging things, that I wondered to find such civilities from a Yahoo. However, I remained silent and sullen; I was ready to faint at the very smell of him and his men. At last I desired something to eat out of my own canoe; but he ordered me a chicken and some excellent wine, and then directed that I should be put to bed in a very clean cabin. I would not undress myself, but lay on the bed-clothes, and in half an hour stole out, when I thought the crew was at dinner, and getting to the side of the ship was going to leap into the sea, and swim for my life, rather than continue among Yahoos. But one of the seamen prevented me, and having informed the captain, I was chained to my cabin.

After dinner Don Pedro came to me, and desired to know my reason for so desperate an attempt: assured me he only meant to do me all the service he was able, and spoke so very movingly, that at last I descended to treat him like an animal which had some little portion of reason. I gave him a very short relation of my voyage, of the conspiracy against me by my own men, of the country where they set me on shore, and of my five years residence there. All which he looked upon as if it were a dream or a vision; whereat I took great offence; for I had quite forgot the faculty of lying, so peculiar to Yahoos in all countries where they preside, and, consequently, the disposition of suspecting truth in others of their own species. I asked him, whether it were the custom of his country to *say the thing that was not*. I assured him I had almost forgot what he meant by falsehood, and if I had lived a thousand years in Houyhnhnmland, I should never have heard a lie from the meanest servant. That I was altogether indifferent whether he believed me or no; but however, in return for his favours, I would give so much allowance to the corruption of his nature as to answer any objection he would please to make, and he might easily discover the truth.

The captain, a wise man, after many endeavours to catch me tripping in some part of my story, at last began to have a better opinion of my veracity. But he added, that since I professed so inviolable an attachment to truth, I must give him my word of honour to bear him company in this voyage without attempting anything against my life, or else he would continue me a prisoner till we arrived in Lisbon. I gave him the promise he required; but at the same time protested that I would suffer the greatest hardships rather than return to live among Yahoos.

Our voyage passed without any considerable accident. In gratitude to the captain I sometimes sat with him at his earnest request, and strove to conceal my antipathy to human kind, although it often broke out, which he suffered to pass without observation. But the greatest part of the day, I confined myself to my cabin, to avoid seeing any of the crew. The captain had often entreated me to strip myself of my savage dress, and offered to lend me the best suit of clothes he had. This I would not be prevailed on to accept, abhorring to cover myself with anything that had been on the back of a Yahoo. I only desired he would lend me two clean shirts, which having been washed since he wore them, I believed would not so much defile me. These I changed every second day, and washed them myself.

We arrived at Lisbon, Nov. 5, 1715. At our landing the captain forced me to cover myself with his cloak, to prevent the rabble from crowding about me. I was conveyed to his own house, and, at my earnest request, he led me up to the highest room backwards.[1] I conjured him to conceal from all persons what I had told him of the Houyhnhnms, because the least hint of such a story would not only draw numbers of people to see me, but probably put me in danger of being imprisoned, or burnt by the Inquisition. The captain persuaded me to accept a suit of clothes newly made, but I would not suffer the tailor to take my measure; however, Don Pedro being almost of my size, they fitted me well enough. He accoutred me with other necessaries all new, which I aired for twenty-four hours before I would use them.

The captain had no wife, nor above three servants, none of which were suffered to attend at meals, and his whole deportment was so obliging, added to very good *human* understanding, that I really began to tolerate his company. He gained so far upon me, that I ventured to look out of the back window. By degrees I was brought into another room, from whence I peeped into the street, but drew my head back in a fright. In a week's time he seduced me down to the door. I found my terror gradually lessened, but my hatred and contempt seemed to increase. I was at last bold enough to walk the street in his company, but kept my nose well stopped with rue, or sometimes with tobacco.

In ten days Don Pedro, to whom I had given some account of my domestic affairs, put it upon me as a point of honour

---

[1] At the rear of the house.

and conscience, that I ought to return to my native country, and live at home with my wife and children. He told me, there was an English ship in the port just ready to sail, and he would furnish me with all things necessary. It would be tedious to repeat his arguments, and my contradictions. He said it was altogether impossible to find such a solitary island as I had desired to live in; but I might command in my own house, and pass my time in a manner as recluse as I pleased.

I complied at last, finding I could not do better. I left Lisbon the 24th day of November, in an English merchantman, but who was the master I never inquired. Don Pedro accompanied me to the ship, and lent me twenty pounds. He took kind leave of me, and embraced me at parting, which I bore as well as I could. During this last voyage I had no commerce with the master or any of his men, but pretending I was sick kept close in my cabin. On the fifth of December, 1715, we cast anchor in the Downs about nine in the morning, and at three in the afternoon I got safe to my house at Redriff.

My wife and family received me with great surprise and joy, because they concluded me certainly dead; but I must freely confess the sight of them filled me only with hatred, disgust and contempt, and the more by reflecting on the near alliance I had to them. For although, since my unfortunate exile from the Houyhnhnm country, I had compelled myself to tolerate the sight of Yahoos, and to converse with Don Pedro de Mendez; yet my memory and imaginations were perpetually filled with the virtues and ideas of those exalted Houyhnhnms. And when I began to consider, that by copulating with one of the Yahoo species I had become a parent of more, it struck me with the utmost shame, confusion, and horror.

As soon as I entered the house, my wife took me in her arms, and kissed me, at which, having not been used to the touch of that odious animal for so many years, I fell in a swoon for almost an hour. At the time I am writing it is five years since my last return to England: during the first year I could not endure my wife or children in my presence, the very smell of them was intolerable; much less could I suffer them to eat in the same room. To this hour they dare not presume to touch my bread, or drink out of the same cup; neither was I ever able to let one of them take me by the hand. The first money I laid out was to buy two young stone-horses,[1] which I keep in a good stable, and next to them the groom is my greatest favourite; for I feel my spirits revived by the smell

[1] Stallions.

he contracts in the stable. My horses understand me tolerably well; I converse with them at least four hours every day. They are strangers to bridle or saddle; they live in great amity with me, and friendship to each other.

CHAPTER XII.

The author's veracity. His design in publishing this work. His censure of those travellers who swerve from the truth. The author clears himself from any sinister ends in writing. An objection answered. The method of planting colonies. His native country commended. The right of the crown to those countries described by the author is justified. The difficulty of conquering them. The author takes his last leave of the reader, proposeth his manner of living for the future, gives good advice, and concludes.

Thus, gentle reader, I have given thee a faithful history of my travels for sixteen years, and above seven months, wherein I have not been so studious of ornament as of truth. I could perhaps like others have astonished thee with strange improbable tales; but I rather chose to relate plain matter of fact in the simplest manner and style, because my principal design was to inform, and not to amuse thee.

It is easy for us who travel into remote countries, which are seldom visited by Englishmen or other Europeans, to form descriptions of wonderful animals both at sea and land. Whereas a traveller's chief aim should be to make men wiser and better, and to improve their minds by the bad as well as good example of what they deliver concerning foreign places.

I could heartily wish a law were enacted, that every traveller, before he were permitted to publish his voyages, should be obliged to make oath before the Lord High Chancellor that all he intended to print was absolutely true to the best of his knowledge; for then the world would no longer be deceived as it usually is, while some writers, to make their works pass the better upon the public, impose the grossest falsities on the unwary reader. I have perused several books of travels with great delight in my younger days; but having since gone over most parts of the globe, and been able to contradict many fabulous accounts from my own observation, it hath given me a great disgust against this part of reading, and some indignation to see the credulity of mankind so impudently abused.

Therefore since my acquaintance were pleased to think my poor endeavours might not be unacceptable to my country, I imposed on myself as a maxim, never to be swerved from, that I would *strictly adhere to truth;* neither indeed can I be ever under the least temptation to vary from it, while I retain in my mind the lectures and example of my noble master, and the other illustrious Houyhnhnms, of whom I had so long the honour to be an humble hearer.

> —— *Nec si miserum Fortuna Sinonem*
> *Finxit, vanum etiam mendacemque improba finget.*[1]

I know very well how little reputation is to be got by writings which require neither genius nor learning, nor indeed any other talent, except a good memory or an exact journal. I know likewise, that writers of travels, like dictionary-makers, are sunk into oblivion by the weight and bulk of those who come last, and therefore lie uppermost. And it is highly probable, that such travellers who shall hereafter visit the countries described in this work of mine, may, by detecting my errors (if there be any), and adding many new discoveries of their own, jostle me out of vogue, and stand in my place, making the world forget that ever I was an author. This indeed would be too great a mortification if I wrote for fame: but, as my sole intention was the PUBLIC GOOD, I cannot be altogether disappointed. For who can read of the virtues I have mentioned in the glorious Houyhnhnms, without being ashamed of his own vices, when he considers himself as the reasoning, governing animal of his country? I shall say nothing of those remote nations where Yahoos preside, amongst which the least corrupted are the Brobdingnagians, whose wise maxims in morality and government it would be our happiness to observe. But I forbear descanting further, and rather leave the judicious reader to his own rmarks and applications.

I am not a little pleased that this work of mine can possibly meet with no censurers: for what objections can be made against a writer who relates only plain facts that happened in such distant countries, where we have not the least interest with respect either to trade or negotiations? I have carefully avoided every fault with which common writers of travels are often too justly charged. Besides, I meddle not the least with any *party*, but write without passion, prejudice, or ill-will against any man or number of men whatsoever. I write for the

[1] See Virgil's *Aeneid*, II, 79–80: "Although vile Fortune has made Sinon wretched, she has not made him false or mendacious."

noblest end, to inform and instruct mankind, over whom I may, without breach of modesty, pretend to some superiority from the advantages I received by conversing so long among the most accomplished Houyhnhnms. I write without any view towards profit or praise. I never suffer a word to pass that may look like reflection, or possibly give the least offence even to those who are most ready to take it. So that I hope I may with justice pronounce myself an author perfectly blameless, against whom the tribe of answerers, considerers, observers, reflecters, detecters, remarkers, will never be able to find matter for exercising their talents.

I confess, it was whispered to me that I was bound in duty, as a subject of England, to have given in a memorial to a secretary of state, at my first coming over; because, whatever lands are discovered by a subject belong to the crown. But I doubt whether our conquests in the countries I treat of would be as easy as those of Ferdinando Cortez over the naked Americans. The Lilliputians, I think, are hardly worth the charge of a fleet and army to reduce them; and I question whether it might be prudent or safe to attempt the Brobdingnagians. Or whether an English army would be much at their ease with the Flying Island over their heads. The Houyhnhnms, indeed, appear not to be so well prepared for war, a science to which they are perfect strangers, and especially against missive weapons. However, supposing myself to be a minister of state, I could never give my advice for invading them. Their prudence, unanimity, unacquaintedness with fear, and their love of their country would amply supply all defects in the military art. Imagine twenty thousand of them breaking into the midst of an European army, confounding the ranks, overturning the carriages, battering the warriors' faces into mummy, by terrible yerks from their hinder hoofs: for they would well deserve the character given to Augustus; *Recalcitrat undique tutus*.[1] But instead of proposals for conquering that magnanimous nation, I rather wish they were in a capacity or disposition to send a sufficient number of their inhabitants for civilizing Europe, by teaching us the first principles of honour, justice, truth, temperance, public spirit, fortitude, chastity, friendship, benevolence, and fidelity. The *names* of all which virtues are still retained among us in most languages, and are to be met with in modern as well as ancient authors; which I am able to assert from my own small reading.

[1] See Horace's *Satires*, II, 1, 20: "He kicks backward, but remains safe on every side."

But I had another reason which made me less forward to enlarge his Majesty's dominions by my discoveries: to say the truth, I had conceived a few scruples with relation to the distributive justice of princes upon those occasions. For instance, a crew of pirates are driven by a storm they know not whither; at length a boy discovers land from the topmast; they go on shore to rob and plunder; they see an harmless people, are entertained with kindness, they give the country a new name, they take formal possession of it for the king, they set up a rotten plank or a stone for a memorial, they murder two or three dozen of the natives, bring away a couple more by force for a sample, return home, and get their pardon. Here commences a new dominion acquired with a title by *divine right*. Ships are sent with the first opportunity, the natives driven out or destroyed, their princes tortured to discover their gold, a free license given to all acts of inhumanity and lust, the earth reeking with the blood of its inhabitants: and this execrable crew of butchers employed in so pious an expedition, is a *modern colony* sent to convert and civilize an idolatrous and barbarous people.

But this description, I confess, doth by no means affect the British nation, who may be an example to the whole world for their wisdom, care, and justice in planting colonies; their liberal endowments for the advancement of religion and learning; their choice of devout and able pastors to propagate Christianity; their caution in stocking their provinces with people of sober lives and conversations from this the mother kingdom; their strict regard to the distribution of justice, in supplying the civil administration through all their colonies with officers of the greatest abilities, utter strangers to corruption: and to crown all, by sending the most vigilant and virtuous governors, who have no other views than the happiness of the people over whom they preside, and the honour of the king their master.

But as those countries which I have described do not appear to have any desire of being conquered, and enslaved, murdered or driven out by colonies, nor abound either in gold, silver, sugar or tobacco; I did humbly conceive they were by no means proper objects of our zeal, our valour, or our interest. However, if those whom it may concern think fit to be of another opinion, I am ready to depose, when I shall be lawfully called, that no European did ever visit these countries before me. I mean, if the inhabitants ought to be believed; unless a dispute may arise about the two Yahoos, said to have been seen many ages ago on a mountain in Houyhnhnmland, from whence the opinion is, that the race of those brutes hath descended; and these, for any thing I know, may have been English, which indeed I was apt to suspect from the lineaments of their posterity's countenances, although very much defaced. But, how far that will go to make out a title, I leave to the learned in colony-law.

But as to the formality of taking possession in my sovereign's name, it never came once into my thoughts; and if it had, yet as my affairs then stood, I should perhaps, in point of prudence and self-preservation, have put it off to a better opportunity.

Having thus answered the *only* objection than can ever be raised against me as a traveller, I here take a final leave of my courteous readers, and return to enjoy my own speculations in my little garden at Redriff; to apply those excellent lessons of virtue which I learned among the Houyhnhnms; to instruct the Yahoos of my own family as far as I shall find them docible animals; to behold my figure often in a glass, and thus if possible habituate myself by time to tolerate the sight of a human creature; to lament the brutality of Houyhnhnms in my own country, but always treat their perons with respect, for the sake of my noble master, his family, his friends, and the whole Houyhnhnm race, whom these of ours have the honour to resemble in all their lineaments, however their intellectuals came to degenerate.

I began last week to permit my wife to sit at dinner with me, at the farthest end of a long table, and to answer (but with the utmost brevity) the few questions I ask her. Yet the smell of a Yahoo continuing very offensive, I always keep my nose well stopped with rue, lavender, or tobacco leaves. And although it be hard for a man late in life to remove old habits, I am not altogether out of hopes in some time to suffer a neighbour Yahoo in my company without the apprehensions I am yet under of his teeth or his claws.

My reconcilement to the Yahoo-kind in general might not be so difficult if they would be content with those vices and follies only which nature hath entitled them to. I am not in the least provoked at the sight of a lawyer, a pickpocket, a colonel, a fool, a lord, a gamester, a politician, a whoremonger, a physician, an evidence, a suborner, an attorney, a traitor, or the like; this is all according to the due course of things: but when I behold a lump of deformity and diseases both in body and mind, smitten with *pride,* it immediately breaks all the measures of my patience; neither shall I be ever able to comprehend how such an animal and such a vice could tally together. The wise and virtuous Houyhnhnms, who abound in all excellencies that can adorn a rational creature, have no name for this vice in their language, which hath no terms to express any thing that is evil, except those whereby they describe the detestable qualities of their Yahoos, among which they were not able to distinguish this of pride, for want of thoroughly understanding human nature, as it showeth itself in other countries, where that animal presides. But I, who had more experience, could plainly observe some rudiments of it among the wild Yahoos.

But the Houyhnhnms, who live under the government of reason, are no more proud of the good qualities they possess, than I should be for not wanting a leg or an arm, which no man in his wits would boast of, although he must be miserable without them. I dwell the longer upon this subject from the desire I have to make the society of an English Yahoo by any means not insupportable; and therefore I here entreat those who have any tincture of this absurd vice, that they will not presume to appear in my sight.

FINIS

Treatises wrote by the same Author, most of them mentioned in the following Discourses; which will be speedily published.

A Character of the present Set of Wits in this Island.

A panegyrical Essay upon the Number THREE.

A Dissertation upon the principal Productions of Grub Street.

Lectures upon a Dissection of Human Nature.

A Panegyric upon the World.

An analytical Discourse upon Zeal, histori-theo-physi-logically considered.

A general History of Ears.

A modest Defence of the Proceedings of the Rabble in all Ages.

A Description of the Kingdom of Absurdities.

A Voyage into England, by a Person of Quality in Terra Australis incognita, translated from the Original.

A critical Essay upon the Art of Canting, philosophically, physically, and musically considered.

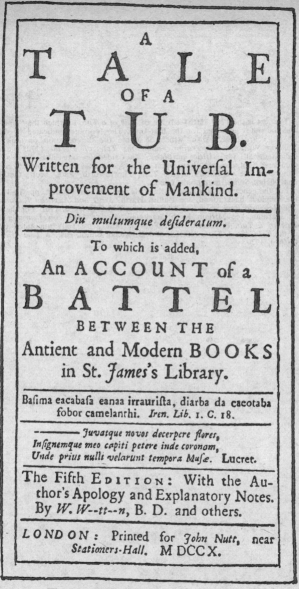

A TALE OF A TUB.

Written for the Univerſal Improvement of Mankind.

Diu multumque deſideratum.

To which is added,

An ACCOUNT of a BATTEL

BETWEEN THE

Antient and Modern BOOKS
in St. *James's* Library.

Baſima eacabaſa eanaa irrauriſta, diarba da caeotaba
fobor camelanthi. *Iren. Lib.* 1. C. 18.

——— *Juvatque novos decerpere flores,*
Inſignemque meo capiti petere inde coronam,
Unde prius nulli velarunt tempora Muſæ. Lucret.

The Fifth EDITION: With the Author's Apology and Explanatory Notes.
By *W. W--tt--n*, B. D. and others.

LONDON : Printed for *John Nutt*, near
Stationers-Hall. MDCCX.

Title-page of the Fifth Edition, 1710

The text is the 1710 (fifth) edition of *Tale of a Tub,* in which the "Apology" and the notes appeared for the first time. The footnotes indicated by devices (* † ||) are Swift's own, which he wrote for the occasion or took from William Wotton's *Observations upon the Tale of a Tub* (1705) and so indicated, all for satiric purposes. The sidenotes are also Swift's. The numbered footnotes are the present editor's, but they are indebted to a long, honorable line of editors of the *Tale:* Hawksworth, Pate, Scott, Guthkelch and Nichol Smith, and Louis Landa.

For the general background to the *Tale,* see the Introduction, pp. 11–12. For the religious background, see Phillip Harth, *Swift and Anglican Rationalism. The Religious Background of "A Tale of a Tub,"* Chicago, 1961. For the satire on learning, see Miriam Kosh Starkman, *Swift's Satire on Learning in A Tale of a Tub,* Princeton, 1950. For the best, most fully annotated edition of the *Tale,* see A. C. Guthkelch and D. Nichol Smith, eds., *A Tale of a Tub,* Oxford, 1920.

AN APOLOGY [1]

For the, &c.

If good and ill nature equally operated upon Mankind, I might have saved my self the trouble of this Apology; for it is manifest by the reception the following discourse hath met with, that those who approve it, are a great majority among the men of taste; yet there have been two or three treatises written expressly against it, besides many others that have flirted at it occasionally, without one syllable having been ever published in its defence or even quotation to its advantage, that I can remember, except by the polite author of a late discourse between a Deist and a Socinian.

Therefore, since the book seems calculated to live at least as long as our language and our taste admit no great alterations, I am content to convey some Apology along with it.

The greatest part of that book was finished above thirteen years since, 1696, which is eight years before it was published. The author was then young, his invention at the height, and his reading fresh in his head. By the assistance of some thinking, and much conversation, he had endeavoured to strip himself of as many real prejudices as he could; I say real ones, because, under the notion of prejudices, he knew to what dangerous heights some men have proceeded. Thus prepared, he thought the numerous and gross corruptions in Religion and Learning might furnish matter for a satire, that would be useful and diverting. He resolved to proceed in a manner that should be altogether new, the world having been already too long nauseated with endless repetitions upon every subject. The abuses in Religion, he proposed to set forth in the Allegory of the Coats and the three Brothers, which was to make up the body of the discourse. Those in learning he chose to introduce by way of digressions. He was then a young gentleman much in the world, and wrote to the taste of those who were like himself; therefore, in order to allure them, he gave a liberty to his pen, which might not suit with maturer years, or graver characters, and which he could have easily corrected with a very few blots, had he been master of his papers, for a year or two before their publication.

Not that he would have governed his judgment by the ill-placed cavils of the sour, the envious, the stupid, and the taste-

[1] For the background of the content of the "Apology," see the Introduction, pp. 13–14.

less, which he mentions with disdain. He acknowledges there are several youthful sallies, which, from the grave and the wise, may deserve a rebuke. But he desires to be answerable no farther than he is guilty, and that his faults may not be multiplied by the ignorant, the unnatural, and uncharitable applications of those who have neither candour to suppose good meanings, nor palate to distinguish true ones. After which, he will forfeit his life, if any one opinion can be fairly deduced from that book, which is contrary to Religion or Morality.

Why should any clergyman of our church be angry to see the follies of fanaticism and superstition exposed, though in the most ridiculous manner; since that is perhaps the most probable way to cure them, or at least hinder them from farther spreading? Besides, though it was not intended for their perusal, it rallies nothing but what they preach against. It contains nothing to provoke them by the least scurrility upon their persons or their functions. It celebrates the Church of England as the most perfect of all others in discipline and doctrine, it advances no opinion they reject, nor condemns any they receive. If the clergy's resentments lay upon their hands, in my humble opinion they might have found more proper objects to employ them on: *nondum tibi defuit hostis;* I mean those heavy, illiterate scribblers, prostitute in their reputations, vicious in their lives, and ruined in their fortunes, who, to the shame of good sense as well as piety, are greedily read, merely upon the strength of bold, false, impious assertions, mixed with unmannerly reflections upon the priesthood, and openly intended against all Religion; in short, full of such principles as are kindly received, because they are levelled to remove those terrors that Religion tells men will be the consequence of immoral lives. Nothing like which is to be met with in this discourse, though some of them are pleased so freely to censure it. And I wish there were no other instance of what I have too frequently observed, that many of that reverend body are not always very nice in distinguishing between their enemies and their friends.

Had the author's intentions met with a more candid interpretation from some whom out of respect he forbears to name, he might have been encouraged to an examination of books written by some of those authors above described, whose errors, ignorance, dullness, and villainy, he thinks he could have detected and exposed in such a manner, that the persons who are most conceived to be infected by them, would soon lay them aside and be ashamed. But he has now given over those thoughts, since the weightiest men in the weightiest stations are pleased to think it a more dangerous point to laugh at those corruptions in Religion, which they themselves must disapprove, than to endeavour pulling up those very foundations, wherein all Christians have agreed.

He thinks it no fair proceeding, that any person should offer determinately to fix a name upon the author of this discourse, who hath all along concealed himself from most of his nearest friends: Yet several have gone a farther step, and pronounced another book * to have been the work of the same hand with this, which the author directly affirms to be a thorough mistake; he having yet never so much as read that discourse: a plain instance how little truth there often is in general surmises, or in conjectures drawn from a similitude of style, or way of thinking.

* *Letter of Enthusiasm* [1]

Had the author writ a book to expose the abuses in Law, or in Physic, he believes the learned professors in either faculty would have been so far from resenting it, as to have given him thanks for his pains, especially if he had made an honourable reservation for the true practice of either science. But Religion, they tell us, ought not to be ridiculed, and they tell us truth; yet surely the corruptions in it may; for we are taught by the tritest maxim in the world, that Religion being the best of things, its corruptions are likely to be the worst.

There is one thing which the judicious reader cannot but have observed, that some of those passages in this discourse, which appear most liable to objection, are what they call parodies, where the author personates the style and manner of other writers, whom he has a mind to expose. I shall produce one instance, it is in the three hundred and seventeenth page. Dryden, L'Estrange,[2] and some others I shall not name, are here levelled at, who, having spent their lives in faction, and apostasies, and all manner of vice, pretended to be sufferers for Loyalty and Religion. So Dryden tells us in one of his prefaces of his merits and sufferings, thanks God that he *possesses his soul in patience;* in other places he talks at the same rate; and L'Estrange often uses the like style; and I believe the reader may find more persons to give that passage an application: but this is enough to direct those who may have overlooked the author's intention.

[1] Written by Lord Shaftesbury in 1708.
[2] Sir Roger L'Estrange (1616–1704), a prolific journalist, pamphleteer, and translator; probably cited by Swift as a type of the Modern hack. For Swift's animus to Dryden, see *Infra, passim.*

There are three or four other passages which prejudiced or ignorant readers have drawn by great force to hint at ill meanings, as if they glanced at some tenets in religion; in answer to all which, the author solemnly protests, he is entirely innocent, and never had it once in his thoughts, that anything he said, would in the least be capable of such interpretations, which he will engage to deduce full as fairly from the most innocent book in the world. And it will be obvious to every reader, that this was not any part of his scheme or design, the abuses he notes being such as all Church of England men agree in; nor was it proper for his subject to meddle with other points, than such as have been perpetually controverted since the Reformation.

To instance only in that passage about the three wooden machines mentioned in the Introduction: in the original manuscript there was a description of a fourth, which those who had the papers in their power, blotted out, as having something in it of satire, that I suppose they thought was too particular; and therefore they were forced to change it to the number Three, from whence some have endeavoured to squeeze out a dangerous meaning, that was never thought on. And, indeed, the conceit was half spoiled by changing the numbers; that of Four being much more cabalistic, and, therefore, better exposing the pretended virtue of Numbers, a superstition there intended to be ridiculed.

Another thing to be observed is, that there generally runs an irony through the thread of the whole book, which the men of taste will observe and distinguish, and which will render some objections that have been made very weak and insignificant.

This Apology being chiefly intended for the satisfaction of future readers, it may be thought unnecessary to take any notice of such treatises as have been writ against this ensuing discourse, which are already sunk into waste paper and oblivion, after the usual fate of common answerers to books, which are allowed to have any merit: they are indeed like annuals, that grow about a young tree, and seem to vie with it for a summer, but fall and die with the leaves in autumn, and are never heard of any more. When Dr. Eachard writ his book about the Contempt of the Clergy, numbers of those answerers immediately started up, whose memory, if he had not kept alive by his replies, it would now be utterly unknown that he were ever answered at all. There is indeed an exception, when any great genius thinks it worth his while to expose a foolish piece; so we still read Marvell's Answer to Parker with pleasure, though the book it answers be sunk long ago; so the Earl of Orrery's *Remarks* will be read with delight, when the *Dissertation* he exposes will neither be sought nor found; but these are no enterprises for common hands, nor to be hoped for above once or twice in an age. Men would be more cautious of losing their time in such an undertaking, if they did but consider, that to answer a book effectually, requires more pains and skill, more wit, learning, and judgment, than were employed in the writing it. And the author assures those gentlemen, who have given themselves that trouble with him, that his discourse is the product of the study, the observation, and the invention of several years; that he often blotted out much more than he left, and if his papers had not been a long time out of his possession, they must have still undergone more severe corrections; and do they think such a building is to be battered with dirt-pellets, however envenomed the mouths may be that discharge them? He hath seen the productions but of two answerers, one of which first appeared as from an unknown hand, but since avowed by a person, who, upon some occasions, hath discovered no ill vein of humour. 'Tis a pity any occasion should put him under a necessity of being so hasty in his productions, which, otherwise, might often be entertaining. But there were other reasons obvious enough for his miscarriage in this; he writ against the conviction of his talent, and entered upon one of the wrongest attempts in nature, to turn into ridicule by a week's labour, a work which had cost so much time, and met with so much success in ridiculing others; the manner how he has handled his subject I have now forgot, having just looked it over when it first came out, as others did, merely for the sake of the title.

The other answer is from a person of a graver character, and is made up of half invective, and half annotation; in the latter of which, he hath generally succeeded well enough. And the project at that time was not amiss, to draw in readers to his pamphlet, several having appeared desirous that there might be some explication of the more difficult passages. Neither can he be altogether blamed for offering at the invective part, because it is agreed on all hands that the author had given him sufficient provocation. The great objection is against his manner of treating it, very unsuitable to one of his function. It was determined by a fair majority, that this answerer had, in a way not to be pardoned, drawn his pen against a certain great man then alive, and universally reverenced for every good quality that could possibly enter into the composition of the most accomplished person; it was observed how he was pleased, and affected to have that noble writer called his adversary; and it was a point of satire well directed; for I have been told Sir W[illiam] T[emple] was sufficiently mortified at the term. All the men of wit and politeness were immediately up in arms through indignation, which prevailed over their contempt, by the consequences they apprehended from such an example; and it grew to be Porsenna's case; *idem trecenti juravimus.* In short, things were ripe for a general insurrection, till my Lord Orrery had a little laid the spirit, and settled the ferment. But his lordship being principally engaged with another antagonist, it was thought necessary, in order to quiet the minds of men, that this opposer should receive a reprimand, which partly occasioned that discourse of *The Battle of the Books;* and the author was farther at the pains to insert one or two remarks on him, in the body of the book.

This Answerer has been pleased to find fault with about a dozen passages, which the author will not be at the trouble of defending, farther than by assuring the reader, that, for the greater part, the Reflecter is entirely mistaken, and forces interpretations which never once entered into the writer's head, nor will, he is sure, into that of any reader of taste and candour; he allows two or three at most, there produced, to have been delivered unwarily: for which he desires to plead the excuse offered already, of his youth, and frankness of speech, and his papers being out of his power at the time they were published.

But this Answerer insists, and says, what he chiefly dislikes, is the design; what that was, I have already told, and I believe there is not a person in England who can understand that book, that ever imagined it to have been anything else, but to expose the abuses and corruptions in Learning and Religion.

But it would be good to know what design this Reflecter was serving, when he concludes his pamphlet with a *Caution to Readers* to beware of thinking the author's wit was entirely his own; surely this must have had some allay of personal animosity, at least mixed with the design of serving the public by so useful a discovery; and it indeed touches the author in a very tender point, who insists upon it, that through the whole book he has not borrowed one single hint from any writer in the world; and he thought, of all criticisms, that would never have been one. He conceived it was never disputed to be an original, whatever faults it might have. However this

Answerer produces three instances to prove this author's wit is not his own in many places. The first is, that the names of Peter, Martin, and Jack, are borrowed from a letter of the late Duke of Buckingham. Whatever wit is contained in those three names, the author is content to give it up, and desires his readers will subtract as much as they placed upon that account; at the same time protesting solemnly, that he never once heard of that letter, except in this passage of the Answerer: so that the names were not borrowed, as he affirms, though they should happen to be the same; which, however, is odd enough, and what he hardly believes, that of Jack being not quite so obvious as the other two. The second instance to show the author's wit is not his own, is Peter's banter (as he calls it in his Alsatia phrase) upon Transubstantiation, which is taken from the same duke's conference with an Irish priest, where a cork is turned into a horse. This the author confesses to have seen about ten years after his book was writ, and a year or two after it was published. Nay, the Answerer overthrows this himself; for he allows the *Tale* was writ in 1697; and I think that pamphlet was not printed in many years after. It was necessary that corruption should have some allegory as well as the rest; and the author invented the properest he could, without inquiring what other people had writ; and the commonest reader will find, there is not the least resemblance between the two stories. The third instance is in these words; 'I have been assured, that the battle in St. James's Library is, *mutatis mutandis,* taken out of a French book, entitled, *Combat des Livres,* if I misremember not.' In which passage there are two clauses observable: 'I have been assured'; and, 'if I misremember not.' I desire first to know whether, if that conjecture proves an utter falsehood, those two clauses will be a sufficient excuse for this worthy critic. The matter is a trifle; but, would he venture to pronounce at this rate upon one of greater moment? I know nothing more contemptible in a writer than the character of a plagiary, which he here fixes at a venture; and this not for a passage, but a whole discourse, taken out from another book, only *mutatis mutandis*. The author is as much in the dark about this as the answerer; and will imitate him by an affirmation at random; that if there be a word of truth in this reflection, he is a paltry, imitating pedant; and the Answerer is a person of wit, manners, and truth. He takes his boldness, from never having seen any such treatise in his life, nor heard of it before; and he is sure it is impossible for two writers, of different times and countries, to agree in their thoughts after such a manner, that two continued discourses shall be the same, only *mutatis mutandis*. Neither will he insist upon the mistake of the title, but let the answerer and his friend produce any book they please, he defies them to show one single particular, where the judicious reader will affirm he has been obliged for the smallest hint; giving only allowance for the accidental encountering of a single thought, which he knows may sometimes happen; though he has never yet found it in that discourse, nor has heard it objected by anybody else.

So that if ever any design was unfortunately executed, it must be that of this Answerer; who, when he would have it observed that the author's wit is not his own, is able to produce but three instances, two of them mere trifles, and all three manifestly false. If this be the way these gentlemen deal with the world in those criticisms, where we have not leisure to defeat them, their readers had need be cautious how they rely upon their credit; and whether this proceeding can be reconciled to humanity or truth, let those who think it worth their while determine.

It is agreed, this Answerer would have succeeded much better if he had stuck wholly to his business as a commentator upon the *Tale of a Tub,* wherein it cannot be denied that he hath been of some service to the public, and has given very fair conjectures towards clearing up some difficult passages; but it is the frequent error of those men (otherwise very commendable for their labours), to make excursions beyond their talent and their office, by pretending to point out the beauties and the faults; which is no part of their trade, which they always fail in, which the world never expected from them, nor gave them any thanks for endeavouring at. The part of Minellius, or Farnaby, would have fallen in with his genius, and might have been serviceable to many readers, who cannot enter into the abstruser parts of that discourse; but *optat ephippia bos piger*. The dull, unwieldy, ill-shaped ox would needs put on the furniture of a horse, not considering he was born to labour, to plough the ground for the sake of superior beings, and that he has neither the shape, mettle, nor speed of that nobler animal he would affect to personate.

It is another pattern of this Answerer's fair dealing to give us hints that the author is dead, and yet to lay the suspicion upon somebody, I know not who, in the country; to which can be only returned, that he is absolutely mistaken in all his conjectures; and surely conjectures are, at best, too light a pretence to allow a man to assign a name in public. He condemns a book, and consequently the author, of whom he is utterly ignorant; yet at the same time fixes in print what he thinks a disadvantageous character upon those who never deserved it. A man who receives a buffet in the dark may be allowed to be vexed; but it is an odd kind of revenge to go to cuffs in broad day with the first he meets with, and lay the last night's injury at his door. And thus much for this *discreet, candid, pious,* and *ingenious* Answerer.

How the author came to be without his papers, is a story not proper to be told, and of very little use, being a private fact of which the reader would believe as little or as much as he thought good. He had, however, a blotted copy by him, which he intended to have writ over, with many alterations, and this the publishers were well aware of, having put it into the bookseller's preface, that they *apprehended a surreptitious copy, which was to be altered,* &c. This, though not regarded by readers, was a real truth, only the surreptitious copy was rather that which was printed; and they made all haste they could, which indeed was needless, the author not being at all prepared; but he has been told the bookseller was in much pain, having given a good sum of money for the copy.

In the author's original copy there were not so many chasms as appear in the book; and why some of them were left, he knows not; had the publication been trusted to him, he should have made several corrections of passages against which nothing hath been ever objected. He should likewise have altered a few of those that seem with any reason to be excepted against; but to deal freely, the greatest number he should have left untouched, as never suspecting it possible any wrong interpretations could be made of them.

The author observes, at the end of the book there is a discourse called *A Fragment,* which he more wondered to see in print than all the rest. Having been a most imperfect sketch, with the addition of a few loose hints, which he once lent a gentleman, who had designed a discourse of somewhat the same subject; he never thought of it afterwards; and it was a sufficient surprise to see it pieced up together, wholly out of the method and scheme he had intended, for it was the groundwork of a much larger discourse, and he was sorry to observe the materials so foolishly employed.

There is one further objection made by those who have answered this book, as well as by some others, that Peter is frequently made to repeat oaths and curses. Every reader observes it was necessary to know that Peter did swear and curse. The oaths are not printed out, but only supposed, and the idea of an oath is not immoral, like the idea of a profane or immodest speech. A man may laugh at the Popish folly of cursing people to hell, and imagine them swearing, without any crime; but lewd words, or dangerous opinions though printed by halves, fill the reader's mind with ill ideas; and of these the author cannot be accused. For the judicious reader will find that the severest strokes of satire in his book are levelled against the modern custom of employing wit upon those topics; of which there is a remarkable instance in the three hundred and fifty-eighth page, as well as in several others, though perhaps once or twice expressed in too free a manner, excusable only for the reasons already alleged. Some overtures have been made by a third hand to the bookseller, for the author's altering those passages which he thought might require it. But it seems the bookseller will not hear of any such thing, being apprehensive it might spoil the sale of the book.

The author cannot conclude this apology without making this one reflection; that, as wit is the noblest and most useful gift of human nature, so humour is the most agreeable; and where these two enter far into the composition of any work, they will render it always acceptable to the world. Now, the great part of those who have no share or taste of either, but by their pride, pedantry, and ill manners, lay themselves bare to the lashes of both, think the blow is weak, because they are insensible; and, where wit hath any mixture of raillery, 'tis but calling it banter, and the work is done. This polite word of theirs was first borrowed from the bullies in White-Friars, then fell among the footmen, and at last retired to the pedants; by whom it is applied as properly to the productions of wit, as if I should apply it to Sir Isaac Newton's mathematics. But, if this bantering, as they call it, be so despisable a thing, whence comes it to pass they have such a perpetual itch towards it themselves? To instance only in the Answerer already mentioned; it is grievous to see him, in some of his writings, at every turn going out of his way to be waggish, to tell us of a *cow that pricked up her tail;* and in his answer to this discourse, he says, *it is all a farce and a ladle;* with other passages equally shining. One may say of these *impedimenta literarum,* that wit owes them a shame; and they cannot take wiser counsel than to keep out of harm's way, or at least not to come till they are sure they are called.

To conclude: with those allowances above required, this book should be read; after which, the author conceives, few things will remain which may not be excused in a young writer. He wrote only to the men of wit and taste, and he thinks he is not mistaken in his accounts, when he says they have been all of his side, enough to give him the vanity of telling his name, wherein the world with all its wise conjectures, is yet very much in the dark; which circumstance is no disagreeable amusement either to the public or himself.

The author is informed, that the bookseller has prevailed on several gentlemen to write some explanatory notes, for the goodness of which he is not to answer, having never seen any of them, nor intends it, till they appear in print; when it is not unlikely he may have the pleasure to find twenty meanings which never entered into his imagination.

June 3, 1709.

POSTSCRIPT

SINCE the writing of this which was about a year ago, a prostitute bookseller [1] hath published a foolish paper, under the name of Notes on the *Tale of a Tub,* with some account of the author: and, with an insolence which, I suppose, is punishable by law, hath presumed to assign certain names. It will be enough for the author to assure the world, that the writer of that paper is utterly wrong in all his conjectures upon that affair. The author farther asserts that the whole work is entirely of one hand, which every reader of judgment will easily discover. The gentleman who gave the copy to the bookseller, being a friend of the author, and using no other liberties besides that of expunging certain passages where now the chasms appear under the name of *desiderata*. But if any person will prove his claim to three lines in the whole book, let him step forth, and tell his name and titles; upon which, the bookseller shall have orders to prefix them to the next edition, and the claimant shall from henceforward be acknowledged the undisputed author.

[1] Edmund Curll (1675–1747), a publisher of very questionable reputation; he published *A Complete Key to the Tale of a Tub,* 1710.

MY LORD,

Though the author has written a large Dedication, yet that being addressed to a prince, whom I am never likely to have the honor of being known to; a person besides, as far as I can observe, not at all regarded, or thought on by any of our present writers; and being wholly free from that slavery which booksellers usually lie under, to the caprices of authors; I think it a wise piece of presumption to inscribe these papers to your lordship, and to implore your lordship's protection of them. God and your lordship know their faults and their merits; for, as to my own particular, I am altogether a stranger to the matter; and though everybody else should be equally ignorant, I do not fear the sale of the book, at all the worse, upon that score. Your lordship's name on the front in capital letters will at any time get off one edition: neither would I desire any other help to grow an alderman, than a patent for the sole privilege of dedicating to your lordship.

I should now, in right of a dedicator, give your lordship a list of your own virtues, and, at the same time, be very unwilling to offend your modesty; but chiefly I should celebrate your liberality towards men of great parts and small fortunes, and give you broad hints that I mean myself. And I was just going on, in the usual method, to peruse a hundred or two of dedications, and transcribe an abstract, to be applied to your lordship; but I was diverted by a certain accident. For, upon the covers of these papers, I casually observed written in large letters the two following words, DETUR DIGNISSIMO; which, for aught I knew, might contain some important meaning. But it unluckily fell out, that none of the authors I employ understood Latin (though I have them often in pay to translate out of that language); I was therefore compelled to have recourse to the curate of our parish, who Englished it thus, *Let it be given to the worthiest:* and his comment was, that the author meant his work should be dedicated to the sublimest genius of the age for wit, learning, judgment, eloquence, and wisdom. I called at a poet's chamber (who

---

[1] John, Lord Somers (1651–1716), one of the Whig lords brought up for impeachment in 1710 by the newly formed Tory ministry. By his *Contests and Dissensions*, in their defense, and by his "Dedication" Swift made a strong bid for Whig support.

works for my shop) in an alley hard by, showed him the translation, and desired his opinion, who it was that the author could mean; he told me, after some consideration, that vanity was a thing he abhorred; but by the description, he thought himself to be the person aimed at; and, at the same time, he very kindly offered his own assistance *gratis* towards penning a dedication to himself. I desired him, however, to give a second guess; why, then, said he, it must be I, or my Lord Somers. From thence I went to several other wits of my acquaintance, with no small hazard and weariness to my person, from a prodigious number of dark, winding stairs; but found them all in the same story, both of your lordship and themselves. Now, your lordship is to understand, that this proceeding was not of my own invention; for I have somewhere heard, it is a maxim, that those to whom everybody allows the second place, have an undoubted title to the first.

This infallibly convinced me, that your lordship was the person intended by the author. But, being very unacquainted in the style and form of dedications, I employed those wits aforesaid to furnish me with hints and materials, towards a panegyric upon your lordship's virtues.

In two days they brought me ten sheets of paper, filled up on every side. They swore to me, that they had ransacked whatever could be found in the characters of Socrates, Aristides, Epaminondas, Cato, Tully, Atticus, and other hard names, which I cannot now recollect. However, I have reason to believe, they imposed upon my ignorance, because, when I came to read over their collections, there was not a syllable there, but what I and everybody else knew as well as themselves: therefore I grievously suspect a cheat; and that these authors of mine stole and transcribed every word, from the universal report of mankind. So that I look upon myself as fifty shillings out of pocket, to no manner of purpose.

If, by altering the title, I could make the same materials serve for another Dedication (as my betters have done) it would help to make up my loss; but I have made several persons dip here and there in those papers, and before they read three lines, they have all assured me plainly, that they cannot possibly be applied to any persons besides your lordship.

I expected, indeed, to have heard of your lordship's bravery at the head of an army; of your undaunted courage in mounting a breach, or scaling a wall; or to have had your pedigree traced in a lineal descent from the house of Austria; or of your wonderful talent at dress and dancing; or your profound knowledge in algebra, metaphysics, and the oriental tongues. But to ply the world with an old beaten story of your wit, and eloquence, and learning, and wisdom, and justice, and politeness, and candor, and evenness of temper in all scenes of life; of that great discernment in discovering, and readiness in favouring deserving men; with forty other common topics; I confess, I have neither conscience nor countenance to do it. Because there is no virtue, either of a public or private life, which some circumstances of your own have not often produced upon the stage of the world; and those few, which for want of occasions to exert them, might otherwise have passed unseen or unobserved by your friends, your enemies have at length brought to light.

'Tis true, I should be very loth, the bright example of your lordship's virtues should be lost to after-ages, both for their sake and your own; but chiefly because they will be so very necessary to adorn the history of a late reign; and that is another reason why I would forbear to make a recital of them here; because I have been told by wise men, that as dedications have run for some years past, a good historian will not be apt to have recourse thither in search of characters.

There is one point, wherein I think we dedicators would do well to change our measures; I mean, instead of running on so far upon the praise of our patrons' liberality, to spend a word or two in admiring their patience. I can put no greater compliment on your lordship's, than by giving you so ample an occasion to exercise it at present. Though perhaps I shall not be apt to reckon much merit to your lordship upon that score, who having been formerly used to tedious harangues, and sometimes to as little purpose, will be the readier to pardon this, especially, when it is offered by one, who is with all respect and veneration,

> My Lord,
>> Your lordship's most obedient,
>> and most faithful servant,
>>> THE BOOKSELLER.

THE
BOOKSELLER
TO THE
READER.

It is now six years since these papers came first to my hand, which seems to have been about a twelvemonth after they were writ; for the author tells us in his preface to the first treatise, that he hath calculated it for the year 1697, and in several passages of that Discourse, as well as the second, it appears they were written about that time.

As to the author, I can give no manner of satisfaction; however, I am credibly informed that this publication is without his knowledge; for he concludes the copy is lost, having lent it to a person, since dead, and being never in possession of it after: so that, whether the work received his last hand, or whether he intended to fill up the defective places, is like to remain a secret.

If I should go about to tell the reader, by what accident I became master of these papers, it would, in this unbelieving age, pass for little more than the cant or jargon of the trade. I therefore gladly spare both him and myself so unnecessary a trouble. There yet remains a difficult question, why I published them no sooner. I forbore upon two accounts: first, because I thought I had better work upon my hands; and secondly, because I was not without some hope of hearing from the author, and receiving his directions. But I have been lately alarmed with intelligence of a surreptitious copy, which a certain great wit had new polished and refined, or, as our present writers express themselves, *fitted to the humor of the age;* as they have already done, with great felicity, to Don Quixote, Boccalini, La Bruyère, and other authors. However, I thought it fairer dealing to offer the whole work in its naturals. If any gentleman will please to furnish me with a key, in order to explain the more difficult parts, I shall very gratefully acknowledge the favour, and print it by itself.

THE EPISTLE DEDICATORY
TO
HIS ROYAL HIGHNESS
PRINCE POSTERITY.*

Sir,

I here present your highness with the fruits of a very few leisure hours, stolen from the short intervals of a world of business, and of an employment quite alien from such amusements as this, the poor production of that refuse of time which has lain heavy upon my hands, during a long prorogation of parliament, a great dearth of foreign news, and a tedious fit of rainy weather; for which, and other reasons, it cannot choose extremely to deserve such a patronage as that of your highness, whose numberless virtues in so few years, make the world look upon you as the future example to all princes, for although your highness is hardly got clear of infancy, yet has the universal learned world already resolved upon appealing to your future dictates with the lowest and most resigned submission; fate having decreed you sole arbiter of the productions of human wit, in this polite and most accomplished age. Methinks, the number of appellants were enough to shock and startle any judge of a genius less unlimited than yours: but in order to prevent such glorious trials, the person (it seems) to whose care the education of your highness is committed, has resolved (as I am told) to keep you in almost an universal ignorance of our studies, which it is your inherent birth-right to inspect.

It is amazing to me, that this person should have assurance in the face of the sun, to go about persuading your highness, that our age is almost wholly illiterate, and has hardly produced one writer upon any subject. I know very well, that when your highness shall come to riper years, and have gone through the learning of antiquity, you will be too curious to neglect inquiring into the authors of the very age before you: and to think that this insolent, in the account he is preparing for your view, designs to reduce them to a number so insignificant as I am ashamed to mention; it moves my zeal and

---

* The Citation out of Irenæus in the title-page, which seems to be all gibberish, is a form of initiation used anciently by the Marcosian Heretics. W. Wotton.

It is the usual style of decried writers to appeal to Posterity, who is here represented as a prince in his nonage, and Time as his governor, and the author begins in a way very frequent with him, by personating other writers, who sometimes offer such reasons and excuses for publishing their works as they ought chiefly to conceal and be ashamed of.

my spleen for the honor and interest of our vast flourishing body, as well as of myself, for whom I know by long experience, he has professed, and still continues a peculiar malice.

'Tis not unlikely, that when your highness will one day peruse what I am now writing, you may be ready to expostulate with your governor upon the credit of what I here affirm, and command him to show you some of our productions. To which he will answer (for I am well informed of his designs) by asking your highness, where they are? and what is become of them? and pretend it a demonstration that there never were any, because they are not then to be found. Not to be found! Who has mislaid them? Are they sunk in the abyss of things? 'Tis certain, that in their own nature they were light enough to swim upon the surface for all eternity. Therefore the fault is in him, who tied weights so heavy to their heels, as to depress them to the center. Is their very essence destroyed? Who has annihilated them? Were they drowned by purges or martyred by pipes? Who administered them to the posteriors of ———? But that it may no longer be a doubt with your highness, who is to be the author of this universal ruin, I beseech you to observe that large and terrible scythe which your governor affects to bear continually about him. Be pleased to remark the length and strength, the sharpness and hardness of his nails and teeth: consider his baneful, abominable breath, enemy to life and matter, infectious and corrupting: and then reflect whether it be possible for any mortal ink and paper of this generation to make a suitable resistance. Oh, that your highness would one day resolve to disarm this usurping *maître du palais* * of his furious engines, and to bring your empire *hors de page*.†

It were endless to recount the several methods of tyranny and destruction, which your governor is pleased to practise upon this occasion. His inveterate malice is such to the writings of our age, that of several thousands produced yearly from this renowned city, before the next revolution of the sun, there is not one to be heard of: unhappy infants, many of them barbarously destroyed, before they have so much as learnt their mother-tongue to beg for pity. Some he stifles in their cradles, others he frights into convulsions, whereof they suddenly die; some he flays alive, others he tears limb from limb. Great numbers are offered to Moloch, and the rest, tainted by his breath, die of a languishing consumption.

* Comptroller.
† Out of guardianship.

But the concern I have most at heart, is for our corporation of poets, from whom I am preparing a petition to your highness, to be subscribed with the names of one hundred thirty-six of the first rate; but whose immortal productions are never likely to reach your eyes, though each of them is now an humble and an earnest appellant for the laurel, and his large comely volumes ready to show for a support to his pretensions. The never-dying works of these illustrious persons, your governor, sir, has devoted to unavoidable death, and your highness is to be made believe, that our age has never arrived at the honor to produce one single poet.

We confess *Immortality* to be a great and powerful goddess; but in vain we offer up to her our devotions and our sacrifices, if your highness's governor, who has usurped the priesthood, must by an unparalleled ambition and avarice, wholly intercept and devour them.

To affirm that our age is altogether unlearned, and devoid of writers in any kind, seems to be an assertion so bold and so false, that I have been some time thinking, the contrary may almost be proved by uncontrollable demonstration. 'Tis true indeed, that although their numbers be vast, and their productions numerous in proportion, yet are they hurried so hastily off the scene, that they escape our memory, and delude our sight. When I first thought of this address, I had prepared a copious list of titles to present your highness as an undisputed argument for what I affirm. The originals were posted fresh upon all gates and corners of streets; but returning in a very few hours to take a review, they were all torn down, and fresh ones in their places. I inquired after them among readers and booksellers, but I inquired in vain; *the memorial of them was lost among men; their place was no more to be found;* and I was laughed to scorn for a clown and a pedant, without all taste and refinement, little versed in the course of present affairs, and that knew nothing of what had passed in the best companies of court and town. So that I can only avow in general to your highness, that we do abound in learning and wit; but to fix upon particulars, is a task too slippery for my slender abilities. If I should venture in a windy day to affirm to your highness, that there is a large cloud near the horizon in the form of a bear, another in the zenith with the head of an ass, a third to the westward with claws like a dragon, and your highness should in a few minutes think fit to examine the truth, 'tis certain they would all be changed in figure and position, new ones would arise, and all we could agree upon would be, that clouds there were, but that I was grossly mistaken in the zoography and topography of them.

But your governor perhaps may still insist, and put the question: what is then become of those immense bales of paper, which must needs have been employed in such numbers of books? Can these also be wholly annihilate, and so of a sudden, as I pretend? What shall I say in return of so invidious an objection? It ill befits the distance between your highness and me, to send you for ocular conviction to a jakes or an oven, to the windows of a bawdy-house, or to a sordid lantern. Books, like men their authors, have no more than one way of coming into the world, but there are ten thousand to go out of it, and return no more.

I profess to your highness, in the integrity of my heart, that what I am going to say is literally true this minute I am writing: what revolutions may happen before it shall be ready for your perusal, I can by no means warrant; however, I beg you to accept it as a specimen of our learning, our politeness, and our wit. I do therefore affirm upon the word of a sincere man, that there is now actually in being a certain poet called John Dryden, whose translation of Virgil was lately printed in a large folio, well bound, and if diligent search were made, for aught I know, is yet to be seen. There is another called Nahum Tate, who is ready to make oath that he has caused many reams of verse to be published, whereof both himself and his bookseller (if lawfully required) can still produce authentic copies, and therefore wonders why the world is pleased to make such a secret of it. There is a third, known by the name of Tom Durfey, a poet of a vast comprehension, an universal genius, and most profound learning. There are also one Mr. Rymer, and one Mr. Dennis, most profound critics. There is a person styled Dr. Bentley, who has written near a thousand pages of immense erudition, giving a full and true account of a certain squabble of wonderful importance between himself and a bookseller: he is a writer of infinite wit and humour; no man rallies with a better grace, and in more sprightly turns. Farther, I avow to your highness, that with these eyes I have beheld the person of William Wotton, B.D., who has written a good sizeable volume against a friend of your governor (from whom, alas! he must therefore look for little favour) in a most gentlemanly style, adorned with utmost politeness and civility; replete with discoveries equally valuable for their

novelty and use; and embellished with traits of wit so poignant
and so apposite, that he is a worthy yokemate to his forementioned friend.

Why should I go upon farther particulars, which might fill
a volume with the just eulogies of my contemporary brethren?
I shall bequeath this piece of justice to a larger work, wherein
I intend to write a character of the present set of wits in our
nation: their persons I shall describe particularly and at
length, their genius and understandings in miniature.

In the meantime, I do here make bold to present your highness with a faithful abstract drawn from the universal body
of all arts and sciences, intended wholly for your service and
instruction. Nor do I doubt in the least, but your highness will
peruse it as carefully, and make as considerable improvements, as other young princes have already done by the many
volumes of late years written for a help to their studies.

That your highness may advance in wisdom and virtue, as
well as years, and at last outshine all your royal ancestors,
shall be the daily prayer of,

  Sir,

   Your Highness's
    Most devoted, &c.

Decemb.
1697.

PREFACE.

THE wits of the present age being so very numerous and penetrating, it seems the grandees of Church and State begin to fall under horrible apprehensions, lest these gentlemen, during the intervals of a long peace, should find leisure to pick holes in the weak sides of Religion and Government. To prevent which, there has been much thought employed of late upon certain projects for taking off the force and edge of those formidable inquirers, from canvassing and reasoning upon such delicate points. They have at length fixed upon one, which will require some time as well as cost to perfect. Meanwhile, the danger hourly increasing, by new levies of wits, all appointed (as there is reason to fear) with pen, ink, and paper, which may at an hour's warning be drawn out into pamphlets, and other offensive weapons, ready for immediate execution, it was judged of absolute necessity, that some present expedient be thought on, till the main design can be brought to maturity. To this end, at a Grand Committee some days ago, this important discovery was made by a certain curious and refined observer: that seamen have a custom when they meet a whale, to fling him out an empty tub by way of amusement, to divert him from laying violent hands upon the ship. This parable was immediately mythologized: the whale was interpreted to be Hobbes's *Leviathan*,[1] which tosses and plays with all other schemes of Religion and Government, whereof a great many are hollow, and dry, and empty, and noisy, and wooden, and given to rotation. This is the *Leviathan* from whence the terrible wits of our age are said to borrow their weapons. The ship in danger is easily understood to be its old anti-type, the Commonwealth. But how to analyze the tub, was a matter of difficulty; when after long enquiry and debate, the literal meaning was preserved; and it was decreed, that in order to prevent these Leviathans from tossing and sporting with the Commonwealth (which of itself is too apt to fluctuate) they should be diverted from that game by a *Tale of a Tub*. And my genius being conceived to lie not unhappily that way, I had the honor done me to be engaged in the performance.

This is the sole design in publishing the following treatise,

[1] Hobbes's *Leviathan* (1651), probably the most controversial work of its time, was a natural target for Swift as a type of Modernity. See p. 372, note 1.

which I hope will serve for an *interim* of some months to employ those unquiet spirits, till the perfecting of that great work, into the secret of which it is reasonable the courteous reader should have some little light.

It is intended that a large Academy be erected, capable of containing nine thousand seven hundred forty and three persons; which by modest computation is reckoned to be pretty near the current number of wits in this island. These are to be disposed into the several schools of this academy, and there pursue those studies to which their genius most inclines them. The undertaker himself will publish his proposals with all convenient speed, to which I shall refer the curious reader for a more particular account, mentioning at present only a few of the principal schools. There is first a large Pæderastic School, with French and Italian masters. There is also the Spelling School, a very spacious building: the School of Looking glasses: the School of Swearing: the School of Critics: the School of Salivation: the School of Hobby-horses: the School of Poetry: the School of Tops: * the School of Spleen: the School of Gaming: with many others too tedious to recount. No person to be admitted member into any of these schools without an attestation under two sufficient persons' hands, certifying him to be a wit.[1]

But, to return, I am sufficiently instructed in the principal duty of a preface, if my genius were capable of arriving at it. Thrice have I forced my imagination to make the tour of my invention, and thrice it has returned empty; the latter having been wholly drained by the following treatise. Not so, my more successful brethren the Moderns, who will by no means let slip a preface or dedication without some notable distinguishing stroke to surprise the reader at the entry, and kindle a wonderful expectation of what is to ensue. Such was that of a most ingenious poet, who soliciting his brain for something new, compared himself to the hangman, and his patron to the patient: this was *insigne, recens, indictum ore alio.***

† *Reading Prefaces, etc.* When I went through that necessary and noble course of study,† I had the happiness to observe many such egregious touches, which I shall not injure the authors by transplanting, because I have remarked, that nothing is so very tender as a modern piece of wit, and

---

* This I think the author should have omitted, it being the very same nature with the School of Hobby-horses, if one may venture to censure one who is so severe a censurer of others, perhaps with too little distinction.

** Horace. Something extraordinary, new and never hit upon before.

[1] Swift's Academy is satirical of the scientific societies projected and set up by the New Science. (For details see Starkman, pp. 64–86.)

which is apt to suffer so much in the carriage. Some things are extremely witty to-day, or fasting, or in this place, or at eight o'clock, or over a bottle, or spoke by Mr. What d'y'call'm, or in a summer's morning: any of which, by the smallest transposal or misapplication, is utterly annihilate. Thus, wit has its walks and purlieus, out of which it may not stray the breadth of an hair, upon peril of being lost. The Moderns have artfully fixed this mercury, and reduced it to the circumstances of time, place, and person. Such a jest there is, that will not pass out of Covent-Garden; and such a one, that is nowhere intelligible but at Hyde-Park Corner. Now, though it sometimes tenderly affects me to consider, that all the towardly passages I shall deliver in the following treatise, will grow quite out of date and relish with the first shifting of the present scene, yet I must need subscribe to the justice of this proceeding: because, I cannot imagine why we should be at expense to furnish wit for succeeding ages, when the former have made no sort of provision for ours; wherein I speak the sentiment of the very newest, and consequently the most orthodox refiners, as well as my own. However, being extremely solicitous, that every accomplished person who has got into the taste of wit calculated for this present month of August, 1697, should descend to the very bottom of all the sublime [1] throughout this treatise, I hold fit to lay down this general maxim: whatever reader desires to have a thorough comprehension of an author's thoughts, cannot take a better method, than by putting himself into the circumstances and postures of life, that the writer was in upon every important passage as it flowed from his pen; for this will introduce a parity and strict correspondence of ideas between the reader and the author. Now, to assist the diligent reader in so delicate an affair, as far as brevity will permit, I have recollected, that the shrewdest pieces of this treatise were conceived in bed in a garret; at other times (for a reason best known to myself) I thought fit to sharpen my invention with hunger; and in general, the whole work was begun, continued, and ended, under a long course of physic, and a great want of money. Now, I do affirm, it will be absolutely impossible for the candid peruser to go along with me in a great many bright passages, unless upon the several difficulties emergent, he will please to capacitate and prepare himself by these directions. And this I lay down as my principal *postulatum*.

---

[1] Swift alludes to Longinus *On the Sublime;* Longinus's equation of art with rapture would naturally strike Swift as Enthusiastic.

Because I have professed to be a most devoted servant of all Modern forms, I apprehend some curious wit may object against me, for proceeding thus far in a preface, without declaiming, according to the custom, against the multitude of writers, whereof the whole multitude of writers most reasonably complains. I am just come from perusing some hundreds of prefaces, wherein the authors do at the very beginning address the gentle reader concerning this enormous grievance. Of these I have preserved a few examples, and shall set them down as near as my memory has been able to retain them.

One begins thus:

For a man to set up for a writer, when the press swarms with, &c.

Another:

The tax upon paper does not lessen the number of scribblers, who daily pester, &c.

Another:

When every little would-be-wit takes pen in hand, 'tis in vain to enter the lists, &c.

Another:

To observe what trash the press swarms with, &c.

Another:

Sir, *It is merely in obedience to your commands that I venture into the public; for who upon a less consideration would be of a party with such a rabble of scribblers,* &c.

Now, I have two words in my own defence against this objection. First, I am far from granting the number of writers a nuisance to our nation, having strenuously maintained the contrary in several parts of the following discourse. Secondly, I do not well understand the justice of this proceeding because I observe many of these polite prefaces to be not only from the same hand, but from those who are most voluminous in their several productions. Upon which I shall tell the reader a short tale.

A mountebank in Leicester-fields had drawn a huge assembly about him. Among the rest, a fat unwieldy fellow, half stifled in the press, would be every fit crying out, Lord! what a filthy crowd is here, pray, good people, give way a little. Bless me! what a devil has raked this rabble together; z—ds! what squeezing is this! honest friend, remove your elbow. At last a weaver that stood next him, could hold no longer. A plague confound you (said he) for an overgrown sloven; and who (in the devil's name) I wonder, helps to make up the crowd half so much as yourself? Don't you consider (with a pox) that you take up more room with that carcass than any five here? Is not the place as free for us as for you? Bring your own guts to a reasonable compass (and be d—n'd) and then I'll engage we shall have room enough for us all.

There are certain common privileges of a writer, the benefit whereof, I hope, there will be no reason to doubt; particularly, that where I am not understood, it shall be concluded, that something very useful and profound is couched underneath; and again, that whatever word or sentence is printed in a different character, shall be judged to contain something extraordinary either of wit or sublime.

As for the liberty I have thought fit to take of praising myself, upon some occasions or none, I am sure it will need no excuse, if a multitude of great examples be allowed sufficient authority. For it is here to be noted, that praise was originally a pension paid by the world; but the Moderns finding the trouble and charge too great in collecting it, have lately bought out the fee-simple; since which time, the right of presentation is wholly in ourselves. For this reason it is, that when an author makes his own eulogy, he uses a certain form to declare and insist upon his title, which is commonly in these or the like words, 'I speak without vanity'; which I think plainly shows it to be a matter of right and justice. Now, I do here once for all declare, that in every encounter of this nature through the following treatise, the form aforesaid is implied; which I mention, to save the trouble of repeating it on so many occasions.

'Tis a great ease to my conscience that I have writ so elaborate and useful a discourse without one grain of satire intermixed; which is the sole point wherein I have taken leave to dissent from the famous originals of our age and country. I have observed some satirists to use the public much at the rate that pedants do a naughty boy ready horsed for discipline: first expostulate the case, then plead the necessity of the rod from great provocations, and conclude every period with a lash. Now, if I know anything of mankind, these gentlemen might very well spare their reproof and correction: for there is not, through all nature, another so callous and insensible a member as the world's posteriors, whether you apply to it the toe or the birch. Besides, most of our late satirists seem to lie under a sort of mistake, that because nettles have the prerogative to sting, therefore all other weeds must do so too. I make not this comparison out of the least design to detract from these worthy writers, for it is well known among mythologists, that weeds have the preeminence over all other vegetables; and therefore the first monarch of this island, whose taste and judgment were so acute and refined, did very wisely root out the roses from the collar of the Order, and plant the thistles in their stead as the nobler flower of the two. For which reason it is conjectured by profounder antiquaries, that the satirical itch, so prevalent in this part of our island, was first brought among us from beyond the Tweed. Here may it long flourish and abound; may it survive and neglect the scorn of the world, with as much ease and contempt, as the world is insensible to the lashes of it. May their own dullness, or that of their party, be no discouragement for the authors to proceed; but let them remember, it is with wits as with razors, which are never so apt to cut those they are employed on, as when they have lost their edge. Besides, those whose teeth are too rotten to bite are best of all others qualified to revenge that defect with their breath.

I am not like other men, to envy or undervalue the talents I cannot reach; for which reason I must needs bear a true honour to this large eminent sect of our British writers. And I hope this little panegyric will not be offensive to their ears, since it has the advantage of being only designed for themselves. Indeed, nature herself has taken order, that fame and honour should be purchased at a better pennyworth by satire, than by any other productions of the brain; the world being soonest provoked to praise by lashes, as men are to love. There is a problem in an ancient author, why dedications, and other bundles of flattery run all upon stale, musty topics, without the smallest tincture of anything new; not only to the torment and nauseating of the Christian reader, but (if not suddenly prevented) to the universal spreading of that pestilent disease, the lethargy, in this island: whereas there is very little satire which has not something in it untouched before. The defects of the former are usually imputed to the want of invention among those who are dealers in that kind; but, I think, with a great deal of injustice; the solution being easy and natural. For the materials of panegyric being very few in number, have been long since exhausted. For, as health is but one thing, and has been always the same, whereas diseases are by thousands, besides new and daily additions; so, all the virtues that have been ever in mankind, are to be counted upon a few fingers, but his follies and vices are innumerable,

and time adds hourly to the heap. Now, the utmost a poor poet can do, is to get by heart a list of the cardinal virtues, and deal them with his utmost liberality to his hero or his patron: he may ring the changes as far as it will go, and vary his phrase till he has talked round; but the reader quickly finds it is all pork,* with a little variety of sauce.   * *Plutarch*
For there is no inventing terms of art beyond our ideas; and when ideas are exhausted, terms of art must be so too.

But though the matter for panegyric were as fruitful as the topics of satire, yet would it not be hard to find out a sufficient reason why the latter will be always better received than the first. For, this being bestowed only upon one or a few persons at a time, is sure to raise envy, and consequently ill words from the rest, who have no share in the blessing; but satire being levelled at all, is never resented for an offence by any, since every individual person makes bold to understand it of others, and very wisely removes his particular part of the burden upon the shoulders of the world, which are broad enough, and able to bear it. To this purpose, I have sometimes reflected upon the difference between Athens and England, with respect to the point before us. In the Attic common-wealth,† it was the privilege and birthright of   † Vide
every citizen and poet to rail aloud and in public,   *Xenophon*
or to expose upon the stage by name, any person they pleased, though of the greatest figure, whether a Creon, an Hyperbolus, an Alcibiades, or a Demosthenes: but on the other side, the least reflecting word let fall against the people in general, was immediately caught up, and revenged upon the authors, however considerable for their quality or their merits. Whereas in England it is just the reverse of all this. Here, you may securely display your utmost rhetoric against mankind, in the face of the world; tell them, 'That all are gone astray: that there is none that doth good, no not one; that we live in the very dregs of time; that knavery and atheism are epidemic as the pox; that honesty is fled with Astræa'; with any other commonplaces equally new and eloquent, which are furnished by the *splendida bilis*.** And when you have ** *Horace*
done, the whole audience, far from being offended, shall return you thanks as a deliverer of precious and useful truths. Nay farther; it is but to venture your lungs, and you may preach in Covent-Garden against foppery and fornication, and something else: against pride, and dissimulation, and bribery, at Whitehall: you may expose rapine and injustice in the Inns of Court Chapel: and in a city pulpit be as fierce

as you please against avarice, hypocrisy, and extortion. 'Tis but a ball bandied to and fro, and every man carries a racket about him to strike it from himself among the rest of the company. But on the other side, whoever should mistake the nature of things so far, as to drop but a single hint in public, how such a one starved half the fleet, and half-poisoned the rest: how such a one, from a true principle of love and honour, pays no debts but for wenches and play: how such a one has got a clap and runs out of his estate: how Paris bribed by Juno and Venus,* loth to offend either party, slept out the whole cause on the bench: or how such an orator makes long speeches in the senate with much thought, little sense, and to no purpose; whoever, I say, should venture to be thus particular, must expect to be imprisoned for *scandalum magnatum;* to have challenges sent him; to be sued for defamation; and to be brought before the bar of the house.

But I forget that I am expatiating on a subject wherein I have no concern, having neither a talent nor an inclination for satire. On the other side, I am so entirely satisfied with the whole present procedure of human things, that I have been for some years preparing materials towards *A Panegyric upon the World;* to which I intended to add a second part, entitled, *A modest Defence of the Proceedings of the Rabble in all Ages.* Both these I had thoughts to publish by way of appendix to the following treatise; but finding my common-place book fill much slower than I had reason to expect, I have chosen to defer them to another occasion. Besides, I have been unhappily prevented in that design by a certain domestic misfortune, in the particulars whereof, though it would be very seasonable, and much in the Modern way, to inform the gentle reader, and would also be of great assistance towards extending this preface into the size now in vogue, which by rule ought to be large in proportion as the subsequent volume is small; yet I shall now dismiss our impatient reader from any farther attendance at the porch, and having duly prepared his mind by a preliminary discourse, shall gladly introduce him to the sublime mysteries that ensue.

---

* Juno and Venus are money and a mistress, very powerful bribes to a judge, if scandal says true. I remember such reflections were cast about that time, but I cannot fix the person intended here.

A TALE
OF A
TUB, &c.

SECTION I.

THE INTRODUCTION.

WHOEVER hath an ambition to be heard in a crowd, must press, and squeeze, and thrust, and climb with indefatigable pains, till he has exalted himself to a certain degree of altitude above them. Now, in all assemblies, though you wedge them ever so close, we may observe this peculiar property, that over their heads there is room enough, but how to reach it is the difficult point; it being as hard to get quit of number, as of hell.

> ———Evadere ad auras,
> Hoc opus, hic labor est.*

To this end, the philosopher's way in all ages has been by erecting certain edifices in the air: but, whatever practice and reputation these kind of structures have formerly possessed, or may still continue in, not excepting even that of Socrates, when he was suspended in a basket to help contemplation, I think, with due submission, they seem to labour under two inconveniences. First, that the foundations being laid too high, they have been often out of sight, and ever out of hearing. Secondly, that the materials, being very transitory, have suffered much from inclemencies of air, especially in these north-west regions.[1]

Therefore, towards the just performance of this great work, there remain but three methods that I can think on; whereof the wisdom of our ancestors being highly sensible, has, to encourage all aspiring adventurers, thought fit to erect three wooden machines for the use of those orators who desire to talk much without interruption. These are, the pulpit, the lad-

---

* But to return, and view the cheerful skies,
  In this the task and mighty labour lies.

[1] Swift refers to an episode in Aristophanes's *Clouds*. But the passage in general expresses Swift's profound mistrust of speculative philosophy.

der, and the stage-itinerant. For, as to the bar, though it be compounded of the same matter, and designed for the same use, it cannot however be well allowed the honor of a fourth, by reason of its level or inferior situation exposing it to perpetual interruption from collaterals. Neither can the bench itself, though raised to a proper eminency, put in a better claim, whatever its advocates insist on. For if they please to look into the original design of its erection, and the circumstances or adjuncts subservient to that design, they will soon acknowledge the present practice exactly correspondent to the primitive institution, and both to answer the etymology of the name, which in the Phœnician tongue is a word of great signification, importing, if literally interpreted, the place of sleep; but in common acceptation, a seat well bolstered and cushioned, for the repose of old and gouty limbs: *senes ut in otia tuta recedant.* Fortune being indebted to them this part of retaliation, that, as formerly they have long talked whilst others slept, so now they may sleep as long whilst others talk.

But if no other argument could occur to exclude the Bench and the Bar from the list of oratorial machines, it were sufficient that the admission of them would overthrow a number which I was resolved to establish, whatever argument it might cost me; in imitation of that prudent method observed by many other philosophers and great clerks, whose chief art in division has been to grow fond of some proper mystical number, which their imaginations have rendered sacred, to a degree, that they force common reason to find room for it in every part of nature; reducing, including, and adjusting every genus and species within that compass, by coupling some against their wills, and banishing others at any rate. Now among all the rest, the profound number THREE is that which hath most employed my sublimest speculations, nor ever without wonderful delight. There is now in the press (and will be published next term) a panegyrical essay of mine upon this number, wherein I have by most convincing proofs not only reduced the senses and the elements under its banner, but brought over several deserters from its two great rivals, SEVEN and NINE.

Now, the first of these oratorial machines in place as well as dignity, is the pulpit. Of pulpits there are in this island several sorts; but I esteem only that made of timber from the *sylva Caledonia,* which agrees very well with our climate. If it be upon its decay, 'tis the better both for conveyance of sound, and for other reasons to be mentioned by and by. The degree of perfection in shape and size, I take to consist in being extremely narrow, with little ornament, and best of all without a cover; (for by ancient rule, it ought to be the only uncovered vessel in every assembly where it is rightfully used) by which means, from its near resemblance to a pillory, it will ever have a mighty influence on human ears.

Of ladders I need say nothing: 'tis observed by foreigners themselves, to the honor of our country, that we excel all nations in our practice and understanding of this machine. The ascending orators do not only oblige their audience in the agreeable delivery, but the whole world in their early publication of these speeches; [1] which I look upon as the choicest treasury of our British eloquence, and whereof I am informed that worthy citizen and bookseller, Mr. John Dunton,[2] hath made a faithful and a painful collection, which he shortly designs to publish in twelve volumes in folio, illustrated with copper-plates. A work highly useful and curious, and altogether worthy of such a hand.

The last engine of orators is the stage itinerant * [3] erected with much sagacity, *sub Jove pluvio, in triviis & quadriviis.*† It is the great seminary of the two former, and its orators are sometimes preferred to the one, and sometimes to the other, in proportion to their deservings, there being a strict and perpetual intercourse between all three.

From this accurate deduction it is manifest, that for obtaining attention in public, there is of necessity required a superior position of place. But although this point be generally granted, yet the cause is little agreed in; and it seems to me, that very few philosophers have fallen into a true, natural solution of this phenomenon. The deepest account, and the most fairly digested of any I have yet met with, is this, that air being a heavy body, and therefore (according to the system of Epicurus ‡) continually descending must ‡ *Lucretius,* needs be more so, when loaden and pressed *Lib. 2.* down by words; which are also bodies of much weight and gravity, as it is manifest from those deep impressions they make and leave upon us; and therefore must be delivered from

---

* Is the mountebank's stage, whose orators the author determines either to the gallows or a conventicle.

† In the open air, and in streets where the greatest resort is.

[1] Condemned criminals were allowed to speak from the gallows before they were hanged; some of their speeches were published for their sensational appeal.

[2] John Dunton was a popular journalist and publisher, who becomes for Swift a type of the Grub Street hack.

[3] The identification of the "stage itinerant" is doubtful; some critics have interpreted it as Grub Street, which stands as one with the hacks who inhabited it.

a due altitude, or else they will neither carry a good aim, nor
fall down with a sufficient force.

Corpoream quoque enim vocem constare fatendum est,
Et sonitum, quoniam possunt impellere sensus.*

Lucr. Lib. 4.

And I am the readier to favour this conjecture, from a common observation, that in the several assemblies of these orators, nature itself hath instructed the hearers to stand with
their mouths open, and erected parallel to the horizon, so as
they may be intersected by a perpendicular line from the zenith
to the center of the earth. In which position, if the audience be
well compact, every one carries home a share, and little or
nothing is lost.

I confess there is something yet more refined in the contrivance and structure of our modern theatres. For, first, the
pit is sunk below the stage with due regard to the institution
above deduced; that whatever weighty matter shall be delivered thence (whether it be lead or gold) may fall plumb into
the jaws of certain critics (as I think they are called) which
stand ready open to devour them. Then, the boxes are built
round, and raised to a level with the scene, in deference to
the ladies, because, that large portion of wit laid out in raising
pruriences and protuberances, is observed to run much upon a
line, and ever in a circle. The whining passions, and little
starved conceits, are gently wafted up by their own extreme
levity, to the middle region, and there fix and are frozen by the
frigid understandings of the inhabitants. Bombastry and buf-
foonery, by nature lofty and light, soar highest of all, and
would be lost in the roof, if the prudent architect had not
with much foresight contrived for them a fourth place, called
the twelve-penny gallery, and there planted a suitable colony,
who greedily intercept them in their passage.

Now this physico-logical scheme of oratorial receptacles or
machines, contains a great mystery, being a type, a sign, an
emblem, a shadow, a symbol, bearing analogy to the spacious
commonwealth of writers, and to those methods by which they
must exalt themselves to a certain eminency above the inferior
world. By the pulpit are adumbrated the writings of our Modern saints in Great Britain, as they have spiritualized and refined them from the dross and grossness of sense and human
reason. The matter, as we have said, is of rotten wood, and
that upon two considerations: because it is the quality of rotten

---

* 'Tis certain then, that voice that thus can wound
  Is all material; body every sound.

wood to give light in the dark; and secondly, because its cavities are full of worms; which is a type with a pair of handles,* having a respect to the two principal qualifications of the orator, and the two different fates attending upon his works.

The ladder is an adequate symbol of faction and of poetry, to both of which so noble a number of authors are indebted for their fame. Of faction, because †   *   *   *Hiatus in MS.
*   *   *   *   *   *   *   *   *   *
*   *   *   *   *   *   *   *   *   *
*   *   *   *   * Of poetry, because its orators do *perorare* with a song; and because climbing up by slow degrees, fate is sure to turn them off before they can reach within many steps of the top: and because it is a preferment attained by transferring of propriety, and a confounding of *meum* and *tuum.*

Under the stage-itinerant are couched those productions designed for the pleasure and delight of mortal man; such as Six-penny-worth of Wit, Westminster Drolleries, Delightful Tales, Compleat Jesters, and the like; by which the writers of and for *Grub Street,* have in these latter ages so nobly triumphed over Time; have clipped his wings, pared his nails, filed his teeth, turned back his hour-glass, blunted his scythe, and drawn the hob-nails out of his shoes. It is under this classis I have presumed to list my present treatise, being just come from having the honor conferred upon me to be adopted a member of that illustrious fraternity.

Now, I am not unaware, how the productions of the Grub Street brotherhood, have of late years fallen under many prejudices, nor how it has been the perpetual employment of two junior start-up societies to ridicule them and their authors, as unworthy their established post in the commonwealth of wit and learning. Their own consciences will easily inform them, whom I mean; nor has the world been so negligent a looker-on, as not to observe the continual efforts made by the societies of Gresham, and of Will's,‡ to edify a name and repu-

---

* The two principal qualifications of a fanatic preacher are, his inward light, and his head full of maggots, and the two different fates of his writings are, to be burnt or worm-eaten.

† Here is pretended a defect in the manuscript, and this is very frequent with our author, either when he thinks he cannot say anything worth reading, or when he has no mind to enter on the subject, or when it is a matter of little moment, or perhaps to amuse his reader (whereof he is frequently very fond) or lastly, with some satirical intention.

‡ Will's coffee-house was formerly the place where the poets usually met, which tho' it be yet fresh in memory, yet in some years may be forgot, and want this explanation.

tation upon the ruin of OURS. And this is yet a more feeling grief to us upon the regards of tenderness as well as of justice, when we reflect on their proceedings not only as unjust, but as ungrateful, undutiful, and unnatural. For how can it be forgot by the world or themselves (to say nothing of our own records, which are full and clear in the point) that they both are seminaries not only of our planting, but our watering too? I am informed, our two rivals have lately made an offer to enter into the lists with united forces, and challenge us to a comparison of books, both as to weight and number. In return to which (with licence from our president) I humbly offer two answers: first, we say, the proposal is like that which Archimedes made upon a smaller affair,* including an impossibility in the practice; for where can they find scales of capacity enough for the first, or an arithmetician of capacity enough for the second? Secondly, we are ready to accept the challenge, but with this condition, that a third indifferent person be assigned, to whose impartial judgment it shall be left to decide, which society each book, treatise, or pamphlet, do most properly belong to. This point, God knows, is very far from being fixed at present; for we are ready to produce a catalogue of some thousands, which in all common justice ought to be entitled to our fraternity, but by the revolted and new-fangled writers, most perfidiously ascribed to the others. Upon all which, we think it very unbecoming our prudence, that the determination should be remitted to the authors themselves; when our adversaries, by briguing and caballing, have caused so universal a defection from us, that the greatest part of our society hath already deserted to them, and our nearest friends begin to stand aloof, as if they were half-ashamed to own us.

> * Viz. *About moving the earth*

This is the utmost I am authorized to say upon so ungrateful and melancholy a subject; because we are extreme unwilling to inflame a controversy, whose continuance may be so fatal to the interests of us all, desiring much rather that things be amicably composed; and we shall so far advance on our side, as to be ready to receive the two prodigals with open arms, whenever they shall think fit to return from their husks and their harlots; which I think from the present course of their studies † they most properly may be said to be engaged in; and like an indulgent parent, continue to them our affection and our blessing.

> † *Virtuoso experiments, and modern comedies*

But the greatest maim given to that general

reception, which the writings of our society have formerly received (next to the transitory state of all sublunary things) hath been a superficial vein among many readers of the present age, who will by no means be persuaded to inspect beyond the surface and the rind of things; whereas wisdom is a fox, who after long hunting will at last cost you the pains to dig out. 'Tis a cheese, which by how much the richer, has the thicker, the homelier, and the coarser coat; and whereof to a judicious palate, the maggots are the best. 'Tis a sack-posset, wherein the deeper you go, you will find it the sweeter. Wisdom is a hen, whose cackling we must value and consider, because it is attended with an egg. But then lastly, 'tis a nut, which unless you choose with judgment, may cost you a tooth, and pay you with nothing but a worm. In consequence of these momentous truths, the Grubæan Sages have always chosen to convey their precepts and their arts, shut up within the vehicles of types and fables, which having been perhaps more careful and curious in adorning, than was altogether necessary, it has fared with these vehicles after the usual fate of coaches over-finely painted and gilt, that the transitory gazers have so dazzled their eyes, and filled their imaginations with the outward lustre, as neither to regard or consider the person or the parts of the owner within. A misfortune we undergo with somewhat less reluctancy, because it has been common to us with Pythagoras, Æsop, Socrates, and other of our predecessors.

However, that neither the world nor our selves, may any longer suffer by such misunderstandings, I have been prevailed on, after much importunity from my friends, to travel in a complete and laborious dissertation upon the prime productions of our society, which, beside their beautiful externals, for the gratification of superficial readers, have darkly and deeply couched under them the most finished and refined systems of all sciences and arts; as I do not doubt to lay open by untwisting or unwinding, and either to draw up by exantlation, or display by incision.

This great work was entered upon some years ago, by one of our most eminent members: he began with the *History of Reynard the Fox*,* but neither lived to publish his essay, nor to proceed farther in so useful an attempt, which is very much to be lamented, because the discovery he made, and commu-

---

* The Author seems here to be mistaken, for I have seen a Latin edition of *Reynard the Fox*, above an hundred years old, which I take to be the original; for the rest it has been thought by many people to contain some satirical design in it.

nicated with his friends, is now universally received; nor do I think any of the learned will dispute that famous treatise to be a complete body of civil knowledge, and the revelation, or rather the apocalypse of all State Arcana. But the progress I have made is much greater, having already finished my annotations upon several dozens; from some of which I shall impart a few hints to the candid reader, as far as will be necessary to the conclusion at which I aim.

[1] The first piece I have handled is that of *Tom Thumb,* whose author was a Pythagorean philosopher. This dark treatise contains the whole scheme of the Metempsychosis, deducing the progress of the soul through all her stages.

The next is *Dr. Faustus,* penned by Artephius, an author *bonæ notæ,* and an *adeptus;* he published it in the nine hundred-eighty-fourth year of his age; * this writer proceeds wholly by reincrudation, or in the *via humida;* and the marriage between Faustus and Helen does most conspicuously dilucidate the fermenting of the male and female dragon.

* He lived a thousand.

Whittington and his Cat is the work of that mysterious rabbi, Jehuda Hannasi, containing a defence of the Gemara of the Jerusalem Mishna, and its just preference to that of Babylon, contrary to the vulgar opinion.

The Hind and Panther. This is the masterpiece of a famous writer now living,† intended for a complete abstract of sixteen thousand schoolmen from Scotus to Bellarmine.

† Viz. in the year 1698.

Tommy Potts. Another piece supposed by the same hand, by way of supplement to the former.

The Wise Men of Gotham, cum appendice. This is a treatise of immense erudition, being the great original and fountain of those arguments, bandied about both in France and England, for a just defence of the Modern learning and wit, against the presumption, the pride, and the ignorance of the Ancients. This unknown author hath so exhausted the subject, that a penetrating reader will easily discover whatever hath been written since upon that dispute, to be little more than repeti-

---

[1] The following six paragraphs contain Swift's most brilliant satire on occultism, which he equates with Modern, Nonconformist Enthusiasm. (See Starkman, pp. 44–56.)

From the tangled web of occultism, Swift untangles the following threads: Pythogoreanism (*Tom Thumb*); alchemy (*Dr. Faustus* by Artephius); Cabalism (*Whittington and his Cat* by Rabbi Jehuda Hannasi); scholasticism (*Hind and the Panther* by John Dryden). To this list Swift adds the ballad of *Tommy Potts,* probably for sheer obfuscation, and, as his final thrust, a Modern encyclopedia, *The Wise Men of Gotham, cum appendice.*

tion. An abstract of this treatise hath been lately published by a worthy member of our society.*

These notices may serve to give the learned reader an idea as well as a taste of what the whole work is likely to produce; wherein I have now altogether circumscribed my thoughts and my studies; and if I can bring it to a perfection before I die, shall reckon I have well employed the poor remains of an unfortunate life.† This indeed is more than I can justly expect from a quill worn to the pith in the service of the state, in *pros* and *cons* upon Popish plots, and meal-tubs,** and exclusion bills, and passive obedience, and addresses of lives and fortunes, and prerogative, and property, and liberty of conscience, and letters to a friend: from an understanding and a conscience thread-bare and ragged with perpetual turning; from a head broken in a hundred places by the malignants of the opposite factions; and from a body spent with poxes ill cured, by trusting to bawds and surgeons, who (as it afterwards appeared) were professed enemies to me and the government, and revenged their party's quarrel upon my nose and shins. Fourscore and eleven pamphlets have I written under three reigns, and for the service of six and thirty factions. But finding the state has no farther occasion for me and my ink, I retire willingly to draw it out into speculations more becoming a philosopher, having, to my unspeakable comfort, passed a long life with a conscience void of offence.

But to return. I am assured from the reader's candor, that the brief specimen I have given, will easily clear all the rest of our society's productions from an aspersion grown, as it is manifest, out of envy and ignorance: that they are of little farther use or value to mankind, beyond the common entertainments of their wit and their style; for these I am sure have never yet been disputed by our keenest adversaries: in both which, as well as the more profound and mystical part, I have throughout this treatise closely followed the most applauded originals. And to render all complete, I have with much thought and application of mind, so ordered that the chief title prefixed to it (I mean, that under which I design it shall pass in the common conversations of court and town) is modelled exactly after the manner peculiar to our society.

* This I suppose to be understood of Mr. W-tt-n's *Discourse of Ancient and Modern Learning.*

† Here the author seems to personate L'Estrange, Dryden, and some others, who after having passed their lives in vices, faction and falsehood, have the impudence to talk of merit and innocence and sufferings.

** In King Charles the Second's time, there was an account of a Presbyterian plot, found in a tub, which then made much noise.

I confess to have been somewhat liberal in the business of titles,* having observed the humor of multiplying them, to bear great vogue among certain writers, whom I exceedingly reverence. And indeed it seems not unreasonable that books, the children of the brain, should have the honor to be christened with variety of names, as well as other infants of quality. Our famous Dryden has ventured to proceed a point farther, endeavouring to introduce also a multiplicity of god-fathers; † [1] *† See Virgil translated, etc.* which is an improvement of much more advantage, upon a very obvious account. 'Tis a pity this admirable invention has not been better cultivated, so as to grow by this time into general imitation, when such an authority serves it for a precedent. Nor have my endeavours been wanting to second so useful an example. But it seems there is an unhappy expense usually annexed to the calling of a god-father, which was clearly out of my head, as it is very reasonable to believe. Where the pinch lay, I cannot certainly affirm; but having employed a world of thoughts and pains to split my treatise into forty sections, and having entreated forty lords of my acquaintance, that they would do me the honor to stand, they all made it a matter of conscience, and sent me their excuses.

SECTION II.

ONCE upon a time, there was a man who had three sons by one wife,** and all at a birth, neither could the midwife tell certainly which was the eldest. Their father died while they were young, and upon his deathbed, calling the lads to him, spoke thus:

'Sons, because I have purchased no estate, nor was born to any, I have long considered of some good legacies to bequeath you; and at last, with much care as well as expense, have provided each of you (here they are) a new coat.‡ Now, you

---

* The title-page in the original was so torn, that it was not possible to recover several titles which the author here speaks of.
** By these three sons, Peter, Martin, and Jack, Popery, the Church of England, and our Protestant dissenters are designed. W. WOTTON.
‡ By his coats which he gave his sons, the garments of the Israelites. W. WOTTON.
An error (with submission) of the learned commentator; for by the coats are meant the doctrine and faith of Christianity, by the wisdom of the Divine Founder fitted to all times, places and circumstances. LAMBIN.[2]
1 Dryden's dedication of the various parts of his translation of Virgil to different patrons provoked considerable comment.
2 A characteristic piece of nonsense with which Swift loads his scholarly apparatus; Lambin, a sixteenth-century French scholar, was dead before *Tale of a Tub* was written.

are to understand, that these coats have two virtues contained in them: one is, that with good wearing, they will last you fresh and sound as long as you live; the other is, that they will grow in the same proportion with your bodies, lengthening and widening of themselves, so as to be always fit. Here, let me see them on you before I die. So, very well; pray children, wear them clean, and brush them often. You will find in my will * (here it is) full instructions in every particular concerning the wearing and management of your coats; wherein you must be very exact, to avoid the penalties I have appointed for every transgression or neglect, upon which your future fortunes will entirely depend. I have also commanded in my will, that you should live together in one house like brethren and friends, for then you will be sure to thrive, and not otherwise.'

Here the story says, this good father died, and the three sons went all together to seek their fortunes.

I shall not trouble you with recounting what adventures they met for the first seven years,[1] any farther than by taking notice, that they carefully observed their father's will, and kept their coats in very good order; that they travelled through several countries, encountered a reasonable quantity of giants, and slew certain dragons.

Being now arrived at the proper age for producing themselves, they came up to town, and fell in love with the ladies, but especially three, who about that time were in chief reputation: the Duchess d'Argent, Madame de Grands Titres, and the Countess d'Orgueil.† On their first appearance, our three adventurers met with a very bad reception; and soon with great sagacity guessing out the reason, they quickly began to improve in the good qualities of the town: they writ, and rallied, and rhymed, and sung, and said, and said nothing: they drank, and fought, and whored, and slept, and swore, and took snuff: they went to new plays on the first night, haunted the chocolate-houses, beat the watch, lay on bulks, and got claps: they bilked hackney-coachmen, ran in debt with shopkeepers, and lay with their wives: they killed bailiffs, kicked fiddlers down stairs, ate at Locket's, loitered at Will's: they talked of the drawing-room, and never came there: dined with lords they never saw: whispered a duchess, and spoke never a word: ex-

---

* The New Testament.
† Their mistresses are the Duchess d'Argent, Mademoiselle de Grands Titres, and the Countess d'Orgueil, i.e., covetousness, ambition, and pride, which were the three great vices that the ancient Fathers inveighed against as the first corruptions of Christianity. W. WOTTON.

[1] The first seven centuries of Christianity.

posed the scrawls of their laundress for billet-doux of quality: came ever just from court, and were never seen in it: attended the Levee *sub dio:* got a list of peers by heart in one company, and with great familiarity retailed them in another. Above all, they constantly attended those Committees of Senators who are silent in the House, and loud in the coffee-house, where they nightly adjourn to chew the cud of politics, and are encompassed with a ring of disciples, who lie in wait to catch up their droppings. The three brothers had acquired forty other qualifications of the like stamp, too tedious to recount, and by consequence were justly reckoned the most accomplished persons in the town. But all would not suffice, and the ladies aforesaid continued still inflexible. To clear up which difficulty I must, with the reader's good leave and patience, have recourse to some points of weight, which the authors of that age have not sufficiently illustrated.

For about this time it happened a sect arose,* whose tenets obtained and spread very far, especially in the *grand monde,* and among everybody of good fashion. They worshipped a sort of idol,† who, as their doctrine delivered, did daily create men by a kind of manufactory operation. This idol they placed in the highest parts of the house, on an altar erected about three foot: he was shown in the posture of a Persian emperor, sitting on a superficies, with his legs interwoven under him. This god had a goose for his ensign; whence it is, that some learned men pretend to deduce his original (from Jupiter Capitolinus.[1] At his left hand, beneath the altar, Hell [2] seemed to open, and catch at the animals the idol was creating; to prevent which, certain of his priests hourly flung in pieces of the uninformed mass, or substance, and sometimes whole limbs already enlivened, which that horrid gulf insatiably swallowed, terrible to behold. The goose was also held a subaltern divinity or *deus minorum gentium,* before whose shrine was sacrificed that creature, whose hourly food is human gore, and who is in so great renown abroad, for being the delight and favourite of the Ægyptian Cercopithecus.** Millions of these

* This is an occasional satire upon dress and fashion, in order to introduce what follows.
† By this idol is meant a tailor.
** The Ægyptians worshipped a monkey, which animal is very fond of eating lice, styled here creatures that feed on human gore.

[1] The goose is ensign of the tailor whose pressing iron, because of the shape of its handle, is called a goose. When the Gauls attempted to sack Rome, the cry of the sacred geese gave warning, and the city was saved.
[2] A tailor's waste box.

animals were cruelly slaughtered every day, to appease the hunger of that consuming deity. The chief idol was also worshipped as the inventor of the yard and the needle; whether as the god of seamen, or on account of certain other mystical attributes, hath not been sufficiently cleared.

The worshippers of this deity had also a system of their belief, which seemed to turn upon the following fundamental. They held the universe to be a large suit of clothes, which invests everything: that the earth is invested by the air; the air is invested by the stars; and the stars are invested by the *primum mobile*. Look on this globe of earth, you will find it to be a very complete and fashionable dress. What is that which some call land, but a fine coat faced with green? or the sea, but a waistcoat of water-tabby? Proceed to the particular works of the creation, you will find how curious Journeyman Nature hath been, to trim up the vegetable beaux; observe how sparkish a periwig adorns the head of a beech, and what a fine doublet of white satin is worn by the birch. To conclude from all, what is man himself but a microcoat,* or rather a complete suit of clothes with all its trimmings? As to his body, there can be no dispute; but examine even the acquirements of his mind, you will find them all contribute in their order towards furnishing out an exact dress. To instance no more: is not religion a cloak; honesty a pair of shoes worn out in the dirt; self-love a surtout; vanity a shirt; and conscience a pair of breeches, which, though a cover for lewdness as well as nastiness, is easily slipt down for the service of both? [1]

These *postulata* being admitted, it will follow in due course of reasoning, that those beings which the world calls improperly suits of clothes, are in reality the most refined species of animals, or to proceed higher, that they are rational creatures, or men. For is it not manifest that they live, and move, and talk, and perform all other offices of human life? Are not beauty, and wit, and mien, and breeding, their inseparable properties? In short, we see nothing but them, hear nothing but them. Is it not they who walk the streets, fill up parlia-

---

* Alluding to the word microcosm, or a little world, as man hath been called by philosophers.

[1] In his satirical system of the tailor worshippers (later known as "the clothes philosophy") Swift plays with the conventional figures of the universe as a series of correspondences between macrocosm and microcosm, and thus sets up his own mad metaphysical system. Implicit in it there may be some satire on the New Logic. Phillip Harth, however, sees this paragraph as a specific parody of the first paragraph of Hobbes's *Leviathan*.

ment-, coffee-, play-, bawdy-houses? 'Tis true indeed, that these animals, which are vulgarly called suits of clothes, or dresses, do according to certain compositions receive different appellations. If one of them be trimmed up with a gold chain, and a red gown, and a white rod, and a great horse, it is called a Lord-Mayor; if certain ermines and furs be placed in a certain position, we style them a Judge; and so an apt conjunction of lawn and black satin we entitle a Bishop.

Others of these professors, though agreeing in the main system, were yet more refined upon certain branches of it; and held that man was an animal compounded of two dresses, the natural and the celestial suit, which were the body and the soul: that the soul was the outward, and the body the inward clothing; that the latter was *ex traduce*,[1] but the former of daily creation and circumfusion. This last they proved by scripture, because in them we live, and move, and have our being; as likewise by philosophy, because they are all in all, and all in every part. Besides, said they, separate these two, and you will find the body to be only a senseless unsavoury carcass. By all which it is manifest, that the outward dress must needs be the soul.

To this system of religion were tagged several subaltern doctrines, which were entertained with great vogue: as particularly, the faculties of the mind were deduced by the learned among them in this manner: embroidery was sheer wit; gold fringe was agreeable conversation; gold lace was repartee; a huge long periwig was humor; and a coat full of powder was very good raillery: all which required abundance of *finesse* and *delicatesse* to manage with advantage, as well as a strict observance after times and fashions.

I have with much pains and reading, collected out of ancient authors, this short summary of a body of philosophy and divinity, which seems to have been composed by a vein and race of thinking, very different from any other systems, either ancient or modern. And it was not merely to entertain or satisfy the reader's curiosity, but rather to give him light into several circumstances of the following story, that knowing the state of dispositions and opinions in an age so remote, he may better comprehend those great events which were the issue of them. I advise therefore the courteous reader to peruse with a world of application, again and again, whatever I have writ-

---

[1] The doctrine of traducianism holds that the body and soul are propagated together.

ten upon this matter. And so leaving these broken ends, I carefully gather up the chief thread of my story and proceed.*

These opinions therefore were so universal, as well as the practices of them, among the refined part of court and town, that our three brother-adventurers, as their circumstances then stood, were strangely at a loss. For, on the one side, the three ladies they addressed themselves to (whom we have named already) were ever at the very top of the fashion, and abhorred all that were below it but the breadth of a hair. On the other side, their father's will was very precise, and it was the main precept in it, with the greatest penalties annexed, not to add to, or diminish from their coats one thread, without a positive command in the will. Now, the coats their father had left them were, 'tis true, of very good cloth, and besides, so neatly sewn, you would swear they were all of a piece; but at the same time very plain, and with little or no ornament; and it happened, that before they were a month in town, great shoulder-knots † came up; straight all the world was shoulder-knots; no approaching the ladies' *ruelles* without the *quota* of shoulder-knots. That fellow, cries one, has no soul; where is his shoulder-knot? Our three brethren soon discovered their want by sad experience, meeting in their walks with forty mortifications and indignities. If they went to the play-house, the door-keeper showed them into a twelve-penny gallery. If they called a boat, says a waterman, I am a first sculler. If they stepped to the Rose to take a bottle, the drawer would cry, Friend, we sell no ale. If they went to visit a lady, a footman met them at the door with, Pray send up your message. In this unhappy case, they went immediately to consult their father's will, read it over and over, but not a word of the shoulder-knot. What should they do? What temper should they find? Obedience was absolutely necessary, and yet shoulder-knots appeared extremely requisite. After much thought, one of the

* The first part of the *Tale* is the history of Peter; thereby Popery is exposed; everybody knows the Papists have made great additions to Christianity; that indeed is the great exception which the Church of England makes against them; accordingly Peter begins his pranks with adding a shoulder-knot to his coat. W. WOTTON.

His description of the cloth of which the coat was made, has a farther meaning than the words may seem to import: 'The coats their father had left them were of very good cloth, and besides so neatly sewn, you would swear it had been all of a piece, but at the same time very plain with little or no ornament.' This is the distinguishing character of the Christian religion. *Christiana religio absoluta et simplex*, was Ammianus Marcellinus's description of it, who was himself a heathen. W. WOTTON.

† By this is understood the first introducing of pageantry, and unnecessary ornaments in the Church, such as were neither for convenience nor edification, as a shoulder-knot, in which there is neither symmetry nor use.

brothers who happened to be more book-learned than the other
two, said, he had found an expedient. ' 'Tis true,' said he,
'there is nothing here in this will, *totidem verbis*,* making
mention of shoulder-knots, but I dare conjecture we may find
them *inclusive*, or *totiden syllabis*.' This distinction was immediately approved by all; and so they fell again to examine
the will. But their evil star had so directed the matter, that the
first syllable was not to be found in the whole writing. Upon
which disappointment, he, who found the former evasion, took
heart and said, 'Brothers, there is yet hopes; for though we
cannot find them *totidem verbis*, nor *totidem syllabis*, I dare
engage we shall make them out, *tertio modo*, or *totidem
literis*.' This discovery was also highly commended, upon
which they fell once more to the scrutiny, and soon picked
out S,H,O,U,L,D,E,R; when the same planet, enemy to their
repose, had wonderfully contrived, that a K was not to be
found. Here was a weighty difficulty! But the distinguishing
brother (for whom we shall hereafter find a name) now his
hand was in, proved by a very good argument, that K was a
modern illegitimate letter, unknown to the learned ages, nor
anywhere to be found in ancient manuscripts. ' 'Tis true,' said
he, 'the word *Calendæ* hath in *Q.V.C.*† been
sometimes writ with a K, but erroneously, for in
the best copies it has been ever spelt with a C.
And by consequence it was a gross mistake in our language to
spell Knot with a K, but that from henceforward he would
take care it should be writ with a C.' Upon this all farther
difficulty vanished; shoulder-knots were made clearly out to be
jure paterno, and our three gentlemen swaggered with as large
and as flaunting ones as the best.

† *Quibusdam
veteribus
codicibus.*

But, as human happiness is of a very short duration, so in
those days were human fashions, upon which it entirely depends. Shoulder-knots had their time, and we must now imagine them in their decline; for a certain lord came just from
Paris, with fifty yards of gold lace upon his coat, exactly
trimmed after the court fashion of that month. In two days all
mankind appeared closed up in bars of gold lace: † whoever
durst peep abroad without his complement of gold lace, was

* When the Papists cannot find any thing which they want in Scripture,
they go to oral tradition: thus Peter is introduced satisfied with the tedious
way of looking for all the letters of any word, which he has occasion for in
the Will, when neither the constituent syllables, nor much less the whole
word, were there *in terminis*. W. WOTTON.

† I cannot tell whether the author means any new innovation by this
word, or whether it be only to introduce the new methods of forcing and
perverting Scripture.

as scandalous as a —, and as ill received among the women.
What should our three knights do in this momentous affair?
They had sufficiently strained a point already in the affair of
shoulder-knots. Upon recourse to the will, nothing appeared
there but *altum silentium*. That of the shoulder-knots was a
loose, flying, circumstantial point; but this of gold lace seemed
too considerable an alteration without better warrant. It did
aliquo modo essentiæ adhærere, and therefore required a positive precept. But about this time it fell out, that the learned
brother aforesaid had read *Aristotelis Dialectica*, and especially that wonderful piece *de Interpretatione*, which has the
faculty of teaching its readers to find out a meaning in everything but itself, like commentators on the Revelations, who
proceed prophets without understanding a syllable of the text.
'Brothers,' said he, 'you are to be informed,* that of wills
duo sunt genera, nuncupatory † and scriptory; that in the
scriptory will here before us, there is no precept or mention
about gold lace, *conceditur:* but, *si idem affirmetur de nuncu-
patorio, negatur.* For brothers, if you remember, we heard a
fellow say when we were boys, that he heard my father's man
say, that he heard my father say, that he would advise his sons
to get gold lace on their coats, as soon as ever they could
procure money to buy it.' 'By G—, that is very true,' cries the
other; 'I remember it perfectly well,' said the third. And so
without more ado they got the largest gold lace in the parish,
and walked about as fine as lords.

A while after there came up all in fashion a pretty sort of
flame-coloured satin ** for linings, and the mercer brought a
pattern of it immediately to our three gentlemen, 'An please
your worships,' said he,‡ my Lord C—and Sir J. W. had linings out of this very piece last night; it takes wonderfully, and

* The next subject of our author's wit is the glosses and interpretations
of Scripture, very many absurd ones of which are allowed in the most
authentic books of the Church of Rome. W. WOTTON.

† By this is meant tradition, allowed to have equal authority with the
scripture, or rather greater.

** This is purgatory, whereof he speaks more particularly hereafter, but
here only to show how Scripture was perverted to prove it, which was done
by giving equal authority with the Canon to Apocrypha, called here a
codicil annexed.

It is likely the author, in every one of these changes in the brothers' dresses,
refers to some particular error in the Church of Rome, though it is not
easy I think to apply them all, but by this of flame-coloured satin, is manifestly intended purgatory; by gold lace may perhaps be understood the lofty
ornaments and plate in the churches; the shoulder-knots and silver fringe are
not so obvious, at least to me; but the Indian figures of men, women and
children plainly relate to the pictures in the Romish churches, of God like
an old man, of the Virgin Mary, and our Saviour as a child.

‡ This shows the time the author writ, it being about fourteen years since
those two persons were reckoned the fine gentlemen of the town.

I shall not have a remnant left enough to make my wife a pin-cushion by to-morrow morning at ten o'clock.' Upon this, they fell again to rummage the will, because the present case also required a positive precept, the lining being held by orthodox writers to be of the essence of the coat. After long search, they could fix upon nothing to the matter in hand, except a short advice of their father's in the will, to take care of fire, and put out their candles before they went to sleep.* This though a good deal for the purpose, and helping very far towards self-conviction, yet not seeming wholly of force to establish a command; and being resolved to avoid farther scruple, as well as future occasion for scandal, says he that was the scholar. 'I remember to have read in wills of a codicil annexed, which is indeed a part of the will, and what it contains hath equal authority with the rest. Now, I have been considering of this same will here before us, and I cannot reckon it to be complete for want of such a codicil. I will therefore fasten one in its proper place very dexterously; I have had it by me some time; it was written by a dog-keeper of my grandfather's,† and talks a great deal (as good luck would have it) of this very flame-coloured satin.' The project was immediately approved by the other two; an old parchment scroll was tagged on according to art, in the form of a codicil annexed, and the satin bought and worn.

Next winter, a player, hired for the purpose by the corporation of fringe-makers, acted his part in a new comedy, all covered with silver fringe,** and according to the laudable custom gave rise to that fashion. Upon which, the brothers consulting their father's will, to their great astonishment found these words; 'Item, I charge and command my said three sons to wear no sort of silver fringe upon or about their said coats,' etc., with a penalty in case of disobedience, too long here to insert. However, after some pause the brother so often mentioned for his erudition, who was well skilled in criticisms, had found in a certain author, which he said should be nameless, that the same word which in the will is called fringe, does also signify a broom-stick, and doubtless ought to have the same interpretation in this paragraph. This, another of the brothers disliked, because of that epithet silver, which could not, be humbly conceived, in propriety of speech be reasonably ap-

---

* That is, to take care of hell, and, in order to do that, to subdue and extinguish their lusts.
† I believe this refers to that part of the Apocrypha where mention is made of Tobit and his dog.
** This is certainly the farther introducing the pomps of habit and ornament.

plied to a broom-stick; but it was replied upon him, that this epithet was understood in a mythological and allegorical sense. However, he objected again, why their father should forbid them to wear a broom-stick on their coats, a caution that seemed unnatural and impertinent; upon which he was taken up short, as one that spoke irreverently of a mystery, which doubtless was very useful and significant, but ought not to be over-curiously pried into, or nicely reasoned about. And in short, their father's authority being now considerably sunk, this expedient was allowed to serve as a lawful dispensation for wearing their full proportion of silver fringe.

A while after was revived an old fashion, long antiquated, of embroidery with Indian figures of men, women, and children.* Here they had no occasion to examine the will. They remembered but too well how their father had always abhorred this fashion, that he made several paragraphs on purpose, importing his utter detestation of it, and bestowing his everlasting curse to his sons whenever they should wear it. For all this, in a few days they appeared higher in the fashion than anybody else in the town. But they solved the matter by saying, that these figures were not at all the same with those that were formerly worn, and were meant in the will. Besides, they did not wear them in that sense, as forbidden by their father, but as they were a commendable custom, and of great use to the public. That these rigorous clauses in the will did therefore require some allowance, and a favourable interpretation, and ought to be understood *cum grano salis*.

But fashions perpetually altering in that age, the scholastic brother grew weary of searching farther evasions, and solving everlasting contradictions. Resolved therefore at all hazards to comply with the modes of the world, they concerted matters together, and agreed unanimously to lock up their father's will in a strong box,† brought out of Greece or Italy (I have forgot which) and trouble themselves no farther to examine it, but only refer to its authority whenever they thought fit. In consequence whereof, a while after it grew a general mode to wear an infinite number of points, most of them tagged with

---

* The images of saints, the blessed Virgin, and our Saviour an infant. *Ibid.* Images in the Church of Rome give him but too fair a handle. The brothers remembered, &c. The allegory here is direct. W. WOTTON.

† The Papists formerly forbade the people the use of scripture in a vulgar tongue; Peter therefore locks up his father's will in a strong box, brought out of Greece or Italy. Those countries are named because the New Testament is written in Greek; and the vulgar Latin, which is the authentic edition of the Bible in the Church of Rome, is in the language of old Italy. W. WOTTON.

silver: upon which the scholar pronounced *ex cathedra*,* that points were absolutely *jure paterno*, as they might very well remember. 'Tis true, indeed, the fashion prescribed somewhat more than were directly named in the will; however, that they, as heirs-general of their father, had power to make and add certain clauses for public emolument, though not deducible, *totidem verbis*, from the letter of the will, or else *multa absurda sequerentur*. This was understood for canonical, and therefore on the following Sunday they came to church all covered with points.

The learned brother so often mentioned was reckoned the best scholar in all that, or the next street to it; insomuch as, having run something behind-hand with the world, he obtained the favour from a certain lord,** to receive him into his house, and to teach his children. A while after the lord died, and he, by long practice of his father's will, found the way of contriving a deed of conveyance of that house to himself and his heirs; upon which he took possession, turned the young squires out, and received his brothers in their stead.

SECTION III.

A DIGRESSION CONCERNING CRITICS.

THOUGH I have been hitherto as cautious as I could, upon all occasions, most nicely to follow the rules and methods of writing laid down by the example of our illustrious Moderns; yet has the unhappy shortness of my memory led me into an error, from which I must immediately extricate myself, before I can decently pursue my principal subject. I confess with shame, it was an unpardonable omission to proceed so far as I have already done, before I had performed the due discourses, expostulatory, supplicatory, or deprecatory, with my good lords the critics. Towards some atonement of this grievous neglect, I do here make humbly bold to present them with a short account of themselves and their art, by looking into

* The popes in their decretals and bulls have given their sanction to very many gainful doctrines which are now received in the Church of Rome that are not mentioned in scripture, and are unknown to the primitive church; Peter accordingly pronounces *ex cathedra*, that points tagged with silver were absolutely *jure paterno*, and so they wore them in great numbers. W. WOTTON.

** This was Constantine the Great, from whom the popes pretend a donation of St. Peter's patrimony, which they have been never able to produce.

Ibid. The bishops of Rome enjoyed their privileges in Rome at first by the favour of emperors, whom at last they shut out of their own capital city, and then forged a donation from Constantine the Great, the better to justify what they did. In imitation of this, Peter having run something behind-hand in the world, obtained leave of a certain lord, &c. W. WOTTON.

the original and pedigree of the word, as it is generally understood among us, and very briefly considering the ancient and present state thereof.

By the word critic, at this day so frequent in all conversations, there have sometimes been distinguished three very different species of mortal men, according as I have read in ancient books and pamphlets. For first, by this term was understood such persons as invented or drew up rules for themselves and the world, by observing which, a careful reader might be able to pronounce upon the productions of the learned, form his taste to a true relish of the sublime and the admirable, and divide every beauty of matter or of style from the corruption that apes it. In their common perusal of books, singling out the errors and defects, the nauseous, the fulsome, the dull, and the impertinent, with the caution of a man that walks through Edinburgh streets in a morning, who is indeed as careful as he can to watch diligently, and spy out the filth in his way; not that he is curious to observe the colour and complexion of the ordure, or take its dimensions, much less to be paddling in, or tasting it; but only with a design to come out as cleanly as he may. These men seem, though very erroneously, to have understood the appellation of critic in a literal sense; that one principal part of his office was to praise and acquit; and that a critic, who sets up to read only for an occasion of censure and reproof, is a creature as barbarous as a judge, who should take up a resolution to hang all men that came before him upon a trial.

Again, by the word critic have been meant the restorers of ancient learning from the worms, and graves, and dust of manuscripts.

Now, the races of these two have been for some ages utterly extinct; and besides, to discourse any farther of them would not be at all to my purpose.

The third, and noblest sort, is that of the TRUE CRITIC, whose original is the most ancient of all. Every true critic is a hero born, descending in a direct line from a celestial stem by Momus and Hybris, who begat Zoilus, who begat Tigellius, who begat Etcætera the Elder; who begat Bentley, and Rymer, and Wotton, and Perrault, and Dennis, who begat Etcætera the Younger.[1]

And these are the critics from whom the commonwealth of

---

[1] This paragraph satirically depicts the truest and noblest critic, the Modern critic. He is descended from Night and Pride, related to the worst of Ancient critics (Zoilus and Tigellius), and begets the Modern English and French Modern critics, Bentley, Rymer, Wotton, Perrault, and Dennis.

learning has in all ages received such immense benefits, that the gratitude of their admirers placed their origin in Heaven, among those of Hercules, Theseus, Perseus, and other great deservers of mankind. But heroic virtue itself hath not been exempt from the obloquy of evil tongues. For it hath been objected, that those ancient heroes, famous for their combating so many giants, and dragons, and robbers, were in their own persons a greater nuisance to mankind, than any of those monsters they subdued; and therefore to render their obligations more complete, when all other vermin were destroyed, should in conscience have concluded with the same justice upon themselves as Hercules most generously did, and hath upon that score procured to himself more temples and votaries than the best of his fellows. For these reasons, I suppose it is, why some have conceived it would be very expedient for the public good of learning that every true critic, as soon as he had finished his task assigned, should immediately deliver himself up to ratsbane, or hemp, or from some convenient altitude; and that no man's pretensions to so illustrious a character should by any means be received, before that operation were performed.

Now, from this heavenly descent of criticism, and the close analogy it bears to heroic virtue, 'tis easy to assign the proper employment of a true ancient genuine critic; which is, to travel through this vast world of writings; to pursue and hunt those monstrous faults bred within them; to drag out the lurking errors like Cacus from his den; to multiply them like Hydra's heads; and rake them together like Augeas's dung. Or else drive away a sort of dangerous fowl, who have a perverse inclination to plunder the best branches of the tree of knowledge, like those Stymphalian birds that ate up the fruit.[1]

These reasonings will furnish us with an adequate definition of a true critic: that he is a discoverer and collector of writers' faults. Which may be farther put beyond dispute by the following demonstration: that whoever will examine the writings in all kinds, wherewith this ancient sect has honoured the world, shall immediately find, from the whole thread and tenor of them, that the ideas of the authors have been altogether conversant and taken up with the faults and blemishes, and oversights, and mistakes of other writers; and let the subject treated on be whatever it will, their imaginations are so entirely possessed and replete with the defects of other pens, that the very quintessence of what is bad does of neces-

---

[1] Hercules's labor was to destroy the Stymphalian birds of prey.

sity distil into their own, by which means the whole appears
to be nothing else but an abstract of the criticisms themselves
have made.

Having thus briefly considered the original and office of a
critic, as the word is understood in its most noble and universal acceptation, I proceed to refute the objections of those
who argue from the silence and pretermission of authors; by
which they pretend to prove, that the very art of criticism, as
now exercised, and by me explained, is wholly Modern; and
consequently, that the critics of Great Britain and France have
no title to an original so ancient and illustrious as I have deduced. Now, if I can clearly make out on the contrary, that
the most ancient writers have particularly described both the
person and the office of a true critic, agreeable to the definition laid down by me, their grand objection, from the silence
of authors, will fall to the ground.

I confess to have for a long time borne a part in this general
error; from which I should never have acquitted myself, but
through the assistance of our noble Moderns; whose most edifying volumes I turn indefatigably over night and day, for the
improvement of my mind, and the good of my country. These
have with unwearied pains made many useful searches into
the weak sides of the ancients, and given us a comprehensive
list of them.* Besides, they have proved beyond *See Wotton,*
contradiction, that the very finest things delivered *Of Ancient
and Modern*
of old, have been long since invented, and *Learning.*
brought to light by much later pens; and that the noblest discoveries those ancients ever made, of art or of nature, have
all been produced by the transcending genius of the present
age. Which clearly shows, how little merit those Ancients can
justly pretend to; and takes off that blind admiration paid
them by men in a corner, who have the unhappiness of conversing too little with present things. Reflecting maturely upon
all this, and taking in the whole compass of human nature, I
easily concluded, that these Ancients, highly sensible of their
many imperfections, must needs have endeavoured from some
passages in their works, to obviate, soften, or divert the cen-
sorious reader, by satire, or panegyric upon the true critics,
in imitation of their masters, the Moderns. Now, in the commonplaces of both these,† I was plentifully in- †*Satire and
panegyric*
structed, by a long course of useful study in pref- *upon critics.*
aces and prologues; and therefore immediately
resolved to try what I could discover of either, by a diligent
perusal of the most ancient writers, and especially those who

treated of the earliest times. Here I found to my great surprise, that although they all entered, upon occasion, into particular descriptions of the true critic, according as they were governed by their fears or their hopes; yet whatever they touched of that kind, was with abundance of caution, adventuring no farther than mythology and hieroglyphic. This, I suppose, gave ground to superficial readers, for urging the silence of authors, against the antiquity of the true critic, though the types are so apposite, and the applications so necessary and natural, that it is not easy to conceive how any reader of a modern eye and taste could overlook them. I shall venture from a great number to produce a few, which I am very confident will put this question beyond dispute.

It well deserves considering, that these ancient writers in treating enigmatically upon the subject, have generally fixed upon the very same hieroglyph, varying only the story according to their affections or their wit. For first, Pausanias is of opinion, that the perfection of writing correct was entirely owing to the institution of critics; and that he can possibly mean no other than the true critic, is, I think, manifest enough from the following description. He says, they were a race of men, who delighted to nibble at the superfluities, and excrescencies of books; which the learned at length observing, took warning of their own accord, to lop the luxuriant, the rotten, the dead, the sapless, and the overgrown branches from their works. But now, all this he cunningly shades under the following allegory; that the Nauplians in Argia * learned the art of pruning their vines, by observing, that when an ASS had browsed upon one of them, it thrived the better, and bore fairer fruit. But Herodotus † holding the very same hieroglyph, speaks much plainer, and almost *in terminis*. He hath been so bold as to tax the true critics of ignorance and malice; telling us openly, for I think nothing can be plainer, that in the western part of Libya, there were ASSES with HORNS: upon which relation Ctesias ** yet refines, mentioning the very same animal about India, adding, that whereas all other ASSES wanted a gall, these horned ones were so redundant in that part, that their flesh was not to be eaten because of its extreme bitterness.[1]

Lib. —.

† *Lib. 4.*

** *Vide excerpta ex eo apud photium.*

[1] This paragraph and the two following are a brilliant parody of the matter and manner of Richard Bentley, particularly of his *Epistles of Phalaris*. The parody is contained in Swift's allusiveness, digressiveness, abstruseness of detail, his play with the leitmotif of the *ass* (which ran throughout the Phalaris controversy), and in his own erudition which rivals Bentley's.

Now, the reason why those ancient writers treated this subject only by types and figures, was, because they durst not make open attacks against a party so potent and so terrible, as the critics of those ages were, whose very voice was so dreadful, that a legion of authors would tremble, and drop their pens at the sound; for so Herodotus tells us expressly in another place,* how a vast army of Scythians was put to flight in a panic terror, by the braying of an ASS. From hence it is conjectured by certain profound philologers, that the great awe and reverence paid to a true critic, by the writers of Britain, have been derived to us from those our Scythian ancestors. In short, this dread was so universal, that in process of time, those authors who had a mind to publish their sentiments more freely, in describing the true critics of their several ages, were forced to leave off the use of the former hieroglyph, as too nearly approaching the prototype, and invented other terms instead thereof that were more cautious and mystical; so Diodorus,† speaking to the same purpose, ventures no farther than to say, that in the mountains of Helicon, there grows a certain weed, which bears a flower of so damned a scent, as to poison those who offer to smell it. Lucretius gives exactly the same relation:

* Lib. 4

† Lib.

> Est etiam in magnis Heliconis montibus arbos,
> Floris odore hominem retro consueta necare.**

Lib. 6.

But Ctesias, whom we lately quoted, hath been a great deal bolder; he had been used with much severity by the true critics of his own age, and therefore could not forbear to leave behind him at least one deep mark of his vengeance against the whole tribe. His meaning is so near the surface, that I wonder how it possibly came to be overlooked by those who deny the antiquity of the true critics. For pretending to make a description of many strange animals about India, he hath set down these remarkable words: 'Amongst the rest,' says he, 'there is a serpent that wants teeth, and consequently cannot bite; but if its vomit (to which it is much addicted) happens to fall upon anything, a certain rottenness or corruption ensues. These serpents are generally found among the mountains where jewels grow, and they frequently emit a poisonous juice

** Near Helicon, and round the learned hill,
Grow trees, whose blossoms with their odour kill.

whereof whoever drinks, that person's brains fly out of his nostrils.'

There was also among the Ancients a sort of critic, not distinguished in species from the former, but in growth or degree, who seem to have been only the tyros or junior scholars; yet, because of their differing employments, they are frequently mentioned as a sect by themselves. The usual exercise of these younger students, was to attend constantly at theatres, and learn to spy out the worst parts of the play, whereof they were obliged carefully to take note, and render a rational account to their tutors. Fleshed at these smaller sports, like young wolves, they grew up in time to be nimble and strong enough for hunting down large game. For it hath been observed both among Ancients and Moderns, that a true critic hath one quality in common with a whore and an alderman, never to change his title or his nature; that a gray critic has been certainly a green one, the perfections and acquirements of his age being only the improved talents of his youth; like hemp, which some naturalists inform us, is bad for suffocations though taken but in the seed. I esteem the invention, or at least the refinement of prologues, to have been owing to these younger proficients, of whom Terence makes frequent and honourable mention, under the name of *malevoli*.

Now, 'tis certain, the institution of the true critics was of absolute necessity to the commonwealth of learning. For all human actions seem to be divided like Themistocles and his company; one man can fiddle, and another can make a small town a great city; and he that cannot do either one or the other, deserves to be kicked out of the creation. The avoiding of which penalty has doubtless given the first birth to the nation of critics, and withal, an occasion for their secret detractors to report, that a true critic is a sort of mechanic, set up with a stock and tools for his trade, at as little expense as a tailor; and that there is much analogy between the utensils and abilities of both: that the tailor's hell is the type of a critic's common-place book, and his wit and learning held forth by the goose; that it requires at least as many of these to the making up of one scholar, as of the others to the composition of a man; that the valour of both is equal, and their weapons near of a size. Much may be said in answer to those invidious reflections; and I can positively affirm the first to be a falsehood: for, on the contrary, nothing is more certain, than that it requires greater layings out, to be free of the crtic's company, than of any other you can name. For, as to be a true beggar, it will cost the richest candidate every groat he is worth; so, before one can commence a true critic, it will cost a man all the good qualities of his mind; which, perhaps, for a less purchase, would be thought but an indifferent bargain.

Having thus amply proved the antiquity of criticism, and described the primitive state of it, I shall now examine the present condition of this empire, and show how well it agrees with its ancient self. A certain author,* whose works have many ages since been entirely lost, does in his fifth book and eighth chapter, say of critics, that their writings are the mirrors of learning. This I understand in a literal sense, and suppose our author must mean, that whoever designs to be a perfect writer, must inspect into the books of critics, and correct his invention there as in a mirror. Now, whoever considers, that the mirrors of the Ancients were made of brass, and *sine mercurio,* may presently apply the two principal qualifications of a true Modern critic, and consequently must needs conclude, that these have always been, and must be for ever the same. For brass is an emblem of duration, and when it is skilfully burnished, will cast reflections from its own superficies, without any assistance of mercury from behind. All the other talents of a critic will not require a particular mention, being included, or easily deducible to these. However, I shall conclude with three maxims, which may serve both as characteristics to distinguish a true modern critic from a pretender, and will be also of admirable use to those worthy spirits, who engage in so useful and honourable an art.

The first is, that criticism, contrary to all other faculties of the intellect, is ever held the truest and best, when it is the very first result of the critic's mind; as fowlers reckon the first aim for the surest, and seldom fail of missing the mark, if they stay not for a second.

Secondly, the true critics are known by their talent of swarming about the noblest writers, to which they are carried merely by instinct, as a rat to the best cheese, or a wasp to the fairest fruit. So when the king is a horse-back, he is sure to be the dirtiest person of the company, and they that make their court best, are such as bespatter him most.

Lastly, a true critic, in the perusal of a book, is like a dog at a feast, whose thoughts and stomach are wholly set upon what the guests fling away, and consequently is apt to snarl most when there are the fewest bones.

* A quotation after the manner of a great author. *Vide* Bentley's *Dissertation, &c.*

Thus much, I think, is sufficient to serve by way of address to my patrons, the true Modern critics, and may very well atone for my past silence, as well as that which I am like to observe for the future. I hope I have deserved so well of their whole body, as to meet with generous and tender usage at their hands. Supported by which expectation, I go on boldly to pursue those adventures already so happily begun.

SECTION IV.

A TALE OF A TUB

I HAVE now with much pains and study conducted the reader to a period, where he must expect to hear of great revolutions. For no sooner had our learned brother, so often mentioned, got a warm house of his own over his head, than he began to look big, and to take mightily upon him; insomuch, that unless the gentle reader out of his great candour will please a little to exalt his idea, I am afraid he will henceforth hardly know the hero of the play, when he happens to meet him, his part, his dress, and his mien being so much altered.

He told his brothers, he would have them to know that he was their elder, and consequently his father's sole heir,[1] nay, a while after, he would not allow them to call him brother, but Mr. PETER; and then he must be styled *Father* PETER; and sometimes, *My Lord* PETER. To support this grandeur, which he soon began to consider could not be maintained without a better *fonde* than what he was born to, after much thought, he cast about at last to turn projector and virtuoso, wherein he so well succeeded, that many famous discoveries, projects, and machines, which bear great vogue and practice at present in the world, are owing entirely to Lord Peter's invention. I will deduce the best account I have been able to collect of the chief amongst them, without considering much the order they came out in, because, I think, authors are not well agreed as to that point.

I hope, when this treatise of mine shall be translated into foreign languages (as I may without vanity affirm, that the labour of collecting, the faithfulness in recounting, and the great usefulness of the matter to the public, will amply deserve that justice) that the worthy members of the several acad-

[1] Swift alludes to the claim that the Roman Catholic was the only legitimate church.

emies abroad, especially those of France and Italy, will favourably accept these humble offers, for the advancement of universal knowledge. I do also advertise the most reverend fathers, the Eastern Missionaries, that I have, purely for their sakes, made use of such words and phrases, as will best admit an easy turn into any of the oriental languages, especially the Chinese. And so I proceed with great content of mind, upon reflecting, how much emolument this whole globe of Earth is like to reap by my labours.

The first undertaking of Lord Peter, was to purchase a large continent,* lately said to have been discovered in *Terra Australis Incognita.* This tract of land he bought at a very great pennyworth from the discoveries themselves (though some pretend to doubt whether they had ever been there) and then retailed it into several cantons to certain dealers, who carried over colonies, but were all shipwrecked in the voyage. Upon which Lord Peter sold the said continent to other customers again, and again, and again, and again, with the same success.

The second project I shall mention, was his sovereign remedy for the worms,† especially those in the spleen.** The patient was to eat nothing after supper for three nights: as soon as he went to bed, he was carefully to lie on one side, and when he grew weary, to turn upon the other. He must also duly confine his two eyes to the same object; and by no means break wind at both ends together, without manifest occasion. These prescriptions diligently observed, the worms would void insensibly by perspiration, ascending through the brain.

A third invention was the erecting of a whispering-office,‡ for the public good and ease of all such as are hypochondriacal, or troubled with the colic; as likewise of all eaves-droppers, physicians, midwives, small politicians, friends fallen out, repeating poets, lovers happy or in despair, bawds, privy-counsellors, pages, parasites and buffoons: in short, of all such as are in danger of bursting with too much wind. An ass's head was placed so conveniently, that the party affected might

* That is, Purgatory.
† Penance and absolution are played upon under the notion of a sovereign remedy for the worms, especially in the spleen, which by observing Peter's prescription would void sensibly by perspiration, ascending through the brain, &c. W. WOTTON.
** Here the author ridicules the penances of the Church of Rome, which may be made as easy to the sinner as he pleases, provided he will pay for them accordingly.
‡ By his whispering-office, for the relief of eaves-droppers, physicians, bawds, and privy-counsellors, he ridicules auricular confession, and the priest who takes it, is described by the ass's head. W. WOTTON.

easily with his mouth accost either of the animal's ears; which he was to apply close for a certain space, and by a fugitive faculty, peculiar to the ears of that animal, receive immediate benefit, either by eructation, or expiration, or evomition.

Another very beneficial project of Lord Peter's was an office of insurance * for tobacco-pipes, martyrs of the modern zeal, volumes of poetry, shadows, ————— and rivers: that these, nor any of these shall receive damage by fire. From whence our friendly societies [1] may plainly find themselves to be only transcribers from this original; though the one and the other have been of great benefit to the undertakers, as well as of equal to the public.

Lord Peter was also held the original author of puppets and raree-shows,† the great usefulness whereof being so generally known, I shall not enlarge farther upon this particular.

But another discovery for which he was much renowned was his famous universal pickle.** For having remarked how your common pickle ‡ in use among housewives, was of no farther benefit than to preserve dead flesh, and certain kinds of vegetables, Peter, with great cost as well as art, had contrived a pickle proper for houses, gardens, towns, men, women, children, and cattle; wherein he could preserve them as sound as insects in amber. Now, this pickle to the taste, the smell, and the sight, appeared exactly the same with what is in common service for beef, and butter, and herring (and has been often that way applied with great success) but for its many sovereign virtues was a quite different thing.) For Peter would put in a certain quantity of his powder *pimperlim pimp*, || after which it never failed of success. The operation was performed by spargefaction in a proper time of the moon. The patient who was to be pickled, if it were a house, would infallibly be preserved from all spiders, rats, and weasels; if the party affected were a dog, he should be exempt from mange, and madness, and hunger. It also infallibly took away all scabs

---

* This I take to be the office of indulgences, the gross abuses whereof first gave occasion for the Reformation.

† I believe are the monkeries and ridiculous processions, &c. among the papists.

** Holy water, he calls an universal pickle, to preserve houses, gardens, towns, men, women, children, and cattle, wherein he could preserve them as sound as insects in amber. W. WOTTON.

‡ This is easily understood to be holy water, composed of the same ingredients with many other pickles.

|| And because holy water differs only in consecration from common water, therefore he tells us that his pickle by the powder of *pimperlimpimp* receives new virtues, though it differs not in sight nor smell from the common pickles, which preserve beef, and butter, and herrings. W. WOTTON.

[1] Insurance companies and benevolent associations.

and lice, and scalled heads from children, never hindering the patient from any duty, either at bed or board.

But of all Peter's rarities, he most valued a certain set of bulls,* whose race was by great fortune preserved in a lineal descent from those that guarded the golden fleece. Though some who pretended to observe them curiously, doubted the breed had not been kept entirely chaste; because they had degenerated from their ancestors in some qualities, and had acquired others very extraordinary, but a foreign mixture. The bulls of Colchos are recorded to have brazen feet; but whether it happened by ill pasture and running, by an allay from intervention of other parents, from stolen intrigues; whether a weakness in their progenitors had impaired the seminal virtue, or by a decline necessary through a long course of time, the originals of nature being depraved in these latter sinful ages of the world; whatever was the cause, 'tis certain that Lord Peter's bulls were extremely vitiated by the rest of time in the metal of their feet, which was now sunk into common lead. However, the terrible roaring, peculiar to their lineage was preserved; as likewise that faculty of breathing out fire from their nostrils; which notwithstanding many of their detractors took to be a feat of art; and to be nothing so terrible as it appeared; proceeding only from their usual course of diet, which was of squibs and crackers.† [1] However they had two peculiar marks which extremely distinguished them from the bulls of Jason, and which I have not met together in the description of any other monster, beside that in Horace:

Varias inducere plumas;
and
Atrum desinit in piscem.

For these had fishes' tails, yet upon occasion could outfly any bird in the air. Peter put these bulls upon several employs. Sometimes he would set them a-roaring to fright naughty boys,** and make them quiet. Sometimes he would send them out upon errands of great importance; where it is wonderful

* The papal bulls are ridiculed by name, so that here we are at no loss for the author's meaning. W. WOTTON.

Ibid. Here the author has kept the name, and means the pope's bulls, or rather his fulminations and excommunications of heretical princes, all signed with lead and the seal of the fisherman.

† These are the fulminations of the pope threatening hell and damnation to those princes who offend him.

** That is, kings who incur his displeasure.

[1] Firecrackers.

to recount, and perhaps the cautious reader may think much to believe it, an *appetitus sensibilis,* deriving itself through the whole family from their noble ancestors, guardians of the golden fleece, they continued so extremely fond of gold, that if Peter sent them abroad, though it were only upon a compliment, they would roar, and spit, and belch, and piss, and fart, and snivel out fire, and keep a perpetual coil, till you flung them a bit of gold; but then, *pulveris exigui jactu,* they would grow calm and quiet as lambs. In short, whether by secret connivance, or encouragement from their master, or out of their own liquorish affection to gold, or both, it is certain they were no better than a sort of sturdy, swaggering beggars; and where they could not prevail to get an alms, would make women miscarry, and children fall into fits, who to this very day, usually call sprites and hobgoblins by the name of bull-beggars. They grew at last so very troublesome to the neighbourhood, that some gentlemen of the north-west got a parcel of right English bull-frogs, and baited them so terribly, that they felt it ever after.

I must needs mention one more of Lord Peter's projects, which was very extraordinary, and discovered him to be master of a high reach, and profound invention. Whenever it happened that any rogue of Newgate was condemned to be hanged, Peter would offer him a pardon for a certain sum of money which when the poor caitiff had made all shifts to scrape up and send, his lordship would return a piece of paper in this form.*

'TO all mayors, sheriffs, jailors, constables, bailiffs, hangmen, &c. Whereas we are informed that A. B. remains in the hands of you, or any of you, under the sentence of death. We will and command you upon sight hereof, to let the said prisoner depart to his own habitation, whether he stands condemned for murder, sodomy, rape, sacrilege, incest, treason, blasphemy, &c., for which this shall be your sufficient warrant: and if you fail hereof, G—d—mn you and yours to all eternity. And so we bid you heartily farewell.

Your most humble

man's man,[1]

Emperor PETER.'

---

* This is a copy of a general pardon, signed *Servus Servorum.*

Ibid. Absolution *in articulo mortis;* and the tax *cameræ apostolicæ,* are jested upon in Emperor Peter's letter. W. WOTTON.

[1] A parody of the papal phrase *servus servorum Dei.*

The wretches trusting to this lost their lives and money too.

I desire of those, whom the learned among posterity will appoint for commentators upon this elaborate treatise, that they will proceed with great caution upon certain dark points, wherein all who are not *verè adepti*, may be in danger to form rash and hasty conclusions, especially in some mysterious paragraphs, where certain *arcana* are joined for brevity sake, which in the operation must be divided. And I am certain, that future sons of art will return large thanks to my memory, for so grateful, so useful an *innuendo*.

It will be no difficult part to persuade the reader that so many worthy discoveries met with great success in the world; though I may justly assure him that I have related much the smallest number; my design having been only to single out such as will be of most benefit for public imitation, or which best served to give some idea of the reach and wit of the inventor. And therefore it need not be wondered, if by this time, Lord Peter was become exceeding rich. But alas, he had kept his brain so long and so violently upon the rack, that at last it shook itself, and began to turn round for a little ease. In short, what with pride, projects, and knavery, poor Peter was grown distracted, and conceived the strangest imaginations in the world. In the height of his fits (as it is usual with those who run mad out of pride) he would call himself God Almighty,* and sometimes monarch of the universe. I have seen him (says my author) take three old high-crowned hats,† and clap them all on his head three story high, with a huge bunch of keys at his girdle,** and an angling rod in his hand. In which guise, whoever went to take him by the hand in the way of salutation, Peter with much grace, like a well-educated spaniel, would present them with his foot,‡ and if they refused his civility, then he would raise it as high as their chops, and give them a damned kick on the mouth, which hath ever since been called a salute. Whoever walked by without paying him their compliments, having a wonderful strong breath, he would blow their hats off into the dirt. Meantime, his affairs at home went upside down; and his two brothers had a

---

* The Pope is not only allowed to be the vicar of Christ, but by several divines is called God upon earth, and other blasphemous titles.

† The triple crown.

** The keys of the church.

Ibid. The Pope's universal monarchy, and his triple crown and fisher's ring. W. WOTTON.

‡ Neither does his arrogant way of requiring men to kiss his slipper escape reflection. W. WOTTON.

wretched time; where his first *boutade* * was, to kick both
their wives one morning out of doors, and his own too,† and
in their stead, gave orders to pick up the first three strollers
could be met with in the streets. A while after he nailed up
the cellar-door, and would not allow his brothers a drop of
drink to their victuals.** Dining one day at an alderman's in
the city, Peter observed him expatiating after the manner of
his brethren, in the praises of his sirloin of beef. Beef, said the
sage magistrate, is the king of meat; beef comprehends in it
the quintessence of partridge, and quail, and venison, and
pheasants, and plum-pudding, and custard. When Peter came
home, he would needs take the fancy of cooking up this
doctrine into use, and apply the precept in default of a sirloin,
to his brown loaf: 'Bread,' says he, 'dear brothers, is the staff
of life; in which bread is contained, inclusive, the quintessence
of beef, mutton, veal, venison, partridge, plum-pudding, and
custard: and to render all complete, there is intermingled a
due quantity of water, whose crudities are also corrected by
yeast or barm, through which means it becomes a wholesome
fermented liquor diffused through the mass of the bread.'
Upon the strength of these conclusions, next day at dinner was
the brown loaf served up in all the formality of a city feast.
'Come brothers,' said Peter, 'fall to, and spare not; here is
excellent good mutton,‡ or hold, now my hand is in, I'll help
you.' At which word, in much ceremony, with fork and knife,
he carves out two good slices of a loaf, and presents each on a
plate to his brothers. The elder of the two not suddenly entering into Lord Peter's conceit, began with very civil language
to examine the mystery. 'My lord,' said he, 'I doubt, with
great submission, there may be some mistake.' 'What,' says
Peter, 'you are pleasant; come then, let us hear this jest your
head is so big with.' 'None in the world, my lord; but unless
I am very much deceived, your lordship was pleased a while
ago to let fall a word about mutton, and I would be glad to
see it with all my heart.' 'How,' said Peter, appearing in
great surprise, 'I do not comprehend this at all.'—Upon

* This word properly signifies a sudden jerk, or lash of a horse, when you
do not expect it.

† The celibacy of the Romish clergy is struck at in Peter's beating his
own and brothers' wives out of doors. W. Wotton.

** The Popes' refusing the cup to the laity, persuading them that the blood
is contained in the bread, and that the bread is the real and entire body of
Christ.

‡ Transubstantiation. Peter turns his bread into mutton, and according to
the popish doctrine of concomitants, his wine too, which in his way he
calls palming his damned crusts upon the brothers for mutton. W. Wotton.

which, the younger interposing to set the business right, 'My lord,' said he, 'my brother, I suppose, is hungry, and longs for the mutton your lordship hath promised us to dinner.' 'Pray,' said Peter, 'take me along with you; either you are both mad, or disposed to be merrier than I approve of; if you there do not like your piece, I will carve you another, though I should take that to be the choice bit of the whole shoulder.' 'What then, my lord,' replied the first, 'it seems this is a shoulder of mutton all this while.' 'Pray, sir,' says Peter, 'eat your victuals and leave off your impertinence, if you please, for I am not disposed to relish it at present.' But the other could not forbear, being over-provoked at the affected seriousness of Peter's countenance. 'By G——, my lord,' said he, 'I can only say, that to my eyes, and fingers, and teeth, and nose, it seems to be nothing but a crust of bread.' Upon which the second put in his word: 'I never saw a piece of mutton in my life so nearly resembling a slice from a twelve-penny loaf.' 'Look ye, gentlemen," cries Peter in a rage, 'to convince you what a couple of blind, positive, ignorant, wilful puppies you are, I will use but this plain argument; by G——, it is true, good, natural mutton as any in Leadenhall market; and G—— confound you both eternally, if you offer to believe otherwise.' Such a thundering proof as this left no farther room for objection: the two unbelievers began to gather and pocket up their mistake as hastily as they could. 'Why, truly,' said the first, 'upon more mature consideration'—'Ay,' says the other, interrupting him, 'now I have thought better on the thing, your lordship seems to have a great deal of reason.' 'Very well,' said Peter. 'Here boy, fill me a beer-glass of claret. Here's to you both with all my heart.' The two brethren much delighted to see him so readily appeased returned their most humble thanks, and said they would be glad to pledge his lordship. 'That you shall,' said Peter, 'I am not a person to refuse you anything that is reasonable; wine moderately taken is a cordial; here is a glass a-piece for you; 'tis true natural juice from the grape; none of your damned vintners brewings.' Having spoke thus, he presented to each of them another large dry crust, bidding them drink it off, and not be bashful, for it would do them no hurt. The two brothers, after having performed the usual office in such delicate conjunctures, of staring a sufficient period at Lord Peter and each other, and finding how matters were like to go, resolved not to enter on a new dispute, but let him carry the point as he pleased; for he was now got into one of his mad fits, and to argue or expostulate further, would only serve to render him a hundred times more untractable.

I have chosen to relate this worthy matter in all its circumstances, because it gave a principal occasion to that great and famous rupture,* which happened about the same time among these brethren, and never afterwards made up. But of that I shall treat at large in another section.

However, it is certain, that Lord Peter, even in his lucid intervals, was very lewdly given in his common conversation, extreme wilful and positive, and would at any time rather argue to the death, than allow himself to be once in an error. Besides, he had an abominable faculty of telling huge palpable lies upon all occasions; and swearing, not only to the truth, but cursing the whole company to hell, if they pretended to make the least scruple of believing him. One time he swore he had a cow † at home, which gave as much milk at a meal, as would fill three thousand churches; and what was yet more extraordinary, would never turn sour. Another time he was telling of an old sign-post ** that belonged to his father, with nails and timber enough on it to build sixteen large men-of-war. Talking one day of Chinese waggons, which were made so light as to sail over mountains: 'Z—nds,' said Peter, 'where's the wonder of that? By G—, I saw a large house of lime and stone ‡ travel over sea and land (granting that it stopped sometimes to bait) above two thousand German leagues.' And that which was the good of it, he would swear desperately all the while, that he never told a lie in his life; and at every word: 'By G—, gentlemen, I tell you nothing but the truth; and the D —l broil them eternally that will not believe me.'

In short, Peter grew so scandalous that all the neighbourhood began in plain words to say, he was no better than a knave. And his two brothers, long weary of his ill usage, resolved at last to leave him; but first they humbly desired a copy of their father's will, which had now lain by neglected

---

* By this rupture is meant the Reformation.

† The ridiculous multiplying of the Virgin Mary's milk among the papists, under the allegory of a cow, which gave as much milk at a meal as would fill three thousand churches. W. WOTTON.

** By this sign-post is meant the cross of our Blessed Saviour.

‡ The chapel of Loretto. He falls here only upon the ridiculous inventions of popery: the Church of Rome intended by these things to gull silly, superstitious people, and rook them of their money; that the world had been too long in slavery, our ancestors gloriously redeemed us from that yoke. The Church of Rome therefore ought to be exposed, and he deserves well of mankind that does expose it. W. WOTTON.

Ibid. The chapel of Loretto, which travelled from the Holy Land to Italy.

time out of mind. Instead of granting this request, he called them damned sons of whores, rogues, traitors, and the rest of the vile names he could muster up. However, while he was abroad one day upon his projects, the two youngsters watched their opportunity, made a shift to come at the will,* and took a *copia vera*, by which they presently saw how grossly they had been abused; their father having left them equal heirs, and strictly commanded, that whatever they got should lie in common among them all. Pursuant to which, their next enterprise was to break open the cellar-door and get a little good drink † to spirit and comfort their hearts. In copying the will, they had met another precept against whoring, divorce, and separate maintenance; upon which their next work ** was to discard their concubines, and send for their wives. Whilst all this was in agitation, there enters a solicitor from Newgate, desiring Lord Peter would please to procure a pardon for a thief that was to be hanged to-morrow. But the two brothers told him, he was a coxcomb to seek pardons from a fellow who deserved to be hanged much better than his client; and discovered all the method of that imposture, in the same form I delivered it a while ago, advising the solicitor to put his friend upon obtaining a pardon from the king.‡ In the midst of all this clutter and revolution, in comes Peter with a file of dragoons || at his heels, and gathering from all hands what was in the wind, he and his gang, after several millions of scurrilities and curses, not very important here to repeat, by main force very fairly kicks them both out of doors || || and would never let them come under his roof from that day to this.

SECTION V.

A DIGRESSION IN THE MODERN KIND.

WE whom the world is pleased to honor with the title of Modern authors, should never have been able to compass our great design of an everlasting remembrance, and never-dying fame, if our endeavours had not been so highly serviceable

---

* Translated the scriptures into the vulgar tongues.
† Administered the cup to the laity at the communion.
** Allowed the marriages of priests.
‡ Directed penitents not to trust to pardons and absolutions procured for money, but sent them to implore the mercy of God, from whence alone remission is to be obtained.
|| By Peter's dragoons is meant the civil power which those princes who were bigoted to the Romish superstition, employed against the reformers.
|| || The Pope shuts all who dissent from him out of the Church.

to the general good of mankind. This, O universe, is the adventurous attempt of me thy secretary: [1]

> ——Quemvis perferre laborem
> Suadet, & inducit noctes vigilare serenas.[2]

To this end, I have some time since, with a world of pains and art, dissected the carcass of human nature, and read many useful lectures upon the several parts, both containing and contained; till at last it smelt so strong, I could preserve it no longer. Upon which, I have been at a great expense to fit up all the bones with exact contexture, and in due symmetry; so that I am ready to show a very complete anatomy thereof to all curious gentlemen and others. But not to digress farther in the midst of a digression, as I have known some authors enclose digressions in one another, like a nest of boxes; I do affirm, that having carefully cut up human nature, I have found a very strange, new, and important discovery, that the public good of mankind is performed by two ways, instruction and diversion. And I have farther proved in my said several readings (which perhaps the world may one day see, if I can prevail on any friend to steal a copy, or on certain gentlemen of my admirers to be very importunate) that, as mankind is now disposed, he receives much greater advantage by being diverted than instructed; his epidemical diseases being fastidiosity, amorphy, and oscitation; whereas in the present universal empire of wit and learning, there seems but little matter left for instruction. However, in compliance with a lesson of great age and authority, I have attempted carrying the point in all its heights; and accordingly throughout this divine treaties, have skillfully kneaded up both together with a layer of *utile,* and a layer of *dulce.*[3]

When I consider how exceedingly our illustrious Moderns have eclipsed the weak glimmering lights of the Ancients, and turned them out of the road of all fashionable commerce, to a degree, that our choice town wits,* of most refined accom-

---

* The learned person here meant by our author, hath been endeavouring to annihilate so many ancient writers, that until he is pleased to stop his hand it will be dangerous to affirm, whether there have been [ever] any ancients in the world.

[1] Swift here satirizes the attempts of the Modern scientists to achieve universal and utilitarian systems of knowledge, and what he takes to be their pride and presumptuousness.

[2] Lucretius, I, 141–2.

[3] The source of Swift's probably Rosicrucian philosopher of O. Brazile and his highly alchemical formula for universal knowledge is either Thomas Vaughan's *Anthroposophia Theomagica* or Samuel Butler's *Character of An Hermetic Philosopher.* The satiric point in context is that Modern foolish pretensions to universal knowledge are best figured forth by a system, an *arcanum,* that is easily foolish and pretentious to begin with.

plishments, are in grave dispute, whether there have been ever any Ancients or no: in which point we are like to receive wonderful satisfaction from the most useful labours and lucubrations of that worthy modern, Dr. Bentley: I say, when I consider all this, I cannot but bewail, that no famous Modern hath ever yet attempted an universal system in a small portable volume of all things that are to be known, or believed, or imagined, or practised in life. I am, however, forced to acknowledge, that such an enterprise was thought on some time ago by a great philosopher of O. Brazile.* The method he proposed was by a certain curious receipt, a nostrum, which after his untimely death, I found among his papers, and do here out of my great affection to the modern learned, present them with it, not doubting it may one day encourage some worthy undertaker.

You take fair correct copies, well bound in calf's skin, and lettered at the back, of all modern bodies of arts and sciences whatsoever, and in what language you please. These you distil in balneo Mariæ, *infusing quintessence of poppy Q.S., together with three pints of* Lethe, *to be had from the apothecaries. You cleanse away carefully the* sordes *and* caput mortuum, *letting all that is volatile evaporate. You preserve only the first running, which is again to be distilled seventeen times, till what remains will amount to about two drams. This you keep in a glass vial, hermetically sealed, for one-and-twenty days. Then you begin your catholic treatise, taking every morning fasting (first shaking the vial), three drops of this* elixir, *snuffing it strongly up your nose. It will dilate itself about the brain (where there is any) in fourteen minutes, and you immediately perceive in your head an infinite number of* abstracts, summaries, compendiums, extracts, collections, medulas, excerpta quædams, florilegias *and the like, all disposed into great order, and reducible upon paper.*[1]

I must needs own, it was by the assistance of this *arcanum,* that I, though otherwise *impar,* have adventured upon so daring an attempt, never achieved or undertaken before, but by a certain author called Homer, in whom, though otherwise a person not without some abilities, and for an Ancient of a

---

* This is an imaginary island, of kin to that which is called the Painters' Wives Island, placed in some unknown part of the ocean, merely at the fancy of the map-maker.

[1] The quick and easy way to knowledge is further satire on the Modern innovations of abstracts, summaries, extracts, abridgments, etc., published by John Dunton, for example, in his *Young Students Library.* Note Swift's *My New Help of Smatterers, or the Art of being Deep-learned and Shallow-read.*

tolerable genius, I have discovered many gross errors, which are not to be forgiven his very ashes, if, by chance any of them are left. For whereas we are assured he designed his work for a complete body of all knowledge,* human, divine, political, and mechanic, it is manifest he hath wholly neglected some, and been very imperfect in the rest. For, first of all, as eminent a cabalist as his disciples would represent him, his account of the *opus magnum* is extremely poor and deficient; he seems to have read but very superficially either Sendivogius, Behmen, or *Anthroposophia Theomagica*.† He is also quite mistaken about the *sphæra pyroplastica*, a neglect not to be atoned for; and (if the reader will admit so severe a censure), *vix crederem autorem hunc, unquam audivisse ignis vocem*. His failings are not less prominent in several parts of the mechanics. For, having read his writings with the utmost application usual among Modern wits, I could never yet discover the least direction about the structure of that useful instrument, a save-all.[1] For want of which, if the Moderns had not lent their assistance, we might yet have wandered in the dark. But I have still behind, a fault far more notorious to tax this author with; I mean, his gross ignorance in the common laws of this realm, and in the doctrine as well as discipline of the Church of England.** A defect indeed, for which both he and all the ancients stand most justly censured, by my worthy and ingenious friend, Mr. Wotton, Bachelor of Divinity, in his incomparable treatise of *Ancient and Modern Learning,* a book never to be sufficiently valued, whether we consider the happy turns and flowings of the author's wit, the great usefulness of his sublime discoveries upon the subject of flies and spittle, or the laborious eloquence of his style. And I cannot forbear doing that author the justice of my public acknowledgments, for the great helps and liftings I had out of his incomparable piece, while I was penning this treatise.

But, besides these omissions in Homer already mentioned, the curious reader will also observe several defects in that author's writings, for which he is not altogether so account-

* *Homerus omnes res humanas poematis complexus est.* —Xenoph in conviv.

† A treatise written about fifty years ago, by a Welsh gentleman of Cambridge; his name, as I remember, was Vaughan, as appears by the answer to it writ by the learned Dr. Henry More; it is a piece of the most unintelligible fustian, that, perhaps, was ever published in any language.

**Mr. Wotton (to whom our author never gives any quarter) in his comparison of ancient and modern learning, numbers divinity, law, &c., among those parts of knowledge wherein we excel the Ancients.

[1] A mechanical contrivance for saving candle ends.

able. For whereas every branch of knowledge has received such wonderful acquirements since his age, especially within these last three years, or thereabouts, it is almost impossible he could be so very perfect in modern discoveries as his advocates pretend. We freely acknowledge him to be the inventor of the compass, of gunpowder, and the circulation of the blood: but I challenge any of his admirers to show me in all his writings a complete account of the spleen. Does he not also leave us wholly to seek in the art of political wagering? What can be more defective and unsatisfactory than his long dissertation upon tea? And as to his method of salivation without mercury, so much celebrated of late, it is to my own knowledge and experience a thing very little to be relied on.

It was to supply such momentous defects, that I have been prevailed on after long solicitation, to take pen in hand; and I dare venture to promise, the judicious reader shall find nothing neglected here, that can be of use upon any emergency of life. I am confident to have included and exhausted all that human imagination can rise or fall to. Particularly, I recommend to the perusal of the learned certain discoveries that are wholly untouched by others; whereof I shall only mention among a great many more: my *New Help of Smatterers, or the Art of being Deep-learned and Shallow-read; A Curious Invention about Mouse-Traps; An Universal Rule of Reason, or Every Man his own Carver;* together with a most useful engine for catching of owls. All which the judicious reader will find largely treated on in the several parts of this discourse.

I hold myself obliged to give as much light as is possible, into the beauties and excellencies of what I am writing, because it is become the fashion and humor most applauded among the first authors of this polite and learned age, when they would correct the ill nature of critical, or inform the ignorance of courteous readers. Besides, there have been several famous pieces lately published both in verse and prose, wherein, if the writers had not been pleased, out of their great humanity and affection to the public, to give us a nice detail of the sublime and the admirable they contain, it is a thousand to one whether we should ever have discovered one grain of either. For my own particular, I cannot deny, that whatever I have said upon this occasion, had been more proper in a preface, and more agreeable to the mode which usually directs it there. But I here think fit to lay hold on that great and honourable privilege of being the last writer. I claim an absolute authority in right, as the freshest Modern, which gives me a despotic power over all authors before me. In the strength of which title, I do utterly disapprove and declare against that pernicious custom, of making the preface a bill of fare to the book. For I have always looked upon it as a high point of indiscretion in monster-mongers and other retailers of strange sights, to hang out a fair large picture over the door, drawn after the life, with a most eloquent description underneath. This hath saved me many a threepence, for my curiosity was fully satisfied, and I never offered to go in, though often invited by the urging and attending orator, with his last moving and standing piece of rhetoric: 'Sir, upon my word, we are just going to begin.' Such is exactly the fate, at this time, of Prefaces, Epistles, Advertisements, Introductions, Prolegomenas, Apparatuses, To-the-Readers.[1] This expedient was admirable at first; our great Dryden has long carried it as far as it would go, and with incredible success. He has often said to me in confidence, that the world would have never suspected him to be so great a poet, if he had not assured them so frequently in his prefaces, that it was impossible they could either doubt or forget it. Perhaps it may be so; however, I much fear, his instructions have edified out of their place, and taught men to grow wiser in certain points, where he never intended they should; for it is lamentable to behold, with what a lazy scorn many of the yawning readers in our age, do now-a-days twirl over forty or fifty pages of preface and dedication (which is the usual Modern stint) as if it were so much Latin. Though it must be also allowed on the other hand that a very considerable number is known to proceed critics and wits, by reading nothing else. Into which two factions, I think, all present readers may justly be divided. Now, for myself, I profess to be one of the former sort; and therefore having the Modern inclination to expatiate upon the beauty of my own productions, and display the bright parts of my discourse, I thought best to do it in the body of the work, where, as it now lies, it makes a very considerable addition to the bulk of the volume, a circumstance by no means to be neglected by a skilful writer.

Having thus paid my due deference and acknowledgment to an established custom of our newest authors, by a long digression unsought for, and an universal censure unprovoked, by forcing into the light, with much pains and dex-

---

[1] The reader will note the way in which Swift's *Tale* exactly parodies these Modern innovations.

terity, my own excellencies and other men's defaults, with great justice to myself and candor to them, I now happily resume my subject, to the infinite satisfaction both of the reader and the author.

SECTION VI.

A TALE OF A TUB.

We left Lord Peter in open rupture with his two brethren; both for ever discarded from his house, and resigned to the wide world, with little or nothing to trust to. Which are circumstances that render them proper subjects for the charity of a writer's pen to work on, scenes of misery ever affording the fairest harvest for great adventures. And in this the world may perceive the difference between the integrity of a generous author and that of a common friend. The latter is observed to adhere close in prosperity, but on the decline of fortune to drop suddenly off. Whereas the generous author, just on the contrary, finds his hero on the dunghill, from thence by gradual steps raises him to a throne, and then immediately withdraws, expecting not so much as thanks for his pains, in imitation of which example, I have placed Lord Peter in a noble house, given him a title to wear, and money to spend. There I shall leave him for some time, returning where common charity directs me, to the assistance of his brothers, at their lowest ebb. However, I shall by no means forget my character of an historian to follow the truth step by step, whatever happens, or wherever it may lead me.

The two exiles, so nearly united in fortune and interest, took a lodging together, where, at their first leisure, they began to reflect on the numberless misfortunes and vexations of their life past, and could not tell on the sudden, to what failure in their conduct they ought to impute them, when, after some recollection, they called to mind the copy of their father's will, which they had so happily recovered. This was immediately produced, and a firm resolution taken between them, to alter whatever was already amiss and reduce all their future measures to the strictest obedience prescribed therein. The main body of the will (as the reader cannot easily have forgot) consisted in certain admirable rules about the wearing of their coats, in the perusal whereof, the two brothers at every period duly comparing the doctrine with the practice, there was never seen a wider difference between two things, horrible downright transgressions of every point. Upon which they both resolved, without further delay, to fall immediately upon reducing the whole, exactly after their father's model.

But here it is good to stop the hasty reader, ever impatient to see the end of an adventure, before we writers can duly prepare him for it. I am to record, that these two brothers began to be distinguished at this time by certain names. One of them desired to be called MARTIN,* and the other took the appellation of JACK.† These two had lived in much friendship and agreement under the tyranny of their brother Peter, as it is the talent of fellow-sufferers to do; men in misfortune being like men in the dark, to whom all colours are the same. But when they came forward into the world, and began to display themselves to each other, and to the light, their complexions appeared extremely different, which the present posture of their affairs gave them sudden opportunity to discover.

But here the severe reader may justly tax me as a writer of short memory, a deficiency to which a true Modern cannot but of necessity be a little subject: because, memory being an employment of the mind upon things past, is a faculty for which the learned in our illustrious age have no manner of occasion, who deal entirely with invention, and strike all things out of themselves, or at least by collision from each other,[1] upon which account, we think it highly reasonable to produce our great forgetfulness, as an argument unanswerable for our great wit. I ought in method to have informed the reader about fifty pages ago of a fancy Lord Peter took, and infused into his brothers, to wear on their coats whatever trimmings came up in fashion; never pulling off any, as they went out of the mode, but keeping on all together, which amounted in time to a medley the most antic you can possibly conceive, and this to a degree, that upon the time of their falling out there was hardly a thread of the original coat to be seen, but an infinite quantity of lace, and ribbons, and fringe, and embroidery, and points (I mean only those tagged with silver,** for the rest fell off). Now this material circumstance having been forgot in due place, as good fortune hath ordered, comes in very properly here, when the two brothers are just

---

* Martin Luther.
† John Calvin.
** Points tagged with silver are those doctrines that promote the greatness and wealth of the church, which have been therefore woven deepest in the body of Popery.
[1] Swift satirizes Modern materialistic subversion of the orthodox faculty psychology, see p. 372, n. 1.

going to reform their vestures into the primitive state, prescribed by their father's will.

They both unanimously entered upon this great work, looking sometimes on their coats, and sometimes on the will. Martin laid the first hand; at one twitch brought off a large handful of points; and with a second pull, stripped away ten dozen yards of fringe. But when he had gone thus far, he demurred a while: he knew very well there yet remained a great deal more to be done; however, the first heat being over, his violence began to cool, and he resolved to proceed more moderately in the rest of the work; having already very narrowly escaped a swinging rent in pulling off the points, which being tagged with silver (as we have observed before) the judicious workman had with much sagacity double sewn, to preserve them from falling. Resolving therefore to rid his coat of a huge quantity of gold lace, he picked up the stitches with much caution, and diligently gleaned out all the loose threads as he went, which proved to be a work of time. Then he fell about the embroidered Indian figures of men, women, and children, against which, as you have heard in its due place, their father's testament was extremely exact and severe: these, with much dexterity and application, were after a while quite eradicated, or utterly defaced. For the rest, where he observed the embroidery to be worked so close, as not to be got away without damaging the cloth, or where it served to hide or strengthen any flaw in the body of the coat, contracted by the perpetual tampering of workmen upon it; he concluded the wisest course was to let it remain, resolving in no case whatsoever, that the substance of the stuff should suffer injury, which he thought the best method for serving the true intent and meaning of his father's will. And this is the nearest account I have been able to collect of Martin's proceedings upon this great revolution.

But his brother Jack, whose adventures will be so extraordinary, as to furnish a great part in the remainder of this discourse, entered upon the matter with other thoughts, and a quite different spirit. For the memory of Lord Peter's injuries produced a degree of hatred and spite, which had a much greater share of inciting him than any regards after his father's commands, since these appeared at best only secondary and subservient to the other. However, for this medley of humor, he made a shift to find a very plausible name, honoring it with the title of zeal; which is perhaps the most significant word that hath been ever yet produced in any language;

as, I think, I have fully proved in my excellent analytical discourse upon that subject; wherein I have deduced a histori-theo-physi-logical account of zeal, showing how it first proceeded from a notion into a word, and from thence in a hot summer ripened into a tangible substance. This work, containing three large volumes in folio, I design very shortly to publish by the Modern way of subscription, not doubting but the nobility and gentry of the land will give me all possible encouragement, having already had such a taste of what I am able to perform.

I record, therefore, that brother Jack, brimful of this miraculous compound, reflecting with indignation upon Peter's tyranny, and farther provoked by the despondency of Martin, prefaced his resolutions to this purpose. 'What,' said he, 'a rogue that locked up his drink, turned away our wives, cheated us of our fortunes, palmed his damned crusts upon us for mutton, and at last kicked us out of doors; must we be in his fashions, with a pox? A rascal, besides, that all the street cries out against.' Having thus kindled and inflamed himself as high as possible, and by consequence, in a delicate temper for beginning a reformation, he set about the work immediately, and in three minutes made more dispatch than Martin had done in as many hours. For (courteous reader) you are given to understand, that zeal is never so highly obliged, as when you set it a-tearing; and Jack, who doated on that quality in himself, allowed it at this time its full swing. Thus it happened, that stripping down a parcel of gold lace a little too hastily, he rent the main body of his coat from top to bottom; and whereas his talent was not of the happiest in taking up a stitch, he knew no better way than to darn it again with packthread and a skewer. But the matter was yet infinitely worse (I record it with tears) when he proceeded to the embroidery: for, being clumsy by nature, and of temper impatient; withal, beholding millions of stitches that required the nicest hand, and sedatest constitutions, to extricate; in a great rage he tore off the whole piece, cloth and all, and flung it into the kennel, and furiously thus continuing his career: 'Ah, good brother Martin,' said he, 'do as I do, for the love of God; strip, tear, pull, rend, flay off all, that we may appear as unlike the rogue Peter as it is possible. I would not for a hundred pounds carry the least mark about me, that might give occasion to the neighbours of suspecting I was related to such a rascal.' But Martin, who at this time happened to be extremely phlegmatic and sedate, begged his brother, of all love, not to damage his coat by any means; for he never would get such another: desired him to consider, that it was not their business to form their actions by any reflection upon Peter's, but by observing the rules prescribed in their father's will. That he should remember, Peter was still their brother, whatever faults or injuries he had committed; and therefore they should by all means avoid such a thought as that of taking measures for good and evil, from no other rule than of opposition to him. That it was true, the testament of their good father was very exact in what related to the wearing of their coats; yet was it no less penal and strict in prescribing agreement, and friendship, and affection between them. And therefore, if straining a point were at all dispensible, it would certainly be so rather to the advance of unity than increase of contradiction.

Martin had still proceeded as gravely as he began, and doubtless would have delivered an admirable lecture of morality, which might have exceedingly contributed to my reader's repose, both of body and mind (the true ultimate end of ethics); but Jack was already gone a flight-shot beyond his patience. And as in scholastic disputes, nothing serves to rouse the spleen of him that opposes, so much as a kind of pedantic affected calmness in the respondent; disputants being for the most part like unequal scales, where the gravity of one side advances the lightness of the other, and causes it to fly up and kick the beam; so it happened here that the weight of Martin's argument exalted Jack's levity, and made him fly out and spurn against his brother's moderation. In short, Martin's patience put Jack in a rage; but that which most afflicted him was, to observe his brother's coat so well reduced into the state of innocence; while his own was either wholly rent to his shirt, or those places which had escaped his cruel clutches, were still in Peter's livery. So that he looked like a drunken beau, half rifled by bullies; or like a fresh tenant of Newgate, when he has refused the payment of garnish; or like a discovered shoplifter, left to the mercy of Exchange women; or like a bawd in her old velvet petticoat, resigned into the secular hands of the mobile. Like any or like all of these, a medley of rags, and lace, and rents, and fringes, unfortunately Jack did now appear: he would have been extremely glad to see his coat in the condition of Martin's, but infinitely gladder to find that of Martin's in the same predicament with his. However, since neither of these was likely to come to pass, he thought fit to lend the whole business another turn, and to dress up necessity into a virtue. Therefore, after as many of the fox's arguments as he could muster up, for bringing Martin to reason, as he called it; or, as he meant it, into his own ragged, bobtailed condition; and observing he said all to little purpose; what, alas, was left for the forlorn Jack to do, but after a million of scurrilities against his brother, to run mad with spleen, and spite, and contradiction. To be short, here began a mortal breach between these two. Jack went immediately to new lodgings, and in a few days it was for certain reported, that he had run out of his wits. In a short time after he appeared abroad, and confirmed the report by falling into the oddest whimseys that ever a sick brain conceived.

And now the little boys in the streets began to salute him with several names. Sometimes they would call him Jack the Bald; * sometimes, Jack with a lantern; † sometimes, Dutch Jack; ** sometimes, French Hugh; ‡ sometimes, Tom the beggar; || and sometimes, Knocking Jack of the north.|| || And it was under one, or some, or all of these appellations (which I leave the learned reader to determine) that he hath given rise to the most illustrious and epidemic sect of Æolists; who with honourable commemoration, do still acknowledge the renowned JACK for their author and founder. Of whose original, as well as principles, I am now advancing to gratify the world with a very particular account.

——Mellæo contingens cuncta lepore.

SECTION VII.

A DIGRESSION IN PRAISE OF DIGRESSIONS.

I HAVE sometimes heard of an *Iliad* in a nutshell; but it hath been my fortune to have much oftener seen a nutshell in an *Iliad*. There is no doubt that human life has received most wonderful advantages from both; but to which of the two the world is chiefly indebted, I shall leave among the curious, as a problem worthy of their utmost inquiry. For the invention of the latter, I think the commonwealth of learning is chiefly obliged to the great Modern improvement of digressions: the late refinements in knowledge, running parallel to those of diet in our nation, which among men of a judicious taste are

* That is, Calvin, from *calvus*, bald.
† All those who pretend to inward light.
** Jack of Leyden, who gave rise to the Anabaptists.
‡ The Huguenots.
|| The Gueuses, by which name some Protestants in Flanders were called.
|| || John Knox, the reformer of Scotland.

dressed up in various compounds, consisting in soups and olios, fricassees, and ragouts.

'Tis true, there is a sort of morose, detracting, ill-bred people, who pretend utterly to disrelish these polite innovations; and as to the similitude from diet, they allow the parallel, but are so bold to pronounce the example itself, a corruption and degeneracy of taste. They tell us that the fashion of jumbling fifty things together in a dish, was at first introduced in compliance to a depraved and debauched appetite, as well as to a crazy constitution: and to see a man hunting through an olio, after the head and brains of a goose, a widgeon, or a woodcock, is a sign he wants a stomach and digestion for more substantial victuals. Farther, they affirm, that digressions in a book are like foreign troops in a state, which argue the nation to want a heart and hands of its own, and often either subdue the natives, or drive them into the most unfruitful corners.

But, after all that can be objected by these supercilious censors, 'tis manifest, the society of writers would quickly be reduced to a very inconsiderable number, if men were put upon making books, with the fatal confinement of delivering nothing beyond what is to the purpose. 'Tis acknowledged, that were the case the same among us, as with the Greeks and Romans, when learning was in its cradle, to be reared and fed, and clothed by invention, it would be an easy task to fill up volumes upon particular occasions, without farther expatiating from the subject than by moderate excursions, helping to advance or clear the main design. But with knowledge it has fared as with a numerous army, encamped in a fruitful country, which for a few days maintains itself by the product of the soil it is on; till provisions being spent, they send to forage many a mile, among friends or enemies, it matters not. Meanwhile, the neighbouring fields, trampled and beaten down, become barren and dry, affording no sustenance but clouds of dust.

The whole course of things being thus entirely changed between us and the Ancients, and the Moderns wisely sensible of it, we of this age have discovered a shorter, and more prudent method, to become scholars and wits, without the fatigue of reading or of thinking. The most accomplished way of using books at present is two-fold: either first, to serve them as some men do lords, learn their titles exactly, and then brag of their acquaintance. Or secondly, which is indeed the choicer, the profounder, and politer method, to get a thorough insight into the index, by which the whole book is governed and turned, like fishes by the tail. For, to enter the palace of learning at the great gate, requires an expense of time and forms; therefore men of much haste and little ceremony are content to get in by the back door. For the arts are all in a flying march, and therefore more easily subdued by attacking them in the rear. Thus physicians discover the state of the whole body, by consulting only what comes from behind. Thus men catch knowledge by throwing their wit on the posteriors of a book, as boys do sparrows with flinging salt upon their tails. Thus human life is best understood by the wise man's rule of regarding the end. Thus are the sciences found like Hercules's oxen, by tracing them backwards. Thus are old sciences unravelled like old stockings, by beginning at the foot.

Besides all this, the army of the sciences hath been of late, with a world of martial discipline, drawn into its close order, so that a view or a muster may be taken of it with abundance of expedition. For this great blessing we are wholly indebted to systems and abstracts, in which the modern fathers of learning, like prudent usurers, spent their sweat for the ease of us their children. For labor is the seed of idleness, and it is the peculiar happiness of our noble age to gather the fruit.

Now the method of growing wise, learned, and sublime, having become so regular an affair, and so established in all its forms, the numbers of writers must needs have increased accordingly, and to a pitch that has made it of absolute necessity for them to interfere continually with each other. Besides, it is reckoned, that there is not at this present, a sufficient quantity of new matter left in nature, to furnish and adorn any one particular subject to the extent of a volume. This I am told by a very skilful computer, who hath given a full demonstration of it from rules of arithmetic.

This, perhaps, may be objected against by those who maintain the infinity of matter, and therefore will not allow that any species of it can be exhausted. For answer to which, let us examine the noblest branch of Modern wit or invention, planted and cultivated by the present age, and which, of all others, hath borne the most and the fairest fruit. For though some remains of it were left us by the Ancients, yet have not any of those, as I remember, been translated or compiled into systems for Modern use. Therefore we may affirm, to our own honor, that it has in some sort, been both invented and brought to a perfection by the same hands. What I mean is, that highly celebrated talent among the Modern wits, of deducing similitudes, allusions, and applications, very surprising, agreeable, and apposite, from the *pudenda* of either sex, together with their proper uses. And truly, having observed how little invention bears any vogue, besides what is derived into these channels, I have sometimes had a thought, that the happy genius of our age and country was prophetically held forth by that Ancient typical description of the Indian pigmies,* whose stature did not exceed above two foot; *sed quorum pudenda crassa, & ad talos usque pertingentia.* Now, I have been very curious to inspect the late productions, wherein the beauties of this kind have most prominently appeared. And although this vein hath bled so freely, and all endeavours have been used in the power of human breath to dilate, extend, and keep it open; like the Scythians,† who had a custom, and an instrument, to blow up the privities of their mares, that they might yield the more milk; yet I am under an apprehension it is near growing dry, and past all recovery; and that either some new *fonde* of wit should, if possible, be provided, or else that we must e'en be content with repetition here, as well as upon other occasions.

* Ctesiæ fragm. apud Photium.

† Herodot. L. 4.

This will stand as an uncontestable argument, that our Modern wits are not to reckon upon the infinity of matter for a constant supply. What remains therefore, but that our last recourse must be had to large indexes, and little compendiums; quotations must be plentifully gathered, and booked in alphabet; to this end, though authors need be little consulted, yet critics, and commentators, and lexicons carefully must. But above all, those judicious collectors of bright parts, and flowers, and observandas, are to be nicely dwelt on, by some called the sieves and boulters of learning, though it is left undetermined, whether they dealt in pearls or meal; and consequently, whether we are more to value that which passed through, or what stayed behind.

By these methods, in a few weeks, there starts up many a writer, capable of managing the profoundest and most universal subjects. For, what though his head be empty, provided his commonplace book be full; and if you will bate him but the circumstances of method, and style, and grammar, and invention; allow him but the common privileges of transcribing from others, and digressing from himself, as often as he shall see occasion; he will desire no more ingredients towards fitting up a treatise, that shall make a very comely figure on a bookseller's shelf; there to be preserved neat and clean for a long eternity, adorned with the heraldry of its title fairly inscribed on a label; never to be thumbed or greased by students, nor bound to everlasting chains of darkness in a library: but when the fulness of time is come, shall happily undergo the trial of purgatory, in order to ascend the sky.

Without these allowances, how is it possible we Modern wits should ever have an opportunity to introduce our collections, listed under so many thousand heads of a different nature? for want of which, the learned world would be deprived of infinite delight, as well as instruction, and we ourselves buried beyond redress in an inglorious and undistinguished oblivion.

From such elements as these, I am alive to behold the day, wherein the corporation of authors can outvie all its brethren in the field. A happiness derived to us with a great many others from our Scythian ancestors, among whom the number of pens was so infinite, that the Grecian * eloquence had no other way of expressing it, than by saying, that in the regions, far to the north, it was hardly possible for a man to travel, the very air was so replete with feathers.

* Herodot. L. 4.

The necessity of this digression will easily excuse the length; and I have chosen for it as proper a place as I could readily find. If the judicious reader can assign a fitter, I do here empower him to remove it into any other corner he pleases. And so I return with great alacrity to pursue a more important concern.

SECTION VIII.

A TALE OF A TUB.

The learned Æolists † [1] maintain the original cause of all things to be wind, from which principle this whole universe was at first produced, and into which it must at last be resolved; that the same breath which had kindled, and blew *up* the flame of nature, should one day blow it *out:*

Quod procul à nobis flectat Fortuna gubernans.

† All pretenders to inspiration whatsoever.

[1] Swift's Aeolist system, a reductive one, is based on wind; it is also an occult system, based on the *Anthroposophia Theomagica* by Thomas Vaughan, alias Eugenius Philalethes. And by means of occultism, or philosophical Enthusiasm, Swift satirizes Nonconformity, or religious Enthusiasm. Both this section of the *Tale* and the following "Digression Concerning Madness" become clearer and more meaningful when read as a unit. (See Starkman, pp. 44–56.)

This is what the *adepti* understand by their *anima mundi;* that is to say, the spirit, or breath, or wind of the world; or examine the whole system by the particulars of nature, and you will find it not to be disputed. For whether you please to call the *forma informans* of man, by the name of *spiritus, animus, afflatus,* or *anima;* what are all these but several appellations for wind, which is the ruling element in every compound, and into which they all resolve upon their corruption? Farther, what is life itself, but as it is commonly called, the breath of our nostrils? Whence it is very justly observed by naturalists, that wind still continues of great emolument in certain mysteries not to be named, giving occasion for those happy epithets of *turgidus* and *inflatus,* applied either to the *emittent* or *recipient* organs.

By what I have gathered out of ancient records, I find the compass of their doctrine took in two-and-thirty points, wherein it would be tedious to be very particular. However, a few of their most important precepts, deducible from it, are by no means to be omitted; among which the following maxim was of much weight: that since wind had the master share, as well as operation in every compound, by consequence, those beings must be of chief excellence, wherein that *primordium* appears most prominently to abound, and therefore man is in highest perfection of all created things, as having by the great bounty of philosophers, been endued with three distinct *animas* or winds, to which the sage Æolists, with much liberality, have added a fourth of equal necessity as well as ornament with the other three, by this *quartum principium,* taking in the four corners of the world; which gave occasion to that renowned cabalist, Bumbastus,* of placing the body of a man in due position to the four cardinal points.

In consequence of this, their next principle was, that man brings with him into the world a peculiar portion or grain of wind, which may be called a *quinta essentia,* extracted from the other four. This quintessence is of a catholic use upon all emergencies of life, is improvable into all arts and sciences, and may be wonderfully refined, as well as enlarged by certain methods in education. This, when blown up to its perfection, ought not to be covetously hoarded up, stifled, or hid under a bushel, but freely communicated to mankind. Upon these reasons, and others of equal weight, the wise Æolists affirm the gift of BELCHING to be the noblest act of a ra-

---

* This is one of the names of Paracelsus; he was called Christophorus, Theophrastus, Paracelsus, Bumbastus.

tional creature. To cultivate which art, and render it more serviceable to mankind, they made use of several methods. At certain seasons of the year, you might behold the priests amongst them, in vast numbers, with their mouths * gaping wide against a storm. At other times were to be seen several hundreds linked together in a circular chain, with every man a pair of bellows applied to his neighbour's breech, by which they blew up each other to the shape and size of a tun; and for that reason, with great propriety of speech, did usually call their bodies, their vessels. When, by these and the like performances, they were grown sufficiently replete, they would immediately depart, and disembogue for the public good a plentiful share of their acquirements, into their disciples' chaps. For we must here observe, that all learning was esteemed among them to be compounded from the same principle. Because, first, it is generally affirmed, or confessed that learning puffeth men up; and, secondly, they proved it by the following syllogism: Words are but wind; and learning is nothing but words; *ergo*, learning is nothing but wind. For this reason, the philosophers among them did, in their schools, deliver to their pupils, all their doctrines and opinions, by eructation, wherein they had acquired a wonderful eloquence, and of incredible variety. But the great characteristic, by which their chief sages were best distinguished, was a certain position of countenance, which gave undoubted intelligence to what degree or proportion the spirit agitated the inward mass. For, after certain gripings, the wind and vapours issuing forth, having first, by their turbulence and convulsions within, caused an earthquake in man's little world, distorted the mouth, bloated the cheeks, and gave the eyes a terrible kind of *relievo*. At which junctures all their belches were received for sacred, the sourer the better, and swallowed with infinite consolation by their meagre devotees. And to render these yet more complete, because the breath of man's life is in his nostrils, therefore the choicest, most edifying, and most enlivening belches, were very wisely conveyed through that vehicle, to give them a tincture as they passed.[1]

Their gods were the four winds, whom they worshipped, as the spirits that pervade and enliven the universe, and as those from whom alone all inspiration can properly be said to proceed. However, the chief of these, to whom they performed the adoration of *latria*, was the *Almighty North*, an

* This is meant of those seditious preachers, who blow up the seeds of rebellion, &c.

[1] See *The Mechanical Operation of the Spirit*.

ancient deity, whom the inhabitants of Megalopolis in Greece had likewise in highest reverence. *Omnium deorum Boream maxime celebrant.** This god, though endued with ubiquity, was yet supposed by the pro-founder Æolists, to possess one peculiar habitation, or (to speak in form) a *cœlum empyræum,* wherein he was more intimately present. This was situated in a certain region, well known to the ancient Greeks by them called Σκοτία, or the Land of Darkness. And although many controversies have arisen upon that matter; yet so much is undisputed, that from a region of the like denomination, the most refined Æolists have borrowed their original, from whence, in every age, the zealous among their priesthood have brought over their choicest inspiration, fetching it with their own hands from the fountain head in certain bladders, and disploding it among the sectaries in all nations, who did, and do, and ever will, daily gasp and pant after it.

* Pausan. L. 8.

Now, their mysteries and rites were performed in this manner. 'Tis well known among the learned, that the virtuosos of former ages had a contrivance for carrying and preserving winds in casks or barrels, which was of great assistance upon long sea voyages; and the loss of so useful an art at present is very much to be lamented, though, I know not how, with great negligence omitted by Pancirollus.† It was an invention ascribed to Æolus himself, from whom this sect is denominated; and who in honour of their founder's memory have to this day preserved great numbers of those barrels, whereof they fix one in each of their temples, first beating out the top. Into this barrel, upon solemn days, the priest enters, where, having before duly prepared himself by the methods already described, a secret funnel is also conveyed from his posteriors to the bottom of the barrel, which admits new supplies of inspiration from a northern chink or cranny. Whereupon, you behold him swell immediately to the shape and size of his vessel. In this posture he disembogues whole tempests upon his auditory, as the spirit from beneath gives him utterance, which, issuing *ex adytis* and *penetralibus* is not performed without much pain and gripings. And the wind in breaking forth deals with his face ** as it does with that of the sea, first blackening, then wrinkling, and at last bursting it into a foam. It is in this guise the sacred Æolist delivers

† An author who writ *De Artibus perditis,* &c., Of Arts lost, and of Arts invented.

** This is an exact description of the changes made in the face by enthusiastic preachers.

his oracular belches to his panting disciples; of whom some are greedily gaping after the sanctified breath, others are all the while hymning out the praises of the winds; and, gently wafted to and fro by their own humming, do thus represent the soft breezes of their deities appeased.

It is from this custom of the priests, that some authors maintain these Æolists to have been very ancient in the world.[1] Because, the delivery of their mysteries, which I have just now mentioned, appears exactly the same with that of other ancient oracles, whose inspirations were owing to certain subterraneous effluviums of wind, delivered with the same pain to the priest, and much about the same influence on the people. It is true indeed, that these were frequently managed and directed by female officers, whose organs were understood to be better disposed for the admission of those oracular gusts, as entering and passing up through a receptacle of greater capacity, and causing also a pruriency by the way, such as with due management hath been refined from a carnal into a spiritual ecstasy. And to strengthen this profound conjecture, it is farther insisted, that this custom of female priests * is kept up still in certain refined colleges of our modern Æolists, who are agreed to receive their inspiration, derived through the receptacle aforesaid, like their ancestors, the Sybils.

And whereas the mind of Man, when he gives the spur and bridle to his thoughts, doth never stop, but naturally sallies out into both extremes of high and low, of good and evil; his first flight of fancy commonly transports him to ideas of what is most perfect, finished, and exalted; till having soared out of his own reach and sight, not well perceiving how near the frontiers of height and depth border upon each other; with the same course and wing, he falls down plumb into the lowest bottom of things, like one who travels the east into the west, or like a straight line drawn by its own length into a circle. Whether a tincture of malice in our natures makes us fond of furnishing every bright idea with its reverse; or whether reason, reflecting upon the sum of things, can, like the sun, serve only to enlighten one half of the globe, leaving the other half, by necessity, under shade and darkness; or, whether fancy, flying up to the imagination of what is highest and best, becomes over-shot, and spent, and weary, and suddenly falls like a dead bird of paradise to the ground. Or

* Quakers who suffer their women to preach and pray.

[1] Note that when Swift connects Aeolism with Antiquity it is only to its most discredited aspects, for example, oracles.

whether after all these metaphysical conjectures, I have not entirely missed the true reason, the proposition, however, which has stood me in so much circumstance, is altogether true; that, as the most uncivilized parts of mankind have some way or other climbed up into the conception of a God, or Supreme Power, so they have seldom forgot to provide their fears with certain ghastly notions, which, instead of better, have served them pretty tolerably for a devil. And this proceeding seems to be natural enough; for it is with men, whose imaginations are lifted up very high, after the same rate as with those whose bodies are so; that, as they are delighted with the advantage of a nearer contemplation upwards, so they are equally terrified with the dismal prospect of the precipice below. Thus, in the choice of a devil, it hath been the usual method of mankind, to single out some being, either in act or in vision, which was in most antipathy to the god they had framed. Thus also the sect of Æolists possessed themselves with a dread, and horror, and hatred of two malignant natures, betwixt whom, and the deities they adored, perpetual enmity was established. The first of these was the chameleon,* sworn foe to inspiration, who in scorn devoured large influences of their god, without refunding the smallest blast by eructation. The other was a huge terrible monster, called Moulinavent, who, with four strong arms, waged eternal battle with all their divinities, dexterously turning to avoid their blows, and repay them with interest.

Thus furnished, and set out with gods, as well as devils, was the renowned sect of Æolists, which makes at this day so illustrious a figure in the world, and whereof that polite nation of Laplanders are, beyond all doubt, a most authentic branch; of whom I therefore cannot, without injustice, here omit to make honourable mention, since they appear to be so closely allied in point of interest, as well as inclinations, with their brother Æolists among us, as not only to buy their winds by wholesale from the same merchants, but also to retail them after the same rate and method, and to customers much alike.

Now, whether this system here delivered was wholly compiled by Jack, or, as some writers believe, rather copied from the original at Delphos, with certain additions and emendations, suited to times and circumstances, I shall not absolutely determine. This I may affirm, that Jack gave it at least a new

---

* I do not well understand what the Author aims at here, any more than by the terrible Monster, mentioned in the following lines, called *Moulinavent*, which is the French word for a windmill.

turn, and formed it into the same dress and model as it lies deduced by me.

I have long sought after this opportunity of doing justice to a society of men for whom I have a peculiar honour, and whose opinions, as well as practices, have been extremely misrepresented and traduced by the malice or ignorance of their adversaries. For I think it one of the greatest and best of human actions, to remove prejudices, and place things in their truest and fairest light: which I therefore boldly undertake, without any regards of my own, beside the conscience, the honour, and the thanks.

SECTION IX.

A DIGRESSION CONCERNING THE ORIGINAL, THE USE, AND IMPROVEMENT OF MADNESS IN A COMMONWEALTH

NOR shall it any ways detract from the just reputation of this famous sect, that its rise and institution are owing to such an author as I have described Jack to be; a person whose intellectuals were overturned, and his brain shaken out of its natural position; which we commonly suppose to be a distemper, and call by the name of madness or phrenzy. For, if we take a survey of the greatest actions that have been performed in the world, under the influence of single men, which are the establishment of new empires by conquest, the advance and progress of new schemes in philosophy, and the contriving, as well as the propagating, of new religions, we shall find the authors of them all to have been persons whose natural reason had admitted great revolutions from their diet, their education, the prevalency of some certain temper, together with the particular influence of air and climate. Besides, there is something individual in human minds, that easily kindles at the accidental approach and collision of certain circumstances, which, though of paltry and mean appearance, do often flame out into the greatest emergencies of life. For great turns are not always given by strong hands, but by lucky adaption, and at proper seasons; and it is of no import where the fire was kindled, if the vapour has once got up into the brain.[1] For the upper region of man is furnished like the middle region of the air; the materials are formed

[1] The theory of vapors, again a reductive theory, explains madness as resulting from the vapors rising to the brain and causing mechanical disturbance. And vapor is no more than wind in another state. Thus Nonconformity is again satirized, but in "A Digression Concerning Madness," through science and philosophy rather than occultism. (See Starkman, pp. 24–44.)

from causes of the widest difference, yet produce at last the same substance and effect. Mists arise from the earth, steams from dunghills, exhalations from the sea, and smoke from fire; yet all clouds are the same in composition as well as consequences, and the fumes issuing from a jakes will furnish as comely and useful a vapour as incense from an altar. Thus far, I suppose, will easily be granted me; and then it will follow, that as the face of nature never produces rain but when it is overcast and disturbed, so human understanding, seated in the brain, must be troubled and overspread by vapours, ascending from the lower faculties to water the invention and render it fruitful. Now, although these vapours (as it hath been already said) are of as various original as those of the skies, yet the crop they produce differs both in kind and degree, merely according to the soil. I will produce two instances to prove and explain what I am now advancing.

A certain great prince * raised a mighty army, filled his coffers with infinite treasures, provided an invincible fleet, and all this without giving the least part of his design to his greatest ministers or his nearest favourites. Immediately the whole world was alarmed; the neighbouring crowns in trembling expectations towards what point the storm would burst; the small politicians everywhere forming profound conjectures. Some believed he had laid a scheme for universal monarchy; others, after much insight, determined the matter to be a project for pulling down the pope, and setting up the reformed religion, which had once been his own. Some, again, of a deeper sagacity, sent him into Asia to subdue the Turk, and recover Palestine. In the midst of all these projects and preparations, a certain state-surgeon,† gathering the nature of the disease by these symptoms, attempted the cure, at one blow performed the operation, broke the bag, and out flew the vapour; nor did anything want to render it a complete remedy, only that the prince unfortunately happened to die in the performance. Now, is the reader exceeding curious to learn from whence this vapour took its rise, which had so long set the nations at a gaze? What secret wheel, what hidden spring could put into motion so wonderful an engine? It was afterwards discovered that the movement of this whole machine had been directed by an absent female, whose eyes had raised a protuberancy, and before emission, she was removed into an enemy's country. What should an unhappy

---

* This was Harry the Great of France.
† Ravillac, who stabbed Henry the Great in his coach.

prince do in such ticklish circumstances as these? He tried in vain the poet's never-failing receipt of *corpora quæque;* for

> Idque petit corpus mens unde est saucia amore;
> Unde feritur, eo tendit, gestitq; coire. — LUCR.

Having to no purpose used all peaceable endeavours, the collected part of the semen, raised and inflamed, became a dust, converted to choler, turned head upon the spinal duct, and ascended to the brain.[1] The very same principle that influences a bully to break the windows of a whore who has jilted him, naturally stirs up a great prince to raise mighty armies, and dream of nothing but sieges, battles, and victories.

> —— Teterrima belli
> Causa ——

The other instance * is what I have read somewhere in a very ancient author, of a mighty king, who, for the space of above thirty years, amused himself to take and lose towns; beat armies, and be beaten; drive princes out of their dominions; fright children from their bread and butter; burn, lay waste, plunder, dragoon, massacre subject and stranger, friend and foe, male and female. 'Tis recorded, that the philosophers of each country were in grave dispute upon causes natural, moral, and political, to find out where they should assign an original solution of this phenomenon. At last the vapour or spirit, which animated the hero's brain, being in perpetual circulation, seized upon that region of the human body, so renowned for furnishing the *zibeta occidentalis,*† and gathering there into a tumor, left the rest of the world for that time in peace. Of such mighty consequence it is where those exhalations fix, and of so little from whence they proceed. The same spirits which, in their superior progress would conquer a kingdom, descending upon the anus, conclude in a fistula.

Let us next examine the great introducers of new schemes in philosophy, and search till we can find from what faculty of the soul the disposition arises in mortal man, of taking it into his head to advance new systems with such an eager zeal, in things agreed on all hands impossible to be known; from what seeds this disposition springs, and to what quality of

---

* This is meant of the present French king.

† Paracelsus, who was so famous for chemistry, tried an experiment upon human excrement, to make a perfume of it, which when he had brought to perfection, he called *zibeta occidentalis,* or western-civet, the back parts of man (according to his division mentioned by the author, pp. 360–61 being the west.)

[1] See *The Mechanical Operation of the Spirit.*

human nature these grand innovators have been indebted for their number of disciples. Because, it is plain, that several of the chief among them, both Ancient and Modern, were usually mistaken by their adversaries, and indeed by all except their own followers, to have been persons crazed, or out of their wits, having generally proceeded in the common course of their words and actions by a method very different from the vulgar dictates of unrefined reason; agreeing for the most part in their several models, with their present undoubted successors in the academy of modern Bedlam (whose merits and principles I shall farther examine in due place). Of this kind were *Epicurus, Diogenes, Appollonius, Lucretius, Paracelsus,*[1] *Descartes,* and others; who, if they were now in the world, tied fast, and separate from their followers, would, in this our undistinguishing age, incur manifest danger of phlebotomy, and whips, and chains, and dark chambers, and straw. For what man in the natural state or course of thinking, did ever conceive it in his power to reduce the notions of all mankind exactly to the same length, and breadth, and height of his own? Yet this is the first humble and civil design of all innovators in the empire of reason. Epicurus modestly hoped, that one time or other, a certain fortuitous concourse of all men's opinions, after perpetual justlings, the sharp with the smooth, the light and the heavy, the round and the square, would by certain *clinamina* unite in the notions of atoms and void, as these did in the originals of all things.[2] Cartesius reckoned to see before he died the sentiments of all philosophers, like so many lesser stars in his romantic system, wrapped and drawn within his own vortex.[3] Now, I would gladly be informed, how it is possible to account for such imaginations as these in particular men, without recourse to my phenomenon of vapours, ascending from the lower faculties to overshadow the brain, and there distilling into conceptions, for which the narrowness of our mother-tongue has not yet assigned any other name besides that of madness or phrenzy. Let us therefore now conjecture how it comes to pass, that none of these great prescribers do ever fail providing themselves and their notions with a number of implicit disciples. And, I think, the reason is easy to be assigned: for there is a peculiar string in the

---

[1] Of this list of mad philosophers, Appollonius (of Tyana) and Paracelsus are included because, Ancient or Modern, they were mystical philosophers.

[2] Epicurus, like Diogenes and Lucretius, is for Swift a Modern philosopher, and hence in Bedlam. In the late seventeenth century neo-Epicurianism had become a Modern system, support and justification of the new materialistic philosophy of Hobbes and Descartes.

[3] Cartesianism, again a reductive system by reason of its vortical explanation of phenomena, was to Swift the very type of Modern, mad philosophy.

harmony of human understanding, which in several individuals is exactly of the same tuning. This, if you can dexterously screw up to its right key, and then strike gently upon it, whenever you have the good fortune to light among those of the same pitch, they will, by a secret necessary sympathy, strike exactly at the same time.[1] And in this one circumstance lies all the skill or luck of the matter; for if you chance to jar the string among those who are either above or below your own height, instead of subscribing to your doctrine, they will tie you fast, call you mad, and feed you with bread and water. It is therefore a point of the nicest conduct to distinguish and adapt this noble talent, with respect to the differences of persons and of times. Cicero understood this very well, when writing to a friend in England, with a caution, among other matters, to beware of being cheated by our hackney-coachmen (who, it seems, in those days were as arrant rascals as they are now) has these remarkable words: *Est quod gaudeas te in ista loca venisse, ubi aliquid sapere viderere.** For, to speak a bold truth, it is a fatal miscarriage so ill to order affairs, as to pass for a fool in one company, when in another you might be treated as a philosopher. Which I desire some certain gentlemen of my acquaintance to lay up in their hearts, as a very seasonable innuendo.

* *Epist. ad. Fam. Trebatio.*

This, indeed, was the fatal mistake of that worthy gentleman, my most ingenious friend, Mr. Wotton: a person, in appearance ordained for great designs, as well as performances; whether you will consider his notions or his looks. Surely no man ever advanced into the public with fitter qualifications of body and mind, for the propagation of a new religion. Oh, had those happy talents misapplied to vain philosophy been turned into their proper channels of dreams and visions, where distortion of mind and countenance are of such sovereign use; the base detracting world would not then have dared to report that something is amiss, this his brain hath undergone an unlucky shake; which even his brother Modernists themselves, like ungrates, do whisper so loud, that it reaches up to the very garret I am now writing in.

Lastly, whosoever pleases to look into the fountains of Enthusiasm, from whence, in all ages, have eternally proceeded such fattening streams, will find the springhead to have been as troubled and muddy as the current. Of such great

[1] Swift's system of indoctrination has several implications: medical (the concept of health as harmony), philosophical (the pre-Epicurean soul as harmony), and scientific (the Modern concept of sympathetic vibration).

emolument is a tincture of this vapour, which the world calls madness, that without its help, the world would not only be deprived of those two great blessings, conquests and systems, but even all mankind would unhappily be reduced to the same belief in things invisible. Now, the former *postulatum* being held, that it is of no import from what originals this vapour proceeds, but either in what angles it strikes and spreads over the understanding, or upon what species of brain it ascends; it will be a very delicate point to cut the feather, and divide the several reasons to a nice and curious reader, how this numerical difference in the brain can produce effects of so vast a difference from the same vapour, as to be the sole point of individuation between Alexander the Great, Jack of Leyden, and Monsieur Des Cartes. The present argument is the most abstracted that ever I engaged in; it strains my faculties to their highest stretch; and I desire the reader to attend with utmost perpensity, for I now proceed to unravel this knotty point.

There is in mankind a certain †   *   *   *   *   *
*   *   *   *   *   *   *   *   *   *   *   *
Hic multa   *   *   *   *   *   *   *   *   *
desiderantur   *   *   *   *   *   *   *   *   *
*   *   * And this I take to be a clear solution of the matter.

Having therefore so narrowly passed through this intricate difficulty, the reader will, I am sure, agree with me in the conclusion, that if the Moderns mean by madness, only a disturbance or transposition of the brain, by force of certain vapours issuing up from the lower faculties, then has this madness been the parent of all those mighty revolutions that have happened in empire, in philosophy, and in religion. For the brain, in its natural position and state of serenity, disposeth its owner to pass his life in the common forms, without any thought of subduing multitudes to his own power, his reasons, or his visions; and the more he shapes his understanding by the pattern of human learning, the less he is inclined to form parties after his particular notions, because that instructs him in his private infirmities, as well as in the stubborn ignorance of the people. But when a man's fancy gets astride on his reason, when imagination is at cuffs with the senses, and common understanding, as well as common sense, is kicked out

---

† Here is another defect in the manuscript, but I think the author did wisely, and that the matter which thus strained his faculties, was not worth a solution; and it were well if all metaphysical cobweb problems were no otherwise answered.

of doors, the first proselyte he makes is himself; and when that is once compassed, the difficulty is not so great in bringing over others; a strong delusion always operating from without as vigorously as from within. For, cant and vision are to the ear and the eye, the same that tickling is to the touch. Those entertainments and pleasures we most value in life, are such as dupe and play the wag with the senses. For, if we take an examination of what is generally understood by happiness, as it has respect either to the understanding or the senses, we shall find all its properties and adjuncts will herd under this short definition: that it is a perpetual possession of being well deceived. And first, with relation to the mind or understanding, 'tis manifest what mighty advantages fiction has over truth; and the reason is just at our elbow; because imagination can build nobler scenes, and produce more wonderful revolutions than fortune or nature will be at expense to furnish. Nor is mankind so much to blame in his choice thus determining him, if we consider that the debate merely lies between things past and things conceived; and so the question is only this: whether things that have place in the imagination, may not as properly be said to exist, as those that are seated in the memory; which may be justly held in the affirmative, and very much to the advantage of the former, since this is acknowledged to be the womb of things, and the other allowed to be no more than the grave. Again, if we take this definition of happiness, and examine it with reference to the senses, it will be acknowledged wonderfully adapt. How fading and insipid do all objects accost us, that are not conveyed in the vehicle of delusion? How shrunk is everything, as it appears in the glass of nature? So that if it were not for the assistance of artificial mediums, false lights, refracted angles, varnish, and tinsel, there would be a mighty level in the felicity and enjoyments of mortal men. If this were seriously considered by the world, as I have a certain reason to suspect it hardly will, men would no longer reckon among their high points of wisdom, the art of exposing weak sides, and publishing infirmities; an employment, in my opinion, neither better nor worse than that of unmasking, which I think has never been allowed fair usage, either in the world or the play-house.[1]

In the proportion that credulity is a more peaceful possession of the mind than curiosity, so far preferable is that wis-

[1] In this paragraph Swift satirizes the Hobbesian subversion of the faculty psychology, an orderly movement from the Senses to the Memory to the Imagination to the Reason. As Swift saw it, Hobbes dethrones Reason, exalts the Imagination, undervalues the Memory, and gives the Senses supreme power.

dom, which converses about the surface, to that pretended philosophy which enters into the depth of things, and then comes gravely back with informations and discoveries, that in the inside they are good for nothing. The two senses, to which all objects first address themselves, are the sight and the touch; these never examine farther than the colour, the shape, the size, and whatever other qualities dwell, or are drawn by art upon the outward of bodies; and then comes reason officiously with tools for cutting, and opening, and mangling, and piercing, offering to demonstrate, that they are not of the same consistence quite through. Now, I take all this to be the last degree of perverting nature; one of whose eternal laws it is, to put her best furniture forward. And therefore, in order to save the charges of all such expensive anatomy for the time to come, I do here think fit to inform the reader, that in such conclusions as these, reason is certainly in the right, and that in most corporeal beings, which have fallen under my cognizance, the outside hath been infinitely preferable to the in; whereof I have been farther convinced from some late experiments. Last week I saw a woman flayed, and you will hardly believe how much it altered her person for the worse. Yesterday I ordered the carcass of a beau to be stripped in my presence, when we were all amazed to find so many unsuspected faults under one suit of clothes. Then I laid open his brain, his heart, and his spleen; but I plainly perceived at every operation, that the farther we proceeded, we found the defects increase upon us in number and bulk: from all which, I justly formed this conclusion to myself; that whatever philosopher or projector can find out an art to sodder and patch up the flaws and imperfections of nature, will deserve much better of mankind, and teach us a more useful science, than that so much in present esteem, of widening and exposing them (like him who held anatomy to be the ultimate end of physic). And he, whose fortunes and dispositions have placed him in a convenient station to enjoy the fruits of this noble art; he that can with Epicurus content his ideas with the films and images that fly off upon his senses from the superficies of things; such a man truly wise, creams off nature, leaving the sour and the dregs for philosophy and reason to lap up. This is the sublime and refined point of felicity, called, the possession of being well deceived; the serene peaceful state of being a fool among knaves.[1]

[1] Using the ethics and the physics of Epicureanism as the material of his paragraph, Swift strikes off a brilliant satirical delineation of the happy, foolish Epicure.

But to return to madness. It is certain, that according to the system I have above deduced, every species thereof proceeds from a redundancy of vapours; therefore, as some kinds of phrenzy give double strength to the sinews, so there are of other species, which add vigor, and life, and spirit to the brain. Now, it usually happens, that these active spirits, getting possession of the brain, resemble those that haunt other waste and empty dwellings, which for want of business, either vanish, and carry away a piece of the house, or else stay at home and fling it all out of the windows. By which are mystically displayed the two principal branches of madness, and which some philosophers not considering so well as I, have mistook to be different in their causes, over-hastily assigning the first to deficiency, and the other to redundance.

I think it therefore manifest, from what I have here advanced, that the main point of skill and address is to furnish employment for this redundancy of vapour, and prudently to adjust the season of it; by which means it may certainly become of cardinal and catholic emolument in a commonwealth. Thus one man, choosing a proper juncture, leaps into a gulf, from whence proceeds a hero, and is called the saver of his country; another achieves the same enterprise, but unluckily timing it, has left the brand of madness fixed as a reproach upon his memory; upon so nice a distinction are we taught to repeat the name of Curtius with reverence and love, that of Empedocles with hatred and contempt. Thus also it is usually conceived, that the elder Brutus only personated the fool and madman for the good of the public; but this was nothing else than a redundancy of the same vapour, long misapplied, called by the Latins, *ingenium par negotiis;* * or (to translate it as nearly as I can) a sort of phrenzy, never in its right element, till you take it up in business of the state.

* *Tacit.*

Upon all which, and many other reasons of equal weight, though not equally curious, I do here gladly embrace an opportunity I have long sought for, of recommending it as a very noble undertaking to Sir Edward Seymour, Sir Christopher Musgrave, Sir John Bowls, John How, Esq.,[1] and other patriots concerned, that they would move for leave to bring in a bill for appointing commissioners to inspect into Bedlam, and the parts adjacent; who shall be empowered to send for persons, papers, and records: to examine into the merits and qualifications of every student and professor; to observe with

[1] Swift enumerates the leading Tories of the House of Commons.

utmost exactness their several dispositions and behaviour, by which means, duly distinguishing and adapting their talents, they might produce admirable instruments for the several offices in a state, * * * * * †, civil, and military, proceeding in such methods as I shall here humbly propose. And I hope the gentle reader will give some allowance to my great solicitudes in this important affair, upon account of that high esteem I have ever borne that honourable society, whereof I had some time the happiness to be an unworthy member.

Is any student tearing his straw in piece-meal, swearing and blaspheming, biting his grate, foaming at the mouth, and emptying his piss-pot in the spectators' faces? Let the right worshipful, the commissioners of inspection, give him a regiment of dragoons, and send him into Flanders among the rest. Is another eternally talking, sputtering, gaping, bawling, in a sound without period or article? What wonderful talents are here mislaid! Let him be furnished immediately with a green bag and papers, and threepence in his pocket,* and away with him to Westminster Hall. You will find a third gravely taking the dimensions *A lawyer's coach-hire.* of his kennel, a person of foresight and insight, though kept quite in the dark; for why, like Moses, *ecce cornuta** erat ejus facies.* He walks duly in one pace, entreats your penny with due gravity and ceremony, talks much of hard times, and taxes, and the whore of Babylon, bars up the wooden window of his cell constantly at eight o'clock, dreams of fire, and shoplifters, and court-customers, and privileged places. Now, what a figure would all these acquirements amount to, if the owner were sent into the city among his brethren! Behold a fourth, in much and deep conversation with himself, biting his thumbs at proper junctures, his countenance checkered with business and design, sometimes walking very fast, with his eyes nailed to a paper that he holds in his hands; a great saver of time, somewhat thick of hearing, very short of sight, but more of memory; a man ever in haste, a great hatcher and breeder of business, and excellent at the famous art of whispering nothing; a huge idolator of monosyllables and procrastination, so ready to give his word to everybody, that he never keeps it; one that has forgot the common meaning of words, but an admirable retainer of the sound; extremely subject to the looseness, for his occasions are perpetually calling him away. If you approach his grate in his familiar intervals, 'Sir,'

† Ecclesiastical.
** Cornutus is either horned or shining, and by this term, Moses is described in the vulgar Latin of the Bible.

says he, 'give me a penny, and I'll sing you a song; but give me the penny first.' (Hence comes the common saying, and commoner practice of parting with money for a song.) What a complete system of court skill is here described in every branch of it, and all utterly lost with wrong application. Accost the hole of another kennel, first stopping your nose; you will behold a surly, gloomy, nasty, slovenly mortal, raking in his own dung, and dabbling in his urine. The best part of his diet is the reversion of his own ordure, which expiring into steams, whirls perpetually about, and at last re-infunds. His complexion is of a dirty yellow, with a thin scattered beard, exactly agreeable to that of his diet upon its first declination, like other insects, who having their birth and education in an excrement, from thence borrow their colour and their smell. The student of this apartment is very sparing of his words, but somewhat over-liberal of his breath; he holds his hand out ready to receive your penny, and immediately upon receipt withdraws to his former occupations. Now, is it not amazing to think, the society of Warwick-lane [1] should have no more concern for the recovery of so useful a member, who, if one may judge from these appearances, would become the greatest ornament to that illustrious body? Another student struts up fiercely to your teeth, puffing with his lips, half squeezing out his eyes, and very graciously holds you out his hand to kiss. The keeper desires you not to be afraid of this professor, for he will do you no hurt; to him alone is allowed the liberty of the antechamber, and the orator of the place gives you to understand, that this solemn person is a tailor run mad with pride. This considerable student is adorned with many other qualities, upon which, at present, I shall not farther enlarge - - - - - - *Hark in your ear* * - - - - - - I am strangely mistaken, if all his address, his motions, and his airs, would not then be very natural, and in their proper element.

I shall not descend so minutely, as to insist upon the vast number of beaux, fiddlers, poets, and politicians, that the world might recover by such a reformation; but what is more material, besides the clear gain redounding to the commonwealth, by so large an acquisition of persons to employ, whose talents and acquirements, if I may be so bold as to affirm it, are now buried, or at least misapplied; it would be a mighty advantage accruing to the public from this inquiry, that all these would very much excel, and arrive at great perfection

* I cannot conjecture what the author means here, or how this chasm could be filled, tho' it is capable of more than one interpretation.

[1] The Royal College of Physicians.

in their several kinds; which, I think, is manifest from what I have already shown, and shall enforce by this one plain instance, that even I myself, the author of these momentous truths, am a person, whose imaginations are hard-mouthed, and exceedingly disposed to run away with his reason, which I have observed from long experience to be a very light rider, and easily shook off,[1] upon which account, my friends will never trust me alone, without a solemn promise to vent my speculations in this, or the like manner, for the universal benefit of human kind; which perhaps the gentle, courteous, and candid reader, brimful of that Modern charity and tenderness usually annexed to his office, will be very hardly persuaded to believe.

SECTION X.

A TALE OF A TUB.

It is an unanswerable argument of a very refined age, the wonderful civilities that have passed of late years between the nation of authors and that of readers. There can hardly pop out a play, a pamphlet, or a poem, without a preface full of acknowledgments to the world for the general reception and applause they have given it,* which the Lord knows where, or when, or how, or from whom it received. In due deference to so laudable a custom, I do here return my humble thanks to his Majesty, and both Houses of Parliament; to the Lords of the King's Most Honourable Privy Council; to the reverend the Judges; to the clergy, and gentry, and yeomanry of this land; but in a more especial manner to my worthy brethren and friends at Will's Coffee-house, and Gresham College, and Warwick Lane, and Moorfields, and Scotland Yard, and Westminster Hall, and Guildhall; in short, to all inhabitants and retainers whatsoever, either in court, or church, or camp, or city, or country, for their generous and universal acceptance of this divine treatise. I accept their approbation and good opinion with extreme gratitude, and to the utmost of my poor capacity, shall take hold of all opportunities to return the obligation.

I am also happy, that fate has flung me into so blessed an

---

* This is literally true, as we may observe in the prefaces to most plays, poems, &c.

[1] Dryden, under the influence of Hobbes, had written in the "Preface to Troilus and Cressida": "No man should pretend to write who cannot temper his fancy with his judgment: nothing is more dangerous to a raw horseman than a hot-mouthed jade without a curb."

age for the mutual felicity of booksellers and authors, whom I may safely affirm to be at this day the two only satisfied parties in England. Ask an author how his last piece hath succeeded: Why, truly, he thanks his stars, the world has been very favourable, and he has not the least reason to complain: and yet, by G—, he writ it in a week at bits and starts, when he could steal an hour from his urgent affairs; as it is a hundred to one you may see farther in the preface, to which he refers you, and for the rest, to the bookseller. There you go as a customer, and make the same question: he blesses his God the thing takes wonderfully, he is just printing a second edition, and has but three left in his shop. You beat down the price: 'Sir, we shall not differ,' and in hopes of your custom another time, lets you have it as reasonable as you please, 'and pray send as many of your acquaintance as you will, I shall upon your account furnish them all at the same rate.'

Now, it is not well enough considered, to what accidents and occasions the world is indebted for the greatest part of those noble writings, which hourly start up to entertain it. If it were not for a rainy day, a drunken vigil, a fit of the spleen, a course of physic, a sleepy Sunday, an ill run at dice, a long tailor's bill, a beggar's purse, a factious head, a hot sun, costive diet, want of books, and a just contempt of learning. But for these events, I say, and some others too long to recite (especially a prudent neglect of taking brimstone inwardly) I doubt, the number of authors and of writings would dwindle away to a degree most woeful to behold. To confirm this opinion, hear the words of the famous Troglodyte philosopher: ' 'Tis certain' (said he) 'some grains of folly are of course annexed, as part of the composition of human nature, only the choice is left us, whether we please to wear them inlaid or embossed; and we need not go very far to seek how that is usually determined, when we remember it is with human faculties as with liquors, the lightest will be ever at the top.'

There is in this famous island of Britain a certain paltry scribbler, very voluminous, whose character the reader cannot wholly be as stranger to. He deals in a pernicious kind of writings, called *Second Parts*, and usually passes under the name of the *Author of the First*. I easily foresee, that as soon as I lay down my pen, this nimble operator will have stole it, and treat me as inhumanly as he hath already done Dr. Blackmore, L'Estrange, and many others who shall here be nameless; I therefore fly for justice and relief into the hands of that great rectifier of saddles, and lover of mankind, Dr. Bentley, begging he will take this enormous grievance into his most Modern consideration; and if it should so happen, that the furniture of an ass, in the shape of a second part, must for my sins be clapped by a mistake upon my back, that he will immediately please, in the presence of the world, to lighten me of the burden, and take it home to his own house, till the true beast thinks fit to call for it.

In the meantime I do here give this public notice, that my resolutions are to circumscribe within this discourse the whole stock of matter I have been so many years providing. Since my vein is once opened, I am content to exhaust it all at a running, for the peculiar advantage of my dear country, and for the universal benefit of mankind. Therefore hospitably considering the number of my guests, they shall have my whole entertainment at a meal; and I scorn to set up the leavings in the cupboard. What the guests cannot eat may be given to the poor, and the dogs * under the table may gnaw the bones. This I understand for a more generous proceeding, than to turn the company's stomach, by inviting them again to-morrow to a scurvy meal of scraps.

If the reader fairly considers the strength of what I have advanced in the foregoing section, I am convinced it will produce a wonderful revolution in his notions and opinions; and he will be abundantly better prepared to receive and to relish the concluding part of this miraculous treatise. Readers may be divided into three classes, the superficial, the ignorant, and the learned: and I have with much felicity fitted my pen to the genius and advantage of each. The superficial reader will be strangely provoked to laughter; which clears the breast and the lungs, is sovereign against the spleen, and the most innocent of all diuretics. The ignorant reader (between whom and the former the distinction is extremely nice) will find himself disposed to stare; which is an admirable remedy for ill eyes, serves to raise and enliven the spirits, and wonderfully helps perspiration. But the reader truly learned, chiefly for whose benefit I wake when others sleep, and sleep when others wake, will here find sufficient matter to employ his speculations for the rest of his life. It were much to be wished, and I do here humbly propose for an experiment, that every prince in Christendom will take seven of the deepest scholars in his dominions, and shut them up close for seven years in seven chambers, with a command to write seven ample commentaries on

---

* By dogs, the author means common injudicious critics, as he explains it himself before in his Digression upon Critics (pp. 335–36).

this comprehensive discourse. I shall venture to affirm, that whatever difference may be found in their several conjectures, they will be all, without the least distortion, manifestly deducible from the text. Meantime, it is my earnest request, that so useful an undertaking may be entered upon (if their Majesties please) with all convenient speed; because I have a strong inclination, before I leave the world, to taste a blessing which we mysterious writers can seldom reach till we have got into our graves. Whether it is, that fame, being a fruit grafted on the body, can hardly grow, and much less ripen, till the stock is in the earth; or whether she be a bird of prey, and is lured, among the rest, to pursue after the scent of a carcass; or whether she conceives her trumpet sounds best and farthest when she stands on a tomb, by the advantage of a rising ground, and the echo of a hollow vault.

'Tis true, indeed, the republic of dark authors, after they once found out this excellent expedient of dying, have been peculiarly happy in the variety, as well as extent of their reputation. For, night being the universal mother of things, wise philosophers hold all writings to be fruitful in the proportion they are dark; and therefore, the true illumi- *A name of* nated * (that is to say, the darkest of all) have *the Rosicru-* met with such numberless commentators, whose *cians.* scholiastic midwifery hath delivered them of meanings, that the authors themselves perhaps never conceived, and yet may very justly be allowed the lawful parents of them, the words of such writers being like seed,† which, however scattered at random, when they light upon a fruitful ground, will multiply far beyond either the hopes or imagination of the sower.

And therefore in order to promote so useful a work, I will here take leave to glance a few innuendoes, that may be of great assistance to those sublime spirits, who shall be appointed to labor in a universal comment upon this wonderful discourse. And first,** I have couched a very profound mystery in the number of O's multiplied by seven, and divided by nine. Also, if a devout brother of the Rosy Cross will pray fervently for sixty-three mornings, with a lively faith, and then transpose certain letters and syllables according to prescription in the second and fifth section, they will certainly reveal into a full receipt of the *opus magnum.* Lastly, whoever will be at

---

† Nothing is more frequent than for commentators to force interpretation, which the author never meant.

** This is what the Cabalists among the Jews have done with the Bible, and pretend to find wonderful mysteries by it.

the pains to calculate the whole number of each letter in this treatise, and sum up the difference exactly between the several numbers, assigning the true natural cause for every such difference, the discoveries in the product will plentifully reward his labour. But then he must beware of Bythus and Sigè,* and be sure not to forget the qualities of Acamoth: *A cujus lacrymis humecta prodit substantia, à risu lucida, à tristitiâ solida, & à timore mobilis,* wherein Eugenius Philalethes † hath committed an unpardonable mistake.

† Vid. Anima magica abscondita.

SECTION XI.

A TALE OF A TUB.

AFTER so wide a compass as I have wandered, I do now gladly overtake, and close in with my subject, and shall henceforth hold on with it an even pace to the end of my journey, except some beautiful prospect appears within sight of my way, whereof though at present I have neither warning nor expectation, yet upon such an accident, come when it will, I shall beg my reader's favour and company, allowing me to conduct him through it along with myself. For in writing, it is as in travelling: if a man is in haste to be at home (which I acknowledge to be none of my case, having never so little business as when I am there), if his horse be tired with long riding and ill ways, or be naturally a jade, I advise him clearly to make the straightest and the commonest road, be it ever so dirty. But then surely we must own such a man to be a scurvy companion at best; he spatters himself and his fellow-travellers at every step: all their thoughts, and wishes, and conver-

* I was told by an eminent divine, whom I consulted on this point, that these two barbarous words, with that of Acamoth and its qualities, as here set down, are quoted from Irenæus. This he discovered by searching that ancient writer for another quotation of our author, which he has placed in the title-page, and refers to the book and chapter; the curious were very inquisitive, whether those barbarous words, *basima eacabasa, &c.* are really in Irenæus, and upon enquiry 'twas found they were a sort of cant or jargon of certain heretics, and therefore very properly prefixed to such a book as this of our author.

† To the above-mentioned treatise, called *Anthroposophia Theomagica*, there is another annexed, called *Anima magica abscondita*, written by the same author, Vaughan, under the name of Eugenius Philalethes, but in neither of those treatises is there any mention of Acamoth or its qualities, so that this is nothing but amusement, and a ridicule of dark, unintelligble writers; only the words, *A cujus lacrymis, &c.* are as we have said, transcribed from Irenæus, though I know not from what part. I believe one of the author's designs was to set curious men a-hunting through indexes, and enquiring for books out of the common road.

sation, turn entirely upon the subject of their journey's end; and at every splash, and plunge, and stumble, they heartily wish one another at the devil.

On the other side, when a traveller and his horse are in heart and plight, when his purse is full, and the day before him, he takes the road only where it is clean or convenient; entertains his company there as agreeably as he can; but upon the first occasion, carries them along with him to every delightful scene in view, whether of art, of nature, or of both; and if they chance to refuse out of stupidity or weariness, let them jog on by themselves and be d—n'd; he'll overtake them at the next town, at which arriving, he rides furiously through; the men, women, and children run out to gaze; a hundred noisy curs * run barking after him, of which, if he honors the boldest with a lash of his whip, it is rather out of sport than revenge; but should some sourer mongrel dare too near an approach, he receives a salute on the chaps by an accidental stroke from the courser's heels (nor is any ground lost by the blow), which sends him yelping and limping home.

I now proceed to sum up the singular adventures of my renowned Jack, the state of whose dispositions and fortunes the careful reader does, no doubt, most exactly remember, as I last parted with them in the conclusion of a former section. Therefore, his next care must be from two of the foregoing to extract a scheme of notions, that may best fit his understanding for a true relish of what is to ensue.

Jack had not only calculated the first revolution of his brain so prudently, as to give rise to that epidemic sect of Æolists, but succeeding also into a new and strange variety of conceptions, the fruitfulness of his imagination led him into certain notions, which, although in appearance very unaccountable, were not without their mysteries and their meanings, nor wanted followers to countenance and improve them. I shall therefore be extremely careful and exact in recounting such material passages of this nature as I have been able to collect, either from undoubted tradition, or indefatigable reading; and shall describe them as graphically as it is possible, and as far as notions of that height and latitude can be brought within the compass of a pen. Nor do I at all question, but they will furnish plenty of noble matter for such, whose converting imaginations dispose them to reduce all things into types; who can make shadows, no thanks to the sun, and then mould them into substances, no thanks to philosophy; whose peculiar tal-

* By these are meant what the author calls the true critics, pp. 336–37.

ent lies in fixing tropes and allegories to the letter, and refining what is literal into figure and mystery.

Jack had provided a fair copy of his father's will, engrossed in form upon a large skin of parchment; and resolving to act the part of a most dutiful son, he became the fondest creature of it imaginable. For although, as I have often told the reader, it consisted wholly in certain plain, easy directions about the management and wearing of their coats, with legacies and penalties, in case of obedience or neglect, yet he began to entertain a fancy that the matter was deeper and darker, and therefore must needs have a great deal more of mystery at the bottom. 'Gentlemen,' said he, 'I will prove this very skin of parchment to be meat, drink, and cloth, to be the philosopher's stone, and the universal medicine.' * In consequence of which raptures, he resolved to make use of it in the most necessary, as well as the most paltry, occasions of life. He had a way of working it into any shape he pleased; so that it served him for a nightcap when he went to bed, and for an umbrella in rainy weather. He would lap a piece of it about a sore toe, or when he had fits, burn two inches under his nose; or if anything lay heavy on his stomach, scrape off, and swallow as much of the powder as would lie on a silver penny; they were all infallible remedies. With analogy to these refinements, his common talk and conversation ran wholly in the phrase of his will,† and he circumscribed the utmost of his eloquence within that compass, not daring to let slip a syllable without authority from thence. Once at a strange house, he was suddenly taken short upon an urgent juncture, whereon it may not be allowed too particularly to dilate; and being not able to call to mind, with that suddenness the occasion required, an authentic phrase for demanding the way to the backside; he chose rather as the more prudent course to incur the penalty in such cases usually annexed. Neither was it possible for the united rhetoric of mankind to prevail with him to make himself clean again; because having consulted the will upon this emergency, he met with a passage ** near the bottom (whether foisted in by the transcriber, is not known) which seemed to forbid it.

* The author here lashes those pretenders to purity, who place so much merit in using Scripture phrases on all occasions.
† The Protestant dissenters use Scripture phrases in their serious discourses and composures more than the Church of England men; accordingly Jack is introduced making his common talk and conversation to run wholly in the phrase of his will. W. WOTTON.
** I cannot guess the author's meaning here, which I would be very glad to know, because it seems to be of importance.

He made it a part of his religion, never to say grace to his meat,* nor could all the world persuade him, as the common phrase is, to eat his victuals like a Christian.†

He bore a strange kind of appetite to snap-dragon,** and to the livid snuffs of a burning candle, which he would catch and swallow with an agility wonderful to conceive; and by this procedure, maintained a perpetual flame in his belly, which issuing in a glowing steam from both his eyes, as well as his nostrils and his mouth, made his head appear in a dark night, like the skull of an ass, wherein a roguish boy had conveyed a farthing candle, to the terror of his Majesty's liege subjects. Therefore, he made use of no other expedient to light himself home, but was wont to say, that a wise man was his own lanthorn.

He would shut his eyes as he walked along the streets, and if he happened to bounce his head against a post, or fall into the kennel (as he seldom missed either to do one or both), he would tell the gibing prentices, who looked on, that he submitted with entire resignation, as to a trip, or a blow of fate, with whom he found, by long experience, how vain it was either to wrestle or to cuff; and whoever durst undertake to do either, would be sure to come off with a swinging fall, or a bloody nose. 'It was ordained,' said he, 'some few days before the creation, that my nose and this very post should have a rencounter; and, therefore, providence thought fit to send us both into the world in the same age, and to make us countrymen and fellow-citizens. Now, had my eyes been open, it is very likely the business might have been a great deal worse; for how many a confounded slip is daily got by man with all his foresight about him? Besides, the eyes of the understanding see best, when those of the senses are out of the way; and therefore, blind men are observed to tread their steps with much more caution, and conduct, and judgment, than those who rely with too much confidence upon the virtue of the visual nerve, which every little accident shakes out of order, and a drop, or a film, can wholly disconcert; like a lanthorn among a pack of roaring bullies when they scour the streets, exposing its owner and itself to outward kicks and buffets, which both might have escaped, if the vanity of appearing

---

* The slovenly way of receiving the sacrament among the fanatics.
† This is a common phrase to express eating cleanlily, and is meant for an invective against that undecent manner among some people in receiving the sacrament, so in the lines before, which is to be understood of the Dissenters refusing to kneel at the sacrament.
** I cannot well find the author's meaning here, unless it be the hot, untimely, blind zeal of enthusiasts.

would have suffered them to walk in the dark. But farther, if we examine the conduct of these boasted lights, it will prove yet a great deal worse than their fortune. 'Tis true, I have broke my nose against this post, because providence either forgot, or did not think it convenient to twitch me by the elbow, and give me notice to avoid it. But let not this encourage either the present age or posterity to trust their noses into the keeping of their eyes, which may prove the fairest way of losing them for good and all. For, O ye eyes, ye blind guides, miserable guardians are ye of our frail noses; ye, I say, who fasten upon the first precipice in view, and then tow our wretched willing bodies after you, to the very brink of destruction; but, alas, that brink is rotten, our feet slip, and we tumble down prone into a gulf, without one hospitable shrub in the way to break the fall; a fall, to which not any nose of mortal make is equal, except that of the giant Laurcalco,* who was lord of the silver bridge. Most properly therefore, O eyes, and with great justice, may you be compared to those foolish lights, which conduct men through dirt and darkness, till they fall into a deep pit or a noisome bog.'

Vide Don Quixote.

This I have produced as a scantling of Jack's great eloquence, and the force of his reasoning upon such abstruse matters.

He was, besides, a person of great design and improvement in affairs of devotion, having introduced a new deity, who hath since met with a vast number of worshippers, by some called Babel, by others Chaos; who had an ancient temple of Gothic structure upon Salisbury plain, famous for its shrine, and celebration by pilgrims.

When he had some roguish trick to play,† he would down with his knees, up with his eyes, and fall to prayers, though in the midst of the kennel. Then it was that those who understood his pranks, would be sure to get far enough out of his way; and whenever curiosity attracted strangers to laugh, or to listen, he would of a sudden with one hand out with his gear, and piss full in their eyes, and with the other, all to bespatter them with mud.

In winter he went always loose and unbuttoned,** and clad as thin as possible, to let *in* the ambient heat; and in summer lapped himself close and thick to keep it *out*.

---

† The villainies and cruelties committed by enthusiasts and fanatics among us were all performed under the disguise of religion and long prayers.
** They affect differences in habit and behaviour.

In all revolutions of government,* he would make his court for the office of hangman general; and in the exercise of that dignity, wherein he was very dextrous, would make use of no other vizard † than a long prayer.

He had a tongue so musculous and subtile, that he could twist it up into his nose, and deliver a strange kind of speech from thence. He was also the first in these kingdoms, who began to improve the Spanish accomplishment of braying; and having large ears, perpetually exposed and arrect, he carried his art to such a perfection, that it was a point of great difficulty to distinguish either by the view or the sound between the original and the copy.

He was troubled with a disease, reverse to that called the stinging of the tarantula; and would run dog-mad at the noise of music,** especially a pair of bagpipes. But he would cure himself again, by taking two or three turns in Westminster Hall, or Billingsgate, or in a boarding-school, or the Royal-Exchange, or a state coffee-house.

He was a person that feared no colours,‡ but mortally hated all, and upon that account bore a cruel aversion to painters; insomuch, that in his paroxysms, as he walked the streets, he would have his pockets loaden with stones to pelt at the signs.

Having from this manner of living, frequent occasion to wash himself, he would often leap over head and ears into the water, though it were in the midst of the winter, but was always observed to come out again much dirtier, if possible, than he went in.

He was the first that ever found out the secret of contriving a soporiferous medicine to be conveyed in at the ears; ‖ it was a compound of sulphur and balm of Gilead, with a little pilgrim's salve.

He wore a large plaister of artificial caustics on his stomach, with the fervor of which, he could set himself a-groaning, like the famous board upon application of a red-hot iron.

He would stand in the turning of a street, and, calling to those who passed by, would cry to one, 'Worthy sir, do me the

---

* They are severe persecutors, and all in a form of cant and devotion.

† Cromwell and his confederates went, as they called it, to seek God, when they resolved to murder the king.

** This is to expose our Dissenters' aversion to instrumental music in churches. W. WOTTON.

‡ They quarrel at the most innocent decency and ornament, and defaced the statues and paintings on all the churches in England.

‖ Fanatic preaching, composed either of hell and damnation, or a fulsome description of the joys of heaven; both in such a dirty, nauseous style, as to be well resembled to pilgrim's salve.

honour of a good slap in the chaps'; * to another, 'Honest friend, pray favour me with a handsome kick on the arse'; 'Madam, shall I entreat a small box on the ear from your ladyship's fair hands?' 'Noble captain, lend a reasonable thwack, for the love of God, with that cane of yours over these poor shoulders.' And when he had by such earnest solicitations made a shift to procure a basting sufficient to swell up his fancy and his sides, he would return home extremely comforted, and full of terrible accounts of what he had undergone for the public good. 'Observe this stroke,' (said he, showing his bare shoulders) 'a plaguy janissary gave it me this very morning at seven o'clock, as, with much ado, I was driving off the great Turk. Neighbours mine, this broken head deserves a plaister; had poor Jack been tender of his noddle, you would have seen the Pope and the French king, long before this time of day, among your wives and your warehouses. Dear Christians, the great Mogul was come as far as White-chapel, and you may thank these poor sides that he hath not (God bless us) already swallowed up man, woman, and child.'

It was highly worth observing the singular effects of that aversion,† or antipathy, which Jack and his brother Peter seemed, even to an affectation, to bear toward each other. Peter had lately done some rogueries, that forced him to abscond; and he seldom ventured to stir out before night, for fear of bailiffs. Their lodgings were at the two most distant parts of the town from each other; and whenever their occasions or humours called them abroad, they would make choice of the oddest unlikely times and most uncouth rounds they could invent, that they might be sure to avoid one another: yet, after all this, it was their perpetual fortune to meet. The reason of which is easy enough to apprehend; for, the phrenzy and the spleen of both having the same foundation, we may look upon them as two pair of compasses, equally extended, and the fixed foot of each remaining in the same center; which, though moving contrary ways at first, will be sure to encounter somewhere or other in the circumference. Besides,

---

* The fanatics have always had a way of affecting to run into persecution, and count vast merit upon every little hardship they suffer.

† The papists and fanatics, tho' they appear the most averse to each other, yet bear a near resemblance in many things, as has been observed by learned men.

Ibid. The agreement of our dissenters and the papists in that which Bishop Stillingfleet called the fanaticism of the Church of Rome, is ludicrously described for several pages together by Jack's likeness to Peter, and their being often mistaken for each other, and their frequent meeting when they least intended it. W. WOTTON.

it was among the great misfortunes of Jack, to bear a huge
personal resemblance with his brother Peter. Their humour
and dispositions were not only the same, but there was a close
analogy in their shape and size, and their mien. Insomuch as
nothing was more frequent than for a bailiff to seize Jack by
the shoulders, and cry, 'Mr. Peter, you are the king's prisoner.'
Or, at other times, for one of Peter's nearest friends to accost
Jack with open arms, 'Dear Peter, I am glad to see thee, pray
send me one of your best medicines for the worms.' This we
may suppose was a mortifying return of those pains and proceedings Jack had laboured in so long; and finding how directly opposite all his endeavours had answered to the sole
end and intention which he had proposed to himself, how
could it avoid having terrible effects upon a head and heart so
furnished as his? However, the poor remainders of his coat
bore all the punishment; the orient sun never entered upon
his diurnal progress, without missing a piece of it. He hired a
tailor to stitch up the collar so close, that it was ready to
choke him, and squeezed out his eyes at such a rate, as one
could see nothing but the white. What little was left of the
main substance of the coat, he rubbed every day for two hours
against a rough-cast wall, in order to grind away the remnants of lace and embroidery, but at the same time went on
with so much violence, that he proceeded a heathen philosopher. Yet after all he could do of this kind, the success continued still to disappoint his expectation. For, as it is the nature of rags to bear a kind of mock resemblance to finery,
there being a sort of fluttering appearance in both, which is
not to be distinguished at a distance, in the dark, or by short-
sighted eyes; so, in those junctures, it fared with Jack and his
tatters, that they offered to the first view a ridiculous flaunting,
which assisting the resemblance in person and air, thwarted
all his projects of separation, and left so near a similitude between them, as frequently deceived the very disciples and followers of both.

* * * * * * * * * * * *
* * * * * * * * * * * *
Desunt non- * * * * * * * *
nulla. * * * * * * * *
* * * * * * * * * * *
* * * * * * * * * * *

The old Sclavonian proverb said well, that it is with men
as with asses; whoever would keep them fast, must find a very

good hold at their ears. Yet I think we may affirm, that it hath been verified by repeated experience, that,

Effugiet tamen hæc sceleratus vincula Proteus.

It is good, therefore, to read the maxims of our ancestors, with great allowances to times and persons; for if we look into primitive records, we shall find, that no revolutions have been so great, or so frequent, as those of human ears. In former days, there was a curious invention to catch and keep them; which, I think, we may justly reckon among the *artes perditæ;* and how can it be otherwise, when in these latter centuries the very species is not only diminished to a very lamentable degree, but the poor remainder is also degenerated so far as to mock our skilfullest tenure? For, if the only slitting of one ear in a stag hath been found sufficient to propagate the defect through a whole forest, why should we wonder at the greatest consequences, from so many loppings and mutilations, to which the ears of our fathers, and our own, have been of late so much exposed? 'Tis true, indeed, that while this island of ours was under the dominion of grace, many endeavours were made to improve the growth of ears once more among us. The proportion of largeness was not only looked upon as an ornament of the outward man, but as a type of grace in the inward. Besides, it is held by naturalists, that if there be a protuberancy of parts in the superiour region of the body, as in the ears and nose, there must be a parity also in the inferior; and therefore in that truly pious age, the males in every assembly, according as they were gifted, appeared very forward in exposing their ears to view, and the regions about them; because Hippocrates tells us,* that when the vein behind the ear happens to be cut, a man becomes a eunuch: and the females were nothing   * Lib. de aëre locis & aquis. backwarder in beholding and edifying by them; whereof those who had already used the means, looked about them with great concern, in hopes of conceiving a suitable offspring by such a prospect; others, who stood candidates for benevolence, found there a plentiful choice, and were sure to fix upon such as discovered the largest ears, that the breed might not dwindle between them. Lastly, the devouter sisters, who looked upon all extraordinary dilatations of that member as protrusions of zeal, or spiritual excrescencies, were sure to honor every head they sat upon, as if they had been marks of grace; but especially that of the preacher, whose ears were usually of the prime magnitude; which upon that account, he was very frequent and exact in exposing with all advantages to the people: in his rhetorical paroxysms turning sometimes to hold forth the one, and sometimes to hold forth the other; from which custom, the whole operation of preaching is to this very day, among their professors, styled by the phrase of *holding forth.*

Such was the progress of the saints for advancing the size of that member; and it is thought the success would have been every way answerable, if in process of time a cruel king * had not arose, who raised a bloody persecution against all ears above a certain standard; upon which some were glad to hide their flourishing sprouts in a black border, others crept wholly under a periwig; some were slit, others cropped, and a great number sliced off to the stumps. But of this more hereafter in my general *History of Ears,* which I design very speedily to bestow upon the public.

From this brief survey of the falling state of ears in the last age, and the small care had to advance their ancient growth in the present, it is manifest, how little reason we can have to rely upon a hold so short, so weak, and so slippery; and that whoever desires to catch mankind fast, must have recourse to some other methods. Now, he that will examine human nature with circumspection enough, may discover several handles whereof the six † senses afford one apiece, beside a great number that are screwed to the passions, and some few riveted to the intellect. Among these last, curiosity is one, and of all others affords the firmest grasp: curiosity, that spur in the side, that bridle in the mouth, that ring in the nose, of a lazy, an impatient, and a grunting reader.[1] By this handle it is, that an author should seize upon his readers; which as soon as he has once compassed, all resistance and struggling are in vain, and they become his prisoners as close as he pleases, till weariness or dullness force him to let go his grip.

† *Including Scaliger's.*

And therefore, I, the author of this miraculous treatise, having hitherto, beyond expectation, maintained by the aforesaid handle a firm hold upon my gentle reader, it is with great reluctance, that I am at length compelled to remit my grasp, leaving them in the perusal of what remains to that natural

* This was King Charles the Second, who at his restoration turned out all the dissenting teachers that would not conform.

[1] Swift here appears to be parodying Hobbes: see *Leviathan,* 1, 6, 8.

oscitancy inherent in the tribe. I can only assure thee, courteous reader, for both our comforts, that my concern is altogether equal to thine, for my unhappiness in losing, or mislaying among my papers the remaining part of these memoirs; which consisted of accidents, turns, and adventures, both new, agreeable, and surprising; and therefore calculated, in all due points, to the delicate taste of this our noble age. But, alas, with my utmost endeavours, I have been able only to retain a few of the heads. Under which, there was a full account, how Peter got a protection out of the King's Bench; and of a reconcilement * between Jack and him, upon a design they had in a certain rainy night, to trepan brother Martin into a spunging-house, and there strip him to the skin. How Martin, with much ado, showed them both a fair pair of heels. How a new warrant came out against Peter; upon which, how Jack left him in the lurch, stole his protection, and made use of it himself. How Jack's tatters came into fashion in court and city; how he got upon a great horse,† and eat custard.** But the particulars of all these, with several others, which have now slid out of my memory, are lost beyond all hopes of recovery. For which misfortune, leaving my readers to condole with each other, as far as they shall find it to agree with their several constitutions; but conjuring them by all the friendship that hath passed between us, from the title-page to this, not to proceed so far as to injure their healths for an accident past remedy; I now go on to the ceremonial part of an accomplished writer, and therefore, by a courtly Modern, least of all others to be omitted.

THE CONCLUSION.

Going too long is a cause of abortion as effectual, though not so frequent, as going too short; and holds true especially

---

* In the reign of King James the Second, the Presbyterians by the king's invitation, joined with the Papists, against the Church of England, and addressed him for repeal of the penal laws and test. The king by his dispensing power gave liberty of conscience, which both Papists and Presbyterians made use of, but upon the Revolution, the Papists being down of course, the Presbyterians freely continued their assemblies, by virtue of King James's indulgence, before they had a toleration by law; this I believe the author means by Jack's stealing Peter's protection, and making use of it himself.

† Sir Humphry Edwyn, a Presbyterian, was some years ago Lord Mayor of London, and had the insolence to go in his formalities to a conventicle, with the ensigns of his office.

** Custard is a famous dish at a Lord Mayor's feast.

in the labors of the brain. Well fare the heart of that noble
Jesuit,* who first adventured to confess in print,
that books must be suited to their several seasons, like dress, and diet, and diversions; and
better fare our noble nation, for refining upon this among
other French modes. I am living fast to see the time, when a
book that misses its tide, shall be neglected, as the moon by
day, or like mackerel a week after the season. No man hath
more nicely observed our climate, than the bookseller who
bought the copy of this work; he knows to a tittle what subjects will best go off in a dry year, and which it is proper to
expose foremost, when the weather-glass is fallen to much
rain. When he had seen this treatise, and consulted his almanack upon it, he gave me to understand, that he had maturely considered the two principal things, which were the
bulk and the subject; and found it would never take but after
a long vacation, and then only in case it should happen to be
a hard year for turnips. Upon which I desired to know, considering my urgent necessities, what he thought might be
acceptable this month. He looked westward, and said, 'I doubt
we shall have a fit of bad weather; however, if you could prepare some pretty little banter (but not in verse) or a small
treatise upon the ——— it would run like wildfire. But, if it
hold up, I have already hired an author to write something
against Dr. Bentley, which, I am sure, will turn to account.'

* Père
d'Orleans.

At length we agreed upon this expedient; that when a customer comes for one of these, and desires in confidence to
know the author, he will tell him very privately, as a friend,
naming whichever of the wits shall happen to be that week
in the vogue; and if Durfey's last play should be in course, I
had as lieve he may be the person as Congreve. This I mention, because I am wonderfully well acquainted with the present relish of courteous readers; and have often observed, with
singular pleasure, that a fly, driven from a honey-pot, will
immediately, with very good appetite alight and finish his
meal on an excrement.

I have one word to say upon the subject of profound writers, who are grown very numerous of late; and I know very
well, the judicious world is resolved to list me in that number.
I conceive therefore, as to the business of being profound,
that it is with writers as with wells; a person with good eyes
may see to the bottom of the deepest, provided any water be
there; and that often, when there is nothing in the world at
the bottom, besides dryness and dirt, though it be but a yard

and half under ground, it shall pass, however, for wondrous deep, upon no wiser a reason than because it is wondrous dark.

I am now trying an experiment very frequent among Modern authors; which is to write upon *Nothing;* when the subject is utterly exhausted, to let the pen still move on; by some called the ghost of wit, delighting to walk after the death of its body. And to say the truth, there seems to be no part of knowledge in fewer hands, than that of discerning when to have done. By the time that an author has writ out a book, he and his readers are become old acquaintants, and grow very loth to part; so that I have sometimes known it to be in writing, as in visiting, where the ceremony of taking leave has employed more time than the whole conversation before. The conclusion of a treatise resembles the conclusion of human life, which hath sometimes been compared to the end of a feast; where few are satisfied to depart, *ut plenus vitæ conviva:* for men will sit down after the fullest meal, though it be only to doze, or to sleep out the rest of the day. But, in this latter, I differ extremely from other writers, and shall be too proud, if by all my labours, I can have any ways contributed to the repose of mankind in times * so turbulent and unquiet as these. Neither do I think such an employment so very alien from the office of a wit as some would suppose. For among a very polite nation in Greece,† there were the same temples built and consecrated to Sleep and the Muses, between which two deities they believed the strictest friendship was established.

† *Trezenii. Pausan. l. 2.*

I have one concluding favour to request of my reader; that he will not expect to be equally diverted and informed by every line or every page of this discourse; but give some allowance to the author's spleen, and short fits or intervals of dullness, as well as his own; and lay it seriously to his conscience, whether, if he were walking the streets, in dirty weather or a rainy day, he would allow it fair dealing in folks at their ease from a window to critic his gait, and ridicule his dress at such a juncture.

In my disposure of employments of the brain, I have thought fit to make invention the master, and give method and reason the office of its lackeys. The cause of this distribution was, from observing it my peculiar case, to be often under a temptation of being witty, upon occasion, where I could be neither wise nor sound, nor anything to the master in hand.

---

* This was writ before the peace of Ryswick.

And I am too much a servant of the Modern way to neglect any such opportunities, whatever pains or improprieties I may be at, to introduce them. For I have observed, that from a laborious collection of seven hundred thirty-eight flowers and shining hints of the best Modern authors, digested with great reading into my book of commonplaces, I have not been able after five years to draw, hook, or force, into common conversation, any more than a dozen. Of which dozen, the one moiety failed of success, by being dropped among unsuitable company; and the other cost me so many strains, and traps, and ambages to introduce, that I at length resolved to give it over. Now, this disappointment (to discover a secret) I must own, gave me the first hint of setting up for an author; and I have since found, among some particular friends, that it is become a very general complaint, and has produced the same effects upon many others. For I have remarked many a towardly word to be wholly neglected or despised in discourse, which has passed very smoothly, with some consideration and esteem, after its preferment and sanction in print. But now, since by the liberty and encouragement of the press, I am grown absolute master of the occasions and opportunities to expose the talents I have acquired, I already discover, that the issues of my *observanda* begin to grow too large for the receipts. Therefore, I shall here pause a while, till I find, by feeling the world's pulse and my own, that it will be of absolute necessity for us both, to resume my pen.

FINIS

A

Full and True Account

OF THE

BATTEL

Fought laſt *FRIDAY*,

Between the

Antient and the *Modern*

BOOKS

IN

St. *JAMES*'s

LIBRARY.

LONDON:

Printed in the Year, MDCCX.

THE
BOOKSELLER
TO THE
READER.

THE following Discourse, as it is unquestionably of the same author, so it seems to have been written about the same time with the former, I mean the year 1697, when the famous dispute was on foot about Ancient and Modern learning. The controversy took its rise from an essay of Sir William Temple's upon that subject, which was answered by W. Wotton, B.D., with an Appendix by Dr. Bentley, endeavouring to destroy the credit of Æsop and Phalaris for authors, whom Sir William Temple had, in the essay before-mentioned, highly commended. In that appendix, the doctor falls hard upon a new edition of Phalaris, put out by the Honourable Charles Boyle (now Earl of Orrery) to which Mr. Boyle replied at large, with great learning and wit; and the doctor voluminously rejoined. In this dispute, the town highly resented to see a person of Sir William Temple's character and methods roughly used by the two reverend gentlemen aforesaid, and without any manner of provocation. At length, there appearing no end of the quarrel, our author tells us, that the Books in St. James's Library, looking upon themselves as parties principally concerned, took up the controversy, and came to a decisive battle; but the manuscript, by the injury of fortune or weather, being in several places imperfect, we cannot learn to which side the victory fell.[1]

I must warn the reader to beware of applying to persons what is here meant only of books in the most literal sense. So, when Virgil is mentioned, we are not to understand the person of a famous poet called by that name, but only certain sheets of paper, bound up in leather, containing in print the works of the said poet, and so of the rest.

[1] See the Introduction, pp. 13–14 for an account of the background of *The Battle of the Books*. For a full account, see Richard Foster Jones, *Ancients and Moderns, A Study of the Background of* The Battle of the Books, 1936. The best annotated edition of the *Battle* is the Guthkelch and Nichol Smith edition.

THE
PREFACE
OF THE
AUTHOR.

Satire is a sort of glass, wherein beholders do generally discover everybody's face but their own; which is the chief reason for that kind of reception it meets in the world, and that so very few are offended with it. But if it should happen otherwise, the danger is not great; and I have learned from long experience never to apprehend mischief from those understandings I have been able to provoke; for anger and fury, though they add strength to the sinews of the body, yet are found to relax those of the mind, and to render all its efforts feeble and impotent.

There is a brain that will endure but one scumming; let the owner gather it with discretion, and manage his little stock with husbandry; but of all things, let him beware of bringing it under the lash of his betters, because that will make it all bubble up into impertinence, and he will find no new supply: wit, without knowledge, being a sort of cream, which gathers in a night to the top, and, by a skilful hand, may be soon whipped into froth; but once scummed away, what appears underneath will be fit for nothing but to be thrown to the hogs.

A FULL AND TRUE
ACCOUNT
OF THE
BATTLE
FOUGHT LAST FRIDAY, &c.

WHOEVER examines with due circumspection into the *Annual Records of Time* * will find it remarked, that war is the child of pride, and pride the daughter of riches. The former of which assertions may be soon granted, but one cannot so easily subscribe to the latter; for pride is nearly related to beggary and want, either by father or mother, and sometimes by both; and to speak naturally, it very seldom happens among men to fall out when all have enough; invasions usually travelling from north to south, that is to say from poverty upon plenty. The most ancient and natural grounds of quarrels are lust and avarice; which, though we may allow to be brethren or collateral branches of pride, are certainly the issues of want. For, to speak in the phrase of writers upon the politics, we may observe in the Republic of Dogs (which in its original seems to be an institution of the many) that the whole state is ever in the profoundest peace after a full meal; and that civil broils arise among them when it happens for one great bone to be seized on by some leading dog, who either divides it among the few, and then it falls to an oligarchy, or keeps it to himself, and then it runs up to a tyranny. The same reasoning also holds place among them in those dissensions we behold upon a turgescency in any of their females. For the right of possession lying in common (it being impossible to establish a property in so delicate a case) jealousies and suspicions do so abound, that the whole commonwealth of that street is reduced to a manifest state of war, of every citizen against every citizen, till some one of more courage, conduct, or for-

* Riches produces pride; pride is war's ground, &c. *Vide Ephem. de Mary Clarke;* [1] opt. edit.

[1] Mary Clarke was the printer of a popular almanac sheet; Swift's citation satirizes its ephemeral quality.

tune than the rest, seizes and enjoys the prize; upon which naturally arises plenty of heart-burning, and envy, and snarling against the happy dog. Again, if we look upon any of these republics engaged in a foreign war, either of invasion or defence, we shall find the same reasoning will serve as to the grounds and occasions of each; and that poverty or want in some degree or other (whether real or in opinion, which makes no alteration in the case) has a great share, as well as pride, on the part of the aggressor.

Now, whoever will please to take this scheme, and either reduce or adapt it to an intellectual state, or commonwealth of learning, will soon discover the first ground of disagreement between the two great parties at this time in arms, and may form just conclusions upon the merits of either cause. But the issue or events of this war are not so easy to conjecture at; for the present quarrel is so inflamed by the warm heads of either faction, and the pretensions somewhere or other so exorbitant, as not to admit the least overtures of accommodation. This quarrel first began (as I have heard it affirmed by an old dweller in the neighbourhood) about a small spot of ground, lying and being upon one of the two tops of the hill Parnassus; the highest and largest of which had, it seems, been time out of mind in quiet possession of certain tenants, called the Ancients, and the other was held by the Moderns. But these disliking their present station, sent certain ambassadors to the Ancients, complaining of a great nuisance; how the height of that part of Parnassus quite spoiled the prospect of theirs, especially towards the *East;* [1] and therefore, to avoid a war, offered them the choice of this alternative; either that the Ancients would please to remove themselves and their effects down to the lower summity, which the Moderns would graciously surrender to them, and advance in their place; or else that the said Ancients will give leave to the Moderns to come with shovels and mattocks, and level the said hill as low as they shall think it convenient. To which the Ancients made answer: how little they expected such a message as this from a colony whom they had admitted out of their own free grace, to so near a neighbourhood. That, as to their own seat, they were aborigines of it, and therefore to talk with them of a removal or surrender, was a language they did not understand. That if the height of the hill on their side shortened the prospect of the Moderns, it was a disadvantage they could not

---

[1] In his *Essay*, Sir William Temple charted the movement of art and science from the East to the West.

help, but desired them to consider, whether that injury (if it be any) were not largely recompensed by the shade and shelter it afforded them. That, as to levelling or digging down, it was either folly or ignorance to propose it, if they did, or did not know, how that side of the hill was an entire rock, which would break their tools and hearts, without any damage to itself. That they would therefore advise the Moderns rather to raise their own side of the hill, than dream of pulling down that of the Ancients, to the former of which they would not only give licence, but also largely contribute. All this was rejected by the Moderns with much indignation, who still insisted upon one of the two expedients; and so this difference broke out into a long and obstinate war, maintained on the one part by resolution, and by the courage of certain leaders and allies; but on the other, by the greatness of their number, upon all defeats, affording continual recruits. In this quarrel whole rivulets of ink have been exhausted, and the virulence of both parties enormously augmented. Now, it must here be understood, that ink is the great missive weapon in all battles of the learned, which conveyed through a sort of engine called a quill, infinite numbers of these are darted at the enemy, by the valiant on each side, with equal skill and violence, as if it were an engagement of porcupines. This malignant liquor was compounded by the engineer who invented it of two ingredients, which are gall and copperas, by its bitterness and venom to suit in some degree, as well as to foment, the genius of the combatants. And as the Grecians, after an engagement, when they could not agree about the victory, were wont to set up trophies on both sides, the beaten party being content to be at the same expense, to keep itself in countenance (a laudable and ancient custom, happily revived of late, in the art of war) so the learned, after a sharp and bloody dispute, do on both sides hang out their trophies too, whichever comes by the worse. These trophies have largely inscribed on them the merits of the cause, a full impartial account of such a battle, and how the victory fell clearly to the party that set them up. They are known to the world under several names; as disputes, arguments, rejoinders, brief considerations, answers, replies, remarks, reflections, objections, confutations. For a very few days they are fixed up in all public places, either by themselves or their representatives,* for passengers to gaze at; from whence the chiefest and largest are removed to certain magazines they call libraries, there to remain in a quarter purposely assigned

*Their title-pages.

them, and from thenceforth begin to be called Books of Controversy.

In these books is wonderfully instilled and preserved the spirit of each warrior, while he is alive; and after his death his soul transmigrates there to inform [1] them. This, at least, is the more common opinion; but I believe it is with libraries as with other cemeteries, where some philosophers affirm that a certain spirit, which they call *brutum hominis,* hovers over the monument till the body is corrupted and turns to dust or to worms, but then vanishes or dissolves. So, we may say, a restless spirit haunts over every book, till dust or worms have seized upon it, which to some may happen in a few days, but to others later; and therefore, books of controversy being, of all others, haunted by the most disorderly spirits, have always been confined in a separate lodge from the rest; and for fear of mutual violence against each other, it was thought prudent by our ancestors to bind them to the peace with strong iron chains. Of which invention the original occasion was this: when the works of Scotus first came out, they were carried to a certain great library and had lodgings appointed them; but this author was no sooner settled than he went to visit his master Aristotle, and there both concerted together to seize Plato by main force, and turn him out from his ancient station among the divines, where he had peaceably dwelt near eight hundred years.[2] The attempt succeeded, and the two usurpers have reigned ever since in his stead; but to maintain quiet for the future, it was decreed, that all polemics of the larger size should be held fast with a chain.

By this expedient, the public peace of libraries might certainly have been preserved, if a new species of controversial books had not arose of late years, instinct with a most malignant spirit, from the war above-mentioned between the learned, about the higher summit of Parnassus.

When these books were first admitted into the public libraries, I remember to have said upon occasion, to several persons concerned, how I was sure they would create broils wherever they came, unless a world of care were taken; and therefore I advised that the champions of each side should be coupled together, or otherwise mixed, that like the blending of contrary poisons their malignity might be employed among themselves. And it seems I was neither an ill prophet nor an ill counsellor; for it was nothing else but the neglect of this

[1] To animate.
[2] In point of fact Aristotle had supplanted Plato among Christian theologians well before the time of Duns Scotus.

caution which gave occasion to the terrible fight that happened on Friday last between the Ancient and Modern books in the King's Library. Now, because the talk of this battle is so fresh in everybody's mouth, and the expectation of the town so great to be informed in the particulars, I, being possessed of all qualifications requisite in an historian, and retained by neither party, have resolved to comply with the urgent importunity of my friends, by writing down a full impartial account thereof.

The guardian of the regal library, a person of great valor, but chiefly renowned for his humanity,[*] had been a fierce champion for the Moderns;[1] and, in an engagement upon Parnassus, had vowed, with his own hands, to knock down two of the Ancient chiefs, who guarded a small pass on the superior rock, but, endeavouring to climb up, was cruelly obstructed by his own unhappy weight, and tendency towards his center, a quality to which those of the Modern party are extreme subject; for, being light-headed, they have in speculation a wonderful agility, and conceive nothing too high for them to mount, but in reducing to practice discover a mighty pressure about their posteriors and their heels. Having thus failed in his design, the disappointed champion bore a cruel rancour to the Ancients, which he resolved to gratify by showing all marks of his favour to the books of their adversaries, and lodging them in the fairest apartments; when at the same time, whatever book had the boldness to own itself for an advocate of the Ancients, was buried alive in some obscure corner, and threatened, upon the least displeasure, to be turned out of doors. Besides, it so happened, that about this time there was a strange confusion of place among all the books in the library; for which several reasons were assigned. Some imputed it to a great heap of learned dust, which a perverse wind blew off from a shelf of Moderns into the keeper's eyes. Others affirmed he had a humour to pick the worms out of the schoolmen, and swallow them fresh and fasting; whereof some fell upon his spleen, and some climbed up into his head, to the great perturbation of both. And lastly, others maintained that by walking much in the dark about the library, he had quite lost the situation of it out of his head; and therefore in

---

[*] The Honourable Mr. Boyle, in the preface to his edition of Phalaris, says he was refused a manuscript by the library keeper, *pro solita humanitate suâ.*

[1] The fact that Richard Bentley was a famous classical scholar does not dispute his Modernity; in respect to the new science of philology he was for Swift a type of the Modern. His "inhumanity" refers to his reputed incivility to Robert Boyle. He was appointed Royal Librarian in 1693.

replacing his books he was apt to mistake, and clap Descartes next to Aristotle; poor Plato had got between Hobbes and the Seven Wise Masters, and Virgil was hemmed in with Dryden on one side and Wither [1] on the other.

Meanwhile those books that were advocates for the Moderns chose out one from among them to make a progress through the whole library, examine the number and strength of their party, and concert their affairs. This messenger performed all things very industriously, and brought back with him a list of their forces, in all fifty thousand, consisting chiefly of light-horse, heavy-armed foot, and mercenaries; whereof the foot were in general but sorrily armed, and worse clad; their horses large, but extremely out of case and heart; however, some few by trading among the Ancients had furnished themselves tolerably enough.

While things were in this ferment, discord grew extremely high, hot words passed on both sides, and ill blood was plentifully bred. Here a solitary Ancient, squeezed up among a whole shelf of Moderns, offered fairly to dispute the case, and to prove by manifest reasons, that the priority was due to them, from long possession, and in regard of their prudence, antiquity, and, above all, their great merits towards the Moderns. But these denied the premises, and seemed very much to wonder how the Ancients could pretend to insist upon their antiquity, when it was so plain (if they went to that) that the Moderns were much the more ancient * [2] of the two. As for any obligations they owed to the Ancients, they renounced them all. ' 'Tis true,' said they, 'we are informed, some few of our party have been so mean to borrow their subsistence from you; but the rest, infinitely the greater number (and especially we French and English) were so far from stooping to so base an example, that there never passed, till this very hour, six words between us. For our horses are of our own breeding, our arms of our own forging, and our clothes of our own cutting out and sewing.' Plato was by chance upon the next shelf, and observing those that spoke to be in the ragged plight mentioned a while ago, their jades lean and foundered, their weapons of rotten wood,

* According to the modern paradox.

[1] George Wither (1588–1667), the poet and pamphleteer, here held in contempt by Swift possibly for his Puritan sympathies as well as the pedestrian quality of his work.

[2] The relative authority of the Ancients vs. the Moderns in the controversy is depicted in the dwarf-giant image, and echoed in the phrases, *antiquitas saeculi juventus mundi* (Bacon) and *C'est nous qui sommes les anciens* (Perrault), by which the Moderns implied that their additions to Ancient knowledge raised the Moderns above the Ancients, since knowledge was cumulative.

their armour rusty, and nothing but rags underneath, he laughed aloud, and in his pleasant way swore, by G— he believed them.

Now, the Moderns had not proceeded in their late negotiation with secrecy enough to escape the notice of the enemy. For those advocates, who had begun the quarrel by setting first on foot the dispute of precedency, talked so loud of coming to a battle, that Temple happened to overhear them, and gave immediate intelligence to the Ancients, who thereupon drew up their scattered troops together, resolving to act upon the defensive; upon which several of the Moderns fled over to their party, and among the rest Temple himself. This Temple, having been educated and long conversed among the Ancients, was, of all the Moderns, their greatest favorite, and became their greatest champion.

Things were at this crisis, when a material accident fell out. For, upon the highest corner of a large window, there dwelt a certain spider, swollen up to the first magnitude by the destruction of infinite numbers of flies, whose spoils lay scattered before the gates of his palace, like human bones before the cave of some giant. The avenues to his castle were guarded with turnpikes and palisadoes, all after the Modern way of fortification. After you had passed several courts, you came to the center, wherein you might behold the constable himself in his own lodgings, which had windows fronting to each avenue, and ports to sally out upon all occasions of prey or defence. In this mansion he had for some time dwelt in peace and plenty, without danger to his person by swallows from above, or to his palace by brooms from below: when it was the pleasure of fortune to conduct thither a wandering bee, to whose curiosity a broken pane in the glass had discovered itself, and in he went; where expatiating a while, he at last happened to alight upon one of the outward walls of the spider's citadel; which, yielding to the unequal weight, sunk down to the very foundation. Thrice he endeavoured to force his passage, and thrice the center shook. The spider within, feeling the terrible convulsion, supposed at first that nature was approaching to her final dissolution; or else that Beelzebub,[1] with all his legions, was come to revenge the death of many thousands of his subjects, whom his enemy had slain and devoured. However, he at length valiantly resolved to issue forth, and meet his fate. Meanwhile the bee had acquitted himself of his toils, and posted securely at some dis-

---

[1] The devil whose name has been identified as "the god of flies."

tance, was employed in cleansing his wings, and disengaging them from the ragged remnants of the cobweb. By this time the spider was adventured out, when beholding the chasms, and ruins, and dilapidations of his fortress, he was very near at his wit's end; he stormed and swore like a madman, and swelled till he was ready to burst. At length, casting his eye upon the bee, and wisely gathering causes from events (for they knew each other by sight), 'A plague split you,' said he, 'for a giddy son of a whore. Is it you, with a vengeance, that have made this litter here? Could you not look before you, and be d—nd? Do you think I have nothing else to do (in the devil's name) but to mend and repair after your arse?' 'Good words, friend,' said the bee (having now pruned himself, and being disposed to droll) 'I'll give you my hand and word to come near your kennel no more; I was never in such a confounded pickle since I was born.' 'Sirrah,' replied the spider, 'if it were not for breaking an old custom in our family, never to stir abroad against an enemy, I should come and teach you better manners.' 'I pray have patience,' said the bee, 'or you will spend your substance, and for aught I see, you may stand in need of it all, towards the repair of your house.' 'Rogue, rogue,' replied the spider, 'yet methinks you should have more respect to a person, whom all the world allows to be so much your betters,' 'By my troth,' said the bee, 'the comparison will amount to a very good jest, and you will do me a favour to let me know the reasons that all the world is pleased to use in so hopeful a dispute.' At this the spider, having swelled himself into the size and posture of a disputant, began his argument in the true spirit of controversy, with a resolution to be heartily scurrilous and angry, to urge on his own reasons, without the least regard to the answers or objections of his opposite, and fully predetermined in his mind against all conviction.

'Not to disparage myself,' said he, 'by the comparison with such a rascal, what art thou but a vagabond without house or home, without stock or inheritance, born to no possession of your own, but a pair of wings and a drone-pipe? Your livelihood is an universal plunder upon nature; a freebooter over fields and gardens; and for the sake of stealing will rob a nettle as easily as a violet. Whereas I am a domestic animal, furnished with a native stock within myself. This large castle (to show my improvements in the mathematics [1]) is all built

---

[1] The Moderns prided themselves on their superiority in mathematics; Temple disputed their claim in his *Essay*. For Swift's detailed satire on the New Mathematics, see *Gulliver*, Book III, chap. 2.

with my own hands, and the materials extracted altogether out of my own person.'

'I am glad,' answered the bee, 'to hear you grant at least that I am come honestly by my wings and my voice; for then, it seems, I am obliged to Heaven alone for my flights and my music; and Providence would never have bestowed me two such gifts, without designing them for the noblest ends. I visit indeed all the flowers and blossoms of the field and the garden; but whatever I collect from thence enriches myself, without the least injury to their beauty, their smell, or their taste. Now, for you and your skill in architecture and other mathematics, I have little to say: in that building of yours there might, for aught I know, have been labor and method enough, but by woful experience for us both, 'tis too plain, the materials are naught, and I hope you will henceforth take warning, and consider duration and matter as well as method and art. You boast, indeed, of being obliged to no other creature, but of drawing and spinning out all from yourself; that is to say, if we may judge of the liquor in the vessel by what issues out, you possess a good plentiful store of dirt and poison in your breast; and, though I would by no means lessen or disparage your genuine stock of either, yet I doubt you are somewhat obliged for an increase of both, to a little foreign assistance. Your inherent portion of dirt does not fail of acquisitions, by sweepings exhaled from below; and one insect furnishes you with a share of poison to destroy another. So that in short, the question comes all to this; which is the nobler being of the two, that which by a lazy contemplation of four inches round, by an overweening pride, feeding and engendering on itself, turns all into excrement and venom, producing nothing at last, but flybane and a cobweb; or that which, by an universal range, with long search, much study, true judgment, and distinction of things, brings home honey and wax.'

This dispute was managed with such eagerness, clamor, and warmth, that the two parties of books in arms below stood silent a while, waiting in suspense what would be the issue, which was not long undetermined, for the bee grown impatient at so much loss of time, fled straight away to a bed of roses, without looking for a reply, and left the spider like an orator, collected in himself and just prepared to burst out.

It happened upon this emergency, that Æsop broke silence first. He had been of late most barbarously treated by a strange effect of the regent's humanity, who had tore off his title-page, sorely defaced one half of his leaves, and chained him fast among a shelf of Moderns.[1] Where soon discovering how high the quarrel was like to proceed, he tried all his arts, and turned himself to a thousand forms. At length in the borrowed shape of an ass, the regent mistook him for a Modern; by which means he had time and opportunity to escape to the Ancients, just when the spider and the bee were entering into their contest, to which he gave his attention with a world of pleasure; and when it was ended, swore in the loudest key, that in all his life he had never known two cases so parallel and adapt to each other, as that in the window, and this upon the shelves. 'The disputants,' said he, 'have admirably managed the dispute between them, have taken in the full strength of all that is to be said on both sides, and exhausted the substance of every argument *pro* and *con*. It is but to adjust the reasonings of both to the present quarrel, then to compare and apply the labors and fruits of each as the bee has learnedly deduced them; and we shall find the conclusions fall plain and close upon the Moderns and us. For pray gentlemen, was ever anything so modern as the spider in his air, his turns, and his paradoxes? He argues in the behalf of you his brethren and himself, with many boastings of his native stock and great genius, that he spins and spits wholly from himself, and scorns to own any obligation or assistance from without. Then he displays to you his great skill in architecture, and improvement in the mathematics. To all this the bee, as an advocate retained by us the Ancients, thinks fit to answer; that if one may judge of the great genius or inventions of the Moderns by what they have produced, you will hardly have countenance to bear you out in boasting of either. Erect your schemes with as much method and skill as you please; yet if the materials be nothing but dirt, spun out of your own entrails (the guts of modern brains) the edifice will conclude at last in a cobweb, the duration of which, like that of other spiders' webs, may be imputed to their being forgotten, or neglected, or hid in a corner. For anything else of genuine that the Moderns may pretend to, I cannot recollect, unless it be a large vein of wrangling and satire, much of a nature and substance with the spider's poison; which, however, they pretend to spit wholly out of themselves, is improved by the same arts, by feeding upon the insects and vermin of the age. As for us the Ancients, we are content with the bee to pretend

---

[1] The authenticity of Æsop as well as of Phalaris was questioned in the Phalaris Controversy.

to nothing of our own, beyond our wings and our voice, that is to say, our flights and our language. For the rest, whatever we have got, has been by infinite labor and search, and ranging through every corner of nature; the difference is, that instead of dirt and poison, we have rather chose to fill our hives with honey and wax, thus furnishing mankind with the two noblest of things, which are sweetness and light.' [1]

'Tis wonderful to conceive the tumult arisen among the books, upon the close of this long descant of Æsop; both parties took the hint, and heightened their animosities so on a sudden, that they resolved it should come to a battle. Immediately the two main bodies withdrew under their several ensigns, to the farther parts of the library, and there entered into cabals and consults upon the present emergency. The Moderns were in very warm debates upon the choice of their leaders; and nothing less than the fear impending from their enemies could have kept them from mutinies upon this occasion.[2] The difference was greatest among the horse, where every private trooper pretended to the chief command, from Tasso and Milton to Dryden and Withers. The light-horse were commanded by Cowley and Despréaux. There came the bowmen under their valiant leaders, Descartes, Gassendi, and Hobbes, whose strength was such that they could shoot their arrows beyond the atmosphere, never to fall down again, but turn like that of Evander,[3] into meteors, or like the cannon-ball, into stars. Paracelsus brought a squadron of stink-pot-flingers from the snowy mountains of Rhætia.[4] There came a vast body of dragoons, of different nations, under the leading of Harvey,[5] their great aga, part armed with scythes, the weapons of death; part with lances and long knives, all steeped in poison; part shot bullets of a most malignant nature, and used white powder which infallibly killed without report.[6] There came several bodies of heavy-armed foot, all mercenaries, under the ensigns of Guicciardini, Davila, Poly-

[1] Swift's phrase "sweetness and light" becomes the crucial image of Matthew Arnold's *Culture and Anarchy* (1869). Swift derived his bee image from Temple's *Essay*.
[2] Swift's alignment of the armies of the Moderns is as follows: the light and heavy horsemen are the lyric and epic poets; the bowmen are the philosophers; the mercenaries are the historians; and the engineers are the scientists.
[3] The arrow should have been ascribed Alcestis (*Aeneid* V, 525–8).
[4] Swift satirizes the alchemical experiment of Paracelsus (born in Switzerland).
[5] The Moderns were curiously oblivious to Harvey's significance; Temple questioned not only the usefulness of his discovery of the circulation of the blood, but its originality.
[6] The identification of the "white powder" is obscure; Browne mentions it in *Vulgar Errors*, II, 5.

dore Virgil, Buchanan, Mariana, Camden, and others.[1] The
engineers were commanded by Regiomontanus and Wilkins.[2]
The rest were a confused multitude, led by Scotus, Aquinas,
and Bellarmine,[3] of mighty bulk and stature, but without
either arms, courage, or discipline. In the last place, came
infinite swarms of calones,* [4] a disorderly rout led by
L'Estrange, rogues and ragamuffins, that follow the camp for
nothing but the plunder, all without coats to cover them.

The army of the Ancients was much fewer in number;
Homer led the horse, and Pindar the light-horse; Euclid was
chief engineer; Plato and Aristotle commanded the bowmen;
Herodotus and Livy the foot; Hippocrates the dragoons. The
allies, led by Vossius [5] and Temple, brought up the rear.

All things violently tending to a decisive battle, Fame, who
much frequented, and had a large apartment formerly assigned her in the regal library, fled up straight to Jupiter, to
whom she delivered a faithful account of all that passed between the two parties below. (For, among the gods, she always
tells truth.) Jove, in great concern, convokes a council in the
Milky Way. The senate assembled, he declares the occasion
of convening them; a bloody battle just impendent between
two mighty armies of Ancient and Modern creatures, called
books, wherein the celestial interest was but too deeply concerned. Momus,[6] the patron of the Moderns, made an excellent speech in their favor, which was answered by Pallas, the
protectress of the Ancients. The assembly was divided in their
affections; when Jupiter commanded the book of fate to be
laid before him. Immediately were brought by Mercury three
large volumes in folio, containing memoirs of all things past,
present, and to come. The clasps were of silver, double gilt;
the covers of celestial turkey leather; and the paper such as
here on earth might almost pass for vellum. Jupiter, having
silently read the decree, would communicate the import to
none, but presently shut up the book.

Without the doors of this assembly, there attended a vast
number of light, nimble gods, menial servants to Jupiter:

* These are pamphlets, which are not bound or covered.
[1] All these are Modern historians of the 16th century.
[2] Both were mathematicians and astronomers.
[3] Bellarmine was a Catholic apologist, whom Swift classes with the
scholastics, Scotus and Aquinas.
[4] By the *calones* (soldier-slaves) is implied the hack-writers, those who
engaged in controversy not by reason of their convictions but for mercenary
reasons.
[5] A Dutch theologian and classical scholar.
[6] Momus as a type of night or carping critic (rather than as the god
of ridicule) is here cited as opposite to Pallas, the goddess of wisdom.

these are his ministering instruments in all affairs below. They travel in a caravan, more or less together, and are fastened to each other like a link of galley-slaves, by a light chain, which passes from them to Jupiter's great toe; and yet in receiving or delivering a message, they may never approach above the lowest step of his throne, where he and they whisper to each other through a long hollow trunk. These deities are called by mortal men accidents or events; but the gods call them second causes. Jupiter having delivered his message to a certain number of these divinities, they flew immediately down to the pinnacle of the regal library, and, consulting a few minutes, entered unseen and disposed the parties according to their orders.

Meanwhile Momus, fearing the worst, and calling to mind an ancient prophecy, which bore no very good face to his children the Moderns, bent his flight to the region of a malignant deity, called Criticism. She dwelt on the top of a snowy mountain in Nova Zembla; there Momus found her extended in her den, upon the spoils of numberless volumes half devoured. At her right hand sat Ignorance, her father and husband, blind with age; at her left, Pride, her mother, dressing her up in the scraps of paper herself had torn. There was Opinion, her sister, light of foot, hoodwinked, and headstrong, yet giddy and perpetually turning. About her played her children, Noise and Impudence, Dulness and Vanity, Positiveness, Pedantry, and Ill-Manners. The goddess herself had claws like a cat; her head, and ears, and voice resembled those of an ass; her teeth fallen out before, her eyes turned inward, as if she looked only upon herself; her diet was the overflowing of her own gall; her spleen was so large, as to stand prominent like a dug of the first rate; nor wanted excrescencies in form of teats, at which a crew of ugly monsters were greedily sucking; and, what is wonderful to conceive, the bulk of spleen increased faster than the sucking could diminish it, 'Goddess,' said Momus, 'can you sit idly here while our devout worshippers, the Moderns, are this minute entering into a cruel battle, and perhaps now lying under the swords of their enemies? Who then hereafter will ever sacrifice or build altars to our divinities? Haste therefore to the British Isle, and, if possible, prevent their destruction, while I make factions among the gods, and gain them over to our party.'

Momus, having thus delivered himself, stayed not for an answer, but left the goddess to her own resentment. Up she rose in a rage, and as it is the form upon such occasions, began a soliloquy: ' 'Tis I' (said she) 'who give wisdom to infants and idiots; by me, children grow wiser than their parents. By me, beaux become politicians, and school-boys judges of philosophy. By me, sophisters debate, and conclude upon the depths of knowledge; and coffeehouse wits, instinct by me, can correct an author's style and display his minutest errors, without understanding a syllable of his matter or his language. By me, striplings spend their judgment, as they do their estate, before it comes into their hands. 'Tis I who have deposed wit and knowledge from their empire over poetry, and advanced myself in their stead. And shall a few upstart Ancients dare oppose me?—But come, my aged parents and you, my children dear, and thou my beauteous sister; let us ascend my chariot, and haste to assist our devout Moderns, who are now sacrificing to us a hecatomb, as I perceive by that grateful smell, which from thence reaches my nostrils.'

The goddess and her train having mounted the chariot, which was drawn by tame geese, flew over infinite regions, shedding her influence in due places, till at length she arrived at her beloved island of Britain; but in hovering over its metropolis, what blessings did she not let fall upon her seminaries of Gresham and Covent Garden?[1] And now she reached the fatal plain of St. James's Library, at what time the two armies were upon the point to engage; where entering with all her caravan unseen, and landing upon a case of shelves, now desert, but once inhabited by a colony of virtuosos, she stayed a while to observe the posture of both armies.

But here the tender cares of a mother began to fill her thoughts, and move in her breast. For, at the head of a troop of Modern Bowmen, she cast her eyes upon her son W-tt-n; to whom the fates had assigned a very short thread. W-tt-n, a young hero, whom an unknown father of mortal race begot by stolen embraces with this goddess. He was the darling of his mother above all her children, and she resolved to go and comfort him. But first, according to the good old custom of deities, she cast about to change her shape, for fear the divinity of her countenance might dazzle his mortal sight, and overcharge the rest of his senses. She therefore gathered up her person into an octavo compass; her body grew white and arid, and split in pieces with dryness; the thick turned into

[1] The irony lies in Swift's association of Gresham's, the home of the Royal Society, with Covent Garden, the area of coffee houses frequented by wits and men of fashion.

pasteboard, and the thin into paper, upon which her parents
and children artfully strewed a black juice, or decoction of
gall and soot, in form of letters; her head, and voice, and
spleen, kept their primitive form, and that which before was
a cover of skin, did still continue so. In which guise she
marched on towards the Moderns, undistinguishable in shape
and dress from the divine B-ntl-y, W-tt-n's dearest friend.
'Brave W-tt-n,' said the goddess, 'why do our troops stand
idle here, to spend their present vigour, and opportunity of
this day? Away, let us haste to the generals, and advise to
give the onset immediately.' Having spoke thus, she took the
ugliest of her monsters, full glutted from her spleen, and
flung it invisibly into his mouth, which, flying straight up
into his head, squeezed out his eye-balls, gave him a distorted
look, and half overturned his brain. Then she privately ordered two of her beloved children, Dulness and Ill-Manners,
closely to attend his person in all encounters. Having thus
accoutred him, she vanished in a mist, and the hero perceived
it was the goddess his mother.

The destined hour of fate being now arrived, the fight
began; whereof, before I dare adventure to make a particular
description, I must, after the example of other authors, petition for a hundred tongues, and mouths, and hands, and pens,
which would all be too little to perform so immense a work.
Say, goddess, that presidest over History, who it was that first
advanced in the field of battle. Paracelsus, at the head of his
dragoons, observing Galen [1] in the adverse wing, darted his
javelin with a mighty force, which the brave Ancient received
upon his shield, the point breaking in the second fold.   *
Hic pauca   *   *   *   *   *   *
desunt. *   *   *   *   *   *   *
*   *   *   *   *   *   *   *

They bore the wounded aga on their shields to his chariot
Desunt *   *   *   *   *   *   *
nonnula *   *   *   *   *   *   *
*   *   *   *   *   *   *   *

Then Aristotle, observing Bacon advance with a furious
mien, drew his bow to the head, and let fly his arrow, which
missed the valiant Modern, and went hizzing over his head.
But Descartes it hit; the steel point quickly found a defect in
his head-piece; it pierced the leather and the pasteboard, and
went in at his right eye. The torture of the pain whirled the

---

[1] The battle over the new medicine was focused in the conflict between
the Ancient Galenists and the Modern Paracelsians.

valiant bowman round, till death, like a star of superior influence, drew him into his own *vortex*.[1]   *   *   *
*   *   *   *   *   *   *   *

Ingens hiatus   *   *   *   *   *   *
hic in MS   *   *   *   *   *   *
*   *   *   *   *   *   *   *

when Homer appeared at the head of the cavalry, mounted
on a furious horse, with difficulty managed by the rider himself, but which no other mortal durst approach; he rode
among the enemy's ranks, and bore down all before him. Say,
goddess, whom he slew first, and whom he slew last. First,
Gondibert [2] advanced against him, clad in heavy armour, and
mounted on a staid sober gelding, not so famed for his speed
as his docility in kneeling, whenever his rider would mount
or alight. He had made a vow to Pallas that he would never
leave the field till he had spoiled Homer * of   * Vid. *Homer.*
his armor; madman, who had never once seen
the wearer, nor understood his strength. Him Homer overthrew, horse and man to the ground, there to be trampled
and choked in the dirt. Then, with a long spear, he slew Denham,† a stout Modern, who from his father's side derived his
lineage from Apollo, but his mother was of mortal race. He
fell, and bit the earth. The celestial part Apollo took, and
made it a star, but the terrestrial lay wallowing upon the
ground. Then Homer slew W-sl-y [3] with a kick of his horse's
heel; he took Perrault by mighty force out of his saddle, then
hurled him at Fontenelle,[4] with the same blow dashing out
both their brains.

On the left wing of the horse, Virgil appeared in shining
armor, completely fitted to his body; he was mounted on a
dapple-gray steed, the slowness of whose pace was an effect
of the highest mettle and vigour. He cast his eye on the adverse wing, with a desire to find an object worthy of his
valour, when behold, upon a sorrel gelding of a monstrous
size, appeared a foe, issuing from among the thickest of the
enemy's squadrons; but his speed was less than his noise; for

† Sir John Denham's poems are very unequal, extremely good, and very
indifferent; so that his detractors said he was not the real author of *Cooper's
Hill.*

[1] Swift repeatedly attacks Descartes' theory of vortices; he seems to
imply its atheistical, or at least materialistic, quality.

[2] An epic by Sir William D'Avenant, often ridiculed by the Ancients as
a type of Modern lack of genius.

[3] Sam Wesley, author of a pedestrian heroic poem, *The Life of Christ,*
and a friend of Swift's.

[4] Fontenelle and Perrault were the two great French spokesmen for the
Modern cause.

his horse, old and lean, spent the dregs of his strength in a
high trot, which though it made slow advances, yet caused a
loud clashing of his armor, terrible to hear. The two cavaliers
had now approached within the throw of a lance, when the
stranger desired a parley, and lifting up the vizor of his helmet, a face hardly appeared from within, which after a pause
was known for that of the renowned Dryden. The brave Ancient suddenly started, as one possessed with surprise and disappointment together; for the helmet was nine times too large
for the head, which appeared situate far in the hinder part,
even like the lady in a lobster,[1] or like a mouse under a
canopy of state, or like a shrivelled beau from within the pent-
house of a modern periwig; and the voice was suited to the
visage, sounding weak and remote. Dryden in a long harangue
soothed up the good Ancient, called him father, and by a
large deduction of genealogies, made it plainly appear that
they were nearly related.[2] Then he humbly proposed an exchange of armor, as a lasting mark of hospitality between
them. Virgil consented (for the goddess Diffidence came unseen, and cast a mist before his eyes) though his was of
gold,* and cost a hundred beeves, the other's
* Vid. Homer. but of rusty iron. However, this glittering armor
became the Modern yet worse than his own. Then they agreed
to exchange horses; but when it came to the trial, Dryden
was afraid, and utterly unable to mount.   *   *   *

*   *   *   *   *   *
*   *   *   *   *   *   *Alter hiatus*
*   *   *   *   *   *   *in MS.*

*   *   *   Lucan appeared upon a fiery horse of
admirable shape, but headstrong, bearing the rider where he
list, over the field; he made a mighty slaughter among the
enemy's horse; which destruction to stop, Blackmore,[3] a
famous Modern (but one of the mercenaries) strenuously opposed himself, and darted a javelin with a strong hand, which
falling short of its mark, struck deep in the earth. Then
Lucan threw a lance; but Æsculpaius came unseen, and
turned off the point. 'Brave Modern,' said Lucan, 'I perceive
some god protects you, for never did my arm so deceive me
before; but what mortal can contend with a god? Therefore,
let us fight no longer, but present gifts to each other.' Lucan

---

[1] "The lady in the lobster" refers to a certain formation in the stomach
of the lobster said to resemble the figure of a woman.
[2] Swift satirizes Dryden's translation of Virgil and his avowal of his
fealty to his two masters, Virgil and Spenser.
[3] Sir Richard Blackmore, a physician and voluminous epic poet.

then bestowed the Modern a pair of spurs, and Blackmore gave Lucan a bridle.   *   *   *   *   *

*   *   *   *   *   *   *   *

Pauca de-   *   *   *   *   *   *
sunt.   *   *   *   *   *   *   *

Creech;[1] but the goddess Dulness took a cloud, formed into the shape of Horace, armed and mounted, and placed it in a flying posture before him. Glad was the cavalier to begin a combat with a flying foe, and pursued the image, threatening loud, till at last it led him to the peaceful bower of his father Ogleby,[2] by whom he was disarmed, and assigned to his repose.

Then Pindar slew —, and —, and Oldham,[3] and —, and Afra the Amazon,[4] light of foot; never advancing in a direct line, but wheeling with incredible agility and force, he made a terrible slaughter among the enemy's light horse. Him when Cowley [5] observed, his generous heart burnt within him, and he advanced against the fierce Ancient, imitating his address, and pace, and career, as well as the vigour of his horse and his own skill would allow. When the two cavaliers had approached within the length of three javelins, first Cowley threw a lance, which missed Pindar, and passing into the enemy's ranks, fell ineffectual to the ground. Then Pindar darted a javelin so large and weighty that scarce a dozen cavaliers, as cavaliers are in our degenerate days, could raise it from the ground; yet he threw it with ease, and it went by an unerring hand singing through the air; nor could the Modern have avoided present death, if he had not luckily opposed the shield that had been given him by Venus. And now both heroes drew their swords, but the Modern was so aghast and disordered, that he knew not where he was; his shield dropped from his hands; thrice he fled, and thrice he could not escape; at last he turned, and lifting up his hands in the posture of a suppliant: 'Godlike Pindar,' said he, 'spare my life, and possess my horse with these arms, besides the ransom which my friends will give when they hear I am alive, and your prisoner.' 'Dog,' said Pindar, 'let your ransom stay with your friends; but your carcass shall be left for the fowls of the air

[1] Thomas Creech (1659–1700), translator of Horace and Lucretius.
[2] John Ogleby (1600–1676), translator of Homer and Virgil.
[3] John Oldham (1653–1683), translator and poet, known for his Pindaric odes.
[4] Aphra Behn (1640–1689), dramatist, novelist, and author of Pindaric odes.
[5] Among the poets Swift mentions as slain by Pindar (the implication being that they were all inept Pindarists) Abraham Cowley was actually the best of his imitators.

and the beasts of the field.' With that he raised his sword, and with a mighty stroke cleft the wretched Modern in twain, the sword pursuing the blow; and one half lay panting on the ground, to be trod in pieces by the horses' feet, the other half was borne by the frighted steed through the field. This Venus * took, washed it seven times in ambrosia, then struck it thrice with a sprig of amaranth; upon which the leather grew round and soft, the leaves turned into feathers, and being gilded before, continued gilded still; so it became a dove, and she harnessed it to her chariot.   *   *   *

*   *   *   *   *   *   *   *
*   *   *   *   *   *Hiatus valdè de-*
*   *   *   *   *   *flendus* in MS.

Day being far spent, and the numerous forces of the Moderns half inclining to a retreat, there issued forth from a squadron of their heavy-armed foot, a captain, whose name was † *The Episode of B-ntl-y and W-tt-n.* B-ntl-y,† in person the most deformed of all the Moderns, tall, but without shape or comeliness, large but without strength or proportion. His armor was patched up of a thousand incoherent pieces, and the sound of it, as he marched, was loud and dry, like that made by the fall of a sheet of lead, which an Etesian wind [1] blows suddenly down from the roof of some steeple. His helmet was of old rusty iron, but the vizor was brass, which, tainted by his breath, corrupted into copperas, nor wanted gall from the same fountain; so that, whenever provoked by anger or labour, an atramentous quality, of most malignant nature, was seen to distil from his lips. In his right hand ** he grasped a flail, and (that he might never be unprovided of an offensive weapon) a vessel full of ordure in his left: thus completely armed, he advanced with a slow and heavy pace where the Modern chiefs were holding consult upon the sum of things; who, as he came onwards, laughed to behold his crooked leg and hump shoulder, which his boot and armor, vainly endeavouring to hide, were forced to comply with and expose. The generals made use of him for his talent of railing, which, kept within government, proved frequently of great service to their cause, but at other times did more mischief than good; for at the least touch of offence, and often without any at all, he would, like a wounded elephant, convert it against his

---

    * I do not approve the author's judgment in this, for I think Cowley's *Pindarics* are much preferable to his *Mistress.*
    ** The person here spoken of is famous for letting fly at everybody without distinction, and using mean and foul scurrilities.
    [1] The northwest wind, referred to in Wotton's *Reflections.*

leaders. Such, at this juncture, was the disposition of B-ntl-y; grieved to see the enemy prevail, and dissatisfied with everybody's conduct but his own. He humbly gave the Modern generals to understand, that he conceived, with great submission, they were all a pack of rogues, and fools, and sons of whores, and d-mnd cowards, and confounded loggerheads, and illiterate whelps, and nonsensical scoundrels; that if himself had been constituted general, those presumptuous dogs,* the Ancients, would long before this have been beaten out of the field. 'You,' said he, 'sit here idle; but when I, or any other valiant Modern, kill an enemy, you are sure to seize the spoil. But I will not march one foot against the foe till you all swear to me, that, whomever I take or kill, his arms I shall quietly possess.' B-ntl-y having spoken thus, Scaliger,[1] bestowing him a sour look: 'Miscreant prater,' said he, 'eloquent only in thine own eyes, thou railest without wit, or truth, or discretion; the malignity of thy temper perverteth nature; thy learning makes thee more barbarous, thy study of humanity[2] more inhuman; thy converse amongst poets, more grovelling, miry, and dull. All arts of civilizing others render thee rude and untractable; courts have taught thee ill manners, and polite conversation has finished thee a pedant. Besides, a greater coward burdeneth not the army. But never despond; I pass my word, whatever spoil thou takest shall certainly be thy own, though, I hope, that vile carcass will first become a prey to kites and worms.'

Vid. Homer, de Thersite.

B-ntl-y durst not reply, but half choked with spleen and rage, withdrew, in full resolution of performing some great achievement. With him, for his aid and companion, he took his beloved W-tt-n; resolving by policy or surprise, to attempt some neglected quarter of the Ancients' army. They began their march over carcasses of their slaughtered friends; then to the right of their own forces; then wheeled northward, till they came to Aldrovandus's[3] tomb, which they passed on the side of the declining sun. And now they arrived with fear towards the enemy's outguards; looking about, if haply they might spy the quarters of the wounded, or some straggling sleepers, unarmed and remote from the rest. As when two mongrel curs, whom native greediness and domestic want pro-

---

[1] Joseph Justus Scaliger (1540–1609), scholar and critic, referred to in Boyle's *Dissertation*.
[2] The humanities, or, as Swift probably meant, classical studies.
[3] Ulisse Aldrovandi (1522–1605), prolific compiler of works on natural history; he became blind.

voke and join in partnership, though fearful, nightly to invade
the folds of some rich grazier, they, with tails depressed, and
lolling tongues, creep soft and slow; meanwhile, the conscious
moon, now in her zenith, on their guilty heads darts perpendicular rays; nor dare they bark, though much provoked at
her refulgent visage, whether seen in puddle by reflection, or
in sphere direct; but one surveys the region round, while
t'other scouts the plain, if haply to discover at distance from
the flock, some carcass half devoured, the refuse of gorged
wolves, or ominous ravens. So marched this lovely, loving
pair of friends, nor with less fear and circumspection; when,
at distance, they might perceive two shining suits of armor
hanging upon an oak, and the owners not far off in a profound sleep. The two friends drew lots, and the pursuing of
this adventure fell to B-ntl-y; on he went, and in his van Confusion and Amaze, while Horror and Affright brought up the
rear. As he came near, behold two heroes of the Ancients'
army, Phalaris and Æsop, lay fast asleep: B-ntl-y would fain
have dispatched them both, and stealing close, aimed his flail
at Phalaris's breast. But then the goddess Affright interposing,
caught the Modern in her icy arms, and dragged him from the
danger she foresaw; for both the dormant heroes happened
to turn at the same instant, though soundly sleeping, and busy
in a dream. For Phalaris * was just that minute dreaming
how a most vile poetaster had lampooned him, and how he
had got him roaring in his bull.[1] And Æsop dreamed, that as
he and the Ancient chiefs were lying on the ground, a wild ass
broke loose, ran about trampling and kicking, and dunging
in their faces. B-ntl-y, leaving the two heroes asleep, seized
on both their armors, and withdrew in quest of his darling
W-tt-n.

He, in the mean time, had wandered long in search of some
enterprise, till at length he arrived at a small rivulet, that
issued from a fountain hard by, called in the language of mortal men, Helicon.[2] Here he stopped, and, parched with thirst,
resolved to allay it in this limpid stream. Thrice with profane
hands he essayed to raise the water to his lips, and thrice it
slipped all through his fingers. Then he stooped prone on his
breast, but ere his mouth had kissed the liquid crystal,

---

* This is according to Homer, who tells the dreams of those who were
killed in their sleep.

[1] Phalaris (c. 570–554 B.C.) was a Sicilian tyrant among whose cruelties
the burning of his victims in a brazen bull figured; Bentley's proof that the
letters showing him a benevolent ruler were spurious was the issue of the
Phalaris controversy.

[2] The mountain in Boeotia sacred to the Muses.

Apollo came, and in the channel held his shield betwixt the Modern and the fountain, so that he drew up nothing but mud. For, although no fountain on earth can compare with the clearness of Helicon, yet there lies at bottom a thick sediment of slime and mud; for so Apollo begged of Jupiter, as a punishment to those who durst attempt to taste it with unhallowed lips, and for a lesson to all not to draw too deep or far from the spring.

At the fountain-head W-tt-n discerned two heroes; the one he could not distinguish, but the other was soon known for Temple, general of the allies to the Ancients. His back was turned, and he was employed in drinking large draughts in his helmet from the fountain, where he had withdrawn himself to rest from the toils of the war. W-tt-n, observing him, with quaking knees, and trembling hands, spoke thus to himself: 'Oh that I could kill this destroyer of our army, what renown should I purchase among the chiefs! But to issue out against him,* man for man, shield against shield, and lance against lance, what Modern of us dare?   * Vid. *Homer.* For he fights like a god, and Pallas or Apollo are ever at his elbow. But, Oh mother! if what Fame reports be true, that I am the son of so great a goddess, grant me to hit Temple with this lance, that the stroke may send him to hell, and that I may return in safety and triumph, laden with his spoils.' The first part of his prayer, the gods granted at the intercession of his mother and of Momus; but the rest by a perverse wind sent from Fate was scattered in the air. Then W-tt-n grasped his lance, and brandishing it thrice over his head, darted it with all his might, the goddess, his mother, at the same time, adding strength to his arm. Away the lance went hissing, and reached even to the belt of the averted Ancient, upon which lightly grazing, it fell to the ground. Temple neither felt the weapon touch him, nor heard it fall; and W-tt-n might have escaped to his army, with the honor of having remitted his lance against so great a leader, unrevenged; but Apollo, enraged that a javelin, flung by the assistance of so foul a goddess, should pollute his fountain, put on the shape of ———, and softly came to young Boyle, who then accompanied Temple. He pointed first to the lance, then to the distant Modern that flung it, and commanded the young hero to take immediate revenge. Boyle, clad in a suit of armor, which had been given him by all the gods, immediately advanced against the trembling foe, who now fled before him. As a young lion in the Libyan plains or Araby desert, sent by his aged sire to hunt for prey, or health, or exercise, he scours along, wishing to meet some tiger from the mountains, or a furious boar; if chance, a wild ass, with brayings importune, affronts his ear, the generous beast, though loathing to distain his claws with blood so vile, yet much provoked at the offensive noise, which Echo, foolish nymph, like her ill-judging sex, repeats much louder, and with more delight than Philomela's song, he vindicates the honor of the forest, and hunts the noisy, long-eared animal. So W-tt-n fled, so Boyle pursued. But W-tt-n, heavy-armed and slow of foot, began to slack his course, when his lover B-ntl-y appeared, returning laden with the spoils of the two sleeping Ancients. Boyle observed him well, and soon discovering the helmet and shield of Phalaris, his friend, both which he had lately with his own hands new polished and gilded, rage sparkled in his eyes, and, leaving his pursuit after W-tt-n, he furiously rushed on against this new approacher. Fain would he be revenged on both; but both now fled differ-

ent ways; and as a woman * in a little house
* Vid. *Homer.* that gets a painful livelihood by spinning, if chance her geese be scattered o'er the common, she courses round the plain from side to side, compelling here and there the stragglers to the flock; they cackle loud, and flutter o'er the champaign. So Boyle pursued, so fled this pair of friends: finding at length their flight was vain, they bravely joined, and drew themselves in phalanx. First B-ntl-y threw a spear with all his force, hoping to pierce the enemy's breast; but Pallas came unseen, and in the air took off the point, and clapped on one of lead, which after a dead bang against the enemy's shield, fell blunted to the ground. Then Boyle observing well his time, took a lance of wondrous length and sharpness; and as this pair of friends compacted stood close side to side, he wheeled him to the right, and with unusual force, darted the weapon. B-ntl-y saw his fate approach, and flanking down his arms close to his ribs, hoping to save his body, in went the point, passing through arm and side, nor stopped or spent its force, till it had also pierced the valiant W-tt-n who, going to sustain his dying friend, shared his fate. As when a skilful cook has trussed a brace of woodcocks, he, with iron skewer, pierces the tender sides of both, their legs and wings close pinioned to their ribs; so was this pair of friends transfixed, till down they fell, joined in their lives, joined in their deaths, so closely joined that Charon would

* This is also after the manner of Homer; the woman's getting a painful livelihood by spinning, has nothing to do with the similitude, nor would be excusable without such an authority.

mistake them both for one, and waft them over Styx for half
his fare. Farewell, beloved loving pair; few equals have you
left behind: and happy and immortal shall you be, if all my
wit and eloquence can make you.

   And, now   *   *   *   *   *   *
*   *   *   *   *   *   *   *
*   *   *   *   *   *   *   *
*   *   *Desunt cætera.*

FINIS.

THE BOOKSELLER'S ADVERTISEMENT.[1]

The following discourse came into my hands perfect and entire. But there being several things in it, which the present age would not very well bear, I kept it by me some years, resolving it should never see the light. At length, by the advice and assistance of a judicious friend, I retrenched those parts that might give most offense, and have now ventured to publish the remainder; concerning the author, I am wholly ignorant; neither can I conjecture whether it be the same with that of the two foregoing pieces, the original having been sent me at a different time, and in a different hand. The learned reader will better determine; to whose judgment I entirely submit it.

[1] Probably written by Swift himself.

A
DISCOURSE

Concerning the

Mechanical Operation

OF THE

SPIRIT.

IN A

LETTER

To a FRIEND.

A

FRAGMENT.

LONDON:
Printed in the Year, MDCCX.

A FRAGMENT.[1]

A DISCOURSE CONCERNING THE

MECHANICAL OPERATION

OF THE SPIRIT, &C.*

For T. H. Esquire, at his chambers in the Academy of
the Beaux Esprits in New-Holland.

SIR,[2]

It is now a good while since I have had in my head something, not only very material, but absolutely necessary to my
health, that the world should be informed in. For, to tell you
a secret, I am able to contain it no longer. However, I have
been perplexed for some time to resolve what would be the
most proper form to send it abroad in. To which end, I have
three days been coursing through Westminster Hall, and St.
Paul's Churchyard, and Fleet Street,[3] to peruse titles; and I
do not find any which holds so general a vogue as that of
A Letter to a Friend: [4] nothing is more common than to meet
with long epistles addressed to persons and places, where, at
first thinking, one would be apt to imagine it not altogether

* This discourse is not altogether equal to the two former, the best parts
of it being omitted; whether the Bookseller's account be true, that he durst
not print the rest, I know not, nor indeed is it easy to determine whether
he may be relied on in anything he says of this, or the former treatises,
only as to the time they were writ in, which, however, appears more from
the discourses themselves than his relation.

[1] The place of this so-called Fragment in the *Tale of a Tub* volume still
remains conjectural; it has been interpreted variously as a true fragment
which should not have been published, or as integrally related to the *Tale*
and *Battle* as a variation of one of their themes—an analysis of Enthusiasm,
like Jack; an Enthusiastic system, like Aeolism; or another attack on
Modernity.

[2] Its epistolary style and scientific manner, as well as references to
virtuosi of foreign lands, suggest that the *Mechanical Operation* is intended
as a parody of communications to the Royal Society.

[3] Booksellers had their shops in these areas.

[4] Swift satirizes Modern style in this and the following phrases. The
Modern manner as well as matter, as in *Tale of a Tub*, is his target.

so necessary or convenient; such as *a neighbor at next door, a mortal enemy, a perfect stranger*, or *a person of quality in the clouds;* and these upon subjects, in appearance, the least proper for conveyance by the post; as, *long schemes in philosophy; dark and wonderful mysteries of state; laborious dissertations in criticism and philosophy, advice to parliaments,* and the like.

Now, Sir, to proceed after the method in present wear. (For, let me say what I will to the contrary, I am afraid you will publish this letter, as soon as ever it comes to your hands.) I desire you will be my witness to the world how careless and sudden a scribble it has been; that it was but yesterday when you and I began accidentally to fall into discourse on this matter; that I was not very well when we parted; that the post is in such haste I have had no manner of time to digest it into order or correct the style; and if any other Modern excuses, for haste and negligence, shall occur to you in reading, I beg you to insert them, faithfully promising they shall be thankfully acknowledged.

Pray, Sir, in your next letter to the Iroquois Virtuosi, do me the favour to present my humble service to that illustrious body, and assure them I shall send an account of those phenomena as soon as we can determine them at Gresham.

I have not had a line from the Literati of Tobinambou [1] these three last ordinaries.

And now, Sir, having dispatched what I had to say of forms, or of business, let me entreat you will suffer me to proceed upon my subject; and to pardon me, if I make no farther use of the epistolary style till I come to conclude.

SECTION I.

'TIS recorded of Mahomet, that upon a visit he was going to pay in paradise, he had an offer of several vehicles to conduct him upwards, as fiery chariots, winged horses, and celestial sedans; but he refused them all, and would be borne to heaven upon nothing but his ass.[2] Now, this inclination of Mahomet, as singular as it seems, hath been since taken up

[1] The Iroquois Virtuosi and the Literati of Tobinambou establish the speaker's relationship to the Modern learned; their immediate source, however, is to be found in epigrams of Boileau, who cited them in his essays, which Swift might have known from Temple.

[2] The "ass" figures prominently in the Phalaris phase of the Ancients and Moderns controversy. It is to be noted, however, that Swift here early begins his elaborate and ingenious series of sexual metaphors and implications, which has led to the conclusion that *Mechanical Operation* turns out to be nothing more than a vast, collective orgasm. The sexual impropriety of the Enthusiastic dissenters was a commonplace in the attacks upon them.

by a great number of devout Christians; and doubtless with very good reason. For, since that Arabian is known to have borrowed a moiety of his religious system from the Christian faith, it is but just he should pay reprisals to such as would challenge them; wherein the good people of England, to do them all right, have not been backward. For, though there is not any other nation in the world so plentifully provided with carriages for that journey, either as to safety or ease, yet there are abundance of us who will not be satisfied with any other machine beside this of Mahomet.

For my own part, I must confess to bear a very singular respect to this animal, by whom I take human nature to be most admirably held forth in all its qualities as well as operations: and therefore, whatever in my small reading occurs, concerning this our fellow-creature, I do never fail to set it down, by way of commonplace; and when I have occasion to write upon human reason, politics, eloquence, or knowledge, I lay my memorandums before me, and insert them with a wonderful facility of application. However, among all the qualifications ascribed to this distinguished brute, by Ancient or Modern authors, I cannot remember this talent, of bearing his rider to heaven, has been recorded for a part of his character, except in the two examples mentioned already; therefore, I conceive the methods of this art to be a point of useful knowledge in very few hands, and which the learned world would gladly be better informed in. This is what I have undertaken to perform in the following discourse. For, towards the operation already mentioned, many peculiar properties are required, both in the rider and the ass; which I shall endeavour to set in as clear a light as I can.

But, because I am resolved, by all means, to avoid giving offense to any party whatever, I will leave off discoursing so closely to the letter as I have hitherto done, and go on for the future by way of allegory, though in such a manner that the judicious reader may without much straining make his applications as often as he shall think fit. Therefore, if you please, from hence forward, instead of the term, *ass*, we shall make use of *gifted*, or *enlightened teacher;* and the word *rider*, we will exchange for that of *fanatic auditory*, or any other denomination of the like import. Having settled this weighty point, the great subject of inquiry before us is to examine by what methods this *teacher* arrives at his *gifts*, or *spirit*, or *light;* and by what intercourse between him and his assembly it is cultivated and supported.

In all my writings, I have had constant regard to this great end, not to suit and apply them to particular occasions and circumstances of time, of place, or of person; but to calculate them for universal nature, and mankind in general. And of such catholic use I esteem this present disquisition: for I do not remember any other temper of body, or quality of mind, wherein all nations and ages of the world have so unanimously agreed, as that of a fanatic strain, or tincture of Enthusiasm; which improved by certain persons or societies of men, and by them practised upon the rest, has been able to produce revolutions of the greatest figure in history; as will soon appear to those who know anything of Arabia, Persia, or China, Morocco and Peru. Farther, it has possessed as great a power in the kingdom of knowledge, where it is hard to assign one art or science which has not annexed to it some fanatic branch: such are the *Philosopher's Stone;* the *Grand Elixir;* * the *Planetary Worlds;* the *Squaring of the Circle;* the *Summum Bonum; Utopian Commonwealths,* with some others of * Some writers hold them for the same, others not. less or subordinate note; which all serve for nothing else but to employ or amuse this grain of Enthusiasm dealt into every composition.[1]

But, if this plant has found a root in the fields of empire, and of knowledge, it has fixed deeper, and spread yet farther upon holy ground. Wherein, though it hath passed under the general name of Enthusiasm, and perhaps arisen from the same original, yet hath it produced certain branches of a very different nature, however often mistaken for each other. The word in its universal acceptation may be defined, *a lifting up of the soul or its faculties above matter.* This description will hold good in general; but I am only to understand it as applied to religion; wherein there are three general ways of ejaculating the soul, or transporting it beyond the sphere of matter. The first is the immediate act of God, and is called *prophecy* or *inspiration.* The second is the immediate act of the devil, and is termed *possession.* The third is the product of natural causes, the effect of strong imagination, spleen, violent anger, fear, grief, pain, and the like. These three have been abundantly treated on by authors, and therefore shall not employ my enquiry. But, the fourth method of religious Enthusiasm, or launching out the soul, as it is purely an effect of artifice and *Mechanick Operation* has been sparingly handled, or not

---

[1] For the connections between Enthusiasm, occultism, and the new science, see *Tale of a Tub,* p. 368, n. 1.

at all, by any writer; [1] because though it is an art of great antiquity, yet having been confined to few persons, it long wanted those advancements and refinements, which it afterwards met with, since it has grown so epidemic, and fallen into so many cultivating hands.

It is therefore upon this *Mechanical Operation of the Spirit* that I mean to treat, as it is at present performed by our British workmen. I shall deliver to the reader the result of many judicious observations upon the matter, tracing, as near as I can, the whole course and method of this trade, producing parallel instances, and relating certain discoveries that have luckily fallen in my way.

I have said that there is one branch of religious Enthusiasm which is purely an effect of nature; whereas the part I mean to handle is wholly an effect of art, which, however, is inclined to work upon certain natures and constitutions more than others. Besides, there is many an operation which, in its original, was purely an artifice, but through a long succession of ages, hath grown to be natural. Hippocrates tells us,[2] that among our ancestors, the Scythians, there was a nation called Longheads*, which at first began by a custom

* *Macrocephali*

among midwives and nurses of molding, and squeezing, and bracing up the heads of infants; by which means nature, shut out at one passage, was forced to seek another, and finding room above, shot upwards, in the form of a sugar-loaf; and being diverted that way, for some generations, at last found it out of herself, needing no assistance from the nurse's hand. This was the original of the Scythian Longheads, and thus did custom, from being a second nature, proceed to be a first. To all which there is something very analogous among us of this nation, who are the undoubted posterity of that refined people. For, in the age of our fathers, there arose a generation of men in this island,

---

[1] It has been suggested that Swift's *Mechanical Operation* owes its origins to Meric Casaubon's *Treatise of Enthusiasme* (1655) and Henry More's *Enthusiasmus Triumphatus* (1656), both of which attacks on Enthusiasm use the phrase "mechanical enthusiasm" and distinguish it from "natural" or "supernatural" enthusiasm. Swift's implication is that, though the founders of Enthusiasm were naturally mad, their followers had to contrive systems to remain so. Philosophically, Swift may be satirizing reductive systems of philosophy, that is, systems which reduce all phenomena to one principle; here it is wind; among the Aeolists it was vapors. (See Phillip Harth, *Swift and Anglican Rationalism. The Religious Background of* A Tale of a Tub, University of Chicago Press, 1961, pp. 74, 75.)

[2] Hippocrates (c. 460–370 B.C.) in *De Aere, Aquis, et Locis*, in which, however, he does not relate the Scythians to the Macrocephali. (For this and many other notes related to the sources of the *Mechnical Operation*, I am indebted to the A. C. Guthkelch and D. Nichol Smith edition of the *Tale of a Tub* volume, Clarendon Press, 1920.)

called Roundheads, whose race is now spread over three king-doms, yet in its beginning was merely an operation of art, produced by a pair of scissors, a squeeze of the face, and a black cap. These heads, thus formed into a perfect sphere in all assemblies, were most exposed to the view of the female sort, which did influence their conceptions so effectually, that nature, at last, took the hint, and did it of herself; so that a Roundhead has been ever since as familiar a sight among us as a Longhead among the Scythians.

Upon these examples, and others easy to produce, I desire the curious reader to distinguish, first between an effect grown from art into nature, and one that is natural from its begin-ning; secondly, between an effect wholly natural, and one which has only a natural foundation, but where the superstruc-ture is entirely artificial. For the first and last of these I under-stand to come within the districts of my subject. And having obtained these allowances, they will serve to remove any ob-jections that may be raised hereafter against what I shall ad-vance.

The practitioners of this famous art proceed in general upon the following fundamental: that *the corruption of the senses is the generation of the spirit;* because the senses in men are so many avenues to the fort of reason, which in this operation is wholly blocked up. All endeavours must be therefore used, either to divert, bind up, stupify, fluster, and amuse the senses, or else to justle them out of their stations; and while they are either absent, or otherwise employed, or engaged in a civil war against each other, the Spirit enters and performs its part.

Now, the usual methods of managing the senses upon such conjectures are what I shall be very particular in delivering, as far as it is lawful for me to do; but having had the honour to be initiated into the mysteries of every society, I desire to be excused from divulging any rites, wherein the profane must have no part.

But here, before I can proceed farther, a very dangerous objection must, if possible, be removed: for it is positively denied by certain critics, that the spirit can by any means be introduced into an assembly of Modern saints, the disparity being so great in many material circumstances, between the primitive way of inspiration, and that which is practised in the present age. This they pretend to prove from the second chapter of the *Acts,* where comparing both, it appears: first, that *the apostles were gathered together with one accord in one place;* by which is meant, an universal agreement in opinion, and form of worship; a harmony (say they) so far from being found between any two conventicles among us, that it is vain to expect it between any two heads in the same. Secondly, the spirit instructed the apostles in the gift of speaking several languages; a knowledge so remote from our dealers in this art, that they neither understand propriety of words, or phrases in their own. Lastly (say these objectors), the Modern artists do utterly exclude all approaches of the Spirit, and bar up its ancient way of entering, by covering themselves so close, and so industriously a top. For, they will needs have it as a point clearly gained, that the cloven tongues never sat upon the apostles' heads while their hats were on.

Now, the force of these objections seems to consist in the different acceptation of the word *Spirit:* which if it be understood for a supernatural assistance, approaching from without, the objectors have reason, and their assertions may be allowed; but the Spirit we treat of here, proceeding entirely from within, the argument of these adversaries is wholly eluded. And upon the same account, our Modern artificers find it an expedient of absolute necessity to cover their heads as close as they can, in order to prevent perspiration, than which nothing is observed to be a greater spender of mechanick light, as we may, perhaps, farther show in convenient place.

To proceed therefore upon the phenomenon of spiritual mechanism, it is here to be noted, that in forming and working up the Spirit, the assembly has a considerable share, as well as the preacher; the method of this arcanum is as follows. They violently strain their eyeballs inward, half closing the lids; then, as they sit, they are in a perpetual motion of see-saw, making long hums at proper periods, and continuing the sound at equal height, choosing their time in those intermissions, while the preacher is at ebb. Neither is this practice, in any part of it, so singular or improbable as not to be traced in distant regions, from reading and observation. For first, the

* *Bernier, Mem. de Mogol.*[1] Jauguis,* or enlightened saints of India, see all their visions by help of an acquired straining and pressure of the eyes. Secondly, the art of see-saw on a beam, and swinging by session upon a cord, in order to raise artificial ecstasies, hath been derived to us from our

† *Guagnini, Hist. Sarmat.*[2] Scythian ancestors,† where it is practised at this day among the women. Lastly, the whole proceeding, as I have here related it, is performed

[1] *Suite des Memoires du Sr. Bernier sur l'Empire du Grand Mogol,* 1671.
[2] Alexander Guagninus, *Sarmatiae Europeae Descriptio,* 1578.

by the natives of Ireland, with a considerable improvement; and it is granted that his noble nation hath, of all others, admitted fewer corruptions, and degenerated least from the purity of the old Tartars. Now it is usual for a knot of Irish, men and women, to abstract themselves from matter, bind up all their senses, grow visionary and spiritual, by influence of a short pipe of tobacco, handed round the company, each preserving the smoke in his mouth, till it comes again to his turn to take in fresh: at the same time, there is a concert of a continued gentle hum, repeated and renewed by instinct, as occasion requires, and they move their bodies up and down, to a degree that sometimes their heads and points lie parallel to the horizon. Meanwhile, you may observe their eyes turned up in the posture of one who endeavours to keep himself awake; by which, and many other symptoms among them, it manifestly appears that the reasoning faculties are all suspended and superseded, that imagination hath usurped the seat, scattering a thousand deliriums over the brain. Returning from this digression, I shall describe the methods by which the Spirit approaches. The eyes being disposed according to art, at first you can see nothing, but after a short pause, a small glimmering light begins to appear, and dance before you. Then, by frequently moving your body up and down, you perceive the vapors to ascend very fast, till you are perfectly dosed and flustered like one who drinks too much in a morning. Meanwhile, the preacher is also at work; he begins a loud hum, which pierces you quite through; this is immediately returned by the audience, and you find yourself prompted to imitate them, by a mere spontaneous impulse, without knowing what you do. The *interstitia* are duly filled up by the preacher, to prevent too long a pause, under which the Spirit would soon faint and grow languid.

This is all I am allowed to discover about the progress of the Spirit, with relation to that part which is born by the assembly; but in the methods of the preacher, to which I now proceed, I shall be more large and particular.

SECTION II.

You will read it very gravely remarked in the books of those illustrious and right eloquent pen-men, the Modern travellers, that the fundamental difference in point of religion between the wild Indians and us, lies in this: that we worship God, and they worship the devil. But, there are certain critics who will by no means admit of this distinction; rather believing that all nations whatsoever adore the true God, because they seem to intend their devotions to some invisible power, of greatest goodness and ability to help them, which perhaps will take in the brightest attributes ascribed to the divinity. Others, again, inform us that those idolaters adore two principles: the principle of good, and that of evil; which, indeed, I am apt to look upon as the most universal notion, that mankind, by the mere light of nature, ever entertained of things invisible. How this idea hath been managed by the Indians and us, and with what advantage to the understandings of either, may well deserve to be examined. To me, the difference appears little more than this, that they are put oftener upon their knees by their fears, and we by our desires; that the former set them a praying, and us a cursing. What I applaud them for is their discretion in limiting their devotions and their deities to their several districts, nor ever suffering the liturgy of the white God to cross or interfere with that of the black. Not so with us, who pretending, by the lines and measures of our reason, to extend the dominion of one invisible power, and contract that of the other, have discovered a gross ignorance in the natures of good and evil, and most horribly confounded the frontiers of both. After men have lifted up the throne of their divinity to the *Coelum Empyraeum,* adorned him with all such qualities and accomplishments as themselves seem most to value and possess: after they have sunk their principle of evil to the lowest center, bound him with chains, loaded him with curses, furnished him with viler dispositions than any rake-hell of the town, accoutered him with tail, and horns, and huge claws, and saucer eyes; I laugh aloud to see these reasoners, at the same time engaged in wise dispute, about certain walks and purlieus, whether they are in the verge of God or the devil, seriously debating whether such and such influences come into men's minds from above or below, or whether certain passions and affections are guided by the evil spirit or the good.

> *Dum fas atque nefas exiguo fine libidinum*
> *Discernunt avidi - - - - -* [1]

Thus do men establish a fellowship of Christ with Belial, and such is the analogy they make between cloven tongues and cloven feet. Of the like nature is the disquisition before us: it

[1] Horace, *Odes,* I, xviii, 10–11.

hath continued these hundred years an even debate, whether the deportment and the cant of our English Enthusiastic preachers were possession or inspiration, and a world of argument has been drained on either side, perhaps, to little purpose. For, I think, it is in life as in tragedy, where, it is held, a conviction of great defect both in order and invention to interpose the assistance of preternatural power, without an absolute and last necessity. However, it is a sketch of human vanity for every individual to imagine the whole universe is interested in his meanest concern. If he hath got cleanly over a kennel, some angel, unseen, descended on purpose to help him by the hand; if he knocked his head against a post, it was the devil, for his sins, let loose from hell, on purpose to buffet him. Who that sees a little paltry mortal droning, and dreaming, and drivelling to a multitude can think it agreeable to common good sense that either heaven or hell should be put to the trouble of influence or inspection upon what he is about? Therefore, I am resolved immediately to weed this error out of mankind, by making it clear that this mystery of venting spiritual gifts is nothing but a trade, acquired by much instruction, and mastered by equal practice and application as others are. This will best appear by describing and deducing the whole process of the operation, as variously as it hath fallen under my knowledge or experience.

* * * * * * * * * *Here the whole scheme of*
* * * * * * * * * *spiritual mechanism was*
* * * * * * * * * *deduced and explained,*
* * * * * * * * * *with an appearance of*
* * * * * * * * * *great reading and observa-*
* * * * * * * * * *tion; but it was thought*
* * * * * * * * * *neither safe nor conven-*
* * * * * * * * * *ient to print it.*
* * * * * * * * * * * * *

Here it may not be amiss to add a few words upon the laudable practice of wearing quilted caps, which is not a matter of mere custom, humour, or fashion, as some would pretend, but an institution of great sagacity and use; these, when moistened with sweat, stop all perspiration, and by reverberating the heat, prevent the Spirit from evaporating any way but at the mouth; even as a skilful housewife, that covers her still with a wet clout, for the same reason, and finds the same effect. For, it is the opinion of choice virtuosi, that the brain is only a crowd of little animals, but with teeth and claws extremely sharp, and, therefore, cling together in the contexture we behold, like the picture of Hobbes's *Leviathan*,[1] or like bees in perpendicular swarm upon a tree, or like a carrion corrupted into vermin, still preserving the shape and figure of the mother animal. That all invention is formed by the morsure of two or more of these animals, upon certain capillary nerves, which proceed from thence, whereof three branches spread into the tongue, and two into the right hand. They hold also, that these animals are of a constitution extremely cold; that their food is the air we attract, their excrement phlegm; and that what we vulgarly call rheums, and colds, and distillations, is nothing else but an epidemical looseness, to which that little commonwealth is very subject, from the climate it lies under. Farther, that nothing less than a violent heat can disentangle these creatures from their hamated station of life, or give them vigor and humour, to imprint the marks of their little teeth. That if the morsure be hexagonal, it produces poetry; the circular gives eloquence; if the bite hath been conical, the person whose nerve is so affected shall be disposed to write upon the politics; and of the rest.

I shall now discourse briefly by what kind of practices the voice is best governed, towards the composition and improvement of the Spirit; for, without a competent skill in tuning and toning each word, and syllable, and letter to their due cadence, the whole operation is incomplete, misses entirely of its effect on the hearers, and puts the workman himself to continual pains for new supplies, without success. For, it is to be understood that in the language of the Spirit, cant and droning supply the place of sense and reason in the language of men: because in spiritual harangues, the disposition of the words according to the art of grammar hath not the least use, but the skill and influence wholly lie in the choice and cadence of the syllables; even as a discreet composer, who in setting a song, changes the words and order so often that he is forced to make it nonsense, before he can make it music. For this reason, it hath been held by some that the art of canting is ever in greatest perfection when managed by Ignorance: which is thought to be enigmatically meant by Plutarch when he tells us that the best musical instruments were made from the bones of an ass. And the profounder critics upon that passage are of opinion the word in its genuine signification means no other than a jaw-bone, though some rather think it to have been the

---

[1] Swift refers to the engraving on the title page of the 1651 edition of Hobbes's *Leviathan;* the implication is that there is little to choose from between Hobbes's system and *Mechanical Operation.*

os sacrum; but in so nice a case, I shall not take upon me to decide; the curious are at liberty to pick from it whatever they please.

The first ingredient towards the art of canting is a competent share of inward light: that is to say, a large memory, plentifully fraught with theological polysyllables, and mysterious texts from Holy Writ, applied and digested by those methods and mechanical operations already related: the bearers of this light resembling lanthorns, compact of leaves from old Geneva Bibles; which invention Sir Humphrey Edwyn,[1] during his mayoralty, of happy memory, highly approved and advanced; affirming the scripture to be now fulfilled, where is says, 'Thy word is a lanthorn to my feet, and a light to my paths.' [2]

Now, the art of canting consists in skilfully adapting the voice to whatever words the Spirit delivers, that each may strike the ears of the audience with its most significant cadence. The force or energy of this eloquence is not to be found, as among ancient orators, in the disposition of words to a sentence, or the turning of long periods; but, agreeable to the Modern refinements in music, is taken up wholly in dwelling and dilating upon syllables and letters. Thus it is frequent for a single vowel to draw sighs from a multitude, and for a whole assembly of saints to sob to the music of one solitary liquid. But these are trifles, when even sounds inarticulate are observed to produce as forcible effects. A master workman shall blow his nose so powerfully as to pierce the hearts of his people, who are disposed to receive the excrements of his brain with the same reverence as the issue of it. Hawking, spitting, and belching, the defects of other men's rhetoric, are the flowers, and figures, and ornaments of his. For, the Spirit being the same in all, it is of no import through what vehicle it is conveyed.

It is a point of too much difficulty to draw the principles of this famous art within the compass of certain adequate rules. However, perhaps I may one day oblige the world with my *Critical Essay upon the Art of Canting, Philosophically, Physically, and Musically Considered.*

But, among all improvements of the Spirit, wherein the

---

[1] Sir Humphrey Edwin was elected Lord Mayor of London in September, 1697. He is referred to in *Tale of a Tub,* and he helps date *Mechanical Operation* as coming after the writing of the religious satire in *Tale of a Tub.*

[2] See Psalm CXIX, 105; Swift also satirizes the "inner light" which the Enthusiasts claimed.

voice hath born a part, there is none to be compared with that
of conveying the sound through the nose, which under the
denomination of snuffling,* 1 hath passed with so great applause in the world. The originals of this institution are very
dark; but having been initiated into the mystery of it, and
leave being given me to publish it to the world, I shall deliver
as direct a relation as I can.

This art, like many other famous inventions, owed its birth,
or at least, improvement and perfection, to an effect of chance,
but was established upon solid reasons, and hath flourished in
this island ever since, with great luster. All agree that it first
appeared upon the decay and discouragement of bag-pipes,
which having long suffered under the mortal hatred of the
brethren, tottered for a time, and at last fell with monarchy.
The story is thus related.

As yet, snuffling was not; when the following adventure
happened to a Banbury saint.2 Upon a certain day, while he
was far engaged among the tabernacles of the wicked, he felt
the outward man put into odd commotions, and strangely
pricked forward by the inward: an effect very usual among
the Modern inspired. For, some think, that the Spirit is apt to
feed on the flesh, like hungry wines upon raw beef. Others
rather there is a perpetual game at leap-frog between both;
and, sometimes the flesh is uppermost and sometimes the
Spirit; adding that the former, while it is in the state of a
rider, wears huge Rippon spurs,3 and when it comes to the
turn of being bearer, is wonderfully headstrong and hard-
mouthed. However it came about, the saint felt his vessel full
extended in every part (a very natural effect of strong inspiration); and the place and time falling out so unluckily, that he
could not have the convenience of evacuating upwards by
repetition, prayer, or lecture, he was forced to open an inferior vent. In short, he wrestled with the flesh so long, that
he at length subdued it, coming off with honourable wounds,
all before. The surgeon had now cured the parts primarily
affected; but the disease driven from its post, flew up into his
head; and, as a skilful general, valiantly attacked in his
trenches, and beaten from the field, by flying marches with-

---

* The snuffling of men, who have lost their noses by lewd courses, is said
to have given rise to that tone which our dissenters did too much affect.
W. WOTTON.

1 The implications of snuffling are manifold: referring primarily to the
whining drone of Enthusiastic preachers, it also has sexual implications, and
suggests the pox which frequently affected the nose.
2 Banbury was known for its saints, by which a fanatic is implied.
3 Rippon was noted for its manufacture of spurs.

draws to the capital city, breaking down the bridges to prevent pursuit; so the disease, repelled from its first station, fled before the rod of Hermes, to the upper region, there fortifying itself; but finding the foe making attacks at the nose, broke down the bridge and retired to the headquarters. Now, the naturalists observe, that there is in human noses an idiosyncrasy, by virtue of which the more the passage is obstructed, the more our speech delights to go through, as the music of a flageolet is made by the stops. By this method, the twang of the nose becomes perfectly to resemble the snuffle of a bagpipe, and is found to be equally attractive of British ears; whereof the saint had sudden experience, by practising his new faculty with wonderful success in the operation of the Spirit. For, in a short time, no doctrine passed for sound and orthodox unless it were delivered through the nose. Straight every pastor copied after this original; and those who could not otherwise arrive to a perfection, spirited by a noble zeal, made use of the same experiment to acquire it. To that, I think, it may be truly affirmed, the saints owe their empire to the snuffling of one animal, as Darius did his, to the neighing of another; and both stratagems were performed by the same art; for we read how the Persian beast * acquired his faculty, by covering a mare the day before.

* *Herodot.*

I should now have done, if I were not convinced that whatever I have yet advanced upon this subject is liable to great exception. For, allowing all I have said to be true, it may still be justly objected that there is in the commonwealth of artificial Enthusiasm some real foundation for art to work upon in the temper and complexion of individuals, which other mortals seem to want. Observe but the gesture, the motion, and the countenance of some choice professors, though in their most familiar actions; you will find them of a different race from the rest of human creatures. Remark your commonest pretender to a light within; how dark and dirty and gloomy he is without; as lanthorns, which the more light they bear in their bodies, cast out so much the more soot, and smoke, and fuliginous matter to adhere to the sides. Listen but to their ordinary talk, and look on the mouth that delivers it; you will image you are hearing some ancient oracle, and your understanding will be equally informed. Upon these, and the like reasons, certain objectors pretend to put it beyond all doubt that there must be a sort of preternatural Spirit, possessing the heads of the Modern saints; and some will have it to be the heat of zeal, working upon the dregs of igno-

rance, as other Spirits are produced from lees, by the force
of fire. Some again think, that when our earthly tabernacles
are disordered and desolate, shaken and out of repair, the
Spirit delights to dwell within them; as houses are said to be
haunted when they are forsaken and gone to decay.

To set this matter in as fair a light as possible, I shall here,
very briefly, deduce the history of fanaticism, from the most
early ages to the present. And if we are able to fix upon any
one material or fundamental point, wherein the chief professors have universally agreed, I think we may reasonably
lay hold on that, and assign it for the great seed or principle
of the Spirit.

The most early traces we meet with of fanatics in ancient
story are among the Egyptians, who instituted those rites,
known in Greece by the names of *Orgya, Panegyres,* and
Dionysia, whether introduced there by Orpheus or Melampus,*
we shall not dispute at present, nor in all likeli-
hood, at any time for the future. These feasts
were celebrated to the honor of Osiris, whom
the Grecians called Dionysius, and is the same
with Bacchus: which has betrayed some superficial readers to
imagine that the whole business was nothing more than a set
of roaring, scouring companions, over-charged with wine; but
this is a scandalous mistake foisted on the world by a sort of
Modern authors, who have too literal an understanding; and
because antiquity is to be traced backwards, do therefore, like
Jews, begin their books at the wrong end, as if learning were
a sort of conjuring. These are the men, who pretend to understand a book by scouting through the index, as if a traveller
should go about to describe a palace when he had seen nothing but the privy; or like certain fortune-tellers in Northern
America, who have a way of reading a man's destiny by peeping in his breech. For at the time of instituting these mysteries,† there was not one vine in all Egypt,[1] the
natives drinking nothing but ale; which liquor
seems to have been far more ancient than wine, and has the
honour of owing its invention and progress, not only to the
Egyptian Osiris,[2] but to the Grecian Bacchus,**
who in their famous expedition carried the receipt of it along with them, and gave it to the
nations they visited or subdued. Besides, Bacchus himself was

*Diod. Sic.
L. 1. Plut. de
Iside &
Osyride.*

†*Herod. L. 2.*

**Diod. Sic.
L. 1 & 3.*

[1] Herodotus, II, 77.
[2] Diodorus Sculus, I, 15; III, 6.

very seldom or never drunk: for it is recorded of him, that he
was the first inventor of the Mitre [*] [1] which
* *Id. L. 4.*
he wore continually on his head (as the whole
company of Bacchanals did) to prevent vapors and the headache after hard drinking. And for his reason (say some) the
scarlet whore, when she makes the kings of the earth drunk
with her cup of abomination, is always sober herself, though
she never balks the glass in her turn, being, it seems, kept
upon her legs by virtue of her triple mitre. Now, these feasts
were instituted in imitation of the famous expedition Osiris
made through the world, and of the company that attended
him,[†] whereof the Bacchanalian ceremonies were
so many types and symbols. From which account,   † *See the Par-*
it is manifest, that the fanatic rites of these   *ticulars in*
bacchanals, cannot be imputed to intoxications   *Diod. Sic. Lib.*
1 & 3.
by wine, but must needs have had a deeper foundation. What
this was, we may gather large hints from certain circumstances in the course of their mysteries. For, in the first place,
there was in their processions an entire mixture and confusion
of sexes; they affected to ramble about hills and deserts; their
garlands were of ivy and vine, emblems of cleaving and clinging; or of fir, the parent of turpentine. It is added, that they
imitated satyrs, were attended by goats, and rode upon asses,
all companions of great skill and practice in affairs of gallantry. They bore for their ensigns certain curious figures,
perched upon long poles, made into the shape and size of the
virga genitalis, with its appurtenances, which were so many
shadows and emblems of the whole mystery, as well as
tropies set up by the female conquerors. Lastly, in a certain
town of Attica, the whole solemnity [**] stripped
of all its types, was performed in *puris naturali-*   ** *Dionysia*
bus, the votaries, not flying in coveys, but sorted   *Brauronia.*
into couples.[2] The same may be farther conjectured from the
death of Orpheus, one of the institutors of these mysteries,
who was torn in pieces of women, because he refused to
communicate his orgies [‡] to them; which others
explained by telling us he had castrated himself   ‡ *Vid. Photium*
upon grief for the loss of his wife.[3]   *in excerptis*
è Conone.

Omitting many others of less note, the next

[1] Ibid., IV, 4.
[2] Swift refers to the *Brauronia,* the celebration in honor of Dionysus at
Brauron.
[3] Photius (c. 820–892), a Greek theologian and churchman included
among his writings quotations from lost Greek works.

fanatics we meet with, of any eminence, were the numerous sects of heretics appearing in the five first centuries of the Christian Era, from Simon Magnus and his followers, to those of Eutyches. I have collected their systems from infinite reading, and comparing them with those of their successors in the several ages since, I find there are certain bounds set even to the irregularities of human thought, and those a great deal narrower than is commonly apprehended. For, as they all frequently interfere, even in their wildest ravings, so there is one fundamental point wherein they are sure to meet, as lines in a center, and that is the community of women: great were their solicitudes in this matter, and they never failed of certain articles in their schemes of worship, on purpose to establish it.

The last fanatics of note were those which started up in Germany, a little after the Reformation of Luther; springing, as mushrooms do at the end of a harvest; such were John of Leyden, David George, Adam Neuster,[1] and many others; whose visions and revelations always terminated in leading about half a dozen sisters, apiece, and making that practice a fundamental part of their system. For, human life is a continual navigation, and, if we expect our vessels to pass with safety through the waves and tempests of this fluctuating world, it is necessary to make a good provision of the flesh, as seamen lay in store of beef for a long voyage.

Now, from this brief survey of some principal sects, among the fanatics in all ages (having omitted the Mahometans and others, who might also help to confirm the argument I am about) to which I might add several among ourselves, such as the Family of Love, Sweet Singers of Israel,[2] and the like: and from reflecting upon that fundamental point in their doctrines, about women, wherein they have so unanimously agreed; I am apt to imagine that the seed or principle, which has ever put men upon visions in things invisible, is of a corporeal nature: for the profounder chemists inform us that the strongest Spirits may be extracted from human flesh. Besides,

---

[1] John of Leyden was the hero of the Munster Anabaptist uprising; he was crowned King of the New Jerusalem, and after his downfall, in 1536 was executed.

David George, a Dutch Anabaptist, was the founder of the Family of Love, or Familist sect.

Adam Neuster was a German theologian who was converted to Mohammedanism.

[2] The Family of Love was a minor Anabaptist sect that flourished in England in the 16th and 17th centuries.

The Sweet Singers of Israel, a sect of Enthusiasts, believed themselves incapable of sinning; they were attacked by John Bunyan.

the spinal marrow, being nothing else but a continuation of the brain, must needs create a very free communication between the superior faculties and those below: and thus the thorn in the flesh serves for a spur to the Spirit. I think it is agreed among physicians that nothing affects the head so much as a tentiginous humour, repelled and elated to the upper region, found by daily practice, to run frequently up into madness. A very eminent member of the faculty assured me, that when the Quakers first appeared, he seldom was without some female patients among them, for the *furor* ———. Persons of a visionary devotion, either men or women, are in their complexion, of all others, the most amorous: for zeal is frequently kindled from the same spark with other fires, and from inflaming brotherly love, will proceed to raise that of a gallant. If we inspect into the usual process of modern courtship, we shall find it to consist in a devout turn of the eyes, called ogling; an artificial form of canting and whining by rote, every interval, for want of other matter, made up with a shrug, or a hum, a sigh, or a groan; the style compact of insignificant words, incoherences and repetition. These I take to be the most accomplished rules of address to a mistress; and where are these performed with more dexterity than by the saints? Nay, to bring this argument yet closer, I have been informed by a certain sanguine brethren of the first class, that in the height and *orgasmus* of their spiritual exercise it has been frequent with them *****; immediately after which, they found the Spirit to relax and flag of a sudden with the nerves, and they were forced to hasten to a conclusion. This may be farther strengthened by observing, with wonder, how unaccountably all females are attracted by visionary or Enthusiastic preachers, though never so contemptible in their outward mien; which is usually supposed to be done upon considerations purely spiritual, without any carnal regards at all. But I have reason to think the sex hath certain characteristics by which they form a truer judgment of human abilities and performings than we ourselves can possibly do of each other. Let that be as it will, thus much is certain, that however spiritual intrigues begin, they generally conclude like all others; they may branch upwards toward heaven, but the root is in the earth. Too intense a contemplation is not the business of flesh and blood; it must by the necessary course of things, in a little time, let go its hold, and fall into matter. Lovers, for the sake of celestial converse, are but another sort of platonics, who pretend to see stars and heavens in ladies' eyes, and to look or think no lower; but the same pit is provided for both; and they seem a perfect moral to the story of that philosopher who, while his thoughts and eyes were fixed upon the constellations, found himself seduced by his lower parts into a ditch.[1]

I had somewhat more to say upon this part of the subject; but the post is just going, which forces me in great haste to conclude.

Sir,
Yours, &c.

Pray, burn this letter as
soon as it comes into
your hands.

FINIS.

[1] Swift probably refers to Thales (c. 636–546 B.C.), a renowned Greek astronomer and philosopher.

AN ARGUMENT

TO PROVE THAT THE
ABOLISHING OF CHRISTIANITY IN ENGLAND.[1]

May, as Things Now Stand, Be Attended with Some Inconveniences, and Perhaps Not Produce Those Many Good Effects Proposed Thereby.

Written in the Year 1708.

I AM very sensible what a weakness and presumption it is to reason against the general humour and disposition of the world. I remember it was with great justice, and a due regard to the freedom both of the public and the press, forbidden upon severe penalties to write, or discourse, or lay wagers against the *Union*,[2] even before it was confirmed by parliament, because that was looked upon as a design to oppose the current of the people, which, besides the folly of it, is a manifest breach of the fundamental law that makes this majority of opinion the voice of God. In like manner, and for the very same reasons, it may perhaps be neither safe nor prudent to argue against the abolishing of Christianity at a juncture when all parties appear so unanimously determined upon the point, as we cannot but allow from their actions, their discourses, and their writings. However, I know not how, whether from the affectation of singularity or the perverseness

---

[1] The *Argument* has a double focus: an attack on Deism, which advocated "natural" as opposed to "revealed" religion, as atheistical and Enthusiastic; and a plea to the Whigs, of whom Swift was still nominally one, to reconsider their support of the abolition of the Test Act of 1673. Designed to keep dissenters and Catholics from public office, the Test Act demanded the acceptance of the sacrament of the Lord's Supper according to the usage of the Church of England. The abolition of the Test Act, Swift felt, endangered both Church and State. But the *Argument* rises above its topical significance and becomes a powerful moralistic plea for real, as opposed to nominal, Christianity. Its satirical method is of a piece with that of Swift's great, belletristic satires.

[2] The Act of Union of 1707, uniting England and Scotland, was feared by Anglicans and Presbyterians both as weakening to the power of their respective churches.

of human nature, but so it unhappily falls out that I cannot be entirely of this opinion. Nay, although I were sure an order were issued out for my immediate prosecution by the Attorney-General, I should still confess that in the present posture of our affairs at home or abroad, I do not yet see the absolute necessity of extirpating the Christian religion from among us.

This perhaps may appear too great a paradox even for our wise and paradoxical age to endure; therefore I shall handle it with all tenderness, and with the utmost deference to that great and profound majority which is of another sentiment.

And yet the curious may please to observe, how much the genius of a nation is liable to alter in half an age. I have heard it affirmed for certain by some very old people, that the contrary opinion was even in their memories as much in vogue as the other is now; and, that a project for the abolishing of Christianity would then have appeared as singular, and been thought as absurd, as it would be at this time to write or discourse in its defence.

Therefore I freely own that all appearances are against me. The system of the Gospel, after the fate of other systems, is generally antiquated and exploded; and the mass or body of the common people, among whom it seems to have had its latest credit, are now grown as much ashamed of it as their betters; opinions, like fashions, always descending from those of quality to the middle sort, and thence to the vulgar, where at length they are dropped and vanish.

But here I would not be mistaken, and must therefore be so bold as to borrow a distinction from the writers on the other side when they make a difference between nominal and real Trinitarians. I hope no reader imagines me so weak to stand up in the defence of *real* Christianity, such as used in primitive times (if we may believe the authors of those ages) to have an influence upon men's belief and actions: to offer at the restoring of that would indeed be a wild project; it would be to dig up foundations; to destroy at one blow *all* the wit and *half* the learning of the kingdom; to break the entire frame and constitution of things; to ruin trade, extinguish arts and sciences with the professors of them; in short, to turn our courts, exchanges, and shops into deserts; and would be full as absurd as the proposal of Horace,[1] where he advises the Romans all in a body to leave their city and seek a new seat in some remote part of the world by way of cure for the corruption of their manners.

[1] The sixteenth Epode.

Therefore I think this caution was in itself altogether unnecessary, (which I have inserted only to prevent all possibility of cavilling) since every candid reader will easily understand my discourse to be intended only in defence of *nominal* Christianity; the other having been for some time wholly laid aside by general consent, as utterly inconsistent with our present schemes of wealth and power.

But why we should therefore cast off the name and title of Christians, although the general opinion and resolution be so violent for it, I confess I cannot (with submission) apprehend the consequence necessary. However, since the undertakers propose such wonderful advantages to the nation by this project, and advance many plausible objections against the system of Christianity, I shall briefly consider the strength of both, fairly allow them their greatest weight, and offer such answers as I think most reasonable. After which I will beg leave to show what inconvenience may possibly happen by such an innovation in the present posture of our affairs.

First, one great advantage proposed by the abolishing of Christianity is, that it would very much enlarge and establish liberty of conscience, that great bulwark of our nation, and of the *Protestant* Religion, which is still too much limited by *priestcraft* notwithstanding all the good intentions of the legislature, as we have lately found by a severe instance.[1] For it is confidently reported that two young gentlemen of great hopes, bright wit, and profound judgment, who upon a thorough examination of causes and effects, and by the mere force of natural abilities, without the least tincture of learning, having made a discovery that there was no God, and generously communicating their thoughts for the good of the public, were some time ago, by an unparalleled severity, and upon I know not what *obsolete* law, broke *only* for blasphemy. And as it hath been wisely observed, if persecution once begins, no man alive knows how far it may reach, or where it will end.

In answer to all which, with deference to wiser judgments, I think this rather shows the necessity of a *nominal* religion among us. Great wits love to be free with the highest objects; and if they cannot be allowed a *God* to revile or renounce, they will *speak evil of dignities,* abuse the government, and reflect upon the ministry; which I am sure few will deny to be

[1] Swift seems to refer to agitation for the abolition of the Test Act in Ireland in 1708.

of much more pernicious consequence, according to the saying of Tiberius, *Deorum offensa diis curæ*.[1] As to the particular fact related, I think it is not fair to argue from one instance, perhaps another cannot be produced; yet (to the comfort of all those who may be apprehensive of persecution) blasphemy we know is freely spoke a million of times in every coffeehouse and tavern, or wherever else *good company* meet. It must be allowed indeed, that to break an English free-born officer only for blasphemy, was, to speak the gentlest of such an action, a very high strain of absolute power. Little can be said in excuse for the general; perhaps he was afraid it might give offence to the allies,[2] among whom, for aught I know, it may be the custom of the country to believe a God. But if he argued, as some have done, upon a mistaken principle, that an officer who is guilty of speaking blasphemy, may some time or other proceed so far as to raise a mutiny, the consequence is by no means to be admitted; for surely the commander of an English army is likely to be but ill obeyed, whose soldiers fear and reverence him as little as they do a deity.

It is further objected against the Gospel System, that it obliges men to the belief of things too difficult for freethinkers,[3] and such who have shaken off the prejudices that usually cling to a confined education. To which I answer, that men should be cautious how they raise objections which reflect upon the wisdom of the nation. Is not every body freely allowed to believe whatever he pleases, and to publish his belief to the world whenever he thinks fit, especially if it serve to strengthen the party which is in the right? Would any indifferent foreigner, who should read the trumpery lately written by Asgill, Tindal, Toland, Coward,[4] and forty more, imagine the Gospel to be our rule of faith, and confirmed by parliaments? Does any man either believe, or say he believes, or desire to have it thought that he says he believes one syllable of the matter? And is any man worse received upon that score, or does he find his want of *nominal* faith a disadvantage to him in the pursuit of any civil or military employment? What if there be an old dormant statute or two against him? Are they not now obsolete, to a degree, that Empson and Dudley [5]

---

[1] The sentence is inexactly quoted and incorrectly ascribed; see Tacitus, *Annals*, I, 73.

[2] In the War of the Spanish Succession.

[3] The Deists, who were opposed to revealed religion, were the freethinkers of their day.

[4] Prominent Deists.

[5] Unscrupulous agents of King Henry VII, ruthless in their collection of taxes and crown penalties.

themselves if they were now alive, would find it impossible to put them in execution?

It is likewise urged that there are, by computation, in this kingdom above ten thousand parsons, whose revenues added to those of my lords the bishops would suffice to maintain at least two hundred young gentlemen of wit and pleasure, and freethinking, enemies to priestcraft, narrow principles, pedantry, and prejudices; who might be an ornament to the Court and Town: and then, again, so great a number of able (bodied) divines might be a recruit to our fleet and armies. This indeed appears to be a consideration of some weight: but then, on the other side, several things deserve to be considered likewise: as, first, whether it may not be thought necessary that in certain tracts of country, like what we call parishes, there should be *one* man at least of abilities to read and write. Then it seems a wrong computation that the revenues of the Church throughout this island would be large enough to maintain two hundred young gentlemen, or even half that number, after the present refined way of living; that is, to allow each of them such a rent, as in the modern form of speech, would make them *easy*. But still there is in this project a greater mischief behind; and we ought to beware of the woman's folly who killed the hen that every morning laid her a golden egg. For, pray what would become of the race of men in the next age, if we had nothing to trust to besides the scrofulous, consumptive productions, furnished by our men of wit and pleasure, when having squandered away their vigour, health and estates, they are forced by some disagreeable marriage to piece up their broken fortunes, and entail rottenness and politeness on their posterity? Now, here are ten thousand persons reduced by the wise regulations of Henry the Eighth,[1] to the necessity of a low diet, and moderate exercise, who are the only great restorers of our breed, without which the nation would in an age or two become but one great hospital.

Another advantage proposed by the abolishing of Christianity is the clean gain of one day in seven, which is now entirely lost, and consequently the kingdom one seventh less considerable in trade, business, and pleasure; beside the loss to the public of so many stately structures now in the hands of the Clergy, which might be converted into theatres, exchanges, market-houses, common dormitories, and other public edifices.

[1] Anglicans still smarted at the injustice of King Henry VIII's dealings with the English Church.

I hope I shall be forgiven a hard word, if I call this a perfect cavil. I readily own there has been an old custom time out of mind for people to assemble in the churches every Sunday, and that shops are still frequently shut, in order as it is conceived, to preserve the memory of that ancient practice, but how this can prove a hindrance to business or pleasure is hard to imagine. What if the men of pleasure are forced one day in the week to game at home instead of the chocolate-house? Are not the taverns and coffeehouses open? Can there be a more convenient season for taking a dose of physic? Are fewer claps got upon Sundays than other days? Is not that the chief day for traders to sum up the accounts of the week, and for lawyers to prepare their briefs? But I would fain know how it can be pretended that the churches are misapplied? Where are more appointments and rendezvouzes of gallantry? Where more care to appear in the foremost box with greater advantage of dress? Where more meetings for business? Where more bargains driven of all sorts? And where so many conveniences or enticements to sleep?

There is one advantage greater than any of the foregoing, proposed by the abolishing of Christianity: that it will utterly extinguish parties among us, by removing those factious distinctions of High and Low Church, of Whig and Tory, Presbyterian and Church of England, which are now so many grievous clogs upon public proceedings, and dispose men to prefer the gratifying themselves, or depressing their adversaries, before the most important interest of the state.

I confess, if it were certain that so great an advantage would redound to the nation by this expedient, I would submit and be silent: but will any man say, that if the words *whoring, drinking, cheating, lying, stealing,* were by act of parliament ejected out of the English tongue and dictionaries, we should all awake next morning chaste and temperate, honest and just, and lovers of truth. Is this a fair consequence? Or, if the physicians would forbid us to pronounce the words *pox, gout, rheumatism* and *stone,* would that expedient serve like so many talismans to destroy the diseases themselves? Are party and faction rooted in men's hearts no deeper than phrases borrowed from religion, or founded upon no firmer principles? And is our language so poor that we cannot find other terms to express them? Are *envy, pride, avarice* and *ambition* such ill nomenclators, that they cannot furnish appelations for their owners? Will not *heydukes* and *mamalukes, mandarins* and *potshaws,* or any other words formed at pleasure, serve to distinguish those who are in the ministry from others who *would be in* it *if they could?* What, for instance, is easier than to vary the form of speech, and instead of the word church, make it a question in politics, whether the Monument be in danger? Because religion was nearest at hand to furnish a few convenient phrases, is our invention so barren, we can find no other? Suppose, for argument sake, that the Tories favoured Margarita, the Whigs Mrs. Tofts, and the Trimmers Valentini,* would not *Margaritians, Toftians* and *Valentinians* be very tolerable marks of distinction? The *Prasini* and *Veneti*,[1] two most virulent factions in Italy, began (if I remember right) by a distinction of colours in ribbons, which we might do with as good a grace about the dignity of the blue and the green, and would serve as properly to divide the Court, the Parliament, and the Kingdom between them, as any terms of art whatsoever borrowed from religion. Therefore, I think, there is little force in this objection against Christianity, or prospect of so great an advantage as is proposed in the abolishing of it.

It is again objected, as a very absurd ridiculous custom, that a set of men should be suffered, much less employed and hired, to bawl one day in seven against the lawfulness of those methods most in use towards the pursuit of greatness, riches and pleasure, which are the constant practice of all men alive on the other six. But this objection is, I think, a little unworthy so refined an age as ours. Let us argue this matter calmly. I appeal to the breast of any polite freethinker, whether in the pursuit of gratifying a predominant passion, he hath not always felt a wonderful incitement by reflecting it was a thing forbidden; and therefore we see, in order to cultivate this taste, the wisdom of the nation hath taken special care that the ladies should be furnished with prohibited silks, and the men with prohibited wine: and indeed it were to be wished that some other prohibitions were promoted, in order to improve the pleasures of the town which for want of such expedients begin already, as I am told, to flag and grow languid, giving way daily to cruel inroads from the spleen.

It is likewise proposed as a great advantage to the public, that if we once discard the system of the Gospel, all religion will of course be banished for ever; and consequently, along with it, those grievous prejudices of education, which under the names of virtue, conscience, honour, justice, and the like,

---

* Italian singers then in vogue.

[1] The principal factions in the Roman chariot races whose rivalry precipitated a war in the reign of Justinian.

are so apt to disturb the peace of human minds, and the notions whereof are so hard to be eradicated by right reason or freethinking, sometimes during the whole course of our lives.

Here, first, I observe how difficult it is to get rid of a phrase which the world is once grown fond of, although the occasion that first produced it be entirely taken away. For several years past if a man had but an ill-favoured nose, the deep-thinkers of the age would some way or other contrive to impute the cause to the prejudice of his education. From this fountain are said to be derived all our foolish notions of justice, piety, love of our country, all our opinions of God, or a future state, Heaven, Hell, and the like: and there might formerly, perhaps, have been some pretence for this charge. But so effectual care has been since taken to remove those prejudices, by an entire change in the methods of education, that (with honour I mention it to our polite innovators) the young gentlemen who are now on the scene seem to have not the least tincture left of those infusions, or string of those weeds; and, by consequence, the reason for abolishing nominal Christianity upon that pretext is wholly ceased.

For the rest, it may perhaps admit a controversy, whether the banishing all notions of religion whatsoever, would be convenient for the vulgar. Not that I am in the least of opinion with those who hold religion to have been the invention of politicians to keep the lower part of the world in awe by the fear of invisible powers; unless mankind were then very different from what it is now: for I look upon the mass or body of our people here in England to be as freethinkers, that is to say as staunch unbelievers, as any of the highest rank. But I conceive some scattered notions about a superior power to be of singular use for the common people, as furnishing excellent materials to keep children quiet when they grow peevish, and providing topics of amusement in a tedious winter-night.

Lastly, it is proposed as a singular advantage, that the abolishing of Christianity will very much contribute to the uniting of Protestants, by enlarging the terms of communion so as to take in all sorts of dissenters, who are now shut out of the pale upon account of a few ceremonies, which all sides confess to be things indifferent: that this alone will effectually answer the great ends of a scheme for comprehension,[1] by opening a large noble gate at which all bodies may enter; whereas the chaffering with dissenters, and dodging about this or the other ceremony, is but like opening a few wickets, and

[1] The proposed unification of the Protestant churches.

leaving them at jar, by which no more than one can get in at a time, and that not without stooping, and sideling, and squeezing his body.

To all this I answer, that there is one darling inclination of mankind, which usually affects to be a retainer to religion, although she be neither its parent, its godmother, or its friend; I mean the spirit of opposition, that lived long before Christianity, and can easily subsist without it. Let us, for instance, examine wherein the opposition of sectaries among us consists; we shall find Christianity to have no share in it at all. Does the Gospel anywhere prescribe a starched, squeezed countenance, a stiff, formal gait, a singularity of manners and habit, or any affected modes of speech different from the reasonable part of mankind? Yet, if Christianity did not lend its name to stand in the gap, and to employ or divert these humours, they must of necessity be spent in contraventions to the laws of the land, and disturbance of the public peace. There is a portion of enthusiasm assigned to every nation which, if it hath not proper objects to work on, will burst out and set all into a flame. If the quiet of a state can be bought by only flinging men a few ceremonies to devour, it is a purchase no wise man would refuse. Let the mastiffs amuse themselves about a sheep's skin stuffed with hay, provided it will keep them from worrying the flock. The institution of convents abroad seems in one point a strain of great wisdom, there being few irregularities in human passions, that may not have recourse to vent themselves in some of those orders, which are so many retreats for the speculative, the melancholy, the proud, the silent, the politic and the morose, to spend themselves, and evaporate the noxious particles; for each of whom we in this island are forced to provide a several sect of religion to keep them quiet. And whenever Christianity shall be abolished, the legislature must find some other expedient to employ and entertain them. For what imports it how large a gate you open, if there will be always left a number who place a pride and a merit in refusing to enter?

Having thus considered the most important objections against Christianity, and the chief advantages proposed by the abolishing thereof, I shall now with equal deference and submission to wiser judgments as before, proceed to mention a few inconveniences that may happen, if the Gospel should be repealed; which perhaps the projectors may not have sufficiently considered.

And first, I am very sensible how much the gentlemen of

wit and pleasure are apt to murmur, and be shocked at the sight of so many daggled-tail parsons, who happen to fall in their way, and offend their eyes: but at the same time, these wise reformers do not consider what an advantage and felicity it is for great wits to be always provided with objects of scorn and contempt, in order to exercise and improve their talents, and divert their spleen from falling on each other or on themselves; especially when all this may be done without the least imaginable *danger to their persons*.

And to urge another argument of a parallel nature: if Christianity were once abolished, how could the free-thinkers, the strong reasoners, and the men of profound learning, be able to find another subject so calculated in all points whereon to display their abilities? What wonderful productions of wit should we be deprived of, from those whose genius by continual practice hath been wholly turned upon raillery and invectives against religion, and would therefore never be able to shine or distinguish themselves upon any other subject. We are daily complaining of the great decline of wit among us, and would we take away the greatest, perhaps the only topic we have left? Who would ever have suspected Asgill for a wit, or Toland for a philosopher, if the inexhaustible stock of Christianity had not been at hand to provide them with materials? What other subject, through all art or nature, could have produced Tindal for a profound author, or furnished him with readers? It is the wise choice of the subject that alone adorns and distinguishes the writer. For, had an hundred such pens as these been employed on the side of religion, they would have immediately sunk into silence and oblivion.

Nor do I think it wholly groundless, or my fears altogether imaginary, that the abolishing of Christianity may perhaps bring the Church in danger, or at least put the senate to the trouble of another securing vote. I desire I may not be mistaken; I am far from presuming to affirm or think that the Church is in danger at present, or as things now stand; but we know not how soon it may be so when the Christian religion is repealed. As plausible as this project seems, there may a dangerous design lurk under it. Nothing can be more notorious, than that the Atheists, Deists, Socinians, Anti-trinitarians, and other subdivisions of freethinkers, are persons of little zeal for the present ecclesiastical establishment: Their declared opinion is for repealing the Sacramental Test; they are very indifferent with regard to ceremonies; not do they hold the *jus divinum* [1] of Episcopacy. Therefore this may be intended as one politic step towards altering the constitution of the Church established, and setting up Presbytery in the stead, which I leave to be further considered by those at the helm.

In the last place, I think nothing can be more plain, than that by this expedient, we shall run into the evil we chiefly pretend to avoid; and that the abolishment of the Christian religion will be the readiest course we can take to introduce popery. And I am the more inclined to this opinion, because we know it has been the constant practice of the Jesuits to send over emissaries, with instructions to personate themselves members of the several prevailing sects among us. So it is recorded, that they have at sundry times appeared in the guise of Presbyterians, Anabaptists, Independents and Quakers, according as any of these were most in credit; so since the fashion hath been taken up of exploding religion, the popish missionaries have not been wanting to mix with the freethinkers; among whom, Toland, the great oracle of the Anti-Christians is an Irish priest, the son of an Irish priest; and the most learned and ingenious author of a book called *The Rights of the Christian Church*,[2] was in a proper juncture reconciled to the Romish faith, whose true son, as appears by an hundred passages in his treatise, he still continues. Perhaps I could add some others to the number; but the fact is beyond dispute, and the reasoning they proceed by is right: for, supposing Christianity to be extinguished, the people will never be at ease till they find out some other method of worship; which will as infallibly produce superstition, as this will end in popery.

And therefore, if notwithstanding all I have said, it shall still be thought necessary to have a bill brought in for repealing Christianity, I would humbly offer an amendment; that instead of the word *Christianity*, may be put *Religion* in general; which I conceive will much better answer all the good ends proposed by the projectors of it. For, as long as we leave in being a God and his providence, with all the necessary consequences which curious and inquisitive men will be apt to draw from such premises, we do not strike at the root of the evil although we should ever so effectually annihilate the present scheme of the Gospel. For, of what use is freedom of thought, if it will not produce freedom of action, which is the sole end, how remote soever in appearance, of all objections

[1] Divine right.
[2] Matthew Tindall (d. 1733); he formally renounced Catholicism in 1688.

against Christianity? And therefore, the freethinkers consider it as a sort of edifice, wherein all the parts have such a mutual dependence on each other, that if you happen to pull out one single nail, the whole fabric must fall to the ground. This was happily expressed by him who had heard of a text brought for proof of the Trinity, which in an ancient manuscript was differently read; he thereupon immediately took the hint, and by a sudden deduction of a long *sorites*, most logically concluded; Why, if it be as you say, I may safely whore and drink on, and defy the parson. From which, and many the like instances easy to be produced, I think nothing can be more manifest, than that the quarrel is not against any particular points of hard digestion in the Christian system, but against religion in general; which, by laying restraints on human nature, is supposed the great enemy to the freedom of thought and action.

Upon the whole, if it shall still be thought for the benefit of Church and State, that Christianity be abolished, I conceive however, it may be more convenient to defer the execution to a time of peace, and not venture in this conjuncture to disoblige our allies, who, as it falls out, are all Christians, and many of them, by the prejudices of their education, so bigoted as to place a sort of pride in the appellation. If upon being rejected by them, we are to trust to an alliance with the Turk, we shall find ourselves much deceived: for, as he is too remote, and generally engaged in war with the Persian emperor, so his people would be more scandalized at our infidelity than our Christian neighbours. Because the Turks are not only strict observers of religious worship, but what is worse, believe a God; which is more than is required of us even while we preserve the name of Christians.

To conclude: whatever some may think of the great advantages to trade by this favourite scheme, I do very much apprehend that in six months' time after the act is passed for the extirpation of the Gospel, the Bank and East-India Stock may fall at least one *percent*. And since that is fifty times more than ever the wisdom of our age thought fit to venture for the *preservation* of Christianity, there is no reason we should be at so great a loss, merely for the sake of *destroying* it.

THE BICKERSTAFF PAPERS.[1]

PREDICTIONS for the Year 1708

Wherein the Month, and Day of the Month, are set down, the Persons named, and the great Actions and Events of next Year particularly related as they will come to pass.

Written to prevent the People of England from being farther imposed on by vulgar Almanack-Makers.

By Isaac Bickerstaff, Esq.*

HAVING long considered the gross abuse of astrology in this kingdom, upon debating the matter with my self, I could not possibly lay the fault upon the art, but upon those gross impostors, who set up to be the artists. I know several learned men have contended, that the whole is a cheat; that it is absurd and ridiculous to imagine the stars can have any influence at all upon human actions, thoughts, or inclinations; and whoever has not bent his studies that way may be excused for thinking so, when he sees in how wretched a manner this noble art is treated, by a few mean, illiterate traders between us and the stars; who import a yearly stock of nonsense, lies, folly, and impertinence, which they offer to the world as genuine

---

* It is said that the author, when he had writ the following paper, and being at a loss what name to prefix to it, passing through Long-Acre, observed a sign over a house where a locksmith dwelt, and found the name Bickerstaff written under it: which being a name somewhat uncommon, he chose to call himself Isaac Bickerstaff. This name was sometime afterward made use of by Sir Richard Steele and Mr. Addison in the *Tatlers;* in which papers, as well as many of the *Spectators,* it is well known, that the author had a considerable part.

[1] The following three (of the four so-called *Partridge Papers*) are *jeux d'esprits* in Swift's most light-hearted vein. Partly they are a joke on John Partridge, a quack and astrologer, author of an annual almanac, *Merlinus Liberatus.* But Partridge, in addition to forecasting coming events, also attacked the English clergy, and hence earned Swift's satire. Partridge challenged his competitors; Swift, in the satiric pose of a fellow astrologer, takes up the challenge in the *Predictions.* In his *Accomplishment,* Swift replies to Partridge's attack in the almanac of 1709. But so effectively had Swift killed him, that the government actually claimed Partridge's publication rights. When Partridge attacked Bickerstaff again, Swift replied in his *Vindication.* Swift treats his astrologer-quack in much the same way he treats all his Modern virtuosi and projectors in *Tale of a Tub* and in *Gulliver's Travels.* (For an excellent account of the controversy, see William A. Eddy, "The Wits vs. John Partridge," *Studies in Philology,* XXIX (1932), 29 ff.)

from the planets, although they descend from no greater a height than their own brains.

I intend, in a short time, to publish a large and rational defence of this art, and therefore shall say no more in its justification at present, than that it hath been in all ages defended by many learned men, and among the rest by Socrates himself, whom I look upon as undoubtedly the wisest of uninspired mortals: to which if we add, that those who have condemned this art, although otherwise learned, having been such as either did not apply their studies this way, or at least did not succeed in their applications; their testimony will not be of much weight to its disadvantage, since they are liable to the common objection of condemning what they did not understand.

Nor am I at all offended, or think it an injury to the art, when I see the common dealers in it, the *Students in astrology*, the *Philomaths*, and the rest of that tribe, treated by wise men with the utmost scorn and contempt; but I rather wonder, when I observe gentlemen in the country, rich enough to serve the nation in Parliament, poring in Partridge's Almanack, to find out the events of the year, at home and abroad; not daring to propose a hunting match, until Gadbury [1] or he hath fixed the weather.

I will allow either of the two I have mentioned, or any other of the fraternity, to be not only astrologers, but conjurers too, if I do not produce an hundred instances in all their Almanacks, to convince any reasonable man, that they do not so much as understand grammar and syntax; that they are not able to spell any word out of the usual road, nor, even in their prefaces, to write common sense, or intelligible English. Then, for their observations and predictions, they are such as will equally suit any age or country in the world. "This month a certain great person will be threatened with death or sickness." This the newspaper will tell them, for there we find at the end of the year, that no month passes without the death of some person of note; and it would be hard, if it should be otherwise, when there are at least two thousand persons of note in this kingdom, many of them old, and the Almanack-maker has the liberty of choosing the sickliest season of the year, where he may fix his prediction. Again, "This month an eminent clergyman will be preferred;" of which there may be some hundreds, half of them with one foot in the grave. Then, "Such a planet in such a house shows great machinations, plots, and conspiracies, that may in time be brought to light:" after which, if we hear of any

[1] John Gadbury, a rival astrologer.

discovery the astrologer gets the honour; if not, his prediction still stands good. And at last, "God preserve King William from all his open and secret enemies, Amen." When, if the king should happen to have died, the astrologer plainly foretold it; otherwise it passes but for the pious ejaculation of a loyal subject: although it unluckily happened in some of their Almanacks, that poor King William was prayed for many months after he was dead, because it fell out, that he died about the beginning of the year.

To mention no more of their impertinent predictions, what have we to do with their advertisements about "pills and drink for the venereal disease," or their mutual quarrels in verse and prose of Whig and Tory, wherewith the stars have little to do?

Having long observed and lamented these, and a hundred other abuses of this art too tedious to repeat, I resolved to proceed in a new way, which I doubt not will be to the general satisfaction of the kingdom. I can this year produce but a specimen of what I design for the future; having employed most part of my time, in adjusting and correcting the calculations I made for some years past, because I would offer nothing to the world, of which I am not as fully satisfied, as that I am now alive. For these two last years I have not failed in above one or two particulars, and those of no very great moment. I exactly foretold the miscarriage at Toulon, with all its particulars; and the loss of Admiral Shovel [1] although I was mistaken as to the day, placing that accident about thirty-six hours sooner than it happened; but upon reviewing my schemes, I quickly found the cause of that error. I likewise foretold the battle at Almanza to the very day and hour, with the loss on both sides, and the consequences thereof. All which I showed to some friends many months before they happened; that is, I gave them papers sealed up, to open at such a time, after which they were at liberty to read them; and there they found my predictions true in every article, except one or two very minute.

As for the few following predictions I now offer the world, I forebore to publish them, till I had perused the several Almanacks for the year we are now entered upon. I found them all in the usual strain, and I beg the reader will compare their manner with mine: and here I make bold to tell the world, that I lay the whole credit of my art upon the truth of these predictions; and I will be content, that Partridge, and the rest

[1] The English Fleet, under Sir Cloudesly Shovel, failed in its attack on Toulon in 1707.

of his clan, may hoot me for a cheat and impostor, if I fail in any single particular of moment. I believe, any man who reads this paper, will look upon me to be at least a person of as much honesty and understanding, as a common maker of Almanacks. I do not lurk in the dark; I am not wholly unknown in the world; I have set my name at length to be a mark of infamy to mankind, if they shall find I deceive them.

In one point I must desire to be forgiven, that I talk more sparingly of home affairs. As it would be imprudence to discover secrets of state, so it might be dangerous to my person; but in smaller matters, and such as are not of public consequence, I shall be very free; and the truth of my conjectures will as much appear from these as the other. As for the most signal events abroad in France, Flanders, Italy, and Spain, I shall make no scruple to predict them in plain terms: some of them are of importance, and I hope I shall seldom mistake the day they will happen; therefore, I think good to inform the reader, that I all along make use of the Old Style [1] observed in England, which I desire he will compare with that of the newspapers, at the time they relate the actions I mention.

I must add one word more: I know it hath been the opinion of several learned persons, who think well enough of the true art of astrology, that the stars do only incline, and not force, the actions or wills of men; and therefore, however I may proceed by right rules, yet I cannot in prudence so confidently assure that the events will follow exactly as I predict them.

I hope I have maturely considered this objection, which in some cases is of no little weight. For example: a man may, by the influence of an over-ruling planet, be disposed or inclined to lust, rage, or avarice, and yet by the force of reason overcome that evil influence. And this was the case of Socrates: but the great events of the world, usually depending upon numbers of men, it cannot be expected they should all unite to cross their inclinations, from pursuing a general design, wherein they unanimously agree. Besides, the influence of the stars reaches to many actions and events, which are not any way in the power of reason; as sickness, death, and what we commonly call accidents, with many more needless to repeat.

But now it is time to proceed to my predictions, which I have begun to calculate from the time that the sun enters into Aries. And this I take to be properly the beginning of the natural year. I pursue them to the time that he enters Libra, or somewhat more, which is the busy period of the year. The

[1] Referring to the Old Calendar in use in England until 1752.

remainder I have not yet adjusted, upon account of several impediments needless here to mention. Besides, I must remind the reader again, that this is but a specimen of what I design in succeeding years to treat more at large, if I may have liberty and encouragement.

My first prediction is but a trifle, yet I will mention it, to show how ignorant those sottish pretenders to astrology are in their own concerns: it relates to Partridge the Almanack-maker; I have consulted the star of his nativity by my own rules, and find he will infallibly die upon the 29th of March next, about eleven at night, of a raging fever; therefore I advise him to consider of it, and settle his affairs in time.

The month of APRIL will be observable for the death of many great persons. On the 4th will die the Cardinal de Noailles, Archbishop of Paris: on the 11th, the young Prince of Asturias, son to the Duke of Anjou: on the 14th, a great peer of this realm will die at his country-house: on the 19th, an old layman of great fame for learning: and on the 23rd, an eminent goldsmith in Lombard Street. I could mention others, both at home and abroad, if I did not consider such events of very little use or instruction to the reader, or to the world.

As to public affairs: On the 7th of this month there will be an insurrection in Dauphine, occasioned by the oppressions of the people, which will not be quieted in some months.

On the 15th will be a violent storm on the south-east coast of France, which will destroy many of their ships, and some in the very harbour.

The 19th will be famous for the revolt of a whole province or kingdom, excepting one city, by which the affairs of a certain prince in the alliance will take a better face.

MAY, against common conjectures, will be no very busy month in Europe, but very signal for the death of the Dauphin, which will happen on the 7th, after a short fit of sickness, and grievous torments with the strangury. He dies less lamented by the court than the kingdom.

On the 9th, a Mareschal of France will break his leg by a fall from his horse. I have not been able to discover whether he will then die or not.

On the 11th will begin a most important siege, which the eyes of all Europe will be upon: I cannot be more particular; for, in relating affairs that so nearly concern the confederates, and consequently this kingdom, I am forced to confine myself, for several reasons very obvious to the reader.

On the 15th, news will arrive of a very surprising event, than which nothing could be more unexpected.

On the 19th three noble ladies of this kingdom will, against all expectation, prove with child, to the great joy of their husbands.

On the 23rd, a famous buffoon of the playhouse will die a ridiculous death, suitable to his vocation.

JUNE. This month will be distinguished at home by the utter dispersing of those ridiculous deluded enthusiasts, commonly called the Prophets; occasioned chiefly by seeing the time come, when many of their prophecies were to be fulfilled, and then finding themselves deceived by contrary events. It is indeed to be admired, how any deceiver can be so weak to foretell things near at hand, when a very few months must, of necessity, discover the imposture to all the world; in this point less prudent than common almanack-makers, who are so wise to wander in generals, talk dubiously, and leave to the reader the business of interpreting.

On the 1st of this month, a French general will be killed by a random shot of a cannon-ball.

On the 6th, a fire will break out in the suburbs of Paris, which will destroy above a thousand houses; and seems to be the foreboding of what will happen, to the surprise of all Europe, about the end of the following month.

On the 10th, a great battle will be fought, which will begin at four of the clock in the afternoon; and last till nine at night, with great obstinacy, but no very decisive event. I shall not name the place, for the reasons aforesaid; but the commanders on each left wing will be killed. ———I see bonfires, and hear the noise of guns for a victory.

On the 14th, there will be a false report of the French king's death.

On the 20th, Cardinal Portocarero will die of a dysentery, with great suspicion of poison; but the report of his intention to revolt to King Charles will prove false.

JULY. The 6th of this month, a certain general will, by a glorious action, recover the reputation he lost by former misfortunes.

On the 12th, a great commander will die a prisoner in the hands of his enemies.

On the 14th, a shameful discovery will be made of a French Jesuit, giving poison to a great foreign general; and when he is put to the torture, will make wonderful discoveries.

In short, this will prove a month of great action, if I might have liberty to relate the particulars.

At home, the death of an old famous senator will happen on the 15th, at his country-house, worn with age and diseases.

But that which will make this month memorable to all posterity, is the death of the French king, Louis the Fourteenth, after a week's sickness, at Marli, which will happen on the 29th, about six o'clock in the evening. It seems to be an effect of the gout in his stomach, followed by a flux. And in three days after, Monsieur Chamillard will follow his master, dying suddenly of an apoplexy.

In this month likewise an ambassador will die in London; but I cannot assign the day.

AUGUST. The affairs of France will seem to suffer no change for a while under the Duke of Burgundy's administration; but the genius that animated the whole machine being gone, will be the cause of mighty turns and revolutions in the following year. The new king makes yet little change either in the army or the ministry; but the libels against his grandfather, that fly about his very court, give him uneasiness.

I see an express in mighty haste, with joy and wonder in his looks, arriving by the break of day on the 26th of this month, having travelled in three days a prodigious journey by land and sea. In the evening I hear bells and guns, and see the blazing of a thousand bonfires.

A young admiral of noble birth does likewise this month gain immortal honour by a great achievement.

The affairs of Poland are this month entirely settled: Augustus resigns his pretensions, which he had again taken up for some time: Stanislaus is peaceably possessed of the throne; and the King of Sweden declares for the Emperor.

I cannot omit one particular accident here at home; that near the end of this month much mischief will be done at Bartholomew Fair, by the fall of a booth.

SEPTEMBER. This month begins with a very surprising fit of frosty weather, which will last near twelve days.

The Pope having long languished last month, the swellings in his legs breaking, and the flesh mortifying, will die on the 11th instant; and in three weeks' time, after a mighty contest, be succeeded by a Cardinal of the imperial faction, but native of Tuscany, who is now about sixty-one years old.

The French army acts now wholly on the defensive, strongly fortified in their trenches; and the young French king sends overtures for a treaty of peace by the Duke of Mantua; which, because it is a matter of state that concerns us here at home, I shall speak no farther of it.

I shall add but one prediction more, and that in mystical terms, which shall be included in a verse out of Virgil:

Alter erit jam Tethys, & altera, quæ vehat, Argo Delectos heroas.[1]

Upon the 25th day of this month, the fulfilling of this prediction will be manifest to everybody.

This is the farthest I have proceeded in my calculations for the present year. I do not pretend that these are all the great events which will happen in this period; but that those I have set down will infallibly come to pass. It may perhaps still be objected, why I have not spoke more particularly of affairs at home, or of the success of our armies abroad, which I might, and could very largely have done. But those in power have wisely discouraged men from meddling in public concerns, and I was resolved by no means to give the least offence. This I will venture to say, that it will be a glorious campaign for the Allies, wherein the English forces, both by sea and land, will have their full share of honour: that Her Majesty Queen Anne will continue in health and prosperity: and that no ill accident will arrive to any in the chief ministry.

As to the particular events I have mentioned, the readers may judge, by the fulfilling of them, whether I am of the level with common astrologers; who, with an old paltry cant, and a few pot-hooks for planets to amuse the vulgar, have, in my opinion, too long been suffered to abuse the world. But an honest physician ought not to be despised, because there are such things as mountebanks. I hope I have some share of reputation, which I would not willingly forfeit for a frolic or humour; and I believe no gentleman who reads this paper, will look upon it to be of the same cast or mould with the common scribbles that are every day hawked about. My fortune has placed me above the little regard of writing for a few pence, which I neither value nor want: therefore, let not wise men too hastily condemn this essay, intended for a good design, to cultivate and improve an ancient art, long in disgrace by having fallen into mean unskilful hands. A little time will determine whether I have deceived others or myself; and I think it is no very unreasonable request, that men would please to suspend their judgments till then. I was once of the

[1] The fourth Eclogue.

opinion with those who despise all predictions from the stars, till in the year 1686, a man of quality showed me, written in his *album,* that the most learned astronomer, Captain Halley, assured him, he would never believe anything of the stars' influence if there were not a great revolution in England in the year 1688. Since that time I began to have other thoughts, and after eighteen years diligent study and application, I think I have no reason to repent of my pains. I shall detain the reader no longer than to let him know, that the account I design to give of next year's events, shall take in the principal affairs that happen in Europe; and if I be denied the liberty of offering it to my own country, I shall appeal to the learned world, by publishing it in Latin, and giving order to have it printed in Holland.

THE ACCOMPLISHMENT
of the First of Mr. Bickerstaff's Predictions.

Being an Account of the Death of Mr. Partridge, the Almanack-Maker, upon the 29th instant,[1] in a Letter to a Person of Honour.

Written in the Year 1708.

MY LORD,

IN obedience to your Lordship's commands, as well as to satisfy my own curiosity, I have for some days past enquired constantly after Partridge the almanack-maker, of whom it was foretold in Mr. Bickerstaff's Predictions, published about a month ago, that he should die the 29th instant, about eleven at night, of a raging fever. I had some sort of knowledge of him when I was employed in the revenue, because he used every year to present me with his almanack, as he did other gentlemen upon the score of some little gratuity we gave him. I saw him accidentally once or twice about ten days before he died; and observed he began very much to droop and languish, although I hear his friends did not seem to apprehend him in any danger. About two or three days ago he grew ill, was confined first to his chamber, and in a few hours after to his bed; where Dr. Case and Mrs. Kirleus * were sent for to visit, and to prescribe to him. Upon this intelligence I sent thrice every day one servant or other to enquire after his health; and yesterday about four in the afternoon, word was brought me that he was past hopes; upon which I prevailed

* Two famous quacks at that time in London.
[1] Swift published the *Vindication* on March 30.

with myself to go and see him, partly out of commiseration, and, I confess, partly out of curiosity. He knew me very well, seemed surprised at my condescension, and made me compliments upon it as well as he could in the condition he was. The people about him said he had been for some hours delirious; but when I saw him, he had his understanding as well as ever I knew, and spoke strong and hearty, without any seeming uneasiness or constraint. After I had told him I was sorry to see him in those melancholy circumstances, and said some other civilities suitable to the occasion, I desired him to tell me freely and ingenuously whether the predictions Mr. Bickerstaff had published relating to his death, had not too much affected and worked on his imagination. He confessed he often had it in his head, but never with much apprehension till about a fortnight before; since which time it had the perpetual possession of his mind and thoughts, and he did verily believe was the true natural cause of his present distemper: for, said he, "I am thoroughly persuaded, and I think I have very good reasons, that Mr. Bickerstaff spoke altogether by guess, and knew no more what will happen this year than I did myself." I told him his discourse surprised me; and I would be glad he were in a state of health to be able to tell me what reason he had to be convinced of Mr. Bickerstaff's ignorance. He replied, "I am a poor ignorant fellow, bred to a mean trade; yet I have sense enough to know, that all pretences of foretelling by astrology are deceits, for this manifest reason, because the wise and the learned, who can only judge whether there be any truth in this science, do all unanimously agree to laugh at and despise it; and none but the poor ignorant vulgar give it any credit, and that only upon the word of such silly wretches as I and my fellows, who can hardly write or read." I then asked him, why he had not calculated his own nativity, to see whether it agreed with Bickerstaff's predictions. At which he shook his head, and said, "O! sir, this is no time for jesting, but for repenting those fooleries, as I do now from the very bottom of my heart." "By what I can gather from you," said I, "the observations and predictions you printed with your almanacks were mere impositions on the people." He replied, "If it were otherwise, I should have the less to answer for. We have a common form for all those things: as to foretelling the weather, we never meddle with that, but leave it to the printer, who takes it out of any old almanack as he thinks fit: the rest was my own invention to make my almanack sell, having a wife to maintain, and no other way to get my bread; for mending old shoes is a poor livelihood; and" (added he, sighing) "I wish I may not have done more mischief by my physic than my astrology; although I had some good receipts from my grandmother, and my own compositions were such, as I thought could at least do no hurt."

I had some other discourse with him, which now I cannot call to mind; and I fear I have already tired your lordship. I shall only add one circumstance, that on his death-bed he declared himself a nonconformist, and had a fanatic preacher to be his spiritual guide. After half an hour's conversation I took my leave, being almost stifled by the closeness of the room. I imagined he could not hold out long, and therefore withdrew to a little coffeehouse hard by, leaving a servant at the house with orders to come immediately and tell me, as near as he could, the minute when Partridge should expire, which was not above two hours after; when looking upon my watch, I found it to be above five minutes after seven: by which it is clear that Mr. Bickerstaff was mistaken almost four hours in his calculation. In the other circumstances he was exact enough. But whether he hath not been the cause of this poor man's death, as well as the predictor, may be very reasonably disputed. However, it must be confessed, the matter is odd enough, whether we should endeavour to account for it by chance or the effect of imagination: for my own part, although I believe no man hath less faith in these matters, yet I shall wait with some impatience, and not without some expectation, the fulfilling of Mr. Bickerstaff's second prediction, that the Cardinal de Noailles is to die upon the 4th of April; and if that should be verified as exactly as this of poor Partridge, I must own I should be wholly surprised, and at a loss, and infallibly expect the accomplishment of all the rest.

A VINDICATION

Of Isaac Bickerstaff, Esq.; against What is Objected to Him by Mr. Partridge, in his Almanack for the present Year 1709.

By the said Isaac Bickerstaff, Esq.

Written in the Year 1709.

MR. PARTRIDGE hath been lately pleased to treat me after a very rough manner, in that which is called his almanack for the present year: such usage is very indecent from one gentleman to another, and doth not at all contribute to the discovery of truth, which ought to be the great end in all disputes of the learned. To call a man fool and villain, and impudent fellow, only for differing from him in a point merely speculative, is, in my humble opinion, a very improper style for a person of his education. I appeal to the learned world, whether in my last year's predictions, I gave him the least provocation for such unworthy treatment. Philosophers have differed in all ages, but the discreetest among them have always differed as became philosophers. Scurrility and passion, in a controversy among scholars, is just so much of nothing to the purpose; and at best a tacit confession of a weak cause: my concern is not so much for my own reputation, as that of the republic of letters, which Mr. Partridge hath endeavoured to wound through my sides. If men of public spirit must be superciliously treated for their ingenuous attempts, how will true useful knowledge be ever advanced? I wish Mr. Partridge knew the thoughts which foreign universities have conceived of his ungenerous proceedings with me; but I am too tender of his reputation to publish them to the world. That spirit of envy and pride, which blasts so many rising geniuses in our nation, is yet unknown among professors abroad: the necessity of justifying myself will excuse my vanity, when I tell the reader, that I have near an hundred honorary letters from several parts of Europe (some as far as Muscovy) in praise of my performance. Beside several others, which, as I have been credibly informed, were opened in the post office, and never sent me. It is true the inquisition in Portugal was pleased to burn my predictions,* and condemn the author and readers of them; but I hope at the same time, it will be considered in how deplorable a state learning lies at present in that kingdom: and with the profoundest veneration for crowned heads, I will presume to add, that it a little concerned his Majesty of Portugal to interpose his authority in behalf of a scholar and a gentleman, the subject of a nation with which he is now in so strict an alliance. But the other kingdoms and states of Europe have treated me with more candour and generosity. If I had leave to print the Latin letters transmitted to me from foreign parts, they would fill a volume, and be a full defence against all that Mr. Partridge, or his accomplices of the Portugal inquisition, will be ever able to object; who, by the way,

---

* This is fact, as the author was assured by Sir Paul Methuen, then ambassador to that crown.

are the only enemies my predictions have ever met with at home or abroad. But I hope I know better what is due to the honour of a learned correspondence, in so tender a point. Yet some of those illustrious persons will perhaps excuse me for transcribing a passage or two in my own vindication. The most learned Monsieur Leibnitz [1] thus addresses to me his third letter:—*Illustrissimo Bickerstaffio astrologiæ instauratori,* &c.* Monsieur Le Clerc,[2] quoting my predictions in a treatise he published last year, is pleased to say, *Ità nuperrime Bicker-staffius, magnum illud Angliæ sidus.* Another great professor writing of me, has these words: *Bickerstaffius, nobilis Anglus, astrologorum hujusce seculi facilè princeps.* Signior Maglia-becchi,[3] the Great Duke's famous library-keeper, spends almost his whole letter in compliments and praises. It is true, the renowned professor of astronomy at Utrecht seems to differ from me in one article; but it is after the modest manner that becomes a Philosopher; as, *pace tanti viri dixerim:* and, page 55, he seems to lay the error upon the printer (as indeed it ought) and says, *vel forsan error typographi, cum alioquin Bickerstaffius vir doctissimus,* &c.

If Mr. Partridge had followed these examples in the controversy between us, he might have spared me the trouble of justifying myself in so public a manner. I believe few men are readier to own their errors than I, or more thankful to those who will please to inform him of them. But it seems this gentleman, instead of encouraging the progress of his own art, is pleased to look upon all attempts of that kind as an invasion of his province. He hath been indeed so wise, to make no objection against the truth of my predictions, except in one single point relating to himself; and to demonstrate how much men are blinded by their own partiality, I do solemnly assure the reader, that he is the only person from whom I ever heard that objection offered; which consideration alone, I think, will take off all its weight.

With my utmost endeavours I have not been able to trace above two objections ever made against the truth of my last year's prophecies: the first is of a Frenchman, who was pleased to publish to the world, that the Cardinal de Noailles was still alive, notwithstanding the pretended prophecy of

---

* The quotations here inserted are in imitation of Dr. Bentley, in some part of the famous controversy between him and Mr. Boyle, Esq., afterwards Earl of Orrery.

[1] Gottfried Wilhelm, Baron von Leibnitz (1646–1716), a German philosopher and mathematician.

[2] Jean Le Clerc (1657–1736), a Swiss theologian.

[3] Antonio Magliabecchi (1633–1714), Florentine scholar and librarian.

Monsieur Biquerstaffe: but how far a Frenchman, a Papist, and an enemy, is to be believed in his own cause, against an English Protestant, who is true to the government, I shall leave to the candid and impartial reader.

The other objection is the unhappy occasion of this discourse, and relates to an article in my predictions, which foretold the death of Mr. Partridge to happen on March 29, 1708. This he is pleased to contradict absolutely in the almanack he hath published for the present year, and in that ungentlemanly manner (pardon the expression) as I have above related. In that work he very roundly asserts, that he is not only now alive, but was likewise alive upon that very 29th of March, when I had foretold he should die. This is the subject of the present controversy between us; which I design to handle with all brevity, perspicuity, and calmness: in this dispute, I am sensible the eyes, not only of England, but of all Europe, will be upon us; and the learned in every country will, I doubt not, take part on that side where they find most appearance of reason and truth.

Without entering into criticisms of chronology about the hour of his death, I shall only prove that Mr. Partridge is not alive. And my first argument is thus: above a thousand gentlemen having bought his almanacks for this year, merely to find what he said against me, at every line they read, they would lift up their eyes, and cry out, betwixt rage and laughter, they were sure no man alive ever writ such damned stuff as this. Neither did I ever hear that opinion disputed; so that Mr. Partridge lies under a dilemma, either of disowning his almanack, or allowing himself to be no man alive. But now, if an uninformed carcass walks still about, and is pleased to call itself Partridge, Mr. Bickerstaff does not think himself anyway answerable for that. Neither had the said carcass any right to beat the poor boy, who happened to pass by it in the street, crying, "A full and true account of Dr. Partridge's death," &c.

Secondly, Mr. Partridge pretends to tell fortunes, and recover stolen goods; which all the parish says he must do by conversing with the devil, and other evil spirits: and no wise man will ever allow he could converse personally with either till after he was dead.

Thirdly, I will plainly prove him to be dead, out of his own almanack for this year, and from the very passage which he produces to make us think him alive. He there says, he is not only now alive, but was also alive upon that very 29th of

March, which I foretold he should die on; by this, he declares his opinion, that a man may be alive now who was not alive a twelvemonth ago. And, indeed, there lies the sophistry of his argument. He dares not assert he was alive ever since that 29th of March, but that he is now alive, and was so on that day: I grant the latter, for he did not die till night, as appears by the printed account of his death, in a letter to a lord; and whether he be since revived, I leave the world to judge. This indeed is perfect cavilling, and I am ashamed to dwell any longer upon it.

Fourthly, I will appeal to Mr. Partridge himself, whether it be probable I could have been so indiscreet, to begin my pre-dictions with the only falsehood that ever was pretended to be in them; and this in an affair at home, where I had so many opportunities to be exact; and must have given such advantages against me to a person of Mr. Partridge's wit and learning, who, if he could possibly have raised one single objection more against the truth of my prophecies, would hardly have spared me.

And here I must take occasion to reprove the above-men-tioned writer of the relation of Mr. Partridge's death, in a Letter to a Lord; who was pleased to tax me with a mistake of four whole hours in my calculation of that event. I must confess, this censure, pronounced with an air of certainty, in a matter that so nearly concerned me, and by a grave judi-cious author, moved me not a little. But although I was at that time out of town, yet several of my friends, whose curi-osity had led them to be exactly informed, (for as to my own part, having no doubt at all in the matter, I never once thought of it,) assured me I computed to something under half an hour; which (I speak my private opinion) is an error of no very great magnitude, that men should raise clamour about it. I shall only say, it would not be amiss, if that author would henceforth be more tender of other men's reputation, as well as his own. It is well there were no more mistakes of that kind; if there had, I presume he would have told me of them with as little ceremony.

There is one objection against Mr. Partridge's death, which I have sometimes met with, although indeed very slightly offered: that he still continues to write almanacks. But this is no more than what is common to all of that profession; Gad-bury, Poor Robin, Dove, Wing, and several others, do yearly publish their almanacks, although several of them have been dead since before the Revolution. Now the natural reason of this I take to be, that whereas it is the privilege of other authors to live after their death, almanack-makers are alone excluded; because their dissertations, treating only upon the minutes as they pass, become useless as these go off. In consideration of which, Time, whose registers they are, gives them a lease in reversion, to continue their works after their death.

I should not have given the public or myself the trouble of this vindication, if my name had not been made use of by several persons to whom I never lent it; one of which, a few days ago, was pleased to father on me a new set of predictions.[1] But I think these are things too serious to be trifled with. It grieved me to the heart, when I saw my labours, which had cost me so much thought and watching, bawled about by common hawkers of Grub-Street, which I only intended for the weighty consideration of the gravest persons. This prejudiced the world so much at first, that several of my friends had the assurance to ask me whether I were in jest? to which I only answered coldly, "that the event will show." But it is the talent of our age and nation, to turn things of the greatest importance into ridicule. When the end of the year had verified all my predictions, out comes Mr. Partridge's almanack, disputing the point of his death; so that I am employed, like the general who was forced to kill his enemies twice over, whom a necromancer had raised to life. If Mr. Partridge has practised the same experiment upon himself, and be again alive, long may he continue so; but that does not the least contradict my veracity; for I think I have clearly proved, by invincible demonstration, that he died at farthest within half an hour of the time I foretold, and not four hours sooner, as the above-mentioned author, in his letter to a lord, has maliciously suggested, with design to blast my credit, by charging me with so gross a mistake.

[1] Possibly, *A Continuation of the Predictions for the Remaining Part of the Year, 1708,* not by Swift, but signed Bickerstaff.

THE EXAMINER[1]

No. 14

November 9, 1710

E quibus hi vacuas implent sermonibus aures,
Hi narrata ferunt alio: mensuraque ficti
Crescit, et auditis aliquid novus adjicit autor,
Illic Credulitas, illic temerarius Error,
Vanaque Laetitia est, consternatique Timores,
Seditioque recens, dubioque autore susurri.[2]

I AM prevailed on, through the importunity of friends, to interrupt the scheme I had begun in my last paper, by an Essay upon the Art of Political Lying.[3] We are told, "the Devil is the father of lies, and was a liar from the beginning"; so that, beyond contradiction, the invention is old: and which is more, his first essay of it was purely political, employed in undermining the authority of his Prince, and seducing a third part of the subjects from their obedience. For which he was driven down from Heaven, where (as Milton expresseth it) he had been viceroy of a great Western province; and forced to exercise his talent in inferior regions among other fallen spirits, or poor deluded men, whom he still daily tempts to his own sin, and will ever do so till he be chained in the bottomless pit.

But although the Devil be the father of lies, he seems, like other great inventors, to have lost much of his reputation, by the continual improvements that have been made upon him.

---

[1] Swift's taking-over of the *Examiner* (with No. 13) began his formal career as a spokesman for the Tory Party. To justify the new ministry, he needed to discredit the old, in its principles and personnel. The *Examiner* papers are largely topical, but they exploit the full range of Swift's satiric gifts. The Earl of Wharton, appointed as Lord Lieutenant of Ireland in 1708, had returned to England in 1710 and attacked the newly formed Tory ministry under Harley and Bolingbroke. Wharton was particularly vulnerable to attack: he had used his private wealth to attain and further his political ambitions, was friendly to the dissenters, disapproved of the Test Act, and had the reputation of a profligate and a blasphemer. Swift's satire on Wharton's system of political lying is similar to his satire on Modern systems in *Tale of a Tub* and in *Gulliver's Travels*.

[2] Ovid, *Metamorphoses*, XII, 56–61.

[3] John Arbuthnot's *Art of Political Lying* was not published until 1712.

Who first reduced lying into an art and adapted it to politics, is not so clear from history, although I have made some diligent enquiries: I shall therefore consider it only according to the Modern system, as it hath been cultivated these twenty years past in the southern part of our own island.

The poets tell us, that after the giants were over-thrown by the gods, the earth in revenge produced her last offspring, which was Fame.[1] And the fable is thus interpreted: that when tumults and seditions are quieted, rumours and false reports are plentifully spread through a nation. So that by this account, *lying* is the last relief of a routed, earth-born, rebellious party in a state. But here, the moderns have made great additions, applying this art to the gaining of power, and preserving it, as well as revenging themselves after they have lost it; as the same instruments are made use of by animals to feed themselves when they are hungry, and bite those that tread upon them.

But the same genealogy cannot always be admitted for *political lying;* I shall therefore desire to refine upon it, by adding some circumstances of its birth and parents. A political lie is sometimes born out of a discarded statesman's head, and thence delivered to be nursed and dandled by the rabble. Sometimes it is produced a monster, and *licked* into shape; at other times it comes into the world completely formed, and is spoiled in the licking. It is often born an infant in the regular way, and requires time to mature it; and often it sees the light in its full growth, but dwindles away by degrees. Sometimes it is of noble birth; and sometimes the spawn of a stock-jobber. *Here,* it screams aloud at opening the womb; and *there,* it is delivered with a whisper. I know a lie that now disturbs half the kingdom with its noise, which although too proud and great at present to own its parents, I can remember in its whisper-hood. To conclude the nativity of this monster: when it comes into the world without a *sting,* it is still-born; and whenever it loses its sting, it dies.

No wonder, if an infant so miraculous in its birth, should be destined for great adventures: and accordingly we see it hath been the guardian spirit of a prevailing party [2] for almost twenty years. It can conquer kingdoms without fighting, and sometimes with the loss of a battle: it gives and resumes employments; can sink a mountain to a mole-hill, and raise a mole-hill to a mountain; hath presided for many years at

---

[1] Fama was the daughter of Terra; see Virgil, *Aeneid,* IV, 173-8.
[2] The Whigs.

committees of elections; can wash a blackamoor white; make a saint of an atheist, and a patriot of a profligate; can furnish foreign ministers with intelligence; and raise or let fall the credit of the nation. This goddes flies with a huge looking-glass in her hands to dazzle the crowd, and make them see, according as she turns it, their ruin in their interest, and their interest in their ruin. In this glass you will behold your best friends clad in coats powdered with *flower-de-luces* and triple crowns,[1] their girdles hung round with chains, and beads, and wooden shoes: and your worst enemies adorned with the ensigns of liberty, property, indulgence, moderation, and a cornucopia in their hands. Her large wings, like those of a flying fish, are of no use but while they are moist; she therefore dips them in mud, and soaring aloft scatters it in the eyes of the multitude, flying with great swiftness; but at every turn is forced to stoop in dirty ways for new supplies.

I have been sometimes thinking, if a man had the art of the second sight for seeing lies, as they have in Scotland for seeing spirits, how admirably he might entertain himself in this town; to observe the different shapes, sizes and colours, of those swarms of lies which buzz about the heads of some people, like flies about a horse's ears in summer: or those legions hovering every afternoon in Exchange Alley, enough to darken the air; or over a club of discontented grandees, and thence sent down in cargoes to be scattered at elections.

There is one essential point wherein a political liar differs from others of the faculty; that he ought to have but a short memory, which is necessary according to the various occasions he meets with every hour, of differing from himself, and swearing to both sides of a contradiction, as he finds the persons disposed, with whom he hath to deal. In describing the virtues and vices of mankind, it is convenient, upon every article, to have some eminent person in our eye, from whence we copy our description. I have strictly observed this rule; and my imagination this minute represents before me a certain great man famous for this talent,* to the constant practice of which he owes his twenty years' reputation of the most skilful head in England, for the management of nice affairs. The superiority of his genius consists in nothing else but an inexhaustible fund of political lies, which he plentifully distributes every minute he speaks, and by an unparalleled gen-

---

* The late Earl of Wharton.

[1] The Tories were suspected of French Jacobite sympathies; the point is that good Tories are turned into bad Jacobites by the art of political lying.

erosity forgets, and consequently contradicts the next half-hour. He never yet considered whether any proposition were true or false, but whether it were convenient for the present minute or company to affirm or deny it; so that if you think to refine upon him, by interpreting every thing he says, as we do dreams by the contrary, you are still to seek, and will find yourself equally deceived, whether you believe or no: the only remedy is to suppose that you have heard some inarticulate sounds, without any meaning at all. And besides, that will take off the horror you might be apt to conceive at the oaths wherewith he perpetually tags both ends of every proposition: although at the same time I think he cannot with any justice be taxed for perjury, when he invokes God and Christ, because he hath often fairly given public notice to the world, that he believes in neither.

Some people may think that such an accomplishment as this, can be of no great use to the owner or his party, after it hath been often practised, and is become notorious; but they are widely mistaken: few lies carry the inventor's mark; and the most prostitute enemy to truth may spread a thousand without being known for the author. Besides, as the vilest writer hath his readers, so the greatest liar hath his believers; and it often happens, that if a lie be believed only for an hour, it hath done its work, and there is no farther occasion for it. Falsehood flies, and Truth comes limping after it; so that when men come to be undeceived, it is too late, the jest is over, and the tale has had its effect: like a man who has thought of a good repartee when the discourse is changed, or the company parted: or, like a physician who hath found out an infallible medicine after the patient is dead.

Considering that natural disposition in many men to lie, and in multitudes to believe, I have been perplexed what to do with that maxim, so frequent in everybody's mouth, that "Truth will at last prevail." Here, has this island of ours, for the greatest part of twenty years lain under the influence of such counsels and persons, whose principle and interest it was to corrupt our manners, blind our understandings, drain our wealth, and in time destroy our constitution both in Church and State; [1] and we at last were brought to the very brink of ruin; yet by the means of perpetual misrepresentations, have never been able to distinguish between our enemies and friends. We have seen a great part of the nation's money got

[1] Swift seems to refer to the abolition of the Test Act. (See *The Abolishing of Christianity in England.*)

into the hands of those, who by their birth, education and merit, could pretend no higher than to wear our liveries. While others, who by their credit, quality and fortune, were only able to give reputation and success to the Revolution, were not only laid aside, as dangerous and useless; but loaden with the scandal of Jacobites, men of arbitrary principles, and pensioners to France; while Truth, who is said to lie in a well, seemed now to be buried there under a heap of stones. But I remember it was a usual complaint among the Whigs, that the bulk of landed men was not in their interests, which some of the wisest looked on as an ill omen; and we saw it was with the utmost difficulty that they could preserve a majority, while the court and ministry were on their side; till they had learned those admirable expedients for deciding elections, and influencing distant boroughs by *powerful motives* from the city.[1] But all this was mere force and constraint, however upheld by most dexterous artifice and management; until the people began to apprehend their properties, their religion, and the monarchy itself in danger; then we saw them greedily laying hold on the first occasion to interpose. But of this mighty change in the dispositions of the people, I shall discourse more at large in some following paper; wherein I shall endeavour to undeceive or discover those deluded or deluding persons, who hope or pretend, it is only a short madness in the vulgar, from which they may soon recover. Whereas I believe it will appear to be very different in its causes, its symptoms, and its consequences; and prove a great example to illustrate the maxim I lately mentioned, that "Truth (however sometimes late) "will at last prevail."

[1] Commercial and financial interests in London.

A

LETTER

TO THE

Shop-Keepers, Tradesmen, Farmers, and Common-People of IRELAND,

Concerning the

Braſs Half-Pence

Coined by

Mr. Woods,

WITH

A DESIGN to have them Paſs in this
KINGDOM.

Wherein is ſhewn the Power of the ſaid PATENT, the Value of the HALF-PENCE, and how far every Perſon may be oblig'd to take the ſame in Payments, and how to behave in Caſe ſuch an Attempt ſhou'd be made by WOODS or any other Perſon.

[Very Proper to be kept in every FAMILY.]

By M. B. Drapier.

Dublin: Printed by J. Harding in Moleſworth's-Court.

THE DRAPIER'S FIRST LETTER.

TO THE SHOPKEEPERS, TRADESMEN, FARMERS, AND COMMON PEOPLE OF IRELAND,[1]

A Letter Concerning the Brass Halfpence Coined by Mr. Woods, with a Design to Have Them Pass in This Kingdom,

Wherein is shown the power of his Patent, the value of the Halfpence, and how far every person may be obliged to take the same in payments, and how to behave himself, in case such an attempt should be made by Woods, or any other person.

(VERY PROPER TO BE KEPT IN EVERY FAMILY)

By M. B. Drapier.

Brethren, Friends, Countrymen, and Fellow-Subjects.

WHAT I intend now to say to you, is, next to your duty to God, and the care of your salvation, of the greatest concern to your selves and your children; your bread and clothing, and every common necessary of life entirely depend upon it. Therefore I do most earnestly exhort you as men, as Christians, as parents, and as lovers of your country, to read this paper with the utmost attention, or get it read to you by others; which that you may do at the less expense, I have ordered the printer to sell it at the lowest rate.

[1] In 1722, William Woods, an English ironmonger, was granted a patent by the English Parliament to coin a large amount of money for use in Ireland, without the approval of the Irish Parliament, or of due safeguards against the debasement of the Irish currency. The Irish people were incensed at this further evidence of their political and economic exploitation. Swift's seven *Drapier's Letters* (1724–1725) both fanned and reflected Irish resentment. By late 1724 the English Privy Council ordered an inquiry into Woods' patent, and by 1725 it was revoked. Swift's fame thereafter as an Irish patriot was secure. As M. B. Drapier, the learned linen draper, Swift had achieved a considerable feat. The first letter, here reprinted, is no less brilliant than many parts of *Tale of a Tub* and *Battle of the Books;* it is a tour de force of exaggeration and invective.

It is a great fault among you, that when a person writes with no other intention than to do you good, you will not be at the pains to read his advices: one copy of this paper may serve a dozen of you, which will be less than a farthing apiece. It is your folly that you have no common or general interest in your view, not even the wisest among you; neither do you know or inquire, or care who are your friends, or who are your enemies.

About four years ago a little book was written, to advise all people to wear the manufactures of this our own dear country. It had no other design, said nothing against the king or parliament, or any person whatsoever; yet the poor printer was prosecuted two years with the utmost violence, and even some weavers themselves, for whose sake it was written, being upon the jury, found him guilty. This would be enough to discourage any man from endeavoring to do you good, when you will either neglect him, or fly in his face for his pains; and when he must expect only danger to himself, and to be fined and imprisoned, perhaps to his ruin.

However, I cannot but warn you once more of the manifest destruction before your eyes, if you do not behave yourselves as you ought.

I will therefore first tell you the plain story of the fact; and then I will lay before you how you ought to act in common prudence, and according to the laws of your country.

The fact is thus; it having been many years since copper halfpence or farthings were last coined in this kingdom, they have been for some time very scarce, and many counterfeits passed about under the name of raps: several applications were made to England, that we might have liberty to coin new ones, as in former times we did; but they did not succeed. At last one Mr. Wood, a mean ordinary man, a hardware dealer, procured a patent under his Majesty's broad seal to coin £108,000 in *copper* for this kingdom; which patent, however, did not oblige anyone here to take them, unless they pleased. Now you must know that the halfpence and farthings in England pass for very little more than they are worth; and if you should beat them to pieces, and sell them to the brazier, you would not lose much above a penny in a shilling. But Mr. Wood made his halfpence of such base metal, and so much smaller than the English ones, that the brazier would not give you above a penny of good money for a shilling of his; so that this sum of £108,000 in good gold and silver, must be given for trash, that will not be worth above eight or nine thousand pounds real value. But this is not the worst; for Mr. Wood, when he pleases, may by stealth send over another £108,000 and buy all our goods for eleven parts in twelve under the value. For example, if a hatter sells a dozen of hats for five shilling apiece, which amounts to three pounds, and receives the payment in Mr. Wood's coin, he really receives only the value of five shillings.

Perhaps you will wonder how such an ordinary fellow as this Mr. Wood could have so much interest as to get his Majesty's broad seal for so great a sum of bad money to be sent to this poor country; and that all the nobility and gentry here could not obtain the same favor, and let us make our own halfpence, as we used to do. Now I will make that matter very plain. We are at a great distance from the king's court, and have nobody there to solicit for us, although a great number of lords and squires, whose estates are here, and are our countrymen, spend all their lives and fortunes there. But this same Mr. Wood was able to attend constantly for his own interest; he is an Englishman, and had great friends,[1] and it seems knew very well where to give money to those that would speak to others that could speak to the king, and would tell a fair story. And his Majesty, and perhaps the great lord or lords who advised him, might think it was for our country's good; and so, as the lawyers express it, the king was deceived in his grant, which often happens in all reigns. And I am sure if his Majesty knew that such a patent, if it should take effect according to the desire of Mr. Wood, would utterly ruin this kingdom, which hath given such great proofs of its loyalty, he would immediately recall it, and perhaps show his displeasure to somebody or other: but a word to the wise is enough. Most of you must have heard with what anger our honorable House of Commons received an account of this Wood's patent. There were several fine speeches made upon it, and plain proofs, that it was all a wicked cheat from the bottom to the top; and several smart votes were printed, which that same Wood had the assurance to answer likewise in print; and in so confident a way, as if he were a better man than our whole parliament put together.

This Wood, as soon as his patent was passed, or soon after, sends over a great many barrels of those halfpence to Cork and other seaport towns; and to get them off, offered a hundred pounds in his coin for seventy or eighty in silver: but

---

[1] The Duchess of Kendall, the King's mistress, was reputed to have sold Woods the patent for £10,000.

the collectors of the king's customs very honestly refused to take them, and so did almost everybody else. And since the parliament hath condemned them, and desired the king that they might be stopped, all the kingdom do abominate them.

But Wood is still working underhand to force his halfpence upon us; and if he can by help of his friends in England prevail so far as to get an order that the commissioners and collectors of the king's money shall receive them, and that the army is to be paid with them, then he thinks his work shall be done. And this is the difficulty you will be under in such a case; for the common soldier, when he goes to the market or alehouse, will offer this money; and if it be refused, perhaps he will swagger and hector, and threaten to beat the butcher or alewife, or take the goods by force and throw them the bad halfpence. In this and the like cases, the shop-keeper or victualer, or any other tradesman, has no more to do, than to demand ten times the price of his goods, if it is to be paid in Wood's money: for example, twenty pence of that money for a quart of ale, and so in all things else, and not part with his goods till he gets the money.

For suppose you go to an alehouse with that base money, and the landlord gives you a quart for four of these halfpence, what must the victualer do? His brewer will not be paid in that coin, or, if the brewer should be such a fool, the farmers will not take it from them for their bere, because they are bound, by their leases, to pay their rents in good and lawful money of England, which this is not, nor of Ireland neither; and the squire, their landlord, will never be so bewitched to take such trash for his land; so that it must certainly stop somewhere or other; and wherever it stops it is the same thing, and we are all undone.

The common weight of these halfpence is between four and five to an ounce; suppose five, then three shillings and fourpence will weigh a pound, and consequently twenty shillings will weigh six pounds butter weight.[1] Now there are many hundred farmers, who pay two hundred pounds a year rent; therefore when one of these farmers comes with his half-year's rent, which is one hundred pounds, it will be at least six hundred pounds weight, which is three horses' load.

If a squire has a mind to come to town to buy clothes and wine and spices for himself and family, or perhaps to pass

---

[1] The weight used in selling butter, roughly 18 ounces to the pound; hence overweight.

the winter here, he must bring with him five or six horses loaden with sacks as the farmers bring their corn; and when his lady comes in her coach to our shops, it must be followed by a car loaded with Mr. Wood's money. And I hope we shall have the grace to take it for no more than it is worth.

They say Squire Conolly [1] has sixteen thousand pounds a year; now if he sends for his rent to town, as it is likely he does, he must have two hundred and fifty horses to bring up his half-year's rent, and two or three great cellars in his house for stowage. But what the bankers will do I cannot tell. For I am assured, that some great bankers keep by them forty thousand pounds in ready cash, to answer all payments; which sum in Mr. Wood's money would require twelve hundred horses to carry it.

For my own part, I am already resolved what to do; I have a pretty good shop of Irish stuffs and silks, and instead of taking Mr. Wood's bad copper, I intend to truck with my neighbors the butchers and bakers and brewers, and the rest, goods for goods; and the little gold and silver I have, I will keep by me like my heart's blood till better times, or until I am just ready to starve, and then I will buy Mr. Wood's money, as my father did the brass money in King James's time, who could buy ten pounds of it with a guinea, and I hope to get as much for a pistole, and so purchase bread from those who will be such fools as to sell it me.

These halfpence, if they once pass, will soon be counter-feited, because it may be cheaply done, the stuff is so base. The Dutch likewise will probably do the same thing, and send them over to us to pay for our goods; and Mr. Wood will never be at rest, but coin on: so that in some years we shall have at least five times £108,000 of this lumber. Now the current money of this kingdom is not reckoned to be above four hundred thousand pounds in all; and while there is a silver sixpence left, these bloodsuckers will never be quiet.

When once the kingdom is reduced to such a condition, I will tell you what must be the end: the gentlemen of estates will all turn off their tenants for want of payment; because, as I told you before, the tenants are obliged by their leases to pay sterling, which is lawful current money of England; then they will turn their own farmers, as too many of them do

---

[1] William Conolly, Speaker of the Irish House of Commons, who supported Woods; his name is used probably to imply the discrepancy between the rich and the poor.

already; run all into sheep [1] where they can, keeping only such other cattle as are necessary; then they will be their own merchants, and send their wool, and butter, and hides, and linen beyond sea for ready money, and wine, and spices, and silks. They will keep only a few miserable cottagers. The farmers must rob or beg, or leave their country. The shopkeepers in this and every other town must break and starve; for it is the landed man that maintains the merchant, and shopkeeper, and handcraftsman.

But when the squire turns farmer and merchant himself, all the good money he gets from abroad, he will hoard up to send for England, and keep some poor tailor or weaver, and the like, in his own house, who will be glad to get bread at any rate.

I should never have done, if I were to tell you all the miseries that we shall undergo, if we be so foolish and wicked as to take this cursed coin. It would be very hard, if all Ireland should be put into one scale, and this sorry fellow Wood into the other; that Mr. Wood should weigh down this whole kingdom, by which England gets above a million of good money every year clear into their pockets: and that is more than the English do by all the world besides.

But your great comfort is, that as his Majesty's patent does not oblige you to take this money, so the laws have not given the Crown a power of forcing the subject to take what money the king pleases; for then by the same reason we might be bound to take pebblestones, or cockleshells, or stamped leather for current coin, if ever we should happen to live under an ill prince; who might likewise by the same power make a guinea pass for ten pounds, a shilling for twenty shillings, and so on; by which he would in a short time get all the silver and gold of the kingdom into his own hands, and leave us nothing but brass or leather, or what he pleased. Neither is anything reckoned more cruel or oppressive in the French government, than their common practice of calling in all their money after they have sunk it very low, and then coining it anew at a much higher value; which however is not the thousandth part so wicked as this abominable project of Mr. Wood. For the French give their subjects silver for silver, and gold for gold; but this fellow will not so

---

[1] To support the woolen trade, England limited the amount of Irish land which could be cultivated, so that the rest could be kept as pasturage for sheep; this policy considerably weakened Irish agriculture.

much as give us good brass or copper for our gold and silver, nor even a twelfth part of their worth.

Having said thus much, I will now go on to tell you the judgments of some great lawyers in this matter, whom I fee'd on purpose for your sakes, and got their opinions under their hands, that I might be sure I went upon good grounds.

A famous lawbook, called *The Mirror of Justice*,[1] discoursing of the charters (or laws) ordained by our ancient kings, declares the law to be as follows: "It was ordained that no king of this realm should change or impair the money, or make any other money than of gold or silver, without the assent of all the counties"; that is, as my Lord Coke[2] says, without the assent of parliament.

This book is very ancient, and of great authority for the time in which it was wrote, and with that character is often quoted by that great lawyer my Lord Coke. By the laws of England the several metals are divided into lawful or true metal, and unlawful or false metal: the former comprehends silver or gold, the latter all baser metals. That the former is only to pass in payments, appears by an act of parliament made the twentieth year of Edward the First, called the *Statute Concerning the Passing of Pence;* which I give you here as I got it translated into English; for some of our laws at that time were, as I am told, written in Latin: "Whoever in buying or selling presumeth to refuse a halfpenny or farthing of lawful money, bearing the stamp which it ought to have, let him be seized on as a contemner of the king's majesty, and cast into prison."

By this statute, no person is to be reckoned a contemner of the king's Majesty, and for that crime to be committed to prison, but he who refuseth to accept the king's coin made of lawful metal; by which as I observed before, silver and gold only are intended.

That this is the true construction of the act, appears not only from the plain meaning of the words, but from my Lord Coke's observation upon it. By this act (says he) it appears, that no subject can be forced to take, in buying or selling or other payments, any money made but of lawful metal; that is, of silver or gold.

The law of England gives the king all mines of gold and

---

[1] Compiled by Andrew Horn.
[2] Lord Edward Coke (1552–1634), one of the greatest jurists in the history of English law. Swift cites his *Institutes*.

silver; but not the mines of other metals: the reason of which prerogative or power, as it is given by my Lord Coke, is because money can be made of gold and silver; but not of other metals.

Pursuant to this opinion, halfpence and farthings were anciently made of silver, which is evident from the act of parliament of Henry the Fourth, chap. 4, whereby it is enacted as follows: "Item, for the great scarcity that is at present within the realm of England of halfpence and farthings of silver, it is ordained and established, that the third part of all the money of silver plate which shall be brought to the bullion, shall be made in halfpence and farthings." This shows that by the words "halfpenny and farthing of lawful money," in that statute concerning the passing of pence, is meant a small coin in halfpence and farthings of silver.

This is farther manifest from the statute of the ninth year of Edward the Third, chap. 3, which enacts "that no sterling halfpenny or farthing be molten for to make vessels, or any other thing, by the goldsmiths, nor others, upon forfeiture of the money so molten" (or melted).

By another act in this king's reign, *black money* was not to be current in England. And by an act made in the eleventh year of his reign, chap. 5, *galley halfpence* were not to pass. What kind of coin these were I do not know; but I presume they were made of base metal. And these acts were no new laws, but further declarations of the old laws relating to the coin.

Thus the law stands in relation to coin. Nor is there any example to the contrary, except one in Davis's Reports, who tells us that in the time of Tyrone's rebellion,[1] Queen Elizabeth ordered money of mixed metal to be coined in the Tower of London, and sent over hither for the payment of the army, obliging all people to receive it; and commanding that all silver money should be taken only as bullion; that is, for as much as it weighed. Davis tells us several particulars in this matter too long here to trouble you with, and that the privy council of this kingdom obliged a merchant in England to receive this mixed money for goods transmitted hither.

But this proceeding is rejected by all the best lawyers, as contrary to law, the privy council here having no such legal power. And besides it is to be considered, that the queen was

---

[1] Hugh O'Neill, 2d Earl of Tyrone, whose surrender to the English in 1603 marked the end of the rebellion of the chiefs and of tribal autonomy in Ireland.

then under great difficulties by a rebellion in this kingdom assisted from Spain. And whatever is done in great exigencies and dangerous times, should never be an example to proceed by in seasons of peace and quietness.

I will now, my dear friends, to save you the trouble, set before you, in short, what the law obliges you to do; and what it does not oblige you to.

First, you are obliged to take all money in payments which is coined by the king, and is of the English standard or weight, provided it be of gold or silver.

Secondly, you are not obliged to take any money which is not of gold or silver; not only the halfpence or farthings of England, but of any other country. And it is merely for convenience, or ease, that you are content to take them; because the custom of coining silver halfpence and farthings hath long been left off; I suppose on account of their being subject to be lost.

Thirdly, much less are we obliged to take those vile halfpence of that same Wood, by which you must loose almost eleven pence in every shilling.

Therefore, my friends, stand to it one and all: refuse this filthy trash. It is no treason to rebel against Mr. Wood. His Majesty in his patent obliges nobody to take these halfpence: our gracious prince hath no such ill advisers about him; or if he had, yet you see the laws have not left it in the king's power to force us to take any coin but what is lawful, of right standard, gold and silver. Therefore you have nothing to fear.

And let me in the next place apply myself particularly to you who are the poorer sort of tradesmen; perhaps you may think you will not be so great losers as the rich, if these halfpence should pass, because you seldom see any silver, and your customers come to your shops or stalls with nothing but brass, which you likewise find hard to be got. But you may take my word, whenever this money gains footing among you, you will be utterly undone. If you carry these halfpence to a shop for tobacco or brandy, or any other thing that you want, the shopkeeper will advance his goods accordingly, or else he must break, and leave the key under the door. Do you think I will sell you a yard of tenpenny stuff for twenty of Mr. Wood's halfpence? No, not under two hundred at least; neither will I be at the trouble of counting, but weigh them in a lump. I will tell you one thing further, that if Mr. Wood's project should take, it will ruin even our beggars;

for when I give a beggar a halfpenny, it will quench his thirst, or go a good way to fill his belly; but the twelfth part of a halfpenny will do him no more service than if I should give him three pins out of my sleeve.

In short, these halfpence are like the accursed thing, which as the Scripture tells us, the children of Israel were forbidden to touch. They will run about like the plague and destroy everyone who lays his hands upon them. I have heard scholars talk of a man who told the king that he had invented a way to torment people by putting them into a bull of brass with fire under it, but the prince put the projector first into his own brazen bull to make the experiment.[1] This very much resembles the project of Mr. Wood; and the like of this may possibly be Mr. Wood's fate; that the brass he contrived to torment this kingdom with, may prove his own torment, and his destruction at last.

N.B. The author of this paper is informed by persons, who have made it their business to be exact in their observations on the true value of these halfpence, that any person may expect to get a quart of twopenny ale for thirty-six of them.

I desire that all families may keep this paper carefully by them, to refresh their memories whenever they shall have farther notice of Mr. Wood's halfpence, or any other the like imposture.

[1] See p. 418, n. 1.

A MODEST PROPOSAL[1]

FOR

PREVENTING THE CHILDREN OF POOR PEOPLE IN IRELAND FROM BEING A BURDEN TO THEIR PARENTS OR COUNTRY, AND FOR MAKING THEM BENEFICIAL TO THE PUBLIC.

IT is a melancholy object to those who walk through this great town, or travel in the country, when they see the streets, the roads and cabin-doors crowded with beggars of the female sex, followed by three, four, or six children, all in rags, and importuning every passenger for an alms.[2] These mothers, instead of being able to work for their honest livelihood, are forced to employ all their time in strolling, to beg sustenance for their helpless infants, who, as they grow up, either turn thieves for want of work, or leave their dear native country to fight for the Pretender in Spain, or sell themselves to the Barbadoes.[3]

I think it is agreed by all parties that this prodigious number of children, in the arms, or on the backs, or at the heels of their mothers, and frequently of their fathers, is in the present deplorable state of the kingdom a very great additional grievance; and therefore whoever could find out a fair, cheap, and easy method of making these children sound and useful

[1] *A Modest Proposal* (1729) is one of a number of tracts urging the necessity for the amelioration of Irish poverty that Swift wrote during this period, but it reaches a unique height. Swift's satiric range and depth are brilliant: his parody of the new political arithmetic, of the new science of economics and of its endless "modest proposals" for the amelioration of one condition or another, its heartless distinction between the "able" and the "impotent" poor, the devastating irony of a project to decimate a population already all but decimated by poverty, and his ironic manipulation of the truism that the wealth of a nation lay in its population; his mad, but logical, deduction that cannibalism is the *summum bonum*, that children are better off dead.

[2] See Swift's *Proposal for Giving Badges to the Beggars in all the Parishes of Dublin*, 1737, for an understanding of the poverty in Ireland at this time.

[3] Poverty led many Irish to enlist in the French and Spanish armies and to emigrate to Barbados.

members of the commonwealth would serve so well of the public as to have his statue set up for a preserver of the nation.

But my intention is very far from being confined to provide only for the children of professed beggars; it is of a much greater extent, and shall take in the whole number of infants at a certain age who are born of parents in effect as little able to support them as those who demand our charity in the streets.

As to my own part, having turned my thoughts for many years upon this important subject, and maturely weighed the several schemes of other projectors, I have always found them grossly mistaken in their computation. It is true a child just dropped from its dam may be supported by her milk for a solar year with little other nourishment, at most not above the value of two shillings, which the mother may certainly get, or the value in scraps, by her lawful occupation of begging, and it is exactly at one year old that I propose to provide for them, in such a manner as, instead of being a charge upon their parents, or the parish, or wanting food and raiment for the rest of their lives, they shall, on the contrary, contribute to the feeding and partly to the clothing of many thousands.

There is likewise another great advantage in my scheme, that it will prevent those voluntary abortions, and that horrid practice of women murdering their bastard children, alas, too frequent among us, sacrificing the poor innocent babes, I doubt, more to avoid the expense than the shame, which would move tears and pity in the most savage and inhuman breast.

The number of souls in Ireland being usually reckoned one million and a half, of these I calculate there may be about two hundred thousand couples whose wives are breeders, from which number I subtract thirty thousand couples who are able to maintain their own children, although I apprehend there cannot be so many under the present distresses of the kingdom, but this being granted, there will remain an hundred and seventy thousand breeders. I again subtract fifty thousand for those women who miscarry, or whose children die by accident or disease within the year. There only remain an hundred and twenty thousand children of poor parents annually born: the question therefore is, how this number shall be reared, and provided for, which, as I have already said, under the present situation of affairs is utterly impossible by all the methods hitherto proposed, for we can neither employ them in handicraft or agriculture; we neither build houses (I mean in the country), nor cultivate land: they can very seldom pick up a livelihood by stealing until they arrive at six years old, except where they are of towardly parts although I confess they learn the rudiments much earlier, during which time they can however be properly looked upon only as probationers, as I have been informed by a principal gentleman in the County of Cavan, who protested to me that he never knew above one or two instances under the age of six, even in a part of the kingdom so renowned for the quickest proficiency in that art.

I am assured by our merchants that a boy or a girl before twelve years old, is no saleable commodity, and even when they come to this age, they will not yield above three pounds, or three pounds and half-a-crown at most on the Exchange, which cannot turn to account either to the parents or the kingdom, the charge of nutriment and rags having been at least four times that value.

I shall now therefore humbly propose my own thoughts, which I hope will not be liable to the least objection.

I have been assured by a very knowing American of my acquaintance in London, that a young healthy child well nursed is at a year old a most delicious, nourishing and wholesome food, whether stewed, roasted, baked, or boiled, and I make no doubt that it will equally serve in a fricassee, or a ragout.

I do therefore humbly offer it to public consideration, that of the hundred and twenty thousand children, already computed, twenty thousand may be reserved for breed, whereof only one fourth part to be males, which is more than we allow to sheep, black-cattle, or swine, and my reason is that these children are seldom the fruits of marriage, a circumstance not much regarded by our savages, therefore one male will be sufficient to serve four females. That the remaining hundred thousand may at a year old be offered in sale to the persons of quality, and fortune, through the kingdom, always advising the mother to let them suck plentifully in the last month, so as to render them plump, and fat for a good table. A child will make two dishes at an entertainment for friends, and when the family dines alone, the fore or hind quarter will make a reasonable dish, and seasoned with a little pepper or salt will be very good boiled on the fourth day, especially in winter.

I have reckoned upon a medium, that a child just born will weigh twelve pounds, and in a solar year if tolerably nursed increaseth to twenty-eight pounds.

I grant this food will be somewhat dear, and therefore very proper for landlords, who, as they have already devoured most of the parents, seem to have the best title to the children.

Infant's flesh will be in season throughout the year, but more plentiful in March, and a little before and after, for we are told by a grave * 1 author, an eminent French physician, that fish being a prolific diet, there are more children born in Roman Catholic countries about nine months after Lent than at any other season; therefore reckoning a year after Lent, the markets will be more glutted than usual, because the number of Popish infants is at least three to one in this kingdom, and therefore it will have one other collateral advantage by lessening the number of Papists among us.

I have already computed the charge of nursing a beggar's child (in which list I reckon all cottagers, labourers, and four-fifths of the farmers) to be about two shillings *per annum*, rags included, and I believe no gentleman would repine to give ten shillings for the carcass of a good fat child, which, as I have said, will make four dishes of excellent nutritive meat, when he hath only some particular friend or his own family to dine with him. Thus the Squire will learn to be a good landlord and grow popular among his tenants, the mother will have eight shillings net profit, and be fit for work until she produces another child.

Those who are more thrifty (as I must confess the times require) may flay the carcass; the skin of which artificially dressed, will make admirable gloves for ladies, and summer boots for fine gentlemen.

As to our city of Dublin, shambles may be appointed for this purpose, in the most convenient parts of it, and butchers we may be assured will not be wanting, although I rather recommend buying the children alive, and dressing them hot from the knife, as we do roasting pigs.

A very worthy person, a true lover of his country, and whose virtues I highly esteem, was lately pleased, in discoursing on this matter to offer a refinement upon my scheme. He said that many gentlemen of this kingdom, having of late destroyed their deer, he conceived that the want of venison

---

* Rabelais.

1 Rabelais (*Gargantua and Pantagruel*, Book V, chap. 19) recommends the Lenten diet as conducive to propagation.

might be well supplied by the bodies of young lads and maidens, not exceeding fourteen years of age, nor under twelve, so great a number of both sexes in every county being now ready to starve, for want of work and service: and these to be disposed of by their parents if alive, or otherwise by their nearest relations. But with due deference to so excellent a friend, and so deserving a patriot, I cannot be altogether in his sentiments. For as to the males, my American acquaintance assured me from frequent experience that their flesh was generally tough and lean, like that of our school-boys, by continual exercise, and their taste disagreeable, and to fatten them would not answer the charge. Then as to the females, it would, I think with humble submission, be a loss to the public, because they soon would become breeders themselves: and besides, it is not improbable that some scrupulous people might be apt to censure such a practice (although indeed very unjustly) as a little bordering upon cruelty, which I confess, hath always been with me the strongest objection against any project, howsoever well intended.

But in order to justify my friend, he confessed that this expedient was put into his head by the famous Psalmanazar,[1] a native of the island Formosa, who came from thence to London, above twenty years ago, and in conversation told my friend that in his country when any young person happened to be put to death, the executioner sold the carcass to persons of quality, as a prime dainty, and that, in his time, the body of a plump girl of fifteen, who was crucified for an attempt to poison the emperor, was sold to his Imperial Majesty's Prime Minister of State, and other great Mandarins of the Court, in joints from the gibbet, at four hundred crowns. Neither indeed can I deny that if the same use were made of several plump young girls in this town who, without one single groat to their fortunes, cannot stir abroad without a chair, and appear at the playhouse and assemblies in foreign fineries, which they never will pay for, the kingdom would not be the worse.

Some persons of a desponding spirit are in great concern about the vast number of poor people, who are aged, diseased, or maimed, and I have been desired to employ my thoughts what course may be taken to ease the nation of so grievous an encumbrance. But I am not in the least pain upon that matter, because it is very well known that they are every day

[1] George Psalmanazar (1679–1763), a literary impostor, author of *An Historical and Geographical Description of Formosa* (1704).

dying, and rotting, by cold, and famine, and filth, and vermin, as fast as can be reasonably expected. And as to the younger labourers they are now in almost as hopeful a condition. They cannot get work, and consequently pine away from want of nourishment, to a degree that if at any time they are accidentally hired to common labour, they have not strength to perform it; and thus the country and themselves are in a fair way of being soon delivered from the evils to come.

I have too long digressed, and therefore shall return to my subject. I think the advantages by the proposal which I have made are obvious and many, as well as of the highest importance.

For first, as I have already observed, it would greatly lessen the number of Papists, with whom we are yearly over-run being the principal breeders of the nation, as well as our most dangerous enemies, and who stay at home on purpose with a design to deliver the kingdom to the Pretender, hoping to take their advantage by the absence of so many good Protestants, who have chosen rather to leave their country than stay at home and pay tithes against their conscience to an idolatrous Episcopal curate.

Secondly, the poorer tenants will have something valuable of their own, which by law may be made liable to distress,[1] and help to pay their landlord's rent, their corn and cattle being already seized, and money a thing unknown.

Thirdly, whereas the maintenance of an hundred thousand children, from two years old, and upwards, cannot be computed at less than ten shillings a piece *per annum,* the nation's stock will be thereby increased fifty thousand pounds *per annum,* besides the profit of a new dish, introduced to the tables of all gentlemen of fortune in the kingdom, who have any refinement in taste, and the money will circulate among ourselves, the goods being entirely of our own growth and manufacture.

Fourthly, the constant breeders, besides the gain of eight shillings sterling *per annum,* by the sale of their children, will be rid of the charge of maintaining them after the first year.

Fifthly, this food would likewise bring great custom to taverns, where the vintners will certainly be so prudent as to procure the best receipts for dressing it to perfection, and consequently have their houses frequented by all the fine gentlemen, who justly value themselves upon their knowledge

---

[1] Seizure (for failure to pay debts).

in good eating; and a skilful cook, who understands how to oblige his guests, will contrive to make it as expensive as they please.

Sixthly, this would be a great inducement to marriage, which all wise nations have either encouraged by rewards, or enforced by laws and penalties. It would increase the care and tenderness of mothers towards their children, when they were sure of a settlement for life, to the poor babes, provided in some sort by the public to their annual profit instead of expense. We should soon see an honest emulation among the married women, which of them could bring the fattest child to the market. Men would become as fond of their wives, during the time of their pregnancy, as they are now of their mares in foal, their cows in calf, or sows when they are ready to farrow, nor offer to beat or trick them (as it is too frequent a practice) for fear of a miscarriage.

Many other advantages might be enumerated. For instance, the addition of some thousand carcasses in our exportation of barrelled beef; the propagation of swine's flesh, and improvement in the art of making good bacon, so much wanted among us by the great destruction of pigs, too frequent at our tables, are no way comparable in taste or magnificence to a well-grown, fat yearling child, which roasted whole will make a considerable figure at a Lord Mayor's feast, or any other public entertainment. But this and many others I omit, being studious of brevity.

Supposing that one thousand families in this city would be constant customers for infants flesh, besides others who might have it at merry meetings, particularly weddings and christenings; I compute that Dublin would take off annually about twenty thousand carcasses, and the rest of the kingdom (where probably they will be sold somewhat cheaper) the remaining eighty thousand.

I can think of no one objection that will possibly be raised against this proposal, unless it should be urged that the number of people will be thereby much lessened in the kingdom. This I freely own, and it was indeed one principal design in offering it to the world. I desire the reader will observe, that I calculate my remedy *for this one individual Kingdom* of Ireland, *and for no other that ever was, is, or, I think, ever can be upon earth*. Therefore let no man talk to me of other expedients: *Of taxing our absentees at five shillings a pound: Of using neither clothes, nor household furniture, except what is of our own growth and manufacture: Of utterly rejecting the materials and instruments that promote foreign luxury: Of curing the expensiveness of pride, vanity, idleness, and gaming in our women: Of introducing a vein of parsimony, prudence, and temperance: Of learning to love our country, wherein we differ even from* Laplanders, *and the inhabitants of* Topinamboo.[1] *Of quitting our animosities and factions, nor act any longer like the* Jews, *who were murdering one another at the very moment their city was taken: Of being a little cautious not to sell our country and consciences for nothing: Of teaching landlords to have at least one degree of mercy towards their tenants.* Lastly, *of putting a spirit of honesty, industry, and skill into our shopkeepers, who, if a resolution could now be taken to buy only our native goods, would immediately unite to cheat and exact upon us in the price, the measure and the goodness, nor could ever yet be brought to make one fair proposal of just dealing, though often and earnestly invited to it.*

Therefore I repeat, let no man talk to me of these and the like expedients, till he hath at least a glimpse of hope that there will ever be some hearty and sincere attempt to put them in practice.

But as to myself, having been wearied out for many years with offering vain, idle, visionary thoughts, and at length utterly despairing of success, I fortunately fell upon this proposal, which as it is wholly new, so it hath something solid and real, of no expense and little trouble, full in our own power, and whereby we can incur no danger in disobliging England. For this kind of commodity will not bear exportation, the flesh being of too tender a consistence to admit a long continuance in salt, *although perhaps I could name a country which would be glad to eat up our whole nation without it.*

After all I am not so violently bent upon my own opinion as to reject any offer, proposed by wise men, which shall be found equally innocent, cheap, easy and effectual. But before some thing of that kind shall be advanced in contradiction to my scheme, and offering a better, I desire the author, or authors, will be pleased maturely to consider two points. First, as things now stand, how they will be able to find food and raiment for a hundred thousand useless mouths and backs? And secondly, there being a round million of creatures in human figure, throughout this kingdom, whose whole subsistence put into a common stock would leave them in debt two millions of pounds sterling; adding those who are beggars

[1] Savages in Brazil.

by profession, to the bulk of farmers, cottagers, and labourers with their wives and children, who are beggars in effect; I desire those politicians who dislike my overture, and may perhaps be so bold to attempt an answer, that they will first ask the parents of these mortals whether they would not at this day think it a great happiness to have been sold for food at a year old, in the manner I prescribed, and thereby have avoided such a perpetual scene of misfortunes as they have since gone through, by the oppression of landlords, the impossibility of paying rent without money or trade, the want of common sustenance, with neither house nor clothes to cover them from the inclemencies of weather, and the most inevitable prospect of entailing the like, or greater miseries upon their breed for ever.

I profess in the sincerity of my heart that I have not the least personal interest in endeavouring to promote this necessary work, having no other motive than the *public good of my country, by advancing our trade, providing for infants, relieving the poor, and giving some pleasure to the rich.* I have no children by which I can propose to get a single penny; the youngest being nine years old, and my wife past child-bearing.

SWIFT'S CORRESPONDENCE.

JOURNAL TO STELLA.[1]

LETTER II.

London, Sept. 9, 1710

I GOT here last Thursday after five days travelling, weary the first, almost dead the second, tolerable the third, and well enough the rest; and now am glad of the fatigue, which has served for exercise; and I am at present well enough. The Whigs were ravished to see me, and would lay hold on me as a twig while they were drowning, and the great men making me their clumsy apologies, &c.[2] But my lord treasurer[3] received me with a great deal of coldness, which has enraged me so, I am almost vowing revenge. I have not yet gone half my circle; but I find all my acquaintance just as I left them. I hear my lady Gifford[4] is much at Court, and Lady Wharton[5] was ridiculing it t'other day; so I have lost a friend there. I have not yet seen her, nor intend it; but I will contrive to see Stella's mother[6] some other way. I writ to the Bishop of Clogher from Chester; and I now write to the Archbishop of Dublin. Everything is turning upside down; every Whig in great office will, to a man, be infallibly put out; and we shall have such a winter as hath not been seen in England. Everybody asks me, how I came to be so long in Ireland, as naturally as if here were my being; but no soul offers to make it so; and I protest I shall return to Dublin, and the Canal at Laracor, with more satisfaction than I ever did in my life. The Tatler[7] expects every day to be turned out of his employ-

---

[1] The series of letters, in the form of journal entries, that Swift wrote to Stella (Esther Johnson) and her companion Rebecca Dingley between September 1710 and June 1713 is known as the *Journal to Stella*. Swift was at his height as a public figure at this period, and his letters are of extraordinary public as well as private interest; the letters are detailed and candid, and Swift's candor has been used against him. The so-called little language Swift occasionally affects is probably a code for a private language Swift had with the two ladies to whom he wrote, with whom his relationship was close and playful.

[2] Swift had been disappointed in his reasonable hopes of preferment by the Whigs. See the Introduction.

[3] Sidney Godolphin.

[4] Sister to Sir William Temple, whom Swift knew well from his sojourns at Moor Park.

[5] Second wife of the Earl of Wharton.

[6] Stella's mother was in the attendance of Lady Gifford.

[7] Richard Steele.

ment; and the Duke of Ormond, they say, will be lieutenant of Ireland. I hope you are now peaceably in Presto's [1] lodgings; but I resolve to turn you out by Christmas; in which time I shall either do my business, or find it not to be done. Pray be at Trim by the time this letter comes to you, and ride little Johnson, who must be now in good case. I have begun this letter unusually, on the post-night, and have already written to the Archbishop; and cannot lengthen this. Henceforth I will write something every day to MD,[2] and make it a sort of journal; and when it is full, I will send it whether MD writes or no; and so that will be pretty; and I shall always be in conversation with MD, and MD with Presto. Pray make Parvisol [3] pay you the ten pounds immediately; so I ordered him. They tell me I am grown fatter, and look better; and on Monday Jervas [4] is to retouch my picture; I thought I saw Jack Temple [5] and his wife pass by me today in their coach; but I took no notice of them. I am glad I have wholly shaken off that family. Tell the provost [6] I have obeyed his commands to the Duke of Ormond; or let it alone if you please. I saw Jemmey Leigh [7] just now at the coffee-house, who asked after you with great kindness; he talks of going in a fortnight to Ireland. My service to the Dean,[8] and Mrs. Walls and her archdeacon.[9] Will Frankland's [10] wife is near bringing to bed, and I have promised to christen the child. I fancy you had my Chester letter the Tuesday after I writ. I presented Dr. Raymond to Lord Wharton at Chester. Pray let me know when Joe gets his money. It is near ten, and I hate to send by the bellman. MD shall have a longer letter in a week, but I send this only to tell I am safe in London; and so farewell, &c.

LETTER L.

Kensington, July 17, 1712.

I am weary of living in this Place, and glad I am to leave it so soon. The Qu— goes on Tuesday to Windsor, and I shall

[1] Swift's name for himself in these letters; a translation of *Swift* into Italian.
[2] MD usually stands for Stella and Rebecca Dingley in the little language, possibly standing for My Dear or My Dears.
[3] Swift's agent at Laracor, his benefice in Ireland.
[4] Charles Jervas, a contemporary portrait painter.
[5] John Temple, nephew to Sir William. Swift's hostility to the Temple family is apparent from the *Journal*.
[6] Benjamin Pratt, Provost of Trinity College, Dublin.
[7] An Irish acquaintance of Swift and the ladies.
[8] John Sterne, Dean of St. Patrick's.
[9] Archdeacon Walls, rector of Castleknock.
[10] Treasurer of the Stamp Office.

follow in 3 or 4 days after. I can do nothing here, going early to London, and coming late from it and supping at Ldy Mashams.[1] I din'd to day with the D. of Argyle at Cue, and would not go to the Court to night because of writing to Md. the Bp of Clogher [2] has been here this fortnight; I see him as often as I can. poor Master Ash has a sad Redness in his Face, it is St Anthony's fire, his face all swelld; and will break in his Cheek, but no danger.—Since Dunkirk has been in our Hands, Grubstreet has been very fruitful: pdfr [3] has writt 5 or 6 Grubstreet papers this last week. Have you seen Toland's Invitation to Dismal, or a Hue & cry after Dismal, or a Ballad on Dunkirk, or an Argument that Dunkirk is not in our Hands Poh, you have seen nothing.—I am dead here with the Hot weathr, yet I walk every night home, & believe it does me good. but my Shouldr is not yet right, itchings, & scratchings, and small akings. Did I tell you that I have made Ford Gazeteer,[4] with 200ll a year Salary, besides Perquisites. I had a Lettr lately from Parvisol, who says my Canal looks very finely; I long to see it; but no Apples; all blasted again. He tells me there will be a Triennial Visitation in August. I must send Raymd another Proxy. So now I will answr ee Rettle N. 33. dated Jun. 17. Ppt [5] writes as well as ever for all her waters I wish I had never come here, as often and as heartily as Ppt, what had I to do here? I have heard of the Bp's making me uneasy, but I did not think it was because I never writt to him. A little would make me write to him; but I don't know what to say. I find I am obliged to the Provost for keeping the Bp from being impertinent.—Yes Maram Dd,[6] but oo would not be content with Letters flom pdfr of 6 lines, or 12 either fais. I hope Ppt will have done with the waters soon, and find benefit by them; I believe if they were as far off as Wexford they would do as much good; For I take the Journy to contribute as much as any thing. I can assure you the Bp of Cloghers being here does not in the least affect my staying or going. I never talkt to Higgins but once in the Street; and I believe he and I shall hardly meet but by chance. What care I whethr my Lettr to Ld Treasr [7] be commended there or no?

[1] Lady Masham, a favorite of Queen Anne, helped, by court intrigue, to secure favor for her cousin Robert Harley.
[2] St. George Ashe, Bishop of Clogher.
[3] Probably one of Swift's designations for himself: poor dear foolish rogue.
[4] Swift helped Ford to secure the editorship of *The London Gazette*, a government journal.
[5] Probably standing for Stella: poppet, or poor pretty thing.
[6] Madam Dingley.
[7] Swift refers to his *A Proposal for Correcting, Improving and Ascertaining the English Tongue*, 1712, cast in the form of a letter to Harley.

why does not somebody among you answer it, as 3 or 4 have done here (I am now sitting with nothing but my Nightgown for heat). Ppt shall have a great Bible. I have put it down in my memlandums, just now. and Dd shall be repaid her tother Book; but patience, all in good time; you are so hasty a dog would &c. So Ppt has neither won nor lost. Why mun, I play sometimes too, at Picket that is Picquett I mean; but very seldom.—Out late, why 'tis onely at Ldy Mashams, and that's in our Town: but I never come late here from London, except once in rain when I could not get a Coach.—We have had very little Thunder here; none these 2 Months; why pray, Madam Philosopher, how did the Rain hinder the Thunder from doing harm, I suppose it ssquencht it.—So here comes ppt aden with her little watry postscript; o Rold, dlunken Srut drink pdfrs health ten times in a molning; you are a whetter, fais I sup Mds 15 times evly molning in milk porridge. lele's fol oo now, and lele's fol ee Rettle, & evly kind of sing,[1] and now I must say something else.—You hear Secty St John is made Vicount Bullinbrook; I could hardly persuade him to take that Title, because the eldest Branch of his Family had it in an Earldom, & it was last Year extinct; If he did not take it I advised him to be Ld Pomfret, wch I think is a noble Title; you hear of it often in the *Chronicles* Pomfret Castle: but we believed it was among the Titles of some other Ld. Jack Hill sent his Sister a Pattern of a head-dress from Dunkirk; it was like our Fashion 20 years ago, onely not quite so high, and lookt very ugly. I have made Trap Chapln to Ld Bullinbroke, and he is mighty happy & thankfull for it.—Mr Addison returnd me my visit this morning; He lives in our Town. I shall be mighty retired and mighty busy for a while at Windsor. Pray why dont Md go to Trim, and see Laracor; and give me an Account of the Garden & the River, & the Holly, & the Cherry trees on the River walk.———

19. I could not send this Lettr last Post, being called away before I could fold or finish it. I dined yestrday with Ld Treasr, satt with him till 10 at night, yet could not find a Minute for some Business I had with him. He brought me to Kensington, and Ld Bulingbrook would not let me go away till 2, and I am now in bed very lazy and sleepy at nine. I must shave head & Face, & meet Ld Bullinbrook at 11; and dine again with Ld Tr. To day there will be another Grub; a Letter

---

[1] These lines probably read: O Lord, drunken slut drink poor dear foolish rogue's health ten times in a morning; you are a whetter, faith I sup my dears 15 times every morning in milk porridge; there's for you now, and there's for your letter, and every kind of thing.

from the Pretendr to a Whig Ld. Grubstreet has but ten days to live, then an Act of Parlmt takes place, that ruins it, by taxing every half sheet at a halfpenny: We have news just come, but not the Particulars, that the Earl of Albermarle at the head of 8 thousd Dutch is beaten lost the greatest part of his men, & himself a Prisoner. This perhaps may cool their Courage, & make them think of a Peace. the D. of Ormd has got abundance of Credit by his good Conduct of Affairs in Flanders. We had a good deal of Rain last night, very refreshing—Tis late & I must rise. Don't play at Ombre in your waters Sollah—Farewel deelest Md Md Md Md FW FW Me Me Me lele lele lele—

Address: To Mrs Dingley, att
                her Lodgings over against St
            Marys Church near Capel street
                        Dublin.
        Ireland

SWIFT TO JOHN GAY [1]

Dublin, January 8, 1722–23.

COMING home after a short Christmas ramble, I found a letter upon my table, and little expected when I opened it to read your name at the bottom. The best and greatest part of my life, until these last eight years, I spent in England: there I made my friendships, and there I left my desires. I am condemned for ever to another country; what is in prudence to be done? I think to be *oblitusque meorum, obliviscendus et illis.* What can be the design of your letter but malice, to wake me out of a scurvy sleep, which however is better than none? I am towards nine years old since I left you, yet that is the least of my alterations; my business, my diversions, my conversations, are all entirely changed for the worse, and so are my studies and my amusements in writing. Yet, after all, this humdrum way of life might be passable enough, if you would let me alone. I shall not be able to relish my wine, my parsons, my horses, nor my garden, for three months, until the spirit you have raised shall be dispossessed. I have sometimes wondered that I have not visited you, but I have been stopped by too many reasons, besides years and laziness, and

[1] John Gay, the poet, with whom Swift was on terms of the closest friendship from the time he met him in 1713 until Gay's death in 1732; he was an important member of the Scriblerus Club.

yet these are very good ones. Upon my return after half a year amongst you, there would be to me, *Desiderio nec pudor nec modus*. I was three years reconciling myself to the scene, and the business, to which fortune has condemned me, and stupidity was what I had recourse to. Besides, what a figure should I make in London, while my friends are in poverty, exile, distress, or imprisonment, and my enemies with rods of iron? Yet I often threaten myself with the journey, and am every summer practising to ride and get health to bear it; the only inconvenience is, that I grow old in the experiment.

Although I care not to talk to you as a divine, yet I hope you have not been author of your colic. Do you drink bad wine, or keep bad company? Are you not as many years older as I? It will not be always: *Et tibi quos mihi dempserit apponet annos*. I am heartily sorry you have any dealings with that ugly distemper, and I believe our friend Arbuthnot will recommend you to temperance and exercise. I wish they would have as good an effect upon the giddiness I am subject to, and which this moment I am not free from. I should have been glad if you had lengthened your letter by telling me the present condition of many of my old acquaintance—Congreve, Arbuthnot, Lewis, etc., but you mention only Mr. Pope, who, I believe, is lazy, or else he might have added three lines of his own. I am extremely glad he is not in your case of needing great men's favour, and could heartily wish that you were in his.

I have been considering why poets have such ill success in making their court, since they are allowed to be the greatest and best of all flatterers. The defect is, that they flatter only in print or in writing, but not by word of mouth: they will give things under their hand which they make a conscience of speaking. Besides, they are too libertine to haunt ante-chambers, too poor to bribe porters and footmen, and too proud to cringe to second-hand favourites in a great family. Tell me, are you not under original sin by the dedication of your Eclogues to Lord Bolingbroke? I am an ill judge at this distance; and besides, am, for my case, utterly ignorant of the commonest things that pass in the world; but if all Courts have a sameness in them, as the parsons' phrase is, things may be as they were in my time, when all employments went to Parliament-men's friends, who had been useful in elections, and there was always a huge list of names in arrears at the Treasury, which would take up at least your seven years' expedient to discharge even one half.

I am of opinion, if you will not be offended, that the surest course would be to get your friend who lodges in your house, to recommend you to the next chief governor who comes over here, for a good civil employment, or to be one of his secretaries, which your Parliament-men are fond enough of, when there is no room at home. The wine is good and reasonable; you may dine twice a week at the Deanery House; there is a set of company in this town sufficient for one man; folks will admire you, because they have read you, and read of you; and a good employment will make you live tolerably in London, or sumptuously here; or if you divide between both places, it will be for your health. The Duke of Wharton settled a pension on Dr. Young. Your landlord is much richer. These are my best thoughts after three days' reflections. Mr. Budgell got a very good office here, and lost it by a great want of common politics. If a [Whig] recommendation be hearty, and the governor who comes here be already inclined to favour you, nothing but *fortuna Trojanae* can hinder the success.

If I write to you once a quarter, will you promise to send me an answer in a week, and then I will leave you at rest till the next quarter-day; and I desire you will leave part of a blank side for Mr. Pope. Has he some *quelque chose* of his own upon the anvil? I expect it from him since poor Homer helped to make him rich. Why have not I your works, and with a civil inscription before it, as Mr. Pope ought to have done to his, for so I had from your predecessors of the two last reigns. I hear yours were sent to Ben Tooke, but I never had them. You see I wanted nothing but provocation to send you a long letter, which I am not weary of writing, because I do not hear myself talk, and yet I have the pleasure of talking to you, and if you are not good at reading ill hands, it will cost you as much time as it has done me. I wish I could do more than say I love you. I left you in a good way both for the late Court, and the successors; and by the force of too much honesty or too little sublunary wisdom, you fell between two stools. Take care of your health and money; be less modest and more active; or else turn parson and get a bishopric here. Would to God they would send us as good ones from your side! I am ever, with all friendship and esteem,

Yours.

Mr. Ford presents his service to Mr. Pope and you. We keep him here as long as we can.

SWIFT TO ALEXANDER POPE [1]

September 29, 1725.

SIR,

I CANNOT guess the reason of Mr. Stopford's management, but impute it at a venture to either haste or bashfulness, in the latter of which he is excessive to a fault, although he had already gone the tour of Italy and France to harden himself. Perhaps this second journey, and for a longer time, may amend him. He treated you just as he did Lord Carteret, to whom I recommended him.

My letter you saw to Lord Bolingbroke has shown you the situation I am in, and the company I keep, if I do not forget some of its contents, but I am now returning to the noble scene of Dublin, into the *grand monde,* for fear of burying my parts, to signalise myself among curates and vicars, and correct all corruptions crept in relating to the weight of bread and butter, through those dominions where I govern. I have employed my time, besides ditching, in finishing, correcting, amending, and transcribing my Travels, in four parts complete, newly augmented, and intended for the press, when the world shall deserve them, or rather when a printer shall be found brave enough to venture his ears. I like the scheme of our meeting after distresses and dispersions; but the chief end I propose to myself in all my labours is to vex the world rather than divert it; and if I could compass that design, without hurting my own person or fortune, I would be the most indefatigable writer you have ever seen, without reading. I am exceedingly pleased that you have done with translations. Lord Treasurer Oxford often lamented that a rascally world should lay you under a necessity of misemploying your genius for so long a time. But since you will now be so much better employed, when you think of the world give it one lash the more at my request. I have ever hated all nations, professions, and communities, and all my love is toward individuals: for instance, I hate the tribe of lawyers, but I love Counsellor Such-a-one, and Judge Such-a-one: so with physicians—I will not speak of my own trade—soldiers, English, Scotch, French, and the rest. But principally I hate and detest that animal called

[1] Swift's long and close friendship with Pope dated from 1713 until the date of Swift's incompetence, 1742. Although Pope may have been guilty of some considerable disloyalty to Swift on two occasions in relationship to publication rights, their correspondence continued until 1740. The letter here reprinted has been used by critics to confirm Swift's misanthropy.

man, although I heartily love John, Peter, Thomas, and so forth. This is the system upon which I have governed myself many years, but do not tell, and so I shall go on till I have done with them. I have got materials toward a treatise, proving the falsity of that definition *animal rationale,* and to show it would be only *rationis capax.* Upon this great foundation of misanthropy, though not in Timon's manner, the whole building of my Travels is erected; and I never will have peace of mind till all honest men are of my opinion. By consequence you are to embrace it immediately, and procure that all who deserve my esteem may do so too. The matter is so clear that it will admit of no dispute; nay, I will hold a hundred pounds that you and I agree in the point.

I did not know your Odyssey was finished, being yet in the country, which I shall leave in three days. I shall thank you kindly for the present, but shall like it three-fourths the less, from the mixture you mention of another hand; however, I am glad you saved yourself so much drudgery. I have been long told by Mr. Ford of your great achievements in building and planting, and especially of your subterranean passage to your garden, whereby you turned a blunder into a beauty, which is a piece of *ars poetica.*

I have almost done with harridans, and shall soon become old enough to fall in love with girls of fourteen. The lady whom you describe to live at court, to be deaf, and no party woman, I take to be mythology, but know not how to moralise it. She cannot be Mercy, for Mercy is neither deaf, nor lives at Court. Justice is blind, and perhaps deaf, but neither is she a Court lady. Fortune is both blind and deaf, and a Court lady, but then she is a most damnable party woman, and will never make me easy, as you promise. It must be Riches, which answers all your description. I am glad she visits you, but my voice is so weak that I doubt she will never hear me.

Mr. Lewis sent me an account of Dr. Arbuthnot's illness, which is a very sensible affliction to me, who, by living so long out of the world, have lost that hardness of heart contracted by years and general conversation. I am daily losing friends, and neither seeking nor getting others. Oh! if the world had but a dozen Arbuthnots in it, I would burn my Travels. But, however, he is not without fault. There is a passage in Bede highly commending the piety and learning of the Irish in that age, where, after abundance of praises he overthrows them all, by lamenting that, alas! they kept Easter at a wrong time of the year. So our Doctor has every quality and virtue that can make a man amiable or useful; but, alas! he has a sort of slouch in his walk. I pray God protect him, for he is an excellent Christian, though not a Catholic, and as fit a man either to live or die as ever I knew.

I hear nothing of our friend Gay, but I find the Court keeps him at hard meat. I advised him to come over here with a Lord Lieutenant. Mr. Tickell is in a very good office. I have not seen Philips, though formerly we were so intimate. He has got nothing and by what I find will get nothing, though he writes little flams, as Lord Leicester called those sorts of verses, on Miss Carteret. It is remarkable, and deserves recording that a Dublin blacksmith, a great poet, has imitated his manner in a poem to the same Miss. Philips is a complainer, and on this occasion I told Lord Carteret that complainers never succeed at Court, though railers do.

Are you altogether a country gentleman, that I must address to you out of London, to the hazard of your losing this precious letter, which I will now conclude, although so much paper is left. I have an ill name, and therefore shall not subscribe it, but you will guess it comes from one who esteems and loves you about half as much as you deserve, I mean as much as he can.

I am in great concern, at what I am just told is in some of the newspapers, that Lord Bolingbroke is much hurt by a fall in hunting. I am glad he has so much youth and vigour left, of which he has not been thrifty, but I wonder he has no more discretion.

SWIFT'S POEMS.

A DESCRIPTION OF THE MORNING.[1]

1709

Now hardly here and there an hackney-coach
Appearing, show'd the ruddy morn's approach.
Now Betty from her master's bed had flown,
And softly stole to discompose her own.
The slipshod prentice from his master's door,
Had par'd the dirt, and sprinkled round the floor.
Now Moll had whirl'd her mop with dext'rous airs,
Prepar'd to scrub the entry and the stairs.

The youth with broomy stumps began to trace
The kennel-edge, where wheels had worn the place.
The small-coal man was heard with cadence deep,
'Till drown'd in shriller notes of chimney-sweep,
Duns at his lordship's gate began to meet,
And brickdust Moll had scream'd through half the street.
The turnkey now his flock returning sees,
Duly let out a-nights to steal for fees:
The watchful bailiffs take their silent stands;
And school-boys lag with satchels in their hands.

A DESCRIPTION OF A CITY SHOWER.[2]

[In Imitation of Virgil's Georgics]

1710

Careful observers may foretell the hour
(By sure prognostics) when to dread a show'r:
While rain depends, the pensive cat gives o'er
Her frolics, and pursues her tail no more.
Returning home at night, you'll find the sink
Strike your offended sense with double stink.
If you be wise, then go not far to dine,

[1] Swift emerges here as a parodist of romantic descriptions of the morning by his combination of a magniloquent tone and homely detail; it stands as one of the most skilful of his early verses.

[2] A companion piece to "A Description of the Morning," the "City Shower" continues to parody clichés of romanticism in the form of a burlesque of Virgil's Eclogues. The last three lines, a triplet of alexandrines, burlesque the manner of Modern heroic poets, possibly of Dryden.

You'll spend in coach-hire more than save in wine.
A coming show'r your shooting corns presage,
Old aches throb, your hollow tooth will rage.
Sauntring in coffee-house is Dulman seen;
He damns the climate, and complains of spleen.

Meanwhile the South rising with dabbled wings,
A sable cloud a-thwart the welkin flings,
That swill'd more liquor than it could contain,
And like a drunkard gives it up again.
Brisk Susan whips her linen from the rope,
While the first drizzling show'r is borne aslope,
Such is that sprinkling which some careless quean
Flirts on you from her mop, but not so clean.
You fly, invoke the gods; then turning, stop
To rail; she singing, still whirls on her mop.
Not yet, the dust had shunn'd th' unequal strife,
But aided by the wind, fought still for life;
And wafted with its foe by violent gust,
'Twas doubtful which was rain, and which was dust.
Ah! where must needy poet seek for aid,
When dust and rain at once his coat invade;
His only coat! where dust confus'd with rain,
Roughen the nap, and leave a mingled stain.

Now in contiguous drops the flood comes down,
Threat'ning with deluge this *devoted* town.
To shops in crowds the daggled females fly,
Pretend to cheapen goods, but nothing buy.
The Templar spruce, while ev'ry spout's a-broach,
Stays till 'tis fair, yet seems to call a coach.
The tuck'd-up sempstress walks with hasty strides,
While streams run down her oil'd umbrella's sides.
Here various kinds by various fortunes led,
Commence acquaintance underneath a shed.
Triumphant Tories, and desponding Whigs,
Forget their feuds, and join to save their wigs.
Box'd in a chair the beau impatient sits,
While spouts run clatt'ring o'er the roof by fits;
And ever and anon with frightful din
The leather sounds, he trembles from within.
So when Troy chair-men bore the wooden steed,
Pregnant with Greeks impatient to be freed,
(Those bully Greeks, who, as the moderns do,

Instead of paying chair-men, run them thro.)
Laocoon struck the outside with his spear,
And each imprison'd hero quaked for fear.

Now from all parts the swelling kennels flow,
And bear their trophies with them as they go:
Filth of all hues and odours seem to tell
What street they sail'd from, by their sight and smell.
They, as each torrent drives, with rapid force
From Smithfield, or St. Pulchre's shape their course,
And in huge confluent join at Snow-hill ridge,
Fall from the conduit prone to Holborn-bridge.
Sweepings from butchers' stalls, dung, guts, and blood,
Drown'd puppies, stinking sprats, all drench'd in mud,
Dead cats and turnip-tops come tumbling down the flood.

VERSES ON THE DEATH OF DR. SWIFT, D.S.P.D.[1]

Occasioned by reading a Maxim in Rochefoucault

*Dans l'adversité de nos meilleurs amis nous trouvons quelque
chose, qui ne nous deplaist pas.*
In the adversity of our best friends, we find something that
doth not displease us.

Written by Himself, November 1731

As Rochefoucault his maxims drew
From nature, I believe 'em true:
They argue no corrupted mind
In him; the fault is in mankind.

This maxim more than all the rest
Is thought too base for human breast;
"In all distresses of our friends
We first consult our private ends,
While nature kindly bent to ease us,
Points out some circumstance to please us."

If this perhaps your patience move
Let reason and experience prove.

We all behold with envious eyes,
Our *equal* rais'd above our *size;*

[1] This poem, among the last of Swift's works, indicates Swift's complete
control of *vers de société;* his concluding estimation of himself is perhaps
more just than that which posterity has been willing to accord him.
The notes to the poem are Swift's own, and come from various editions
published in Swift's lifetime.

Who wou'd not at a crowded show
Stand high himself, keep others low?
I love my friend as well as you,
But would not have him stop my view;
Then let me have the higher post;
I ask but for an inch at most.

If in a battle you should find,
One, whom you love of all mankind,
Had some heroic action done,
A champion kill'd or trophy won;
Rather than thus be over-topt,
Would you not wish his laurels cropt?

Dear honest Ned is in the gout,
Lies rackt with pain, and you without:
How patiently you hear him groan!
How glad the case is not your own!

What poet would not grieve to see,
His brethren write as well as he?
But rather than they should excel,
He'd wish his rivals all in hell.

Her end when emulation misses,
She turns to envy, stings and hisses:
The strongest friendship yields to pride,
Unless the odds be on our side.

Vain human kind! Fantastic race!
Thy various follies, who can trace?
Self-love, ambition, envy, pride,
Their empire in our hearts divide:
Give others riches, power, and station,
'Tis all on me an usurpation.
I have no title to aspire;
Yet, when you sink, I seem the higher.
In Pope, I cannot read a line,
But with a sigh, I wish it mine:
When he can in one couplet fix
More sense than I can do in six:
It gives me such a jealous fit,
I cry, pox take him, and his wit.

Why must I be outdone by Gay,
In my own hum'rous biting way?

Arbuthnot is no more my friend,
Who dares to irony pretend;
Which I was born to introduce,
Refin'd it first, and shew'd its use.

St. John, as well as Pultney knows,
That I had some repute for prose;
And till they drove me out of date,
Could maul a minister of state:
If they have mortify'd my pride,
And made me throw my pen aside;
If with such talents heav'n hath blest 'em
Have I not reason to destest 'em?

To all my foes, dear fortune, send
Thy gifts, but never to my friend:
I tamely can endure the first,
But, this with envy makes me burst.

Thus much may serve by way of proem,
Proceed we therefore to our poem.

The time is not remote, when I
Must by the course of nature die:
When I foresee my special friends,
Will try to find their private ends:
Tho' it is hardly understood,
Which way my death can do them good,
Yet, thus methinks, I hear 'em speak;
"See, how the Dean begins to break:
Poor gentleman, he droops apace,
You plainly find it in his face:
That old vertigo in his head,
Will never leave him, till he's dead:
Besides, his memory decays,
He recollects not what he says;
He cannot call his friends to mind;
Forgets the place where last he din'd:
Plyes you with stories o'er and o'er,
He told them fifty times before.
How does he fancy we can sit,
To hear his out-of-fashion'd wit?
But he takes up with younger fokes,
Who for his wine will bear his jokes:

Faith, he must make his stories shorter,
Or change his comrades once a quarter:
In half the time, he talks them round;
There must another set be found.

"For poetry, he's past his prime,
He takes an hour to find a rhime:
His fire is out, his wit decay'd,
His fancy sunk, his muse a jade.
I'd have him throw away his pen;
But there's no talking to some men."

And, then their tenderness appears
By adding largely to my years:
"He's older than he would be reckon'd
And well remembers Charles the Second.

"He hardly drinks a pint of wine;
And that, I doubt, is no good sign.
His stomach too begins to fail:
Last year we thought him strong and hale;
But now, he's quite another thing;
I wish he may hold out till spring."

Then hug themselves, and reason thus;
"It is not yet so bad with us."

In such a case they talk in tropes,
And, by their fears express their hopes,
Some great misfortune to portend,
No enemy can match a friend.
With all the kindness they profess,
The merit of a lucky guess
(When daily howd'y's come of course,
And servants answer; worse and worse)
Wou'd please 'em better than to tell,
That, God prais'd, the Dean is well.
Then he who prophecy'd the best,
Approves his foresight to the rest:
"You know, I always fear'd the worst,
And often told you so at first":
He'd rather chuse, that I should die,
Than his prediction prove a lie.
Not one foretells I shall recover;
But, all agree, to give me over.

Yet shou'd some neighbour feel a pain,
Just in the parts, where I complain;
How many a message would he send?
What hearty prayers that I should mend?
Enquire what regimen I kept;
What gave me ease, and how I slept?
And more lament, when I was dead,
Than all the sniv'llers round my bed.

My good companions, never fear,
For though you may a mistake a year;
Though your prognostics run too fast,
They must be verify'd at last.

Behold the fatal day arrive!
"How is the Dean? He's just alive.
Now the departing prayer is read:
He hardly breathes. The Dean is dead."
Before the passing-bell begun,
The news thro' half the town has run.
"O, may we all for death prepare!
What has he left? And who's his heir?
I know no more than what the news is,
'Tis all bequeath'd to public uses.
To public use! A perfect whim!
What had the public done for him!
Mere envy, avarice, and pride!
He gave it all:—But first he dy'd.
And had the Dean, in all the nation,
No worthy friend, no poor relation?
So ready to do strangers good,
Forgetting his own flesh and blood?"

Now Grub-street wits are all employ'd,
With elegies, the town is cloy'd:
Some paragraph in ev'ry paper,
To curse the Dean or bless the Drapier.[1]

The doctors tender of their fame,
Wisely on me lay all the blame:
"We must confess his case was nice:

[1] The author supposes that the scriblers of the prevailing party, which he always opposed, will libel him after his death; but that others who remember the service he had done to Ireland, under the name of M. B. Drapier, by utterly defeating the destructive project of Wood's half-pence, in five Letters to the People of Ireland, at the time read universally, and convincing every reader, will remember him with gratitude.

But he would never take advice:
Had he been rul'd, for ought appears,
He might have liv'd these twenty years:
For when we open'd him we found,
That all his vital parts were sound."

From Dublin soon to London spread,
'Tis told at Court, the Dean is dead.[2]
Kind Lady Suffolk [3] in the spleen,
Runs laughing up to tell the Queen,
The Queen so gracious, mild, and good,
Cries, "Is he gone? 'Tis time he shou'd.
He's dead you say; Why, let him rot;
I'm glad the medals were forgot.[4]
I promis'd him, I own, but when?
I only was a Princess then;
But now as consort of a king
You know 'tis quite a different thing."

Now, Chartres [5] at Sir Robert's levee,
Tells, with a sneer, the tidings heavy:
"Why, is he dead without his shoes?
(Cries Bob [6]) "I'm sorry for the news;

[2] The Dean supposeth himself to dye in Ireland.

[3] Mrs. Howard, afterwards Countess of Suffolk, then of the Bedchamber to the Queen, professed much favour for the Dean. The Queen then Princess, sent a dozen times to the Dean (then in London) with her command to attend her; which at last he did, by advice of all his friends. She often sent for him afterwards, and always treated him very graciously. He taxed her with a present worth ten pounds, which she promised before he should return to Ireland, but on his taking leave, the medals were not ready.

[4] The medals were to be sent to the Dean in four months, but she forgot, or thought them too dear. The Dean being in Ireland sent Mrs. Howard a piece of plaid made in that kingdom, which the Queen seeing took it from her and wore it herself, and sent to the Dean for as much as would clothe herself and children—desiring he would send the charge of it. He did the former; it cost 35l. but he said he would have nothing except the medals: he went next summer to England and was treated as usual, and she being then Queen, the Dean was promised a settlement in England but return'd as he went, and instead of receiving of her intended favours or the medals hath been ever since under her Majesty's displeasure.

[5] Chartres is a most infamous, vile scoundrel, grown from a foot-boy, or worse, to a prodigious fortune both in England and Scotland: he had a way of insinuating himself into all Ministers under every change, either as pimp, flatterer, or informer. He was tried at seventy for a rape, and came off by sacrificing a great part of his fortune (he is since dead, but this poem still preserves the scene and time it was writ in.)

[6] Sir Robert Walpole, Chief Minister of State, treated the Dean in 1726, with great distinction, invited him to dinner at Chelsea, with the Dean's friends chosen on purpose; appointed an hour to talk with him of Ireland, to which kingdom and people the Dean found him no great friend; for he defended Wood's project of half-pence, &c. The Dean would see him no more; and upon his next year's return to England, Sir Robert on an accidental meeting, only made a civil compliment, and never invited him again.

Oh, were the wretch but living still,
And, in his place my good friend Will; [7]
Or, had a mitre on his head
Provided Bolingbroke [8] were dead."

Now, Curl [9] his shop from rubbish drains;
Three genuine tomes of *Swift's Remains*.
And then, to make them pass the glibber,
Revis'd by Tibbalds, Moore, and Cibber.[10]
He'll treat me as he does my betters.
Publish my will, my life, my letters.[11]
Revive the libels born to die;
Which Pope must bear, as well as I.

Here shift the scene, to represent
How those I love, my death lament.
Poor Pope will grieve a month; and Gay
A week; and Arbuthnot a day.

St. John himself will scarce forbear,
To bite his pen, and drop a tear.
The rest will give a shrug, and cry,
I'm sorry; but we all must die.
Indifference clad in wisdom's guise,
All fortitude of mind supplies:
For how can stony bowels melt,
In those who never pity felt;

[7] Mr. William Pultney, from being Mr. Walpole's intimate friend, detesting his administration, became his mortal enemy, and joyned with my Lord Bolingbroke, to expose him in an excellent paper, called the *Craftsman*, which is still continued.

[8] Henry St. John, Lord Viscount Bolingbroke, Secretary of State to Queen Anne of blessed memory. He is reckoned the most universal genius in Europe; Walpole dreading his abilities, treated him most injuriously, working with King George who forgot his promise of restoring the said lord, upon the restless importunity of Sir Robert Walpole.

[9] Curl hath been the most infamous bookseller of any age or country; his character in part may be found in Mr. Pope's *Dunciad*. He published three volumes all charged on the Dean, who never writ three pages of them; he hath used many of the Dean's friends in almost as vile a manner.

[10] Three stupid verse writers in London, the last to the shame of the Court, and the highest disgrace to wit and learning, was made Laureat. Moore, commonly called Jemmy Moore, son of Arthur Moore, whose father was jaylor of Monaghan in Ireland. See the character of Jemmy Moore, and Tibbalds, Theobald in the *Dunciad*.

[11] Curl is notoriously infamous for publishing the Lives, Letters, and last Wills and Testaments of the nobility and Ministers of State, as well as of all the rogues, who are hanged at Tyburn. He hath been in custody of the House of Lords for publishing or forging the letters of many peers; which made the Lords enter a resolution in their Journal Book, that no life or writings of any lord should be published without the consent of the next heir at law, or licence from their House.

When *We* are lash'd, *They* kiss the rod;
Resigning to the will of God.

    The fools, my juniors by a year,
Are tortur'd with suspence and fear.
Who wisely thought my age a screen,
When death approach'd, to stand between:
The screen remov'd, their hearts are trembling,
They mourn for me without dissembling.

    My female friends, whose tender hearts,
Have better learn'd to act their parts,
Receive the news in doleful dumps,
"The Dean is dead, (and what is trumps?)
Then Lord have mercy on his soul.
(Ladies I'll venture for the vole.)
Six deans they say must bear the pall.
(I wish I knew what king to call.)
Madam, your husband will attend
The funeral of so good a friend.
No madam, 'tis a shocking sight,
And he's engag'd to-morrow night!
My Lady Club wou'd take it ill,
If he shou'd fail her at quadrill.
He lov'd the Dean. (I led a heart.)
But dearest friends, they say, must part.
His time was come, he ran his race;
We hope he's in a better place."

    Why do we grieve that friends should die?
No loss more easy to supply.
One year is past; a different scene;
No further mention of the Dean;
Who now, alas, no more is missed,
Than if he never did exist.
Where's now this fav'rite of Apollo?
Departed; and his words must follow:
Must undergo the common fate;
His kind of wit is out of date.
Some country Squire to Lintot [12] goes,
Enquires for SWIFT in Verse and Prose:
Says Lintot, "I have heard the name:
He dy'd a year ago." The same.

[12] Bernard Lintot, a bookseller in London, *Vide* Mr. Pope's *Dunciad.*

He searches all his shop in vain;
"Sir you may find them in Duck-Lane: [13]
I sent them with a load of books,
Last Monday, to the pastry-cooks.
To fancy they cou'd live a year!
I find you're but a stranger here.
The Dean was famous in his time;
And had a kind of knack at rhyme:
His way of writing now is past;
The town hath got a better taste:
I keep no antiquated stuff;
But, spick and span I have enough.
Pray, do but give me leave to shew'em,
Here's Colley Cibber's Birth-day poem.
This ode you never yet have seen,
By Stephen Duck, upon the Queen.
Then, here's a Letter finely penn'd
Against the Craftsman and his friend;
It clearly shews that all reflection
On ministers, is disaffection.
Next, here's Sir Robert's *Vindication*,[14]
And Mr. Henly's last Oration: [15]
The hawkers have not got 'em yet,
Your Honour please to buy a set?

"Here's Woolston's [16] tracts, the twelfth edition;
'Tis read by ev'ry politician:
The country members, when in town,
To all their boroughs send them down:
You never met a thing so smart;
The courtiers have them all by heart:
Those Maids of Honour (who can read)
Are taught to use them for their creed.
The rev'rend author's good intention,
Hath been rewarded with a pension:

[13] A place where old books are sold in London.
[14] Walpole hath a set of party scriblers, who do nothing else but write in his defence.
[15] Henly is a clergyman who wanting both merit and luck to get preferment, or even to keep his curacy in the Established Church, formed a new conventicle, which he calls an Oratory. There, at set times, he delivereth strange speeches compiled by himself and his associates, who share the profit with him: every hearer pays a shilling each day for admittance. He is an absolute dunce, but generally reputed crazy.
[16] Woolston was a clergyman, but for want of bread, hath in several treatises, in the most blasphemous manner, attempted to turn Our Saviour and his miracles into ridicule. He is much caressed by many great courtiers, and by all the infidels, and his books read generally by the Court Ladies.

He doth an honour to his gown,
By bravely running priest-craft down:
He shews as sure as God's in *Gloc'ster*,
That Jesus was a grand impostor:
That all his miracles were cheats,
Perform'd as jugglers do their feats:
The Church had never such a writer:
A shame, he hath not got a mitre!"

Suppose me dead; and then suppose
A club assembled at the Rose;
Where from discourse of this and that,
I grow the subject of their chat:
And, while they toss my name about,
With favour some, and some without;
One quite indiff'rent in the cause,
My character impartial draws.

"The Dean, if we believe report,
Was never ill receiv'd at Court.
As for his Works in Verse and Prose,
I own my self no judge of those:
Nor, can I tell what critics thought 'em;
But, this I know, all people bought 'em;
As with a moral view design'd
To cure the vices of mankind;
His vein, ironically grave,
Expos'd the fool, and lash'd the knave:
To steal a hint was never known,
But what he writ, was all his own.

"He never thought an honour done him,
Because a duke was proud to own him:
Would rather slip aside, and chuse
To talk with wits in dirty shoes:
Despis'd the fools with Stars and Garters,
So often seen caressing Chartres: [17]
He never courted men in station,
Nor persons had in admiration;
Of no man's greatness was afraid,
Because he sought for no man's aid.
Though trusted long in great affairs,
He gave himself no haughty airs:

[17] See the notes before on Chartres.

Without regarding private ends,
Spent all his credit for his friends:
And only choose the wise and good;
No flatt'rers; no allies in blood;
But succour'd virtue in distress,
And seldom fail'd of good success;
As numbers in their hearts must own,
Who, but for him, had been unknown.

"With princes kept a due decorum,
But never stood in awe before 'em:
He follow'd David's lesson just,
In Princes never put thy Trust.
And, would you make him truly sour;
Provoke him with a slave in power:
The Irish Senate, if you nam'd,
With what impatience he declaim'd!
Fair LIBERTY was all his cry;
For her he stood prepar'd to die;
For her he boldly stood alone;
For her he oft expos'd his own.
Two kingdoms, just as faction led,
Had set a price upon his head; [18]
But, not a traitor cou'd be found.
To sell him for six hundred pound.

"Had he but spar'd his tongue and pen,
He might have rose like other men:
But, power was never in his thought;
And, wealth he valu'd not a groat:
Ingratitude he often found,
And pity'd those who meant the wound:
But, kept the tenor of his mind,
To merit well of human kind:
Nor made a sacrifice of those
Who still were true, to please his foes.
He labour'd many a fruitless hour

[18] In the Year 1713, the late Queen was prevailed with by an Address of the House of Lords in England, to publish a Proclamation, promising three hundred pounds to whatever person would discover the author of a pamphlet called *The Publick Spirit of the Whiggs;* and in Ireland, in the year 1724, my Lord Carteret at his first coming into the Government, was prevailed on to issue a Proclamation for promising the like reward of three hundred pounds, to any person who could discover the author of a pamphlet called, *The Drapier's Fourth Letter,* &c. writ against that destructive project of coining half-pence for Ireland; but in neither kingdoms was the Dean discovered.

To reconcile his friends in power; [19]
Saw mischief by a faction brewing,
While they pursu'd each others ruin.
But, finding vain was all his care,
He left the court in mere despair.

"And, oh! how short are human schemes!
Here ended all our golden dreams.
What St. John's skill in state affairs,
What Ormond's valour, Oxford's cares,
To save their sinking country lent,
Was all destroy'd by one event.
Too soon that precious life was ended,[20]
On which alone, our weal depended.

"When up a dangerous faction starts,[21]
With wrath and vengeance in their hearts;
By solemn League and Cov'nant bound,
To ruin, slaughter, and confound;
To turn religion to a fable,
And make the Government a Babel:
Pervert the law, disgrace the gown,
Corrupt the senate, rob the crown;
To sacrifice old England's glory,
And make her infamous in story.
When such a tempest shook the land,
How could unguarded virtue stand?

"With horror, grief, despair the Dean
Beheld the dire destructive scene:
His friends in exile, or the Tower,

[19] Queen Anne's Ministry fell to variance from the first year after their Ministry began: Harcourt the Chancellor, and Lord Bolingbroke the Secretary, were discontented with the Treasurer Oxford, for his too much mildness to the Whig Party; this quarrel grew higher every day till the Queen's death: the Dean, who was the only person that endeavoured to reconcile them, found it impossible; and thereupon retired to the country about ten weeks before that fatal event: upon which he returned to his Deanry in Dublin, where for many years he was worryed by the new people in power, and had hundreds of libels writ against him in England.

[20] In the height of the quarrel between the Ministers, the Queen died.

[21] Upon Queen Anne's death the Whig faction was restored to power, which they exercised with the utmost rage and revenge; impeached and banished the chief leaders of the Church party, and stripped all their adherents of what employments they had, after which England was never known to make so mean a figure in Europe: the greatest preferments in the Church in both kingdoms were given to the most ignorant men. Fanatics were publicly caressed; Ireland utterly ruined and enslaved; only great Ministers heaping up millions; and so affairs continued to this 3rd. of May 1732, and are likely to remain so.

Himself within the frown of power; [22]
Pursu'd by base envenom'd pens,
Far to the land of slaves and fens; [23]
A servile race in folly nurs'd,
Who truckle most, when treated worst.

"By innocence and resolution,
He bore continual persecution;
While numbers to preferment rose;
Whose merits were, to be his foes.
When, ev'n his own familiar friends
Intent upon their private ends;
Like renegadoes now he feels,
Against him lifting up their heels.

"The Dean did by his pen defeat
An infamous destructive cheat. [24]
Taught fools their int'rest how to know;
And gave them arms to ward the blow.
Envy hath own'd it was his doing,
To save that helpless land from ruin;
While they who at the steerage stood,
And reapt the profit, sought his blood.

"To save them from their evil fate,
In him was held a crime of state.
A wicked monster on the bench, [25]
Whose fury blood could never quench;
As vile and profligate a villain,
As modern Scroggs, or old Tressilian; [26]

[22] Upon the Queen's death, the Dean returned to live in Dublin, at his Deanry-house: numberless libels were writ against him in England, as a Jacobite; he was insulted in the street, and at nights he was forced to be attended by his servants armed.

[23] The Land of slaves and fens, is Ireland.

[24] One Wood, a hardware-man from England, had a patent for coining copper half-pence in Ireland, to the sum of £108,000 which in the consequence, must leave that kingdom without gold or silver (See *Drapier's Letters.*)

[25] One Whitshed was then Chief Justice: he had some years before prosecuted a printer for a pamphlet writ by the Dean, to perswade the people of Ireland to wear their own manufactures. Whitshed sent the jury down elevent times, and kept them nine hours until they were forced to bring in a special verdict. He sat as judge afterwards on the tryal of the printer of the *Drapier's Fourth Letter;* but the jury, against all he could say or swear, threw out the bill: all the kingdom took the Drapier's part, except the courtiers, or those who expected places. The Drapier was celebrated in many poems and pamphlets: his sign was set up in most streets in Dublin (where many of them still continue) and in several country towns.

[26] Scroggs was Chief Justice under King Charles the Second: his judgment always varied in state tryals, according to directions from Court. Tressilian was a wicked judge, hanged above three hundred years ago.

Who long all justice had discarded,
Nor fear'd he God, nor man regarded;
Vow'd on the Dean his rage to vent,
And make him of his zeal repent;
But Heav'n his innocence defends,
The grateful people stand his friends:
Nor strains of law, nor judges frown,
Nor topics brought to please the crown,
Nor witness hir'd, nor jury pick'd,
Prevail to bring him in convict.

"In exile [27] with a steady heart,
He spent his life's declining part;
Where folly, pride, and faction sway,
Remote from St. John,[28] Pope, and Gay.

"His friendship there to few confin'd,[29]
Were always of the midling kind:
No fools of rank, a mungril breed,
Who fain would pass for Lords indeed;
Where titles give no right or power,
And peerage is a wither'd flower,[30]
He would have held it a disgrace,
If such a wretch had known his face.
On rural squires, that kingdom's bane,
He vented oft his wrath in vain:
Biennial squires, to market brought; [31]
Who sell their souls and votes for naught;
The nation stripp'd go joyful back,
To rob the Church, their tenants rack,
Go snacks with rogues and rapparees [32]
And, keep the peace, to pick up fees:

[27] In Ireland, which he had reason to call a place of exile; to which country nothing could have driven him, but the Queen's death, who had determined to fix him in England, in Spight of the Dutchess of Somerset, &c.
[28] Henry St. John, Lord Viscount Bolingbroke, mentioned before.
[29] In Ireland the Dean was not acquainted with one single Lord Spiritual or Temporal. He only conversed with private gentlemen of the clergy or laity, and but a small number of either.
[30] The peers of Ireland lost their jurisdiction by one single Act, and tamely submitted to the infamous mark of slavery without the least resentment or remonstrance.
[31] The Parliament, as they call it, in Ireland meet but once in two years, and after having given five times more than they can afford return home to reimburse themselves by all country jobs and oppressions of which some few only are mentioned.
[32] The highwaymen in Ireland, are, since the late wars there, usually called Rapparees, which was a name given to those Irish soldiers who in small parties used at that time to plunder Protestants.

In every job to have a share,
A jail or barrack to repair; [33]
And turn the tax for public roads
Commodious to their own abodes.

"Perhaps I may allow, the Dean
Had too much satire in his vein;
And seem'd determin'd not to starve it,
Because no age could more deserve it.
Yet, malice never was his aim;
He lash'd the vice, but spar'd the name.
No individual could resent,
Where thousands equally were meant.
His satire points at no defect,
But what all mortals may correct:
For he abhorr'd that senseless tribe,
Who call it humour when they jibe:
He spar'd a hump, or crooked nose,
Whose owners set not up for beaux.
True genuine dullness mov'd his pity,
Unless it offer'd to be witty.
Those, who their ignorance confess'd,
He ne'er offended with a jest;
But laugh'd to hear an idiot quote,
A verse from Horace, learn'd by rote.

"He knew an hundred pleasant stories,
With all the turns of Whigs and Tories:
Was cheerful to his dying day,
And friends would let him have his way.

"He gave the little wealth he had,
To build a house for fools and mad:
And shew'd by one satiric touch,
No nation wanted it so much:
That kingdom [34] he hath left his debtor,
I wish it soon may have a better."

[33] The army in Ireland are lodged in barracks, the building and repairing whereof and other charges have cost a prodigious sum to that unhappy kingdom.
[34] Meaning Ireland, where he now lives, and probably may dye.

ON POETRY: A RHAPSODY.[1]

All human race would fain be Wits
And millions miss, for one that hits.
Young's universal Passion, Pride,
Was never known to spread so wide.
Say, Britain, could you ever boast,
Three Poets in an age at most?
Our chilling climate hardly bears
A sprig of Bays in fifty years:
While every fool his claim alleges,
As if it grew in common hedges.
What reason can there be assigned
For this perverseness in the mind?
Brutes find out where their talents lie:
A bear will not attempt to fly;
A foundered horse will oft debate,
Before he tries a five-barred gate;
A dog by instinct turns aside,
Who sees the ditch too deep and wide.
But man we find the only creature,
Who, led by folly, fights with Nature;
Who, when she loudly cries, Forbear,
With obstinacy fixes there;
And where his Genius least inclines,
Absurdly bends his whole designs.

Not Empire to the rising sun,
By valour, conduct, fortune won;
Nor highest wisdom in debates
For framing laws to govern states;
Nor skill in sciences profound,
So large to grasp the circle round;
Such heavenly influence require,
As how to strike the Muses' lyre.

Not beggar's brat, on bulk begot;
Nor bastard of a pedlar Scot;
Nor boy brought up to cleaning shoes,
The spawn of Bridewell, or the stews;

1 Published on Dec. 31, 1733. "On Poetry: a Rhapsody," one of Swift's
best and longest poems, constitutes his *Essay on Criticism* and his *Dunciad*.
The similarity of several of its themes—literary, political, and scientific—to
those of *Gulliver* and the *Tale* indicates how much of a piece Swift's
thinking was throughout his lifetime.

Nor infants dropped, the spurious pledges
Of Gypsies littering under hedges,
Are so disqualified by Fate
To rise in Church, or Law, or State,
As he, whom Phoebus in his ire
Hath blasted with poetic fire.

What hope of custom in the fair,
While not a soul demands your ware?
Where you have nothing to produce
For private life, or public use?
Court, city, country want you not;
You cannot bribe, betray, or plot.
For poets, law makes no provision:
The wealthy have you in derision.
Of state affairs you cannot smatter,
Are awkward when you try to flatter.
Your portion, taking Britain round,
Was just one annual hundred pound.*
Now not so much as in remainder
Since Cibber [1] brought in an attainder;
For ever fixt by right divine,
(A monarch's right) on Grubstreet line.
Poor starveling bard, how small thy gains:
How unproportioned to thy pains:

And here a simile comes pat in:
Though chickens take a month to fatten,
The guests in less than half an hour
Will more than half a score devour.
So, after toiling twenty days,
To earn a stock of pence and praise,
Thy labours, grown the critic's prey,
Are swallowed o'er a dish of tea;
Gone, to be never heard of more,
Gone, where the chickens went before.

How shall a new attempter learn
Of different spirits to discern,
And how distinguish, which is which,

* Paid to the Poet Laureate, which place was given to one *Cibber*,
a Player.
[1] Colley Cibber, appointed Poet Laureate in 1750, was also one of Pope's
targets in the *Dunciad*.

The Poet's vein, or scribbling itch?
Then hear an old experienced sinner
Instructing thus a young beginner.

Consult yourself, and if you find
A powerful impulse urge your mind,
Impartial judge within your breast
What subject you can manage best;
Whether your genius most inclines
To satire, praise, or hum'rous lines;
To elegies in mournful tone,
Or prologue sent from hand unknown.
Then rising with Aurora's light,
The Muse invoked, sit down to write;
Blot out, correct, insert, refine,
Enlarge, diminish, interline;
Be mindful, when invention fails,
To scratch your head, and bite your nails.

Your poem finished, next your care
Is needful, to transcribe it fair.
In Modern Wit all printed trash is
Set off with numerous breaks—and dashes—

To statesmen would you give a wipe,
You print it in italic type.
When letters are in vulgar shapes,
'tis ten to one the Wit escapes;
But when in capitals expresst,
The dullest reader smokes the jest:
Or else perhaps he may invent
A better than the poet meant,
As learned commentators view
In Homer more than Homer knew.

Your poem in its modish dress,
Correctly fitted for the press,
Convey by penny-post to Lintot,[1]
But let no friend alive look into't.
If Lintot thinks 'twill quit the cost,
You need not fear your labour lost:
And, how agreeably surprised
Are you to see it advertised:

[1] Bernard Lintot, the publisher, was also satirized in Pope's *Dunciad*.

The hawker shows you one in print,
As fresh as farthings from the mint:
The product of your toil and sweating;
A bastard of your own begetting.

Be sure at Will's [1] the following day,
Lie snug, and hear what critics say.
And if you find the general vogue
Pronounces you a stupid rogue;
Damns àll your thoughts as low and little,
Sit still, and swallow down your spittle.
Be silent as a politician,
For talking may beget suspicion:
Or praise the judgment of the town,
And help yourself to run it down.
Give up your fond paternal pride,
Nor argue on the weaker side;
For poems read without a name
We justly praise, or justly blame;
And critics have no partial views,
Except they know whom they abuse.
And since you ne'er provoked their spite,
Depend upon't their judgment's right;
But if you blab, you are undone;
Consider what a risk you run.
You lose your credit all at once;
The town will mark you for a dunce:
The vilest doggerel Grubstreet sends,
Will pass for yours with foes and friends.
And you must bear the whole disgrace,
'Till some fresh blockhead takes your place.

Your secret kept, your poem sunk,
And sent in quires to line a trunk,
If still you be disposed to rhyme,
Go try your hand a second time.
Again you fail, yet safe's the word,
Take courage, and attempt a third.
But first with care employ your thoughts,
Where critics marked your former faults.
The trivial turns, the borrowed wit,
The similes that nothing fit;

[1] Will's Coffee House, a center for the wits of the period, which Swift,
in the *Tale*, satirizes as the Society of the Grub Street hacks.

The cant which every fool repeats,
Town-jests, and coffee-house conceits;
Descriptions tedious, flat and dry,
And introduced the Lord knows why;
Or where we find your fury set
Against the harmless alphabet;
On A's and B's your malice vent,
While readers wonder whom you meant.
A public, or a private robber;
A statesman, or a South-Sea jobber.
A prelate who no God believes;
A —, or den of thieves.
A pick-purse at the bar, or bench;
A duchess, or a suburb-wench.
Or oft when epithets you link,
In gaping lines to fill a chink,
Like stepping stones to save a stride,
In streets where kennels are too wide;
Or like a heel-piece to support
A cripple with one foot too short;
Or like a bridge that joins a marish
To moorlands of a different parish.
So have I seen ill-coupled hounds,
Drag different ways in miry grounds.
So geographers in Afric-maps
With savage pictures fill their gaps,
And o'er uninhabitable downs
Place elephants for want of towns.

But though you miss your third essay,
You need not throw your pen away.
Lay now aside all thoughts of fame,
To spring more profitable game.
From party-merit seek support;
The vilest verse thrives best at court.
A pamphlet in Sir Rob's defence
Will never fail to bring in pence;
Nor be concerned about the sale,
He pays his workmen on the nail.

A Prince the moment his is crowned,
Inherits every virtue round,
As emblems of the sovereign power,
Like other baubles of the Tower,

Is generous, valiant, just and wise,
And so continues 'till he dies.
His humble Senate this professes,
In all their speeches, votes, addresses.
But once you fix him in a tomb,
His virtues fade, his vices bloom;
And each perfection wrong imputed
Is folly, at his death confuted.
The loads of poems in his praise,
Ascending make one funeral-blaze.
As soon as you can hear his knell,
This God on earth turns Devil in hell.
And lo, his ministers of state,
Transformed to imps, his levee wait.
Where, in this scene of endless woe,
They ply their former arts below.
And as they sail in Charon's boat,
Contrive to bribe the judge's vote.
To Cerberus they give a sop,
His tiple-barking mouth to stop;
Or in the Ivory gate of dreams,
Project * * * and .* * * * * * *:
Or hire their party-pamphleteers,
To set Elysium by the ears.

Then Poet, if you mean to thrive,
Employ your Muse on kings alive;
With prudence gathering up a cluster
Of all the virtues you can muster:
Which formed into a garland sweet,
Lay humbly at your monarch's feet;
Who as the odours reach his throne,
Will smile, and think 'em all his own:
For Law and Gospel both determine
All virtues lodge in royal ermine.
(I mean the oracles of both,
Who shall depose it upon oath.)
Your garland in the following reign,
Change but their names will do again.

But if you think this trade too base,
(Which seldom is the dunce's case)
Put on the critic's brow, and sit
At Will's the puny judge of Wit.

A nod, a shrug, a scornful smile,
With caution used, may serve a while.
Proceed no further in your part,
Before you learn the terms of art:
(For you may easy be too far gone,
In all our Modern Critics jargon.)
Then talk with more authentic face,
Of Unities, in Time and Place.
Get scraps of Horace from your friends,
And have them at your fingers' ends.
Learn Aristotle's Rules by rote,
And at all hazards boldly quote:
Judicious Rymer [1] oft review;
Wise Dennis,[2] and profound Bossu.[3]
Read all the Prefaces of Dryden,
For these our critics much confide in,
(Though merely writ at first for filling
To raise the volume's price, a shilling.)

A forward critic often dupes us
With sham quotations *Peri Hupsous:* * [4]
And if we have not read Longinus,
Will magisterially out-shine us.
Then, lest with Greek he over-run ye,
Procure the book for love or money,
Translated from Boileau's Translation,†
And quote quotation on quotation.

At Wills you hear a poem read,
Where Battus [5] from the table-head,
Reclining on his elbow-chair,
Gives judgment with decisive air.
To whom the tribe of circling Wits,
As to an oracle submits.
He gives directions to the town,
To cry it up, or run it down.

---

* A famous Treatise of Longinus.
† By Mr. Welsted.
[1] Thomas Rymer (1641–1713), a critic, whom Swift considered the type of the Grub Street hack. (See *Tale.*)
[2] John Dennis (1657–1734), a critic who, as one of Dryden's circle at Will's, is target for Swift's satire.
[3] Rene le Bossu (1631–1680), notable for a treatise on epic poetry which was admired by Dryden.
[4] Swift refers to the essay on the sublime attributed, erroneously, to Longinus. It was translated into French by Boileau, and an English translation was published by Leonard Welsted.
[5] Dryden.

(Like courtiers, when they send a note,
Instructing members how to vote.)
He sets the stamp of bad and good,
Though not a word be understood.
Your lesson learnt, you'll be secure
To get the name of *conoisseur*.
And when your merits once are known,
Procure disciples of your own.

Our poets (you can never want 'em,
Spread through *Augusta Trinobantum*) [1]
Computing by their pecks of coals,
Amount to just nine thousand souls.
These o'er their proper districts govern,
Of wit and humour, judges sovereign.
In every street a city-bard
Rules, like an alderman his ward.
His undisputed rights extend
Through all the lane, from end to end.
The neighbours round admire his shrewdness,
For songs of loyalty and lewdness.
Outdone by none in rhyming well,
Although he never learnt to spell.

Two bordering Wits contend for glory:
And one is Whig, and one is Tory.
And this, for epics claims the bays,
And that, for elegiac lays.
Some famed for numbers soft and smooth,
By lovers spoke in Punch's booth.
And some as justly fame extols
For lofty lines in Smithfield drolls.
Baevius in Wapping gains renown,
And Maevius [2] reigns o'er Kentish-town;
Tigellius [3] placed in Phoebus' car,
From Ludgate shines to Temple-bar.
Harmonius Cibber entertains
The Court with annual birthday strains;
Whence Gay was banished in disgrace, [4]

---

[1] London.
[2] See Virgil, Eclogue, iii, 90: *"Qui Bavium non odit, amet tua carmina, Maevi."*
[3] Tigellius, a favorite of Julius Caesar, is satirized in *Tale of a Tub* as one of the ancestors of a True Modern Critic.
[4] Gay's opera, *Polly,* was banned in 1728.

Where Pope will never show his face;
Where Y——— must torture his invention,[1]
To flatter knaves, or lose his pension.

But these are not a thousandth part
Of jobbers in the poet's art,
Attending each his proper station,
And all in due subordination;
Through every alley to be found,
In garrets high, or under ground:
And when they join their pericranies,
Out skips a Book of Miscellanies.
Hobbes clearly proves that every creature
Lives in a state of war by Nature.
The greater for the smallest watch,
But meddle seldom with their match.
A whale of moderate size will draw
A shoal of herrings down his maw.
A fox with geese his belly crams;
A wolf destroys a thousand lambs.
But search among the rhyming race,
The brave are worried by the base.
If, on Parnassus' top you sit,
You rarely bite, are always bit:
Each poet of inferior size
On you shall rail and criticize;
And strive to tear you limb from limb,
While others do as much for him.

The vermin only tease and pinch
Their foes superior by an inch.
So, naturalists observe, a flea
Hath smaller fleas that on him prey,
And these have smaller fleas to bite 'em,
And so proceed *ad infinitum:*
Thus every poet in his kind,
Is bit by him that comes behind;
Who, though too little to be seen,
Can tease, and gall, and give the Spleen;
Call dunces, fools, and sons of whores,
Lay Grubstreet at each others' doors;
Extol the Greek and Roman masters,
And curse our modern poetasters.

[1] In 1726 Walpole awarded Young a pension of £200.

Complain, as many an ancient bard did,
How Genius is no more rewarded;
How wrong a taste prevails among us;
How much our ancestors out-sung us;
Can personate an awkward scorn
For those who are not poets born;
And all their brother dunces lash,
Who crowd the press with hourly trash.

O, Grubstreet: how do I bemoan thee,
Whose graceless children scorn to own thee:
Their filial piety forgot,
Deny their country like a Scot:
Though by their idiom and grimace
They soon betray their native place:
Yet *thou* hast greater cause to be
Ashamed of them, than they of thee.
Degenerate from their ancient brood,
Since first the Court allowed them food.

Remains a difficulty still,
To purchase fame by writing ill:
From Flecknoe [1] down to Howard's [2] Time,
How few have reached the *low Sublime?*
For when our high-born Howard died,
Blackmore [3] alone his place supplied:
And lest a chasm should intervene,
When death had finished Blackmore's reign,
The leaden crown devolved to thee,
Great poet of the hollow-tree.*
But, oh, how insecure thy throne:
A thousand bards thy right disown:
They plot to turn in factious zeal,
Duncenia to a common-weal;
And with rebellious arms pretend
An equal privilege to descend.

In bulk there are not more degrees,
From elephants to mites in cheese,

---

* Lord G——.[4]

[1] Richard Flecknoe (1620–1678?), subject of Dryden's satire, *MacFlecknoe.*
[2] Edward Howard, a very minor poet and playwright.
[3] Sir Richard Blackmore had served Swift as a type of the Grub Street hack as early as the *Tale of a Tub.*
[4] William Luckyn Grimston, later Viscount Grimston, author of a play, *The Lawyer's Fortune, or Love in a Hollow Tree,* 1705.

Than what a curious eye may trace
In creatures of the rhyming race.
From bad to worse, and worse they fall,
But, who can reach the worst of all?
For, though in Nature depth and height
Are equally held infinite,
In Poetry the height we know;
'Tis only infinite below.
For instance: When you rashly think,
No Rymer can like Welsted sink.*
His merits balanced you shall find,
That Fielding [1] leaves him far behind.
Concannen,[2] more aspiring bard,
Climbs downwards, deeper by a yard;
Smart Jemmy Moor [3] with Vigor drops,
The rest pursue as thick as hops:
With heads to points the gulf they enter,
Linkt perpendicular to the centre;
And as their heels elated rise,
Their heads attempt the nether skies.

O, what indignity and shame
To prostitute the Muse's name,
By flattering—whom Heaven designed
The plagues and scourges of mankind.
Bred up in ignorance and sloth,
And every vice that nurses both.

Fair Britain in thy Monarch blest,
Whose virtues bear the strictest test;
Whom never faction could bespatter,
Nor minister, nor poet flatter.
What justice in rewarding merit?
What magnanimity of spirit?
What lineaments divine we trace
Through all the features of his face;
Though peace with olive bind his hands,
Confesst the conquering hero stands.
Hydaspes, Indus, and the Ganges,
Dread from his hand impending changes.

* *Vide The Treatise on the Profound,* and Mr. Pope's *Dunciad.*

[1] Probably Swift did not use "Fielding" here, inasmuch as he regarded
him highly. The name may have been inserted by the publisher.
[2] Matthew Concannen (1701–1749), a political hack writer.
[3] James Moore Smythe (1702–1734), a minor playwright, also satirized in
Pope's *Dunciad.*

From him the Tartar, and Chinese,
Short by the knees entreat for peace.
The consort of his throne and bed,
A perfect goddess born and bred.
Appointed sovereign judge to sit
On learning, eloquence and wit.
Our eldest hope, divine Iulus,
(Late, very late, O, may he rule us.)
What early manhood has he shown,
Before his downy beard was grown:
Then think, what wonders will be done
By going on as he begun;
An heir for Britain to secure
As long as Sun and Moon endure.

The remnant of the royal blood,
Comes pouring on me like a flood.
Bright goddesses, in number five;
Duke William,[1] sweetest prince alive.

Now sing the Minister of State,[2]
Who shines alone, without a mate.
Observe with what majestic port
This Atlas stands to prop the Court:
Intent the public debts to pay,
Like prudent Fabius * by delay.
Thou great Vicegerent of the King,
Thy praises every Muse shall sing.
In all affairs thou sole director,
Of wit and learning chief protector;
Though small the time thou hast to spare,
The Church is thy peculiar care.
Of pious prelates what a stock
You choose to rule the sable-flock.
You raise the honour of the peerage,
Proud to attend you at the steerage.
You dignify the noble race,
Content yourself with humbler place.
Now learning, valour, virtue, sense
To titles give the sole pretence.
St. George beheld thee with delight,

---

* *Unus Homo nobis Cunctando resituit rem.*

[1] William Augustus, Duke of Cumberland.
[2] Swift's satire of Walpole in the following section is reminiscent of similar satire in *Gulliver*.

Vouchsafe to be an azure knight,
When on thy breast and sides Herculean,
He fixt the Star and String Cerulean.

Say, Poet, in what other nation,
Shone ever such a constellation.
Attend ye Popes, and Youngs, and Gays,
And tune your harps, and strow your bays.
Your panegyrics here provide,
You cannot err on flattery's side.
Above the stars exalt your style,
You still are low ten thousand mile.
On Lewis all his bards bestowed,
Of incense many a thousand load;
But Europe mortified his pride,
And swore the fawning rascals lied:
Yet what the world refused to Lewis,
Applied to ——— [1] exactly true is:
Exactly true: Invidious Poet:
'Tis fifty thousand times below it.

Translate me now some lines, if you can,
From Virgil, Martial, Ovid, Lucan;
They could all power in Heaven divide,
And do no wrong to either side:
They'll teach you how to split a hair,
Give ——— [2] and Jove an equal share.*
Yet, why should we be laced so straight;
I'll give my * * * * * [3] butter-weight.
And reason good; for many a year
——— never intermeddled here:
Nor, though his priests be duly paid,
Did ever we desire his aid:
We now can better do without him,
Since Woolson gave us arms to rout him.
* * * * * Caetera desiderantur * * * * *

* *Divisum Imperium cum Jove Caesar habet.*
[1] Here one may well supply "George."
[2] Here, too, one may supply "George."
[3] Here one may supply "Monarch."

CHRONOLOGY

1667	Born in Dublin.
1673–1682	At Kilkenny School.
1682	Entered Trinity College, Dublin.
1686	B.A.
1686–1689	In residence at Trinity, studying for M.A.
1689	Departed for England.
1689–1699	Intermittently at Moor Park and Ireland.
1692	M.A. from Oxford.
1694	Ordained a deacon.
1695	Ordained a priest; appointed to Kilroot.
1696–1698	Wrote *Tale of a Tub, Battle of the Books* (pub. 1704).
1696	Resigned Kilroot.
1699–1710	The period of Swift's Whig activities; alternately in Ireland and England.
1699	Death of Sir William Temple; appointed chaplain to Lord Berkeley.
1700	Appointed to Laracor and surrounding parishes.
1701	Received D.D. from Dublin University.
1704	*Tale of a Tub* volume published.
1707–1709	In England negotiating remission of First Fruits; member of Addison and Steele circle; *Bickerstaff Papers*.
1710–1714	The period of Swift's activities in Tory politics.
1710–1711	*Examiner Papers*.
1710–1713	*Journal to Stella*.
1713	Appointed Dean of St. Patrick's Cathedral.
1714	Meetings with Scriblerus Club; death of Queen Anne and fall of the Tories.
1724	*Drapier's Letters*.
1726	*Gulliver's Travels* published.
1729	*A Modest Proposal* published.
1742	Declared incompetent.
1745	Died in Dublin.

SELECTED BIBLIOGRAPHY

TEXTS

BALL, F. ELRINGTON (ed.). *The Correspondence of Jonathan Swift, D.D.* 6 vols. London, 1910–1914.

DAVIS, HERBERT (ed.). *The Prose Works of Jonathan Swift.* 13 vols. Oxford, 1939—(in progress).

GUTHKELCH, A. C., and SMITH, D. NICHOL (eds). *A Tale of a Tub to which is added The Battle of the Books and the Mechanical Operation of the Spirit, by Jonathan Swift.* Oxford, 1942.

LANDA, LOUIS (ed.). *Jonathan Swift, Gulliver's Travels and Other Writings.* Boston, 1960.

WILLIAMS, HAROLD (ed.). *The Poems of Jonathan Swift.* 3 vols. Oxford, 1937, 1958.

CRITIQUES

CASE, ARTHUR E. *Four Essays on Gulliver's Travels.* Princeton, 1945.

EDDY, WILLIAM A. *Gulliver's Travels, A Critical Study.* Princeton, 1923.

HARTH, PHILLIP. *Swift and Anglican Rationalism. The Religious Background of A Tale of a Tub.* Chicago, 1961.

JONES, RICHARD FOSTER. "Ancients and Moderns," *Washington University Studies.* St. Louis, Missouri, 1936.

NICOLSON, MARJORIE H. *Science and Imagination.* Ithaca, New York, 1956.

PRICE, MARTIN. *Swift's Rhetorical Art: A Study in Structure and Meaning.* New Haven, 1953.

QUINTANA, RICARDO. *The Mind and Art of Jonathan Swift.* London, 1936.

STARKMAN, MIRIAM KOSH. *Swift's Satire on Learning in A Tale of a Tub.* Princeton, 1950.

Bantam Book Catalog

It lists over a thousand money-saving best-sellers originally priced from $3.75 to $15.00 —bestsellers that are yours now for as little as 60¢ to $2.95!

The catalog gives you a great opportunity to build your own private library at huge savings!

So don't delay any longer—send us your name and address and 25¢ (to help defray postage and handling costs).

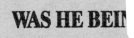

Cam could see Lacey's uneasiness gradually being replaced with trust and he wasn't sure he deserved that trust. He was deliberately setting out to convince her that he was harmless. Which didn't reflect reality at all. In fact, there were times when he felt downright predatory.

It wasn't as if he were planning anything that would hurt her in any way. Yes, he *was* deliberately seducing her, but it was his sincere belief that the end result would be as satisfying to her as it would be to him. They were married. If they really wanted this marriage to work, then, sooner or later, they were going to sleep together. Was it really so terrible of him to soothe her uneasiness? To make the path a little smoother?

ABOUT THE AUTHOR

Thirtieth birthdays do strange things to people,
indeed. Last year, as that auspicious day
approached, Dallas Schulze conceived of the idea
for this book. However, unlike Lacey Newton,
Dallas has been happily married for *many* years.
She and her husband live in Southern California,
where Dallas enjoys quilting and doll-making.

Books by Dallas Schulze
HARLEQUIN AMERICAN ROMANCE

Don't miss any of our special offers. Write to us at the
following address for information on our newest releases.

Harlequin Reader Service
901 Fuhrmann Blvd., P.O. Box 1397, Buffalo, NY 14240
Canadian address: P.O. Box 603,
Fort Erie, Ont. L2A 5X3

THE MORNING AFTER

DALLAS SCHULZE

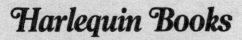

Harlequin Books

TORONTO • NEW YORK • LONDON
AMSTERDAM • PARIS • SYDNEY • HAMBURG
STOCKHOLM • ATHENS • TOKYO • MILAN

Published July 1989

First printing May 1989

ISBN 0-373-16302-9

Chapter One

"An old maid. I've raised a daughter who's going to spend her life as an old maid." Mamie Newton's voice was filled with despair.

"Nobody uses that term anymore, Mother." Lacey smiled to take the edge off the words, wondering if Mamie would notice that her voice was a little too tight.

"What else can you call it?" Mamie looked at her daughter, her beautiful blue eyes reproachful. "Here you are. You're thirty years old and you aren't married. You don't even have a man in your life. Don't you want to get married, have children?"

Lacey took a swallow of tea, aware that her fingers were knotted around the fragile bone-china cup. It took a conscious effort to loosen them and smile.

"Of course I want that, Mother, but until it comes along, I'm leading a full, productive life. I have my shop and I have friends. I'm hardly living like a hermit."

Mamie didn't return her smile. She stared at Lacey as if trying to understand where she'd gone wrong in raising her only child. Lacey said nothing, keeping her expression calm, slightly amused. It wouldn't do to let Mamie know she'd struck a nerve. If she'd learned one thing in thirty years, it was that her delicate Southern belle of a mother had the tenacity of a bulldog. She never meant to be cruel, but if she had the least suspicion that Lacey was anything but content, she'd prod and push and poke until she had all the reasons laid out in front of her, and then she'd start looking for ways to fix whatever she thought the problem was.

The problem was that Lacey herself wasn't sure why her life didn't seem quite as full as it should have. Until she'd worked it out to her own satisfaction, she wasn't going to lay herself open to her mother's tender mercies.

"I just don't understand, Lacey. Sometimes I wonder if maybe your daddy dying when you were so young didn't affect you more than I thought. Maybe I should have remarried. A child should have a father in her life."

Mamie picked up a cucumber sandwich—thin white bread, the crusts removed, of course—and nibbled at it, her expression mournful.

Lacey watched her, torn between the urge to laugh and the urge to scream. Only the laughter would have had a hysterical edge and, if she started screaming, she might not stop.

"Mother, I'm thirty, not ninety. Lots of women wait to have families these days. It's no big deal."

Mamie sighed and swallowed the last of the tiny sandwich before wiping her fingertips on a snow-white linen napkin. If the world itself depended on it, Mamie would never speak with her mouth full.

"I don't mean to be a pushy mother, Lacey, but I worry about you. I never would have thought you'd get to your thirtieth birthday without at least being engaged a time or two. You don't even have a special man in your life."

"Having a man in your life doesn't guarantee happiness. Look at the divorce rate these days."

"You can't dwell on the negative, honey. It's just a matter of finding the right man, that's all." Thirty years in Southern California had not taken the Georgia from Mamie's voice. The tea table, the perfectly decorated room, her mother's soft lavender dress—all of it could have come out of a modern-day Tara. The rest of the world might have embraced "casual" as a way of life, but Mamie Newton believed that the finer things were what made life worth living.

Lacey stared at her beautiful refined mother and wondered how it was possible that she'd missed all the changes in the world around her. Lacey's father had died when she was barely four. What her life might have been like if he'd lived, Lacey would never know. Mamie had chosen to stay in Southern California, but she'd raised her daughter as if they were in the Deep South.

Lacey had worn dresses when other little girls wore jeans. She knew just how to crook her pinky while sipping tea. She was the only woman she knew who actually owned a pair of white gloves for church. To this day, she felt underdressed walking into a church without them. How did she go about explaining to her mother that life wasn't lived on the simple terms Mamie thought it should be?

"When I find the right man, I'll be more than happy to latch on to him."

"Well, you aren't going to find him by shutting yourself up in that stuffy little boutique of yours, getting ink all over your fingers from doing the books and all."

"You've been reading too much Dickens. I have a computer to help me with the books. And Lacey's Lovelies isn't stuffy. It's very chic, and my customers know they can get the best there. I notice you don't hesitate to buy from me."

Mamie waved her fingers, dismissing the shop. "I didn't mean to criticize what you've done, sugar. I'm real proud of you, and your daddy would have been, too. But you take my word for it. A store just doesn't make up for not having a man in your life. And I'm not talkin' about the bedroom, neither. It's important to have somebody there to lean on, someone to share the good times and the bad."

Lacey reached for her tea, trying to ignore the twinge of pain her mother's words brought. "That sounds great, Mother, but wonderful men aren't hanging around like ripe peaches just waiting to be picked."

"Well, you aren't going to find one the way you're going at it. When was the last time you had a date?"

"As a matter of fact, I had lunch with a charming man last week."

She could almost see Mamie's ears perk up. "You did? What's his name?"

"Brad. He's nice, good-looking, and we had a wonderful time." She sipped her tea to hide a grin. She hadn't told a lie. Brad was all those things. He was also gay, but she didn't have to mention an irrelevant detail like that. She also wouldn't mention the fact that he had been trying to sell her an insurance package. For now, Mamie was distracted.

An hour later, she stifled a stab of guilt as she kissed her mother goodbye. Tucked into her purse was an exquisite pair of diamond earrings, Mamie's birthday gift to her only child.

The problem with her mother was that it was impossible to get too angry with her meddling. Mamie genuinely wanted nothing but Lacey's happiness. It was hard to get mad at someone who had your best interests at heart. Still, Mamie's constant concern about her daughter's single state did get on Lacey's nerves.

She settled behind the wheel of her car and started the engine, lifting her hand to wave to her mother before backing out of the driveway. She flicked the radio on, setting it to a station that was playing old rock and roll. The quick rhythms and silly lyrics rarely failed to raise her spirits. Today they failed abysmally. She shut the radio off as she turned onto Foothill Boulevard and headed toward Pasadena.

Thirty. She was thirty years old today. She'd never thought that she was going to be one of those people who was depressed by the big three-o. But here it was, and boy, was she depressed. Her thirties stretched in front of her, endless and empty. No, not empty! She made the correction angrily, her fine brows drawing together.

She'd accomplished a lot in thirty years. She had her own very successful shop and she loved the work. Lacey's Lovelies was proving to be a major success in one of Pasadena's terribly with-it neighborhoods. She'd bought before the prices climbed out of sight, and she was now in a remarkably secure position. She'd even been thinking about opening another shop.

There. Her life was hardly a barren wasteland. But the defiant thought didn't do much to lift her spirits. Neither did the bright California sunshine. In fact, she couldn't remember the last time she'd been so depressed.

Thirty. It sounded so...old. All the magazine articles described it as the prime of a woman's life—the time when she really came into her own. But right now Lacey didn't feel particularly prime. She felt slightly dusty and a little unwanted.

She flipped on a signal and turned into the parking garage beneath her apartment building. The elevator whisked her to the fourth floor and she stepped onto thick carpeting. Her apartment was sleek, charming, beautifully decorated. She was proud of it. So why was it that it looked so...empty? Maybe she should get a cat. Having someone to greet her when she came home would cheer the place up a bit.

Dropping her purse on the breakfast bar, she sank onto a stool and stared at nothing in particular. A cat. The classic symbol of the old maid.

"Next thing, I'll be wearing a doily on my head and talking to myself. All I need is a nice hot bath and some good company. Then I'll see how ridiculous this whole thirty thing is." She stopped suddenly. "Oh, my God, I am talking to myself!"

She laughed, hearing the sound disappear in the big room. Damn Mamie for making her feel like a dinosaur. There was nothing wrong with being unmarried at thirty. There were more things in a woman's life than husbands and children—not that those things wouldn't be nice, but they weren't the be-all and end-all.

She stood up, straightening her shoulders and forcing a smile. She was going to go out tonight, just as she'd planned. She and her friends were going to have a wonderful time celebrating her thirtieth birthday.

"Thirty. I'm thirty." There. She'd said it out loud, and she didn't feel anything awful happen to her. It was no big deal. It was just another birthday.

She walked briskly into the bathroom and turned the water on in the tub, adjusting it to just below scalding. While the tub was filling, she went into the bedroom and stripped off her skirt and blouse. After hanging them up, she caught a glimpse of herself in the mirror, and she paused to study her reflection.

Without giving herself time to think, she stripped off the pale peach camisole and tap pants and faced the mirror squarely. Her eyes were anxious as she studied herself. Her skin still looked firm and supple. She turned sideways, tightening her buttocks. Maybe they weren't quite as firm as they'd been when she was seventeen, but they weren't too bad.

She put her fingertips on the skin over her breasts and pulled upward. Her frown deepened. Were they sagging more than they had a year ago? Maybe she should get one of those things that you squeezed with your hands. They were supposed to build up the pectoral muscles, weren't they? Pectorals. Lord, it sounded like some prehistoric bird.

She leaned closer to the mirror and studied her face. It looked much the same to her. The same delicate bones, inherited from her mother. The same mouth, the lower lip just a bit too full. Her eyes were her best feature, wide set and a clear green. She smiled experimentally, counting the lines at the corners of her eyes. Was she aging too quickly? She'd given up the sun years ago, afraid of having her skin turn to saddle leather. But maybe those careless teenage days at the beach had done too much damage...

She frowned and then quickly erased the expression. Frowning gave you lines. How many times had Mamie told her that? But so did smiling and no one ever suggested that you stop smiling. Lacey stepped back and studied her reflection. No, the signs of deterioration weren't too obvious yet, but she had the gloomy feeling that they were lurking just below the surface, ready to leap out and cause her to wrinkle and sag overnight.

Maybe it wasn't on the birthday itself that all the hideous changes occurred. Maybe it was the day after the birthday. Maybe she was going to wake up tomorrow morning looking like the portrait of Dorian Grey.

The thought should have made her laugh, but she didn't even feel like smiling. Maybe she'd call Jimbo and tell him she really didn't feel like going out tonight. Somehow, turning thirty didn't seem like something to celebrate. She turned away from the mirror and walked into the bathroom. If she called to cancel, he'd want to know why and he'd think she was an idiot. She'd known Jimbo for almost five years now. Despite the considerable age difference, they'd hit it off immediately. But one thing he wasn't, was tactful. No, she'd just have to go tonight and pretend she didn't mind leaving her youth behind.

Sinking into the steaming water, she leaned her head back, staring at the tiled wall. Old maid. At the moment, the description sounded depressingly accurate.

CAMERON MCCLEARY smoothed the fine sandpaper carefully across the wood. Willie Nelson rasped out a tune from the radio in the corner, the only sound in the garage-turned-workshop besides the smooth hiss of the sandpaper. Cam paused and studied the piece in front of him, his eyes critical.

One of his better pieces, if he did say so himself. The fine grain of the oak suited the sweeping lines of the cradle. He brushed a bit of sawdust off the top edge, running his thumb along the curve, testing its smoothness. The wood felt warm and strong under his hand. The Martins would be able to rock more than one baby in this cradle. He'd built it to last for generations.

He picked up a rag and began wiping the sawdust from the delicate carvings that marked the head and foot of the cradle. It wasn't hard to picture an infant asleep in the sturdy oak. The image brought a peculiar pang to his chest.

What would it be like to build a cradle for his own child? The rag stroked gently over the oak, picking up a fine coating of dust and leaving the wood satin smooth. The thought of his own child held safe and protected by the work of his hands was appealing. More than appealing. But while the infant was easy to picture, its mother was something else.

He hadn't gotten to thirty-six without knowing a fair number of women. Once or twice he'd even thought he might be in love but, somehow, the relationships had never quite developed into the kind of commitment that went with marriage and children.

His brows came together, overshadowing his summer-blue eyes. Over the past year, he'd begun to feel a strange restlessness, a sense of something missing in his life. He finally had all the work he could handle, his life was in order, and yet there was something missing. Something indefinable. There was a gap.

Stroking the rag over the cradle, he began to sense what the gap was. He wanted a family. His mouth tilted into a smile. He had to be crazy. After growing up in a family of seven, any sane person would be glad for a little peace and quiet. But he liked the chaos that went with a family—the noise, the arguments, the clutter...the love.

Still, you didn't just walk out and buy a family. It was something that grew out of a commitment to a woman and her commitment to you. Sighing, he tossed the rag aside. These days, that commitment seemed to be a little hard to come by.

Cam stretched and reached for the cup of coffee that had grown cold while he worked. Grimacing at the bitter taste, he set the cup down, promising himself that he was going to buy a Thermos so he could manage hot coffee while he was in the shop.

"Hey, not bad." Cam turned, startled, as the voice boomed out from the doorway. He relaxed, giving a half smile when he saw who it was.

James Robinson—Jimbo as long as Cam had known him—matched his voice. Average height but barrel-chested, so that he seemed shorter than he was, Jimbo was the epitome of the hail-fellow-well-met type. His mouth seemed destined to snap out witty comments, and his eyes viewed the world with a combination of good humor and cynicism.

"Come right in." Jimbo grinned at Cam's halfhearted sarcasm.

"You didn't answer the doorbell and the gate was open. I figured you'd be in the shop."

"Maybe I didn't answer the door because I didn't want to be disturbed."

"Nah. I knew you wouldn't mind me dropping in. You didn't answer the door because you didn't hear it."

Jimbo walked into the converted garage, studying the nearly completed cradle. Cam watched him, knowing before the words were out just what Jimbo was going to say.

"The best thing I've seen you do."

"You said that about the last six things you saw."

Jimbo shrugged. "What can I say? You just keep getting better."

Cam grinned. "Flattery will get you nowhere. What do you want?"

"Me?" Jimbo's eyes were the very picture of injured friendship. "Why do you assume I want something?"

"Because you usually do." Cam leaned against the edge of the workbench, studying his friend with good-natured skepticism. "Three weeks ago, you wanted to borrow my car. A month before that, you wanted me to cover for you on a date you couldn't make. So, what is it this time?"

Jimbo gave him a hurt look. "You wound me, you really do. I come here with an invitation for you, and you practically throw it back in my face even before I can say anything."

Cam ignored the exaggerated expression of pain. "What kind of an invitation?"

"Dinner. Tonight. It's a friend's birthday. Lacey. You've heard me mention her."

"Sure. But I don't see why I'm invited. I've never met her."

"No. But this would be a great opportunity. Lacey is a great gal. You'd like her. Besides, we're going out for Mexican. Picture it—enchiladas swimming in sauce, burritos stuffed to the brim with shredded beef and cheese, margaritas."

Cam held up his hand, groaning. "Stop with the bribery. It sounds great, but I really can't."

"Why not? It looks like you've got this project about done. I know you well enough to know you're not going to start on another project right away."

"No, but—"

"You're becoming a hermit, Cam. When was the last time you went out to dinner with a beautiful woman?"

"Last week."

"Yeah, and I bet it was your mother or one of your sisters."

Cam grinned, lifting his shoulders. "Guilty."

"Come on. This is going to be a great evening. Frank and Lisa are going to be there and I'm taking Betts."

"Look, this Lacey isn't going to want a stranger along on her birthday dinner. Maybe another time."

"Lacey wouldn't mind a bit. In fact, she's been anxious to meet you." He caught the dubious look Cam threw him and amended the statement. "Well, I know she'd be interested. Besides, this way we'll have even numbers in case we go dancing. I don't want Lacey to feel like the odd man out at her own birthday."

"I don't think it's such a hot idea."

"I do. Come on, Cam. You owe me. Didn't I drive all thirty of your brothers and sisters to Disneyland?"

"There's only six of them and that was almost ten years ago."

"Well, it seemed like thirty, and my nerves still haven't recovered. Come on, it will do you good to get out of the house. You work too hard."

Cam looked at him, recognizing the gleam in his friend's eye. If he didn't agree, Jimbo was fully prepared to hound him until he gave up and said yes. Jimbo was nothing if not persistent. Besides, he *had* been feeling restless. Maybe Jimbo was right. Maybe he did need to get out of the house for a while.

"All right. But if it's a disaster, don't say I didn't warn you."

Jimbo grinned, rubbing his hands together. "It'll be fun. You'll see. This is going to be a night to remember."

Cam looked less enthused. "As long as it's not a night to regret."

Chapter Two

Lacey pulled into the parking lot of Los Arcos and slowed the car to a near halt as she looked for a parking place. She edged into a spot that looked more suited to a motorcycle than a car and then realized that she was going to be lucky if she could get her door open. The door did open—barely.

She hesitated, debating the wisdom of finding another place to park, but the lot looked pretty full. She'd been lucky to find the spot she had. It seemed par for the course that she had to squeeze uncomfortably through an opening that would have challenged Houdini.

Considering the way her day had gone so far, it shouldn't have surprised her that, when she slammed the car door and tried to take a step, her skirt was caught. Jerked to an abrupt halt when her dress refused to move with her, Lacey looked over her shoulder with more resignation than irritation.

She wasn't particularly disturbed. It was a reasonably simple matter to open the door and release the swatch of pale green cotton. And if the dress was ruined, that was only to be expected. So far, her thirtieth birthday was turning out to be a day full of unpleasant surprises. A ruined dress barely rated any concern. She started to turn and felt her resignation slip. The skirt was full enough to catch in the door but not full enough to allow her the room to turn so she could get the key in the door. She turned left and then she turned right, but the door remained stubbornly out of reach.

She stopped and stood next to her car, smiling vaguely at a group of people going into the restaurant. They smiled back. One of them even went so far as to comment that it looked like it might rain. Lacey nodded, keeping her smile pinned in place until the door closed behind them. It faded the minute they were out of sight. It was easy for them to smile. She'd be willing to bet that not one of them was over twenty-five. What did they know about turning thirty? Just wait until they reached that day.

She twisted again, reaching for the door handle. Her fingertips just brushed it but there was no way she could get the key in the lock. She stood still, staring at the parking lot. The light was fading. Soon it would be dark and she'd still be standing here, like some bizarre form of modern art. *Woman and Car.*

Remembering the comment about rain, Lacey glanced up at the sky. A few gray clouds scudded overhead. Rain. Great. Just what she needed to top off a fun-filled birthday. She could stand in the rain and catch pneumonia just like that little girl in *Jane Eyre.*

She twisted quickly with some vague idea of surprising the door into letting her go. It didn't work. She nodded to an elderly couple and bent her head over her purse as if she were looking for something terribly important.

She could take off her dress. Then she'd be able to reach the door and release it. Of course, in the meantime, she'd probably draw quite a crowd. Admittedly, Southern Californians were notoriously blasé but she'd be willing to bet that a woman stripping to her skivvies in the parking lot of a Glendale restaurant was going to draw a crowd. It might not get much attention in Hollywood, but Glendale was a bit more conservative.

She could call for help. She abandoned that option almost as soon as she thought of it. If she called for help, she'd have to explain what had happened, and there *was* no explanation. Turning thirty was not a valid excuse for losing all of one's coordination and shutting part of one's person in a car door.

She stood between the two cars and considered the possibilities. None of them looked reasonable. No. She might as well face the fact that she was doomed to grow old and die trapped in the parking lot of a Mexican restaurant. Years from now, they'd find her moldering form lying on the macadam and they'd never know what happened, because by then her skirt would have rotted loose, freeing her at last from the deadly grip of the door.

The image was so absurd that she couldn't help but laugh. It started as a smile and turned into a full-throated chuckle.

"Excuse me. Are you aware that your dress is caught in the car door?"

The voice cut through Lacey's laughter and she turned her head, looking over her shoulder to see its owner. The light had faded to the point where it was difficult to make out much beyond a pair of very broad, very masculine shoulders and the faint gleam of a smile.

"No kidding." Her smile took any sarcasm from the words. "I thought my dress was shrinking."

She felt his eyes sweep down to where her dress was caught and then back up to her face. She sensed the smile in them. "No, it's definitely caught. Can I help?"

"Well, that all depends. If you can reach the lock, you could open the door so that I can move."

He seemed to consider the idea for a moment and then nodded. "I think I can manage that. Do you have the key?"

"Fat lot of good it's done me so far." She handed the key back to him and heard the click as he slid it into the lock. A moment later, he had the door open and her skirt was free.

"Thank you."

"No problem. Any damage?"

Lacey brushed at her skirt and then looked up, wishing she could see more of his face. His voice was wonderfully deep and mellow, making her want to know what he looked like.

"Nothing permanent. I can always have the dress cleaned. Before you came along I was beginning to wonder if I was destined to die there."

"I'm glad I could help."

"Not as glad as I am, I'll bet." They were walking toward the restaurant as they talked, and Lacey wasn't sure whether she was glad or sorry when he opened the door and they stepped into the brightly lit restaurant. She wanted to know what her rescuer looked like, but it was going to be extremely depressing if he turned out to be a twenty-two-year-old weightlifter.

Her first reaction was relief that he wasn't young enough to be her grandchild. Her second reaction was that he was almost too handsome. His features were all-American perfect—strong chin, beautiful mouth, wide brow and eyes the color of the bluest skies. His hair was light brown, sun-streaked and casually combed. This was a man a woman would cheerfully kill for. He was also well on the far side of thirty. Thirty-five or six, at a guess.

The knowledge didn't make her feel much better. A man this good-looking could have his pick of women, most of them younger and prettier than she was. Not that she was particularly interested in him, of course. Heaven knew, she'd grown past the stage of wanting to date a man just because he happened to be quite possibly the most attractive specimen of masculinity she'd ever seen.

She flushed when she realized that he was studying her with just as much interest as she was studying him. She resisted the urge to run her hand over her hair. Surely, as of today she had left behind some of the insecurities of her twenties.

"Well, thanks again."

"You're welcome." His eyes were intense, and Lacey had the impression that he wanted to say something else, though she wasn't sure she wanted to hear it.

"I think I'll visit the ladies' room before I meet my friends. See if I can repair some of the damage." She gestured to her skirt and smiled vaguely, moving away before he could say anything more.

By the time she'd wiped away as much of the mark on her dress as she could, she was cursing herself. The man was gorgeous. And he seemed nice. Why hadn't she waited to see what he wanted to say? He might have asked her for a date. Not that she was given to picking up strange men in parking lots, but she could have made an exception just this once.

She studied her reflection in the washroom mirror. God knows, she might as well make hay while she could. In the relentless fluorescent lighting, every line or hint of a line showed up perfectly. She grimaced. Somebody ought to make a law that said all mirrors had to be lit with candlelight.

With a sigh and one last thought of her rescuer, she left the bathroom. There was no sense in putting this off. Jimbo had insisted on celebrating her birthday in style, and celebrate they would. After all, what was so bad about turning thirty? The small pep talk did not have much effect on her spirits.

Los Arcos was packed on Friday nights, and this was no exception. Lacey stared at the crowd of people and felt her spirits sink. They all looked like they were having so much fun. Couples, families—no one was here alone. And they looked young. Everyone in the place looked like they ought to be eating pablum.

She considered turning and slinking out, but it was too late. Jimbo had seen her and with his usual subtlety was waving his arms to attract her attention. The movements were so attention-getting that Lacey wouldn't have been surprised to see a 747 land on top of him, mistaking his gestures for a signal to land.

She smiled and edged her way through the crowd to the table, feeling as if every eye in the place was on her and every one of them knew it was her thirtieth birthday. They were probably trying to count the wrinkles.

"Lacey! Happy birthday! We were beginning to think you weren't going to show."

"I'm not *that* late." Lacey accepted his hug and smiled at Frank and Lisa. "Hi."

"Lacey, I want you to meet Betts. I did her taxes for her this year."

Lacey's heart sank. If Betts was with Jimbo that must mean that the other man at the table was unattached. And the only empty seat was right next to him. She'd kill Jimbo for this. She'd kill him and enjoy every minute of it.

"Nice to meet you, Betts. Jimbo's done a great job on my taxes."

Jimbo gave the two women a moment to exchange smiles before making the final introduction. "And this is Cameron McCleary. Cam, this is Lacey."

She really looked at the other man for the first time since arriving at the table, and she felt her color rise until her cheeks were on fire. The man who was slowly unfolding himself from the table was none other than her parking-lot rescuer.

"Hello again." He held out his hand, and Lacey put hers into it, oddly reluctant. His palm felt hard and warm, calloused as if he worked with his hands. Her eyes met his and her flush deepened.

"Hi."

"You two know each other?" Jimbo's sharp eyes went from one to the other, missing nothing.

"Not exactly." It was Cam who answered, since Lacey couldn't seem to find her voice. "Lacey was having some trouble with her car and I helped a bit." He shrugged, dismissing the incident as too minor to discuss, and Lacey gave him a grateful smile. She was feeling a little too vulnerable tonight to want everyone to know what a stupid predicament he'd found her in.

"I hope you don't mind that I've sort of crashed your birthday celebration. Jimbo was pretty insistent." Cam's smile made her feel as if he saw only her in the entire room. Lacey warned herself against reading too much into it. Some men were just born knowing how to make a woman feel important.

Her smile was a masterpiece of casual as she said, "He was probably downright obnoxious."

Jimbo shrugged, not in the least disturbed. He returned to his chair, leaving Lacey to settle herself next to

Cam. She tried not to notice how close his thigh was, how large he seemed.

Frank leaned forward, his sandy hair falling into a question mark over one eyebrow. "So, Lacey, how does thirty feel? You going to survive?"

She shrugged, forcing a grin. "I haven't kicked the bucket yet. It's about to kill my mother, though. She thinks I'm doomed to be an old maid."

Everyone laughed, but Cam threw her a quick look, his eyes sharp, and Lacey wondered if he'd heard something in her voice that shouldn't have been there. She leaned back as the waiter set an enormous margarita in front of her, the salty rim a pale contrast to the icy yellow contents of the glass.

"Okay. Time for a birthday toast." Jimbo reached for his glass and everyone followed suit. "To Lacey. May all your birthdays be spent in such charming company." He grinned and reached across the table to touch his glass to hers. Lacey couldn't help but smile at him. It was impossible to stay mad at Jimbo, no matter how irritated she was that he had dragged Cam along as a semi-date for her.

Everyone touched their glasses to hers, adding their good wishes. Cam was the last. As their glasses touched, Lacey met his eyes. His expression seemed to say that he knew exactly what she was feeling. She wanted to look away. He made her uneasy, as if he was seeing too much. But she couldn't look away.

"To the prettiest old maid I've ever met." His quiet tone soothed in some indefinable way, taking the sting out of her mother's words.

"Thank you, I think." She took a sip of her margarita, tasting the salty-sweet tang of it, her eye still on Cam's, and somehow, the evening didn't seem so bad.

It was impossible to stay depressed when everyone else was in such high spirits. The food was hot and spicy, the *salsa* brought tears to her eyes, but so did the laughter. She couldn't have said if it was the tequila in the margaritas or the company, but her depression lifted and suddenly turning thirty wasn't such a big deal.

She ate too much, drank more than she usually did and tried not to stare at Cam. The man was really much too handsome. The fact that he was also a nice guy made him almost too perfect a package.

Somewhere during the course of the evening, she forgot that she'd only just met him. There was something about him that made it impossible to stay uptight. He was warm and friendly and had a quiet sense of humor that blended surprisingly well with the more raucous humor of Jimbo. And it didn't hurt that he looked at her as if he found her as attractive as she found him. In the condition Lacey's ego was in, she needed the boost.

"We should go out and do something exciting." That was Lisa, her voice ever-so-slightly slurred. Her husband looked at her, his expression indulgent.

"Like what?"

"Well, I don't know." She crunched a tortilla chip. "Something different. We should do something fun. After all, a woman only turns thirty once."

"I don't know. I seem to recall you turned thirty three or four times." Frank ducked the playful swat she aimed at him. Everyone laughed, and Lacey tried to ignore the envy that crept over her as she watched them.

"We should go to Las Vegas." Betts's breathy voice cut through the laughter. Everyone turned to look at her.

"Las Vegas?" Lacey didn't know who spoke but the tone expressed her feelings precisely. Nobody went to Las Vegas on a whim.

"Sure. Why not? Las Vegas is really exciting. We could have loads of fun and really celebrate Lacey's birthday in style. I mean, a woman really ought to go all out on her thirtieth." She blinked her soft, slightly owlish blue eyes at the rest of the table. "I think Las Vegas would be loads of fun. Don't you, Lacey?"

All eyes turned to Lacey. She stared at her friends. Nobody drove all that way for no reason but to celebrate a birthday. You made plans for something like that. You spent the weekend. It was an absurd idea.

"I have an aunt in Las Vegas. She's a terrible gossip. I avoid her at all costs."

Everyone considered the matter solemnly. "You don't have to go see her." Frank offered the solution and everyone nodded.

Lacey considered. If she said no, they might all decide to go home. And then she'd have to go home. And there'd be nobody there but that awful mirror that made her look like a hag. And Cam would go home and she might not see him again for years—maybe not ever. The tequila made her thinking slightly fuzzy, but she knew she didn't want to go home.

"Las Vegas sounds great."

It seemed as if her agreement was all they'd been waiting for. Suddenly everyone thought Las Vegas was a great idea. If she'd had more time, Lacey might have changed her mind, but no one gave her a chance. Before she knew what was happening, she was wedged into the back seat of Jimbo's 1955 Cadillac convertible and they were on their way to Nevada.

Jimbo was behind the wheel, the only one of the group who was stone-cold sober, since he never drank. Betts was snuggled up next to him, leaving most of the front seat empty. It was the back seat that was a trifle crowded, with four.

It had started out that Lisa was going to sit in front and Frank was going to sit in the back. That was why Lacey had gotten into the back seat next to Cam. At the last minute, Lisa changed her mind, deciding that she wanted to sit next to her husband. The end result was that Lacey had ended up practically in Cam's lap—a surprisingly comfortable spot. It didn't occur to any of them that Cam or Lacey could have moved to the front seat.

Halfway across the desert, Jimbo started to sing, his scratchy baritone murdering "Happy Days Are Here Again." The rest of the drive was filled with Top 40 songs from the past forty years. No one was safe. Everyone from Gershwin to Huey Lewis was offered up to the clear desert sky.

Lacey found herself snuggling closer to Cam, perfectly content to have his arm around her shoulders, his thigh pressed against hers. Funny, she'd always kept a bit of a distance physically between herself and other people. She wasn't the back-slapping, hugging type. She'd only met Cam a few hours ago, but it felt right to have his long body so close. In fact, it felt rather nice.

Somewhere in the back of her mind, a warning bell sounded, but she ignored it. Tonight she wasn't going to think about anything but having a good time.

"You know, my mother thinks there's something wrong with me." Lacey waved a limp French fry for emphasis.

Lisa heaved a sigh. "Don't all parents think there's something wrong with their kids? My mother refuses to speak to me until I have a baby. I'll fool her, though. If I do have a kid, I'm going to teach it to bite my mother."

Frank shook his head, his expression solemn. "Be easier to get a dog. That's the thing. We'll get a dog and teach it to bite your mother."

Lisa gave him a fuzzy glare. "You never have liked my mother."

"So? Neither do you." The discussion might have degenerated into a fight, but Betts provided a timely interruption.

"My mother never understood why I wanted to be an actress. She wanted me to be a doctor."

Lacey and Lisa looked at Betts. Even after one too many drinks, it was impossible to imagine Betts—of the platinum-blond hair and breathy voice and big blue eyes—having a bedside manner. She was enough to give a male patient a coronary, and any female patient would simply die of despair.

"That's a shame." Frank's sympathy might have been more believable if his gaze hadn't been firmly fixed on her ample cleavage. Lisa's elbow in his ribs recalled his wandering gaze.

"I tried to explain to her that it wasn't a big deal these days to be unmarried at thirty." Lacey's attention hadn't wandered from the original subject.

They were seated in a shiny red vinyl booth in the back of a restaurant that was connected—inevitable in Las Vegas—to one of the casinos. At three in the morning, the casino was still lively, full of people determined to go home winners despite the odds against them.

Arriving in Las Vegas, they'd agreed that food was the first order of business before they decided on just how to finish celebrating Lacey's birthday. The food was mediocre but cheap. The management wanted to encourage people to spend their money at the gaming tables rather than on the dining tables.

Lacey dunked another French fry in catsup and chewed it, feeling a vague melancholy threatening to creep over her.

"Does your mother hassle you because you're not married?" she asked Cam. If she'd been more alert, she might have noticed the strange gentleness in his eyes. But alert was not something she had great quantities of in the wee hours of the morning after a few too many drinks.

"She prods a little once in a while," he admitted.

Lacey shook her head sadly. "Parents are all alike. They think marriage leads to eternal happiness."

"You know, Lacey, you and Cam should get married. That would solve all your problems." It was Jimbo who made the suggestion, his eyes bright and sharp.

There was a moment's silence, and then everyone at the table laughed, long and hard. Nobody could joke quite like Jimbo.

"Come on. We came here to celebrate Lacey's birthday. I think we should go dancing." Frank's suggestion was greeted with unanimous agreement and the restaurant was abandoned for a livelier atmosphere.

Half an hour later Lacey discovered that Cam's arms felt every bit as strong as they looked. Crowded onto the tiny dance floor, he held her close and she didn't object. It felt wonderful to rest her cheek on the soft cotton of his shirt. She could feel the beat of his heart just under her ear, and that felt wonderful, too.

She tilted her head back, her eyes meeting his in the dim light. "You're a good dancer."

"Thanks. You're pretty good yourself. I got a lot of practice dancing with my sisters."

"Sisters? How many?"

"Three sisters and three brothers."

Lacey's brow furrowed. "That's six." She was pleased with herself for coming up with the figure.

"Seven, counting me."

"There's only one of me." She frowned. "Maybe that's why my mother worries about me so much. Although I can't really blame her. Do you know what the probabilities are of a woman my age getting married?"

"Thirty doesn't seem that old."

She ignored his attempt to alleviate harsh reality. "I read this article once that said that a woman has a better chance of being struck by lightning *twice* than she does of getting married after she's thirty." She looked at him solemnly.

Cam grinned, his eyes a bright and shining blue. "Twice, huh? Those are pretty slim odds."

Lacey nodded. The margaritas and the wine she'd had before they danced combined to make her melancholy a distant and not totally unpleasant experience. Somehow, held close to Cam's broad chest, she just couldn't be depressed.

"I'll probably die an old maid."

"I don't think so."

She stared up at him, blinking owlishly. "No? Why not?"

"Gut feeling. You just don't look destined for old maidhood."

"Thank you."

The music was a slow romantic ballad that talked of love forever lost. Cam's hand moved slowly up her back. Lacey felt a slow shiver work its way up her spine, an awareness she'd never felt before. His feet barely moved, keeping up a pretense of dancing. Lacey couldn't drag her eyes from his. The room, the day, everything faded away, lost in the brilliant blue of his eyes.

As his head lowered, she noticed vaguely that there appeared to be something wrong with her breathing. But it didn't seem important. Her fingers tightened on his shoulders, her lips parting in soft anticipation.

When his mouth touched hers, it felt so right, so perfect. It was as if they'd kissed before, as if he'd held her before. Her arms slid upward to circle his neck as her mouth softened beneath the pressure of his.

He tasted of wine. His mouth was warm and firm, coaxing, hungry, demanding, promising. Lacey's head spun with the pleasure of it. Tomorrow she might blame her reaction on too much wine, but tonight she had a sense of destiny. Fate. This moment, this kiss, had to happen.

Her lashes fluttered and her eyes opened slowly as Cam drew away. On the dark dance floor no one seemed to have noticed what had just happened. No one else seemed to feel the ground rocking under their feet. Lacey stared up at Cam, feeling as if she was falling into the bright, bright blue of his eyes. Falling further and further until she could never climb out.

But then, she couldn't imagine ever wanting to.

After that, the night grew hazier. When she tried to recall it afterward, her memories came in sporadic bits, like glimpses of a countryside seen through train windows.

They'd danced some more. Another stolen kiss or two had followed that first devastating assault on her senses. There'd been more wine and a great deal of laughter. Then a sharp clear memory of a bouquet of flowers—neon flowers. There was a volley of cheers and applause, and she had a vague sense that she was the center of this approval, and then the noise and lights were gone.

She and Cam were alone, somewhere dim and private. A small bell had rung in the back of her mind, a warning Lacey ignored. She was floating on a sea of pleasure. No cares, no responsibilities, just these wonderful liquid sensations that filled her, sweeping everything else aside. She was drowning in them, but she wasn't frightened. There was someone with her. Someone strong and warm who held her, kept her safe.

She'd drifted to sleep, aware that everything had changed. Not in the way her life usually changed, which was only after careful thought on her part. No, this was a sudden, cataclysmic change that swept away everything before it.

She might regret it later, but at the moment all she was aware of was that she'd never felt quite so content.

Chapter Three

The noise sounded like a sonic rendition of hell. It boomed through her aching head with relentless force, dragging her away from the oblivion of sleep and forcing her to move. Movement was not a good idea.

Lacey groped for the source of the hideous sound, some distant part of her mind telling her that the noise could be stopped—and she had the power to stop it. Her hand connected with something smooth and cool. She fumbled with it, her fingers curling around a handle and pulling. The bells stopped and she sighed with relief.

The phone. That was it. The phone had been making that awful noise. But when you picked up a receiver, the person on the other end expected you to say hello. She dragged the receiver toward her.

"Hello?" Her voice sounded as thick and fuzzy as she felt.

"Lacey? Honey, is that you? Darlin', this is your mother. Are you there?" The words sounded muffled, and it took Lacey a moment to realize it was because there was a sheet between her and the receiver.

"Just a minute, Mother." She clawed at the sheet, pulling it away from her face, and dragged herself into a sitting position. The pain in her head intensified. It seemed to be centered right behind her eyes, radiating outward from there to make her entire body ache.

"Hello?" She tried again, this time turning the receiver so that the mouthpiece was next to her mouth instead of her ear. It made a remarkable difference in the sound.

"Lacey? Darlin', is that you? I know I shouldn't have called, but I just couldn't wait to scold you." Mamie's tone did not sound like a scold. She sounded as if she was about to burst with pleasure. Lacey tuned out the ecstatic ramblings, uncertain of their cause. She studied her surroundings through slitted eyes.

A hotel room. This was definitely a hotel room. A luxurious hotel room. She shifted her legs and was rewarded with a rolling sensation that didn't feel anything like a nice solid mattress. She was in a water bed. What on earth would she be doing in a water bed in a hotel room? She hated water beds.

A niggling sense of disaster gnawed at the back of her mind. There was something she should remember. She looked down and was surprised to find that she was nude. That was odd. She never slept in the nude.

A muffled sound penetrated her absorption and she froze, feeling her heart nearly stop. Mamie's voice droned on in her ear, but Lacey was no longer listening. She had more important things on her mind. More important than anything her mother might be saying. More important than where she was or what she wasn't wearing. Someone had just groaned. Someone very nearby. Someone in the same bed.

Lacey turned her head stiffly, the phone still held to her ear. There was someone else in the bed, someone whose tanned back contrasted with the snowy white sheets. Tanned, muscular and very bare. Her wide eyes traveled the entire length of it before stopping at the sheet that was draped low on a pair of masculine hips.

A man. There was a man in bed with her.

She squeaked and grabbed for the sheet, drawing it up over her bare breasts. She couldn't drag her eyes away from the bed's other occupant. Bits and pieces of the previous evening and night flashed through her aching head. Her dress caught in the car door, the Mexican restaurant, drinks, the mad drive to Las Vegas, more drinks, and then things became blurrier. She remembered dancing with a man, a man whose eyes had been bluer than a summer sky.

And there were other memories, a little mistier, a little harder to recapture. But they were enough to drive the last tinges of color from her cheeks.

There was another groan, and the bed's other occupant turned over, exposing an endless expanse of bare chest. His lashes flickered and then lifted. His eyes were still blue, but now they were bloodshot. Lacey stared at him, speechless. She was in Las Vegas, in bed—naked—with a man she'd known less than twenty-four hours, and unless she was delirious, they'd done more than just sleep together. And, as the final insanity, her mother was on the phone sounding as if she'd just won the lottery.

Cam stared at Lacey for a long silent moment. He shut his eyes and then opened them again as if hoping she would turn out to be a figment of his imagination. He couldn't possibly wish it as fervently as Lacey did. But nothing had changed when he opened his eyes again. He looked at her and then shut his eyes, groaning as he buried his face in the pillow.

Lacey knew just how he felt.

"Lacey? Honey? Are you there?" Mamie's voice was taking on a worried edge and Lacey responded automatically.

"I'm here, Mother." The words brought another groan from her unwanted bedmate.

"Oh, sweetheart, I'm so happy for you I could just cry. Why didn't you tell me about him? Phoebe says he's just the handsomest thing. What's his name, sugar?"

"Name? His name?" The ache in her head intensified. What on earth was her mother talking about? What did her awful Aunt Phoebe have to do with any of this? She'd made it a point to avoid the woman for years. She had a vague memory of someone telling her that they wouldn't visit her aunt. And why did Mamie want to know his name?

"Cam . . . er . . . Cam . . ."

"Cameron McCleary, for what it's worth." The words were muffled by the pillow, but distinguishable.

"Cameron McCleary, for what—" She parroted the answer into the receiver, catching herself at the last minute.

"Oh, honey, that's a lovely name."

Lacey pulled the receiver away from her ear and stared at it. Why was Mamie so happy about her only daughter being in bed with a total stranger? It was a dream. No, make that a nightmare. That was the only possible explanation. This was all some awful, horrible nightmare. And she'd wake up in her own bed and find that none of this had happened.

"You'll bring him to meet me when you get home, won't you?"

"Ah . . . if you'd like."

"If I'd like? Don't be silly, sugar. I'm dyin' to meet him. We'll have a wonderful reception just as soon as you're settled."

"Of course." Lacey gave up trying to make any sense out of it. If this was all a dream, then none of it would make sense anyway. She'd stop fighting it and just pretend she knew what was going on. "I really have to go now, Mother."

"Of course. I know I shouldn't have called, but I just couldn't wait to congratulate you."

"Talk to you soon."

She fumbled behind her for the phone, finding it more by accident than design, and set the receiver down. Her eyes didn't leave Cam's large form. The room was amazingly still. Nobody moved, nobody spoke. Lacey was still hoping to wake up and find that none of this had happened.

She jumped when Cam suddenly rolled over and sat up. He groaned, burying his head in his hands. He was too large, too bare, too male. Lacey edged toward the side of the bed.

"I'm going to die." He made the announcement with calm certainty. For an instant she felt a twinge of sympathy. She knew just what he meant. Her own head still felt as if it might roll off her shoulders at any moment.

Cam turned his head, his eyes catching hers, and Lacey jumped like a startled doe. She stared at him, trying to think of something witty to say, something to make it clear that she wasn't in the least disturbed to find herself in this situation. Nothing came to mind.

He didn't say anything. He just looked at her for a long silent moment and then returned his head to his hands, his fingers burrowing into tousled brown hair, his shoulders hunched, his whole position indicative of great pain.

Clearly someone had to take charge of the situation. They couldn't sit here all day. Lacey didn't need to look at herself to know that she was not dressed for taking charge. A sheet clutched to her chest was certainly not in any dress-for-success handbook. Her eyes skittered around the room, looking for her clothes.

Her cheeks flushed as she took in their location— scattered across the carpet, intimately entwined with a pair of jeans, a shirt and some decidedly masculine underwear. It was not how she was accustomed to seeing her clothes. Besides, they were well out of reach.

She glanced at her companion and then looked away. This was going to require some cooperation.

"Don't open your eyes."

"If I open my eyes, they're going to fall out of my head." Cam's voice was muffled, but there was no doubting his sincerity.

Lacey swung her feet off the bed, trying to keep one eye on Cam and one on what she was doing. It wasn't easy. Her right foot came down on thick carpeting, but her left landed on something crackly. Tucking the sheet behind her to make sure that nothing vital was exposed, she leaned down and picked up a sheet of heavy parchment paper. With a quick glance at Cam to make sure he hadn't opened his eyes while she wasn't looking, she glanced at the paper.

Her muffled shriek echoed in Cam's pounding head. He clutched at his ears, squeezing his eyes tightly shut, trying to keep the pain at a manageable level. A thousand small children wearing tap shoes were dancing behind his eyes. There was a pause and then a muffled moan from Lacey's direction.

Aware of his promise to keep his eyes shut, he opened them warily. If she was being attacked by a burglar, she surely wouldn't expect him not to look. Of course, in his current condition, he wasn't sure what good he'd be in the event of an attack by anything much larger than a gerbil.

Lacey was sitting on the side of the bed, and despite his pain, Cam couldn't help running an appreciative eye over the smooth length of her back. He was even capable of a vague twinge of regret when he got to where the sheet cut off his view.

She moaned again and he brought his eyes back up, noting the slump to her shoulders. "What's wrong?"

She jumped as if she'd forgotten his presence. It was a measure of how upset she was that she didn't automatically reach behind her to check the position of the sheet. Circumstances had gone beyond worry over modesty.

Lacey turned slowly and handed him the sheet of paper. Cam took it, his eyes on her face. She was pale, her eyes wide green pools of shocked disbelief.

"Read it." She sounded like the voice of doom.

Cam lowered his eyes to the paper, convinced he didn't want to see what was written on it. He was right.

It was a printed form, black ink on thick ivory paper. At the top, in elaborate script were written the words: Little Chapel of Happiness in the Desert Dell. What the hell was Desert Dell, he thought. Then he squeezed his eyes shut and then opened them again, focusing on the rest of the form.

Under ordinary circumstances, it wouldn't have taken him more than a moment to read and assimilate the information on the form. But these were far from ordinary circumstances, and he didn't want to take a chance on misinterpreting anything. Unfortunately, it was pretty hard to misinterpret what he was seeing. It was all quite straightforward.

He was holding a marriage certificate. A simple piece of paper that united two people in the bonds of holy matrimony. Even more unfortunate was the fact that the names were clear and easily read. Cameron David McCleary. Lacey Anne Newton. It took several seconds for the significance of those names to sink in.

When it did, he shut his eyes, absorbing the impact. A marriage certificate with those names on it could mean only one thing. He was married. Married to the woman who was sharing this bed—*reluctantly* sharing this bed.

He opened his eyes and looked at Lacey, seeing the same questions and answers in her eyes. He dropped the certificate, letting it float to the rumpled covers.

"Good morning, Mrs. McCleary." The joke was weak, but it didn't deserve the appalled expression that crept over her delicate features.

She looked at him, skimming over his bare chest to where the sheet rested at his waist. She didn't have to see any farther to know he didn't have a stitch on. His shorts were lying on the carpet in intimate proximity to her silk panties. She didn't have anything on. He didn't have anything on. The implications boggled the mind.

Cam's thoughts were following a similar path. Looking at the provocative pairing of their clothing, he had a sudden vivid memory of skin even softer than the silk that covered it. A sweet response that had seemed so right, so inevitable at the time. And something else. He closed his eyes, feeling the pain in his head intensify.

"Look, I—"

"Obviously, that's a fake of some sort." Lacey pointed to the form he held.

If she knew what he'd been about to say, it was clear she didn't want to talk about it right now. Cam allowed the change of subject, at least momentarily. He glanced down at the certificate and shrugged. "Looks pretty authentic to me."

"Well, it can't be authentic. I mean we wouldn't have—*I* wouldn't have just—" She waved her hand at the paper, unable to get the words out.

"Gotten married?" Cam finished helpfully and was rewarded with her glare.

"Right. People just don't do that, no matter how much they've had to drink."

"Oh, I don't know. People have done stranger things."

"Well, *I* haven't done stranger things. I don't do things like that or like this." She waved her hand, indicating herself, the bed and—most of all—him.

Cam grinned, beginning to enjoy himself despite the headache that gnawed at the back of his eyes. Maybe he was still feeling the effects of overindulgence. Whatever it was, he had a slightly light-headed feeling that things weren't as black as they looked. "You mean you don't wake up in strange hotel rooms with men you barely know?"

"No, I don't."

"That's good to know. I'd hate to think that I'd married a woman of loose moral character and easy virtue."

Lacey's eyes turned frosty. "We are not married. And my virtue is—was—unimpeachable." Each word was bitten off, separate and distinct from the others so that there could be no mistaking their meaning.

Cam sobered. God knows, the latter was the truth. It was the first item that was still in question.

"This says we're married." He nodded to the paper in his hand and wished he hadn't. The movement got the children tap-dancing again.

"Obviously that's a fake." She spoke firmly, as if that would be enough to make it true.

Cam shrugged, resisting the urge to argue further. Maybe he was still drunk, but somehow this situation didn't upset him as much as it should have. Whether the marriage certificate was real or fake, he couldn't seem to work up any real anxiety about it.

"If you'll close your eyes," she said, "I could get my clothes." She didn't look at him, and Cam felt a twinge of guilt. He could see she didn't share his sanguine attitude toward the situation. He was acting too insensitively.

"Sure. I won't look."

Lacey hesitated, throwing a quick glance at his face. His eyes were tightly shut, but that didn't mean he couldn't open them again.

"Go on. I won't look. I promise."

Surprisingly she believed him. Something about Cameron McCleary made her trust him—which probably said something about her sanity, considering the current situation.

She eased off the bed and hurried across the carpet to her clothes. The air-conditioning felt chilly on her bare body, but the goose bumps that rose on her skin were caused more by nerves than the temperature. She snatched up her clothes, trying to avoid touching any of Cam's garments.

Throwing one last glance over her shoulder, she scurried into the bathroom and shut the door behind her with a feeling of relief. The bathroom was as luxurious as the bedroom, all pale green tile and chrome. But decor was not a prime consideration to Lacey at the moment. All that mattered was that she be alone, with a door between her and the rest of the world. Although, right now, the only part of the world that concerned her was what lay just beyond the door she was leaning against.

She drew a deep breath and forced herself to walk to the sink and turn on the tap. If she still retained some hope that this was going to turn out to be a dream, it was shattered when splashing cold water on her face didn't wake her up.

Lacey raised her head reluctantly, meeting her eyes in the mirror. She was really here, in this hotel room, with a man she'd apparently spent the night with. A man whose name was next to hers on a marriage certificate. It didn't bear thinking about. No matter how she looked at it, she couldn't quite figure out how it had happened.

She closed her eyes, trying to piece together the memories of the night before. She'd caught her dress in the car door and he'd helped her free it. Then he'd been sitting at the table and Jimbo had introduced them. Everyone had been having a great time, and someone had suggested they go to Las Vegas.

She groaned and splashed more water on her face, scrubbing at her skin. She should have known she was drunk when Las Vegas didn't sound like such a bad idea. Right then and there, she should have called a cab to take her home. Thirtieth birthday or not, there was no excuse for this insanity. Las Vegas, for crying out loud!

The marriage certificate had to be a fake. That's all there was to it. It wasn't possible that she'd actually married a man she'd just met. On the heels of the thought came a dim memory of someone saying that she and Cam ought to get married, that it would solve all their problems. Everyone had laughed, but after a few glasses of wine, maybe the idea hadn't sounded so funny.

Lacey sank down on the edge of the tub, one arm resting on the sink, her fingers trailing in the cold water. She stared at the fluffy white rug at her feet. Other memories were creeping in. They'd played the slot machines for a while and then they'd gone dancing. She didn't remember much about the music, but she recalled looking into his eyes and thinking that she'd never seen anything quite such a deep, clear blue.

She closed her own eyes, resting her forehead on her arm. He'd kissed her. That was surprisingly vivid. She could remember the way he'd tasted, the scent of him. She could also remember the way her body had tingled and how right his arms had felt around her.

After that, things grew considerably more fuzzy until there was a sudden, sharp image of a neon bouquet of flowers hanging over a pale pink altar and a solemn-faced man looking at her, looking at *them*.

Lacey swallowed a sob. She'd really done it. She'd actually married Cameron McCleary—a man she'd met only hours ago, a man she knew nothing about. And as if marrying him wasn't enough, she'd slept with him. Made love with him. Her memories on that point were even more vague, but they were enough.

She leaned her forehead against the cold tile, squeezing her eyes shut to hold back the tears. Crying wasn't going to solve anything now. What was done was done. Drunk or not, how could she have done something so stupid, so irresponsible? You'd think that, after thirty years, a certain kind of behavior would be ingrained enough to survive even the assault of too many margaritas.

A solitary tear, which escaped to trail forlornly down her cheek, was impatiently dashed away. She stood up, drawing in a deep breath before facing her reflection again in the mirror.

She straightened the slump of her shoulders and took another deep breath. One thing she'd learned by the ripe old age of thirty: there was no erasing what had already been done. You just had to learn to live with it.

Obviously this situation had to be straightened out. Sitting in the bathroom moping about it wasn't going to get them anywhere. They'd had too much to drink, and they'd done something stupid. Those were the facts and there was no changing them. What was done was done. But it could be undone.

Lacey might have felt a little better if she'd been able to read Cam's thoughts on the situation. The moment she was safely out of sight, he swung his legs out of bed and reached for his underwear and jeans. His calm facade cracked in several places, helped along by a steady stream of muttered curses.

A man didn't get to the ripe old age of thirty-six without doing some stupid things, things he shouldn't have done, but this certainly took the cake as far as he was concerned. He jerked the jeans on, trying to figure out just how this situation had happened. There wasn't an answer, and he cursed some more as he reached for his shirt.

He strode to the window and stared out at the sprawl that was Las Vegas. In daylight, it lacked the glitter that made it seem almost magical at night. Now it was just a sprawling desert town with little to recommend it unless you wanted to gamble.

God knows, he'd done enough gambling while he was here, even if it wasn't the kind that emptied his pockets. He turned his back to the window and stared at the bathroom door. What was Lacey thinking? Lacey. The woman he'd made love to last night. His wife.

Lacey steeled herself and reached for the doorknob. She smoothed her hair again, wishing for a brush. The best she'd been able to do was finger-comb the tangles out. While she was in the wishing department, she might as well wish that she was home safe and sound in her own bed, she thought, and that none of this had happened.

The situation had gone beyond wishing. She opened the door and stepped into the bedroom, hoping she looked like a calm adult and not like the nervous wreck she really was.

Cam was standing by the window, and he swung around as she stepped onto the plush gray carpeting. Lacey forgot how to breathe. He'd pulled on his jeans, which were zipped but unbuttoned. His shirt hung open, exposing his chest. His feet were still bare, but he didn't seem to feel as if that put him at any disadvantage. Of course, when you were six foot two, maybe it took more than being barefoot.

"Hi."

"Hi." She had to clear her throat before she could get the word out. It was nerves. It had nothing to do with the pattern of golden brown curls that swirled over his chest.

"How's your head?"

"Okay. It's not hurting much. How's yours?"

"Better." His mouth twisted in a self-deprecating smile. "I haven't had a hangover in a long time. I'd forgotten how awful they are. I guess that will teach me not to drink too much."

"Me, too." Lacey edged her way into the room, trying not to look at his bare chest, trying not to notice the way his jeans clung to his legs, trying to look as if she did this sort of thing every day.

Cam slanted her a shrewd glance, and she had the feeling that he saw through her casual facade to the trembling little girl inside.

Lacey looked around the room, seeking something to distract her from him. She flushed when she saw her panty hose neatly laid out on the foot of the bed, her shoes lying drunkenly beneath them. Cam followed her glance.

"They were under my jeans." The minute he said the words, he wished he'd kept his mouth shut. He'd been trying for a casual approach that would ease some of her obvious embarrassment, but it would have been better to say nothing. Lacey's flush deepened to a fiery red as she snatched up the offending hose and stuffed it into the pocket of her dress.

"Thanks." The word was hardly audible. She didn't look at him.

Cam studied her averted face and gave a quiet sigh. He wished there was something he could say that would reassure her, but the situation was what it was and there wasn't much he could do about it. The pounding behind his eyes had eased, but his brain still felt as if it was functioning at half power.

Just beyond Lacey, on the bed, he could see the corner of the marriage certificate—their marriage certificate. If it was genuine, of course. He didn't really doubt that it was. So, he was married. He felt detached, as if he were watching a play. But this wasn't a play, this was his life—his and Lacey's. And there were things they had to talk about.

"Lacey—"

"We need—"

They both started at the same moment and then stopped. Cam gestured with one hand.

"Ladies first."

She hesitated a moment, her eyes flickering over his chest. She looked away, staring at a point just over his shoulder. "I was just going to say that I think we need to talk."

"Funny, that's exactly what I was going to say."

His tone invited her to relax, but the best she could manage was a weak half smile. Cam studied her, wishing he could think of something to say that would put her at ease.

A knock on the door made them both jump. Cam cocked his eyebrow at Lacey, but she shook her head.

"Who is it?"

"Room service." The voice that answered Cam's inquiry was muffled but understandable.

Cam shrugged in answer to Lacey's questioning glance. *He* hadn't called room service. He walked to the door and pulled it open. Standing outside was a waiter in a crisp white jacket, a room-service trolley in front of him. He smiled at Cam, his expression bright and helpful.

"Your coffee and croissants, Mr. McCleary." He wheeled the cart in as Cam backed away, but Cam wasn't paying any attention to him. Behind the waiter was another visitor, his broad face wreathed in a cheerful smile, his stocky figure encased in a crisp shirt and jeans, a newspaper tucked under one arm.

Jimbo grinned, his eyes full of sly amusement. "So, how's the happy couple?"

Chapter Four

"You!" Cam made the word sound like a curse.

He pounced—there was no other word for it. His long fingers closed over Jimbo's heavy shoulder as if afraid that, without physical restraint, the other might try to escape. Jimbo's grin didn't waver as Cam all but dragged him into the room.

"You low-life scum. You did this on purpose. I suppose you think it's funny."

The waiter backed away from the table, his eyes uneasy, but Jimbo wasn't fazed by Cam's fierce tone. His grin widened, if possible. He took the bill from the waiter, who hadn't been quite nervous enough to leave without it and a tip, and signed it with a flourish, then handed it back with a crisp greenback. He waited until the man was gone before answering Cam's accusation.

"Funny? What should I think is funny? And by the way, it's customary to offer a greeting beyond 'low-life scum.' Something along the lines of 'Good morning' or 'How's tricks' might be appropriate. Good morning, Lacey."

"Good morning." She responded automatically. Courtesy was as ingrained in her as brushing her teeth. From the time Lacey was tiny, Mamie had drilled into her only child the belief that bad manners were one of the cardinal sins. The good Lord had just forgotten to add them to the list.

"There. You see, Cam? That's how it's done. You really should work on it."

"The only thing I feel like working on right now is beating you to a pulp."

Jimbo blinked, widening his eyes in an expression of exaggerated innocence. "Why are you upset with me? I didn't tell you to order those last two scotches. I didn't force them down you. It's hardly my fault if you've got a hangover. You should have some coffee. It'll improve your mood."

The casual comment broke the spell that had been holding Lacey speechless. All the panic she'd been trying to hold back swept over her in a wave.

"Improve his mood? Improve his mood?" Her voice rose to something perilously close to a shriek. "What about *my* mood? How do you think I feel? *We* feel?" She waved one hand, linking herself and Cam with the gesture. "I woke up this morning in bed with a man I'd just met. I had to talk to my mother before I'd figured out what was going on and then—then I step on this."

She snatched the marriage certificate off the bed and waved it in Jimbo's face. "Do you know what this is? *This* is a marriage certificate with my name on it. My name and his. I didn't even know what his last name was when my mother asked.

"And that's another thing. How could you call my mother and tell her about this...insanity? Do you realize she thinks all this is real? How am I supposed to explain this to her?"

"I didn't call your mother," Jimbo told her, calm in the face of her rage.

"Ha! If you didn't call her, how did she find out about it?"

"Well, my guess would be that maybe someone saw the picture and called her with the news."

"Picture? What picture?" It was Cam who asked the question. Lacey seemed to have lost her voice.

"The one in the newspaper. I brought you a copy. I knew you'd want one for your wedding album."

The look Cam gave him should have fried him to a cinder on the spot. Lacey was beyond even a weak frown. She looked down at the paper Jimbo held out. It was folded in half and in the lower left-hand corner was a photograph. She thought longingly of the blurred newspaper pictures that were often such a vital part of her favorite mystery novels. Why wasn't this photo one of those vague images of shadowy figures? Why did this one have to be so clear and sharp?

The flash had caught them in a moment of laughter. Her head was tilted back against Cam's shoulder, her eyes smiling up into his. He was in profile as he looked down at her, the perfect masculine contrast to her femininity.

The picture was charming, romantic, and made Lacey want to scream. The headline above the photo stated: Love Blooms in the Desert. She moaned and closed her eyes.

"Why did they print this photo?" Cam's question was suspicious, but Jimbo shrugged, the picture of innocence.

"Newspapers call it human interest. It's a change from all the bad news. Give me a break, Cam. I didn't bribe the photographer to take the picture."

"This still doesn't explain how Lacey's mother found out about this mess." Lacey glanced up at Cam, surprised and rather pleased by the protective tone of his voice.

"How should I know?" Jimbo shrugged. "Didn't you say you had an aunt in town?"

Lacey shut her eyes. "God, yes. Aunt Phoebe. A hideous woman, and Mother did mention her this morning. I was just too groggy to make the connection."

"I bet your aunt saw the picture and called your mother."

"It's just the kind of thing she'd do." Lacey sighed and rubbed at her aching forehead. "I keep thinking this is all some kind of a nightmare and I'm going to wake up any minute safe in my own bed."

"This is hardly my idea of good fun, either," Cam told her sharply.

"Do I smell trouble in paradise so soon?" Jimbo's arch tone brought two pairs of slightly bloodshot eyes to bear on him. They were neither amused nor friendly.

"If you want to live to see another day, James, I suggest you resist the urge to make any more smart remarks. I'm barely restraining my desire to tear you limb from limb as it is."

Lacey nodded, showing her approval of Cam's bloodthirsty feelings.

"Hey, why do I get the blame?"

"Because you were the only one who was sober last night. You should have put a stop to this whole absurd mess before it got to this point." Cam pinched the bridge of his nose, trying to ease the pain that throbbed behind his eyes.

"I tried. Believe me, I tried." Jimbo moved to the table and poured two cups of coffee, handing one to each of his companions.

"You didn't try hard enough," Cam told him sourly, his disposition not visibly improved by a sip of the steaming black liquid.

"What was I supposed to do? Knock you out? You were bound and determined that getting married was a great idea. The only thing I could do was offer my services as best man." He took a sip of his own coffee. "It was a lovely service."

Cam did not look impressed. "What about everybody else? Why didn't Frank do something, or Lisa, or your friend, what's-her-name?"

Jimbo shook his head. "They were all as drunk as you two. Betts cried a lot. Weddings do that to her. Frank and Lisa thought it was so romantic that they renewed their vows right there on the spot."

"Oh, God." Lacey's gasp brought both men's attention to her. Her gaze skittered from Jimbo to Cam and then away. She didn't want to look at Cam. Looking at him reminded her of waking up in bed with him this morning. It reminded her that she was married to this man. Married, for heaven's sake. She paced to the window and then back again, her fingers knotted around the thick porcelain coffee cup.

Cam watched her quietly, his expression unreadable. Jimbo watched them both, his eyes bright with interest. Lacey started to speak, met Cam's eyes and stopped. She continued to pace.

Cam's gaze wandered to the soft swishing motion of her skirt. There was something so essentially feminine in the gentle sway of her hips. He remembered the way she'd looked earlier, the sheet clutched to her chest, her hair a golden tangle on her shoulders, her wide green eyes full of shock at finding him in the bed beside her. Not even a hangover could dim the delicate beauty of her.

He was glad to see that his taste was impeccable, even when drunk. He pushed the frivolous thought away. This was a serious matter. Marriage was a serious matter. He should be horrified and appalled that he'd jumped into something so important in a moment of drunken stupidity. Yet he didn't feel particularly horrified.

Maybe it was the lingering effects of the scotch. Maybe it was the children who still tap-danced behind his eyes with malicious delight. Whatever it was, the situation just didn't seem as appalling as it should have.

Lacey paced back toward the two men and stopped. Her fingers gripped the coffee cup so tightly that Cam half expected to see it crack beneath the pressure. Her eyes reflected all the distress he should be feeling and wasn't.

"What's done is done. We're married and that's all there is to it. There's no sense in trying to place the blame." Her eyes settled on Jimbo and he shrugged his innocence. She took a deep breath and continued, "Obviously, what we need to do now is to figure out how to undo this mess. It shouldn't be a problem. We'll just get an annulment. That's simple enough."

Her announcement was greeted with total silence. Cam stared at her, his eyes a cool reflective blue, giving no clue to his thoughts. She glanced at him and then away. Every time she looked at him, she remembered too much. Things she had no business remembering about a man who was a total stranger. The ripple of sleek muscle beneath her palms; the feel of crisply curling hair against her breasts. She brought her thoughts to a skidding halt. She'd deal with that aspect of the debacle later.

"Why?" Jimbo's question echoed in the quiet room.

"Why what?" Lacey asked. Cam said nothing.

"Why get an annulment?" Jimbo spoke slowly and precisely, as if to let the impact of each word be felt separately.

Lacey's mouth dropped open, her eyes wide with disbelief. "Why? Are you nuts? The reasons are obvious."

"To whom?" Jimbo sipped his coffee, his expression calm, his English ever correct.

"To whom? To whom? To anyone with half a brain!" Lacey gestured wildly, splashing lukewarm coffee onto her wrist. Cam reached out, taking the cup from her and handing her a napkin. "You explain it to him, Cam. It's obvious."

Jimbo forestalled Cam's reply. "I don't think it's obvious at all. Think about it. What's so awful about being married? Don't tell me you weren't attracted to each other last night. It was obvious, even to someone with half a brain." He lifted his cup in Lacey's direction. "It would get your mother off your back. You're married. She doesn't have to worry about you anymore."

"We hardly know each other. Has that occurred to you?" Lacey looked to Cam for help, but he was staring at Jimbo.

Jimbo shrugged. "So what? You get to know each other after the wedding. People used to get married all the time to people they didn't know."

"This isn't the eighteenth century." She turned to Cam, her eyes fierce. "Why don't you say something? Why am I the one doing all the arguing? Why don't you tell him how ridiculous this whole idea is?"

Cam's eyes, cool blue and enigmatic, met hers. His broad shoulders lifted in a shrug. "We might as well hear what he has to say."

"But this is crazy. You don't want to stay married to me, do you?" When he didn't respond immediately, she repeated the question, her voice rising. "Do you?"

"I don't know yet." The simple response silenced Lacey. She stared at him, unable to believe what she was hearing.

Jimbo grinned and reached out to pick up a croissant. "I'll leave you two to talk. But think about it. It might not be such a bad arrangement. Besides, I think you're perfect for each other."

The door shut behind him, leaving Cam and Lacey alone.

"You were kidding, right?" Lacey's tone pleaded with him to agree. "You can't possibly be serious about this. I mean, we don't know each other. We can't stay married."

"We can do anything we want. Have some more coffee. I don't know about you, but my head still feels like it belongs to somebody else."

Lacey took the cup from him automatically. He gestured to one of the chairs the waiter had pulled up near the table, and she sat down, feeling as if she could use the support. Cam settled himself in the other chair, stretching his long legs out in front of him.

Lacey stared at his feet. They were still bare. She tucked her own bare toes back under the chair, feeling an absurd sense of intimacy that they were sitting here in this hotel room with no shoes on. The rumpled bed was only a few feet away, Cam's shirt was still unbuttoned, but somehow, their bare toes seemed much too intimate.

"How are you feeling?" His tone was so gentle that Lacey felt tears sting her eyes.

"Stupid. Confused. Like a total fool. You may not believe this, but I'm not in the habit of waking up in bed with a complete stranger."

"I know that." His tone was so easy that Lacey dared to look at his face. He was watching her, his expression difficult to read. But there was certainly no judgment or criticism there.

She drew a breath, feeling calmer. Things could have been worse. He could have been a real jerk about the whole thing, instead of doing what he could to put her at ease. Still, they had to decide how to go about getting out of this crazy situation. Preferably as quickly as possible so that she could start picking up the pieces of her life.

"I know you were only kidding," Lacey said, "about us staying in this situation. Jimbo can be hard to deal with."

"True. But I wasn't kidding. I think we should talk about our options. *All* our options." He looked up, catching Lacey's openmouthed surprise, and his lips twitched in a smile. "Is it so awful to contemplate being married to me?"

"To you? No. I mean, I hardly know you." She stopped, trying to gather her wits, aware that she was blushing like a bride. No, that was the wrong simile. She wasn't a bride. Well, she was a bride, but not really. She shook her head sharply, clearing the tangle of her thoughts.

"It's nothing personal." She spoke slowly and carefully, trying to sound as reasonable as possible under the circumstances. "But we don't know each other. People who don't know each other don't get married."

"Usually, they don't. But we've already done it. Don't you think it might be fate? Kismet?"

"How about too much to drink?" Lacey's tone was all the firmer for the fact that, looking into those blue eyes, she found herself wanting to believe in kismet.

"Maybe. But now that it's done, we should think about it before we go off half-cocked again."

Lacey took a quick swallow of coffee. He was actually suggesting that they stay married. The idea was incredible. Ridiculous. It made absolutely no sense at all. And she was going to tell him that.

Just as soon as they got over the shock of discovering that it wasn't as appalling as it should be.

"Think about it, Lacey. Is it really such an awful idea? I don't know about you, but I haven't had a whole lot of luck finding someone I want to share my life with."

"Yes, but this isn't the way to do it." *Why was he beginning to sound so rational?*

"Why not? I'm thirty-six. You're thirty. We're both still alone."

"That's not so old."

"No. But we're not kids anymore, and nothing's come along so far. Now, here we are, already married. Why not explore the possibilities?"

Lacey pushed her hair back from her face, wishing for a hair band. Wishing for fresh clothes and a hot shower. Wishing that she was home safe and sound in her own bed.

Her lonely bed.

She stole a glance at Cam. He looked so relaxed sprawled in the chair. Could he really be so calm? Didn't this thing bother him at all? He looked as if nothing ever disturbed him.

You could really lean on a man like that.

She didn't need anyone to lean on. She was a strong woman, proud of her independence. She was running a successful business. Had a home of her own. The day was long past when a woman married a man because she couldn't make it on her own.

But wouldn't it be nice to have someone to come home to?

She scowled into her coffee cup. She was actually considering this madness. Was it possible that the coffee was drugged? She'd done something incredibly stupid last night, but that didn't mean she had to stick by it. No one could expect that.

She shook her head. "No. No, it would never work. It's an interesting idea, but it would never work."

"Why don't you think about it before you make up your mind?"

She shook her head again. "No. I don't need to think about it. The idea is nuts."

Cam drew in a deep breath, letting it out slowly. "I think we need to talk about something."

"We really don't need to," Lacey said quickly. She had the feeling that, whatever it was he wanted to say, she didn't want to hear it. "Let's just get ourselves out of this situation as quickly as possible. An annulment shouldn't be hard to get."

"An annulment is only possible when a marriage hasn't been consummated."

Cam's quiet words struck her with the force of a blow. She didn't know if what he'd said was true, but she was too embarrassed to pursue it. It was the first reference either of them had made to the fact that they'd done more than just share a bed the night before. She'd been holding onto the vague hope that Cam's memory was even hazier than hers.

"Okay, a divorce then." She had the feeling she was hearing someone else's voice. It sounded so calm. "If we could get married on a moment's notice, we ought to be able to get divorced almost as fast.''

"Lacey." Cam's voice was quiet, but something in it drew her eyes to his face. He looked concerned, regretful, but there was an iron set to his jaw that said that he wasn't going to just drop the subject.

"What?" She sounded sullen but there was nothing she could do about it. She'd never felt so humiliated in her life. What must he think of her? That she fell into bed with every man she met? She could hardly blame him if that's what he thought.

"Lacey, we really need to talk about this. I'm not in the habit of marrying a woman, making love to her and then divorcing her the next day. It's just not my style."

He paused, as if waiting for some response. There wasn't one and he sighed before continuing, his voice gentle. "Especially not when that woman happens to have been a virgin."

Lacey's eyes jerked up to his and then away. She felt her skin flush and then pale. She didn't want to deal with this. She didn't want to deal with anything. She just wanted to go home to her own safe, lonely bed and bury her head under the covers and stay there for the next five or ten years.

But she couldn't do that. At least not until she'd dealt with the current situation. Cam was watching her, waiting for her to say something.

"It's no big deal." As soon as the mumbled words were out, she felt like a fool. No big deal? Couldn't she have come up with something a little more adult?

"No big deal?" Cam questioned. "Lacey, the first time a person makes love is generally a fairly big deal. The fact that you've waited this long means it must have been important to you."

"Waited this long?" She flared up defensively. "You mean, there must be something wrong with me because I was still a . . ." She stumbled over the words. "A . . . you know. . . at thirty? Well, there's nothing wrong with me."

Cam caught the hand she'd been waving for emphasis. "I don't think there's anything wrong with you. All I'm saying is that it must have meant something to you."

Lacey tugged on her hand but he ignored her, watching her with those damned eyes that were so sympathetic. She stopped struggling, her anger leaving her abruptly. It wasn't his fault that they were in this situation. That was the annoying part of it. It wasn't really anyone's fault.

How was she supposed to explain why she hadn't slept with a man in all of her thirty years? It wasn't that she hadn't been tempted a time or two. There'd been that boy in college, but something had made her hold back, and she wasn't sorry she had. Now she could barely remember his face.

She'd just never found someone who made her want to make that commitment. And as the years passed, it had begun to seem like more of a commitment than it had when she was eighteen. When she slept with a man, she wanted to at least feel as if there was a possibility of a lasting relationship. And she'd never felt that with any of the men she'd dated.

She became aware that Cam was still watching her, still holding her hand. She shrugged, trying to look casual.

"I didn't avoid going to bed with a man out of some deep religious conviction, if that's what you meant by it meaning something to me."

"That's not what I had in mind, but I'm relieved to know you weren't considering entering a convent."

"I'm not." She tugged her hands loose, wanting to end the conversation. "Look, I don't see why we're talking about this. It's over and done with and it can't be changed."

"No, but maybe we could build on it."

"You don't build on a drunken marriage."

"Why not? Lacey, we must have felt something for each other, or drunk or not, we wouldn't have gotten married last night. Come on, tell me you didn't feel an attraction between us when we met."

"An attraction, yes, but that doesn't mean I wanted to marry you!" she cried.

"So, we didn't plan it very carefully. But we might have ended up here anyway."

"In a sleazy hotel room in the world's sleaziest city? I don't think so."

"I mean, we might have ended up married," he said quietly.

Lacey opened her mouth to deny the possibility and found herself without a thing to say. She *had* been attracted to Cam, more attracted than she liked to admit. Was it possible he was right? Might their relationship have headed in that direction? She shook her head.

"No. It's crazy. Besides, that's not a good excuse to stay together."

"Why not?" Cam persisted. "Why not give it a shot now that we've gone this far? We could get to know each other just as well after the marriage as we could have before."

"No." But she was weakening. She could hear it. So could Cam.

"Lacey, you slept with me last night. We made love. That's clearly not something you do casually."

"I was drunk!"

"So was I, but maybe that just means our defenses were down. Maybe it made it possible for us to skip all the preliminary garbage and get right to the heart of things."

"You sound like a cross between Sigmund Freud and a liquor salesman."

Cam grinned, hearing the softening in her tone. "Come on, Lacey, take a chance. Let's give it a try."

Lacey shot to her feet. "I can't believe I'm even considering this! This is the most ridiculous idea I've ever heard. We might not even like each other once we get to know each other.

"And what about the practical problems? I don't know where you live. You don't know where I live. Who's going to move in with whom? What if you're a slob and leave your dirty socks all over the place? What if you hate my mother? Oh, God, my mother! How am I going to explain this to her?"

Cam stood up, taking her hands and holding them between his palms. Lacey was aware of the warmth of his skin, the calluses on his fingers, the strength that radiated from him. "I already like you," he said. "I don't think I'm going to change my mind on closer acquaintance. As for the practical problems—I'm reasonably neat, no dirty socks. I have a house in upper Glendale. There's plenty of room for you to move in. I must admit that my moving would be a bit of a problem since my workshop is in the garage, but if you hate the place, we can work something out.

"I'm sure I'll like your mother but if I don't, I can still manage to be civil. Lots of people don't like their in-laws, and it doesn't mean the marriage is doomed. And there's nothing to explain to your mother. You can tell her that we just couldn't resist the chance to get married when we found ourselves surrounded by the romance of the slot machines and blackjack tables. Overcome with emotion, we decided that only marriage would do, and we rushed to the nearest chapel to pledge our troth beneath the light of a neon bouquet."

His description drew a reluctant chuckle. He made it all sound so reasonable, as if this wasn't the craziest thing she'd ever done in her entire life. Besides, Mamie was just enough of a romantic sucker to fall for his corny story.

Her smile faded and she shook her head, staring at their linked hands.

"I don't know. It almost sounds reasonable when you say it, but I know it's crazy."

"It doesn't have to be crazy. We're sane adults. If we go about this right, it could work." His tone grew more serious. "Lacey, I wouldn't expect anything from you until you were ready for it. My house has a spare bedroom and I wouldn't pressure you."

She blushed, keeping her eyes down. She appreciated his reassurance, but she was surprised to find that she hadn't needed it. She trusted him. Despite everything, she trusted him.

"It's nuts." She was weakening.

"But it's worth a try, isn't it?" he coaxed. "Nothing ventured, nothing gained. No pain, no gain."

"No pain, no gain?" she questioned. "I'm not sure that one is relevant here."

Cam shrugged. "I always get my clichés confused." His fingers tightened around hers. "Come on, Lacey. Let's give it a try."

She looked at him, trying to read something beneath his calm facade. *It had to be a facade.* No one could really be that calm at a time like this. But there was nothing visible beneath the still blue of his eyes. *Still wa-*

ters run deep. She had the feeling the phrase applied to Cameron McCleary.

"You really want this, don't you?"

"Yes, I do."

"Why?"

Something flickered in his eyes, gone too quickly for her to identify. His fingers tightened on hers and then dropped away as he sat back in his chair.

"My mother always told me that I have a bad habit of refusing to admit when I've made a mistake. Maybe that's why I want to give this a try."

Reaching for her coffee cup, Lacey stared at the film of liquid in the bottom as if the answer to all her problems could be found there.

It was a crazy idea, and yet ... She was thirty and she hadn't even come close to getting married. Now here she was, married to a man who seemed like the answer to a dream. Not only was he attractive, he was nice, intelligent and considerate. He had a sense of humor.

She'd always planned her life so carefully, looking before she leapt, trying to see what lay ahead before she chose any one path. She had a successful business, friends, a nice apartment. Everything she'd planned to have. Careful planning had gotten her exactly what she wanted.

Hadn't it?

In the end, the answer wasn't in her coffee cup. It wasn't even in her head. It was in her heart. She wanted to jump without looking just once in her life. Maybe she'd known exactly what she was doing last night when she married a total stranger. A few drinks had smothered the practicality that had been threatening to choke the life out of her life.

Maybe it wasn't the smartest thing to do. She might live to regret it, but if she walked away without giving this insanity a chance, she knew she'd spend the rest of her life wondering if it might have worked.

Lacey took a deep breath and looked at Cam. He was watching her, something in the set of his shoulders telling her that her answer was important.

"Okay." She couldn't seem to get out anything beyond that one word. Okay. Such a silly word to use to change her entire life.

"Great." Cam gave her a slow smile that made her knees quiver. "We'll make it work, Lacey. I've got a feeling about this."

Her laughter was shaky. "So do I, but I doubt if it's the same one. I must be crazy to even consider this."

He held his hand out. Lacey stared at it for a long moment before putting her hand in his. Cam's fingers closed around hers, warm and strong. Her eyes widened as the grip on her hand drew her forward until only inches separated them.

"The groom should always kiss the bride," he told her, his voice husky.

"Don't you think you did that last night?" She swallowed, keeping her eyes on his chest.

"That doesn't count. This is our real beginning." He slipped a hand beneath her chin, tilting her head back until her eyes met his. "Do you mind if I kiss you, Lacey?"

She swallowed hard and shook her head, unable to drag her eyes from his.

His mouth touched hers gently, asking more than demanding. Lacey's hands came up to rest against his chest, crisp whorls of hair tickling her palms. Cam's arms circled her back, pulling her closer. She felt surrounded but not trapped. Sheltered in his strength. It was a kiss of exploration, as if he understood that they needed time to get to know each other.

But there was passion underlying the gentleness. Lacey could feel it quivering in her bones like a sound that lay just beneath the level of hearing, more felt than heard. She heard a soft sigh of protest as Cam moved back and was only distantly aware it was her own.

Her lashes quivered a moment and then lifted, staring up into eyes the color of a summer day. His look was questioning, his eyes full of warm hunger. A hunger that reflected her own.

Her gaze dropped away from his. She hadn't expected that response. Hadn't planned on melting against him like that. She wasn't sure if it was lust or insanity that made her suddenly feel more hopeful about this crazy plan.

Chapter Five

"Are you sure we shouldn't try and find the others? At least Frank and Lisa. They'll worry about us."

Lacey's anxious question was addressed to Cam's broad back as he moved ahead of her. He glanced over his shoulder as he opened the door marked Stairs.

"They'll just assume we did exactly what we're doing and left without them. Believe me, this is the safest way. Do you want to face Jimbo and tell him we've decided to take his advice and give this a try?"

"No." She didn't have to think about her answer, but she was still frowning as she followed him into the cement stairwell. "But do you really think sneaking down the stairs is necessary? We're on the eighth floor."

"It would be just like Jimbo to have arranged some kind of a welcoming party at the elevators. He's probably found some old shoes to drape around our necks and a pile of rice to throw at us."

"But how is he going to know we're on our way down?" Lacey was growing a little breathless as they descended what seemed like endless flights of stairs.

Cam paused on the landing next to a door marked with a five. "I called down to check out, remember? He could have asked the desk to let him know when we checked out."

She swallowed a moan of protest as he started downward again. Aerobics three times a week were clearly not enough.

"Don't you think you're being a little paranoid? He's not the CIA."

Cam threw her a quick look over his shoulder without pausing. "You can't have known Jimbo as long as I have, or you'd know just how devious he can be. He wouldn't have to threaten the desk clerk. He could spin him a story about us having just been married and he wants to congratulate us."

Lacey scowled, but she didn't argue anymore. For one thing, she didn't have enough breath. And for another, she did know Jimbo quite well, and the scenario Cam had just painted would be typical of him. Besides, they only had two more flights to go.

Cam opened the door to the lobby and they tried to step out as inconspicuously as possible. The continual clanging of slot machines mingled with the usual hustle and bustle of a big hotel. Palm trees filled an atrium in the middle of the lobby.

Cam reached out to take her hand, and Lacey wondered if he felt the little spark of electricity when they touched. She was so distracted by the tingling sensation that it took her a moment to register what he was saying.

"I told you he'd be lurking in the underbrush."

She looked in the direction he indicated. Lurking in the underbrush wasn't entirely accurate, but there was no mistaking Jimbo's stocky frame hovering on the other side of the planters. He was facing the elevators, clearly waiting. Lacey's fingers tightened around Cam's in silent gratitude that she'd been spared whatever loud and probably embarrassing greeting their friend had in mind.

Cam grinned down at her, waggling his eyebrows in a way that made her want to giggle. "Act natural and we may escape detection."

He moved toward the front doors, shortening his stride to match hers. Act natural. Now why did he have to say that? She felt as if she was wearing a neon sign that begged for attention. Everyone within a fifty-yard radius must surely be looking at them. She was vividly aware of her bare legs, her rumpled dress, the fact that the only makeup she had on was a pale lipstick she'd found in the bottom of her purse.

How many people had seen that stupid picture in the paper? Unconsciously, her hand tightened around Cam's, but she needn't have worried. People who came to Las Vegas had other things on their minds. They slipped out the front door without incident.

The hot dry air was a shock after the hotel's air-conditioning. A line of taxis waited to the left, and it took Lacey a moment to realize that Cam wasn't heading in that direction. His grip on her hand pulled her to the right.

"Cam, the taxis are over there." She tugged against his hold, but he shook his head.

"We're not going to need a taxi. I've got a better idea."

To the right of the hotel was the parking lot. She'd seen it from the window of their room, but she didn't see how the parking lot was going to offer them a better idea than a taxi. At least she didn't see until she realized where Cam was headed.

There was no mistaking the lines of the big black car he was approaching. The Cadillac was Jimbo's pride and joy. He'd restored it from the ground up, and Lacey had learned far more about the art of restoration than she'd ever had any desire to know. It was all he'd talked about for months. Three years after it was complete, he still treated the car as if it were made of porcelain.

"What are you planning on doing?" Her voice was hushed, though there was no one within listening distance.

"I'm going to steal us a ride to the airport." He said it so calmly, as if grand theft was an everyday part of his life.

"You're going to steal Jimbo's car?" Her voice rose to an incredulous squeak before disappearing altogether.

"Sure. Why not?" The top was still down, and Cam opened the door, his movements so casual she might have believed it was his car. Only she knew it wasn't.

"Do you know what Jimbo is going to do when he finds it gone? He's going to report it to the police and they're going to be watching for it. It's not like it's an easy car to miss. And when they catch us, they'll throw us in jail, which will just put the perfect cap on my birthday celebration."

Cam had slid into the driver's seat and was fumbling under the dash, his expression intent. Lacey wasn't even sure he'd heard her dire predictions. The engine suddenly turned over, catching with a well-bred roar. Cam grinned in triumph.

"Some things you just don't forget. Get in. And you don't have to worry about the police. We're going to make sure Jimbo knows exactly what happened to his car."

Lacey hesitated a moment longer before walking around to the passenger side and climbing in. Maybe it was Cam's smile. Maybe it was the look in those incredible eyes. Or maybe turning thirty had brought on insanity.

She closed her eyes as he backed the big car out of the parking space. She half expected to hear the wail of a siren and see the long arm of the law coming at her. But nothing happened. The car responded to Cam's touch just as it always had to Jimbo's. Looking out over half a mile of hood, she didn't see any Bonnie-and-Clyde-style roadblocks. She dared to relax a little.

"How are you going to let Jimbo know that we've got his car so he doesn't sic the FBI on us?"

"Watch."

They circled the back of the hotel, coming up in front of the entryway. Cam pulled the car to a halt but left it idling. A gray-coated valet hurried forward, but Cam waved him back. He leaned on the horn and the unmistakable, three-note blare echoed against the building. Lacey realized what he was doing. If Jimbo was still lurking in the lobby, he couldn't help but hear the horn.

She turned toward the doors just as they slid open to reveal Jimbo's stocky form. He took one look at the car and his face dropped.

"Hey!" He started down the steps at a pace that threatened to send him rolling down rather than walking.

"Hey, yourself," Cam called as he put the car in gear. "Have a nice trip home."

"McCleary!" Jimbo's bellow was probably audible halfway to the coast, but Cam didn't ease his foot off the accelerator. Lacey turned to look out the back as they pulled away from the hotel. Jimbo came to a screeching halt in the middle of the driveway. For a moment, she thought he might be contemplating his chance of catching them on foot, but he must have rated it about as low as she did. He stood there watching them, his hands on his hips, frustration quivering in every line of his body.

The car turned onto the road and Jimbo disappeared from sight. Lacey turned to face the front.

"He looked really upset."

"I know." Cam's grin took on a positively wicked edge.

"You should have told him that we were leaving the car at the airport. What if he thinks we're driving it back to L.A.?"

"He should at least think of the airport. I'll park it in some nice obvious place and bribe a guard to keep an eye on it. Besides, he deserves anything he gets. I may not remember much by way of details of what went on last night, but gut feeling tells me that Jimbo had a lot more to do with things than he's going to admit.

"Nothing would make me happier than for him to get back to Los Angeles, only to find that his precious toy is still in Las Vegas." He spoke with such good-natured malice that Lacey laughed.

THE FLIGHT to Los Angeles was quiet. The closer they got to home, the more surreal the past twenty-four hours seemed. It was hard to believe that this wasn't all some strange dream from which she'd awaken at any moment.

Lacey stole a quick glance at Cam. He looked so calm. He seemed to be taking this whole situation in stride, as if he woke up married to a stranger every day.

She turned her head to look out the window. The sky beyond was a clear pale blue broken by an occasional puff of cloud. The drifting shadows created dark patches on the featureless expanse of tan desert.

Was she crazy to give this marriage a try? Her logical
mind shouted yes. Marriage was tough enough when two
people knew and loved each other. It took a certain
amount of blind optimism even then. But to go into it
with a man she didn't know, had only just met—that had
to be the height of insanity.

If she had any sense at all, she'd tell him right now that
she was going to apply for an annulment—she'd see
about this consummation thing—as soon as she set foot
in Los Angeles. He'd probably be relieved.

But she didn't turn her head, didn't say anything.
Weighed next to every logical argument against this
marriage was a gut-level feeling that she'd regret it the
rest of her life if she backed out now. She didn't know
why but this was something she had to do. And buried
deep inside was a building excitement, an anticipation
that she wasn't ready to acknowledge. There was a feeling that Cam McCleary might be just what she needed to
turn her life upside down and give it a thorough shake.

Once they arrived in Los Angeles, it didn't take long to
rent a car. Cam drove, for which Lacey was grateful. Her
thoughts were still too scattered, jumping from one thing
to another. She was grateful she didn't have to try to
concentrate on negotiating the freeway traffic.

They'd spoken very little since boarding the plane in
Las Vegas. She wondered if Cam was feeling the same
doubts and uncertainties that plagued her. As he eased
the car into the heavy traffic on the San Diego Freeway
she found herself watching his hands. A quick flash of
memory reminded her of just what those hands had felt
like on her skin.

"You know, I don't even know what you do for a living." She spoke abruptly, as much to interrupt her own

train of thought as anything else. "You said something about a shop in your home?"

"I'm a carpenter, more or less. I make furniture, cabinets, that sort of thing."

"It sounds interesting." Her tone was a little overenthused. Privately, she wondered if it was possible to earn a living that way. Some of her doubt must have shown. Cam's mouth quirked into a half smile.

"I make a decent living. Enough to support a wife."

"I don't need anyone to support me, thank you. I make a very good living on my own. Besides, we don't have that kind of marriage."

"What kind is that?" he inquired politely.

"A real one and, even if we did, I would still keep my shop."

"Why wouldn't you? I gather your shop does very well."

"Yes, it does." Lacey spoke without arrogance but with a definite note of pride in her voice.

"Maybe I should give up my work and let you support me in the manner to which I'd like to become accustomed." He grinned, inviting her to share his amusement. Lacey smiled reluctantly. There was something wrong with this picture. They shouldn't be talking and laughing like old friends. Where was all the angst and uncertainty? Didn't he ever worry about anything?

"You know, you really didn't have to drive me home," she said, "I know Pasadena is out of your way."

Cam slanted her a look of amusement. "It's practically next door. Besides, my mother taught me that a gentleman always sees a lady home after a date."

"This has sure been one hell of a date. Oh, my God."

"What?" Cam lifted his foot off the gas pedal in response to Lacey's horror-struck tone. "What's wrong?"

"Your mother."

"My mother?" He glanced in the mirror and stepped on the gas again to avoid being swallowed whole by a semi.

"I'd forgotten all about her."

"I didn't know you were supposed to remember her."

"She's going to hate me."

The light dawned, and Cam smiled. "Mom is going to love you."

"How could she love me? She doesn't know me and everyone knows that mothers always hate the woman their son marries."

Cam grinned. "My mother isn't the possessive type."

"All mothers are possessive," she said gloomily. "I was worried about how you were going to deal with my mother, but at least I know she's going to love you. She'd love any man I married."

"Gee, thanks. You make me feel so special." He made the transition to the Ventura Freeway before glancing at her again. "Take my word for it. My mother will like you. Anyway, you don't have to worry about her for a while. She lives in Virginia."

"What about the rest of your family? Didn't you say there were ten or twelve of you?"

"Only seven. And most of them are scattered across the country. The only one you're likely to meet is Claire. She lives in the Simi Valley. We usually all manage to get together for Christmas, but that's quite a ways off, so I don't think you need to panic yet."

Somehow that knowledge did little to allay Lacey's concerns.

IT SEEMED TYPICAL of Cam that he found a parking place right outside her apartment building. They were usually as rare as hens' teeth. Her steps were slow as she led the way into the building. She'd started trying to imagine Cam's reaction to her home even before they'd pulled off the freeway. Somehow, Cam's tall form and her intensely modern decorating refused to connect in her mind.

Not that it really mattered, of course. It was none of his business how she'd decorated her home. She certainly didn't care what he thought. The elevator came to a halt on her floor and they stepped out into the carpeted hall. Lacey's steps slowed still further, but she could delay the inevitable only so long. Once they stopped in front of her door, they could hardly stand there staring at it. She fished the key out of her purse and unlocked the door, throwing it back with an air of defiance that caused Cam to give her a puzzled look.

She'd spent months fixing this place, studying magazines, getting just the right feel, the proper air of chic. It had cost a small fortune, but it looked exactly like a picture in *House and Garden*. She looked at the rich scarlet and gold tones and then looked at Cam.

"You hate it, don't you?"

"No. No. I mean, it's very... nice. It looks nice."

Lacey looked at the sofa that had cost her a month's profits, the carpet that had been carefully dyed to match the wallpaper, the rather malevolent-looking metal sculpture that dominated one corner of the room.

"Nice?"

"Well, I mean interesting nice. Really interesting nice. My place isn't anything like this." Cam studied the metal sculpture, tilting his head to the side as if wondering if the piece was upside down. "Nothing like this at all."

Lacey looked at him and then looked at the room and her mouth quivered. He looked so out of place. No, the

room looked out of place. Funny, she'd lived with this for
almost three years and had never realized how superficial it was, how little she actually liked it. Cam glanced
at her and misread her expression.

"It really is very nice, Lacey. It's obvious you've
worked hard to make it look this way," he told her earnestly.

The quiver became a chuckle. He so obviously hated
it and he was trying so hard to be complimentary. Cam
cocked one eyebrow.

"Is it something I said?"

"Sort of. You really hate this place, don't you?"

He looked around and then looked back at her, reading the amusement in her eyes. His shoulders lifted in a
sheepish shrug. "It's really not my cup of tea, but it does
look like you spent a lot of time on it. After seeing this,
I'm not sure you're going to like my place. It's very different. Simpler."

"You mean it's not gaudy?"

"I didn't say that. This isn't gaudy. It's just
very...bright." Lacey laughed out loud and he shrugged
again. "Sorry. Like I said, it's not my cup of tea."

"I'm not all that sure it's mine. Would you like some
coffee or something to eat?"

"No, thanks." Cam ran his fingers through his hair. "I
guess I ought to be going. I could use a hot shower and
you'd probably like some time alone."

"I...yes, I guess I would." She couldn't explain, even
to herself, why the idea didn't hold more appeal. Heaven
knew, after the last twenty-four hours, being alone must
be exactly what she needed. But once she was alone, she'd
have to think about what she'd done, what she'd agreed
to.

"You won't change your mind, will you?"

Her eyes swept up to meet Cam's. She felt swallowed in their intense blue. Slowly she shook her head. "I won't change my mind."

And she knew she wouldn't. No matter how crazy this whole idea was, she was committed to it.

"Good. Listen, why don't I pick you up for lunch tomorrow and we can discuss the particulars of our living arrangements?"

"Okay." She was surprised by the strength of her desire to see him again. She gave him the address of the shop and then followed him to the door. Cam hesitated in the doorway, his eyes skimming over her tousled hair and lingering on her mouth. For a moment, Lacey thought he was going to kiss her. She wasn't sure whether or not to be disappointed when he didn't. With a quick smile, he strode down the hallway toward the elevator. Lacey watched him until he turned the corner and then shut the door slowly and leaned against it.

She'd been longing for a hot shower and clean clothes, but she didn't move. Married. She was actually married. It didn't seem real. In fact, the last twenty-four hours didn't seem real. Had it really been only yesterday that she'd sat in Mamie's living room, listening to her lament her daughter's single state?

She shook her head, moving away from the door and heading toward the bedroom. How quickly things had changed. She glanced around the living room, thinking about all the time and money she'd spent decorating it. Funny, she didn't feel so much as a twinge of regret at the thought of leaving the place. Seeing it through Cam's eyes had made her realize how little she really liked it. It was striking, but it lacked warmth. It was about as far from the elegant clutter she'd grown up with as it was possible to get.

Maybe she'd been making some kind of statement. But she was a little old for defiant statements. She was thirty now, whether she liked it or not. And a married woman, whether she liked it or not. Wedded and bedded. The old phrase came to mind and she blushed.

She might be going crazy, but she felt a definite twinge of anticipation at the thought of being married to Mr. Cameron McCleary. Shaking her head, she pushed open the bedroom door and headed for the shower. It had certainly been one hell of a day.

"YOU REALIZE, of course, that I could have had you arrested for grand theft."

Cam glanced up. Jimbo stood in the doorway, the late-afternoon sun silhouetting his stocky body. Cam returned his attention to the workbench. "You realize, of course, that I could shoot you and any judge would call it justifiable homicide," he suggested conversationally.

"Shoot me? Shoot me!" Jimbo stepped farther into the shop, his voice rising on an incredulous note. "I'm not the one who stole his best friend's car and left it parked in a dingy corner of a parking lot, just waiting to be stolen."

"It wasn't a dingy corner. I parked it right next to the guard shack. Besides, no one would steal that thing. No one but an accountant could afford the gas it guzzles."

"What about the mental anguish I suffered?" Jimbo reached out and picked up a handful of pretzels from a bowl on the bench, crunching into one to punctuate his complaint.

"Any mental anguish you suffered was well deserved," Cam told him.

"For what? What did I do?" Jimbo's round face was the very picture of cherubic innocence. Cam was not impressed. He set down the plane he'd been using to shave thin strips of oak from a board and leaned one hip against the bench, fixing his friend with an implacable gaze.

"You set us up. I haven't figured out quite how, and I'm not totally sure about the why, but I *know* you set us up."

"Us? You mean you and Lacey? I told you, there was nothing I could do. You were hell-bent on marriage. I tried to talk you out of it, but there was just no changing your minds."

"Sure. The day hasn't arrived when you couldn't talk someone out of something. Like I said, you set us up."

"Look, I'm not denying that I think the two of you would make a great couple. But the only setting up I did was in arranging for you to meet. I admit to that much, but anything beyond that was purely your own idea. What could I do?"

He lifted his hands and shrugged, but Cam didn't look impressed. He picked up the plane again and turned his attention to the wood. Some people might have taken it as a hint, but Jimbo had never been much inclined to take hints. He lingered, crunching another handful of pretzels.

"So, how'd it go?"

Cam hid a smile. He'd known that Jimbo's curiosity wouldn't be restrained for long.

"How did what go?" He carefully planed another fraction of an inch from the board.

"You and Lacey."

"What about me and Lacey?"

"How did it go? What did you decide?"

"About what?" Jimbo fairly danced with impatience, and Cam bit the inside of his lip, enjoying the moment.

"What did you decide about staying married? Are you going to give it a try or what?"

Cam looked up, widening his eyes in apparent surprise. "Are you kidding? Nobody in their right mind would try and make a go of marriage to a total stranger."

Jimbo's shoulders slumped. "I thought, when you two left like that, that maybe you'd decided to give it a try."

"We did." Cam spoke so calmly that it took several seconds for the meaning of his words to sink in. Jimbo stiffened, staring at him.

"You did?"

"Lacey is moving in here tomorrow."

Jimbo's grin threatened to split his face in two. "Why didn't you tell me? It's been almost a week. I knew you were perfect for each other. I knew it."

"Well, that remains to be seen," Cam pointed out with a dry smile.

"You're perfect for each other. I'm never wrong about these things."

"It must be nice to be right all the time."

"Yes, it is," Jimbo agreed modestly.

Cam laughed. It was impossible to remain even mildly annoyed with Jimbo.

"You wait and see. You and Lacey are going to be great together."

"I hope you're right."

In fact, he'd never hoped anything quite so much in his entire life. Jimbo lingered a little while longer, but Cam's heart wasn't really in the conversation and he was just as glad to see him go.

Lacey was moving in tomorrow. As of tomorrow, he was going to have to start learning how to be a husband. It was hard to believe that a life could change so completely in a week. Would he have let Jimbo talk him into joining Lacey's birthday celebration if he'd known where it was going to lead? It was impossible to say.

It wasn't that he was exactly happy to find himself married to a woman he barely knew. But he wasn't precisely unhappy, either. He'd been thinking that he needed something to shake up his life. Maybe Lacey Newton was just the ticket.

Chapter Six

Cam's home was, as he'd promised, nothing like Lacey's apartment. It was a large house set in the foothills above Glendale. White stucco and a red-tile roof made a gesture toward the area's Spanish heritage.

Lacey turned her car into the brick driveway, parking under the branches of the huge live oak that dominated the front yard. She turned off the engine but made no effort to get out of the car.

She was really here. Over the past week, she'd never quite believed she'd get to this point. Even while she was packing her clothes into boxes and loading them in the car, it hadn't felt real. Now that she was here, she was seized by a sudden attack of nerves. What was she doing here?

Before she had a chance to answer that question, she saw Cam walking toward her. Lacey watched him, her hands still gripping the steering wheel. It had only been a few days since she'd seen him, but she'd almost managed to convince herself that she'd imagined the effect he had on her breathing.

"Are you coming in, or are you going to stay there permanently?" He rested one hand on top of the car and leaned down to look through the window, one of his brows raised inquiringly.

Lacey pried her hands off the steering wheel and gave him what she hoped was a casual smile. "I was just getting a feel for the place."

"It's not huge but it's quiet. Like I said, if you don't like it, we'll work something out." Cam opened the car door and Lacey stepped out of the car, feeling as if she were taking an irrevocable step—as if marrying the man hadn't been irrevocable enough.

"It's a pretty neighborhood. Have you lived here long?" Great. She sounded like a ten-year-old at a tea party.

"Eight years. My grandparents left it to me. I thought about selling, but the garage was already set up as a workshop and it was a good location, so I stayed."

"I'm sure I'll like it."

"I hope so." There was no mistaking the sincerity in his words, and she felt some of her tension fade. He'd reminded her that she wasn't in this alone.

"You can't have brought much with you." Cam eyed her small blue compact car as if trying to imagine how a human being could fit inside. Considering his size, he'd have to wear the car rather than sit in it. The image made Lacey smile as she bent to push the front seat forward and reach for her suitcase.

"Mostly just clothes. Since the shop isn't far from the apartment, I thought it would be easier to move a little bit at a time. I've still got three months to go on my lease, anyway."

And with her apartment still available, she'd have an escape if she needed it. If the thought occurred to Cam, he didn't say anything. He reached past her and lifted the suitcase out easily. For a moment, Lacey was caught between him and the open car door. How could she have forgotten how large he was?

He was wearing jeans and a blue chambray shirt. She stared at the wedge of skin exposed by his open collar. She had a sudden memory of waking up next to him, of warm muscles and tanned skin. Her eyes swept up to meet his, and she wondered if it was her imagination that put the same memories in his gaze. She looked away. Cam stepped back and the moment was gone. But not forgotten.

"I fixed up a room for you."

"Thanks." Lacey had to clear her throat to get the word out. She shut the car door and followed him up the brick walk to the door. He tugged open the screen door and stepped back, waiting for her to enter.

She paused on the threshold, wondering if he was thinking the same thing she was. Under other circumstances, he would be carrying her into her new home. But that was hardly appropriate now. Not that she was in the least disappointed. The last thing she wanted was romantic folderol.

Taking a deep breath, she stepped into the small hallway and looked at her new home. She took in the polished hardwood floors, white plaster walls and chunky leather furniture that filled the living room. A fireplace with a rustic wooden mantel dominated one wall, and windows filled two more. Maple cabinets flanked the fireplace, hand-forged wrought-iron hardware setting off the warm wood.

"Think you can live with it?" Cam's question was light, but she heard the underlying concern. He really cared what she thought.

She nodded slowly. "I like it a lot." And no one could have been more surprised than she was to find that it was the truth. A high ceiling with exposed beams kept the modest-sized room from being overwhelmed by the bulky furniture. The huge expanse of windows further lightened the room. It was plain, almost stark, but there was something very soothing in its simplicity.

"It's very... honest. Nothing fussy or overdone."

"I'm glad you like it." The words were simple, but glancing over her shoulder, Lacey saw the pleasure in his eyes. The knowledge warmed her.

"I'll show you your room and then we can take the grand tour, if you'd like." Before she could reply, there was a strange scrabbling noise she couldn't identify. It grew rapidly closer and she threw Cam a questioning glance.

"Derwent." That was all he had time for before a furry bundle hurtled around a corner and rushed toward them. Lacey took an involuntary step backward. For a moment, she couldn't identify a head or a tail. Even the species was in doubt. All she could see was a tawny-colored mop. Derwent skidded to a halt, nails slipping on the smooth floors. A sharp high-pitched bark clarified that it was a dog. Cam set Lacey's suitcase down and bent to scoop up the animal in one hand.

"This is Derwent. He actually owns this house, or so he'd have you believe. I hope you like dogs."

"I don't know. I've never had much to do with them."

"Well, Derwent is spoiled rotten, but he's friendly."

Lacey studied Derwent doubtfully. Now that she saw him at closer range, she could see a pair of bright button eyes under the ratty beige bangs that spilled over his face. He was regarding her with the same curiosity she was displaying. A pink tongue lolled over sharp little teeth.

"What is he?"

"A Yorkshire Terrier. They're very smart."

She reached out and tentatively scratched behind one ear. Derwent's eyes closed and his tiny body quivered with pleasure in Cam's hold.

"He'll probably be your slave for life. Actually, he likes just about everybody. Except Jimbo. He terrorizes Jimbo."

"A dog with good taste," Lacey commented dryly. She still hadn't forgiven Jimbo for his part in this insane situation. She stepped back, looking at the picture Cam and Derwent made, and her mouth curved in an irrepressible smile. The tiny dog sprawled comfortably in one of Cam's hands, his short legs dangling contentedly. "You know, he's not exactly the kind of dog I'd have pictured you with. I'd have thought you'd have had something a little more . . . in proportion."

Cam's grin showed that he shared her humor. "I know. An Irish Setter maybe, or a Lab. But Derwent followed me home one day and simply refused to go away. I guess the proportions don't bother him." He bent to set the dog on the floor, and Derwent took off at a dead run down the hallway.

"Does he ever walk anywhere?" Lacey asked as the furry little body disappeared.

"Not often. I think when your legs are as short as his, you pretty well have to run to keep up with the rest of the world." Then he added, "By the way, Jimbo came by yesterday."

"Did he find his car?"

"Actually, he came by to threaten me with arrest."

Lacey ran her finger along the edge of a chunky missionary-style bench. "Did you threaten him with murder?"

"Yup." Cam bent to pick up her suitcase again, and she followed him toward the rear of the house.

"Did you tell him we were going to give things a try?" she asked.

"I told him. He said he was sure we were made for each other." Cam pushed open a door and set her bag down in the room before turning to look at her. "He said he's always right about things like that."

"Maybe he should hang out a shingle. Matchmaker With Excellent Track Record. Heaven knows, Southern California has enough palm readers and channelers. We could probably use a good old-fashioned matchmaker."

Lacey slipped by him and into the bedroom. The room wasn't large, but it had the same restful feel that characterized the rest of the house, a feeling she was beginning to associate with Cameron McCleary.

"Do you suppose he'll ask us for a testimonial?" Cam leaned in the doorway, watching her.

Lacey looked at him, trying to ignore the way her pulse seemed to pick up speed when he was around.

"I don't know. I suppose he'll have to wait and see if he was right again."

"I suppose we all will." Cam grinned and stood away from the door. "I'll give you a chance to settle in. I'm going to go start dinner."

"Do you need help?"

"I think I can manage tonight. But don't worry, I'll let you take your turn in the kitchen."

"Gee, thanks."

Cam grinned at her dry tone, but he didn't linger. He lifted a hand and disappeared back the way they'd come. Lacey looked around the room that was to be hers for who knew how long. Until she moved into the master bedroom? Until she moved back to her apartment?

With a sigh, she lifted her suitcase onto the bed and opened it. Just take one day at a time. That's what she'd promised herself she'd do. It was the only thing she *could* do.

"I HOPE YOU LIKE fried chicken." Cam turned from the stove as Lacey stepped into the kitchen.

"Are you kidding? My mother is from Georgia. Fried chicken is practically the national dish in the South."

"Then maybe I should rephrase the question. I hope you like *my* fried chicken."

"I'm sure I will. Is there anything I can do to help?"

"Just sit down and relax. Tonight is my treat." He turned back to the stove. "Is your room okay?"

"It's beautiful. Did you make the dresser that's in there?"

"One of my early efforts."

"It's lovely."

"Thanks." He scooped chicken pieces out of the sizzling oil and set them on a layer of towels to drain. Lacey watched him, realizing it was the first time she'd ever seen a man cook, except at a barbecue. He seemed to be perfectly at home as he drained oil from the pan and set about making a thick gravy.

Outside, a light rain was falling, making the little house a cozy shelter from the elements. The chicken was perfectly cooked, as were the accompaniments, and despite herself, Lacey began to relax. Maybe it was the food. It was difficult to be on guard while you were licking your fingers. Or maybe it was the company. Cam seemed to take the whole situation in stride. It made it hard to worry about what she'd gotten herself into.

They talked while they ate, nothing heavy or full of meaning, just light dinner conversation. Cam wanted to know how she'd come to start Lacey's Lovelies, and Lacey found herself telling him the joys and problems of running her own business. He was a good listener. Halfway through the meal, she stopped and apologized self-consciously.

"I should have warned you about my tendency to ramble on about the shop. I'm inclined to be a bit of a bore about it."

"I wasn't bored. You've obviously worked very hard. You should be proud."

Lacey pushed a crumb around the edge of her plate with the tip of one pale pink fingernail. "I am proud of it. I've worked very hard to make it a success."

"Success usually doesn't come without a lot of work."

"My mother thinks I've worked too hard. She thinks I've put my personal life on hold."

"Have you?"

She glanced up, reading the question in his eyes. Question, but no judgment. She shrugged.

"I don't know. I suppose I have. Not consciously, but it's hard to have a personal life when you're getting a business started."

"And it's easier to deal with business problems than relationships," Cam said quietly. Lacey's eyes jerked to his face, but there was no criticism there. Or, if there was, it was self-directed. His eyes met hers and his mouth twisted in a half smile. "I've done the same thing myself. Business is a lot safer than people."

Lacey's eyes dropped from his, but she nodded slowly. "I suppose it is."

They sat without speaking for a few moments. Outside, the rain continued to drizzle gently, a soft counterpoint to the quiet inside. Derwent stirred restlessly in his bed near the door, his short legs twitching in some canine dream. The scene was one of cozy domesticity.

Cam moved first, breaking the spell. "Here's to two cowards thrust into the middle of commitment by the divine hand of the Little Chapel in the Desert Dell." He grinned, lifting his glass. Lacey hesitated, and then lifted her glass to his. She'd never expected to toast her marriage with a glass of milk, but the lack of champagne didn't bother her.

Meeting Cam's eyes, she was seized by a sudden, foolish sense of optimism. Somehow the situation didn't seem quite as mad as it had. It seemed possible—almost—that this marriage might actually work.

CAM PAUSED in the kitchen doorway, giving himself time to savor the scene before him. Lacey had her back to him, her attention on something she was doing at the counter. Her hair was pulled into a ponytail, a spill of golden blond that brushed her shoulders as she moved. She was wearing faded jeans that molded the smooth lines of her hips in a way that invited a man's hand to test those same curves. A red-and-gray striped top completed the outfit. She looked casual, comfortable and deliciously attractive.

He was surprised by the strength of his pleasure in seeing her so at home in his kitchen. There was something so right about the picture, as if she was just what the house had been waiting for to make it complete.

When he'd picked up on Jimbo's suggestion that they remain married, he'd been acting more from guilt than anything else. Despite what he'd told Lacey, he was well aware that the odds against this marriage succeeding were high. But seducing innocent women and leaving them high and dry was not something he wanted to add to a life that had already had its share of misdeeds.

He felt a strong sense of responsibility for what had occurred between them. It had nothing to do with the few years' difference in their ages; thirty to thirty-six wasn't that big of a jump. But there was something about Lacey that spoke of a certain innocence, as if maybe some of life's harsher realities had passed her by. He didn't want to see that innocence disappear, at least not because of him.

Besides, there was no denying the strong attraction that lay between them. And he did believe in fate. It had played a strong enough part in his life. Maybe this odd marriage was a gesture from fate. Whether it was a gift or a gag remained to be seen.

He must have made some sound, or perhaps Lacey felt his eyes on her, because she turned suddenly and their eyes met. She had a smear of flour on one cheek, her hands were covered in the same substance, and the front of her top was dusted with it. Cam couldn't imagine how she could have looked more attractive.

"Good morning," he said, his voice still husky with sleep.

"Good morning." Her face was flushed. She brushed self-consciously at the flour on her cheek, only succeeding in adding to it. "I heard the shower and thought I'd make some breakfast. I hope you don't mind me making myself at home."

"This *is* your home. Besides, I'd have to be a fool to complain about you making breakfast. I usually make do with a slice of toast and some coffee. That looks like biscuits."

He crossed the room as he spoke, and Lacey had to control the urge to back away. He was so large and...male. It was almost too much for her nerves to take at this hour of the morning.

"Biscuits," she confirmed a bit breathlessly.

"I haven't had real biscuits in ages. Where did you get the recipe?"

Lacey turned back to the counter and finished rolling out the soft dough, using a water glass in place of the rolling pin she hadn't been able to find. "I don't need a recipe. Mother taught me to make biscuits before she taught me how to read. A Southern lady should always know how to cook." Unconsciously, her voice took on a soft drawl in imitation of Mamie's speech.

She turned the glass upside down and deftly cut biscuits, transferring them to a baking sheet. Cam watched her, wondering why he'd never realized how sexy making biscuits could be.

"You seem very California."

Lacey's laughter held a touch of sadness. "I am, but Mother did her best to drum the old South into me. I can play piano and cook and sew. I know precisely how to hold a teacup and I can make a cucumber sandwich. All accomplishments that a lady should acquire."

"Cucumber sandwich? Sounds peculiar."

"You'll probably get a chance to try one this afternoon. Mother is bound to have made them for us. Unless you've changed your mind about going to meet her. I love her dearly, but I have to admit that she can be a little hard to take sometimes. She's very good at pushing you around. Very politely, of course. She's always polite."

She looked sincerely worried that her mother might be more than he could handle. Cam grinned down at her, reaching out to brush the flour from her cheek.

"I think I can stand up to a little polite pushiness. I'm tougher than I look."

Lacey was not completely reassured. Cam had never seen her mother in action. Throughout her teenage years, she'd squirmed with embarrassment every time she brought a date home to meet her mother. Mamie would pump the unsuspecting boy for information, everything from his family background to his future plans. That her dates never realized what was going on hadn't made Lacey feel any better. The fact that her mother was subtle didn't make the interrogation any easier to take.

Lacey didn't have much to say during the drive to her mother's home in San Marino. She was aware of Cam glancing at her, his look questioning, but she was careful not to catch his eyes. How could she explain her feelings? He'd think she was worrying over nothing, especially once he met her mother. Men adored Mamie, and the feeling was mutual.

She wasn't worried about whether her mother and her new husband would like each other. That was practically a foregone conclusion. Mamie would adore Cam because he was male and presentable and he'd rescued her daughter from spinsterhood. Cam would adore Mamie because men always adored Mamie.

What bothered Lacey was the idea of watching her mother twist Cam around her little finger the way she had always done with anything male. It hadn't mattered much in the past, but somehow, with Cam, it did. She didn't want to see him falling hook, line and sinker for her mother's sweet Southern charm. She didn't want to watch Mamie extract information he didn't even know he was giving.

"Relax." She hadn't been aware that her fingers were knotted together in her lap until Cam's hand covered them. "It can't be that bad. I'm sure your mother and I are going to get along just fine."

Lacey sighed softly. "I'm sure you will."

Cam wanted to ask her why that prospect seemed to depress her. He opened his mouth and then closed it without saying anything. Maybe he was safer not knowing. Despite his reassurances to the contrary, he was growing a little uneasy about this meeting.

Was Mamie Newton a dragon lady? He was beginning to picture her as a cross between Bette Davis and Irene Dunne—genteel bitchiness mixed with a touch of the scatterbrained. Despite her warnings, he didn't doubt that Lacey loved her mother. But he was beginning to doubt that he would feel the same. What kind of a woman made her daughter so uneasy?

Of course, he wasn't really in a position to judge. His childhood had hardly been conducive to developing a deep understanding of parent/child relationships. By the time Mary and David Martin had taken him in, it had been more a case of taming a small animal than raising a child.

"This is it."

Lacey pointed to a brick driveway on the left, and Cam shook himself out of his thoughts as he turned the nose of the small truck into it.

Well, for better or worse, they'd arrived, and he was about to have his first meeting with his new mother-in-law. He could only hope that it wasn't going to turn out as badly as Lacey seemed to expect.

Chapter Seven

The rain the day before had left the air sparkling clean, a rare circumstance in Southern California. Two houses away an elderly man pushed an old-fashioned reel mower over the wide sweep of lawn. The gentle whir of the blades fit right into the neighborhood. The homes were large, and there was a quiet elegance to them that spoke of money.

As he walked up the brick path beside Lacey, Cam studied the house with interest. This was where Lacey had grown up. Flower beds flanked the front porch, filled with a bright profusion of tulips and ranunculuses. The flowers were backed by the creamy stucco of the house, and colonial-blue shutters were paired at each window.

The overall feeling was one of controlled gaiety, welcoming but just a little restrained. The house presented a bright front to the street, yet somehow managed to hint that the best it had to offer lay out of sight.

He was aware of Lacey's tension as they stepped onto the porch. She pushed the bell and stood staring at the front door. Cam's brow arched, thinking of the open-door policy at Mary's and David's home. It would never have occurred to him to ring the doorbell there.

They had only a moment to wait before the door swung open. He'd half expected to see a giant of a woman with a rolling pin in one hand and a book of etiquette in the other. He hadn't envisioned the petite woman who was pushing open the screen door.

"Lacey! Honey, it's so good to see you." Mamie hugged her daughter and then turned bright blue eyes on Cam. "You must be Cameron. I can't tell you how pleasured I am to meet you." She held out her arms, and Cam stepped forward to embrace his mother-in-law.

"Now y'all come in. I've got a little bite prepared. Nothing fancy, mind you."

Amused, Cam followed the two women into the house, wondering if Mamie was aware that she hadn't allowed him to say a word.

"Cameron, you just settle yourself on the sofa. It should be comfortable enough for a man of your size. Lacey, you sit next to him. I want to look at the two of you together."

Cam's eyes danced as he sat on the sofa. He could see what Lacey meant. In the nicest possible way, Mamie reminded him of a general positioning his troops.

"Now, tell me all about how the two of you met. I've already told Lacey what I think of her keeping this from me. You knew nothin' would make me happier than to see you married, darlin'. And I can see Cameron is a fine man, so you had no cause for hidin' him."

"I'm afraid that's my fault, Mrs. Newton," Cameron said easily, realizing that if he didn't jump into the conversation now, Mamie would probably carry it all by herself. "I was a little uneasy about meeting Lacey's family. Now that I've met you, I'm sorry we didn't meet sooner. You're just as Lacey described you."

Lacey's arm twitched where it rested against his. She was probably remembering exactly what she'd said about her mother. But Mamie saw nothing wrong with his words. Her soft features colored at the subtle compliment.

"Well, I'm just glad we've had a chance to meet at last. Lacey was always such a secretive child. I suppose I shouldn't be surprised that she kept you to herself. But I must admit I was more than a little surprised when she got married without even telling me." Her words held gentle reproach and Cam could feel the guilt practically oozing out from Lacey.

"Mother—"

"I'll have to take the blame for that, too, Mrs. Newton." Cam didn't have any qualms at all about interrupting. When it came to her mother, it was clear that Lacey needed some help. "I'm the one who convinced Lacey that we should get married the way we did. There we were in Las Vegas, and the chance just seemed too good to pass up. I bullied her shamefully."

He slid his arm around Lacey's rigid shoulders, hugging her close. He didn't dare look at her face, fearing what he might see there. They should have discussed what they were going to tell her mother before they got here, but they hadn't, and so he was winging it.

"You must call me Mamie, Cameron. I hope the ceremony wasn't too stark. I'd always pictured Lacey in a white dress walkin' down the aisle at church." Her eyes were suspiciously bright as she looked at her daughter.

"Well, it wasn't quite that romantic, but we'll always treasure the memories, won't we, Lacey?"

Since neither of them had a clear memory of the event in question, Lacey was hard put to manage anything more than a nod. She hoped her mother would take her flushed face as a sign of her adoration for Cam and not of what it really was. She'd been holding her breath so much during this conversation that she was surprised she was still conscious.

Cam's judicious stretching of the truth seemed to be enough to satisfy Mamie. Lacey was grateful when the conversation moved away from the subject of their wedding. As the afternoon wore on, she allowed herself to relax. Incredible though it seemed, it looked like Mamie had met her match.

Her genteel probing was met with polite response, but it was clear that Cam was telling her only what he chose to tell her. If she fished for more information than he was willing to give, he turned her questions away with as much subtlety as she asked them.

"When do the two of you plan on starting a family?" Mamie asked as she passed around a plate of delicate little sandwiches. Lacey's teacup hit the saucer with a loud clink. Cam took two sandwiches, apparently undisturbed by the question.

"Mother, we just got married." Lacey laughed, wondering if it sounded as false to the others as it did to her. "Give us a little time."

"You don't always have the time you think you're goin' to have, Lacey, honey. Look at your daddy and me. We'd planned to have a big ol' family, but he died before we had more'n you. I've always regretted that I didn't have another baby right away. That way you wouldn't have had to grow up all alone, the way you did. You listen to me, and don't put things off."

There could be no doubting Mamie's sincerity. Her eyes sparkled with tears and her voice shook. As usual when dealing with her mother, Lacey was torn between two opposing emotions: guilt and resentment. She was consumed with guilt and the need to reassure her mother she'd been perfectly happy as an only child, and she wanted to say that she and Cam were starting a family immediately, anything to take that look from Mamie's eyes. At the same time, she felt a tremendous resentment. Why couldn't her mother keep her nose out of things that were none of her business? For heaven's sake, she and Cam hardly even knew each other. How could Mamie be bringing up children?

"Mother—"

Cam's hand closed over hers, squeezing gently. "We've got plenty of time to decide what we want to do about children, Mamie. I think it's a mistake to rush into something like that. Besides, Lacey and I want some time to ourselves, don't we, honey?"

"Honey" nodded. She was incapable of anything more. Cam was looking at her in a way that made speech impossible. She reminded herself that it was all for her mother's benefit, but the look of tender affection in his eyes was so real.

"Well, I can see your point, Cameron. But don't you go waitin' too long. I'm anxious to hold a grandbaby."

"I think you're going to be a wonderful grandmother when the time comes, Mamie, though you look much too young."

Mamie flushed with pleasure. The compliment could have sounded glib, but Cam's tone made it impossible to doubt his sincerity. Lacey stared at her teacup. How did he manage it? For thirty years she'd been trying to find a way to distract her mother. In the space of an afternoon, he'd apparently managed to find the key to directing the conversation where *he* wanted it to go instead of where Mamie chose to take it. And Mamie was loving every minute of it.

She wasn't sure whether to be delighted or annoyed that he accomplished so easily what had always been impossible for her. She scowled at the inoffensive china cup. Why wasn't she happier that everything was going so well?

Beside her, Cam could feel her tension. He wondered at its source. True, he could see that Mamie needed a little managing if you didn't want her to manipulate you into answering questions better left unasked. But under the subtle manipulation, her affection for her only child was obvious.

He took a sip of coffee, listening with half an ear as Mamie and Lacey discussed some new silk scarves that had recently come in to Lacey's shop. He was fascinated by his surroundings. Having seen Lacey's apartment, he'd never have guessed that the home she'd grown up in would be so diametrically opposed in style.

Mamie's home was impeccably decorated in a style that could have seemed dated, yet somehow managed to look timeless. Elegant mahogany furniture settled perfectly into the large living room. Exquisite crocheted doilies created delicate patterns on the dark wood. A baby grand piano sat in one corner, framed by tall windows draped in ivory silk. His attention settled on the neatly arranged photos that covered the piano.

Taking his cup with him, he left Lacey and her mother to their discussion and wandered over to the piano. Sunshine pooled on the gleaming wood, catching on the shiny silver frames. He wasn't surprised to see that most of the pictures were of Lacey. But it wasn't the Lacey he knew.

Picking up a photo, he felt the weight of the silver frame—no aluminum here. The girl in the picture was probably about twelve, but she didn't look like any twelve-year-old he'd ever known. She was seated on a straight-backed chair, her legs neatly crossed at the ankles, her hands clasped in her lap. Her hair—a paler shade of blond then—was drawn back from her face on top and allowed to cascade in neat curls onto her shoulders. A pale pink dress fell over her lap, almost meeting the tops of her white knee-length socks. Black Mary-Janes gleamed on her feet. And her hands were encased in short lace gloves.

Cam had a sudden memory of his foster sisters at that same age. As he recalled, jeans had been the general rule. He doubted if they would have sat still long enough to have their pictures taken in all this finery, and he knew for a fact that not one of them had ever owned a pair of white lace gloves.

He set the photo down, his eyes thoughtful. He was beginning to understand what Lacey had meant when she said that her mother raised her to be a Southern lady. Looking around this house, remembering the maid who'd wheeled in the tea cart—God, who had a tea cart in this day and age, let alone a maid?—he wondered if Lacey wasn't going to find life with him a little too primitive.

"That's one of my favorite pictures of Lacey. She was almost thirteen there." Mamie's voice interrupted his thoughts, and Cam turned to smile at her. Behind her, he could see that Lacey was gone, leaving the two of them alone.

"She was a very pretty little girl."

"Yes, she was." Mamie's expression was tender as she looked at the parade of portraits that marched across the piano top.

"It must have been difficult for you, raising a child on your own."

"It wasn't easy." She reached out to touch a picture of a Lacey barely out of diapers. "When her daddy died, I was so frightened. I'd never really been on my own, you see. I lived with my parents until I married, and then Doug took care of me. There I was with hardly a lick of sense and a little girl who had no one but me.

"I grew up real quick. It was lucky Doug left us well-off, because I sure didn't have a job skill to my name. I made Lacey my job, and I did my best to bring her up in a manner befittin'."

She looked up at him, her eyes full of pride. "I couldn't be any prouder of her. She's made a real success with her shop. I worried that maybe she was puttin' off a personal life, but I guess maybe she was just playin' it close to the vest. I hope the two of you are goin' to be real happy."

"I hope so, too."

Lacey entered the room again, her eyes anxious when she saw the two of them talking. Cam grinned at her and gave her a thumbs-up sign behind Mamie's back. It seemed to reassure her.

He felt as if he was beginning to understand a little more about the woman he'd married. She'd been raised with one foot in both worlds. The modern, ever-changing world of Southern California and the gentler, more refined world her mother held dear.

It must have created quite a conflict for the dainty little girl in the picture. How did you walk a line between being the little lady your mother wanted and the more laid-back, casual life her friends had undoubtedly lived? It explained some of the contradictions he'd seen.

The strong woman who had created a successful business by the time she was thirty. And the woman who seemed slightly uncertain when it came to dealing with other people. The woman who was still a virgin at thirty.

He found himself liking her all the more for the way she'd tried to balance her two selves. A lot of people would have taken the easy road and turned their back on the world Mamie had presented.

He sat down next to Lacey on the sofa, listening with half an ear to Mamie's plans for the reception she insisted they had to have. Reaching out, he took Lacey's hand in his. She turned her head, startled by the casual gesture, but Cam didn't release her fingers. He smiled at her, feeling her hand relax in his.

He was beginning to think that, drunk, he'd had more sense than he might have laid claim to sober.

"I LIKED YOUR MOTHER," Cam said. The car slipped neatly into the stream of westbound traffic.

"You certainly know how to handle her." Lacey couldn't help the twinge of illogical resentment she felt, but she struggled to keep it out of her voice. The look he slanted in her direction told her that she hadn't been completely successful.

"Are you sorry we got along?"

"Of course not." She reached up to flip the visor down to shield her eyes from the late-afternoon sun. Her reflection greeted her in the mirror, and she met her own eyes, full of mixed emotions. She was behaving like a nitwit.

"No, of course I'm not sorry." She sighed. "I'm glad you liked her and I'm glad she liked you and I'm glad the visit went so well. Really I am."

"So what is it you're not glad about?" There was a hint of amusement in his tone but no sarcasm.

Lacey sighed again, feeling like an idiot. "It's really stupid, but in thirty years I've never been able to handle my mother as neatly as you did today. I guess I feel a little outclassed."

Cam grinned, but his glance held understanding, as well as amusement. "The fact that I didn't have any problem with your mother doesn't really have anything to do with how you deal with her. You've got a lot of emotional history with her. That makes it harder. Besides, I think your mother was determined to like me and get along with me. She wants to see you happy. She loves you."

"I know." Lacey scowled. "I love her, too."

Cam laughed and reached over to squeeze her knee. "Cheer up. Now that I've saved you from spinsterhood, that's one bone of contention gone. She won't have to worry about you wasting away all by yourself. That should make her happy."

"Maybe. More than likely, she'll just turn her attention to something else. She's probably going to start worrying about us starting a family. She'll dig up all kinds of statistics about my biological time clock running out." Her mouth quirked in a rueful smile. "At least it will be a change of subject."

Cam smiled, but his eyes were thoughtful. "Do you want children, Lacey?"

The simple question seemed to catch at her throat, choking off her voice. She stared at the freeway ahead of them, oblivious to the traffic. Her answer, when it came, was straight from the heart.

"Yes. Yes, I do want children."

"So do I."

Cam didn't say anything more. He didn't have to. Those few simple words had given Lacey more than enough to think about. Children. Just thinking about them made this marriage seem real. Children meant forever; they meant commitment.

Lying alone in her bed that night, Lacey stared up at the ceiling, trying to picture herself as a mother. The image was a little fuzzy around the edges. She'd never really given children a lot of thought, always putting it off until some unspecified later date. Now it was hard to imagine herself with an infant.

Cam was another story. The picture of him as a father was sharp and clear. He'd be a good father. She didn't have any doubts about that. She might not have known him very long, but she was sure he'd be good with children.

And how did she feel about the idea of having Cam's child?

She closed her eyes as a wave of heat washed over her. One hand pressed against her stomach as she tried to imagine what it would feel like to hold another life inside her. The idea of carrying Cam's child was disturbing, all the more so because it held a definite appeal. Especially when she thought about creating that child.

Her memory of their wedding night was hazy, but when she tried to conjure it up, she was left with an impression of pleasure. Somehow she knew that drunk or not, Cam had been a considerate lover. She only wished she could remember the pleasurable details. Especially since it had been her first time. In her teens she'd often wondered what it would be like to be made love to. Whatever she'd thought then it would be, for sure it would be an experience she'd always remember. But...

She turned over, suddenly restless. Willing her mind to other, less dangerous thoughts, Lacey took deep, slow breaths, forcing herself to relax. Around her, the house was quiet. Cam had no doubt gone to sleep ages ago. Derwent would be snoring away in his bed in the kitchen. And they both showed a great deal more sense than she did.

The thing to do was to take this marriage one day at a time. It was foolish to think too far ahead. And children were a long, long way in the future. If they could make this marriage work—and that was a pretty big if—then they could talk about children.

LACEY GLANCED at the door as the shop bell rang, her face relaxing in a smile when she saw who it was.

"Lisa!" She wove her way around the tables of scarves and silken dainties to hug her friend. "Where have you been? I haven't seen you since—" She stopped, remembering just exactly when they'd last seen each other.

"Since Las Vegas." Lisa returned the hug and then stepped back, studying her friend carefully. "I've been in New York on business. I just got back yesterday and Frank told me what happened. Lacey, I just can't believe it."

"Frank told you what happened? Didn't you remember?"

Lisa shook her head, setting her pale brown page-boy swinging. "Not a thing. I swear to God, Lacey, I haven't been that drunk since the night you and I soaped the dean's windows. The last thing I remember about you and Cam is seeing the two of you dancing. Then Frank suggested we go somewhere a little more private, and I don't remember much of anything after that. We flew home the next day—God, what a miserable flight—and I left for New York that afternoon. I could just kill Frank for not telling me about this. Of course, our schedules never meshed well enough for us to talk directly, but he could have left a message with a secretary or something, don't you think?''

"Maybe he didn't want to distract you," Lacey offered as she led the way back to her tiny office. She signaled to Margaret, her assistant, that she was going to be unavailable. Not that she really needed to let her know. Margaret generally knew what was going on in the shop before Lacey did, anyway.

"Are you kidding? There's nothing Frank would love more than a chance to distract me." Lisa flung herself into the chair across from Lacey's desk while Lacey sat down behind the desk. "He hates my job. He's been bugging me for months to slow down."

"Well, you have been working really hard."

"I know that. But he just doesn't understand. I've got a really important deal in the works right now. Once this is settled, I'll be able to take a little time off."

Lisa had been saying that she was going to take "a little time off" ever since she left college. So far, she'd never found the right time, and Lacey didn't see any reason this time should be any different.

"Frank loves you. Maybe he wants to see a little more of you."

"Don't you start in on me, too." Lisa reached for her cigarettes, lighting one with fingers that seemed a little too tense. She drew in a lungful of smoke and let it out with a sigh, meeting Lacey's eyes across the desk. "I'm sorry, Lace. I didn't mean to snap at you. Frank and I have been going at it a bit too often lately. And what with this deal dragging on like this, I guess my nerves are a little ragged."

"It's okay."

"No, it's not okay." Lisa stubbed out the cigarette. "But I didn't come here to unload my problems on you. What's going on with you and Cam?"

Lacey shrugged. "Well, we got married in Las Vegas."

"I know that much. What I don't know is what's going on now. Frank said you'd moved in with Cam?"

"That's right."

"You mean, you're going to go through with this?" Lisa sounded incredulous.

"What's wrong with that?" Lacey asked defensively. In all the years she and Lisa had been friends, Lisa had never lost her ability to put her on the defensive.

Lisa shrugged. "Well, nothing, I suppose. I just never thought of you as that much of a gambler. You were always inclined to play it safe."

"Well, maybe I got tired of playing it safe."

"Good for you. I must say, Cam is one very attractive hunk of manhood. And nice, too. How goes the gamble so far?"

"Okay, I guess." Lacey picked up a pencil and began to doodle on the back of an invoice. "I only moved in about a week ago, so we're still doing a lot of adjusting."

"That stage never really ends." Lisa tilted her head to one side, studying Lacey as if she was seeing her for the first time. "You know, I'd never have expected you to do something like this. You're the one who always plans your life so carefully. You don't even like to go out to dinner unless you've made reservations in advance. I just wouldn't have pictured you jumping into marriage like this."

Lacey gave a short laugh. "Believe me, it's not the way I'd pictured starting my marriage."

"No, I don't imagine it is," Lisa said thoughtfully. "So, having started out rather unconventionally, how's it going?"

"I told you. We're still making a lot of adjustments."

Lisa waved one hand in a dismissing gesture. "Besides that. How are the two of you getting along? Are you madly in love with him yet? Or at least madly in lust?"

Lacey flushed, wishing Margaret would turn up with some small emergency that she just *had* to attend to herself. But the ever efficient Margaret didn't appear in the doorway, and Lisa didn't look as if she had any intention of disappearing in a puff of smoke.

"I haven't really had time to be madly in love with Cam."

"Okay. Then how about the lust part? Come on. With a man that gorgeous, you can't tell me you don't have a major case of the hots for him."

"I find Cam very attractive," Lacey said. She knew immediately that her tone was repressive, but it was too late to change it.

"Very attractive?" Lisa gave a hoot of laughter. "Lacey, the man is a hunk. A bona fide hunk. I think he deserves something a little stronger than very attractive."

"All right. He's a hunk. But there's more to marriage than that."

"Not as much as you might think." Lisa's tone held an edge of bitterness that surprised Lacey. Before she could question it, Lisa glanced at her watch and gave a quick exclamation. "Good grief. I've got a dinner appointment in less than an hour and I still have to go home and change."

She stood up. Lacey circled the desk and reached for the door, but Lisa's hand on her arm made her pause.

"You know, all I want is for you to be happy. I really do wish you and Cam the best. You know that, don't you?"

"I know." Lacey hugged her. There were times when Lisa drove her crazy, but twenty years of friendship lay behind them. There'd been an awful lot of good times in those twenty years.

She saw Lisa out the door and wandered back to her office. The store would be closing soon, and they weren't likely to be swamped by a sudden rush of customers. If they were, Margaret could call her.

She settled down behind her desk, thinking about Lisa's visit, the look in her eyes that said she wasn't happy with her life. It made Lacey look at her own life more closely, and she was surprised to find that she was happy. She hadn't realized how dull and predictable her life had gotten until Cameron McCleary appeared in it and threw it on its ear.

It wasn't even that everything had gone perfectly since she'd moved in. What she'd told Lisa was true. They were still trying to adjust to each other and there'd been a few snags along the way. But they'd been minor snags.

Like the night she'd fixed chicken curry for dinner. Cam had taken one whiff and turned a delicate shade of green. Curry was one thing he simply couldn't face. He'd once had a landlord who cooked curry twenty-four hours a day, and the smell had permanently destroyed Cam's interest in even trying the food. He'd been as tactful as it was possible to be while opening windows to try to air the house out.

And then there was Cam's taste in music. He adored Willie Nelson. In Lacey's opinion, Willie Nelson had no business calling himself a singer—a musician, maybe, but not a singer. To her ears his whiny tones were like nails on a blackboard. On the other hand, Cam referred to Bach as elevator music. So far, they'd found a shaky common ground with big-band music from the forties and rock and roll from the fifties and sixties.

She smiled suddenly, leaning back in her chair. She supposed that, when it came right down to it, much could be forgiven a man who was a bona fide hunk. Even Willie Nelson and a dislike of curry.

Chapter Eight

"Are you sure I shouldn't have worn something a little dressier?" Lacey smoothed the jade-green skirt over her knees, her eyes going to Cam. He glanced away from the road long enough to inventory the simple cotton dress with the extravagantly full skirt and soft fitted top, and the simple low-heeled pumps. She'd pulled her hair back in a chignon contrived to make her look both elegant and casual.

He faced the windshield again, his fingers tightening on the steering wheel. Did she have any idea how utterly desirable she looked? It was all he could do to resist the urge to pull off the road and kiss her thoroughly.

"Cam?" She interpreted his silence as a negative. "It's not dressy enough, is it? Your sister is going to think I didn't care enough to dress up to meet her," she said with despair.

"You look fine."

If the answer was a little abrupt, it reflected the way he felt. He'd never considered what a strain this arrangement was going to be. Living with an attractive, desirable woman who just happened to be his wife and who he'd promised not to lay a hand on was not his idea of a pleasant, relaxing way to spend his time.

The vague memories he'd retained of their wedding night didn't make things any easier. The fogginess that cloaked them only made them seem more enticing. Was it a fantasy, or had it really been one of the more incredible experiences of his life? Not knowing was enough to drive him crazy.

The only way to find out what was truth and what was fantasy was to try it again without an excess of margaritas. But of course that was going to have to wait until Lacey was ready. And she wasn't. He had only to look at the way she still watched him with that half-wary expression to know she wasn't ready. Not that he blamed her. When you got right down to it, they hadn't known each other all that long. It was an odd quirk on his part that made him feel as if he'd known her forever.

Lacey reached up to fuss with the neckline of the dress. "First impressions are important. I don't— What are you doing?"

With a mumbled curse, Cam switched on the right turn signal and began cutting across the lanes of traffic. He ignored her question, easing into the emergency lane and pulling to a stop.

"What's wrong?"

"You need something to think about besides your dress."

Cam unbuckled his seat belt and then leaned over to do the same to hers. He reached for her, but Lacey hung back against the door, reddening as her eyes met his and his meaning became clear.

"This is nuts. You can't do this."

"I've just done it." His hands closed over her shoulders, drawing her forward. There was a wicked gleam in his eyes that brought an unexpected flutter to her heart.

"Cam, there are laws."

"Against a man kissing his wife?" His breath feathered over her cheek.

"Against using the emergency lane for anything but an emergency," Lacey told him, wondering at the breathlessness that seemed to have stolen her voice.

"This is an emergency." Lacey couldn't have argued the point even if she'd been so inclined. His mouth took the last of her breath.

Her hands slid upward from their half-protesting position against his chest to cling to his shoulders. His fingers settled against the back of her head, mussing the careful chignon, but Lacey didn't care. Tilting her head to allow the kiss to deepen, she wasn't aware of anything but the warm pool of heat that seemed to spread outward from her mouth until her whole body was flushed.

It wasn't the first time he'd kissed her, nor the first time she'd felt this heat. But this time, the warmth seemed to spread a little farther, demand a little more. And Lacey was finding that demand increasingly exciting. She wanted more. She wanted Cam to want more. Each night when he said good-night, it was harder to go off to her lonely bed, knowing he was so close.

His tongue edged along her mouth and she opened to him. His free hand slid upward from the curve of her waist until his palm rested against the side of her breast. She'd forgotten where they were, where they were going. All that really mattered was the feel of Cam's mouth on hers.

The raucous blast of a truck's horn broke the sweet spell. Cam's mouth lifted from hers slowly, as if relinquishing something precious. Lacey felt dazed as she looked up at him. Never in her life had any man made her tremble with just a kiss. Cam looked at her for a long moment, something in his eyes that she couldn't quite read, and then he turned away to put the car in gear.

"Fasten your seat belt."

Lacey's fingers fumbled with the mechanism. Fasten her seat belt? She felt as if she'd just taken a short roller-coaster ride without a seat belt. It seemed a little late to be fastening it now.

Cam pulled the car back onto the freeway, continuing their interrupted journey as if nothing unusual had happened. Lacey stole a quick look at him, but his attention was all on the surrounding traffic. At least so she thought until his eyes flicked toward her and he gave her a quick grin.

"Not worried about your dress anymore, are you?"

She shook her head, coloring slightly as she lifted her hands to her hair, repairing the damage his fingers had done. No, she certainly wasn't worried about her clothes anymore.

Claire's home was on a half acre of land in the Simi Valley. The hills around the property were covered with chaparral, a soft green at this time of year, though in summer they would change to a dull, fire-prone brown.

The car had barely come to a standstill in the gravel drive when the front door of the house burst open and what seemed to be at least a hundred children clattered down the steps, all shouting at the top of their lungs. Lacey blinked once or twice and the hundred children sorted themselves into four or five. It was impossible to get an accurate count because the mini-mob kept moving around.

The shouts of "Uncle Cam! Uncle Cam!" were near to deafening, but Cam didn't seem to mind. He was laughing as he scooped up the two smallest members of the group, settling one on each hip.

The screen door opened again, but closed more genteelly this time. The woman who approached them was lovely. Skin the color of pale coffee was stretched over sculpted cheekbones that made Lacey wish she'd spent more time with blusher and a contour brush. Though her dark eyes remained watchful, the woman smiled at Lacey.

Cam fought his way free of the children long enough to make the introductions. "Lacey, this is my sister Claire. Claire, this is Lacey, who was kind enough to marry me."

Lacey blinked, her eyes unconsciously widening a bit, but Mamie's years of teaching had not been in vain. Her smile was natural as she stretched out a hand to Claire. Claire's grip was as straightforward as her words.

"I take it Cam didn't tell you that we're all adopted."

"I— No, he didn't." Claire's face softened as she looked at her brother, who was kneeling to exclaim over the bandage that decorated his niece's dusty knee. "I think he forgets most of the time. We grew up in a mixed bag of a family. It's easy to forget that other people may be shocked."

"I wasn't shocked." Lacey was quick to correct that impression. "It's just that— Well, you don't look much alike, do you?"

Claire laughed, her eyes lighting with amusement. "No, I guess we don't."

Lacey watched as Claire waded into the group surrounding Cam and proceeded to detach them from their uncle with calm efficiency. Freed of his small entourage, Cam moved over to Lacey, taking her hand and drawing her toward the house.

The house was larger than it looked from the outside, the rooms big and airy. The decor had a simple elegance that reminded Lacey of her hostess. Taupe and black tones were lightened with an occasional shock of burnt orange or peacock blue. It might have looked contrived, but instead the effect was one of hominess. It wasn't hard to imagine children running through these rooms.

Lacey noticed the decor only peripherally. Her attention was on the two men who sat near the fireplace. The taller of the two was clearly Claire's husband. One of them stood up, approaching with a quick stride that she was to learn was characteristic of Claire's husband. Joe was a total contrast to his wife, quick and impatient where she was slower and calmer. He shook Lacey's hand, giving her a wide smile.

"So, you're the lady who finally caught Cam. His mother will be delighted he's no longer on the loose. She's been telling him he needed a wife for at least ten years now."

"Twelve," Cam muttered with feeling. Joe laughed, taking Cam's hand and shaking it with the same fervor he'd shown Lacey.

She heard Claire and the children come in and shut the door, but her attention had shifted over Joe's shoulder to the man now standing up. His eyes met hers uneasily, and it was all Lacey could do to keep from laughing out loud.

"Hi, Lacey."

"Jimbo." She kept her tone neutral. There was no reason to let him off the hook too soon. Though Cam had told her about Jimbo's visit, it was the first time she'd seen him since that eventful night in Las Vegas, and she was enjoying watching him squirm. Not that she blamed him for the fact that she and Cam had gotten married. But it wasn't often that she had a chance to see Jimbo humble.

"You look really nice."

Lacey's chin quivered. He was throwing himself on his knees, at least verbally. She ought to let him grovel, but Mamie'd taught her better. "Thank you."

Jimbo saw the humor in her eyes and he grinned, his relief obvious. "I knew you wouldn't be able to hold a grudge."

"I should." Lacey held out her hand, and Jimbo took it, pulling her into a hug.

The evening turned out to be a great deal more fun and a lot less stressful than Lacey had expected. Claire's entertaining style was relaxed. She allowed her guests to amuse themselves rather than try to force the evening into any set pattern.

The children were everywhere. Even though Lacey had sorted them into only four small bodies, two boys and two girls ranging from ten years old down to three, they still seemed to form a mini-horde. If there was ever a moment when she couldn't see a child, she had only to seek Cam out. Chances were that at least one of his nieces and nephews was somewhere nearby. They all seemed to think that Uncle Cam was one of the best entertainments life had to offer.

Lacey found herself watching him, marveling at his ability to handle the children. He seemed to know just how to talk to them, never condescending and never talking over their heads. She watched him pick up the littlest one, a girl whose precarious balance had been upset by the passage of her older brother. Cam's hands were gentle, smoothing the ruffles on her powder-blue dress and, at the same time, soothing the damage to her dignity. She leaned her head against his chest, sticking her thumb in her mouth as she watched the bustle from the safe haven of her uncle's arms.

As if sensing Lacey's gaze, Cam looked up, his eyes meeting hers. There was a moment when the rest of the room faded away and they might have been all alone. Just the two of them in some place where nothing mattered but each other. She didn't know if he could see the sudden vulnerability she felt, but she saw his eyes darken. He moved as if to come to her, but then Joe was asking Cam's opinion on an armoire he was thinking of buying. Cam stared at her an instant longer, something in his eyes she couldn't quite read, and then he turned to answer Joe and the moment was gone.

"He'll make a good father."

Jimbo's comment followed her own thoughts so closely that Lacey felt as if he must have read her thoughts. "Yes, he will." She reached for her glass of wine, hoping her expression was as calm as her tone.

Claire was in the kitchen, taking care of some last-minute details. Joe and Cam were absorbed in a discussion of the finer points of furniture making. For all intents and purposes, she and Jimbo were alone.

"You know, I've known Cam a lot longer than you have."

Lacey glanced at Jimbo, lifting one eyebrow. "Almost anybody could qualify for that statement."

"I mean, I've known him a lot longer than a lot of people."

"I know the two of you have been friends for a long time."

It was clear he had something he wanted to say. It was so unusual to see Jimbo at any kind of a loss for words that Lacey's attention sharpened. She turned so that she faced him more fully.

"Has Cam told you much about his past?" Jimbo asked.

"No. I didn't even know he was adopted until tonight."

"He doesn't talk about it much, but if it hadn't been for his foster parents, he'd probably be behind bars right now, or dead maybe."

Lacey choked on her wine. Her eyes jerked to where Cam and Joe were talking and then came back to Jimbo. "Cam? You've got to be kidding. Mr. Calm-and-steady?"

But Jimbo didn't look like he was kidding. His square face was set in unusually serious lines. "I met Cam when I was working in a program to help gang members."

Gang members? Lacey was beyond a verbal protest. She stared at Jimbo, her eyes reflecting her disbelief.

"I know it's hard to believe. Cam would probably murder me if he knew I was telling you this, but he'll never say anything, and it might help you understand him a little."

Lacey knew that she should probably open her mouth and say that she didn't want him to tell her anything Cam didn't want her to know, but she couldn't have spoken to save her soul. Now that Jimbo had said this much, she had to know the rest.

"Cam was only thirteen or so, but he was one tough kid. He'd been on the streets for a couple of years and he'd figured out that a gang offered him a way to survive. The police picked him on a robbery charge, and I just happened to get the assignment to talk to him.

"I was only nine or ten years older than he was and he took one look at me and announced I wasn't old enough to be telling him how to live."

Jimbo smiled, his eyes seeing things Lacey could only imagine. "When I met him, he gave me a look that just dared me to try and help him, but there was something in his eyes that made me think maybe it wasn't too late for him. I knew about Mary and David Martin. They'd taken in three or four troubled kids by then. God, Cam was hostile.

"His father was dead and his mother just left him one day and never came back. He was convinced that adults were the enemy in his own private war. He had the most explosive temper I've ever seen in my life. Even though he was just a kid, he could be pretty frightening when he was in a temper.

"But Mary and David took him in as foster parents and convinced him that not every adult was a rat. It took a while to track down his grandparents, since Cam wasn't sure of his mother's maiden name—his paternal grandparents were long dead. By the time they were found, he'd settled in so well with Mary and David that they left him where he was."

"I'd never have guessed," Lacey murmured.

"He'd never tell you, but I know that calm of his can be a little hard to take sometimes. I thought it might help if you understood where it came from."

"It does. It really does." She looked at Cam, trying to see that angry little boy in the man. He glanced up, caught her eye and smiled. Lacey smiled back, but she was glad for the distraction Claire provided by returning to announce dinner. Jimbo had given her a lot to consider.

She was still considering it as they drove home a few hours later. Was it possible she'd imagined the whole conversation? There'd certainly been nothing in Jimbo's manner to indicate that they'd spoken of anything more serious than the next day's weather. He'd been his usual jovial, off-the-wall self, joking with Cam, playing with the children.

She studied Cam surreptitiously. In the light from the dashboard, he looked the same as he always did. But she was seeing him in a different way. She was seeing an angry little boy who'd had no one but himself to depend on.

"Have I got dirt on my nose?" Cam's quiet question made Lacey jump. "You've been staring at me for the last twenty minutes."

"Sorry." She shifted her gaze to the empty freeway ahead. "I was thinking, I guess."

"About what?"

"You. Us. I was thinking that we haven't known each other very long at all."

"True. Does that bother you?"

"I don't know. I guess maybe that's the whole purpose of our living together like we are—to give us a chance to get to know each other."

"Do you feel like we're not making progress?" Lacey felt Cam glance at her, but she didn't return it.

"I don't know. Do you think we're getting to know each other?"

"You must have taken Psych 101 in college. Answering a question with a question. 'And what do you think of this, Mrs. Smith?' I always thought that was a way for the psychiatrist to stall while he was trying to figure out just what Mrs. Smith's dreams of talking pigs really meant.

"But to answer the questions—I think we're getting to know each other. At least, I feel as if I'm getting to know you."

"You don't talk about yourself very much."

Out the corner of her eye, she saw his hands tighten on the wheel and then relax. With the new insight she'd been given, she realized that Cam's control was not as effortless as she'd always assumed.

"I wondered why Jimbo was talking to you so earnestly. Telling you about my misspent youth, was he?"

Lacey shrugged, sorry she'd brought the subject up, even in such an oblique way.

"He told me a little."

Cam laughed, though the sound didn't hold much humor. "I should have known he wouldn't be able to resist."

"He was concerned about us. He said he thought it might help me to understand you."

"And does it?"

"I think so," Lacey said quietly. There was a new tension in the car that she didn't understand.

"It isn't that simple. That's another lesson Psych 101 teaches you: that you can get to know somebody by knowing their past. It doesn't work that way in real life, Lacey. In real life it takes a lot of time and effort to get to know a person. And you have to get to know them in the here and now. You see how the past shaped them by looking at what they've become. When you look at their past and then try to see how it affected them, you're going at it backward."

"Don't you think the two go hand in hand? That you can get to know someone by knowing both their past and their present?"

"No. I think that can just confuse things." She felt his glance though she didn't look at him. "Take this situation. Now that Jimbo has told you all about my pathetic past, you're looking at me in a different way."

"Of course I am. I've just learned something about you."

"No. You've learned something about who I *was*. I'm not that screwed-up little boy anymore. I haven't been for a very long time."

"I didn't say you were," Lacey protested. This conversation wasn't going at all the way she'd hoped. Instead of being able to express her sympathy for what he'd gone through, she'd apparently managed to offend him.

Cam drew in a quick hard breath. "I'm sorry. I didn't mean to jump all over you. I guess you touched on a bit of a sore spot."

"I just wanted you to know that I was sorry you'd had to go through that," she told him softly.

"I know." He reached out, taking her hand in his. "I don't talk about those days because I've gotten past them. I've moved on, and I don't want you looking at me and feeling sorry for what I was. I want you to see what I *am*."

"I do, but I can't help but admire the fact you've pulled yourself up the way you have." Lacey turned her hand in his, her fingers curling around his hard palm. "A lot of people never manage to get away from a start like that."

"I had a lot of help. Jimbo, for one, though I may murder him after this latest routine."

"I really think he was trying to help," Lacey offered.

"I think he was poking his nose where it doesn't belong."

Cam didn't sound too upset. The cold note that had been so unnerving was gone from his voice. He sounded the way he usually did, calm and in control. Still, Lacey had had a glimpse of what lay beneath that control.

They didn't talk much during the remainder of the drive. Cam drew her hand to his leg and pressed it there before returning his own hand to the wheel. She could have drawn away then, but she didn't. No matter what Cam thought, knowing his past did change the way she saw him. It made him more human.

She remembered that moment when their eyes had met and she'd felt so connected to him, as if she was seeing a part of herself that had been missing for a long time.

"Claire liked you."

"I liked her." Lacey shifted, drawing herself straighter in the seat. She would have moved her hand, but Cam's fingers closed over hers, a silent request, and so she left her hand where it was, resting on the hard muscles of his thigh.

"Abby told me she thought you were a very pretty lady."

Abby? It took Lacey a moment to remember that Abby was Claire's youngest, the toddler who'd clung so determinedly to Cam's leg.

She felt as if there were two conversations being carried on. The one on the surface that was safe and comfortable and another that lay underneath and was anything but.

By the time Cam pulled the car into the driveway, several miles of silence lay between them. Midnight hovered just around the corner, and the neighborhood was still, the houses dark.

Lacey was vividly aware of Cam following her up the walkway to the door. The lock snicked beneath the pressure of his key, and they stepped into the silent house. Derwent ran in from the kitchen, and Lacey bent to scratch one ear, glad of the small distraction.

She wasn't quite sure why a distraction was desirable. Nothing had happened. Nothing had been said. This was just a night like any of the other nights she'd spent in this house. But it didn't feel like any other night. There was something different in the air, something she couldn't put her finger on, and she didn't think it was her imagination.

Derwent swiped at her hand with a wet tongue and then turned and headed back toward his bed in the kitchen. Lacey stood up, drawing in a deep breath. She was being ridiculous. There was nothing different about tonight except that her imagination was working overtime. It was late, she was tired, she'd spent too much time worrying about meeting Cam's sister, and her nerves were still a little overstretched. That's all it was.

She cleared her throat. "Well, it's pretty late. I think I'll go to bed."

"Good idea," Cam said. Lacey glanced at him, wondering if his words had a hidden meaning. But there was nothing in his expression to indicate that he'd meant anything more than just what he'd said.

What's wrong with me tonight?

"Well, good night." She hesitated a moment and then took a step closer. Their good-night kiss was a well-established ritual. Why did tonight feel different?

Cam's hand came up, cupping her cheek as his head bent to hers. Lacey could feel the gentle rasp of his callused skin against hers. She could catch the merest whiff of some cologne she couldn't identify, a vague woodsy scent she associated with Cam.

Her gaze lifted as he lowered his head. That look was in his eyes again. The one she'd seen this evening. The one that set her pulse to beating at a faster rate. And she was no closer to defining that look than she had been. Or maybe she was afraid to define it. His thumb stroked her cheekbone, the faint roughness strangely inviting. Lacey's lashes lowered as if drawn by gentle weights.

His mouth was warm, molding to hers in a way that was both demand and appeal. And she had to answer both. She'd been right in sensing that tonight was different. It was as if there'd been something in the air they'd been breathing. Something that had caused a subtle shift, leaving them almost but not quite the same.

His hand slid from her cheek to cradle her throat, his thumb resting in the hollow at its base. Lacey wondered if he could feel the accelerated beat of her pulse. His other arm slipped around her back, drawing her closer as the kiss deepened. Lacey's fingers wove into the thickness of his hair. From somewhere deep inside, need swept over her, warm and hungry.

Her mouth opened to his, inviting—no, demanding—his possession. His tongue slid inside, fencing with hers in an ancient duel that had no winner, no loser. His hand swept her closer still, until not even a shadow could have fit between them. Lacey rose on her toes, molding herself to him, as eager for the contact as he was.

This was what she'd been missing. All her life she'd been only half-complete and she hadn't realized it until now. Everything had been leading up to this moment, this place, this man.

Cam's fingers found the pins that held her hair, pulling them loose. They hit the floor with faint clicks that seemed unnaturally loud in the quiet of the house. Lacey's hair spilled over his hand, a cascade of honey-gold silk. The feel of it against his skin seemed to loosen his control another notch. He tilted her head, deepening the kiss still further as his other hand swept down her back, tracing the gentle hollows at the base of her spine before flattening over the swell of her buttocks and pressing her into the cradle of his hips.

Lacey could feel the pressure of his arousal through the layers of fabric that separated them. A warm, liquid weight seemed to settle in her stomach. She'd never wanted anything in her life more than she wanted Cam in that moment. Her very skin ached with the need for him.

But the strength of that need frightened her. It was as if, in giving in to that need, she might lose something of herself, something she'd never get back. She wasn't ready for this. The realization had to fight its way into her consciousness. She didn't want to acknowledge it, didn't want to give up the sweet sensations pouring through her. But it wouldn't be denied. With each passing moment, her desire grew, but so did her uneasiness. It was too soon. Too much, too soon.

Her hands moved to his shoulders, clinging for a moment in helpless response to the desire still rocketing through her. If this continued, she'd regret it. With an effort she dragged her mouth away from his, drawing in a deep lungful of air.

"No."

The word was hardly more than a whisper. For a moment, she wasn't sure if he'd heard her. His hands continued to hold her close. She could feel the hunger in him, and she knew that if he chose to insist, there'd be nothing she could do to stop him. Looking into his eyes, she saw the same awareness there.

He wouldn't have to use force. Her own need would work against her. He could surely feel it in the way she still pressed so close against him.

His hands tightened their hold on her, and her heart gave a quick leap. For an instant, only an instant, she knew he was tempted to ignore her protest. Time was suspended; even her breathing seemed to stop. And then his eyes closed, and she felt the quick hard breath he drew before his hands moved away.

She stepped back, feeling as if she'd left a piece of herself behind. Cam didn't say anything, and the silence in the little hall grew thick with things unspoken.

"I'm sorry." Lacey's voice was hushed, and she avoided looking at him.

"Don't be. I shouldn't have pushed." But there was a rasp in his voice that told her just how tightly he was holding on to his control.

"No, really. I shouldn't have—"

"Lacey." She'd never realized that the sound of her name could cut across a sentence so neatly. She stopped, staring up at him, her eyes wide. In the dim light she saw his chest rise and fall as he took a quick breath.

"Just go to bed, Lacey. And don't start feeling guilty. I'm a big boy. Cold showers are good for me." His mouth twisted in a half smile that didn't quite reach his eyes, but it was enough to tell her that he wasn't upset with her.

Maybe he was right. It had been a long eventful day. First the visit from Lisa, and then meeting Claire and her family. Jimbo's revelations about Cam's past and now this. She was tired and probably exaggerating the day's events.

"Good night."

"Good night, Lacey."

She turned slowly, fighting the urge to turn back and throw herself into his arms.

Chapter Nine

During the following week, Lacey learned the true meaning of sexual tension. If she'd thought she was aware of Cam before, it was nothing compared to the acute awareness she felt now. It didn't seem possible that one kiss could have changed things so much, but she couldn't deny the results.

If Cam walked into the room, she knew it. She didn't even have to see him. She could *feel* his presence, like a feather being drawn slowly up her spine, bringing all her nerve endings to tingling life.

And it wasn't just the physical awareness that was suddenly so vivid. She felt a new awareness of him as a person. Despite what he'd said, the past did make a difference. Now when she looked at him, she saw where he'd come from, as well as where he was now. And she had to admit that she liked what she saw. Past, present and, she hoped, future. She liked Cameron McCleary. There were moments when she thought it might be more than merely liking, but she wasn't quite ready to debate that issue with herself. For now it was enough that she liked the man she'd married. Love could come later, when she was more prepared for it.

Cam obviously felt the change, too, intangible as it was. He seemed to watch her more. But it wasn't just that. Kisses were no longer limited to a semi-chaste goodnight gesture. He kissed her when they met in the morning. He kissed her when she left for the shop. He kissed her when she got home. And sometimes he kissed her for no reason at all.

At first Lacey was thrown off balance, questioning the reason for each small contact, analyzing her own reactions, wondering if a larger demand was to follow. But when he didn't push any further, she gradually relaxed, enjoying the small attentions.

Cam wondered if he was being totally ethical. He could see Lacey's uneasiness gradually being replaced with trust, and he wasn't sure he deserved that trust. He was deliberately setting out to convince her he was harmless. Which didn't reflect reality at all. In fact, there were times when he felt downright predatory. He'd once watched a cat stalk a sparrow, first acting casual, as if the presence of the bird was of no interest at all, and then pouncing.

Pouncing was exactly what he felt like doing. He didn't think Lacey had any idea of just how desirable she was. If she had, maybe she wouldn't have trusted him so readily.

It wasn't as if he was planning anything that would hurt her in any way, he argued with his conscience. Yes, he was deliberately seducing her, but it was his sincere belief that the end result would be as satisfying to her as it would be to him. They were married. If they really wanted this marriage to work, then sooner or later they were going to have to sleep together. Was it really so terrible of him to soothe her uneasiness? To make the path just a little smoother?

Besides, it wasn't as if all he wanted from her was a quick tumble in the hay. He wanted a lot more than that. For the first time in a very long time, he wanted to build something important with someone else.

He hadn't been entirely honest with her when he'd told her that his past was the past. He knew, better than anyone else, just how long the scars lingered. He'd learned early in life that trusting people was likely to get him hurt, and he hadn't trusted many people since. Maybe that was why he'd never married, never even come close.

But now, here he was, married to a woman he not only desired, but liked. He liked the way she looked in the morning, with her eyes still heavy with sleep. He liked the drive and determination that had made her successful in business. In fact, he liked just about everything about her.

So really, when you looked at it from that angle, there wasn't anything wrong with what he was planning. It was all for the best. Right?

MAMIE'S HOUSE was brightly lit, throwing out a welcoming glow into the dusk. Cam pulled the car into the drive and got out, coming around to open Lacey's door for her. She took his hand, though she didn't really need any help getting out of the car. What she did need was a little moral support. Cam's strong grip provided that.

"Are you sure you don't mind Mother throwing this party? I tried to talk her out of it."

Cam looked down at her, his expression difficult to read in the near dark. "I don't mind a bit. After all, we missed the reception and the usual round of showers, didn't we?"

"Mother just wants to show you off to everyone. I think she wants to prove that I really did get married."

"Nothing wrong with that. You know, you worry too much about your mother's motivations. If you'd just accept her at face value, I think you'd find her a lot easier to get along with."

"Maybe," she muttered. "But you haven't known her as long as I have. She may look like a helpless flower, but she has a knack for getting what she wants."

"Well, then look at it this way. She's already *got* what she wants. We're married. So, what do you think she's after with this party?"

It was a reasonable question. Lacey hesitated, staring at the brightly lit house. "Maybe you're right. Maybe she just wants to do a victory dance now that she's successfully married me off."

Cam laughed. "Your mother can hardly take credit for that."

"You don't know my mother." She reached up to smooth her hair, checking to make sure that none of the pins had come loose. Cam's hand caught hers, drawing it down to her side.

"You look terrific. Stop fussing." Somehow, the casual compliment reassured her in a way more flowery words couldn't have. She laughed as they went up the walkway.

"I guess I'm inclined to be a little paranoid about my mother."

"Just a little." But his tone was more amused than critical. They'd arrived on the front step and he reached out to ring the doorbell. Lacey drew a deep breath, but she didn't get a chance to let it out as Cam's head suddenly dipped and his mouth caught hers. Off balance, she clutched at his shoulders. Thus, her mother opened the door to find her son-in-law kissing her daughter quite thoroughly. Whether he'd planned it or not, Cam couldn't have come up with anything more likely to put Mamie in a good mood.

"Stop it, you two. A doorstop is no place to be kissin' your wife, Cameron." But there was a pleased note in her voice that made it clear she was delighted by this evidence of cordiality in her daughter's marriage.

Cam took his time releasing Lacey. He lifted his head, his eyes meeting hers. Despite the rushing in her ears, Lacey caught the wicked gleam that sparked his eyes to sapphire. He turned away to greet her mother, and she wondered if she'd imagined that look. Lifting a hand to her mouth, she didn't think so.

As she stepped into the living room, Lacey saw that she and Cam were just about the last arrivals. Such tardiness would ordinarily have earned her a scold, but she didn't think Mamie had any such thing in mind. She was too delighted to have Cam to introduce to those of her friends who'd begun to hint that Lacey might never marry.

Lifting a glass of champagne from a table, Lacey edged away, leaving Cam to her mother's tender mercies. She ignored the pleading look he threw her. Served him right for kissing her like that. But there was a faint curve to her mouth as she went to inspect the food.

"You realize you're one of the few people in the world for whom I'd stuff myself into one of these things."

Lacey turned as Jimbo spoke from behind her. Her smile became a full grin. He did look remarkably uncomfortable in the tailored dinner jacket. With his stocky build, the resemblance to a penguin was marked.

"You look like a penguin I saw on a *National Geographic* special one time. Only he looked more comfortable." She reached for a stuffed mushroom and bit into it with obvious pleasure.

"Heartless wench." But reproach was absent from Jimbo's voice. His eyes had gone past her. Lacey turned to see what had caught his attention. Cam and Mamie were standing with a small group of guests. Cam was speaking, and though it was impossible to hear what he was saying, it was apparently amusing because his listeners began to laugh.

"Looks like Cam and Mother are getting along." Lacey turned back to the buffet table, wondering why the thought didn't please her more. Not that she wasn't glad he'd made a hit with Mamie. But she had to admit she might have been a bit gladder if Mamie hadn't made such a hit with Cam. It was great that he liked her mother, but did he have to like her quite so much? She sighed, recognizing the absurdity of her thinking.

"Why didn't you tell me that your mother was so beautiful?" Jimbo's attention was still on the other group. The question surprised her. Beautiful? Her mother?

She turned, trying to look at Mamie through a stranger's eyes. Yes, she supposed she could be called beautiful. She had the fine bone structure that she'd bestowed on her daughter, and it carried age gracefully. Her skin was still smooth and lovely. The years had laid only the gentlest of hands on her. Her pale hair carried more than a few lengths of silver, but they threaded through the strands in a way that seemed to highlight the gold, rather than overpower it.

She answered Jimbo's question after a long pause. "You didn't ask." It seemed to take a conscious effort for him to drag his attention back to her.

"I guess I should have known she'd be beautiful. After all, look at her daughter."

Lacey raised one brow at his exaggeratedly unctuous tone. "Flattery isn't going to get you anything. I've already forgiven you for your part in the whole Vegas thing."

"I'm not sure there's anything to forgive." He reached for a cracker and spread it with a healthy layer of Brie. "It looks to me like you and Cam are doing just fine. If you weren't married to him, would you really be happier?" The look he gave her demanded honesty, as if her answer meant as much to him as it would to her.

Lacey stopped, a shrimp halfway to her mouth, an arrested look in her eyes. Trust Jimbo to ask the wrong question. Or was it the right one? Would she be happier now if she hadn't married Cam?

"Don't try to wiggle out of your responsibility," she told Jimbo absently. She bit into the shrimp, trying to throw off the uneasy feeling that something significant had just happened.

Jimbo's eyes went past her. Even before she turned she knew who was approaching. The back of her neck tingled with awareness.

"Cam. Mother."

"Honey, did I tell you how pretty you look?" Mamie slid her arm through Lacey's in an affectionate gesture, her eyes sparkling with pleasure.

"Since you bought me this dress, Mother, you're somewhat obligated to think it looks nice." She took a sip of champagne, trying not to notice the way Cam's shoulders filled out his jacket.

"Well, since you mention it, I do think I did a good job. That color is perfect for you. Don't the two of you think she looks nice?" Mamie's eyes moved from Cam to Jimbo, a teasing light in them. Lacey felt her cheeks warm, but she didn't say anything. Later, she'd throttle her mother, but for now she'd remember her manners.

"I've already told Lacey my opinion." Cam's voice held a deep note that stroked her like a physical caress. Lacey's eyes swept up to meet his. There was a warmth in his gaze that brought heat to her skin. She looked away, taking a quick swallow of champagne.

"It's easy to see where Lacey gets her looks, Mrs. Newton." Jimbo's tone drew Lacey's attention, and she looked at him sharply, wondering if she was imagining the way he was looking at her mother.

"Please, call me Mamie. And I believe your given name is James. May I?"

"I'd be honored, Mamie." The formal words should have sounded silly, especially coming from Jimbo. Only they didn't sound silly at all. Lacey looked at Cam, her uncertainty about him forgotten in the light of this new development. He raised his brows, his half smile expressing the same surprise she felt.

Jimbo was looking at her mother as if he'd just been granted a glimpse of heaven. He might have been looking at an angel, judging from the expression in his eyes. And her mother... That one was harder to assess. There was a hint of delicate color in Mamie's cheeks, and her eyes seemed to sparkle a bit brighter. But Lacey had seen that look before. There was nothing her mother loved quite so much as a little genteel flirtation. It was impossible to judge whether she saw Jimbo as anything more than a pleasant divertissement.

"Lacey tells me you're an accountant, James. Let me introduce you to Harry Lapin. He has a little business, and he was just sayin' he'd give his right arm to find a good accountant. Now, I don't think you want Harry's right arm, you havin' a perfectly good one of your own and all. But a little of Harry's business might be welcome.''

The two of them moved off, Mamie's hand set gently on the aforementioned right arm, Jimbo's head bent over hers as if every word she spoke was a jewel beyond price.

''What do you think?'' Cam asked, his gaze following the odd couple just as Lacey's had.

''I don't know. Jimbo certainly seems smitten. It's a little harder to tell about Mother. She always told me that Southern women are born knowing how to flirt. That may be all it is.'' She set down her empty glass and moved down the table to pick up a fresh one.

''Were you?''

She turned at Cam's question, raising one brow. ''Was I what?''

''Born knowing how to flirt?'' His eyes met hers over his own glass, and Lacey felt the familiar flush of heat.

''To Mother's everlasting regret, that's a gift apparently given only to those actually born on the sacred soil of the South. And Southern California doesn't count. I'm afraid flirting is not one of my better talents.''

''You have talents all your own.''

Now why did his statement seem to have a double meaning? Her eyes dropped from his to stare into her champagne. The bubbles clung lazily to the side, giving the pale liquid a frivolous look. She only wished her mood could match them. She took a deep swallow, trying not to notice how close Cam was standing.

''You really do look beautiful tonight, Lacey.'' His voice slid over her skin, leaving warmth in its wake. Despite telling herself that it was only a compliment, Lacey's hand was trembling slightly as she smoothed it over the fragile silk of her skirt. The fabric caught the light, revealing threads of gold and blue woven through the jade green. If you watched it long enough, it seemed to change colors, shifting with every change of light.

Not unlike the man who stood beside her. Sometimes he appeared as harmless as that silly dog of his. But then, some shift of light would show a new side, and she'd find her pulse beating a little too fast, her breathing too shallow. She was beginning to realize that Cameron McCleary was more complex than he seemed.

"Do you always go mute when someone gives you a compliment?" he asked teasingly.

Lacey's head jerked up. She hadn't realized how the silence was stretching. "Sorry. I guess I forgot where I was. Thank you. I'm glad you like the dress. Mother bought the fabric on a trip to Japan and had it made for me."

"It suits you. Your mother was right. The color's perfect for you."

"Thank you." She looked up at him, forcing herself to meet his eyes without blushing. "You know, Cam, if I didn't know better, I might think you were flirting with me."

"And what if I am?"

"It seems a bit of a waste. Flirting with your wife, I mean. I thought men were supposed to flirt with other women when they go to a party."

"Why would I want to flirt with another woman? I came with the most beautiful woman here. Besides, we're not thoroughly married yet, are we?"

The look in his eyes brought a rush of color to her cheeks, despite her best efforts to look calm. She knew exactly what he was talking about. They didn't sleep together. It wasn't hard to guess that he'd be more than willing to change that part of their arrangement.

She tried to whip up some annoyance that he'd brought up such a personal matter at a party. But the teasing look made it impossible. He wasn't reproaching her or complaining.

Before she could think of a suitable reply, Mamie interrupted them.

"Now I know the two of you haven't been married all that long, but that's no excuse for ignorin' your guests. Lacey, honey, your Aunt Phoebe wants to talk to you. Now, don't look like that." This was in answer to her daughter's grimace of distaste. "I know she's gettin' a little old and maybe she's a mite crotchety, but she's your great-aunt, sugar, and you should say hello at least."

"Aunt Phoebe was born crotchety, Mother. You and I both know it. The woman makes Godzilla look like a pleasant dinner companion."

Mamie ignored Cam's snort of laughter. "That may be so, but she's come all the way from Las Vegas to see you and meet Cameron, and I think you can make the effort to be polite to her."

"Why? *She* never made the effort to be polite to anyone." But Lacey's comment was muttered into her champagne glass. Her mother had taught her too well. No matter how much she disliked her Aunt Phoebe, she knew that she'd have to find the old bat and try to make polite conversation with her. Just the thought was enough to make her down the last of her champagne and reach for a fresh glass.

Mamie was leading Cam off. Lacey shrugged in answer to the look he threw over his shoulder. There was nothing she could do to rescue him from Mamie's clutches. Once her mother had her mind set on something, she usually got it. Cam wouldn't be set loose until

Mamie was satisfied that he'd met everyone he was supposed to meet.

"Lacey?" She turned, smiling.

"Lisa? I thought you were going to be in New York and couldn't make this shindig." She reached out to catch the other woman's hand, her eyes searching. She hadn't forgotten Lisa's strange mood the last time they'd spoken.

Lisa shrugged. "A meeting was canceled and I decided that I really ought to make my best friend's reception, even if it is a little late."

"You know Mother. I told her that you couldn't have a reception this long after the wedding, but she insisted that it wouldn't be a proper wedding without a reception. I think she just wanted an excuse to throw a party."

"Well, when Mamie throws a party, she certainly does a great job. This place looks wonderful. And the food is fabulous."

Lisa set her champagne glass down and took another from a waiter. Lacey watched her uneasily. She had the feeling that Lisa had had more than her share already.

"Where's Frank?"

"Oh, he's around somewhere." Lisa didn't seem concerned or even particularly interested. "Last I saw, he was talking to a redhead whose dress appeared to have been applied with a brush."

"Sounds like Sally. Don't worry, she's harmless. Believe it or not, she's a devoted wife and mother. She's probably boring Frank to tears with stories about her kids."

"Great. Just what I need." Lisa downed her champagne, her mouth set in an unhappy twist. "Frank is all hot and heavy to have kids now. He's probably lapping up her descriptions of the delightful little darlings."

"Lisa." Lacey reached out to catch her friend's hand just as Lisa was about to pick up another glass of champagne. "Is something wrong? With you and Frank, I mean? I always thought the two of you were so much in love."

"In love?" Lisa stared down at their linked hands, her hair swinging forward to conceal her expression. "I suppose we were. Maybe we still are, but it's not easy to keep a marriage strong these days. We seem to be going in different directions."

She lifted her head suddenly, her eyes intent on Lacey's. "You take advantage of every good time you and Cam have. Because they don't last as long as you think they will. Don't put things off because you think you'll have time later."

Before Lacey could question Lisa's meaning, Mamie returned to make sure that Lacey mingled properly. Lacey had only a moment to tell Lisa that they'd talk later, but when later came, she found that Frank and Lisa had already left.

The conversation lingered in the back of her mind. She'd always thought that Lisa and Frank had a perfect marriage. They'd been so much in love when they'd gotten married. And they'd seemed to be perfectly suited to each other; similar interests, Frank's easygoing personality a perfect balance to Lisa's more frantic ways. If Frank and Lisa couldn't make their marriage work, how could she and Cam possibly hope to succeed?

Her eyes sought Cam's tall figure. He was talking to her awful aunt Phoebe, bent slightly to listen to whatever she was telling him. Just the sight of his broad shoulders was enough to soothe some of Lacey's doubts. He looked so solid. Next to him, every other man she'd known was vague and shadowy. He must have felt her gaze because he turned, his eyes sweeping over the room until he found her.

He didn't smile or wave. He simply looked at her, and she could feel her chest grow tight, leaving her breathless. Someone said something to her and she dragged her eyes from Cam's, reluctant to break the small contact. With an effort, she forced herself to concentrate on the conversation.

But the awareness built as the evening wore on. Lisa's warning to take advantage of every moment niggled at the back of her mind. She'd taken a big gamble by jumping into this marriage, a bigger one by deciding to stick with it. It was a little too late to chicken out now. She wanted Cam, not just because he was physically attractive, but because she'd grown to like him. Maybe even— She shied away from acknowledging anything more than that. For the moment, it was enough that she liked him.

They'd made love once. The fact that her memories of that night were vague didn't change the events. If she was honest, she wanted more than vague memories. But it was such a commitment. Yet the marriage itself was surely an even greater commitment. And if she wanted that to work, didn't she have to throw herself into it wholeheartedly?

And she did want it to work. She wanted to see if what she felt for Cam now would deepen. She wanted to know if the attraction she'd felt from the first moment she saw him had had its roots in some deep recognition of their belonging together.

Her eyes caught Cam's again. He must have read something in her expression, because he excused himself from the conversation he was in and made his way across the room toward her. Now that he was approaching,

Lacey was caught in a sudden attack of nerves. She barely knew this man, marriage or not.

"Have I mentioned that you look particularly beautiful tonight?" Cam took a glass of champagne from a waiter and pressed it into her hand.

"I think you mentioned it," she managed, her voice husky.

"I've been watching you all night."

"Have you?" From somewhere inside, she felt a sudden bubble of giddiness explode upward. She lowered her lashes, looking at Cam from beneath their fragile shelter. "You should be careful. My husband might catch you."

Cam's eyes widened and the slow smile that curved his mouth set off tingles all the way to her toes. "Is your husband the jealous type?"

"I don't know. You see, we have a marriage of convenience." She experimented with batting her lashes a little and was rewarded by the look in his eyes.

"Oh, really." He braced himself against the wall behind her, cutting her off from the rest of the party with the breadth of his shoulders. "It seems to me that any man married to you wouldn't be able to keep it a marriage of convenience for long. You're much too beautiful."

"Thank you." She batted her lashes again, allowing her mouth to curve in a small smile. This kind of flirtation was new to her, but perhaps her mother was right and it was something in the blood.

"I bet he lies awake at night thinking of you lying only a few feet away, your body all warm and soft under the covers. I bet he falls asleep imagining you in the bed next to him, your skin against his."

Lacey stared up at him, unable to drag her eyes from the heated blue of his. His words warmed her skin like a slow-burning fire, setting nerves quivering in places she hadn't even known she had nerves.

"Do you think so?" The words came out more breathless than she'd intended.

"I know so." Was it possible for a man to seduce with his voice alone? Lacey was beginning to think it was. Cam reached out, taking her hand in his, running his thumb over the sensitive skin at the base of her palm.

"Now, I know you're still newlyweds, but that doesn't mean you get to just ignore your guests." Mamie's voice was like a dash of cold water in the face. Lacey blinked, shaking her head and trying to drag herself out of the spell Cam had woven.

Before she could say anything, Cam turned his most charming smile on her mother. "You know, it's getting kind of late, and Lacey and I have to get up early tomorrow. I'm sure you'll understand if we leave a little bit early."

"Well, I . . ." Mamie didn't look as if she understood at all. It wasn't part of her game plan to have the guests of honor leave at ten o'clock. But Cam didn't give her a chance to protest. He had Lacey's wrap in hand and was ushering her out the door before Mamie could marshal her arguments.

Lacey giggled as he opened the car door and saw her seated. It was the first time in years that she'd seen someone so completely outmaneuver her mother. As Cam settled in the driver's seat, she laughed out loud, feeling suddenly wonderfully wicked and wild. He turned to look at her, arching one brow.

"You didn't let her get a word in edgewise," Lacey marveled. "You didn't even tell her why we were leaving."

"I didn't think it was good politics to tell her I wanted to take my wife home to seduce her."

Lacey's breath caught in the brief moment of silence before he turned the key in the ignition. The low roar of the engine filled the car, shutting out the world outside. She could only stare at him, incapable of protest or agreement—and uncertain which response reflected her feelings.

Cam's hand cupped the back of her neck, and Lacey's head tilted back as his mouth lowered on hers. It wasn't a long kiss, but what it lacked in duration, it more than made up for in passion. When his mouth lifted, Lacey couldn't have uttered a protest even if she'd wanted to, which she didn't.

The drive home wasn't long, but each second seemed to increase the awareness that lay between them. By the time Cam pulled into the driveway, Lacey felt as if every inch of her skin was sensitized, attuned to him.

Neither of them spoke as they walked the short distance to the doorway. They'd left a lamp on in the living room, and light spilled into the hallway in dim patches. Cam shut the door behind them and slowly, deliberately, turned to her.

Lacey also turned slowly, feeling as if something hung in the balance. Cam's face was shadowy, impossible to read. But she could feel his eyes on her, as vivid as a physical caress.

He reached out to cup her cheek, and her lashes seemed suddenly much too heavy. His thumb stroked, the callused skin rasping gently. Warmth quivered to life somewhere deep inside her.

"You look so beautiful tonight."

His fingers shifted downward, brushing along the side of her neck. "I couldn't stand being there any longer, with all those people. I had to be alone with you. Tell me you wanted that, too."

His palm settled on the top of her shoulder, sweeping outward, taking the wide strap of her dress with it. Lacey's breath caught in the back of her throat, but she didn't protest. The strap draped just above her elbow. She caught a glimpse of his eyes, blue fire in the shadows, and then his mouth touched the outermost edge of her shoulder. Her eyes fell shut.

He nibbled the soft skin, inhaling the gentle scents of perfume and woman. Lacey's hands came up, fumbling to find his shoulders, as if without them to balance her, she'd tumble helplessly backward. Cam's arms slipped around her, bracing her without drawing her any closer, and she gave herself up to that support.

"Lacey, tell me you want me as much as I want you."

The words were half demand, half plea and wholly irresistible. Her eyes opened slowly to stare up into his. His thumb had replaced his mouth, sliding restlessly over the top of her shoulder. She felt drunk, but she knew it wasn't the champagne.

"Lacey?" He made her name a question. She knew what he was asking.

She needed time to think. It wasn't a decision to be made lightly. She had to think. But how could she when he was standing so close? How could she when her body wanted only to lean into his? Without willing them, her fingers lifted to touch his face, the sensitive line of his mouth, the strength of his jaw. Cam stood still under her light exploration, but she could feel the tension in the hand that lay across her back, see it in the glitter of his eyes.

And the answer was simple after all.

"Yes." The one whispered word was all she could manage, but it was all he needed to hear.

His head lowered, his mouth capturing hers in a kiss that sent shock waves all the way to Lacey's toes. Her zipper slid downward beneath his fingers, and his hand flattened against the warm skin of her back. All the need, all the hunger they had been denying for so long, was suddenly freed of the restraints they'd been holding so tight.

Shirt buttons seemed to slip magically open, and her hands were pressed against the hard muscles of his chest. He eased her a fraction away and the silk dress fell to the floor with barely a whisper of sound. His mouth caught her soft moan of pleasure as the softness of her breasts met the hard warmth of his chest.

Bending, he caught her behind the knees and swept her into his arms. For an instant, Lacey had the dizzying sensation that the world was spinning around her, and she clutched at him.

"I won't let you go." Cam's voice was husky. Lacey tilted her head back to meet his eyes, but she couldn't hold them for long. There was something so intense in his gaze that she had to look away. She buried her face against his chest as he carried her into the bedroom.

Cam set her on the bed, following her down so that she was pressed into the pillows. She was surrounded by him, his warmth, his scent, the sheer masculinity of him. She'd never felt more protected, yet more threatened, in her life. She wanted him, but the very intensity of her desire frightened her.

She slid her fingers into the silky hair at the back of his head, drawing him closer, wanting to lose herself in him. She'd think about the right and wrong of this tomorrow. For now she wanted to think only of how good it felt to be in his arms.

This was right. This was meant to be.

Chapter Ten

Lacey woke slowly, aware of feeling warm and content. She snuggled deeper into the pillow. There was something special about this morning. She couldn't remember what it was, but she knew it was special. It was the same feeling she'd had when she was a little girl waking up on her birthday.

Her mouth curved in a soft smile and she lay in sleepy contentment, not really trying to remember what made this day special. It was enough to savor the feeling.

There was a movement behind her, and a long, definitely masculine arm fell across the curve of her waist. Her eyes flew open. The contentment fled abruptly, replaced with awareness.

Cam. How could she have forgotten, even for a moment, just why today was different? They'd made love last night. More than once, as a matter of fact.

Lacey stared at the patterns of sunlight on the wooden floor. Memories of the night just past slipped uninvited into her mind. Cam's hands, so sure and knowing on her body. His mouth finding erogenous zones she hadn't known existed.

But he hadn't been the only one to take an active part in their lovemaking. Her cheeks warmed as she remembered that she'd made more than a few explorations of her own. Her fingers tingled with the memory of heated skin and firm muscles.

She'd learned more about her own potential for passion last night than she had in all the years that had gone before. Cam was a wonderful lover, strong and considerate, not afraid to take the lead, yet confident enough to lie back and allow her to direct their path. Lacey flushed deeper. She'd taken advantage of that confidence. She'd been shameless last night. And she'd enjoyed every minute of it.

But that had been last night. This morning, the sunlight seemed to cast a slightly different light on things. Their marriage was no longer just writing on a piece of paper. It was real by any standard she cared to name. And now that it was too late, she wasn't sure she was ready for that reality.

She eased the covers back and then lifted Cam's arm, so that she could slip out from beneath it. The floor was cool beneath her bare feet, but it was a pleasant contrast to the heat that seemed to cover her from head to toe. Her own clothes were no doubt still in the hall where they'd been left last night, but Cam's shirt was lying on the floor. She picked it up, wrapping it around her body, wishing that it came to her ankles instead of ending at mid-thigh. Still, it was better than nothing.

Cam rolled onto his stomach, and Lacey hesitated, poised for flight but unable to resist the urge to look at him. The sheet was draped at his waist, baring a width of muscled shoulders and a length of strong back. She didn't need to close her eyes to remember the feel of that back under her hands.

For a moment, the urge to crawl back into bed beside him was strong. She wavered. But she had a shop to open. Besides, she felt too vulnerable, too fragile right now. She needed a little time to gather herself before she faced Cam again.

CAM ROLLED OVER as the door shut behind Lacey. Her scent lingered in the bed, and he almost got up to follow her to her room, which he hoped would become the guest room again. He wanted to take her in his arms and coax her back to bed, but instinct told him that wouldn't be a wise move.

He propped himself up on the pillows, staring at the blank panel of the door as if some message were written upon it. Lacey's stealthy departure from the bed had awakened him, and he'd almost pulled her back down beside him. But it had been so obvious that she was trying to get out of the room before he woke. So he'd forced himself to lie still, allowing her to make her getaway.

He didn't want to press her too hard. Last night they'd taken an enormous step. If she needed a little breathing room after that, he could give it to her.

But not too much. He didn't want her to start thinking of reasons this couldn't possibly work. She would be on her way to the shop. But even the owner had to take a lunch break.

LACEY'S LOVELIES was a success because its owner had worked like a dog to make it so. Looking around the small shop, Lacey was justifiably proud of her efforts. She didn't have the room to carry a large stock, but she didn't need to. She only carried the very best, whether it was handmade leather bags from Italy or lingerie made of a silk so fine that it could literally be drawn through a wedding band. Elbow-length suede gloves in rich jade nestled beside an embroidered fuchsia silk camisole.

Her clientele appreciated the best, and they were willing to pay for it. She also provided them with a luxurious atmosphere, the pale gray-and-peach decor a quiet contrast to the season's current spill of bright colors. Coffee and tea were always available, the rich scent of Jamaican beans adding a last fillip of luxury.

Ordinarily Lacey had no trouble concentrating on business. Surrounded by the evidence of the success of her hard work, she felt inspired to keep going throughout the day.

Today was different. Today her thoughts showed an uncontrollable tendency to wander to the night before. Or to wonder what Cam had thought when he woke to find her gone. Or to wonder what Cam was doing right at that particular moment.

Luckily she wasn't handling the shop by herself today. If she had been, she would probably have managed to lose half the customers who came in. Her mind simply wasn't on the here and now. But Margaret had worked for her for nearly three years, and she was more than capable of running the place on her own. Sensibly Lacey let her do just that.

She retreated to her tiny office behind the fitting rooms and tried to concentrate on updating the accounts. She didn't get very far with that, either. Cam's face kept intruding between her and the columns of figures, making her fingers fumble on the keys of her calculator. She looked up gratefully when Margaret stuck her head in the doorway. She'd just added the same column twice, coming up with impossible sums both times. An interruption was more than welcome.

"Problem?" Lacey asked, almost hoping there was one. Anything to take her mind off Cam. But Margaret was shaking her head.

"You've got a visitor. I do believe it's your husband."
She waggled her eyebrows, her comfortably middle-aged
face settling into an exaggerated expression of apprecia-
tion. "If I had something like that at home, I certainly
wouldn't be spending my days here."

"You've got Stanley." Lacey stood up, fussing with a
stack of papers and keeping her head bent over the task,
trying to conceal the color in her cheeks. Her husband.
Odd, the words made it all seem so real. As if last night
hadn't already made it real.

"I love Stanley dearly, but you're comparing French
fries to potatoes Anna." Margaret's voice called Lacey
back to the present. She smiled at the joke, her thoughts
only half on the conversation. She smoothed a hand over
her hair and then tugged at her skirt, making sure that the
seam was precisely aligned down the front.

Cam wasn't hard to find. His height alone made him
impossible to miss. He towered over the racks and low
tables. But that wasn't the only thing that drew the eye.
That he was a male in a decidedly feminine setting was
part of it. He was wearing a soft blue chambray shirt and
a pair of crisp blue jeans. The contrast between his simple work clothes and the silks and laces of her stock was
vivid.

Oddly enough, he didn't look uncomfortable. Lacey
was beginning to wonder if the situation existed that
could throw Cameron McCleary off his stride. He looked
perfectly at home, standing next to a table of sensual lingerie.

Drawing in a deep breath, Lacey threaded her way
through the racks of garments. He turned as she halted
beside him, his face creasing in a smile that caused a
quick bump in her chest.

"Hi."

"Hi." She had to clear her throat before she could return the simple greeting. Had he gotten even handsomer since this morning? Or had she simply forgotten just how attractive he was?

"I hope you don't mind my just dropping in."

"No, no. I don't mind." She cleared her throat again. "It's good to see you." *Great, nitwit. You sound like a sixteen-year-old on a blind date.*

"It's a beautiful store."

"Thank you."

"I particularly like some of your stock." His smile took on a wicked glint, and Lacey's gaze dropped to what he held. Draped across his palm was an ivory teddy made of a silk Charmeuse so fine it was almost transparent. Coffee-toned lace decorated the silk, emphasizing the high-cut legs and low-cut bodice. Lying across his callused hand, the garment looked wickedly sexy and frivolous.

The color that rose in Lacey's cheeks threatened to scorch her skin, but she struggled to maintain a calm facade.

"I've sold quite a few of those. They're imported from France."

Cam stroked the silk, his eyes on her face. "I always did say that the French really know how to live."

Lacey dragged her eyes from the hypnotic motion of his fingers on the silk only to meet the equally dangerous look in his eyes. Was it possible for blue eyes to look so warm? She reached out to take the garment from him, folding it with brisk motions that concealed the trembling of her fingers.

"Some of our best products come from France." She set the teddy back on the table and looked at him again, clasping her hands together in front of her. "Did you come in for something specific?"

The question came out a little more abrupt than she'd intended, but he'd thrown her so totally off balance, she hardly knew what she was saying.

"I thought you might like to join me for lunch."

Lunch? What a mundane thought. She wasn't sure what she'd been expecting, but she definitely hadn't expected that.

"I really should stay here. A lot of our customers do their shopping during the lunch hour."

"Oh, don't worry about that, Lacey." Margaret's smile was so wide that it threatened to split her face in two. She'd been casually straightening some stock that didn't need straightening not far from where Cam and Lacey stood. Now she decided it was time to add her helpful two bits to the conversation.

"I can manage the shop just fine. I've done it before and there's no reason today should be any different. It's not like we're having a sale or anything." Her wide smile indicated that they would undoubtedly appreciate her help.

"What do you say, Lacey?" Cam was leaving the decision up to her. Lacey nodded slowly, not sure why she was so reluctant. Heaven knew, what they'd shared last night was considerably more intimate than lunch.

"Sure. That would be nice. There's a great café just down the street."

Cam waited while she made a last—unnecessary—check of the office and got her purse, and then he held the door for her to step out onto the sidewalk. Once outside he reached for her hand. The casual touch sent tingles up Lacey's arm, and she suppressed the urge to pull away.

"This place doesn't serve nouvelle cuisine, does it?" Cam asked, following Lacey's lead through the light pedestrian traffic.

"Not really. It's more California cuisine."

"California cuisine? Does that mean all they serve are goat-cheese salads barely big enough to fill a thimble?"

"Well, they do have goat-cheese salads, but they also have other things, and the servings are a reasonable size."

They were a little early, avoiding the worst of the lunch crowd, and they were lucky enough to get a table by the window. The spring sunshine spilled across the patio outside, which was already getting some use despite the lingering coolness in the air.

They didn't talk beyond discussing the menu until the waiter had taken their orders. Once that was done, there were no obvious distractions. Tension was a knot in the pit of her stomach. She felt irritable, irrationally annoyed with Cam, though she couldn't have said why.

She avoided looking at him and stared at the table, her fingers twisting the small bread plate around and around on the checked cloth. Cam's hand came out, his fingers closing over hers, stilling the restless movement. Lacey looked up, meeting his eyes. His mouth was quirked in a half smile, but his eyes held understanding.

"I don't bite, you know."

"I know." She shrugged, pulling her fingers away from his, twisting them together in her lap. "I guess I'm just a little nervous."

"Because of last night?"

"I . . . yes."

Cam leaned back as the waiter set small salads, complete with goat cheese, down in front of them. Cam looked at Lacey, his eyebrows raised, and despite her nervousness, her mouth twitched in a smile.

"Well, at least this is only the first course," he said. "Why are you nervous about last night?" The question was so casually asked that it left her momentarily without words.

"Just being stupid, I suppose," she snapped on a wave of irritation. Dammit! Didn't anything throw him off balance?

Cam winced. "Sorry. I didn't mean to get too nosy."

"No, I'm the one who should be sorry." It wasn't his fault she was so uptight. It wasn't even his fault that he wasn't equally uptight. "I guess I just got up on the wrong side of the bed this morning."

"Or the wrong bed entirely?" Something in his tone made her look at him sharply. Maybe he wasn't quite as unaffected as he'd have her believe. The thought made her feel a little better.

"I'm not sorry," she told him.

"Are you sure?"

Why, he needed reassurance just as much as she did.

"I'm sure." Her color might be a little high, but her voice was steady. "What about you?" She hadn't meant to ask the question, but now that it was out, she held her breath, waiting for his answer.

"Regrets? Me?" He seemed surprised. "You've got to be kidding. How could I possibly regret one of the greatest nights of my life?"

She couldn't doubt his sincerity and something eased inside her. Perhaps, unconsciously, she'd been afraid that last night hadn't proved satisfying for him, that she'd failed to measure up in some way. She smiled at him, the first completely natural smile she'd given. There was a subtle relaxing of tension between them.

She took a bite of her salad, barely tasting the tart dressing on the romaine. Looking around the restaurant, she saw that couples occupied several of the tables. Some of them were obvious business acquaintances, absorbed in discussions of profit and loss. But two or three looked like their meeting might be more personal. How would someone else label her and Cam after just a casual glance at their table? Did they look like a married couple? Just what did a married couple look like, anyway?

"What are you thinking about, Lacey?"

"Nothing all that interesting." She set down her fork, pushing the salad bowl to the side. "I was just wondering how we look to other people."

"Other people?" Cam glanced around the small restaurant. "These other people?"

She nodded, feeling a little foolish now that she'd voiced her thoughts.

"It's a habit of mine," she told him. "Wondering what other people are doing in their lives, wondering how they see me."

"And how do you think they see us?"

"I don't know. Do you think we look married?"

"How does married look?" he asked.

"I'm not sure."

"Well, if there's a look to it, I'm sure we'll develop it, given enough time."

"Are we going to have enough time?" The question was barely audible, and her eyes avoided his.

"I think we're going to have all the time we need. Don't you?"

"I hope so." She looked up, meeting his calm gaze and wishing she felt as sure as he seemed. "I guess I just can't help wondering where we're going to go from here. I mean, we've been sort of living together without spend-

ing a lot of time together. How do we know we're going
to be compatible over the long run?''

''We don't. But nobody does until they try. Why don't
we make it a point to spend more time together? It takes
time to get to know someone. But even if we'd been engaged for five years, we'd still have to spend time learning how to live together. We're just doing things in
reverse order, that's all.''

''I suppose.'' The waiter arrived with their main
courses and the conversation was temporarily halted.
Lacey picked at her boneless chicken breast for a moment. ''But what if—''

''Lacey.'' Cam stopped her before she could finish the
question. ''Let's not borrow trouble. We'll take this one
day at a time, just like everybody else does. Don't look
too far ahead. Okay?''

She nodded slowly. He was right. No one could predict the future and there was no sense in trying. One day
at time. It wasn't a bad philosophy.

THEIR MARRIAGE SHIFTED into a new phase. Lacey no
longer slept alone in the guest room. Cam's bed was more
than big enough for the two of them. No matter what the
stresses of the day had been, they were put aside once the
bedroom door shut behind them.

But it sometimes seemed as if that was the only place
they'd made any progress. Their attempts to spend more
time together met with mixed success. Lacey's visit to his
workshop could hardly be deemed a big step forward in
their relationship.

It might have worked out a little better if she hadn't
happened to show up just after Cam had misjudged the
pressure necessary to shape a thin piece of facing to a

curved shelf. The facing snapped with a pop that paled in comparison to the curse that followed it.

"Hello?"

Cam spun around at the sound of Lacey's tentative greeting, the pieces of facing clenched in his fists. She was standing in the open door, her expression as uncertain as her voice.

"Is this a bad time?"

Cam took a deep breath, forcing himself to relax. "No. It's not a bad time. Aren't you home early?" He set the ruined facing down and crossed the cement floor to where she stood. Lacey lifted her face to his, and Cam felt some of the day's frustrations slide away as her mouth softened under his.

"It sounded like you were having some problems," she commented as they drew apart.

Cam remembered the rather vivid curse and shrugged. "Sorry about that. It hasn't been the greatest day. What are you doing home? Nothing wrong at the shop, is there?"

"No. I've got some things I wanted to do around here, so I'm letting Margaret close tonight."

"Things? What kind of things?"

"Nothing major. Just some cleaning."

"I thought the place couldn't get much cleaner. Don't you think you're working a little too hard?"

"I enjoy it. Is this where you do all your work?"

Cam was willing to let the subject of housework drop for the moment. "It's not huge, but I don't really need a whole lot of room."

"It's a little cluttered, isn't it?" She looked around the shop, trying to sort out some recognizable pattern to the stacks of wood, boxes of tools and half-finished pieces of furniture.

"I know where everything is." Cam eyed her warily. She'd already reorganized the house, but his shop was in exactly the right state of chaotic order.

Lacey caught his eye and laughed. "Don't worry, I'm not going to try and straighten out your hammers and nails and whatever else you have in here."

"Good."

His relief was so obvious that she laughed again. "Coward."

Cam threw his arm around her shoulders, drawing her close. He never tired of the feel of her against him, the scent of her. It never failed to make his heart beat a little faster.

"So what do you do with all these tools?" Lacey's voice carried a hint of nervousness and his mouth curved in a smile. She was a passionate partner in the privacy of their bedroom, but outside the safety of those four walls, she was inclined to shy away.

Cam pulled her closer, turning her so that her hands were caught between them. "Do you really want to talk about carpentry right now?" He murmured the question against the soft skin behind her ear, feeling the shiver of response that ran through her.

But Lacey was nothing if not determined. "I think what you do is very interesting, and I don't really know anything about it."

With a sigh, Cam released her and she sidled away, picking up a chisel and studying it as if it was the most interesting thing she'd seen in weeks.

"Unless you're thinking of adding carpentry to your list of accomplishments, there's really not much to explain. The basics of building furniture are pretty straightforward. It's the details that change a few pieces of wood into a potential Chippendale."

"It must have taken you a long time to learn how to create those details."

Cam picked up a piece of wood, his long fingers caressing the subtle grain. "My grandfather taught me most of what I know. I didn't meet him until I was almost fifteen. My mother had quarreled with her parents and left home to marry my father. My grandparents told me that they had a share in the decisions she'd made, keeping me from them. But I never really believed it."

Lacey watched his face, seeing the old hurts, wondering if he was aware of the pain that drew lines between his brows when he spoke of his past.

"Do you remember much of your mother?" She asked the question tentatively, uncertain of the ground she was treading.

"Sure." Cam laughed, a sound without humor. "I remember a succession of strangers who took care of me a lot better though. She breezed in once in a while, either showering me with presents or sneaking me out without paying the bill, depending on which way her fortunes had gone. She was a shallow vain woman with a soul smaller than her heart.

"I don't remember my father at all, but I never really blamed him for leaving her. I'd have left her if I'd had a choice. Of course, in the end, she made the decision for both of us. Looking back, I'm surprised she kept me with her as long as she did."

"Maybe she loved you in her own way," Lacey offered hesitantly, uncertain of the best way to handle the kind of bitter memories her question had called up.

Cam laughed again. "No. She didn't love anybody but herself."

There was no arguing with his certainty, though Lacey found it hard to comprehend a woman not loving her own child.

"It must have been very hard for you." The platitude seemed woefully inadequate.

"It was hell," Cam said simply. He lifted another piece of wood, weighing it in one hand. "But it all worked out in the end. I was lucky that Jimbo saw something that made him think I might be worth trying to save. He wasn't much more than a kid himself. God knows what he saw in the obnoxious little punk I was then. And Mom and Dad took an even bigger risk. Hell, I half expected me to turn out to be an ax murderer, but they kept insisting there was something worth saving. They believed in me so strongly that I just had to try and prove them right.

"And then they found my grandparents, and I got a chance to see something of my roots. I'm glad I did. It made it easier to straighten out when I saw that they were good people. I could believe that I didn't have to turn out like my mother. I could try and be like my grandparents instead. That's the way my mind worked."

Lacey crossed the few feet that separated them and stood next to him, looking at the wood he was holding.

"Is that why you decided to go into carpentry, because that's what your grandfather did?"

"Not really." He stroked his fingers over the smooth grain. "The minute he handed me a piece of wood, I felt as if I'd found something I'd been missing for a long time. I never wanted to do anything else from that moment on."

There was a long moment when there didn't seem to be anything more to say. Cam broke the somber mood, dropping the small board with a crash that made Lacey jump.

"Enough of all this solemn talk. You're looking much too beautiful to be spending your time in a shop. Let's go out to dinner."

"But I had things I planned to do." Lacey struggled to adjust her thinking from Cam's past to the idea of a dinner out.

"The house will still be dirty when we get back." Cam dismissed her arguments with a wave of his hand, shepherding her out of the shop and shutting the door with a finality that made her wonder if he wasn't shutting the door to his memories.

Chapter Eleven

Cam stroked the plane across the surface of the wood, shaving off fragrant curls of cedar. Approaching summer meant the sunlight lingered till later in the day, and it spilled across the workbench now, painting vivid patterns of light and shadow across the pale wood.

If he looked out the garage door, he could see the light shining from the kitchen window. But he didn't raise his head. Lacey was probably in there preparing some meal guaranteed to set new standards of epicurean excellence. The thought should have delighted him. God knew, it would certainly be enough to delight most men. He hadn't eaten so well in years. He straightened, patting his stomach absently. He'd had to add another mile a day to his run just to keep from developing a bulge.

But that wasn't what bothered him. And it wasn't that he minded Lacey spending her time making fantastic meals. Not if that was what she really enjoyed doing. But he didn't think she was spending so much time in the kitchen out of a passionate love of cooking.

She seemed to be trying to prove something. But what and to whom, he couldn't figure out. He shook his head. He was probably looking for trouble where it didn't exist. Maybe Lacey secretly envied Julia Child. Maybe she was just going through a phase.

After glancing at his watch, he put away the tools, leaving everything ready for the morning. Cam stretched, enjoying the cool of the early-evening air. Spring in Southern California was too brief to be fully enjoyed. Summer's heat followed hard on its heels, making the pavement sizzle and leaving the air a visible presence in the L.A. basin. He enjoyed summer's heat, but it didn't have the innocence of spring.

He opened the back door and came to a dead stop. The rich scent of spices mixed with the pungent and unmistakable aroma of ammonia. In the middle of the floor, on her hands and knees, Lacey tilted her head back to look at him.

"Oh, dear. I should have told you I was going to be stripping the floor. Dinner isn't going to be done for about an hour, and it seemed like a good time to get it done. You'll have to go around to the front door."

Cam leaned his shoulder against the doorjamb, trying to rein in the inexplicable surge of anger that threatened to find voice. Her hair was caught back in a ponytail, the golden blond darkened by perspiration around her face. Her faded jeans and sleeveless top were not complemented by the elbow-length rubber gloves that protected her hands.

"Did you get home early?"

Lacey looked up at him, her expression distracted. "No. I got home about half an hour ago. Why?" She scrubbed another square of tile with the brush she held.

"Well, it seems to me that you must be pretty tired after working all day. And then to come home and start dinner and tackle stripping the kitchen floor is a bit of overkill, don't you think?"

She either didn't hear or chose to ignore the subtle tightness in his voice. "I'm not tired. And the floor really was getting to look grungy. Wax builds up on it so quickly, you know."

"Lacey." He waited until she stopped scrubbing and looked at him again. "It really isn't essential that I be able to literally eat off the floor. A little wax buildup is not fatal."

"I know, but Claire is coming to dinner next week, and I want the house to be really clean for them."

Cam knew when he was licked. He backed out of the doorway and circled around the house, coming in the front door. He went straight to the bedroom, stripping off his clothes on the way to the shower. It was stupid to get annoyed. If he had any common sense, he'd just sit back and enjoy the clean house, the meals, her presence in his bed.

He twisted the shower on. The problem was, he didn't want Suzy Homemaker. He wanted a companion. Someone to talk to, someone who wanted to spend an occasional evening reading the paper together, or watching a movie. And Lacey never seemed to have the time for any of that.

No, that wasn't entirely fair. They *had* been spending more time together. There'd been a trip to the zoo. They'd spent a day at the beach. Cam's mouth curved, remembering Lacey's sunburned nose.

No, he couldn't really say they hadn't been getting to know each other. The more time he spent with her the more things he discovered he liked. Sometimes he thought it was more than liking, but he wasn't quite ready to make that decision.

The warm water pounded down on his back, easing some of the tension from his muscles. He stretched out his arms and placed his hands against the tiled wall, closing his eyes and letting the water wash over him. Slowly a smile covered his mouth, and then he laughed softly.

This marriage business wasn't as easy as he'd thought it would be. He was acting like an idiot. Getting upset over something as ridiculous as the fact that Lacey had a passion for spotless floors and big meals. If she liked to clean house and cook, it was nothing to complain about.

So he complimented Lacey on the floor, ate twice as much as he wanted and refused to be annoyed when she waxed the floor after dinner. He bided his time until they went to bed. At least in bed, she could neither cook nor clean.

Cam lay in bed listening to the sound of the shower. Marriage might not have been as simple as he'd planned, but it definitely had its moments. Such as watching Lacey walk out of the bathroom, her skin lustrous with lingering moisture, her hair tumbling onto her shoulders in honey-colored waves. She was wearing a pair of gray silk pajamas that looked like something Marlene Dietrich might have worn. There was a playful element in their sexiness.

She sat down on the side of the bed to kick off her slippers, and Cam saw the tired slump of her shoulders. It was her own fault she was so exhausted. If she'd stop trying to be superwoman, life would be a lot easier for both of them. But he couldn't resist the vulnerability he saw in her. He sat up, his hands settling on her shoulders.

She tensed under his hands, but only for a moment. His thumbs found the tight muscles at the base of her neck and she went limp.

"You're working too hard," he told her, his voice soft in the dim room.

"I'm enjoying myself." She shifted under his hands so that he could get to a particularly tense spot. "Besides, I want everything to be perfect for the dinner party next week. You know, it will be the first time our families meet."

"That doesn't mean the house has to gleam. No one is going to look behind the stove."

"You never can tell. I just feel better knowing it's clean."

"I think you're taking on more than you should," he insisted, kneading the taut muscles of her shoulders. "You can't do everything."

"It's not that big a deal. Besides, I've watched my mother do this hundreds of times. She always managed without a problem."

"Well, it's no skin off my nose. Let me know what I can do to help."

His hands left her shoulders. Lacey reached up to turn off the lamp as she slid under the covers. She relaxed back against the pillows with a sigh as tired muscles felt the support of the mattress.

"You know, a funny thing happened today." Her voice was quiet in the darkness.

Cam put his arm around her shoulders, drawing her against his chest. He draped his other arm over the curve of her waist.

"What happened today?" These quiet moments before they fell asleep were strangely rewarding. Cam felt more married in this little space of time than he did at any other. There was something so cozy and intimate about lying in bed in a darkened room, hushed voices talking about the little unimportant things that made up most days.

"Jimbo came to the shop."

"Oh, yeah? What did he want?"

"Well, that was what was strange. He never did say what he wanted, but he kept bringing the conversation around to my mother. I invited him to dinner next week, and when I told him she was going to be here, he looked like he'd just been invited to the White House. You don't suppose he's interested in her, do you?"

"I don't know. Why not?"

"Well, she's my mother and she's older than Jimbo, and Jimbo is— Well, Jimbo. They aren't a very likely couple."

"I've seen more unlikely combinations succeed."

"True. Look at us."

"Hey!" Lacey giggled as Cam's fingers found a ticklish spot on her side. It was a measure of how far they'd come that they felt safe enough to tease each other. They might have a long way yet to go, but at moments like this, it was easy to believe that they were going to make it.

"LACEY, THE TABLE looks fine. Will you stop fussing with it?" Despite his efforts to sound teasing, Cam was aware of the bite that had crept into his tone.

Lacey turned away from the table and gave him an apologetic smile. "Sorry. It's just that I want everything to be perfect."

"It looks great. You look great. In fact, you look positively edible." He slipped his arms around her waist. She returned his kiss, but it was obvious that her thoughts were elsewhere. With a resigned sigh, Cam released her. Until this damned dinner party was over with, he might as well resign himself to living with an android.

Well, at least this was the last night he had to worry about it. In a few minutes people would start arriving. Surely, once this was over, she'd relax a little. She'd been wound so tight this past week that he'd felt as if the slightest touch or the wrong word would be enough to send her flying apart in a million pieces.

"Do I look all right?" Lacey asked the question as if it was the first time it had been asked. Cam forced himself to forget the fact he'd already answered it at least three times in the past hour. He looked at her carefully, though he didn't really need to. The ivory silk dress was the essence of elegant simplicity. With a bright fuchsia scarf cinched around her waist and her hair caught back from her face with fuchsia silk bows she looked like she'd stepped off the pages of *Vogue*.

"You look fantastic. The dress is perfect." His reassurance appeared to soothe her anxieties, at least momentarily. Her expression relaxed into a smile.

"Thank you. You look very nice, yourself." Her eyes skimmed his tobacco-brown slacks and light blue shirt. The color of the shirt echoed his eyes, making them seem even bluer than usual.

"We strive to please." But Lacey's attention had already returned to a nervous examination of her table settings. Cam didn't bother to try to distract her again. Maybe when people began to arrive, she'd relax a little. She was so uptight now, she was making him uneasy.

The evening started out just fine. Lacey's mother arrived first, followed almost immediately by Jimbo. So immediately that Cam half suspected he'd been lurking in the underbrush awaiting her arrival. Mamie settled into a chair, a ladylike finger of bourbon beside her, "Because you know, Cameron, that bourbon is the only truly civilized drink. Wine is hardly worth the effort."

Jimbo leaned against the mantel, which just happened to put him close enough to Mamie to catch a whiff of her perfume. From the way his old friend was looking at his new mother-in-law, Cam didn't think there was any real need to speculate on the direction that relationship was going to take, at least if Jimbo had anything to say about it.

Claire and Joe arrived a few minutes late, full of apologies and explanations of the difficulties of getting a houseful of youngsters and a baby-sitter in the same place at the same time.

Cam's hopes that Lacey would relax once the evening was under way were met, at least for a while. Mamie clearly liked Claire and Joe and the feeling was mutual. And Jimbo could always be counted on to keep the conversation going if things began to flag. Lacey was the perfect hostess, relaxed yet in control. Halfway through the hour before dinner she'd planned for everyone to chat, she glanced across the room and caught his eye. The smile she gave him was dazzling, and Cam found it easy to forget the minor stresses and strains of the past couple of weeks.

Twenty minutes before dinner was to be served, Lacey excused herself and disappeared into the kitchen. She'd spent the previous few days making schedules, ones that rivaled those that launched D day. She knew to the second how long each dish was to take and in exactly what order they were to be prepared.

As Cam watched her go he took a sip of his bourbon, glad the anticipated night had finally arrived and was off to a smashing start. A few more hours and this would all be behind them.

His complacency was shattered by a muffled shriek from the direction of the kitchen. Conversations broke off and all heads turned toward the sound. Cam was already on his feet, waving the others back.

"Don't worry about it. I'm sure it's no big deal."

Lacey's expression told him that, whatever was wrong, it was a very big deal indeed. She was standing in front of the counter staring at a roasting pan wherein rested two large chickens—capons, Cam corrected himself. He'd picked the birds up himself the day before, paying an exorbitant sum for what looked to him like a pair of hens with steroid problems.

"What's wrong?"

Lacey didn't even look at him. She simply pointed to the capons, her face set in lines of horrified disbelief. Cam moved closer, not sure what he was supposed to be looking for. The birds appeared to be just fine, their legs neatly tied, their skin pale and smooth. Pale? He looked from the birds to Lacey and then looked away, biting his cheek to keep from laughing.

"I forgot to put them in the oven." She said it as if she were announcing a capital crime.

"It could happen to anyone," he said, trying very hard to look sympathetic.

She turned her head slowly, as if it took a great effort, and looked at him. Her eyes were dark green and full of such tragedy that Cam's urge to laugh faded. "Everything else is done and everyone is out there waiting to be fed, and I forgot to put the damned birds in the oven. How could I be so stupid!"

"Lacey, it could happen to anyone."

"No, it couldn't. It could only happen to someone who's a complete and total idiot."

She looked heartbroken. Cam searched for some consolation and couldn't find one. The fact of the matter was that the dinner she'd planned for the past two weeks was sitting on the counter in front of her completely raw. Her guests were waiting to be fed and her meal was now several hours away from being done.

"I'll tell you what. Why don't we send out for some pizza? I could call Dominic's. We could order a couple of large pizzas. Nobody will mind."

He trailed off as Lacey's gaze changed from near shock to something that looked a great deal like pure loathing.

"Pizza? You want me to throw a dinner party so our families can meet and then serve pizza? I'd sooner serve them live ants. I'd rather—" But he wasn't meant to hear what else she'd rather serve. She broke off, looking past him, her expression a mixture of dread and embarrassment. "Mother."

"Lacey, honey, is everythin' all right? When Cam didn't come back, I thought you might have hurt yourself."

"I'm fine, Mother." She paused and Cam could feel the effort she made to dredge up a smile. "I'm afraid we have a small problem with dinner, however." She gestured to the capons. "I forgot to put dinner in the oven."

"Oh, dear." Mamie laughed. "Don't look so tragic, sugar. We can fix it in no time at all."

"Fix what?" Jimbo appeared behind Mamie, taking in the situation in a glance. "You've got to remember that you're supposed to serve *beef* rare, Lacey. Not chicken."

"Thanks." Irony lay thick in her tone. "Cam just suggested that we could send out for pizza." Despite her best efforts the word came out sounding obscene, giving Cam final evidence—if he'd needed it—of just what she thought of his suggestion. Still, as a good hostess, she was determined that her guests wouldn't starve, and if pizza was all she could offer them, she'd at least make the effort.

"Pizza!" That was Claire, who'd appeared next to Mamie. She gave her brother a disgusted look. "If that isn't just like you to think of pizza. I always knew you had no class."

Cam shrugged sheepishly. He didn't see what was so bad about pizza. He liked it. Besides, hadn't some study decided that pizza was a nutritionally complete food? Or at least not as bad as it looked. It wasn't as if he'd suggested they eat sawdust.

"You know, sugar, it seems to me that you've got the makin's for a good ol' Southern dinner right here." Mamie had approached the capons, and she now poked one with a perfectly manicured nail. "If we cut these chickens up, dredge them in a bit of flour and drop them in a pan of hot oil, I don't think anybody would starve."

"Fried chicken?" It was obvious that, as far as Lacey was concerned, it was only a notch above the despised pizza.

"I haven't had homemade fried chicken in ages." That was Claire. "I'm afraid we usually rely on the Colonel. And the children are all such little plebeians, they'd never notice the difference."

"I'm a mean hand with a butcher knife," Jimbo offered. Cam wouldn't have been surprised to find that he'd never cut up a chicken in his life. He was just looking for an excuse to stay close to Mamie.

No one seemed to miss the more elaborate dinner Lacey had planned, and the fried capon disappeared at a rate that indicated no one was going hungry.

But Lacey picked at her food, while keeping up her end of the conversations that flew across the table. Her heart wasn't really in it. Her exquisite capons reduced to something that could have been bought in a red-and-white bucket. Of course she was lucky there'd been a way to salvage the meal. And it could have been worse. Pizza. She still simmered when she thought about that.

Aside from the near disaster, the evening went well. Everyone liked everyone else, conversation was lively, and she could honestly feel that her first dinner party was a success. Her first dinner party as Cam's wife. Standing next to him in the doorway, waving as their guests left, she realized how married she felt. It was not an unpleasant feeling.

Cam shut the door and the house was suddenly very quiet.

"I think it went pretty well, don't you?" Lacey wandered back into the living room and began stacking cups and saucers.

"Everyone had a great time." Cam followed her into the living room, flopping onto the sofa. "Why don't you leave those till morning?"

"It won't take that much time to throw them in the dishwasher, and then I won't have to worry about them tomorrow."

Cam stifled a yawn, watching her out of sleepy eyes. "Leave them till morning and I'll take care of them."

"That's not necessary."

"Who said anything about necessity?"

"Really, it won't take long. I can— Cam!" His name came out on a shriek as his arm hooked around her waist. She had only an instant to set down the stack of saucers she was holding before he pulled her off her feet to land in an untidy heap on top of him.

"I said leave them till morning." His mouth nuzzled the sensitive skin behind her ear, sending dangerous tingles up her spine.

"Cam, I don't think—"

"That's right. Don't think." He twisted, and her head spun as she found herself suddenly beneath him, pressed into the sofa cushions by the weight of his body. His eyes seemed dangerously blue, warm and slumbrous.

"Cam—" She wasn't sure what she'd planned to say, for he didn't give her a chance to get it out. His mouth settled over hers, scattering her thoughts in a hundred different directions. It wasn't a lengthy kiss, but it was a thorough one.

"You know what your problem is, Lacey Mc-Cleary?" Her lashes lifted slowly. She barely remembered her name.

"What?" She had to clear her throat to get the one word out.

"You think too much." His teeth nibbled at one earlobe, and Lacey felt her toes curl.

"Do I?" she asked breathlessly, hardly aware of what she was saying.

"You do." His tongue traced a heated pattern around the curve of her ear and her fingers dug into his shoulders, seeking something solid to cling to.

"I'll have to try to do less of it."

Cam braced himself on his elbow, his hand seeking out the tiny gold buttons that ran down the front of her dress. His eyes were intent on hers.

"Do less of what?"

"Thinking," she whispered, her breath catching as his hand slipped inside to find the softness of her breast.

"Too much thinking can be dangerous," he breathed, his head lowering.

"Dangerous," she agreed.

But it wasn't thinking that was dangerous. It was feeling. Feeling something so strongly that it threatened to wash away everything else. You could get lost in feelings that strong.

His fingers whispered over her skin, the faint roughness of his work-roughened skin a contrast to the softness of her breast. She closed her eyes, her skin flushing a delicate rose as he spread the dress open so that she lay nearly bare beneath him. The lace and silk of her teddy could hardly be considered a decent covering.

They'd been lovers for weeks now. Certainly he'd seen even more of her than this. But that had always been in the safe darkness of their bedroom. There was something so decadent about this. Lying on the sofa with all the lamps lit. Decadent, and exciting.

Cam's mouth found the nipple of one breast through the pale silk. She arched upward, feeling the gentle tugging sensation deep inside, a warm pool of need spreading outward from the pit of her stomach.

Forcing her hands between them, she struggled with the buttons on his shirt. They resisted stubbornly, but at last gave way beneath her increasingly frantic efforts to tug the shirt open, so that she could bury her fingers in the crisp dark hair that covered his chest. His head left her breast, but only to return to her mouth.

Strong fingers slid into her hair, tilting her face upward as his chest settled over hers. Lacey moaned against his mouth as the firm muscles pressed against her. Passion was no longer played out in a languorous progression from one step to the next. It had become a demanding, urgent presence.

Cam's knee thrust between hers, pressing upward against the heart of her need. Lacey's fingers flexed against his shoulder, a response and a demand. She arched into his knee, wordlessly pleading for more. Cam dragged his mouth away from hers, taking in a great lungful of air.

He stared into her eyes for a moment before pulling himself up and away. She started a protest that ended on a pleased murmur when she saw that he was standing up only so he could strip away the rest of his clothes. She watched him, her eyes half-lidded, her expression vaguely feline. He jerked his shirt off and reached for his belt buckle, his hands freezing as she reached up to cup him through the fabric of his slacks.

Never in all her life had she done anything so blatantly sexual. But then, no one else had ever made her feel the way Cam did. He made her feel like a warm, sensual woman, not the rather reticent, business-oriented Lacey she'd always thought she knew.

Cam groaned as her fingers moved, gently caressing him.

"Lacey, you're driving me crazy."

"You told me I thought too much, so I'm not thinking anymore. I'm feeling. Only feeling."

"I think I'm the one who's feeling." His voice held a strained note that pleased her enormously. He stepped back and Lacey's hand dropped away. Her mouth pursed in a moue, only to soften into a pleased smile when Cam all but ripped off the rest of his clothes.

She could hardly believe she was lying here, on the sofa, with all the lamps lit. Looking at Cam's muscled body, she felt a deep aching throb, a need stronger than any she could remember. She lifted her arms to him in a wordless invitation as old as time. And Cam didn't hesitate to respond. Her teddy was disposed of with a quick tug that threatened the fragile silk. Lacey wouldn't have cared if he'd taken it from her in shreds. All that mattered was her need to feel him against her.

She opened to him, cradling him between her knees, her body arching to that first slow thrust. For a moment, the fire was banked, the emptiness filled, but it was only for a moment.

There was an urgency in her tonight that she didn't understand. A powerful need that was all consuming. When Cam started to move, she responded hungrily. Each movement sent ripples of pleasure through her until she was drowning in sensation. Her hands slid down the sweat-dampened length of his back, feeling the ripple of muscle and sinew.

Cam's mouth found hers, his tongue thrusting inside to tangle with hers, swallowing her soft whispers. Lacey felt as if she couldn't possibly get enough of him. She wanted this feeling to go on forever, and yet the pleasure was so intense that it had to end soon or she'd shatter into a million pieces.

The pleasure built higher until she was aware of nothing but Cam, the scent of him, his weight on hers, the intense ecstasy of their joining. And then the pleasure crested, washing over her, sending her tumbling into pure sensation. From somewhere a long way away, she heard Cam's muffled groan of completion.

It was a long time before either of them moved or spoke. Cam shifted at last, lifting his weight from her. Lacey murmured a protest, reaching up to clutch at his shoulders.

"Sweetheart, this couch ain't big enough for the two of us." She heard his words, but she could also feel them where his chest still rested against hers. It took a great effort to lift her lashes.

"I don't mind," she mumbled, lost in the blue of his eyes.

"Well, I do. I want you somewhere where I can hold you properly." He pushed himself upright and then bent to scoop her off the sofa.

Lacey looped her arms around his neck, leaning her head against his shoulder. "I didn't get the dishes cleared up."

Cam's soft chuckle vibrated through her. "I thought I'd distracted you from that. Apparently I didn't do a very good job."

"You did a wonderful job. I was just making an observation." Her prim tone didn't fit very well with the fact that neither of them had a stitch of clothing on. Cam laughed again, carrying her out of the living room and toward their bedroom.

He set her on the bed and followed her down, sweeping her against him, holding her close. "I'm sure I could do an even better job of distracting you if I had a little more room and a little more time."

"More time? Who said you didn't have all the time in the world?" She placed soft kisses along the line of his collarbone.

"You did. How was I supposed to take my time and show you all my best techniques when you were driving me crazy?"

"Sorry." She didn't feel in the least sorry. In fact, she felt very pleased with herself. Even more pleased when she felt an unmistakable stirring against her thigh. "Is that a gun in your pocket or are you just happy to see me?"

"I don't have any pockets."

"Then I guess you must be happy to see me."

Cam buried his hand in her hair, tilting her head back until their eyes met. Lacey's pulse sped at the look of glittering hunger in his gaze. She'd never felt so completely feminine, so totally desirable.

"Hussy." He made the word a caress. "I'll show you just how happy I am to see you." His mouth came down on hers, stifling any reply she might have made.

But Lacey didn't protest. Tonight was not about words. Sometimes a touch could speak far louder than any words ever could. She had the feeling there was something to be learned in the way Cam touched her, held her. Some message that was important, if only she knew how to interpret it.

But the meaning stayed just out of her grasp.

Chapter Twelve

The television was not turned up particularly loud, but the sound of it grated on Lacey's nerves like fingernails on a blackboard. Cam was sprawled in front of the glowing box, his long legs stretched untidily across the floor. The floor she'd mopped just yesterday.

Not that he seemed to care if the floor had been mopped yesterday or three months ago. She stabbed the needle through the button and into her finger. Jerking her hand from under the fabric, she saw a bright drop of blood welling on the tip of her finger. It only added to her annoyance.

"Yeah!"

She jumped at Cam's loud exclamation. Slightly tinny-sounding cheers issued from the speaker. A home run or an out. She stifled the urge to ask what had happened. She'd enjoyed baseball a time or two herself, but she wasn't in the mood for it right now.

She jabbed the needle through the button again, securing it to the fabric. Her frown deepened as she stared at the inoffensive fabric. Only it wasn't inoffensive. At the moment, it offended her mightily. The faded chambray made her grind her teeth. It was a beautiful sunny Sunday afternoon and she was sitting here doing mending. Not even her own mending, at that. It seemed as if Cam lost buttons off his shirts every time he wore one.

And if she wasn't mending *his* shirts, she was cleaning *his* house or cooking *his* meals. All this while she was trying to run a profitable business. It wasn't that she minded cooking and cleaning and mending. After all, that was part of being married. But she did mind the fact that Cam didn't seem to appreciate all the work she put into making a home.

Oh, he'd comment on the fact that the house looked nice, or he'd tell her that he'd enjoyed a meal she'd just spent two hours cooking only to have it gone in twenty minutes. He'd even suggested on a few occasions that she was working too hard. But he didn't *really* appreciate the amount of work she was doing.

She jabbed at the button again. Maybe it was impossible for men to understand the amount of work that went into making a house a home. Maybe they weren't genetically programmed to understand. But he could at least make an effort.

It was Cam's mistake that he chose that particular moment to speak to her.

"Why don't you come over here and watch the game with me?"

"There's nowhere to sit." She didn't lift her head from the shirt, though she'd looped the thread through the button so many times that nothing short of a nuclear blast could have detached it.

"You could sit on my lap. Or we could move the television so we could both sit on the couch. Come on, Lacey. You haven't stopped working since you got up this morning. It's making me tired just watching you."

"Well, pardon me for trying to get something done," she snapped. Folding the shirt with jerky movements, she stood up, injury in every line of her body. "I'll just go somewhere else so that my working won't bother you."

"What on earth?" Cam's eyes widened as she turned to stalk out of the room. He stood up, taking a quick step forward to catch her arm. "What's wrong?"

Lacey stared at his chest, refusing to lift her eyes any higher. The fact that he could even ask that proved he was the insensitive clod she'd begun to suspect.

"Nothing's wrong."

"Lacey, something's obviously eating at you. Spit it out."

The inelegant command did nothing to soothe her anger. "I told you, there's nothing wrong."

"Does it bother you that I'm watching the baseball game? I asked if you wanted to go for a drive, but you said you had things to do around the house today. I didn't think a little television would bother you."

"Of course it doesn't bother me," she said woodenly, still without looking at him.

"Look, why don't we go for a drive? It's a beautiful day. We could head for the coast and drive up 101."

"I can't. I have too much to do here."

Cam's fingers tightened on her arm a moment before dropping away. He took a deep breath, and she had the feeling he was trying to take hold of his patience. Though what he had to be impatient about, she couldn't imagine.

"Forget about whatever you've got in mind. Let's get out of here. You work too hard."

It was as if he'd lit a match to a Roman candle. How dared he act as if she worked as hard as she did out of choice! Did he think she liked slaving?

"Well, if I don't do it, it's not going to get done, now is it? You obviously have more important things to do."

She gestured contemptuously at the television. There was a moment of dead silence broken only by the electronic roar of the crowd, and then even that was silenced as Cam reached out to snap the set off.

"Don't let me interrupt you," she went on. "This is undoubtedly an important game. Heaven forbid you should miss it." *My God, I sound like a harpy.* But she couldn't seem to stop the flow of rage now that it had been turned loose.

Cam stepped back, folding his arms over his chest. "You want to tell me what the hell this is all about?"

"Nothing. Absolutely nothing." Lacey twisted the shirt between her hands, all the pent-up anger of weeks boiling inside her, seeking a way out.

"Bull," he said bluntly. "You've been acting like Joan of Arc on her way to the stake for days now. I thought it was a passing mood, but obviously it goes deeper than that. You want to tell me what's bugging you?"

"Joan of Arc?" She stared at him, her voice failing her. He returned the look impassively. "Are you implying that I've been acting like a martyr?"

"The thought had crossed my mind."

"Why you . . . you . . . male chauvinist pig!" The insult didn't nearly express her feelings, but it was the best she could come up with in the midst of her anger. He didn't seem in the least disturbed, which only made her angrier.

"Why don't you get it off your chest, Lacey? You'll feel a lot better."

"I'm not going to feel better until I can be reasonably sure I won't ever have to see you again. You are the most inconsiderate, oblivious man I've ever known in my life."

"What have I been inconsiderate and oblivious about?"

How could he remain so calm when she felt like she might explode at any minute? It wasn't fair and it only went to prove her point. He didn't have an ounce of sensitivity in his body.

"It doesn't matter what I do around here—you never notice. I've developed housewife's knees and a permanent bend in my back. I've ruined my fingernails. I've cooked and I've cleaned and I've mended your damned clothes until I feel like a slave, and you sit in front of that damned television watching a stupid baseball game. And then you have the nerve to act like you can't imagine why I'm upset. You—"

"Who asked you to?" The calm question broke into the middle of her tirade. Lacey stopped, bewildered.

"Who asked me to what?"

"Who asked you to cook and clean and mend my damned shirts?"

"I— You—" she stammered, her train of thought broken.

"Oh, no. Don't try to pin this on me. I haven't asked you to do any of that stuff. *You're* the one who's been running around here like the pope was going to come to visit any minute."

This conversation wasn't going at all the way she'd imagined it would. He was supposed to be apologetic and appreciative. He didn't look like either. In fact, he looked more angry than anything else. "But I—"

"But nothing. Have I once said to you, 'Lacey, why don't you wear the grain off the floors with a scrub brush?' Or 'Lacey, why don't you cook like Julia Child every night?' Or 'Lacey, why don't you mend my damned shirts?'"

She jumped as he jerked the shirt out of her hands, throwing it into a corner of the room. The violence in the small act told her that his emotions were every bit as riled as hers.

"You didn't ask maybe, but it was obvious that—"

"No, it wasn't," he interrupted flatly. "The only thing that's been obvious is that you've got a Donna Reed complex. I never asked, implied or hinted that I expected you to take on the sole responsibility for running this place."

"Well, if I don't do it, who will?" There. She had him on that one.

"Lacey, it may not have occurred to you before, but I lived alone for quite a few years. I didn't starve to death, the house didn't vanish in a mound of filth, and my shirts all had buttons. I may not be an immaculate house-keeper, but I'm not Pigpen, either. I'm perfectly capable of taking care of things myself. At the very least, we could share the work."

"Well, then why haven't you? Why have you let me do everything myself?"

"When have you given me a chance to do anything? Every time I suggested doing something, you told me you'd rather do it yourself. When I tried to do laundry, you acted like I was incapable of pushing the right buttons. You pick my damned socks up almost before I get them off my feet. I've been afraid to set foot in the kitchen for fear a spill of flour would send you into a cleaning frenzy. Just what do you suggest I do? Fight you for the privilege of mopping the floor?"

She stared at him, grasping at the anger she was sure she still felt and finding nothing. Had she really been like that? Surely he was exaggerating. Yet, looking back, she could remember a number of instances where he'd offered to do something and she'd immediately denied the need for any help.

"I guess maybe I have been a little compulsive about it," she murmured, trying to absorb this new picture of her own behavior. "It's just that I wanted everything to be perfect."

"Lacey, this is real life. Who needs a perfectly clean house or gourmet meals every night, especially when it cuts into time that could be better spent on other things?"

"Why didn't you say something before?" she asked.

"I've been telling you ever since before the dinner party, but you didn't seem to agree, and I didn't want to push it." He shrugged. "I thought maybe you really liked all that cooking and cleaning. You were so determined to do it."

"My mother always kept the house immaculate and we always had beautiful meals. And she never forgot to put the capon in the oven, let me tell you. That's the image I grew up with of a properly run home. I just wanted to do the same."

"Lacey, honey, think about it. Your mother didn't work full-time. She may have spent a lot of time doing volunteer work and managing your father's investments, but she didn't hold a full-time job, let alone run a business of her own. She had a lot more time to spend on the house. Besides, from what you've told me, Mamie has always had a maid. Did it ever occur to you that the maid had a lot to do with cleaning the house and putting those beautiful meals on the table?"

Lacey shook her head slowly. It was stupid, but she'd never thought of that. All these years, she'd looked at the way her mother ran her home and she'd felt inadequate, sure that she could never do half as well. And these past few weeks had seemed to confirm that. The cooking, the cleaning, the dinner party—all had left her exhausted, with none of the cool elegance that characterized her mother.

But it had never once occurred to her that Mamie hadn't taken on so many roles at one time. She'd never tried to do everything all at once. It was a revolutionary thought.

"I don't know. Maybe you're right."

"Of course I'm right." He reached out, taking her shoulders and drawing her close. "Haven't you figured out yet that I'm always right?"

Lacey managed a smile. "Hardly."

"Close enough." His hand circled the back of her neck, warm and strong. "Between the *two* of us, I don't see any reason why anyone should die of ptomaine poisoning or disappear into a cloud of dust. We may not be able to eat off the floors, but I think we can keep the place in reasonably good shape."

"I'm sorry I snapped at you about watching the game."

"No big deal. You can make it up to me by sitting down and watching the rest of it."

"I really should—" He cut off her protest with a quick, thorough kiss.

"You really should sit down and relax. Come on, admit it. There's nothing you have to do right this minute."

"No, I suppose not." She let him draw her forward to join him on the sofa. She'd halfway planned on making fresh bread. But that was part of the old Lacey. The one who'd been trying to do it all. And she wasn't going to do that anymore, right?

Right. Only it was easier said than done.

If anyone had told her that she'd find it difficult to do less, she wouldn't have believed them. But it was a fact that she felt somewhat lost when she didn't have tasks to fill her every waking moment.

The first time Lacey came home to find that Cam had already fixed dinner, she could barely eat it. When he started sending things to the laundry, just as he'd done before they were married, she almost hoped that his shirts would come back in shreds.

It was ridiculous. She'd never fancied herself as a candidate for Housewife of the Year. And heaven knew, she'd been working herself into the ground. But she felt a niggling resentment with each task that was shifted from her shoulders. Resentment and a vague feeling of failure.

It was one thing to acknowledge that her mother had always had a servant. It was another thing to really let that penetrate and dissolve long-held notions. All the years she'd been growing up, she'd measured herself against her mother and frequently come up wanting. Maybe it was because she'd never known her father. She didn't have two parents to divide her attention between, so her mother had gotten more than her fair share.

Mamie might drive her crazy but she was still a role model, an unattainable goal. And no matter what logic said, Lacey still felt as if she'd failed to measure up in some way. There was a feeling that her mother would have been able to manage everything somehow. She would have run the shop and cleaned the house and cooked and mended and done it all so easily that Cam would never have questioned the fairness of it.

And she couldn't even be mad at Cam. He was concerned about her. The knowledge should have made her feel good. It did make her feel good. But it also made her feel threatened.

She was beginning to wonder if the reason she hadn't married before she was thirty was that she wasn't really suited to the institution. Not that there weren't pleasant aspects of it. It was nice to come home and talk to someone about what had happened during her day. Cam was wonderful company.

In fact, Cam was wonderful about almost everything. And that was a large part of her problem.

The man didn't seem to have any faults.

Lacey's hands paused in their task of folding a pile of batiste camisoles, and she stared at the mirror that hung over the table without seeing anything it reflected. Usually, the image of the quiet elegance of the shop was enough to draw at least a smile. But not today.

Today, nothing seemed able to lift her spirits. She'd been feeling restless and moody for days now. One minute, the world seemed like a pretty terrific place to be, and the next she was wondering if it wasn't time to join a nice convent so that she'd never have to deal with the real world again.

She'd awakened in a gloomy mood this morning. It hadn't helped to find that Cam was already up and had prepared breakfast for her. As she'd poked moodily at her scrambled eggs and bacon, she'd wondered if there was anything the man couldn't do. What did he need a wife for, anyway?

And now, here she was wondering the same thing, when she should have been concentrating on the best way to display this stack of very expensive garments.

"Boy, you look about as cheerful as I feel."

Lacey started, dropping the camisole she held as she turned toward the voice. "Lisa! What are you doing here?"

Lisa shrugged. "I thought maybe you might like to go out for lunch."

"Lunch? You drove all the way from downtown L.A. to see if I wanted to have lunch with you?"

Her friend shrugged again. "It's been a while since we got together. Did I catch you at a bad time?"

"No, of course not." Lacey shook herself out of her gloom, noticing the way Lisa's eyes avoided hers, the dark circles under her eyes that no amount of makeup could completely disguise. "Margaret can take care of the shop for me."

If Margaret hadn't been there, she'd have done the unthinkable and closed Lacey's Lovelies. Lisa obviously needed to talk. But Margaret was there, and Lacey didn't have to worry about losing any business.

She and Lisa walked to a restaurant a couple of blocks away. Lacey deliberately steered clear of the café she and Cam had gone to the day after they'd first made love; right now, memories of Cam were not what she wanted.

They were lucky enough to get a table right away. Lacey waited until they were seated and their orders given before fixing Lisa with a look that demanded honesty.

"What's wrong?"

"It's that obvious, is it?"

Lisa's laugh showed a tendency to waver in the middle and Lacey felt her uneasiness grow stronger. This was something serious.

"It's obvious to me. But I've known you for a long time."

"Yeah. Since before I met Frank." Lisa moved her water glass in small circles, her eyes on the damp loops it left on the polished table.

"Since a long time before you met Frank," Lacey agreed, thinking it was an odd comment to make.

"Well, it looks like you're going to know me *after* I don't know Frank anymore." The flip words broke at the end.

Lacey drew a quick hard breath. "Are you and Frank having more problems?" The idea was inconceivable, despite the evidence she'd already seen. Frank and Lisa were the perfect couple. Everyone who knew them knew they were meant for each other.

"No. No more problems." Lisa shook her head, still not looking at her friend. "In fact, we have no problems at all. He moved out last week and we're filing for divorce."

Lacey felt the world spin around her for a moment before it settled into a new pattern. "Divorce," she whispered. "Lisa, you can't be getting a divorce. You and Frank love each other. Everybody knows that."

"Well, everybody forgot to tell Frank that." Lisa laughed, a bitter sound that carried pain.

Around them, the restaurant was full of people talking to their companions, the clink of silverware on plates. But their table might have been on another plane of reality.

"What happened?" Lacey asked at last.

Lisa shrugged. "Damned if I know. At least not for sure."

"Is it another woman?" Perhaps she shouldn't have asked the question. But this was Lisa. They'd known each other for too long for her to feel as if she was sticking her nose in where it wasn't wanted.

"No," Lisa said and then laughed again, still with that same bitter note. "If it was another woman, I might not feel like such a total failure."

"Don't be an idiot." Lacey reached across the table, catching Lisa's hand in hers and holding it until the other woman met her eyes. The pain in Lisa's was so deep, Lacey could feel it in her own soul. "Whatever happened, you're not a failure. Marriage is a two-way street, Lisa. You're not alone in its success or failure."

"Look who's talking," Lisa jeered. "Are you an expert on the subject now?"

Lacey withdrew her hand, her face tightening. "I'm sorry. You're right. I didn't mean to sound preachy."

"Oh, hell. I'm sorry, Lace. That was nasty and you don't deserve it. I want to shred Frank into little pieces and feed him to a pit bull, but I've got no right to take it out on you. Forgive me? Please?"

She reached out her hand, and Lacey's hesitation was only momentary before she extended her own.

"That's okay. I know you must be in a lot of pain. And I suppose I did sound a bit like a cheap marriage counselor." She squeezed Lisa's fingers before drawing away. The waiter appeared with their food, and the conversation halted until he'd left again.

"You want to tell me what happened?" Lacey's tone gave Lisa permission to say as much or as little as she wished.

"I'm not sure I know what happened." Lisa poked at her salad, her gaze on things Lacey couldn't see. "I guess maybe I haven't been as observant as I should have been. I've been so busy. Concentrating on my career." She laughed. "My career. Well, at least I'll have something to occupy my time."

"Lisa, what happened? What did Frank say? Did he just announce that he was moving out and that was that?"

"More or less."

"But he must have said something, given you some reason."

"He said we didn't seem to need each other very much anymore. He said I seemed to be doing just fine without him." Lisa put her fork down next to her untouched food and rubbed her fingers over her forehead as if soothing an ache. "Remember I told you that he asked me to cut down on my hours a few months ago? That he wanted to start a family?" At Lacey's nod she went on, "I promised him then that we'd talk about it again when I finished the project I was working on."

"And did you?" Lacey asked quietly.

"No. By the time that project was through, there was another in the works and I thought Frank had forgotten about it. And I didn't want to remind him, at least not right away."

"Can't you talk to him, explain that you didn't mean you wanted to wait forever?"

"Oh, Lacey, I don't think he wants to listen anymore." Lisa's voice broke on a sob. "You didn't see the way he looked at me. It wasn't like he was angry. He wasn't even cold. He looked at me like I was someone he'd known once a long time ago. I *tried* to talk to him. I practically begged him to talk. But he said it was too late. He said it was obvious we didn't need each other anymore and there was no sense in staying together.

"But I still need him, even if I haven't shown it lately. Knowing that Frank was there was what kept me going. I don't know how I'm going to manage without him. Don't ever fall in love, not even with Cam. It hurts too damned much when you lose them. Just too damned much."

She stopped talking, her breathing rapid as she fought the threatening tears. Lacey stared at the table, trying to control the panic about to wash over her. This couldn't be true. Not Lisa and Frank. They were so perfect for each other. They'd been so much in love. If their marriage couldn't survive, how could anyone's? Especially one begun on shaky foundations.

Like her own.

Later, she had little memory of what she said to Lisa. She tried to offer comfort and she kept emphasizing that this couldn't be the end of it. Lisa and Frank would talk and they'd realize that they had built too much together to let it go like this. She couldn't be sure if she was trying to convince Lisa or herself.

By the time Lisa left her at the shop, Lisa seemed to have regained her control. Her eyes were red-rimmed, and they held a haunted look that made Lacey ache for her. There were one or two customers, but she left them to Margaret to handle and shut herself in her tiny office.

Seated behind the desk that took up most of the room, she didn't even pretend she was going to accomplish anything. Picking up a pen, she began to doodle aimlessly on the back of an invoice.

Frank and Lisa getting a divorce. What would Cam say when she told him? Would he see things as clearly as she did? It seemed as if this was almost an omen, pointing out how foolish they were to think they could make this marriage work.

We didn't seem to need each other very much anymore. Lisa's words echoed in her mind. Surely needing each other was an important ingredient in any marriage. An ingredient she and Cam didn't have. And they didn't seem likely to develop a sudden dependency on each other, either. After all, how could they? They'd both lived alone a long time. They'd proven they could make it without anyone else.

"Lacey?" Margaret's quiet knock preceded her person by only a moment. Lacey looked up, pulling a stack of papers toward her as if she had been interrupted in the midst of something important.

"Yes?"

"Maude Higgins is here. She says you told her we were going to be getting some new silk scarves, and she wants to see them."

"We didn't get them in yet."

"That's what I told her, but I don't think she believes me. She asked for you." Margaret rolled her eyes, expressing her opinion of Mrs. Higgins. Lacey privately agreed. The last thing she wanted to do right now was deal with a neurotic customer. But Maude Higgins was a very rich and loyal neurotic customer, she reminded herself. And no matter what was going on in her personal life, she had a responsibility to her clientele. Even the annoying ones.

By the time she'd convinced Maude that the scarves truly hadn't come in and promised, again, that she would personally call the moment they arrived, Lacey had managed to put thoughts of Lisa's marriage and her own on a back burner.

But they simmered there, threatening to boil over by the time she pulled into the driveway at home. Cam's home, she reminded herself, suddenly feeling as if it could never be hers. Cam's truck was gone, and she remembered that he was supposed to deliver a desk to someone in Santa Monica. That meant she was alone. She wasn't sure whether she was sorry or glad.

Certainly, with Cam gone, she'd have time to think. But that might not be all to the good. There was an almost inaudible voice in her head that suggested maybe she was overreacting to Lisa's news. Logic struggled to point out that her friend's failed marriage didn't necessarily spell doom for her own.

Part of her wanted Cam to come home and make her believe that everything was going to work out. It was his calm confidence that had taken their marriage this far. He'd made it seem so reasonable. Like it could actually work.

But it couldn't work.

She hurried through the house, giving Derwent an absent pat on her way down the hallway. She was aware of him watching her, his head cocked to one side as if puzzled. It had become a small ritual that she took time to play with him each evening when she came home. But she wasn't in the mood to play tonight.

Right now she had a mission. She suddenly knew what she had to do: end this travesty of a marriage before it was too late. That they hadn't fallen in love was all she was grateful for. If Lisa was right, love would have only brought more pain.

Her movements took on a frantic edge as she dragged her suitcase down from the top of the closet. Lacey's hands were shaking as she reached for her clothes. The sight of Cam's shirts hanging next to her dresses almost destroyed her resolve. But just because their clothes looked good together, didn't mean she and Cam belonged together. She drew out a handful of hangers, stripping the blouses from them and folding them roughly before dropping them into the open suitcase.

This was the right thing to do. She was sure of it. At least, she thought she was sure of it. And it wasn't talking to Lisa today that made her feel that way. That had just been the final little push.

She'd been having doubts for weeks now. Had there ever been a time when she didn't have doubts? She should have recognized her mood swings for what they were—a clear sign that it was time to end this whole foolish experiment.

She packed quickly, wanting nothing so much as to be out of the house before Cam got home. It was cowardly, but she didn't want to face him. She didn't want to listen to his arguments about their marriage being viable. She'd made her decision, and now she just wanted to act on it without anyone trying to talk her out of it.

But luck wasn't with her. She'd just finished putting the last of her toiletries in a small tote when the bedroom door swung open and Cam stopped in the doorway. Lacey froze, the very picture of guilt. Cam's eyes went from her pale face to the full suitcase.

"What's going on?"

Chapter Thirteen

Lacey stared at him, her vocal cords paralyzed. She couldn't look away from him and she couldn't find the voice to answer him, so she said nothing. Cam stared at the suitcase a long moment before his gaze moved back to her, a frown drawing his brows together.

"Lacey? Why are you packing a suitcase?"

She dragged her eyes away from his face, staring at a point somewhere to his left. Just a few more minutes and she'd have been out of here. She could have explained it all in a note. But that was no longer an option. She was going to have to explain it to him face-to-face. How did you go about telling a man you were leaving him?

"I'm leaving." In the end, the bare words were all she could find.

"Leaving?" He stared at her, apparently trying to absorb the meaning of her words. "For good?" He said it as if he couldn't believe her, as if he misunderstood her.

"For good." It sounded appallingly blunt, but she couldn't think of any way to soften it.

Cam thrust his fingers through his hair, ruffling it into pale brown waves. His expression seemed more bewildered than anything else.

"Why?" The simple question was the one she'd been dreading. She understood why her leaving was the right thing to do, but it wasn't something she could explain. Still, he'd asked and she had to try.

"I saw Lisa today."

"Great. What does Lisa have to do with this?" Cam waved one hand, indicating the suitcase.

"She and Frank have separated. They're talking about a divorce."

"I'm sorry to hear that. They seemed to be suited to each other. But I don't see what that has to do with you moving out."

"Don't you see what it means?"

"No." He obviously didn't see at all.

"Lisa and Frank *were* suited. They were so much in love. They fell in love at first sight, did you know that?"

"No. But I—"

"They married before Lisa was out of college and I've never seen a couple more in love. Really in love."

"Well, that's great but—"

"And now they're splitting up. Don't you see?"

Cam frowned, showing the first sign of irritation. "I'm beginning to think I may see what you're getting at, but why don't you explain it to me just to make sure."

"Cam, if Frank and Lisa can't make it when they started out with everything going for them, how can we expect to do any better when we started out with nothing going for us?"

She looked at him, pleading with him to understand. But it wasn't understanding that turned his eyes to a stormy blue.

"Do you mean to tell me you're leaving me because Frank and Lisa couldn't hold their marriage together?"

"Not because they couldn't hold it together, but because of what their breakup represents."

"It represents that they had problems they couldn't work out. It has nothing—absolutely nothing—to do with us."

"Yes, it does. Cam, they loved each other, really loved each other."

"So what?" he burst out, exasperated.

"So, that wasn't enough. We don't even have that much. All we've got is a wedding neither of us remembers, a piece of paper we don't remember signing and a crazy idea that we could make something out of nothing. Well, we can't, and I'm leaving before we end up hurting each other."

She snapped the suitcase shut, but before she could pick it up, Cam's hand slammed down, pinning it to the bed. She jumped, looking up into eyes that burned with anger.

"That is the stupidest argument I've ever heard in my life." He bit each word off. "I could just as well argue that, since Lisa and Frank started out with love on their side, their separation makes it obvious that that's the wrong way to go about marriage."

Lacey closed her ears to the logic in his argument. This was how they'd gotten into this situation. He could make anything seem reasonable.

"Cam, if you're honest, you'll admit that this whole idea was crazy from the start. People don't get married to people they don't know."

"It seems to me that we've muddled along pretty well for the past couple of months. Lacey, don't do this."

"We've muddled along because we both worked at it, but it's not going to work in the end. Take my word for it."

"No! I damn well won't take your word for it." His palm hit the suitcase with a sharp explosion, and then he spun away from her, running his fingers through his hair again. He hunched his shoulders, stretching the fabric of his shirt across the hard muscles.

"Cam, I'm sorry. I didn't mean to hurt you."

"If I understood your reasoning, I might be able to understand why you think you have to do this. But I don't understand it. I'm not even sure you understand it." He turned to face her and Lacey winced away from his blazing eyes.

"I just don't want either of us to get hurt, and I believe that if we go on with this we're both going to regret it."

"Thanks loads for protecting me." He didn't bother to disguise his sarcasm.

Lacey set her chin. She'd made this decision and she wasn't going to change her mind.

"I'm doing what I think is best."

"You're doing what you think is safest. You're a coward, Lacey." Cam's blunt declaration hurt more than she liked to admit. "You're afraid you might be hurt, so you're running away. Let's call it like it is."

"You can think what you like."

"You want to know what I think? I think you're a quitter. When I first met you, I admired your spirit. I thought you faced life head-on and met its challenges, but you don't. You'd rather live in a safe little cocoon than take a chance.

"Oh, you'll take chances on your business, but that's safe enough. What are you going to lose? Money can be replaced. But you're not going to risk your emotions. You've been fighting them ever since Las Vegas.

"You're falling in love with me, but that scares the hell out of you. So you're going to run away. Well, you go ahead and quit, Lacey. Because I'm through fighting to get you to see what we could have. Run away. Lock yourself in that safe little world. I hope you'll be happy there. Alone."

He turned on his heel and strode out. A moment later Lacey heard the front door slam and then the roar of the truck's engine. She sat down on the edge of the bed, aware that her knees were not quite steady. She'd never seen Cam so angry. Angry and hurt.

Still, this was the right thing to do. She was sure of that.

Wasn't she?

ONCE SHE'D LOADED her suitcase in her car, there didn't seem to be any question about where she was going. She still held the lease on her old apartment. It would be empty, but she considered that possibility for only a moment. Those cold, empty rooms weren't home. Maybe they'd never been home.

It was after dark when she pulled into the driveway of the house she'd grown up in. Light spilled from the windows, creating welcoming patterns on the neatly mowed lawn. Lacey rang the doorbell, shivering as she waited for her mother to answer. The air still held a portion of the day's warmth, yet she felt chilled.

She was going to ask if she could spend the night here. Tomorrow, she'd go and open up her apartment. But tonight she didn't feel like dealing with the inevitable dust and stuffiness. She'd very calmly tell Mamie that she'd left Cam and that she didn't want to talk about it. After all, she was an adult now. The day was long past when she felt the need to spill her private difficulties into her mother's ear.

There was the quick tap of heels on the tiled floor and then Mamie was opening the door. Light poured out to embrace Lacey like a warm blanket.

"Why, sugar, what are you doin' here? Is Cameron with you?"

"Mother." Lacey's voice quivered on the word, and her eyes stung with tears.

"Lacey, honey, what's wrong?" Mamie reached out, catching Lacey's hand and pulling her inside. The door shut behind them, shutting the world out and shutting Lacey back in the world that had been so safe when she was a child. A world in which there'd been nothing her mother couldn't fix.

"Can I stay here tonight?" Despite her struggle to sound calm, her voice broke abruptly. She lifted her hand, pressing the back of her fingers against her mouth to stifle the sob that threatened to break through.

"You know you can always stay here, honey. You're pale, sugar. Come on in the livin' room and I'll get you a dash of bourbon. Put a little color in those cheeks."

Lacey let Mamie seat her on the sofa, watching without really seeing as she poured a small dose of amber liquid into a crystal shot glass and brought it back. She took the glass automatically, her fingers numb as they curled around it.

"Now you drink that down. You'll feel better."

Lacey obeyed mechanically, her eyes stinging as the fiery liquid hit the back of her throat. It burned all the way down and she gasped for air as it hit bottom. Mamie patted her back, her fine brows puckered in a concerned frown.

"There now. There's not much that a bit of bourbon can't help. You want to tell me what's wrong, sugar?"

She didn't want to tell her mother what was wrong. She didn't want to tell anyone. She wanted to go somewhere and find a dark corner to crawl into.

"I—I've left Cam."

"Oh, Lacey, honey, why?" Mamie's tone expressed her shocked concern.

"Because it wasn't a real marriage." The top of her head felt light, as if it might float off at any moment. She stared at the bottom of the shot glass, and it occurred to her that she hadn't had anything to eat since breakfast. That would explain why the bourbon seemed to be affecting her so strongly.

"Not a real marriage? Lacey, what are you talkin' about?"

"It was a marriage of convenience. Or maybe inconvenience would be a better description."

Mamie reached out to take the shot glass from her daughter, studying it as if it might contain an explanation for her bizarre behavior.

"Sugar, you're not makin' much sense. You want to tell me what's happened between you and Cameron? You seemed so happy together. Did you quarrel with him?"

"No, we didn't quarrel." Lacey leaned back, suddenly very tired. "At least not until I told him I was leaving. And I'm not falling in love with him." She stopped, closing her eyes for a moment, as if she could shut out the past months. "Oh, Mama, I've been so stupid."

"You just tell me what's happened and we'll see what we can do about it. There's no problem that can't be fixed, Lacey. Tell me what's gone wrong."

There was something in her that responded to her mother's brisk tone. She might be long past the age of believing that her mother could solve all her problems, yet there was enough of the child left in her that she couldn't help but half believe that something could be salvaged out of the tangled mess she'd created.

"It started off all wrong. Maybe things would've been different if it hadn't started off so wrong." She told her mother the true story from beginning to end.

As she sat in the quiet elegance of the living room she'd grown up in, the story behind her marriage seemed even more bizarre. The trip to Las Vegas, waking up in bed with Cam—it was all like something out of a movie. A bad movie.

The hardest part was trying to explain just why they'd decided to give the marriage a try. It had seemed so crazy at the time and the fact that it had almost worked didn't make it any more reasonable.

Her calm control began to crack again when she got to her decision to leave. She'd been right to leave. She knew she was right. But she hadn't expected it to hurt so much. Her voice dissolved into tears as she told her mother about Cam's reaction, how he'd called her a coward and then stormed out.

Mamie reached for her daughter, wrapping one arm around Lacey's trembling shoulders and pulling her close. With a sob, Lacey turned, burying her face in her mother's shoulder just as she'd done when she was a little girl. The simple comfort still had the power to make the world seem a little less bleak.

She cried until she didn't have the breath to cry anymore. Mamie held her, murmuring softly, not saying anything in particular. She didn't speak until Lacey's sobs turned into deep shuddering breaths.

"We're not going to talk about this anymore tonight. You're tuckered out and you're goin' straight to bed."

"I can't sleep."

"Yes, you can," Mamie told her in a brisk tone that brooked no argument. "You're goin' to sleep till mornin' and then we'll talk about this."

"There's nothing to talk about. I've left Cam and that's all there is to it." She sounded sulky and she knew it.

"We'll see. Now, I want you to go take a nice warm shower while I get your room ready."

It was easier to do as she was told than to try to make any decisions of her own. Lacey stood under the shower, keeping her mind a careful blank. The water pounded down, washing over her. She wished it could somehow wash away all her hurt and confusion.

Fresh tears came to her eyes when she stepped into her old bedroom. The paint and wallpaper were different, but this was the room where she'd spent her childhood. She'd played with her dolls here, then played with makeup. She'd studied at the desk in the corner and worked out her first plans for the shop there. The room held a lot of memories. And at the moment, it felt safe.

It was that feeling of safety that made it possible to climb into bed and fall asleep almost immediately. She slept deeply, waking the next morning to bright sunshine, which failed to reflect her mood. Despite the long sleep, she was tired. But maybe that was to be expected. A recovery was going to take more than a few hours' rest.

Mamie was in the kitchen when Lacey left her bedroom. The shop was open only half days on Thursdays, so she had a few hours before she had to go in. She was glad of the extra time. She needed it to pull herself together.

Mamie looked up as Lacey stepped into the kitchen. She was seated at the table wearing a pale yellow blouse and a pair of tailored gray slacks. Lacey ran her hands over her own worn jeans and faded T-shirt. She probably looked like the wrath of God, but she couldn't get up the energy to care.

"There's some coffee on the counter. You look like you could use some."

Lacey started toward the pot and then changed her mind. The smell of the coffee made her stomach turn over. After yesterday's upset it was no wonder. She poured herself a glass of milk instead. Sitting down across from Mamie, she picked up a doughnut from the plate on the table and bit into it.

"How'd you sleep?" Mamie asked, her eyes going over her daughter with maternal concern.

"Good, actually. I was surprised I slept at all."

"A dab of bourbon will help every time." Mamie took a swallow of her coffee, her eyes never leaving Lacey. Lacey shifted uneasily.

"I'm sorry I made such a scene last night."

"Don't be silly, sugar. That's what I'm here for. I'm just glad you came to me. Are you ready to talk about things?"

Lacey felt a quick spurt of panic. She didn't want to talk about anything. She'd made her decision and acted on it, and that was the end of it. On the other hand, she knew that look in her mother's eye. Mamie had made up her mind that there were things to be said, and nothing short of a nuclear blast was likely to change her mind. Still, she tried.

"Actually, Mother, I really should get to the shop."

"You don't open till one o'clock. That gives you a couple of hours before you even need to get dressed."

"Well, we got this shipment in yesterday and I really should work on the books."

"Lacey, you and I have known each other a long time. Why don't you just sit down and let me speak my piece."

Lacey sank back down into the chair. It was true that in the long run it would be simpler to let Mamie get whatever she wanted to say off her chest. She was going to do so sooner or later, anyway.

"All right, Mother. What is it you want to say?"

"It's real simple. Cameron was absolutely right when he said you were actin' like a coward. You're actin' like a scared little rabbit, Lacey, and I think you know it."

"I don't know anything of the kind," Lacey said with dignity. "It seems to me that after I realized that there was no future in our marriage, I would have been pretty dumb to have stayed in it."

"Who says there's no future?"

"Well, it's pretty obvious. I mean, we hardly know each other. The way our marriage started was ridiculous. How can we build anything on a beginning like that?"

"Those aren't real reasons," Mamie told her. "It doesn't matter how long you've known a man before you marry him. You still get most of the knowin' after the weddin'. Do you think if you'd known Cameron for years, you wouldn't have had any doubts after you were married?

"And as for the way your marriage started out, I don't see what the problem is. I think it's a lot more interestin' than a big church weddin' would have been. Think of what a story it would be to tell your children."

"Well, there aren't going to be any children because there isn't going to be a marriage," Lacey declared. Her mother's words were so close to the things Cam had said that she almost suspected a conspiracy between the two of them.

Mamie went on as if she hadn't spoken. "I think the real problem is that you're afraid of gettin' hurt. You're afraid of lovin' someone. But, darlin', everyone is afraid of that."

Lacey stared at the table, trying not to hear the truth in her mother's words. "It's different when it's someone you know. Then you can have some confidence that they aren't going to hurt you."

"Honey, that's just not true. We all hurt the people we love. It's a part of livin'. We don't mean to hurt them, but it happens. No matter how long you've known someone or how much you love them, it's no guarantee that they're not going to break your heart. Do you think your father and I didn't have our share of problems?"

"No, of course not," Lacey said impatiently. "I'm not so naive that I think you can have a relationship without some conflicts, but it's different when you know you love that person and you know he loves you."

"It's not that much different." Mamie shifted her coffee cup back and forth between her hands, her eyes on the aimless movement. "You know, maybe I made a mistake in not remarryin'. You never had a chance to see a relationship close up, all the give and take that goes into makin' a marriage work. After your father died, I just never found someone else I wanted to share my life with."

"I know you loved him very much."

"I loved him. And he loved me, but that didn't mean things were always smooth for us. We fought, sometimes over silly things, sometimes over big things." Mamie looked up, fixing her clear blue eyes on Lacey. "I almost left him once. I never told you that."

"No, you didn't." Lacey looked away, absorbing the shock of her mother's statement. She'd always pictured her parents' marriage as idyllic. Perhaps because she had no memories of them together, she'd painted a picture in her mind of what the perfect marriage was and decided that was what they'd had.

"What happened?"

"I thought he was having an affair."

"Was he?" If she'd expected a quick denial, Lacey was disappointed. Mamie hesitated and then shook her head slowly. "I don't think so."

"You don't think so?" Lacey demanded incredulously.

"Well, I reckon I decided that he wasn't." Her smile held a hint of self-deprecation. "I loved him."

"But if he was having an affair..." Lacey's entire concept of her father had shifted drastically in a matter of seconds. She stared at her mother. "How could you forgive him?"

"Well, like I said, I wasn't even sure there was anything to forgive. And in the end I forgave him because I loved him enough to want to keep our marriage together.

"We'd been fightin' somethin' fierce, sugar. And there was this woman who worked for him. She was real pretty, and I guess maybe I'd been jealous of her for a long time. When I accused your father of cheatin' on me with her, he just looked at me real still and he told me to believe what I wanted. He wasn't goin' to argue with me.

"I realized I could either pack my bags and go home to Georgia, or I could believe that he'd been faithful and stay. And I loved him enough to stay."

"But didn't it spoil things between you?" Lacey was still groping to accept this altered portrait.

Mamie laughed softly. "I reckon it didn't spoil things too much. You were born just a year later. We still fought, but I think we'd both learned that we meant a lot to each other."

Lacey shook her head, staring at her empty milk glass and the half-eaten doughnut in front of her. "I don't see what this has to do with Cam and me. After all, doesn't it just prove my point? You two loved each other when you got married and you still came close to losing each other."

LACEY'S EMOTIONS were so raw a few days later that she began to wonder if she wasn't coming down with one of the throat infections that had been the bane of her childhood. She hadn't had one in years, but the exhaustion she was feeling was a typical symptom. She made an appointment with her doctor; in the meantime she tried to stave it off with vitamins.

But the vitamins didn't do anything to lift her spirits, which had sunk so low she sometimes wondered if they'd ever lift again.

She didn't hear a word from Cam, and she told herself that was exactly the way she wanted it. After all, there was no reason to flog a dead horse—obviously she'd convinced him that their marriage was just that. She was glad he'd accepted it. Very glad.

Which of course didn't explain why she lunged for the phone every time it rang. Why each ring of the brass bell on the shop door brought her head around. It wasn't that she was expecting anyone in particular. It was just that her nerves were strung a little tight these days. Nothing more.

By the time a week had gone by, she'd calmed down so that she no longer jumped when the phone rang or someone entered the shop. It was becoming clear that Cam wasn't going to try to contact her. Which was just the way she wanted it.

It was late morning when the shop bell announced the arrival of Mamie.

"Mother. You didn't tell me you were going to be in town." She glanced at her watch. "Did you want to go for lunch?"

To her surprise, Mamie flushed a delicate shade of pink.

"Well, actually, I already have plans for lunch. I just came in to see if you had a scarf that would look nice with this suit."

Lacey looked at the classic silk suit that fit her mother's trim figure as if it had been tailored especially for her, which it probably had. The delicate ivory was set off perfectly by a warm coral blouse.

"I think I've got something that might look good." She led the way to a table across the shop. "You don't really need anything with that, you know. It looks just about perfect as it is." She began shifting a stack of silk scarves, looking for one that was a blend of just the right shades.

"I don't want to look 'just about' perfect." Mamie fussed with the gold clasp on her purse and Lacey paused in her search, leaning against the table to fix her mother with a searching look. For the first time in a week, something took precedence over her own miseries.

"Just who is this lunch date?"

"Well, it's someone who's become rather important to me."

"Oh, really. Anyone I know?"

Mamie looked away, her skin taking on a tinge of pink. "Well, as a matter of fact—"

The shop bell rang again and Lacey looked up automatically. Jimbo stepped through the door, his stocky form encased in a neat blue suit, complete with tie. Lacey stared at him for a moment. Jimbo never wore a suit—unless he was meeting an important client. And if he was meeting an important client, what was he doing here?

He turned and saw the two of them, and his eyes skimmed over Lacey to settle on Mamie. His face lit up as if he'd just been given a glimpse of the Holy Grail. Lacey looked from him to her mother, surprising a look she'd never seen, a mixture of shy pleasure and coquetry.

She looked at her mother incredulously. "Jimbo?" Her voice was hushed as he began to make his way toward them.

Mamie threw her daughter a quick look that held a touch of defiance. "He's a very nice man."

"Well, sure, but—" She didn't get a chance to finish her sentence. Jimbo stopped in front of them, reaching out to clasp the hand Mamie offered. Her hand looked so tiny, lost on his broad palm. Lacey had to admit there was something very sweet about the way the two of them were looking at each other. For a moment, she felt very old, as if she and Mamie had reversed positions and she was suddenly the mother.

"Mamie. You look exquisite as always."

"Why, thank you, James. You look very handsome in that suit."

To Lacey's amusement, Jimbo blushed, though she wasn't sure if it was pleasure or embarrassment that caused the reaction.

"Hello, Jimbo." She had the strong feeling that if she didn't remind them of her presence, they might forget she was there altogether. Jimbo dragged his eyes from Mamie with obvious effort to focus on Lacey, his expression cooling.

"Hello, Lacey. I hope you know you're an absolute fool."

"Well, I guess I know it now, even if I didn't before. It's nice to see you, too." She carefully didn't ask why he thought she was a fool. She didn't have to be psychic to know the reason involved Cam. Maybe Jimbo would take a hint and let it go at that. She should have known better. Subtlety had never been his strong suit. This time was no exception.

"You realize how dumb this whole thing is, of course. Cam's miserable. You're miserable. And there's no reason it has to be this way."

So Cam was miserable without her. Lacey's heart gave a hard bump, but she kept her expression calm, disinterested. "Did Cam tell you that?"

"Hell, no. Talking to him is like talking to the great stone face these past few days. All he said was that you'd left. He also told me to mind my own business."

"You don't seem inclined to take his advice," Lacey commented dryly.

"I don't see any sense in minding my own business when two of my best friends are miserable."

"Just stay out of it. Cam and I know what we're doing."

"Hah!" Jimbo's inelegant snort exploded out of him, making Lacey jump and drawing the attention of two customers. "You don't have a clue about what you're doing. If you did, you wouldn't be hiding yourself in this place and Cam wouldn't be burying himself in the shop."

"Jimbo—" Lacey's voice held a warning, and Mamie reached out, setting her hand on his sleeve.

"James, I'm not sure we should try and interfere in this. After all, Cameron and Lacey are adults."

"I'm sorry, Mamie, but I can't just stand here and watch them make the biggest mistake of their lives. Any idiot can see that they're head over heels in love with each other."

"Aren't you going to be late for lunch or something?" Lacey chose to ignore his words, knowing that any response she gave him would only encourage him to continue arguing. And this wasn't something she wanted to argue about.

Jimbo glowered at her a moment longer, but he must have realized he was up against a stone wall. He shrugged. "I give up. I suppose the Constitution guarantees you the right to act like an idiot."

"Thank you."

Lacey watched the two of them leave. There was still something incongruous about that pairing. Jimbo's bull-like body and boisterous personality didn't seem to fit with Mamie's delicacy and refinement. Still, she couldn't remember the last time she'd seen her mother look so happy.

She turned back to the table of scarves, and the room suddenly spun around her. Grabbing at the table for balance, she closed her eyes, waiting for the dizzy spell to pass. Damn Jimbo. He had to dredge up the past and call up memories of Cam she'd been trying to bury. See what they did to her? She knew she was right: this marriage was no good.

Chapter Fourteen

Lacey managed to put off thinking about Jimbo's words for several hours. But now, seated in the doctor's waiting room, she found herself thumbing through a magazine and seeing nothing in it.

Head over heels in love with each other. The phrase superimposed itself over an article lamenting the drought in the Midwest. *Cam is miserable* appeared while she was looking at an ad for underwear featuring an impossibly thin model.

In love with each other? Impossible. She'd know if she was in love with Cam, even if she didn't know his feelings. Surely, you couldn't be in love and not know it. No, she wasn't in love with him. But she did miss him.

The knowledge slid into her mind, startling her. Okay, so she missed him. The admission was sulky. There was nothing wrong with missing him. He was a nice guy and she liked him. Liking was a long way from loving. And there was nothing strange in missing someone you liked. In fact, if she was totally honest, she also missed his house and his ditzy dog.

With a muttered curse, she shut the magazine and stared at the wall. Just missing someone wasn't a good enough reason to be married to them. Not even when you missed them so much it felt like a piece of yourself was gone.

She absently dog-eared the pages of the magazine, her eyes focused elsewhere. Cam had said she was a coward, that she was afraid of commitment, afraid of getting hurt, and her mother had agreed with him. *Was* she a coward?

A week ago, it had seemed so clear, so obvious. Now her reasoning seemed a little foggy and blurred around the edges. What had been so obvious was now obscure. Why had she panicked when Lisa told her that she and Frank were splitting up?

But before she could come up with an answer to that question, the nurse called her into the inner office.

"WELL, YOU WERE certainly right about your throat." Dr. Riteman studied her over the top of his glasses. "It's been quite a while since you had one of these infections, hasn't it?"

"A few years," Lacey answered.

"Well, you've got a pretty good one now." He studied the folder he had balanced on his knee, frowning absently. "I see you recently got married. Congratulations."

"Thank you," Lacey murmured, wondering what he'd say if she told him she was likely to be divorced before too long.

He made some notes on the chart, the scrape of his fountain pen audible in the small examining room.

"Well, a round of antibiotics should take care of that throat of yours. Is there any chance you're pregnant?"

"No, I—" She stopped, feeling a sudden tightness in her throat that had nothing to do with infected tonsils. The routine question had caught her off guard. He'd always asked it, drawing blushes when she was sixteen. She didn't feel like blushing now. She felt more like fainting.

It wasn't possible. They'd been careful. Except that night after the party, when they'd made love on the sofa... Only that one time. One careless moment couldn't possibly—

"No," she repeated, as much for herself as the doctor. "No, I'm not pregnant."

Shrewd blue eyes regarded her over the glasses. "Are you sure, Lacey? Because, if there's any doubt, any doubt at all, we don't want to endanger the baby."

"I..." She started to tell him that she was sure, but she couldn't get the words out. The fact was, she wasn't sure at all.

Her eyes filled with quick tears and she looked down, blinking rapidly. "I don't think I'm pregnant." But the words didn't carry any conviction.

"When was your last menstrual period?"

"I don't know." She tried to think. "I'm late, I guess. But I've been under a lot of stress."

"Do you have any other symptoms? Nausea, dizziness, lack of appetite, tiredness?"

"I— All of those."

Her voice was shaking, and Dr. Riteman reached out to put his hands over hers, stilling the restless twisting of her fingers. His eyes were kind. "I'll tell you what. Why don't we take a urine sample and check. Just to make sure. How does that sound?"

She wanted to scream at him that it was an awful idea. It was an unnecessary idea. She wasn't pregnant. She couldn't be pregnant.

Lacey nodded slowly. "Thank you, doctor. I'd appreciate that."

"It's no problem. Better safe than sorry and, this way, you'll know for sure."

It wasn't possible. It just wasn't possible.

BUT TWO HOURS later she walked out of the office with a handful of booklets that said that it was more than possible. It was a reality.

Just the early stages, but it was never too soon to start taking care of herself, the doctor had told her in a tone that was much too cheerful for Lacey's distraught mind.

When she got in her car, she didn't start it right away. She just sat, staring out at the beautiful summer day, trying to absorb this sudden drastic change in her life.

She was carrying a child. Cam's child. The thought brought a confusing rush of emotions tumbling after it. She'd always planned to have children. In the back of her mind, there'd always been the image of one or two small people who were a part of her. The father had been a vague figure, there, but not very real.

Until Cam. Since the odd beginnings of their marriage, she'd unconsciously substituted him for the amorphous masculine image in her mind. There'd even been a time or two when she'd specifically fantasized about the kind of father he'd make. But she'd been thinking of some distant time, so far in the future that it was safe to dream about.

Only now it wasn't a dream anymore. It was reality. Pregnant. Her hands settled on her stomach. It was still flat, giving no sign of the momentous changes taking place inside. A child was growing within. A son or a daughter who'd hold a little of herself and a little of Cam and blend those bits into a totally new and unique person.

Cam. Lacey drew in a quick breath as a wave of longing swept over her, bringing tears to her eyes. She wanted nothing as much in the world as to go to him and tell him her news. She wanted to feel his arms around her, hear him say that he was happy, that everything was going to be all right.

But she couldn't do that. She'd shut that door; slammed it, in fact. How could she go to Cam now and tell him that she wanted to give their marriage a try after all? He'd take her back when he found out about the child—she didn't doubt that for a moment. He had a strong sense of responsibility. And she knew he'd want to be a part of his child's life.

But she didn't want him to take her back because of the baby. She wanted him to take her back because he loved her, because he didn't want to live without her, any more than she wanted to live without him. The realization took her breath away.

She was in love with Cameron McCleary.

She'd been such a fool, an unforgivable fool. She'd let her own fears and doubts blind her to the incredible gift that had been dropped into her lap.

Mamie was in the living room when Lacey came in. She looked up from a handful of knitting the color of a summer sky, her smile welcoming.

"You're home a bit early, sugar. There's some tea, if you'd like. Janey fixed it before she left for the day. Those cookies are absolutely divine. That girl has the lightest touch with anything baked. I've been tryin' to talk her into startin' a bakery of her own. I'd finance it. I do believe it would be a good investment. I think I've almost got her talked into it."

Lacey sat down, pouring a cup of tea and reaching for a cookie. Her appetite had been almost nonexistent for the past couple of weeks, but she was suddenly ravenous. Maybe having a reason for the way she'd been feeling had restored her hunger. She bit into the cookie, feeling it nearly melt in her mouth.

"Aren't those just the best things?"

"How was your lunch with Jimbo?" Lacey reached for another cookie. She still hadn't decided whether she wanted to tell Mamie her own news.

"James and I had a lovely meal. The fish was divine."

"The two of you seem pretty close," Lacey said casually.

"He's a charmin' man and he knows how to treat a lady." Mamie's color was a little high and her tone held just a touch of defiance.

"Well, if you're happy, then I'm happy for you."

"Thank you, Lacey. That means a lot to me. Now, all we need to do is work on your bein' happy."

Lacey shrugged, doing her best to discourage her mother from continuing. It worked better with Mamie than it had with Jimbo. Mamie's lips tightened and she shook her head, despairing of Lacey's common sense, but she didn't say anything more.

Lacey munched another cookie, her eyes on the swift movements of the knitting needles. It crept over her gradually that these past few days with her mother were some of the best they'd ever spent together. For the first time she was seeing her mother as a person apart from her role as a mother. Mamie was a woman with hopes and dreams just like everyone else.

Lacey wasn't sure just what had effected the change. Maybe it was turning thirty, or maybe it was getting married. Whatever, she knew she'd never look at her mother in quite the same way again.

"Mother?"

"Yes, sugar?"

"Have I told you lately that I love you?"

Mamie looked up, startled, and Lacey felt a twinge of shame that her words should come as a surprise.

"I guess I don't tell you often enough, do I?"

Mamie shook her head. "I know you love me, Lacey. You don't always have to say the words."

"Maybe they should be said once in a while."

"Maybe they should," Mamie agreed. "In that case, I should tell you that I love you, too. You're just about the best thing to come into my life."

"Do you ever regret that you raised me alone?"

"Well, I always regretted that you didn't get a chance to know your daddy and that he didn't get a chance to know you. But I never regretted having you, if that's what you're asking. If it hadn't been for you, I just can't imagine where my life would have gone."

"But didn't you ever resent having a kid around? I mean, you were very young. Didn't you ever think of the things you could have done?"

"No. There was nothing I wanted to do that I didn't do. You'll understand when you have children of your own."

Lacey took a sip of her tea then cleared her throat nervously. "How do you feel about being a grandmother?"

Mamie shrugged, without looking up from her knitting. "I won't mind when the time comes. It would be nice to have a little one around the place. A house without a child in it once in a while is a pretty dull place.

"Of course, at the rate you're going, it's likely to be quite some time before I have a grandchild," she added sternly.

Lacey smiled, aware that her lips showed a definite tendency to quiver.

"Mama? I'm going to have a baby."

The knitting needles came to a halt, but Mamie didn't look up. The silence stretched. Then she lifted her head, her eyes reflecting her shock.

"You're havin' a baby?" Lacey nodded, biting her lip nervously. "I'm going to be a grandma?"

"Do you mind?"

"Mind? Do I mind? Have you taken leave of your senses, child?" She leaned forward, and Lacey took the hands she held out. "A baby. Do you know how long I've waited to see you rockin' my grandchild? Oh, sugar, this is about the best news I've had in a month of Sundays!"

Lacey laughed, her eyes sparkling with bright tears. She hadn't realized how real telling someone about it was going to make her pregnancy seem.

Mamie's face sobered abruptly. "You are goin' to tell Cameron." It was a statement, but her tone made it half a question. Lacey's gaze dropped away from her mother's and she shrugged.

"I don't know yet."

Mamie's fingers tightened demandingly on her daughter's. "You listen to me, Lacey. Cameron has a right to know he's goin' to be a daddy. You got no right keepin' it from him."

"I know, I know." She tugged her hands away, twisting them together in her lap. "I'll have to tell him, but not right now. I just found out about it myself, and I need a little time to adjust to the idea. And I need to pick the right time to tell him."

"If you hadn't done such a damn fool thing and left the man, you wouldn't need to pick the right time to tell him," Mamie told her with asperity.

"Mother, please. Don't make me sorry I told you."

Mamie glared at her a moment longer and then softened. "All right. I won't scold you anymore tonight. We should do something to celebrate. I think there's some apple cider in the refrigerator. Why don't I get us a couple of glasses? We'll toast the newest member of the family."

So they toasted the baby with cider served in fluted champagne glasses. They laughed and talked, planning out the child's life right through college. In some ways, it was one of the most wonderful evenings Lacey had ever spent.

But she cried herself to sleep that night. No matter how much fun they'd had, Mamie was not Cam. Right now, no one in the world could reconcile her to the unhappy fact that he wasn't here to share these first few hours of excitement. And it didn't make it any easier that it was her own actions that had shut her away from him.

GOING INTO THE SHOP the next day, Lacey found her concentration at an all-time low. If she wasn't thinking about the baby, she was thinking about its father, wondering how she would break the news to him, wondering what his reaction would be.

Cam was so much on her mind that it was hardly a surprise when the bell pinged and she looked up to see his tall figure step through the door. She'd been kneeling on the floor, checking some stock in a low drawer, and he didn't see her at first. It was a small mercy but one Lacey appreciated. It gave her a moment to grab hold of the composure that threatened to slip away.

She stood up slowly, feeling the impact of Cam's eyes when he saw her. She wanted to run to him, throw herself into his arms and tell him that she'd been a fool. But she didn't. If there was any way to salvage something of the mess she'd made of their relationship, it was going to take time and care. It wasn't something that could be fixed in a few brief moments.

"Hello, Lacey." Cam spoke as she came near, his voice soft, though they were alone in the shop.

"Hello, Cam." She started to hold out her hand and then stopped before the move had a chance to be completed. Shaking hands seemed a little absurd.

"You look beautiful." His eyes didn't miss anything, from the top of her neatly pinned chignon, over her pale green silk dress to the toes of her neat pumps. Lacey had to restrain the urge to put her hands over her stomach as if he could somehow see the new life that was hidden there. But of course he couldn't possibly notice anything.

"Thank you. You look very well." God, she sounded so stilted. She could have been taking a class in manners.

"Thank you."

The silence extended, threatening to grow to unmanageable proportions. Lacey could feel her nerves stretching thin. If only a customer would come in. Anything to break the tension.

"So, did you come in for something in particular?" The words came out too bald, too shrill, as if she felt his presence needed an explanation. Cam's face tightened.

"No. I guess I've caught you at a bad time." He half turned, reaching for the door. In a moment he'd be gone, thinking she didn't want to see him. Lacey's hand caught at his arm.

"Wait. I'm sorry. I didn't mean to sound so abrupt. I guess I'm a little nervous." She felt the muscles tighten in his arm as he slowly turned back to her. His eyes met hers and it wasn't hard to read his doubt.

"Are you sure? I know you've probably got a lot to do here."

Lacey laughed nervously, releasing his arm to wave an eloquent hand at the empty shop. "As you can see I am swamped with customers, but I think I can spare a few minutes."

Cam glanced around and then looked back at her, and she could feel his tension ease.

"Slow day?"

"Slow season. Come summer, all my customers depart for St. Moritz and St. Thomas. It's always the slowest time of year."

"Well, you seem to be busy enough the rest of the year to weather a couple of slow months."

"We are. To tell the truth, it's nice to be able to take a bit of a break."

"I'll bet."

Silence fell between them again, but this time, Lacey spoke before it had a chance to build into something awkward.

"How have you been? Are you keeping busy?"

"Busy enough. I finished the desk."

"The one with all the inlays? It looked gorgeous while you were working on it."

"I'm happy with it. And so were the Masdens. They've asked me to make a matching secretary."

"Are you going to do it?" she asked.

"I think so. I've already told them it would be quite a few months before I could start on it. I've got other things in line ahead of them. It depends on whether or not they want to wait."

"They obviously appreciate the best. They'll wait."

Cam smiled, the first truly relaxed expression she'd seen. "I should hire you to run a PR department for me."

"Well, it's true."

His smile faded, replaced by a searching expression. "How have you been?"

She shrugged. "Okay. How have you been?"

"Okay, I guess. Derwent misses you. He sulked for two full days. He even refused to eat."

"Poor baby." Had Cam missed her, too? *Tell me you missed me. Ask me to come home.*

But he didn't say anything for a moment, and when he did, it was on a different subject. "I hope you don't mind my dropping by like this."

"No, of course not." If only he knew how much she'd missed him, how hungry she'd been for the sight of him.

"I'd hate to think that we couldn't still be friends."

"I would too." Friends? She didn't want to be his friend. Not unless she could also be his wife, his lover, the center of his life.

He stuck his hands into his pockets and then pulled them out again, staring at them for a moment as if he wasn't quite sure what they were doing on the ends of his arms.

"Well, I guess I'd better get going. I need to pick up some things."

Tell him, you nitwit. Tell him how you feel. Tell him how much you miss him, how much you want to come back to him.

She bit her lip against the urge to beg him to take her home with him. How could she tell him she'd changed her mind? What if he still wanted her and then found out about the baby? He'd think that was the only reason she'd changed her mind. And if she told him about the baby first, she'd never be sure if that wasn't the only reason he'd wanted her back.

So she didn't say anything. She murmured a goodbye and watched him leave, the bell jingling merrily behind him. Her hands were clenched into fists at her sides, her nails biting into her palms.

Well, Lacey, you certainly managed to make a royal mess of things this time.

WELL, I CERTAINLY blew that one. Cam stalked along the sidewalk, long angry strides eating up the distance to his truck.

He hadn't said anything he'd wanted to say. He'd probably looked like a total fool, standing there gawking at her.

"I hope we can still be friends." He mimicked his own words under his breath in a tone so savage that a little old lady who'd been about to walk by him quickly turned and went into a men's shoe store.

He'd given her some time. So okay, it was less than two weeks, but the house felt so damned empty without her. He'd come here, half thinking that he'd ask her to reconsider, give their marriage another try. Instead he'd stood there like a mentally deficient gorilla and exchanged a bit of casual conversation with her. Brilliant.

Why didn't you tell her how you felt?

He snarled at the small voice inside, causing a mother with two toddlers to decide that she'd really rather walk on the other side of the street.

How could he tell Lacey that his life was empty without her, that he was in love with her, when it was obvious that she didn't feel anything of the kind for him? It was one thing to take emotional chances. It was something else to throw himself at the mercy of someone who so clearly wasn't interested. Still, he couldn't quite believe it was going to end here. Maybe that was only because it hurt too much to think an end to their relationship was possible.

"No, dammit!" He shoved the key into the door of the truck with such force it threatened to bend. They felt too right together, too perfect for it to be a figment of his imagination. Lacey would feel it, too. She *had* to feel it. Anything else was unthinkable. All he needed to do was give her some time.

Just a little time.

"JAMES IS COMING to dinner, sugar. I hope you don't mind." Even if Lacey had been inclined to object, she wouldn't have said anything to take the excitement from her mother's eyes.

"Of course not. Shall I make myself scarce?" she asked teasingly.

Mamie blushed, looking as young as her daughter. "Don't be silly. Besides, if we wanted to be alone, there're always motels." The look she threw Lacey was pure mischief.

"Mother! I'm shocked and horrified. You're talking like a hussy."

"I know," Mamie said complacently. "Ain't it fun?"

The dinner proved to be more pleasant than she might have expected, considering her last encounter with Jimbo. She didn't know if Mamie had said something to him, or if he'd simply decided that tact might work better than the frontal attack he'd tried before.

Cam's name didn't even come up until dessert was served.

"Have you seen Cam lately, Lacey?" her mother asked.

"As a matter of fact, he stopped by the shop yesterday."

"Lacey, you didn't tell me you'd seen Cameron. Did you tell him—" Mamie broke off abruptly.

"Tell him what?" Jimbo looked from one to the other as his fork sank into the apple pie Mamie had baked especially for him.

"Nothing," Lacey said, without any hope of being believed.

"It doesn't sound like nothing." He lifted a bite of pie to his mouth.

"It's certainly not nothing," Mamie said. She caught her daughter's eye and lifted her chin. "Well, you're not going to be able to keep it a secret forever."

"Mother, I really don't think that this is the time."

"Oh, come on," Jimbo said. "Now you've got to tell me what's going on. I'll die of curiosity." He picked up his coffee cup.

"Mother—"

"I think James should know. He's practically family, after all."

Lacey threw her hands up. There was simply no stopping her mother once she got her teeth into something. It was a wonder she hadn't already told Cam.

"So tell me. My imagination's running wild."

"Lacey's goin' to have a baby."

Jimbo inhaled a mouthful of hot coffee and then choked, gasping for air. He coughed, his eyes watering with the pain of his scalded throat.

"You're what?" He squeezed the words out.

"I'm pregnant."

"Oh, my God."

Lacey raised her brows. She wasn't sure what response she'd expected, but this certainly wasn't it. He looked as if she'd just told him that the world was coming to an end.

"Whatever happened to 'Congratulations, Lacey?'"

Jimbo ignored her mild sarcasm. "Have you told Cam?"

"I don't think that's any of your business."

"Then you haven't told him. Oh, God." He ran his fingers through his short hair, making it stand up on top of his head like a bizarre hat.

"James, what's the matter?"

He gave Mamie a distracted look. "Nothing's the matter. I was just surprised, that's all." He looked at his watch. "Good grief. Look how late it is. I'd forgotten I had an appointment."

"At nine o'clock?" Mamie asked incredulously.

"An eccentric client," he told her, giving her a quick smile. "Sorry I've got to eat and run. The meal was wonderful."

"Jimbo—"

But Lacey was speaking to thin air. He'd already vanished from the dining room, and a minute later the front door closed behind him. Raising her eyebrows questioningly she turned to look at her mother.

Mamie looked as confused as Lacey did. "I have no idea. He seemed upset, didn't he?"

"He seemed demented."

Chapter Fifteen

Summer had truly arrived. The temperatures were creeping into the eighties, and the sun was shining down out of a sky not yet marred by the smog that would descend a little later in the season. In fact, it was an extravagantly beautiful day.

Cam was not in the mood to notice it. He was sitting in front of his workbench, ostensibly working. Except his hands weren't moving. Derwent sat next to the open garage door, apparently on guard, though Cam couldn't have guessed what he thought he was guarding against. Still, at least the dog was acting productive. Cam hadn't managed that much in several days.

The first few days after Lacey left, sheer rage had sustained him. He'd been so angry at her leaving that he hadn't really noticed the hurt. But the anger had trickled away, leaving a void that was too quickly filled with loneliness.

He'd lived alone for years and never felt the least bit lonely. When he developed a craving for companionship, he could always call a friend. But this was a different kind of craving. He didn't want company. He wanted Lacey. There was an empty space inside him that only she could fill.

He should have told her that he loved her. He should have told her weeks ago. He'd accused her of being a coward, but he was certainly no better. He'd known weeks ago that this trial marriage had become very real, at least for him. He should have said something then. But he'd been afraid to lay himself open to the hurt he'd feel if Lacey didn't return his feelings.

And now she was gone. But not for good. He was going to figure out some way to convince her that, despite its crazy beginning, this marriage was the best thing that had ever happened to either one of them.

Derwent growled low in his throat, distracting Cam from his thoughts. He glanced up, not surprised to see Jimbo standing a few feet away from the small dog.

"Kill, Derwent," he ordered without much force. Derwent grumbled, but he didn't attack. Jimbo kept one eye on him as he sidled into the shop.

"I don't know why he doesn't like me," he complained.

"Well, they do say that an animal's instinct is often far superior to a human's. Maybe he knows something about you I don't. Have a seat." Cam turned and leaned back against the bench, watching as Jimbo found himself a stool and sat down.

Once settled, Jimbo didn't say anything. He sat staring at the concrete floor, his expression somewhere between guilt and depression. Cam dragged his attention away from his own problem and studied his friend with a sharper eye.

"You look like the Grinch just stole your Christmas. What's wrong?"

"I want to remind you, Cam, that we have many years of friendship behind us." Cam arched his brows at this apparent irrelevancy.

"That's true. Did you run into my car?"

"No." Jimbo stared at the floor again and then heaved a sigh. "I saw Lacey last night."

Cam sat up straight so suddenly that the stool rocked on its feet. "Is she all right?"

"She's fine. Really, she's just fine."

Cam relaxed slowly, aware that his pulse was faster. "Don't scare me like that."

"Sorry. I didn't mean to upset you prematurely."

"Prematurely?" Cam stiffened again. "Why don't you just spit it out, Jimbo? What's wrong with Lacey?"

"Well, it's not really anything wrong. I mean, it's not like she's sick or anything."

Cam stood up and Jimbo slid off his stool, facing the much larger man with a nervous expression. "Remember our friendship."

"If you don't tell me what the hell you're trying to get out, the only thing left of our friendship is going to consist of my being one of your pallbearers."

"Okay, okay." Jimbo made soothing motions with his hands as he backed slightly away. "I probably shouldn't be saying anything at all, but under the circumstances—which no one else knows at this point—I sort of thought I ought to tell you. Even though Lacey will probably never forgive me."

"Jimbo—" Cam's tone was ominous as was the step he took toward the other man.

"Lacey's pregnant." Jimbo blurted out the announcement and then waited.

Cam stared at him, feeling as if he'd just stepped off a stair onto a floor that wasn't there.

"What did you say?" The voice that asked the question wasn't his. He heard it from far away, much too hoarse and barely audible.

"Lacey's pregnant."

Cam stared at him, but he wasn't seeing Jimbo. He was remembering the night of the dinner party, Lacey's sweet demand matching his own. There'd been no thought of practicalities that night, no thought beyond the heat and scent of her.

"My God."

"Funny, that was my reaction," Jimbo said.

"Why hasn't she told me? Does she plan on keeping it from me? What the hell is going on in her head?" His tone grew more forceful with each question, but he wasn't looking for answers. Derwent, sensing Cam's mood, jumped to his feet and barked sharply, his button eyes focused on Jimbo, who seemed the most likely source of the disturbance.

"I don't know what she plans on doing," Jimbo said, keeping one eye on Cam and one eye on the dog.

"Well, I know what I damn well plan on doing. I'm going to find her and get her to listen to reason, even if I have to kidnap her to do it." Cam turned and strode out of the garage, punching the automatic opener as he went. Jimbo ducked under the closing door, barely escaping a bash on the head.

"Cam, I really think we should talk before you go anywhere." He had to increase his speed to a near trot to keep up with Cam's longer stride. Derwent hurried along beside them, his tongue lolling like a tiny pink warning flag.

"The only person I want to talk to right now is Lacey. Dammit! Why didn't she tell me? How could she keep something like this from me? I'm her husband, for God's sake."

"Well, you see, that's what I think we should talk about."

But Cam wasn't listening. He strode into the house, his entourage of two following close behind.

"We lived together for almost three months." He crossed the kitchen into the hall, grabbing his keys from the small table before reaching for the front door.

"Cam, I really think we need to talk," Jimbo managed a little breathlessly.

"Later. Shut the door, would you?" Jimbo pulled the door shut but not before Derwent had managed to slip through, apparently anxious to see the finale to all this unusual excitement.

"Cam." He hurried down the steps and trotted across the lawn.

Cam turned at the door of the car, but it wasn't because he'd heard Jimbo. "You know, I would have thought that she'd gotten to know me well enough to feel she could come to me with this. We may not have gotten off to a conventional start, but I really thought we had established a relationship. Why wouldn't she tell me she was pregnant? I'm her husband. You'd think I'd be the first person she'd tell, no matter what the circumstances."

"No, you're not." Jimbo leaned one hand on the hood of the car, trying to catch his breath.

Cam looked at him, making a real effort to focus his attention on something besides his burning need to see Lacey. "I appreciate your telling me this. This may be just what we need to straighten things out between us. There's more than just the two of us to consider now. Maybe I can convince Lacey to give our marriage another try."

"No, you can't."

"What?" He finally had Cam's full attention. "What do you mean, I can't? I can't what?"

"You can't convince Lacey to give your marriage *another* try."

"Why not?"

Jimbo pulled himself away from the car and straightened, his expression a mixture of remorse and defiance. Cam felt an uneasy stirring in the pit of his stomach.

"Why can't I convince Lacey to give our marriage another try, Jimbo?"

"Look, Cam, I did it for the best possible reasons. I really thought you two belonged together and I was just trying to see that you got a chance to get to know each other."

Cam stepped away from the car door. "What did you do?"

"It seemed like a really good idea at the time." Jimbo took an uneasy step back, his eyes on Cam's suddenly looming figure.

"Jimbo—" Cam's tone held a warning. "*What* seemed like a good idea at *what* time?"

"Well, this goes back a ways. It's really kind of funny when you think about it, like something out of an old movie."

Cam didn't look in a laughing mood. Jimbo cleared his throat uneasily and went on. "Well, you remember the night of Lacey's birthday?"

"Yes." The one word had an ominous tone.

Jimbo cleared his throat again. "Well, you know, you and Lacey had quite a bit to drink."

"Jimbo, I don't need a postmortem on the night we got married. I just want to know what you did."

"Well, actually, it's not exactly what I did. It's more what you didn't do."

Cam stared at him, a terrible realization creeping over him. "Just what didn't I do?"

His voice had dropped to something between a whisper and a growl. Derwent, sensing the new element in the atmosphere, ranged himself beside his master, his sturdy little body bristling with dislike as he looked at Jimbo. The pairing of very large man and very small dog might have been comical, but Jimbo was not really in a laughing mood.

"Look, I want you to remember that we've been friends a long time, and I really did think it was a good idea at the time."

"Jimbo!" Cam barked the name out, his patience clearly at an end.

"You and Lacey aren't really married." He rushed the words out so quickly that they slurred together, but Cam clearly didn't have any trouble understanding him.

"You son of a—" Jimbo didn't even try to dodge the fist when he saw it coming. Cam's blow got him squarely on the chin, rocking him back off his feet. The lawn that looked so soft didn't feel nearly as plush when he hit it. For an instant he saw stars, and he had a vague hope that maybe he'd been knocked out, but he wasn't that lucky.

"Get up. Get up so I can kill you." Jimbo's vision cleared enough to reveal Cam standing over him, his hands clenched into fists, his stance murderous.

"No, I don't think I will. Not that I don't deserve to be killed, mind you, but I don't want you to have my death on your conscience."

"My conscience can take the pressure. How could you do this to me? To Lacey? My God, when did you plan on telling us?"

Jimbo pushed himself up on one elbow, careful not to rise any higher for fear Cam wouldn't be able to contain his wrath. "I hadn't really thought things out. There the two of you were. You were the ones who decided to get married. And I did try to talk you out of it. But you were both convinced it was a great idea. Well, I couldn't let you get married in that condition.''

"Gee, thanks." Cam's tone lacked any sincere element of gratitude.

"So I set up a fake ceremony, got a fake certificate. But then the two of you disappeared, and I didn't find you till the next morning. You seemed upset enough about the idea of being married. I figured that finding out you weren't really married might be even worse at that point. Besides, it was obvious you were perfect for each other. So I just let things lie for a while.''

"With friends like you, a guy sure as hell doesn't need enemies. Does Lacey know?''

"No. When I found out she was pregnant, I decided maybe it was time to let you know the whole story.''

Cam growled. There was no other word for it. His eyes blazed with a murderous blue light, and the sound that came out of his throat could only be called a growl.

"I wish you'd get up so I could beat you to a pulp.''

Jimbo shook his head, fingering the tender skin on his jaw. "I'm not that stupid. Besides, you don't have time to beat me up. You've got to talk to Lacey.''

"Lacey. My God, how am I going to tell her this?'' Worrying about it distracted him momentarily, but then his gaze sharpened on the prone man again. "You're right. I don't have time to kill you. But you'd better stay out of my sight for the next seventy or eighty years or I swear I'll tear you apart with my bare hands.''

Jimbo was careful not to move until the car had pulled out of the driveway. Well, he'd done his best. Cam would forgive him eventually, and Lacey wasn't inclined to hold a grudge. He wasn't so sure about Mamie. She wasn't going to be very pleased when she found that he'd been partially responsible for her daughter's living in sin.

A low growl brought his attention to Derwent, who was still watching him, stiff-legged and bristling with hostility.

"Oh, shut up. Cam already decked me. There's no reason for you to add insult to injury. Besides, you're too little to take me on."

Derwent promptly proved him wrong by sinking a set of very sharp little teeth into his ankle.

LACEY WAS NOT HAVING a good day. She hadn't slept well. Dreams of Cam and his reaction to finding out about his imminent fatherhood had kept her tossing and turning most of the night. And then she'd awakened to discover the real meaning of morning sickness.

Mamie had nagged her to tell Cam about the baby, her car had coughed and sputtered all the way to the shop, threatening to die at any moment and leave her stranded on the freeway. She'd made it without having to resort to hitchhiking, but that one small blessing hadn't done much to restore her mood.

The shop was unusually busy for a Tuesday morning, which was good for the ledger but not so good when it came to her need to take some time off and put her feet up. It was nearly eleven before she got a chance to pour herself a cup of coffee, and then it sat and got cold while she helped a portly matron select a scarf to go with a particularly hideous dress. Lacey restrained the urge to suggest that a large silk tent would be the only thing that could improve the effect.

When the bell over the door rang and she looked up to see Cam walking in, it seemed like the perfect touch to a day that was going rapidly downhill. The last thing she wanted to deal with right now was Cam. Her emotions were too raw, too close to the surface. She knew she was going to have to tell him about the baby, but she wanted to choose her own time and place. This wasn't it.

Cam saw her and started toward her. There was something in the set of his shoulders that made her uneasy. He didn't look like he was here for a casual hello or an invitation to lunch.

"Lacey, I need to talk to you." He didn't bother with a greeting, and her uneasiness increased. He looked upset, and her mind flew immediately to the child she carried. But he couldn't know about that. Jimbo wouldn't have said anything, would he?

"Cam, this really isn't a very good time." She gestured to the half-dozen customers browsing behind him. "Maybe tomorrow."

"No." Cam barely glanced at the customers. "We've got to talk now."

"Cam, I really can't talk to you now." She started to move away, but his hand caught her wrist, holding her gently but implacably where she was.

"We've got to talk right now. Why don't we move into your office."

Lacey felt a wave of panic. He had to know about the baby. That was the only thing that could have brought him here like this. She wasn't ready to talk to him. She wouldn't talk to him.

"Later." She gave him a tight smile, aware that one or two of the customers were watching them, sensing drama.

"Lacey, we can talk here or we can talk in your office or we can talk on the sidewalk, but we are going to talk now. This can't wait."

"You're being obnoxious, Cam." She smiled at a woman with shockingly red hair. "Don't make a scene."

"I'm not going to make a scene. I don't think it's unreasonable to want to talk to the woman who's carrying my child."

His final words came during a lull in the piped-in music, and they seemed to echo around the room. If Lacey thought it was her imagination, she had only to look at the women in the shop to know that they'd heard every word.

She'd known that her pregnancy had to be what he'd come to talk about, but she still wasn't prepared for the impact of his words. The fact that Cam knew about the baby threw her completely off balance. Foolishly she still tried to avoid the inevitable.

"Let's talk about this later, Cam. Maybe over dinner tonight?" She affected a relaxed, proper tone so as not to draw further attention from the customers.

His fingers tightened over her wrist, not painfully but demandingly. "Lacey, this isn't something you talk about over steak tartare and a glass of cabernet. Why didn't you tell me?"

"I haven't known that long myself. I was just trying to adjust to the idea before discussing it with you."

"So you *did* plan on telling me."

"Of course I did." This time she gritted the words out, then smiled at the portly matron in the ghastly dress.

"We've got to talk about this."

"Later. Margaret won't be in until this afternoon, and I've got a business to run."

"Now. There are things we have to talk about now that are more important than business."

"Cam, just because you're my husband doesn't mean I have to jump when you say jump. Times have changed."

Cam moved closer, his expression intent. "Look, I don't mean to be pushy about this, but I talked to Jimbo this morning—"

"I gathered as much. That worm. I should have guessed he wouldn't be able to keep his mouth shut. I'd like to knock his teeth out."

"I already did, more or less."

"You punched Jimbo?" For the first time since he'd entered the shop, she looked at him with something approaching pleasure. "Good. I hope he has to spend months in a dentist's chair while they repair the damage."

Cam grinned at her bloodthirsty attitude, but the expression was quickly gone. "Look, we need to talk about what he told me."

"I really can't talk about it now."

"You don't understand. Jimbo told me something that we really have to—"

"Cam, please. Come back this afternoon." She was vividly aware that most of the customers had stopped even trying to pretend they weren't listening. "We can talk about this after—"

"Lacey, we're not married."

She stared at him. She was hearing things. Was that a symptom of pregnancy? She hadn't seen it mentioned in any of the books Dr. Riteman had given her, but that was the only possible explanation.

"What?" she got out.

"Jimbo told me that we're not really married. The certificate was a fake. We're not married."

There was no mistaking his words this time. And no doubting that he'd really said them. Not married. Cam wasn't her husband. She wasn't his wife. The realization washed over her. Her lower lip began to tremble. This whole crazy arrangement hadn't ever existed. They hadn't had a marriage of convenience or inconvenience or anything else. They hadn't had a marriage at all.

Cam watched her eyes fill with tears and felt his heart crack. His hand slid up her arm to her shoulder, and he pulled her closer, bending to brush a quick kiss over her shaking mouth.

"Don't cry, honey. It's not a tragedy. We'll get married. For real this time."

She stiffened and pulled away from him, her spine rigid with pride. "No. I don't want you to marry me just because I'm pregnant. I don't need that kind of charity."

"It's not charity." He drew a deep breath but found that the words were easy to say after all. "I love you. I've been in love with you for weeks."

"You're just saying that because of the baby." She wanted to believe him. She ached to believe him. She wanted it so much that she didn't dare believe him.

"No, I'm not. I love you, Lacey."

"If you love me, then why didn't you tell me before this? Why are you only saying it now that you know about the baby?"

"I was scared. I accused you of being a coward, but I was the one who was afraid."

Her eyes searched his, trying to find the truth. She'd had one marriage for the wrong reasons—or so she'd thought. She wasn't going to go into another one for anything less than love.

"I'd believe him, honey. He looks sincere to me."

The voice came from one of the customers, a buxom and bejeweled blonde who was leaning on a rack of thoroughly risqué camisoles, her eyes fixed firmly on them.

"I agree. He looks like a guy who'd tell the truth." That was the woman with the shockingly red hair.

"I don't know, you can't trust a man." This from the matron in the terrible dress. "They're sneaky by nature."

Lacey looked up at Cam, wanting with all her heart to believe him. "Are you sure?"

"I love you more than I can ever tell you. These past couple of weeks without you, I've been empty. I need you and I love you."

"You'll never hear a prettier speech, honey. A man who can talk like that is worth taking a chance on." The buxom blonde threw her opinion into the ring, but Lacey wasn't listening to her. She was listening to her own heart, which was telling her to believe, to take another chance.

"It's not just because of the baby?"

"With or without the baby, Lacey, I want you in my life. I love you."

She drew a deep breath and let it out in a rush. "I love you, too."

Cam's mouth captured the last word as it left her. Lacey threw her arms around his neck, feeling his arms enfold her, holding her close, holding her safe. She'd finally taken the biggest gamble of all, and it felt wonderful.

The sound of applause broke them apart. Cam's arms loosened just enough to allow her to turn and face their small but enthusiastic audience. He bowed slightly, grinning at the watching women. Lacey blushed but smiled. She felt as if she'd never stop smiling.

"If you'll excuse us, ladies, we have a wedding to arrange. Las Vegas?" He looked down at Lacey, cocking one brow in question.

"Where else? We'll do it right this time."

"We did it right the first time," he told her. Looking into the loving blue of his eyes, she had to agree.

Their marriage of inconvenience had turned out to be very right indeed.

COMING IN AUGUST

Janet **DAILEY**

SOMETHING EXTRA

Jolie was ready for adventure after finishing college, and
going to Louisiana to find her family's ancestral home
looked more exciting than returning to the family farm.
Finding the house was wonderful; finding its new owner,
Steve Cameron, was an added bonus. Jolie fell in love with
Steve so quickly that his reputation as a womanizer barely
registered—but his beautiful girlfriend Claudine was quite
another matter....

Watch for this bestselling Janet Dailey favorite, coming in
August from Harlequin.

Also watch for *Sweet Promise* this October.

HARLEQUIN
American Romance®

COMING NEXT MONTH

#305 MOTHER KNOWS BEST by Barbara Bretton

Author of the "Mother Knows Best" helpful-hints column, Diana had a master plan: finish her book, lose ten pounds and on Labor Day, begin the Great Husband Hunt. But then a month at seaside Gull Cottage fell in her lap, and two months early, at exactly the wrong time, Diana met Mr. Right. Don't miss the second book in the GULL COTTAGE series.

#306 FRIENDS by Stella Cameron

As children, Tom, Shelly and Ben had been inseparable. Then they became adults and their friendship faced a challenge. Ben was destined for fame, while Tom and Shelly were destined for love. But would their love break the bonds of an unbreakable friendship?

#307 ONE MAN'S FOLLY by Cathy Gillen Thacker

Diana Tomlinson was justice of the peace in Libertyville, Texas, but her life was far from peaceful. Newcomer Mike Harrigan was insistent about his foster ranch—even though the town was up in arms, all hell had broken loose and there had been a rash of burglaries. Diana knew that where there was a will there was a way—but as she got to know Mike and his trio of boys she found her will rapidly fading....

#308 WHITE MOON by Vella Munn

Lynn Walker was a championship barrel rider without a horse—her dream was just out of reach. Then Bryan Stone found her a mare to match her spirit and her strength: proof that he believed in her and her dream. There are many ways to say "I love you," and White Moon was Bryan's.

Harlequin American Romance.

Gull Cottage

SUMMER.

The sun, the surf, the sand...

One relaxing month by the sea was all Zoe, Diana and Gracie ever expected from their four-week stays at Gull Cottage, the luxurious East Hampton mansion. They never thought they'd soon be sharing those long summer days—or hot summer nights—with a special man. They never thought that what they found at the beach would change their lives forever. But as Boris, Gull Cottage's resident mynah bird said: "Beware of summer romances...."

Join Zoe, Diana and Gracie for the summer of their lives. Don't miss the GULL COTTAGE trilogy in American Romance: #301 *Charmed Circle* by Robin Francis (July 1989), #305 *Mother Knows Best* by Barbara Bretton (August 1989) and #309 *Saving Grace* by Anne McAllister (September 1989).

GULL COTTAGE—because a month can be the start of forever...
